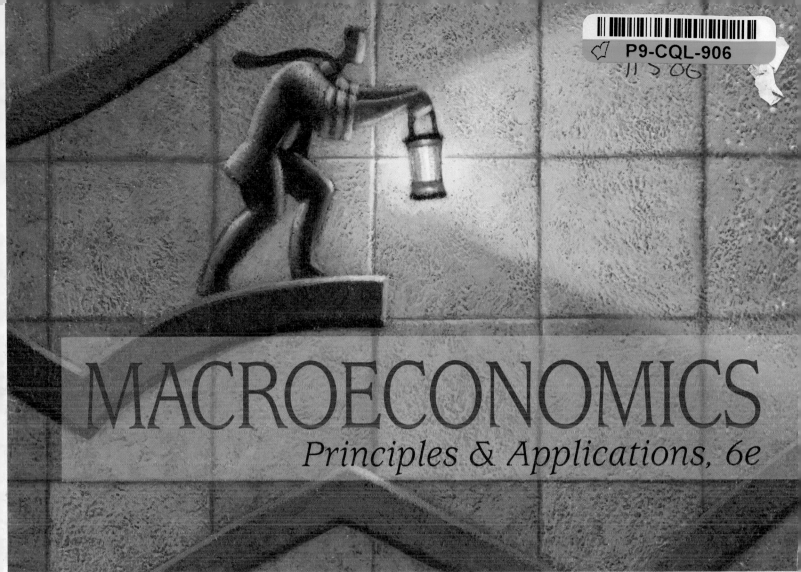

MACROECONOMICS
Principles & Applications, 6e

Robert E. **HALL**

Department of Economics, Stanford University

Marc **LIEBERMAN**

Department of Economics, New York University

SOUTH-WESTERN
CENGAGE Learning·

Australia · Brazil · Japan · Korea · Mexico · Singapore · Spain · United Kingdom · United States

SOUTH-WESTERN
CENGAGE Learning·

Macroeconomics: Principles & Applications, 6th Edition

Robert E. Hall and Marc Lieberman

Vice President of Editorial, Business: Jack W. Calhoun

Publisher: Joe Sabatino

Executive Editor: Michael Worls

Senior Developmental Editor: Susanna C. Smart

Senior Marketing Manager: John Carey

Senior Marketing Communications Manager: Sarah Greber

Senior Content Project Manager: Tim Bailey

Media Editor: Sharon Morgan

Manufacturing Planner: Kevin Kluck

Production Service: MPS Limited, a Macmillan Company

Senior Art Director: Michelle Kunkler

Cover and Internal Designer: jen2design

Cover Image: © Images.com/Corbis

Rights Acquisitions Specialist, Text: Deanna Ettinger

Rights Acquisitions Specialist, Text: Sam Marshall

For product information and technology assistance, contact us at **Cengage Learning Customer & Sales Support, 1-800-354-9706**

For permission to use material from this text or product, submit all requests online at **www.cengage.com/permissions**
Further permissions questions can be emailed to **permissionrequest@cengage.com**

Exam *View*® is a registered trademark of eInstruction Corp. Windows is a registered trademark of the Microsoft Corporation used herein under license.

Library of Congress Control Number: 2011941986

ISBN-13: 978-1-111-82235-4

ISBN-10: 1-111-82235-2

South-Western
5191 Natorp Boulevard
Mason, OH 45040
USA

Cengage Learning products are represented in Canada by Nelson Education, Ltd.

For your course and learning solutions, visit **www.cengage.com**

Purchase any of our products at your local college store or at our preferred online store **www.cengagebrain.com**

Printed in the United States of America
1 2 3 4 5 6 7 16 15 14 13 12

BRIEF CONTENTS

CONTENTS

© IMAGES.COM/CORBIS

Part III: Macroeconomics: Basic Concepts

Part IV: Long-Run Macroeconomics

Part V: The Short-Run Model and Fiscal Policy

Part VI: Expanding the Model: Money, Prices, and the Global Economy

Macroeconomics: Principles and Applications is about economic principles and how economists use them to understand the world. It was conceived, written, and for the sixth edition, substantially revised to help your students focus on those basic principles and applications.

We originally decided to write this book because we thought that existing texts tended to fall into one of three categories. In the first category are the encyclopedias—the heavy tomes with a section or a paragraph on every topic or subtopic you might possibly want to present to your students. These books are often useful as reference tools. But because they cover so many topics—many of them superficially—the central themes and ideas can be lost in the shuffle.

The second type of text we call the "scrapbook." In an effort to elevate student interest, these books insert multicolored boxes, news clippings, interviews, cartoons, and whatever else they can find to jolt the reader on each page. While these special features are often entertaining, there is a trade-off: These books sacrifice a logical, focused presentation of the material. Once again, the central themes and ideas are often lost.

Finally, a third type of text, perhaps in response to the first two, tries to do less in every area—a *lot* less. But instead of just omitting extraneous or inessential details, these texts often throw out key ideas, models, and concepts. Students who use these books may think that economics is overly simplified and unrealistic. After the course, they may be less prepared to go on in the field, or to think about the economy on their own.

A DISTINCTIVE APPROACH

Our approach is very different. We believe that the best way to teach principles is to present economics as a coherent, unified subject. This does not happen automatically. On the contrary, principles students often miss the unity of what we call "the economic way of thinking." The principles course then appears to be just "one thing after another," rather than the coherent presentation we aim for. For example, without proper guidance, students may view the analysis of goods markets, labor markets, and financial markets as entirely different phenomena, rather than as a repeated application of the same methodology with a new twist here and there.

CAREFUL FOCUS

Because we have avoided the encyclopedic approach, we have had to think hard about what topics are most important. As you will see:

We Avoid Nonessential Material

When we believed a topic was not essential to a basic understanding of economics, we left it out. However, we have striven to include core material to *support* an instructor who wants to present special topics in class. So, for example, we do not have separate chapters on environmental economics, agricultural economics, urban economics, health care economics, or comparative systems. But instructors should find in the text a good foundation for building any of these areas—and many others—into their courses. And we have included examples from each of these areas as *applications* of core theory where appropriate throughout the text.

We Avoid Distracting Features

This text does not have interviews, news clippings, or boxed inserts with only distant connections to the core material. The features your students *will* find in our book are there to help them understand and apply economic theory itself, and to help them avoid common mistakes in applying the theory (the Dangerous Curves feature).

We Explain Difficult Concepts Patiently

By freeing ourselves from the obligation to introduce every possible topic in economics, we can explain the topics we *do* cover more thoroughly and patiently. We lead students, step-by-step, through each aspect of theory, through each graph, and through each numerical example. In developing this book, we asked other experienced teachers to tell us which aspects of economic theory were hardest for their students to learn, and we have paid special attention to these trouble spots.

We Use Concrete Examples

Students learn best when they see how economics can explain the world around them. Whenever possible, we develop the theory using real-world examples. You will find numerous references to real-world corporations and government policies throughout the text. We often use real-world data on our conceptual graphs. When we employ hypothetical examples because they illustrate the theory more clearly, we try to make them realistic. In addition, almost every chapter ends with a thorough, extended application (the "Using the Theory" section) focusing on an interesting real-world issue.

FEATURES THAT REINFORCE

To help students see economics as a coherent whole, and to reinforce its usefulness, we have included some important features in this book.

The Three-Step Process

Most economists, when approaching a problem, begin by thinking about buyers and sellers, and the markets in which they come together to trade. They move on to characterize a market equilibrium, and then explore how the equilibrium changes when conditions change. To understand what economics is about, students need to understand this process and see it in different contexts. To help them do so, we have identified and stressed a "three-step process" that economists use in analyzing problems. The three key steps are:

1. **Characterize the Market.** Decide which market or markets best suit the problem being analyzed, and identify the decision makers (buyers and sellers) who interact there.
2. **Find the Equilibrium.** Describe the conditions necessary for equilibrium in the market, and a method for determining that equilibrium.
3. **Determine What Happens When Things Change.** Explore how events or government policies change the market equilibrium.

The steps themselves are introduced toward the end of Chapter 3. Thereafter, the content of most chapters is organized around this three-step process. We believe this helps students learn how to think like economists, and in a very natural way. And they come to see economics as a unified whole, rather than as a series of disconnected ideas.

Dangerous Curves

Anyone who teaches economics for a while learns that, semester after semester, students tend to make the same familiar errors. In class, in office hours, and on exams, students seem pulled, as if by gravity, toward certain logical pitfalls. We've discovered in our own classrooms that merely explaining the theory properly isn't enough; the most common errors need to be *confronted,* and the student needs to be shown *specifically* why a particular logical

path is incorrect. This was the genesis of our "Dangerous Curves" feature—boxes that anticipate the most common traps and warn students just when they are most likely to fall victim to them. We've been delighted to hear from instructors how effective this feature has been in overcoming the most common points of confusion for their students.

Using the Theory

This text is full of applications that are woven throughout the narrative. In addition, almost every chapter ends with an extended application ("Using the Theory") that pulls together several of the tools learned in that chapter. These are not news clippings or world events that relate only tangentially to the material. Rather, they are step-by-step presentations that are rich with real-world detail. The goal is to show students how the tools of economics can explain things about the world—things that would be difficult to explain without those tools.

Content Innovations

In addition to the special features just described, you will find some important differences from other texts in topical approach and arrangement. These, too, are designed to make the theory stand out more clearly, and to make learning easier. These are not pedagogical experiments, nor are they innovation for the sake of innovation. The differences you will find in this text are the product of years of classroom experience.

Scarcity, Choice, and Economic Systems (Chapter 2)

This early chapter, while covering standard material such as opportunity cost, also introduces some central concepts much earlier than other texts. Most importantly, it introduces the concept of *comparative advantage,* and the basic principle of *specialization and exchange.* We have placed them at the front of our book, because we believe they provide the foundation for understanding how economies are organized and what they accomplish.

Working with Supply and Demand (Chapter 4)

Our Chapter 4—in addition to analyzing price ceilings and floors—introduces two concepts not often found in principles texts, but which have become increasingly relevant. The first is how supply and demand can be used for *stock variables,* and not just flow variables. In the chapter, we treat housing as a stock variable, and then apply the model to the recent housing boom and bust. We also believe that teaching the stock-flow distinction early—with the rather intuitive case of housing—makes it easier to think about stock variables later, when students learn about the money market, the behavior of asset prices during the recent financial crisis, and the impact of falling asset prices on banks' balance sheets.

The second concept introduced in this chapter is *leverage*. Although it has been at the heart of recent economic turmoil, it has not been part of the traditional principles pedagogy. We've introduced leverage in a simple, intuitive way in the body of Chapter 4. We then delve a bit deeper in the short appendix to that chapter, which explains the concept of owners' equity (in a home), and presents a simple *leverage ratio* that students can work with. Teaching this concept early creates a fresh connection to current policy debates, and lays the foundation for later applications in the text. Students will see how leverage contributed to the recent housing boom and bust (in Chapter 4); the recession of 2008–2009 (Chapter 11); the problems of bank and non-bank insolvency (Chapter 13); and the Fed's response (Chapter 14).

Long-Run Macroeconomics (Chapters 8 and 9)

Our text presents long-run growth before short-run fluctuations. Chapter 8 develops the long-run, classical model at a level appropriate for introductory students, mostly using supply and demand. Chapter 9 then *uses* the classical model to explain the causes—and costs—of economic growth in both rich and poor countries. We believe it is better to treat the long run before the short run, for two reasons. First, the long-run model makes full use of the tools of supply and demand, and thus allows a natural transition from the preliminary chapters (1 through 4) into macroeconomics. Second, we believe that students can best understand economic fluctuations by understanding *how* and *why* the long-run model breaks down over shorter time periods. This, of course, requires an introduction to the long-run model first.

Economic Fluctuations (Chapter 10)

This unique chapter provides a bridge from the long-run to the short-run macro model, rather than just moving from one to the other with mere assertions about when they are used. This chapter explains *why* the long-run model doesn't work in the short run and paves the way for the short-run focus on spending as a driving force behind economic fluctuations.

Fiscal Policy (Chapter 12)

Our fiscal policy chapter confronts the debate over fiscal stimulus head on, treating both short-run and long-run controversies as seen by mainstream economists. Discussions of fiscal policy can easily become a thicket of confusion. We've tried to organize the material coherently to ensure that students can understand the issues at stake, and we use real-world data to enrich the theory.

Money, Banks, and the Federal Reserve (Chapter 13)

This chapter on the financial system is unusual in two respects. First, we put more emphasis on balance sheets and bank solvency than most other texts. This enables students to understand the financial crisis, and provides an important bridge from the principles class to the ongoing debate about financial system reform. Second, we introduce the "shadow banking system," and carefully explain its role in the crisis.

Monetary Policy (Chapter 14 & 16)

We've divided our presentation of monetary policy into two chapters. This first one (Chapter 14) begins by presenting the traditional money market analysis, but quickly shifts to a more modern approach that de-emphasizes money and focuses on *interest rates*. We pay particular attention to unconventional policy at the zero lower bound. We also discuss the central problem of interest rate spreads without (we hope) adding undue complexity. In a second chapter (Chapter 16: Inflation and Monetary Policy), we go deeper, with discussions about hawks versus doves, monetary policy with ongoing inflation, and asset bubbles.

Aggregate Demand and Aggregate Supply (Chapter 15)

One of our pet peeves about some introductory texts is the too-early introduction of aggregate demand and aggregate supply curves, *before* teaching where these curves come from. Students then confuse the *AD* and *AS* curves with their microeconomic counterparts, requiring corrective action later. In this text, the *AD* and *AS* curves do not appear until Chapter 15, where they are fully explained. Our treatment of aggregate supply is based on a very simple mark-up model that our students have found easy to understand.

Exchange Rates and Macroeconomic Policy (Chapter 17)

Many students find international macroeconomics the most interesting topic in the course, especially the material on exchange rates and what causes them to change. Accordingly, you will find unusually full coverage of exchange rate determination in this chapter. This treatment is kept simple and straightforward, relying exclusively on supply and demand. And it forms the foundation for the discussion of the trade deficit that ends the chapter.

ORGANIZATIONAL FLEXIBILITY

We have arranged the contents of each chapter, and the table of contents as a whole, according to our recommended order of presentation. But we have also built in flexibility.

- Instructors wishing to move rapidly to macro models— and willing to spend less time on macroeconomic measurement issues—can cut large chunks of material out of Chapter 6 (Production and Employment) and Chapter 7 (The Price Level and Inflation) with no loss of continuity. The only *essential* requirements for later chapters are the identity of output and income in Chapter 6, and translating nominal to real variables in Chapter 7.

- Instructors who would like to move rapidly to the short-run model can skip (or postpone) Chapter 9 (Economic Growth) without any loss of continuity. And for those who want to *sprint* to the short run, Chapters 8, 9, and 10 could all be moved toward the end of the course. (In the latter case, students will come across occasional references to Chapters 8 and 10 in the chapters that follow, but they will still have all the analytical tools necessary to keep moving forward.)

Finally, we have included only those chapters that we thought were both essential and teachable in a year-long course. But not everyone will agree about what is essential. While we—as authors—cringe at the thought of a chapter being omitted in the interest of time, we have allowed for that possibility. Nothing in Chapter 9 (Economic Growth), Chapter 10 (Economic Fluctuations), Chapter 16 (Inflation and Monetary Policy), or Chapter 17 (Exchange Rates and Macroeconomic Policy) is essential to any of the other chapters in the book. Skipping any of these should not cause continuity problems.

NEW TO THE SIXTH EDITION

Our previous (fifth) edition was our most significant revision yet. This will not surprise anyone who was teaching an economics principles course during or after September 2008, when the financial crisis hit its peak. One of us (Lieberman) was teaching macro principles at the time and had the daily task of integrating the flood of unprecedented events into the course. When the semester was over, the two of us thought long and hard about what worked, what didn't, and how the principles course—both micro and macro—should respond to the changes we had seen.

In planning this new edition, we were gratified that the major pedagogical changes we had made in the fifth edition still seemed, in retrospect, to be the right ones. So you will not find any radical changes in approach this time. For faculty preparing lectures, this will be welcome news: Very few adjustments will be needed to present core concepts and models. For students, however, we think this revision will make a huge difference.

Our main goal in this edition was to provide students with a *smoother ride* through the text. Valuable suggestions from dozens of users—both instructors and students—were incorporated into every chapter. We paid particular attention to sections that were bogging students down, either deleting them or clarifying them. Many sections were rewritten from scratch to introduce a more careful, step-by-step approach. We removed some of the more complex Dangerous Curves boxes, trimmed down many others, and added about a dozen new ones. And, of course, we brought our examples and Using the Theory sections up to date, to engage with recent economic events.

Changes That May Be of Interest

Aside from the general updating and streamlining mentioned above, we want to call attention to a few changes that *might* affect lectures for some instructors.

Chapter 2 has a new section on markets, ownership, and the invisible hand, as well as a discussion of mixed economies. Chapter 3's Using the Theory section on oil markets is now a much simpler supply-and-demand analysis.

Chapter 6 (Production and Employment) includes new material on alternative labor market measures and some simplifications of GDP measurement. We've also dealt with the endless confusion over the term "recession" by introducing a new bolded term, *slump*, for periods of below-normal output. In our textbook, a recession is a contraction.

Chapter 10 (Economic Fluctuations) reorganizes some of the material on why the classical model cannot explain recessions, and adds a discussion of downward wage rigidity. Chapter 11 (The Short-Run Macro Model) has a brief discussion of Keynesian equilibrium with services, developed further in an end-of-chapter problem. Those who prefer to dispense with inventories entirely might want to reframe Keynesian equilibrium using this approach.

In Chapter 12 (Fiscal Policy), apart from the obvious revisions based on recent fiscal developments, we've changed a few topics. In the short-run section, we've added material on the balanced-budget multiplier, and we've relegated Ricardian equivalence to an end-of-chapter problem. In the long-run section, we've streamlined our discussion of long-run fiscal burdens, and we've made extensive use of some new terms (*debt ratio*, *burden of the debt*, and *basic debt guideline*).

Chapter 13 (Money, Banks, and the Federal Reserve) has one major pedagogical change: When explaining changes in the money supply, we've abandoned our experiment with the "one-bank town," and returned to the story where reserves flow from bank to bank (although in a clearer way than in previous editions). We've also moved our general discussion of the shadow banking system into the body of the chapter, focusing the Using the Theory on the financial crisis itself.

In Chapter 14 (Monetary Policy), we've been careful to introduce the distinction between nominal and real interest rates, which better prepares students for unconventional policy at the zero lower bound. And we've replaced the appendix on feedback effects with a briefer discussion in the chapter, followed up with optional end-of-chapter problems.

In Chapter 15 (Aggregate Demand and Aggregate Supply), we've been more careful to explain the constant-money-supply assumption behind the *AD* curve, and to put that assumption in context. Interest rate targeting (already discussed in Chapter 14) is brought back into the *AS-AD* model in Chapter 16 (Inflation and Monetary Policy).

Chapter 17 (Exchange Rates and Macroeconomic Policy) includes new material on the euro and the recent crisis in the euro zone.

Finally, for those who incorporate the end-of-chapter problems into their courses, we should point out that these, too, have undergone changes: Some deleted, and dozens substantially revised or entirely new.

For the Instructor

- The *Instructor's Manual* is revised by Dell Champlin, Oregon State University. The manual provides chapter outlines, teaching ideas, experiential exercises for many chapters, and solutions to all end-of-chapter problems.
- The *Instructor Companion Site* on the *Product Support Web Site*. This site at **http://login.cengage.com** features the essential resources for instructors, password-protected, in downloadable format: the *Instructor's Manual* in Word, the test banks in Word, and PowerPoint lecture and exhibit slides.
- The *Macroeconomics Test Bank* is revised by Kenneth Slaysman of York College of Pennsylvania. It contains more than 2,500 multiple-choice questions. The test questions have been arranged according to chapter headings and subheadings, making it easy to find the material you need to construct examinations.
- *ExamView Computerized Testing Software.* Exam-View is an easy-to-use test creation package compatible with both Microsoft Windows and Macintosh client software, and it contains all of the questions in all of the printed test banks. You can select questions by previewing them on the screen, by number, or randomly. Questions, instructions, and answers can be edited, and new questions can easily be added.
- *PowerPoint Lecture and Exhibit Slides.* Available on the Web site and the IRCD, the PowerPoint presentations are revised by Andreea Chiritescu, Eastern Illinois University. These consist of speaking points in chapter outline format, accompanied by numerous key graphs and tables from the main text, many

with animations to show movement of demand and supply curves.

- *CengageCompose.* With CengageCompose, you can create your own print text to meet specific course learning objectives. Gather what you need from our vast library of market-leading course books and enrichment content, or add original material. Build your book the way you want it organized, personalized to your students. Publish your title with easy-to-use tools that guarantee you will get what you designed. For more information, contact your sales rep or go to **http://www.cengage.com/custom/**
- *WebTutor Toolbox.* WebTutor Toolbox provides instructors with links to content from the book companion Web site. It also provides rich communication tools to instructors and students, including a course calendar, chat, and e-mail. For more information about the WebTutor products, please contact your local Cengage sales representative.
- *CengageNOW* Ensure that your students have the understanding they need of procedures and concepts they need to know with CengageNOW. This integrated, online course management and learning system combines the best of current technology to save time in planning and managing your course and assignments. You can reinforce comprehension with customized student learning paths and efficiently test and automatically grade assignments with reports that correspond to AACSB standards. For your convenience, CengageNOW is also compatible with WebCT® and Blackboard®. For more information, visit **http://cengage.com/cengagenow.**

For the Student

- *Hall/Lieberman CourseMate* Multiple resources for learning and reinforcing principles concepts are now available in one place!

CourseMate is your one-stop shop for the learning tools and activities to help students succeed. Available for a minimal additional cost, CourseMate provides a wealth of resources that help study and apply economic concepts. As students read and study the chapters, they can access video tutorials with *Ask the Instructor Videos.* They can review with *Flash Cards* and the *Graphing Workshop,* as well as check their understanding of the chapter with *interactive quizzing.*

CourseMate gives you BBC News videos, Econ-News articles, Economic Debates, Links to Economic Data, and more, organized by chapter to help your students get the most from *Macroeconomics:*

Principles and Applications, sixth edition, and from your lectures.

Students can access CourseMate through Cengagebrain at **www.cengagebrain.com.**

- *Global Economic Watch.* A global economic crisis need not be a teaching crisis.

Students can now learn economic concepts through examples and applications using the most current information on the global economic situation. The Global Economic Resource Center includes:

- A 32-page eBook that gives a general overview of the events that led up to the current situation, written by Mike Brandl of the University of Texas, Austin
- A Blog and Community Site updated daily by an economic journalist and designed to allow you and your colleagues to share thoughts, ideas, and resources
- Thousands of articles from leading journals, news services, magazines, and newspapers revised four times a day and searchable by topic and key term
- Student and instructor resources such as Power-Point® decks, podcasts, and videos
- Assessment materials allowing you to ensure student accountability

This resource can be bundled at no charge with this textbook. Visit **www.cengage.com/thewatch** for more information.

- *Tomlinson Economics Videos.* "Like Office Hours 24/7" Award winning teacher, actor, and professional communicator, Steven Tomlinson (PhD, economics, Stanford) walks students through all of the topics covered in principles of economics in an online video format. Segments are organized to follow the organization of the Hall/Lieberman text and most videos include class notes that students can download and quizzes to test their understanding. Find out more at **www.cengage.com/economics/tomlinson.**
- *Aplia.* Founded in 2000 by economist and Stanford professor Paul Romer, Aplia is dedicated to improving learning by increasing student effort and engagement. The most successful online product in economics by far, Aplia has been used by more than 1,000,000 students at more than 850 institutions. Visit **www.aplia.com/cengage** for more details. For help, answers, or a live demonstration, please contact Aplia at **support@aplia.com.**

ACKNOWLEDGMENTS

Our greatest debt is to the many reviewers who carefully read the book and provided numerous suggestions for improvements. While we could not incorporate all their ideas, we did carefully evaluate each one of them. We are especially grateful to the participants in our survey who helped us with the revision for this sixth edition. To all of these people, we are most grateful:

Sindy Abadie	Southwest Tennessee Community College
Eric Abrams	Hawaii Pacific University
Ljubisa Adamovich	Florida State University
Mehdi. Afiat	College of Southern Nevada
Brian A'Hearn	Franklin and Marshall College
Ali Akarca	University of Illinois, Chicago
Rashid Al-Hmoud	Texas Tech University
David Aschauer	Bates College
Richard Ballman	Augustana College
Gayle Bolash	Kent State University
James T. Bang	Virginia Military Institute
Chris Barnett	Gannon University
Parantap Basu	Fordham University
Tom Bernardin	Smith College
Tibor Besedes	Rutgers University
Gautam Bhattacharya	University of Kansas
Maharukh Bhiladwalla	New York University
Margot B. Biery	Tarrant County College
Edward Blackburne	Sam Houston State University
Sylvain Boko	Wake Forest University
Barry Bomboy	J. Sargeant Reynolds Community College
John L. Brassel	Southwest Tennessee Community College
Bruce Brown	Cal Poly Pomona and Santa Monica College
Mark Buenafe	Arizona State University
Steven Call	Metropolitan State College
Dell Champlin	Oregon State University
Kevin Carey	American University
Cheryl Carleton	Villanova University
Siddharth Chandra	University of Pittsburgh
Steven Cobb	Xavier University
Christina Coles	Johnson & Wales University
Maria Salome E. Davis	Indian River State College
Dennis Debrecht	Carroll College
Arthur M. Diamond, Jr.	University of Nebraska, Omaha
Selahattin Dibooglu	University of St. Louis, Missouri
James E. Dietz	California State University, Fullerton
Ferdinand DiFurio	Tennessee Tech University
Erol Dogan	New York University
Khosrow Doroodian	Ohio University

John Duffy	University of Pittsburgh
Debra S. Dwyer	SUNY, Stony Brook
Stephen Erfle	Dickinson College
Barry Falk	Iowa State University
James Falter	Mount Mary College
Sasan Fayazmanesh	California State University, Fresno
William Field	DePauw University
Lehman B. Fletcher	Iowa State University
Richard Fowles	University of Utah
Mark Frascatore	Clarkson College
Mark Funk	University of Arkansas at Little Rock
James R. Gale	Michigan Technological University
Sarmila Ghosh	University of Scranton
Satyajit Ghosh	University of Scranton
Michelle Gietz	Southwest Tennessee Community College
Scott Gilbert	Southern Illinois University, Carbondale
Susan Glanz	St. John's University
Michael J. Gootzeit	University of Memphis
John Gregor	Washington and Jefferson University
Jeff Gropp	DePauw University
Arunee C. Grow	Mesa Community College
Ali Gungoraydinoglu	The University of Mississippi
Rik Hafer	Southern Illinois University
Robert Herman	Nassau Community College
Michael Heslop	Northern Virginia Community College
Paul Hettler	California University of Pennsylvania
Roger Hewett	Drake University
Andrew Hildreth	University of California, Berkeley
Nathan Himelstein	Essex County College
Stella Hofrenning	Augsburg College
Shahruz Hohtadi	Suffolk University
Daniel Horton	Cleveland State
Jack W. Hou	California State University-Long Beach
Ann Horn-Jeddy	Medaille College
Thomas Husted	American University
Jeffrey Johnson	Sullivan University
James Jozefowicz	Indiana University of Pennsylvania
Jack Julian	Indiana University of Pennsylvania
Farrokh Kahnamoui	Western Washington University
Leland Kempe	California State University, Fresno
Jacqueline Khorassani	Marietta College
Philip King	San Francisco State University
Scott Kjar	University of Minnesota Duluth
Frederic R. Kolb	University of Wisconsin, Eau Claire
Kate Krause	University of New Mexico
Brent Kreider	Iowa State University
Eric R. Kruger	Thomas College
Viju Kulkarni	San Diego State University
Matthew Lang	Xavier University
Nazma Latif-Zaman	Providence College
Teresa Laughlin	Palomar College
Bruce Madariaga	Montgomery College
Judith Mann	University of California, San Diego
Thomas McCaleb	Florida State University
Mark McCleod	Virginia Tech University
Michael McGuire	University of the Incarnate Word
Steve McQueen	Barstow Community College
William R. Melick	Kenyon College
Arsen Melkumian	West Virginia University
Samuel Mikhail	Indian River State College
Frank Mixon	University of Southern Mississippi
Shahruz Mohtadi	Suffolk University
Gary Mongiovi	St. John's University
Joseph R. Morris	Broward Community College-South Campus
Paul G. Munyon	Grinnell College
Rebecca Neumann	University of Wisconsin, Milwaukee
Chris Niggle	University of Redlands
Emmanuel Nnadozie	Truman State University
Nick Noble	Miami University, Ohio
Farrokh Nourzad	Marquette University
Lee Ohanian	University of California, Los Angeles
Andrew Paizis	New York University
Jim Palmieri	Simpson College
Zaohong Pan	Western Connecticut State University
Yvon Pho	American University
Thomas Pogue	University of Iowa
Gregg Pratt	Mesa Community College
Scott Redenius	Bryn Mawr College
Michael Reksulak	Georgia Southern University

Teresa Riley — Youngstown State University
William Rosen — Cornell University
Alannah Rosenberg — Saddleback College
Jeff Rubin — Rutgers University
Rose Rubin — University of Memphis

Thomas Sadler — Pace University
Jonathan Sandy — University of San Diego
Ramazan Sari — Texas Tech University
Mustafa Sawani — Truman State University
Edward Scahill — University of Scranton
Robert F. Schlack — Carthage College
Pamela M. Schmitt — U.S. Naval Academy
Mary Schranz — University of Wisconsin, Madison
Gerald Scott — Florida Atlantic University
Peter M. Shaw — Tidewater Community College
Alden Shiers — California Polytechnic State University

William Shughart — University of Mississippi
Kevin Siqueira — Clarkson University
William Doyle Smith — University of Texas, El Paso
Kevin Sontheimer — University of Pittsburgh
Mark Steckbeck — Campbell University
Richard Steinberg — Indiana University, Purdue University, Indianapolis
K. Strong — Baldwin-Wallace College
Martha Stuffler — Irvine Valley College
Mohammad Syed — Miles College

Manjuri Talukdar — Northern Illinois University
Kiril Tochkov — Binghamton University

John Vahaly — University of Louisville
Mikayel Vardanyan — Oregon State University

Thomas Watkins — Eastern Kentucky University
Hsinrong Wei — Baruch College, CUNY
Toni Weiss — Tulane University
Robert Whaples — Wake Forest University
Glen Whitman — California State University, Northridge
Michael F. Williams — University of St. Thomas
Melissa Wiseman — Houston Baptist University

Dirk Yandell — University of San Diego

Petr Zemcik — Southern Illinois University, Carbondale
Xiaodan Zhao — College of Saint Benedict and Saint John's University

We appreciate their input.

We also wish to acknowledge the talented and dedicated group of instructors who helped put together a supplementary package that is second to none. Dell Champlin, Oregon State University, revised the *Instructor's Manual,* and the test banks were carefully revised by Kenneth Slaysman of York College of Pennsylvania.

The beautiful book you are holding would not exist except for the hard work of a talented team of professionals. Book production was overseen by Tim Bailey, senior content project manager at Cengage Learning South-Western and undertaken by Lindsay Schmonsees, project manager at MPS Content Services. Tim and Lindsay showed remarkable patience, as well as an unflagging concern for quality throughout the process. We couldn't have asked for better production partners. Three former NYU students helped to locate and fix the few remaining errors: Madeline Merin, Joshua Savitt, and Matthew Weiner. The overall look of the book and cover was planned by Michelle Kunkler and executed by Jennifer Lambert. Deanna Ettinger managed the photo program, and Kevin Kluck made all the pieces come together in his role as manufacturing planner. We are especially grateful for the hard work of the dedicated and professional South-Western editorial, marketing, and sales teams. Mike Worls, executive editor, has once again shepherded this text through publication with remarkable skill and devotion. John Carey, senior marketing manager, has done a first-rate job getting the message out to instructors and sales reps. Susan Smart, who has been senior development editor on several editions, once again delved into every chapter and contributed to their improvement. She showed her typical patience, flexibility, and skill in managing both content and authors. Sharon Morgan, media editor, has put together a wonderful package of media tools, and the Cengage Learning South-Western sales representatives have been extremely persuasive advocates for the book. We sincerely appreciate all their efforts!

A Request

Although we have worked hard on the six editions of this book, we know there is always room for further improvement. For that, our fellow users are indispensable. We invite your comments and suggestions wholeheartedly. We especially welcome your suggestions for additional "Using the Theory" sections and Dangerous Curves. You may send your comments to either of us in care of South-Western.

Robert E. Hall

Marc Lieberman

© IMAGES.COM/CORBIS

Robert E. Hall

© SUSAN WOODWARD

Robert E. Hall is the Robert and Carole McNeil Joint Professor of Economics at Stanford University and Senior Fellow at Stanford's Hoover Institution. His research focuses on the overall performance of the U.S. economy, including unemployment, capital formation, financial activity, and inflation. He has served as president, vice president, and Ely Lecturer of the American Economic Association and is a Distinguished Fellow of the association. Hall is an elected member of the National Academy of Sciences and Fellow of the American Academy of Arts and Sciences, the Society of Labor Economists, and the Econometric Society. He is director of the Research Program on Economic Fluctuations and Growth of the National Bureau of Economic Research. He was a member of the National Presidential Advisory Committee on Productivity. For further information about his academic activities, visit his Stanford Web site by googling "Robert E. Hall."

Marc Lieberman

© GEOFF JEHLE/MARC LIEBERMAN

Marc Lieberman is Clinical Professor of Economics at New York University. He received his PhD from Princeton University. Lieberman has taught graduate and undergraduate courses in microeconomics, macroeconomics, econometrics, labor economics, and international economics. He has taught Principles of Economics at Harvard, Vassar, the University of California at Santa Cruz, the University of Hawaii, and New York University. He has won NYU's Golden Dozen teaching award three times, and also the Economics Society Award for Excellence in Teaching. He was coeditor and contributor to *The Road to Capitalism: Economic Transformation in Eastern Europe and the Former Soviet Union*. Lieberman has consulted for Bank of America and for the Educational Testing Service. In his spare time, he is a professional screenwriter, and teaches screenwriting at NYU's School of Continuing and Professional Studies.

CHAPTER 1

What Is Economics?

© ISTOCKPHOTO.COM/JOŠT GANTAR

conomics. The word conjures up all sorts of images: manic stock traders on Wall Street, an economic summit meeting in a European capital, an earnest television news anchor announcing good or bad news about the economy. . . . You probably hear about economics several times each day. What exactly *is* economics?

First, economics is a *social science.* It seeks to explain something about *society,* just like other social sciences, such as psychology, sociology, and political science. But economists generally ask different questions about society than other social scientists do, such as:

- Why are some countries poor and others rich? How can we help the worst-off countries escape extreme poverty?

- When a nation is struck by a natural disaster—such as a hurricane or earthquake—how are people's jobs, incomes, and living standards affected?

- Why do Americans who graduate from college earn so much more than those who don't?

- What determines how much we pay for the things we buy every month? What happens when governments try to change these prices?

- Why do the prices of financial assets like stocks, bonds, and foreign currency fluctuate so widely? Can these price movements be predicted?

- What causes economies to occasionally go haywire, suffering months or years of falling production and sustained joblessness? How should governments respond?

In this book, you'll learn how economics can help us answer these and many other questions. You'll also see that the answers share a common starting point: an exploration of how individuals and societies make decisions when they are faced with scarcity.

In fact, a good definition of economics, which stresses its differences from other social sciences, is:

> *Economics is the study of choice under conditions of scarcity.*

Economics The study of choice under conditions of scarcity.

This definition may appear strange to you. Where are the familiar words we ordinarily associate with economics: "money," "stocks and bonds," "prices," "budgets," and so on? As you will soon see, economics deals with all of these things and more. But first, let's take a closer look at two important ideas in this definition: scarcity and choice.

1

SCARCITY AND INDIVIDUAL CHOICE

Think for a moment about your own life. Is there anything you don't have that you'd *like* to have? Anything you'd like *more* of? If your answer is "no," congratulations! You are well advanced on the path of Zen self-denial. The rest of us, however, feel the pinch of limits to our material standard of living. This simple truth is at the very core of economics. It can be restated this way: We all face the problem of **scarcity**.

Scarcity A situation in which the amount of something available is insufficient to satisfy the desire for it.

At first glance, it may seem that you suffer from an infinite variety of scarcities. There are so many things you might like to have right now—a larger room or apartment, a new car, more clothes . . . the list is endless. But a little reflection suggests that your limited ability to satisfy these desires is based on two more basic limitations: scarce *time* and scarce *spending power*.

> As individuals, we face a scarcity of time and spending power. Given more of either, we could each have more of the goods and services that we desire.

The scarcity of spending power is no doubt familiar to you. We've all wished for higher incomes so that we could afford to buy more of the things we want. But the scarcity of time is equally important. So many of the activities we enjoy—seeing movies, taking vacations, making phone calls—require time as well as money. Just as we have limited spending power, we also have a limited number of hours in each day to satisfy our desires.

Because of the scarcities of time and spending power, each of us is forced to make *choices*. We must allocate our scarce *time* to different activities: work, play, education, sleep, shopping, and more. We must allocate our scarce *spending power* among different goods and services: housing, food, furniture, travel, and many others. And each time we choose to buy something or do something, we also choose *not* to buy or do something else.

In fact, what we choose *not* to buy or do—"the road not taken" as the poet Robert Frost put it—leads to an interesting way of thinking about *cost*.

The Concept of Opportunity Cost

What does it cost you to go to the movies? If you answered 9 or 10 dollars because that is the price of a movie ticket, then you are leaving out a lot. Most of us are used to thinking of "cost" as the money we must pay for something. Certainly, the money we pay for goods or services is a *part* of its cost. But economics takes a broader view of costs. The true cost of any choice we make—buying a car, reading a book, or even taking a nap—is everything we must *give up* when we make that choice. This cost is called the *opportunity cost* of the choice because we give up the opportunity to enjoy other desirable things or experiences.

Opportunity cost What is given up when taking an action or making a choice.

> The **opportunity cost** of any choice is what we must forego when we make that choice.

Opportunity cost is the most accurate and complete concept of cost—the one we should use when making our own decisions or analyzing the decisions of others.

Suppose, for example, it's 8 P.M. on a weeknight, and you're spending a couple of hours reading this chapter. As authors, that thought makes us very happy.

We know there are many other things you could be doing: going to a movie, having dinner with friends, playing ping-pong, earning some extra money, watching TV. . . . But—assuming you're still reading and haven't run out the door because we've given you better ideas—let's relate this to opportunity cost.

What *is* the opportunity cost of reading this chapter? Is it *all* of those other possibilities we've listed? Not really, because in the time it takes to read this chapter, you'd probably be able to do only *one* of those other activities. You'd no doubt choose whichever one you regarded as best. So, by reading, you sacrifice only the *best* choice among the alternatives that you could be doing instead.

> *When the alternatives to a choice are mutually exclusive, only the next best choice—the one that would actually be chosen—is used to determine the opportunity cost of the choice.*

For many choices, the opportunity cost consists mostly of the money you actually pay out. If you spend $100 on a new pair of shoes, the most important thing you give up is $100, which is money you could spend on something else. But for other choices, money payments may be only a small part, or no part, of what is sacrificed. Doing a spring cleaning of your home, for example, will take you a lot of time, but very little money.

Economists often attach a monetary value to the time that we give up for a choice. This allows us to express a choice's opportunity cost in dollars—the number of dollars actually paid out plus the dollar value of the time given up. To see how this works, let's see how we might calculate the opportunity cost (in dollars) of an important choice you've already made: to attend college.

An Example: The Opportunity Cost of College

What is the opportunity cost of attending college for an academic year (9 months)? A good starting point is to look at the actual monetary costs—the annual out-of-pocket expenses borne by you or your family. Table 1 shows the College Board's estimates of these expenses for the average student (ignoring scholarships). For example, the third column of the table shows that the average in-state resident at a four-year state college pays $7,605 in tuition and fees, $1,137 for books and supplies, $8,535 for room and board, and $3,062 for transportation and other expenses, for a total of $20,339 per year.

TABLE 1

Average Out-of-Pocket Cost of a Year of College, 2010–2011

Type of Institution	Two-Year Public	Four-Year Public	Four-Year Private
Tuition and fees	$2,713	$7,605	$27,293
Books and supplies	$1,133	$1,137	$1,181
Room and board	$7,259	$8,535	$9,700
Transportation and other expenses	$3,532	$3,062	$2,302
Total out-of-pocket costs	$14,637	$20,339	$40,476

Source: *Trends in College Pricing*, 2010, The College Board, New York, NY.

Notes: Averages are enrollment-weighted by institution to reflect the average experience among students across the United States. Average tuition and fees at public institutions are for in-state residents only. Room and board charges are for students living on campus at four-year institutions and off-campus (but not with parents) at two-year institutions. Four-year private includes nonprofit only.

So, is that the average opportunity cost of a year of college at a public institution? Not really. Even if that is the amount you or your family actually pays out for college, this is not the dollar measure of the opportunity cost.

First, the $20,339 your family pays in this example most likely includes some expenses that are *not* part of the opportunity cost of college. These are payments you'd make whether or not you were in college. Let's suppose that if you *didn't* go to college, you would have lived in an apartment, and your expenses for rent and food would be equal to their college amounts: $8,535. Let's also suppose that you'd have transportation and other expenses equal to their college amounts: $3,062. Then these payments must be deducted from the opportunity cost of choosing college. Table 2 shows that when we deduct these payments, we're left with the additional dollars you pay out of pocket *because* you chose to attend college: $8,742. These dollars—spent on tuition and fees and books and supplies—are the only part of your money payments that are part of the opportunity cost. Money payments that are part of opportunity cost are called **explicit costs**. So your explicit costs of attending college are $8,742.

But college also has **implicit costs**—sacrifices for which no money changes hands. The biggest sacrifice in this category is *time*. But what is that time worth? That depends on what you *would* be doing if you weren't in school. For many students, the alternative would be working full-time at a job. If you are one of these students, attending college requires the sacrifice of the income you *could* have earned at a job—a sacrifice we call *foregone income*.

How much income is foregone when you go to college for a year? In 2010, the average yearly income of an 18- to 24-year-old high school graduate who worked full-time was about $24,000. If we assume that only nine months of work must be sacrificed to attend college (that is, you'd still work full-time in the summer), then foregone income is about 3/4 of $24,000, or $18,000. This is the implicit cost of a year of college.

Summing the explicit and implicit costs gives us a rough estimate of the opportunity cost of a year in college, as shown in Table 2. For a public institution, we have $8,742 in explicit costs and $18,000 in implicit costs, giving us an opportunity cost of $26,742 per year. Notice that this is even greater than the total charges estimated by the College Board we calculated earlier. When you consider this opportunity cost for four years, its magnitude might surprise you. Without financial aid in the form of tuition grants or other fee reductions, the average in-state resident will sacrifice about $107,000 over four years at a state college. At a private college, we'd find (using calculations similar to those in Table 2) a total opportunity cost of about $186,000.

Explicit cost The dollars sacrificed—and actually paid out—for a choice.

Implicit cost The value of something sacrificed when no direct payment is made.

TABLE 2

Sample Opportunity Cost Calculation for In-State Public University

Total out-of-pocket payments:	**$20,339**	
minus $\begin{cases} \text{out-of-pocket expenses} \\ \text{you'd have without college} \end{cases}$	− $8,535 (room and board)	
	− $3,062 (transportation and other)	
= **Explicit cost of college**	= **$8,742**	
plus implicit cost	+ $18,000 (9 months foregone income)	
= **Opportunity cost of 1 year of college**	= **$26,742**	

FIGURE 1 | Education, Earnings and Employment

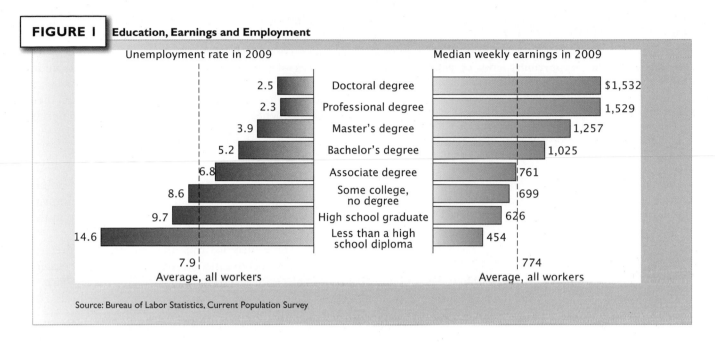

Unemployment rate in 2009		Median weekly earnings in 2009
2.5	Doctoral degree	$1,532
2.3	Professional degree	1,529
3.9	Master's degree	1,257
5.2	Bachelor's degree	1,025
6.8	Associate degree	761
8.6	Some college, no degree	699
9.7	High school graduate	626
14.6	Less than a high school diploma	454
7.9 Average, all workers		774 Average, all workers

Source: Bureau of Labor Statistics, Current Population Survey

Our analysis of the opportunity cost of college is an example of a general, and important, principle:

The opportunity cost of a choice includes both explicit costs and implicit costs.

A Brief Digression: Is College the Right Choice?

Before you start questioning your choice to be in college, there are a few things to remember. First, for many students, scholarships reduce the costs of college to less than those in our example. Second, in addition to its high cost, college has substantial *benefits*, including financial ones.

Figure 1 shows two examples of these financial benefits for the year 2009. The right side of the figure shows that full-time workers with bachelor's degrees earned substantially higher incomes ($1,025 per week) than those with only a high-school diploma ($626 per week). Moreover, as seen in the left side, college graduates were more likely to find full-time jobs; the unemployment rate of those with bachelor's degrees (5.2%) was substantially lower than for high-school graduates (9.7%). These advantages in earnings and employment prospects are seen year after year, in good times and bad. In spite of its high cost, attending college appears to be one of the best *financial* investments you can make.[1]

Finally, remember that we've left out of our discussion many non-financial benefits of attending college. These may be harder to estimate in dollar terms, but they could be very important to you. Do you enjoy taking classes and learning new things more than you'd enjoy working at the job you would have gotten

[1] If you are studying microeconomics, you'll learn more about the value of college as an investment and how economists value future earnings in a later chapter.

© SUSAN VAN ETTEN (BASED ON AN IMAGE IN ECONOCLASS.COM © LORI ALDEN, 2005)

WHAT'S WRONG WITH THIS PICTURE?

We're sending some money to you!

50 CENTS CASH BACK

OFFICAL REBATE MAIL-IN REDEMPTION FORM

Please complete the following information:
Name_____
Address:_____
City:_____State:_____Zip:_____

Please mail this card along with the original UPC code and a copy of the receipt to the address on the back. Please allow 6-8 weeks to receive your rebate check.

⚠ DANGEROUS CURVES

If you think the opportunity cost of your time is zero . . . What if you can't work extra hours for additional pay, so you cannot *actually* turn time into money? Does this mean that the opportunity cost of your time is zero?

If you think the answer is yes, the authors of this textbook would like to hire you for help with some household chores for 25 cents per hour. Does this sound like a good deal to you? It would, if the opportunity cost of your time really had no value. If it doesn't sound like a good deal, then the time you'd be giving up must have some positive value to you. If pressed, you could state that value in money terms—and it would no doubt exceed 25 cents per hour.

© AXL/SHUTTERSTOCK.COM

instead? Do you have a more interesting social life in college than you'd otherwise have? In the future, will you get more satisfaction—above and beyond the extra earnings—from the jobs that will become available to you because of your college degree?

If you answered yes to any of these questions, then the full benefits of college are greater than the purely financial gains.

Time Is Money

Our analysis of the opportunity cost of college points out a general principle, one understood by economists and non-economists alike. It can be summed up in the expression, "Time is money."

For some people, this maxim applies directly: When they spend time on something, they *actually* give up money—money they *could* have earned during that time. Consider Jessica, a freelance writer with a backlog of projects on which she can earn $25 per hour. For each hour Jessica spends *not* working, she sacrifices $25.

What if Jessica decides to see a movie? What is the opportunity cost in dollar terms? Suppose the ticket costs $10, and the entire activity takes three hours—including time spent getting there and back. And suppose that working is Jessica's next best alternative to seeing the movie. The opportunity cost is the sum of the explicit cost ($10 for the ticket) and the implicit cost ($75 for three hours of forgone income), making the total opportunity cost $85.

The idea that a movie "costs" $85 might seem absurd to you. But if you think about it, $85 is a much better estimate than $10 of what the movie actually costs Jessica. To see the movie, Jessica does indeed sacrifice $85.

Our examples about the cost of college and the cost of a movie point out an important lesson about opportunity cost:

> *The explicit (direct money) cost of a choice may only be a part—and sometimes a small part—of the opportunity cost of a choice.*

SCARCITY AND SOCIAL CHOICE

Now let's think about scarcity and choice from *society's* point of view. What are the goals of our society? We want a high standard of living for our citizens, clean air, safe streets, good schools, and more. What is holding us back from accomplishing all of these goals in a way that would satisfy everyone? You already know the answer: scarcity. In society's case, the problem is a scarcity of **resources**—the things we use to make goods and services that help us achieve our goals.

Resources The labor, capital, land (including natural resources), and entrepreneurship that are used to produce goods and services.

The Four Resources

Resources are the most basic elements used to make goods and services. We can classify resources into four categories:

Labor The time human beings spend producing goods and services.

- **Labor**—the time human beings spend producing goods and services.
- **Capital**—any long-lasting tool that is itself produced and helps us make other goods and services.

Capital A long-lasting tool that is used to produce other goods.

More specifically, **physical capital** consists of things like machinery and equipment, factory buildings, computers, and even hand-tools like hammers and screwdrivers. These are all long-lasting *physical* tools that we produce to help us make other goods and services.

Another type of capital is **human capital**—the skills and knowledge possessed by workers. These satisfy our definition of capital: They are *produced* (through education and training), they help us produce *other* things, and they last for many years, typically through an individual's working life.

Note the word *long-lasting* in the definition. If something is used up quickly in the production process—like the flour a baker uses to make bread—it is generally *not* considered capital. A good rule of thumb is that capital should last at least a year, although most types of capital last considerably longer.

The **capital stock** is the total amount of capital at a nation's disposal at any point in time. It consists of all the capital—physical and human—created in previous periods that is still productively useful.

- **Land**—the physical space on which production takes place, as well as the useful materials—*natural resources*—found under it or on it, such as crude oil, iron, coal, or fertile soil.
- **Entrepreneurship**—the ability (and the willingness to *use* it) to combine the *other* resources into a productive enterprise. An entrepreneur may be an *innovator* who comes up with an original idea for a business or a *risk taker* who provides her own funds or time to nurture a project with uncertain rewards.

Anything *produced* in the economy comes, ultimately, from some combination of these four resources.

Think about the last lecture you attended at your college. Some resources were used *directly*: Your instructor's labor and human capital (his or her knowledge of economics); physical capital (the classroom building, a blackboard or projector); and land (the property on which your classroom building sits). Somebody played the role of entrepreneur, bringing these resources together to create your college in the first place. (If you attend a public institution, the entrepreneurial role was played by your state government.)

Many other inputs—besides those special inputs we call resources—were also used to produce the lecture. But these other inputs were themselves produced from resources, as illustrated in Figure 2. For example, the electricity used to power the lights in your classroom is an input, not a resource. But electricity is itself produced from resources, including crude oil, coal, or natural gas (land and natural resources); coal miners or oil riggers (labor); and electricity-generating turbines and power cables (capital).

Opportunity Cost and Society's Trade-offs

For an individual, opportunity cost arises from the scarcity of time and money. But for society as a whole, opportunity cost arises from the scarcity of *resources*. Our desire for goods is limitless, but we have limited resources to produce them. Therefore,

> *virtually all production carries an opportunity cost: To produce more of one thing, society must shift resources away from producing something else.*

© AXL/SHUTTERSTOCK.COM

Physical capital The part of the capital stock consisting of physical goods, such as machinery, equipment, and factories.

Human capital The skills and training of the labor force.

Capital stock The total amount of capital in a nation that is productively useful at a particular point in time.

Land The physical space on which production takes place, as well as the natural resources that come with it.

Entrepreneurship The ability and willingness to combine the *other* resources—labor, capital, and land—into a productive enterprise.

Input Anything (including a resource) used to produce a good or service.

DANGEROUS CURVES

Resources versus inputs The term *resources* is often confused with another more general term—**inputs**. An input is *anything* used to make a good or service. Inputs include not only resources but also many other things made from them (cement, rolled steel, electricity), which are, in turn, used to make goods and services. *Resources*, by contrast, are the *special* inputs that fall into one of four categories: labor, land, capital, and entrepreneurship. They are the ultimate source of everything that is produced.

FIGURE 2   Resources and Production

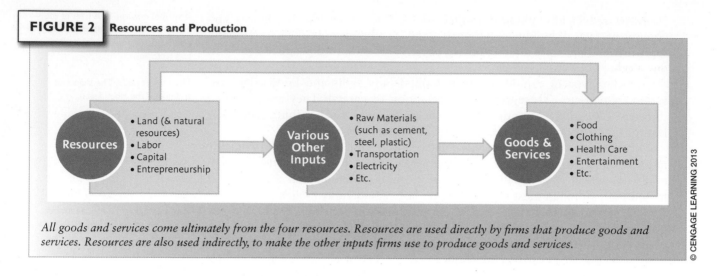

All goods and services come ultimately from the four resources. Resources are used directly by firms that produce goods and services. Resources are also used indirectly, to make the other inputs firms use to produce goods and services.

For example, we'd all like better health for our citizens. What would be needed to achieve this goal? Perhaps more frequent medical checkups for more people and greater access to top-flight medicine when necessary. These, in turn, would require more and better-trained doctors (labor and human capital), and more hospital buildings, laboratories, and high-tech medical equipment (physical capital). In order to produce more health care, we would have to pull resources—land, labor, capital, and entrepreneurship—out of producing other things that we also enjoy. We'd have more health care, but fewer movies, personal computers, cars, or other goods and services that would otherwise have been produced. The opportunity cost of improved health care, then, consists of those other goods and services we would have to do without.

THE WORLD OF ECONOMICS

The field of economics is surprisingly broad. It ranges from the mundane (why does a pound of steak cost more than a pound of chicken?) to the personal (how do couples decide how many children to have?) to the profound (could we ever have another Great Depression in the United States, with tens of millions plunged into sudden poverty?). With a field this broad, it is useful to have some way of classifying the different types of problems economists study and the different methods they use to analyze them.

Microeconomics and Macroeconomics

Microeconomics The study of the behavior of individual households, firms, and governments; the choices they make; and their interaction in specific markets.

The field of economics is divided into two major parts: microeconomics and macroeconomics. **Microeconomics** comes from the Greek word *mikros*, meaning "small." It takes a close-up view of the economy, as if looking through a microscope. Microeconomics is concerned with the behavior of *individual* actors on the economic scene—households, business firms, and governments. It looks at the choices they make and how they interact with each other when they come together to trade *specific* goods and services. What will happen to the cost of movie tickets over the next five years? How many management-trainee jobs will open up for college graduates? These are microeconomic questions because they analyze individual *parts* of an economy rather than the *whole*.

Macroeconomics—from the Greek *makros*, or "large"—takes an *overall* view of the economy. Instead of focusing on the production of carrots or computers, macroeconomics lumps all goods and services together and looks at the economy's *total output*. Instead of focusing on employment of management trainees or manufacturing workers, it considers *total employment* in the economy. Macroeconomics focuses on the big picture and ignores the fine details.

Macroeconomics The study of the behavior of the overall economy.

Positive and Normative Economics

The micro versus macro distinction is based on the level of detail we want to consider. Another useful distinction has to do with our *purpose* in analyzing a problem. **Positive economics** explains how the economy works, plain and simple. If someone says, "The decline in home prices during 2008 and 2009 was a major cause of the recent recession," he or she is making a positive economic statement. A statement need not be accurate or even sensible to be classified as positive. For example, "Government policy has no effect on our standard of living" is a statement that virtually every economist would regard as false. But it is still a positive economic statement. Whether true or not, it's about how the economy works and its accuracy can be tested by looking at the facts—and just the facts.

Positive economics The study of how the economy works.

Normative economics *prescribes solutions* to economic problems. It goes beyond just "the facts" and tells us what we should *do* about them. Normative economics requires us to make judgments about different outcomes and therefore depends on our values.

Normative economics The practice of recommending policies to solve economic problems.

If an economist says, "We should cut total government spending," he or she is engaging in normative economic analysis. Cutting government spending would benefit some citizens and harm others, so the statement rests on a value judgment. A normative statement—like "We should cut government spending"—cannot be proved or disproved by the facts alone.

Positive and normative economics are intimately related in practice. For one thing, we cannot properly argue about what we should or should not do unless we know certain facts about the world. Every normative analysis is therefore based on an underlying positive analysis. And a new understanding of positive economics often changes one's views on normative economics.

Why Economists Disagree about Policy

Suppose the country is suffering from a serious recession—a significant, nationwide decrease in production and employment. Two economists are interviewed on a cable news show.

Economist A says, "We should increase government spending on roads, bridges, and other infrastructure. This would directly create jobs and help end the recession." Economist B says, "No, we should cut taxes instead. This will put more money in the hands of households and businesses, leading them to spend more and create jobs that way." Why do they disagree?

The disagreement might be based on *positive* economics—different views about how the economy works. Economist A might think that government spending will create more jobs, dollar for dollar,

© AXL/SHUTTERSTOCK.COM

DANGEROUS CURVES ⚠️

Seemingly positive statements Be alert to statements that may *seem* purely positive, but contain hidden value judgments. Here's an example: "If we want to reduce greenhouse gas emissions, our society will have to use less gasoline." This may *sound* positive because it seems to refer only to a fact about the world. But it's also at least partly normative. Why? Cutting back on gasoline is just *one* policy among many that could reduce emissions. To say that we *must* choose this method makes a value judgment about its superiority to other methods. A purely positive statement on this topic would be, "Using less gasoline—with no other change in living habits—would reduce greenhouse gas emissions."

Similarly, be alert to statements that use vague terms that hide value judgments. An example: "All else equal, the less gasoline we use, the better our quality of life." Whether you agree or disagree, this is *not* a purely positive statement. People will disagree over the meaning of the phrase "quality of life" and what would make life better. This disagreement could not be resolved just by looking at the facts.

than will tax cuts. Economist B might believe the reverse. Positive differences like these can arise because our knowledge of how the economy works—while always improving—remains imperfect.

But the disagreement might also stem from a difference in values—specifically, what each economist believes about government's proper role in the economy. Those toward the left of the political spectrum tend to believe that government should play a larger economic role. They tend to view increases in government spending more favorably. Those toward the political right tend to believe that government's role should be smaller. They would prefer tax cuts that result in more private, rather than government, spending. This difference in values can explain why two economists—even if they have the same *positive* views about the outcome of a policy—might disagree about its wisdom.

> *Policy differences among economists arise from (1) positive disagreements (about the outcomes of different policies), and (2) differences in values (how those outcomes are evaluated).*

Policy disputes among economists are common. But on *some* policy issues, most economists agree. For example, in microeconomics there is wide agreement that certain types of goods and services should be provided by private business firms and that certain others are best provided by government.

In macroeconomics, almost all economists agree that some of the government policies during the Great Depression of the 1930s were mistakes that worsened and prolonged the economic downturn. When U.S. and global economies sank into a deep recession in 2008 and 2009, many feared a repeat of the Great Depression. Economists had some important disagreements about what the initial response of the U.S. and other governments should be. But they were virtually united in warning against repeating the mistakes of the 1930s.

Most governments heeded these warnings. Although the economic slump continued through 2010 and into 2011, another Great Depression was avoided. You will learn more about these areas of agreement among economists—as well as some important disagreements—in the chapters to come.

WHY STUDY ECONOMICS?

If you've read this far into the chapter, chances are you've already decided to allocate some of your scarce time to studying economics. We think you've made a wise choice. But it's worth taking a moment to consider what you might gain from this choice.

Why study economics?

To Understand the World Better

Applying the tools of economics can help you understand global and catastrophic events such as wars, famines, epidemics, and depressions. But it can also help you understand much of what happens to you locally and personally—the salary you will earn after you graduate or the rent you'll pay on your apartment. Economics has the power to help us understand these phenomena because they result, in large part, from the choices we make under conditions of scarcity.

Economics has its limitations, of course. But it is hard to find any aspect of life about which economics does not have *something* important to say. Economics cannot explain why so many Americans like to watch television, but it *can* explain how TV networks decide which programs to offer. Economics cannot protect you from a robbery, but it *can* explain why some people choose to become thieves and why no society has chosen to eradicate crime completely. Economics will not improve your love life, resolve unconscious conflicts from your childhood, or help you overcome a fear of flying, but it *can* tell us how many skilled therapists, ministers, and counselors are available to help us solve these problems.

To Achieve Social Change

If you are interested in making the world a better place, economics is indispensable. There is no shortage of serious social problems worthy of our attention—unemployment, hunger, poverty, disease, climate change, drug addiction, violent crime. Economics can help us understand the origins of these problems, explain why previous efforts to solve them haven't succeeded, and help us to design new, more effective solutions.

To Help Prepare for Other Careers

Economics has long been a popular college major for individuals intending to work in business. But it has also been popular among those planning careers in politics, international relations, law, medicine, engineering, psychology, and other professions. This is for good reason: Practitioners in each of these fields often find themselves confronting economic issues. For example, lawyers increasingly face judicial rulings based on the principles of economic efficiency. And doctors need to understand how new technologies or changes in health care policy can affect their practices.

To Become an Economist

Only a tiny minority of this book's readers will decide to become economists. This is welcome news to the authors, and after you have studied labor markets in your *microeconomics* course you will understand why. But if you do decide to become an economist—obtaining a master's degree or a PhD—you will find many possibilities for employment. The economists with whom you have most likely had personal contact are those who teach and conduct research at colleges and universities. But as many economists work outside of colleges and universities as work inside them. Economists are hired by banks to assess the risk of investing abroad; by manufacturing companies to help them determine new methods of producing, marketing, and pricing their products; by government agencies to help design policies to fight crime, disease, poverty, and pollution; by international organizations to help create and reform aid programs for less developed countries; by the media to help the public interpret global, national, and local events; and by nonprofit organizations to provide advice on controlling costs and raising funds more effectively.

THE METHODS OF ECONOMICS

One of the first things you will notice as you begin to study economics is the heavy reliance on *models*.

You have no doubt encountered many models in your life. As a child, you played with model trains, model planes, or model people (dolls). You may have also seen architects' cardboard models of buildings. These are all physical models, three-dimensional replicas that you can pick up and hold. Economic models, by contrast, are built with words, diagrams, and mathematical statements.

What, exactly, is a model?

> A *model* is an abstract representation of reality.

Model An abstract representation of reality.

The two key words in this definition are *abstract* and *representation*. A model is not supposed to be exactly like reality. Rather, it *represents* reality by *abstracting* or *taking from* the real world. By including some—but not all—of the details of the real world, a model helps us understand the world more clearly.

The Art of Building Economic Models

When you build a model, how do you know which real-world details to include and which to leave out? There is no simple answer to this question. The right amount of detail depends on your purpose in building the model in the first place. There is, however, one guiding principle:

> *A model should be as simple as possible to accomplish its purpose.*

This means that a model should contain only the *necessary* details.

To understand this a little better, think about a map. A map is a model that represents a part of the earth's surface. But it leaves out many details of the real world. First, a map leaves out the third dimension—height—of the real world. Second, maps always ignore small details, such as trees and houses and potholes. But when you download a map, how much detail do you want it to have?

Suppose you're in Columbus, Ohio, and you want to drive from Port Columbus International Airport to the downtown convention center. You will need a zoomed-in, detailed street map, as on the left side of Figure 3. The zoomed-out highway map on the right doesn't show any streets, so it wouldn't do at all.

But if you instead wanted to find the best driving route from Columbus to Boston, you would want to zoom out to the highway map. The view with individual streets would have too much detail and be harder to use.

The same principle applies in building economic models. The level of detail that would be just right for one purpose will usually be too much or too little for another. When you feel yourself objecting to an economic model because something has been left out, keep in mind the purpose for which the model is built. In introductory economics, the purpose is entirely educational—to help you understand some simple yet powerful principles about how the economy operates. Keeping the models simple makes it easier to see these principles at work and remember them later.

FIGURE 3 | **Maps as Models**

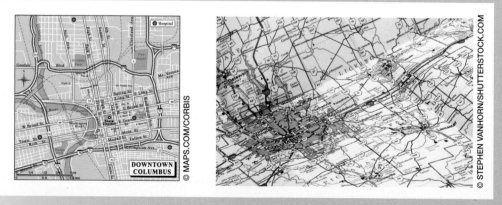

These maps are models. But each would be used for a different purpose.

Assumptions and Conclusions

Every economic model makes two types of assumptions: *simplifying* assumptions and *critical* assumptions.

A **simplifying assumption** is just what it sounds like—a way of making a model simpler without affecting any of its important conclusions. A road map, for example, makes the simplifying assumption, "There are no trees." Having trees on a map would only get in the way. Similarly, in an economic model, we might assume that there are only two goods that households can choose from or that there are only two nations in the world. We make such assumptions *not* because we think they are true, but because they make a model easier to follow and do not change any of the important insights we can get from it.

A **critical assumption**, by contrast, is an assumption that affects the conclusions of a model in important ways. When you use a road map, you make the critical assumption, "All of these roads are open." If that assumption is wrong, your conclusion—the best route to take—might be wrong as well.

In an economic model, there are always one or more critical assumptions. You don't have to look very hard to find them because economists like to make them explicit right from the outset. For example, when we study the behavior of business firms, our model will assume that firms try to earn the highest possible profit for their owners. By stating this critical assumption up front, we can see immediately where the model's conclusions spring from.

Simplifying assumption Any assumption that makes a model simpler without affecting any of its important conclusions.

Critical assumption Any assumption that affects the conclusions of a model in an important way.

Math, Jargon, and Other Concerns

Economists often express their ideas using mathematical concepts and a special vocabulary. Why? Because these tools enable economists to express themselves more precisely than with ordinary language. For example, when conflict raged across Libya in early 2011, someone who never studied economics might say, "Oil prices rose because there was a shortage of oil." That statement might not bother you right now. But in a few weeks, you'll be saying it something like this: "Oil prices rose because the supply curve for oil shifted leftward, while the demand curve continued to shift rightward."

Does the second statement sound strange to you? It should. First, it uses special terms—*demand curve* and *supply curve*—that you've yet to learn. Second, it uses a mathematical concept—*shifting curves*—with which you might not be familiar. But the first statement might mean a number of different things, some of which were *not* true at the time. The second statement—as you will see in Chapter 3—can mean only *one* thing. By being precise, we can steer clear of unnecessary confusion.

If you are worried about the special vocabulary of economics, you can relax. After all, you may never have heard the term "opportunity cost" before, but now you know what it means. New terms will be defined and carefully explained as you encounter them. Indeed, this textbook does not assume you have any special knowledge of economics. It is truly meant for a "first course" in the field.

But what about the math? Here, too, you can relax. While professional economists often use sophisticated mathematics to solve problems, only a little math is needed to understand basic economic *principles*. And virtually all of this math comes from high-school algebra and geometry.

Still, if you have forgotten some of your high-school math, a little brushing up might be in order. This is why we have included an appendix at the end of this chapter. It covers some of the most basic concepts—such as interpreting graphs, the equation for a straight line, and the concept of a slope—that you will need in this course. You may want to glance at this appendix now, just so you'll know what's there. Then, from time to time, you can go back to it when you need it.

HOW TO STUDY ECONOMICS

As you read this book or listen to your instructor, you may find yourself following along and thinking that everything makes perfect sense. Economics may even seem easy. Indeed, it *is* rather easy to *follow* economics, as it's based so heavily on simple logic. But *following* and *learning* are two different things. You will eventually discover (preferably *before* your first exam) that to learn economics, you must study it actively, not passively.

If you are reading these words while you are lying back on a comfortable couch, a phone in one hand and a remote in the other, you are going about it in the wrong way. Active studying means reading with a pencil in your hand and a blank sheet of paper in front of you. It means closing the book periodically and *reproducing* what you have learned. It means listing the steps in each logical argument, retracing the flow of cause and effect in each model, and drawing the graphs. It does require some work, but the payoff is a good understanding of economics and a better understanding of your own life and the world around you.

SUMMARY

Economics is the study of choice under conditions of scarcity. As individuals—and as a society—we have unlimited desires for goods and services. Unfortunately, our ability to satisfy those desires is limited, so we must usually sacrifice something for any choice we make.

The correct measure of the cost of a choice is not just the money price we pay, but the *opportunity cost*: what we must give up when we make a choice.

At the individual level, opportunity cost arises from the scarcity of time or money. For society as a whole, it arises from the scarcity of *resources*. The four types of resources are *land, labor, capital,* and *entrepreneurship*. All of the *inputs* we use to produce goods and services are either resources themselves or are made from resources. Therefore, to produce and enjoy more of one thing, society must shift resources away from producing something else. Every

society must choose which desires to satisfy and how to satisfy them. Economics provides the tools that explain those choices.

The field of economics is divided into two major areas. *Microeconomics* studies the behavior of individual households, firms, and governments as they interact in specific markets. *Macroeconomics*, by contrast, concerns itself with the behavior of the entire economy. It considers variables such as total output and total employment.

Economics makes heavy use of *models*—abstract representations of reality—to help us understand how the economy operates. All models are simplifications, but a good model will have just enough detail for the purpose at hand. The *simplifying* assumptions in a model just make it easier to use. The *critical* assumptions are the ones that affect the model's conclusions.

PROBLEM SET

Answers to even-numbered Problems can be found on the text Web site through www.cengagebrain.com

1. Discuss whether each statement is a purely positive statement, or whether it also contains normative elements and/or value judgments:
   a. An increase in the personal income tax will slow the growth rate of the economy.
   b. The goal of any country's economic policy should be to increase the well-being of its poorest, most vulnerable citizens.
   c. The best way to reduce the national poverty rate is to increase the federal minimum wage.

   d. The 1990s were a disastrous decade for the U.S. economy. Income inequality increased to its highest level since before World War II.

2. For each of the following, state whether economists would consider it a *resource*, and, if they would, identify which of the four types of resources the item is.
   a. A computer used by an FBI agent to track the whereabouts of suspected criminals.
   b. The office building in which the FBI agent works.

c. The time that an FBI agent spends on a case.
d. A farmer's tractor.
e. The farmer's knowledge of how to operate the tractor.
f. Crude oil.
g. A package of frozen vegetables.
h. A food scientist's knowledge of how to commercially freeze vegetables.
i. The ability to bring together resources to start a frozen-food company.
j. Plastic bags used by a frozen-food company to hold its product.

3. Suppose you are using the second map in Figure 3, which shows main highways only. You've reached a conclusion about the best way to drive from the Columbus city center to an area south of the city. State whether each of the following assumptions of the map would be a *simplifying* or *critical* assumption for your conclusion, and explain briefly. (Don't worry about whether the assumption is true or not.)
   a. The thicker numbered lines are major highways without traffic lights.
   b. The earth is two-dimensional.
   c. When two highways cross, you can get from one to the other without going through city traffic.
   d. Distances on the map are proportional to distances in the real world.

4. Suppose that you are considering what to do on an upcoming weekend. Here are your options, from least to most preferred: (1) study for upcoming midterms; (2) fly to Colorado for a quick ski trip; (3) go into seclusion in your dorm room and try to improve your score on a computer game. What is the opportunity cost of a decision to play the computer game all weekend? (Your answer will not be in dollars.)

5. Use the information in Table 1 (as well as the assumption about foregone income made in the chapter) to calculate the average opportunity cost of a year in college for a student at a four-year private institution under each of the following special assumptions:
   a. The student receives free room and board at home at *no* opportunity cost to the parents.
   b. The student receives an academic scholarship covering all tuition and fees (in the form of a grant, not a loan or a work-study aid).
   c. The student works half-time while at school (assume for this problem that the leisure or study time sacrificed has no opportunity cost).

6. Use the information in Table 1 (as well as the assumption about foregone income made in the chapter) to compare the opportunity cost of attending a year of college for a student at a two-year public college, under each of the following special assumptions:
   a. The student receives free room and board at home at *no* opportunity cost to the parents.
   b. The student receives an academic scholarship covering all tuition and fees (in the form of a grant, not a loan or a work-study aid).
   c. The student works half-time while at school (assume for this problem that the leisure or study time sacrificed has no opportunity cost).

TABLES AND GRAPHS

A brief glance at this text will tell you that graphs are important in economics. Graphs provide a convenient way to display information and enable us to immediately *see* relationships between variables.

Suppose that you've just been hired at the advertising department of Len & Harry's—an up-and-coming manufacturer of high-end ice cream products located in Texas. You've been asked to compile a report on how advertising affects the company's sales. It turns out that the company's spending on advertising has changed repeatedly in the past, so you have lots of data on monthly advertising expenditure and monthly sales revenue, both measured in thousands of dollars.

Table A.1 shows a useful way of arranging this data. The company's advertising expenditures in different months are listed in the left-hand column, while the right-hand column lists total sales revenue ("sales" for short) during the same months. Notice that the data in this table is organized so that spending on advertising increases as we move down the first column. Often, just looking at a table like this can reveal useful patterns. In this example, it's clear that higher spending on advertising is associated with higher monthly sales. These two variables—advertising and sales—have a *positive relationship*. A rise in one is associated with a rise in the other. If higher advertising had been associated with *lower* sales, the two variables would have a *negative* or *inverse relationship*: A rise in one would be associated with a fall in the other.

We can be even more specific about the positive relationship between advertising and sales: Logic tells us that the association is very likely *causal*. We'd expect that sales revenue *depends on* advertising outlays, so we call sales our *dependent variable* and advertising our *independent variable*. Changes in an independent variable cause changes in a dependent variable, but not the other way around.

To explore the relationship further, let's graph it. As a rule, the *independent* variable is measured on the *horizontal* axis and the *dependent* variable on the *vertical* axis. In economics, unfortunately, we do not always stick to this rule, but for now we will. In Figure A.1, monthly advertising expenditure—our independent variable—is measured on the horizontal axis. If we start at the *origin*—the corner where the two axes intersect—and move rightward along the horizontal axis, monthly advertising spending increases from $0 to $1,000 to $2,000 and so on. The vertical axis measures monthly sales—the dependent variable. Along this axis, as we move upward from the origin, sales rise.

The graph in Figure A.1 shows six labeled points, each representing a different pair of numbers from our table. For example, point *A*—which represents the numbers in the first row of the table—shows us that when

TABLE A.1		
Advertising and Sales at Len & Harry's	**Advertising Expenditures ($1,000 per Month)**	**Sales ($1,000 per Month)**
	2	24
	3	27
	6	36
	7	39
	11	51
	12	54

FIGURE A.1 | **A Graph of Advertising and Sales**

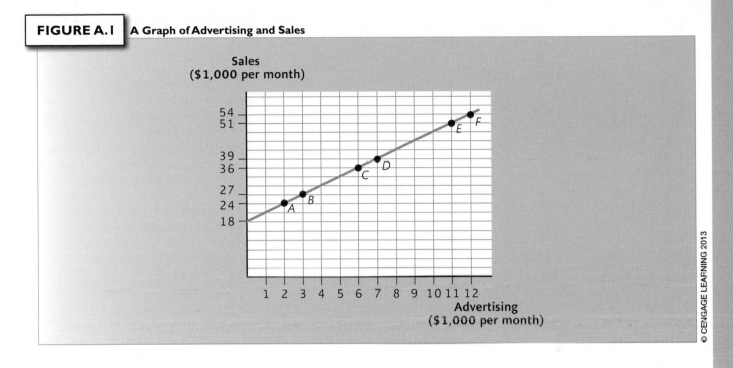

the firm spends $2,000 on advertising, sales are $24,000 per month. Point B represents the *second* row of the table, and so on. Notice that all of these points lie along a *straight line*.

Straight-Line Graphs

You'll encounter straight-line graphs often in economics, so it's important to understand one special property they possess: The "rate of change" of one variable compared with the other is always the same. For example, look at what happens as we move from point A to point B: Advertising rises by $1,000 (from $2,000 to $3,000), while sales rise by $3,000 (from $24,000 to $27,000). If you study the graph closely, you'll see that anywhere along this line, whenever advertising increases by $1,000, sales increase by $3,000. Or, if we define a "unit" as "one thousand dollars," we can say that every time advertising increases by one unit, sales rise by three units. So the "rate of change" is three units of sales for every one unit of advertising.

The rate of change of the *vertically* measured variable for a one-unit change in the *horizontally* measured variable is also called the *slope* of the line. The slope of the line in Figure A.1 is three, and it remains three no matter where along the line we measure it. For example, make sure you can see that from point C to point D, advertising rises by one unit and sales rise by three units.

What if we had wanted to determine the slope of this line, by comparing points D and E which have advertising rising by four units instead of just one? In that case, we'd have to calculate the rise in one variable *per unit* rise in the other. To do this, we divide the change in the vertically measured variable by the change in the horizontally measured variable.

$$\text{Slope of a straight line} = \frac{\text{Change in vertical variable}}{\text{Change in horizontal variable}}.$$

We can make this formula even simpler by using two shortcuts. First, we can call the variable on the vertical axis "Y" and the variable on the horizontal axis "X." In our case, Y is sales, while X is spending on advertising. Second, we use the Greek letter Δ ("delta") to denote the words "change in." Then, our formula becomes:

$$\text{Slope of a straight line} = \frac{\Delta Y}{\Delta X}.$$

Let's apply this formula to get the slope as we move from point D to point E, so that advertising (X) rises from 7 units to 11 units. This is an increase of 4, so $\Delta X = 4$. For this move, sales rise from 39 to 51, an increase of 12, so $\Delta Y = 12$. Applying our formula,

$$\text{Slope} = \frac{\Delta Y}{\Delta X} = \frac{12}{4} = 3.$$

This is the same value for the slope that we found earlier. Not surprising, since it's a straight line and a straight line has the same slope everywhere. The particular pair of points we choose for our calculation doesn't matter.

Curved Lines

Although many of the relationships you'll encounter in economics have straight-line graphs, many others do not. Figure A.2 shows *another* possible relationship between advertising and sales that we might have found from a different set of data. As you can see, the line is curved. But as advertising rises, the curve gets flatter and flatter. Here, as before, each time we spend another $1,000 on advertising, sales rise. But now, the rise in sales seems to get smaller and smaller. This means that the *slope* of the curve is *itself changing* as we move along this curve. In fact, the slope is getting smaller.

How can we measure the slope of a curve? First, note that since the slope is different at every point along the curve, we aren't really measuring the slope of "the curve" but the slope of the curve *at a specific point along it*. How can we do this? By drawing a *tangent line*—a straight line that touches the curve at just one point and that has the same slope as the curve at that point. For example, in the figure, a tangent line has been drawn for point B. To measure the slope of this tangent line, we can compare any two points on it, say, H and B, and calculate the slope as we would for any straight line. Moving from point H to point B, we are moving from 0 to 3 on the horizontal axis ($\Delta X = 3$) and from 21 to 27 on the vertical axis ($\Delta Y = 6$). Thus, the slope of the tangent line—which is the same as the slope of the curved line at point B—is

$$\frac{\Delta Y}{\Delta X} = \frac{6}{3} = 2$$

This says that, at point B, the rate of change is two units of sales for every one unit of advertising. Or, going back to dollars, the rate of change is $2,000 in sales for every $1,000 spent on advertising.

The curve in Figure A.2 slopes everywhere upward, reflecting a positive relationship between the variables. But a curved line can also slope downward

---

FIGURE A.2 | **Measuring the Slope of a Curve**

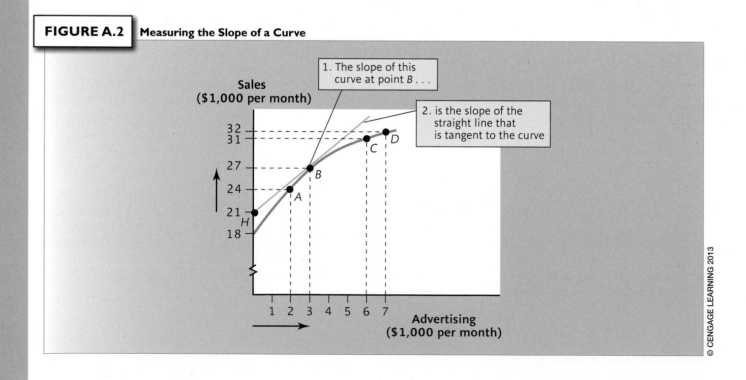

© CENGAGE LEARNING 2013

to illustrate a negative relationship between variables, or it can slope first one direction and then the other. You'll see plenty of examples of each type of curve in later chapters, and you'll learn how to interpret each one as it's presented.

LINEAR EQUATIONS

Let's go back to the straight-line relationship between advertising and sales, as shown in Table A.1. What if you need to know how much in sales the firm could expect if it spent $5,000 on advertising next month? What if it spent $8,000 or $9,000? It would be nice to be able to answer questions like this without having to pull out tables and graphs to do it. As it turns out, anytime the relationship you are studying has a straight-line graph, it is easy to figure out an equation for the entire relationship—a *linear equation*. You then can use the equation to answer any such question that might be put to you.

All straight lines have the same general form. If Y stands for the variable on the vertical axis and X for the variable on the horizontal axis, every straight line has an equation of the form

$$Y = a + bX,$$

where a stands for some number and b for another number. The number a is called the vertical *intercept* because it marks the point where the graph of this equation hits (intercepts) the vertical axis; this occurs when X takes the value zero. (If you plug $X = 0$ into the equation, you will see that, indeed, $Y = a$.) The number b is the slope of the line, telling us how much Y will change every time X changes by one unit. To confirm this, note that when $X = 0$, the equation tells us that $Y = a$. When $X = 1$, it tells us that $Y = a + b$. So as X increases from 0 to 1, Y goes from a to $a + b$. The number b is therefore the change in Y corresponding to a one-unit change in X—exactly what the slope of the graph should tell us.

If b is a positive number, a one-unit increase in X causes Y to *increase* by b units, so the graph of our line would slope upward, as illustrated by the line in the upper left panel of Figure A.3. If b is a negative number, then a one-unit increase in X will cause Y to *decrease* by b units, so the graph would slope downward, as the line does in the lower left panel. Of course, b could equal zero. If it does, a one-unit increase in X causes no change

in Y, so the graph of the line is flat, like the line in the middle left panel.

The value of a has no effect on the slope of the graph. Instead, different values of a determine the graph's position. When a is a positive number, the graph will intercept the vertical Y-axis above the origin, as the line does in the upper right panel of Figure A.3. When a is negative, however, the graph will intercept the Y-axis *below* the origin, as the line in the lower right panel does. When a is zero, the graph intercepts the Y-axis right at the origin, as the line does in the middle right panel.

Let's see if we can figure out the equation for the relationship depicted in Figure A.1. There, X denotes advertising and Y denotes sales. Earlier, we calculated that the slope of this line, b, is 3. But what is a, the vertical intercept? In Figure A.1, you can see that when advertising outlays are zero, sales are $18,000. That tells us that $a = 18$. Putting these two observations together, we find that the equation for the line in Figure A.1 is

$$Y = 18 + 3X.$$

Now if you need to know how much in sales to expect from a particular expenditure on advertising (both in thousands of dollars), you would be able to come up with an answer: You'd simply multiply the amount spent on advertising by 3, add 18, and that would be your sales in thousands of dollars. To confirm this, plug in for X in this equation any amount of advertising in dollars from the left-hand column of Table A.1. You'll see that you get the corresponding amount of sales in the right-hand column.

HOW STRAIGHT LINES AND CURVES SHIFT

So far, we've focused on relationships where some variable Y depends on a single other variable X. But in many of our theories, we recognize that some variable of interest to us is actually affected by more than just one other variable. When Y is affected by both X and some third variable, changes in that third variable will usually cause a *shift* in the graph of the relationship between X and Y. This is because whenever we draw the graph between X and Y, we are holding fixed every other variable that might possibly affect Y.

FIGURE A.3 Straight Lines with Different Slopes and Vertical Intercepts

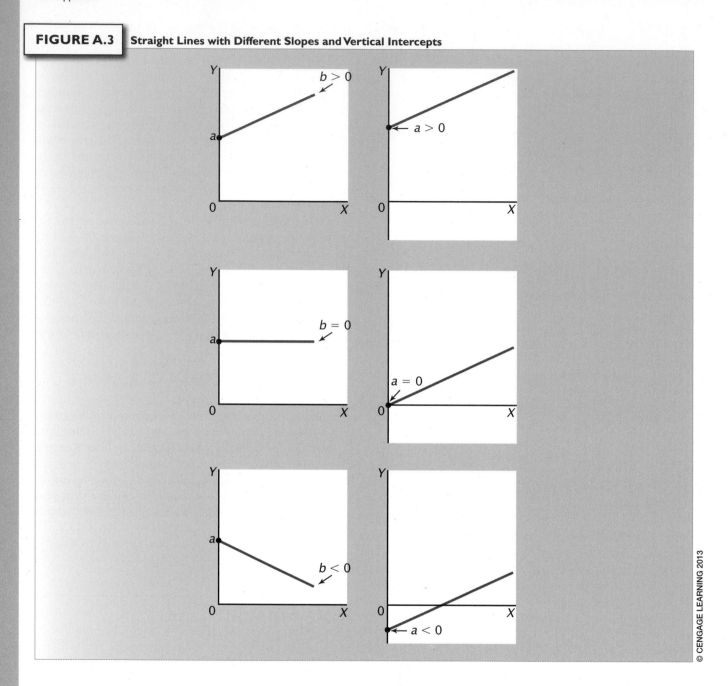

A graph between two variables X and Y is only a picture of their relationship when all other variables affecting Y are held constant.

But suppose one of these other variables *does* change? What happens then?

Think back to the relationship between advertising and sales. Earlier, we supposed sales depended only on advertising. But suppose we make an important discovery: Ice cream sales are *also* affected by how hot the weather is. What's more, all of the data in Table A.1 on which we previously based our analysis turns out to have been from the month of June in different years, when

FIGURE A.4	Shift in the Graphs of Advertising and Sales

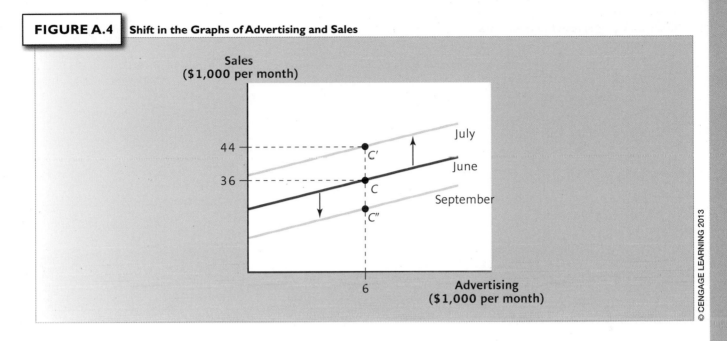

the average temperature in Texas is 80 degrees. What's going to happen in July, when the average temperature rises to 100 degrees?

In Figure A.4 we've redrawn the graph from Figure A.1, this time labeling the line "June." Often, a good way to determine how a graph will shift is to perform a simple experiment like this: Put your pencil tip anywhere on the graph labeled June—let's say at point C. Now ask the following question: If I hold advertising constant at $6,000, do I expect to sell more or less ice cream as temperature rises in July? If you expect to sell more, then the amount of sales corresponding to $6,000 of advertising will be *above* point C, at a point such as C′ (pronounced "C prime"), representing sales of $44,000. From this, we can tell that the graph will *shift upward* as temperature rises. In September, however, when temperatures fall, the amount of sales corresponding to $6,000 in advertising would be less than it is at point C. It would be shown by a point such as C″, (pronounced "C double-prime"). In that case, the graph would shift downward.

The same procedure works well whether the original graph slopes upward or downward and whether it is a straight line or a curved one. Figure A.5 sketches two examples. In panel (a), an increase in some third variable, Z, increases the value of Y for each value of X, so the graph of the relationship between X and Y shifts upward as Z increases. We often phrase it this way: "An increase in Z causes an increase in Y, *at any value of* X." In panel (b), we assume that an increase in Z *decreases* the value of Y, at any value of X, so the graph of the relationship between X and Y shifts *downward* as Z increases.

You'll notice that in Figures A.4 and A.5, the original line is darker, while the new line after the shift is drawn in a lighter shade. We'll often use this convention—a lighter shade for the new line—after a shift.

Shifts versus Movements Along a Line

If you look back at Figure A.1, you'll see that when advertising increases (say, from $2,000 to $3,000), we *move along* our line, from point A to point B. But you've just learned that when average temperature changes, the entire line *shifts*. This may seem strange to you. After all, in both cases, an independent variable changes (either advertising or temperature). Why should we move *along* the line in one case and *shift* it in the other?

The reason for the difference is that in one case (advertising), the independent variable is *in our graph*, measured along one of the axes. When an independent variable in the graph changes, we simply move along the line. In the other case (temperature), the independent variable does *not* appear in our graph. Instead, it's been in the background, being held constant.

FIGURE A.5 | Shifts of Curved Lines

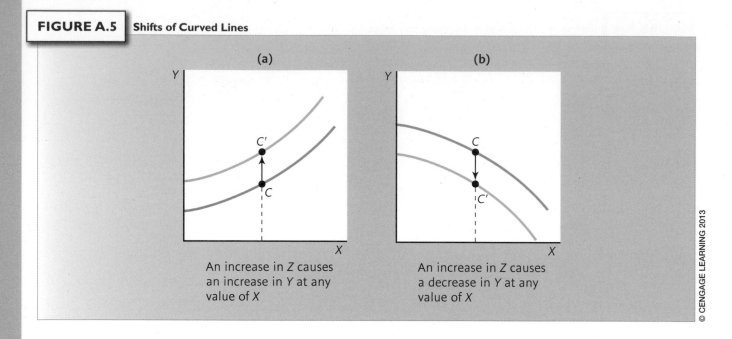

(a)

An increase in *Z* causes an increase in *Y* at any value of *X*

(b)

An increase in *Z* causes a decrease in *Y* at any value of *X*

Here's a very simple—but crucial—rule:

> *Suppose Y is the dependent variable, which is measured on one of the axes in a graph. If the independent variable measured on the other axis changes, we move along the line. But if any other independent variable changes, the entire line shifts.*

Be sure you understand the phrase "any other independent variable." It refers to any variable that actually *affects* Y but is *not* measured on either axis in the graph.

This rule applies to straight lines as well as curved lines. And it applies even in more complicated situations, such as when *two different* lines are drawn in the same graph and a shift of one causes a movement along the other. (You'll encounter this situation in Chapter 3.) But for now, make sure you can see how we've been applying this rule in our example, where the three variables are total sales, advertising, and temperature.

SOLVING EQUATIONS

When we first derived the equation for the relationship between advertising and sales, we wanted to know what level of sales to expect from different amounts of advertising. But what if we're asked a slightly different question?

Suppose, this time, you are told that the sales committee has set an ambitious goal of $42,000 for next month's sales. The treasurer needs to know how much to budget for advertising, and you have to come up with the answer.

Since we know how advertising and sales are related, we ought to be able to answer this question. One way is just to look at the graph in Figure A.1. There, we could first locate sales of $42,000 on the vertical axis. Then, if we read over to the line and then down, we find the amount of advertising that would be necessary to generate that level of sales. Yet even with that carefully drawn diagram, it is not always easy to see just exactly how much advertising would be required. If we need to be precise, we'd better use the equation for the graph instead.

According to the equation, sales (*Y*) and advertising (*X*) are related as follows:

$$Y = 18 + 3X.$$

In the problem before us, we know the value we want for sales, and we need to solve for the corresponding amount of advertising. Substituting the sales target of $42 for *Y*, we need to find that value of *X* for which

$$42 = 18 + 3X.$$

In this case, *X* is the unknown value for which we want to solve.

Whenever we solve an equation for one unknown, say, X, we need to *isolate* X on one side of the equal sign and everything else on the other side of the equal sign. We do this by performing identical operations on both sides of the equal sign. Here, we can first subtract 18 from both sides, getting

$$24 = 3X.$$

We can then divide both sides by 3 and get

$$8 = X.$$

This is our answer. If we want to achieve sales of $42,000, we'll need to spend $8,000 on advertising.

Of course, not all relationships are linear, so this technique will not work in every situation. But no matter what the underlying relationship, the idea remains the same:

> To *solve for* X *in any equation, rearrange the equation, following the rules of algebra, so that* X *appears on one side of the equals sign and everything else in the equation appears on the other side.*

CHAPTER 2

Scarcity, Choice, and Economic Systems

In 2010, the U.S. Congress did something controversial: It voted to approve the Patient Protection and Affordable Care Act, which President Obama signed into law. The new law would eventually require most Americans to purchase health insurance or face a fine. It imposed new regulations on insurance companies and made many other changes in the way medical care would be provided and paid for. In the year leading up to the Act's passage, public opinion had been divided. The debate in Congress was intense. Even after the Act was passed, the controversy didn't die. Democrats in Congress were proud of the new law, while Republicans called it a disaster and vowed to repeal it or defeat it in the courts.

The debate over health care reform, like so many other public disagreements, was a debate about how society's resources should be used and about who should be making the decisions. How much of our resources should be used to produce medical services? How much should be devoted to national defense or education? Or to consumer goods that individuals choose for themselves? What are the consequences of these decisions, and how should they be made?

In this chapter, you'll learn a new framework for thinking about society's resources. Opportunity cost—which you learned about in the last chapter—plays a central role in this framework. So let's start with a simple model of opportunity cost for society's choices.

SOCIETY'S PRODUCTION CHOICES

Let's consider a specific choice that faces every society: how much of its resources to allocate toward national defense versus how much to use for civilian production. To make this choice more concrete, we'll make a simplifying assumption: In the economy we're studying, there is one kind of military good (tanks) and one kind of civilian good (wheat).

Table 1 lists some possible combinations of yearly tank production and yearly wheat production that this society could manage, given its available resources and the currently available production technology. For example, the first row of the table (choice A) tells us what would happen if all available resources were devoted to wheat production and no resources at all to producing tanks. The resulting quantity of wheat—1 million bushels per year—is the most this society could possibly produce. In the second row (choice B), society moves enough resources into tank production to make 1,000 tanks per year. This leaves fewer resources for wheat production, which now declines to 950,000 bushels per year.

TABLE 1

Production of Tanks and Wheat

© CENGAGE LEARNING 2013

Choice	Tank Production (number per year)	Wheat Production (bushels per year)
A	0	1,000,000
B	1,000	950,000
C	2,000	850,000
D	3,000	700,000
E	4,000	400,000
F	5,000	0

As we continue down the table, moving to choices C, D, and E, tank production increases by increments of 1,000. Finally, look at the last row (choice F). It shows us that when society throws all of its resources into tank production (with none for wheat), tank production is 5,000 and wheat production is zero.

The table gives us a quantitative measure of opportunity cost for this society. For example, suppose this society currently produces 1,000 tanks per year, along with 950,000 bushels of wheat (choice B). What would be the opportunity cost of producing another 1,000 tanks? Moving down to choice C, we see that producing another 1,000 tanks (for a total of 2,000) would require wheat production to drop from 950,000 to 850,000 bushels, a decrease of 100,000 bushels. Thus, the opportunity cost of 1,000 more tanks is 100,000 bushels of wheat. The opportunity cost of having more of one good is measured in the units of the other good that must be sacrificed.

The Production Possibilities Frontier

We can see opportunity cost even more clearly in Figure 1, where the data in Table 1 has been plotted on a graph. In the figure, tank production is measured along the horizontal axis, and wheat production along the vertical axis. Each of the six points labeled A through F corresponds to one of society's choices in the table. For example, point B represents 1,000 tanks and 950,000 bushels of wheat.

When we connect these points with a smooth line, we get a curve called society's **production possibilities frontier (PPF)**. Specifically, this PPF tells us the maximum quantity of wheat that can be produced for each quantity of tanks produced. Alternatively, it tells us the maximum number of tanks that can be produced for each different quantity of wheat.

Points outside the frontier are unattainable with the technology and resources at the economy's disposal. For example, locate the point (not marked in the figure) that would correspond to 4,000 tanks and 700,000 bushels of wheat, and label it "G." Point G would be unobtainable because if we were producing 4,000 tanks, we'd have enough resources left over to produce only 400,000 bushels of wheat, not 700,000. Producing at point G would require more land, labor, capital, and entrepreneurship than this economy has. Society's choices are limited to points on or inside the PPF.

Now recall our earlier example of moving from choice B to choice C in the table. When tank production increased from 1,000 to 2,000, wheat production decreased from 950,000 to 850,000. In the graph, this change would be represented by a movement along the PPF from point B to point C. We're moving rightward

Production possibilities frontier (PPF) A curve showing all combinations of two goods that can be produced with the resources and technology currently available.

FIGURE 1   The Production Possibilities Frontier

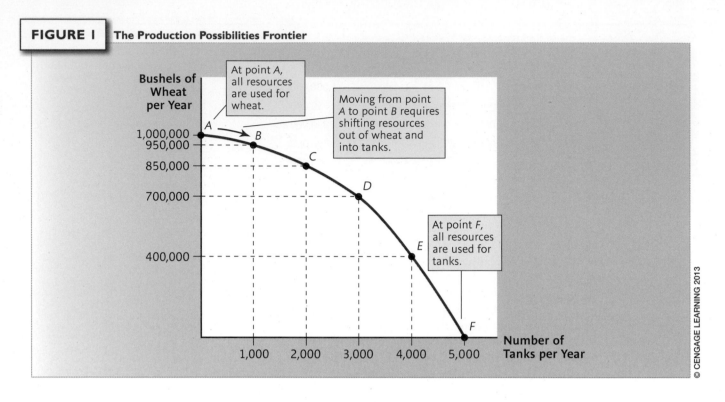

Bushels of Wheat per Year

At point *A*, all resources are used for wheat.

Moving from point *A* to point *B* requires shifting resources out of wheat and into tanks.

At point *F*, all resources are used for tanks.

Number of Tanks per Year

(1,000 more tanks) and also downward (100,000 fewer bushels of wheat). Thus, the opportunity cost of 1,000 more tanks can be viewed as the vertical drop along the PPF as we move from point *B* to point *C*.

Increasing Opportunity Cost

Suppose we have arrived at point *C*, and society then decides to produce still more tanks. Once again, resources must be shifted into tank production to make an additional 1,000 of them, moving from point *C* to point *D*. This time, however, there is an even *greater opportunity cost*: Production of wheat falls from 850,000 to 700,000 bushels, a sacrifice of 150,000 bushels. The opportunity cost of 1,000 more tanks has risen. Graphically, the vertical drop along the curve is greater for the same move rightward.

Figure 2 shows that as we continue to increase tank production by increments of 1,000—moving from point *C* to point *D* to point *E* to point *F*—the opportunity cost of producing an additional 1,000 tanks keeps rising, until the last 1,000 tanks costs us 400,000 bushels of wheat. (You can also see this in the table, by running down the numbers in the right column. Each time tank production rises by 1,000, wheat production falls by more and more.)

The behavior of opportunity cost described here—the more tanks we produce, the greater the opportunity cost of producing still more—applies to a wide range of choices facing society. It can be generalized as the *law of increasing opportunity cost*.

> *According to the law of increasing opportunity cost, the more of something we produce, the greater the opportunity cost of producing even more of it.*

FIGURE 2 | Increasing Opportunity Cost

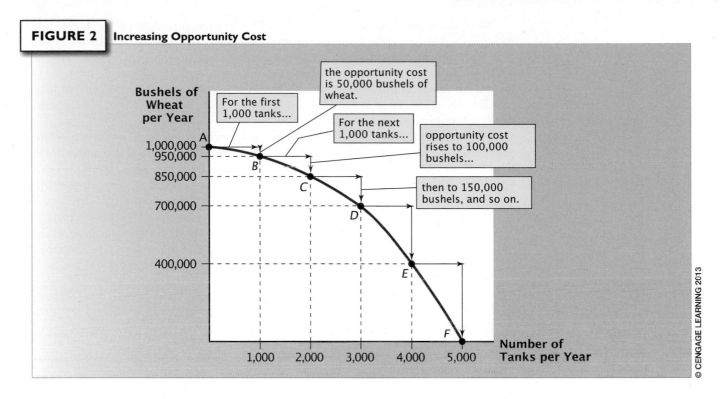

The law of increasing opportunity cost causes the PPF to have a concave (upside-down bowl) shape, becoming steeper as we move rightward and downward. That's because the slope of the PPF—the change in the quantity of wheat divided by the change in the quantity of tanks—can be interpreted as the change in wheat *per additional tank*. For example, moving from point *C* to point *D*, we give up 150,000 bushels of wheat to get 1,000 more tanks, or *150 bushels of wheat per tank*. Thus, the slope of the PPF between points *C* and *D* is approximately −150. (We say approximately because the PPF is curved, so its slope changes slightly as we move along the interval from *C* to *D*.) If we remove the minus sign from this slope and consider just its absolute value, it tells us the opportunity cost of *one more tank*.

Now—as we've seen—this opportunity cost increases as we move rightward. Therefore, the absolute value of the PPF's slope must rise as well. The PPF grows increasingly steeper, giving us the concave shape we see in Figure 1: 150 bushels of wheat.[1]

The Reason for Increasing Opportunity Cost

Why does opportunity cost increase as we move along a PPF? Because most resources—by their very nature—are better suited to some purposes than to others. If the economy were operating at point *A*, for example, we'd be using *all* of our resources for wheat, even those that are much better suited to making tanks. People who would be better at factory work than farming would nevertheless be pressed into working on farms. And we'd be growing wheat on all the land available, even land that would be fine for a tank factory but awful for growing crops.

---

[1] You might be wondering if the law of increasing opportunity cost applies in both directions. That is, does the opportunity cost of producing more wheat increase as we produce more of it? The answer is yes, as you'll be asked to show in an end-of-chapter problem.

Now, as we move rightward along the PPF, say from *A* to *B*, we would *first* shift those resources *best suited* to tank production—and least suited for wheat. So the first thousand tanks cause only a small drop in wheat production. This is why, at first, the PPF is very flat: a small vertical drop for the rightward movement.

As we continue moving rightward, however, we must shift resources to tanks that are less and less suited to tanks and more and more suited to wheat. As a result, the PPF becomes steeper.

The principle of increasing opportunity cost applies to most of society's production choices, not just that between wheat and tanks. If we look at society's choice between food and oil, we would find that some land is better suited to growing food, and other land is better suited to drilling for oil. As we continue to produce more oil, we would find ourselves drilling on land that is less and less suited to producing oil, but better and better for producing food. The opportunity cost of producing additional oil will therefore increase. The same principle applies if we want to produce more health care, more education, more automobiles, or more computers: The more of something we produce, the greater the opportunity cost of producing still more.

THE SEARCH FOR A FREE LUNCH

This chapter has argued that every decision to produce *more* of something requires us to pay an opportunity cost by producing less of something else. Nobel Prize–winning economist Milton Friedman summarized this idea in his famous remark, "There is no such thing as a free lunch." Friedman's point was that, even if a meal is provided free of charge to someone, society still uses up resources to provide it. Therefore, a "free lunch" is not *really* free: Society pays an opportunity cost by not producing other things with those resources. *Some* members of society will have less of something else.

The same logic applies to other supposedly "free" goods and services. From society's point of view, there is no such thing as a free sample at a supermarket or free medical care, even if people don't pay directly. Providing any of these things requires a sacrifice of *other* things, as illustrated by a movement along society's PPF.

But what if an economy is *not* living up to its productive potential, and is operating *inside* its PPF? For example, in Figure 3, suppose we are currently operating at point *W*, where we are producing 2,000 tanks and 400,000 bushels of wheat. Then we could move from point *W* to point *E* and produce 2,000 more tanks, with no sacrifice of wheat. Or, starting at point *W*, we could move to point *C* (more wheat with no sacrifice of tanks), or to a point like *D* (more of *both* wheat and tanks).

When we are operating inside the PPF, a "free lunch" may be possible, because we can have more of one thing (such as wheat or tanks) with no opportunity cost. However, in modern economies, these free lunches are not as easy to find or exploit as you may think. To see why, let's explore some reasons why an economy might be operating inside its PPF in the first place.

Productive Inefficiency

One reason we might be operating inside the PPF is that resources are not being used in the most productive way. Suppose, for example, that many people who could be outstanding wheat farmers are instead making tanks, and many who would be great at tank production are instead stuck on farms. Then switching people from one job

FIGURE 3   **Operating Inside the Production Possibilities Frontier**

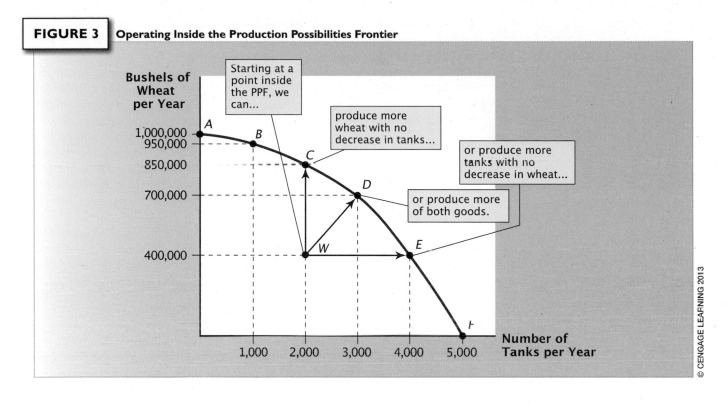

to the other could enable us to have more of *both* tanks *and* wheat. That is, because of the mismatch of workers and jobs, we would be *inside* the PPF at a point like W. Creating better job matches would then move us to a point *on* the PPF (such as point *E*).

Economists use the phrase *productive inefficiency* to describe this type of situation that puts us inside our PPF.

> *A firm, an industry, or an entire economy is **productively inefficient** if it could produce more of at least one good without producing less of any other good.*

Productively inefficient A situation in which more of at least one good can be produced without sacrificing the production of any other good.

The phrase *productive efficiency* means the absence of any productive *in*efficiency.

No firm, industry, or economy is ever 100 percent productively efficient. But in a well-functioning economy, cases of gross inefficiency are not as common as you might think. Business firms have strong incentives to identify and eliminate productive inefficiency, since any waste of resources increases their costs and decreases their profit. When one firm discovers a way to eliminate waste, others quickly follow.

For example, empty seats on an airline flight represent productive inefficiency. Since the plane is making the trip anyway, filling the empty seat would enable the airline to fly more people (produce more transportation services) without using any additional resources (other than the trivial resources of in-flight snacks). Therefore, more people could fly without sacrificing any other good or service. When American Airlines developed a computer model in the late 1980s to fill its empty seats by altering schedules and fares, the other airlines followed its example very rapidly. And when—in the late 1990s—Priceline.com enabled airlines to auction off empty seats on the Internet, several airlines jumped at the chance

© ISTOCKPHOTO.COM/SHANE SHAW

and others quickly followed. As a result, a case of productive inefficiency in the airline industry—and therefore in the economy—was eliminated.

Starbucks provides another example. The company routinely uses efficiency experts to look for ways to increase the number of drinks served with a given amount of labor. In 2009, for example, it found that just by moving the whipped cream and caramel drizzle closer to where the drinks are handed to customers reduced preparation time from 45 seconds per drink to 37 seconds. Starbucks made these changes to save on labor costs and increase the company's profits. But from society's perspective, resource-saving efforts by Starbucks and other business firms free up labor time that can be used to produce other things.

Economists, logistics experts, business managers, and engineers are continually identifying and working to eliminate the most obvious and important cases of productive inefficiency. As a result, many of the "free lunches" we might think we can enjoy by eliminating productive inefficiency have already been served and eaten.

Recessions

Another reason an economy might operate inside its PPF is a *recession*—a slowdown in overall economic activity. During recessions, many resources are idle. For one thing, there is widespread *unemployment*—people who *want* to work but are unable to find jobs. In addition, factories shut down, so we are not using all of our available capital. An end to the recession would move the economy from a point *inside* its PPF to a point *on* its PPF—using idle resources to produce more goods and services without sacrificing anything.

This simple observation can help us understand an otherwise confusing episode in U.S. economic history. During the early 1940s, after the United States entered World War II and began using massive amounts of resources to produce military goods and services, the standard of living in the United States did *not* decline as we might have expected but actually improved slightly. Why?

When the United States entered the war in 1941, it was still suffering from the Great Depression—the most serious and long-lasting economic downturn in modern history, which began in 1929 and hit most of the developed world. As we joined the Allied war effort, the economy also recovered from the depression. (Indeed, for reasons you will learn when you study macroeconomics, U.S. participation in the war may have accelerated the depression's end.) So, in Figure 4, this moved our economy from a point like A, *inside* the PPF, to a point like B, *on* the frontier. Military production, such as tanks, increased, but so did the production of civilian goods, such as wheat. Although there were shortages of some consumer goods, the overall result was a rise in total production and an increase in the material well-being of the average U.S. citizen.

⚠ DANGEROUS CURVES

False benefits from employment Often, you'll hear an evaluation of some economic activity that includes "greater employment" as one of the benefits. For example, an article in the online magazine *Slate*, after discussing the costs of e-mail spam, pointed out that spam also has "a corresponding economic payoff. Anti-spam efforts keep well-paid software engineers employed."[2]

This kind of thinking is usually incorrect. True, when the economy is in recession, an increase in any kind of employment can be regarded as a benefit—especially to those who get the jobs. But this is a special, temporary situation. Once a recession ends, the software engineers—if not for the spam—would be employed elsewhere. At that point, employment in the spam-fighting industry—far from being a benefit—is actually part of the *opportunity cost* of spam: We sacrifice the goods and services these spam-fighting engineers would otherwise produce.

© AXL/SHUTTERSTOCK.COM

[2] Jeff Merron, "Workus Interruptus," *Slate*, Posted March 16, 2006, 12:06 PM ET.

FIGURE 4   **Production and Unemployment**

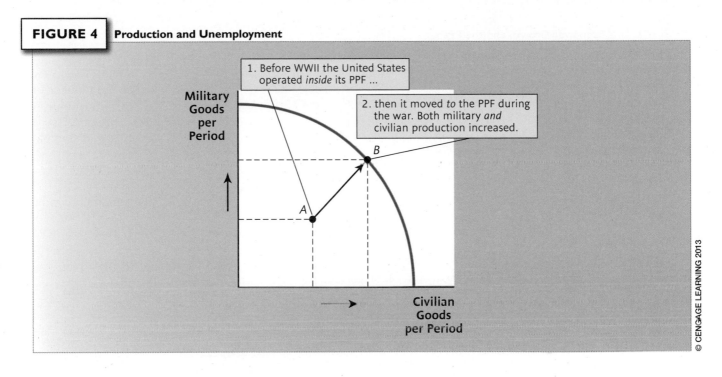

1. Before WWII the United States operated *inside* its PPF ...

2. then it moved *to* the PPF during the war. Both military *and* civilian production increased.

Military Goods per Period

Civilian Goods per Period

No government would ever *choose* war as a purely economic policy to end a downturn because other, economically superior policies could accomplish the same goal. But do these other methods of promoting recovery give us a free "lunch"? Yes... and no. When you study macroeconomics you'll learn that policies to cure or avoid recessions have risks and costs of their own. Indeed, when the Obama administration used some of these policies in 2009 and 2010 to help the economy recover from a deep recession, a heated debate broke out about whether the costs and risks were worth it.

Economic Growth

What if the PPF itself were to change? Couldn't we then produce more of everything? This is exactly what happens when an economy's productive capacity grows.

One way that productivity capacity grows is by an increase in available resources. Historically, the resource that has contributed most to rising living standards is capital. More physical capital (factory buildings, tractors, and medical equipment) or more human capital (skilled doctors, engineers, and construction workers) can enable us to produce more of *any* goods and services that use these tools.

The other major source of economic growth is *technological change*—the discovery of new ways to produce more from a given quantity of resources. The development of the Internet, for example, enabled people to find information in a few minutes that used to require hours of searching through printed documents. As a result, a variety of professionals—teachers, writers, government officials, attorneys, and physicians—can produce more of their services with the same amount of labor hours.

Figure 5 shows three examples of how economic growth can change the PPF. Panel (a) illustrates a change that initially affects only wheat production—say, the acquisition of more tractors (usable in wheat farming but not in tank-making) or the discovery of a new, higher-yielding technique for growing wheat. If we used *all* of our resources to produce wheat, we could now produce more of it than before. For

FIGURE 5 Economic Growth and the PPF

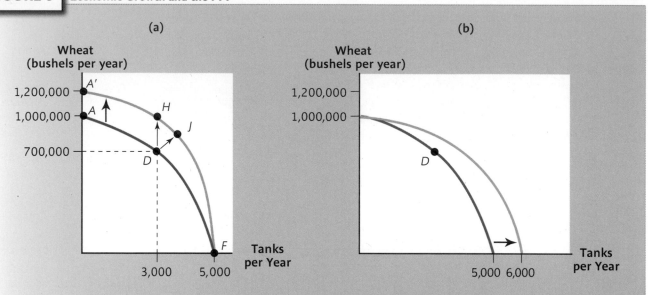

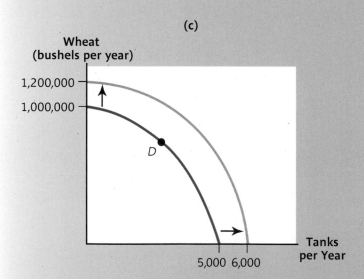

All three panels show economic growth from an increase in resources or a technological change. In panel (a), the additional resources or technological advance directly affect only wheat production. However, society can choose to have more wheat and more tanks if it desires, such as at point J. In panel (b), the additional resources or technological advance directly affect only tank production. But once again, society can choose to have more of both goods. In panel (c), the additional resources or technological advance directly affect production of both goods.

that reason, the vertical intercept of the PPF rises from point *A* to a point like *A'*, where the economy could produce a maximum of 1,200,000 bushels per year. But the horizontal intercept of the PPF remains at point *F*, because the changes we're considering apply only to wheat. If we were to use all of our resources in tank production, we'd be able to produce the same number of tanks as before. So the final effect is to stretch the PPF upward along the vertical axis.

Suppose we were originally operating at point *D* on the old PPF. Then, with our new PPF, we could choose to produce more wheat and the same number of tanks (point *H*). Or we could produce more of *both* goods (point *J*). We could even choose to produce more tanks and the same amount of wheat as before. (See if you can identify this point on the new PPF.)

But wait . . . how can having more tractors or a new technique for growing wheat—changes that directly affect only the wheat industry—enable us to produce more tanks? The answer is: After the change in the PPF, society can choose to shift some resources out of wheat farming and have the same amount of wheat as before at point *D*, on the original PPF. The shifted resources can be used to increase tank production.

Panel (b) illustrates the opposite type of change in the PPF—from a technological change in producing tanks, or an increase in resources usable only in the tank industry. This time, the *horizontal* intercept of the PPF increases, while the vertical intercept remains unchanged. (Can you explain why?) As before, we could choose to produce more tanks, more wheat, or more of both. (See if you can identify points on the new PPF in panel [b] to illustrate all three cases.)

Finally, panel (c) illustrates the case where technological change occurs in both the wheat and the tank industries, or there is an increase in resources (such as workers or capital) that could be used in either. Now both the horizontal and the vertical intercepts of the PPF increase. But as before, society can choose to locate anywhere along the new PPF, producing more tanks, more wheat, or more of both.

Panels (a) and (b) can be generalized to an important principle about economic growth:

> *A technological change or an increase in resources, even when the direct impact is to increase production of just one type of good, allows us to choose greater production of all types of goods.*

This conclusion certainly *seems* like a free lunch. But is it?

Yes . . . and no. True, comparing the new PPF to the old, it looks like we can have more of something—in fact, more of everything—without any sacrifice. But Figure 4 tells only part of the story. It leaves out the sacrifice that creates the change in the PPF in the first place.

Consumption versus Growth

Suppose we want more capital, in order to shift the PPF outward as in the three panels of Figure 5. First, note that capital plays two roles in the economy. On the one hand, capital is a *resource* that we use to produce goods and services. On the other hand, capital is *itself* a good and is produced . . . using resources! A tractor, for example, is produced using land, labor, and *other* capital (a tractor factory and all of the manufacturing equipment inside the factory).

Each year, we must choose how much of our available resources to devote to producing capital, as opposed to other things. On the plus side, the more capital we produce this year, the more capital we'll have in the future to produce other things.

FIGURE 6 How Current Production Affects Economic Growth

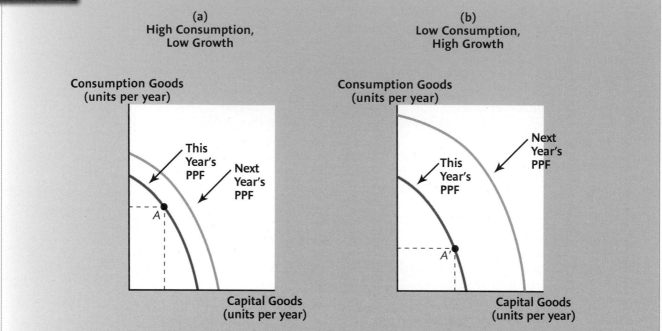

(a)
High Consumption, Low Growth

(b)
Low Consumption, High Growth

In panel (a), production is tilted toward current consumption goods, with relatively few resources devoted to production of capital goods. As a result, in the future, there will not be much of an increase in capital, so the PPF will not shift out much in the future. In panel (b), production is tilted more toward capital goods, with a greater sacrifice of current consumption. As a result, there will be a greater increase in capital, so the PPF will shift out more in the future.

(Remember: Capital, once produced, is a long-lasting tool.) But there's a trade-off: Any resources used to produce capital this year are *not* being used to produce *consumer goods*—food, health care, and other things that we can enjoy right now.

Figure 6 illustrates this trade-off. In each panel, the total quantity of capital goods is measured on the horizontal axis, and consumption goods on the vertical axis. In each panel, the darker curve is *this year's* PPF. In the left panel, point *A* shows one choice we could make this year: relatively high production of consumer goods and low production of capital goods. We'd have a relatively high standard of living this year (lots of consumer goods), but we'd be adding little to our total stock of capital during the year. As a result, *next year's* PPF—the lighter curve—will be shifted outward somewhat (because we'll have a bit more capital next year than we had this year), but not by much.

The right panel shows a different choice for the same economy. If we are situated at point *A'* on this year's PPF, we sacrifice more consumption goods now and produce more capital goods than at point *A* in the left panel. Living standards are lower this year. But next year, when we have considerably more capital, the PPF will have shifted outward even more. We can then choose a point on next year's PPF with greater production of consumer goods than we could have had if we had chosen point *A*. So, choosing point *A'* rather than *A* can lead to a greater rise in living standards next year, but requires greater sacrifice of consumer goods this year.

A similar trade-off exists when technological change drives growth. New technologies don't just "happen"—resources must be used *now* for research and development. These resources could have been used to produce other things that we'd enjoy today. For example, doctors who work at developing new drugs in pharmaceutical companies could instead be providing health care to patients right now. We could show this using the same PPFs as in Figure 6. But on the horizontal axis, instead of "capital goods," we'd have some measure of "research and development activities." And we'd come to the same conclusion about technological change that we came to earlier about having more capital:

> *In order to produce more goods and services in the future, we must shift resources toward R&D and capital production, and away from producing things we'd enjoy right now.*

We must conclude that although economic growth—at first glance—*appears* to be a free lunch, someone ends up paying the check. In this case, the bill is paid by those who will have to make do with less in the present.

ECONOMIC SYSTEMS

As you read these words—perhaps sitting at home or in the library—you are experiencing a very private moment. It is just you and this book; the rest of the world might as well not exist. Or so it seems. . . .

Actually, even in this supposedly private moment, you are connected to others in ways you may not have thought about. In order for you to be reading this book, the authors had to write it. Someone had to edit it, to help make sure that all necessary material was covered and explained as clearly as possible. Someone else had to prepare the graphics.

And there's more. If you are reading a physical book (rather than reading online), people had to manufacture all kinds of goods: paper and ink, the computers used to keep track of inventory, and so on. And still others had to pack the book, ship it, unpack it, put it on a store shelf, and then sell it to you. It is no exaggeration to say that thousands of people were involved in making this book available to you.

Take a walk in your town or city, and you will see even more evidence of our economic interdependence: People are collecting garbage, helping schoolchildren cross the street, transporting furniture across town, constructing buildings, repairing roads, painting houses. Everyone is producing goods and services for *other people*.

Why is it that so much of what we consume is produced by other people? Why are we all so heavily dependent on each other for our material well-being? Why don't we all—like Robinson Crusoe on his island—produce our own food, clothing, housing, and anything else we desire? And how did it come about that *you*—who most likely did not produce any of these things yourself—are able to consume them?

These are all questions about our *economic system*—the way our economy is organized. Ordinarily, we take our economic system for granted, like the water that runs out of our faucets. But now it's time to begin looking at the plumbing—to learn how our economy serves so many millions of people, enabling them to survive and prosper.

Specialization and Exchange

If we were forced to, many of us could become economically *self-sufficient*. We could stake out a plot of land, grow our own food, make our own clothing, and build our own homes. But in no society is there such extreme self-sufficiency. On the contrary, every society has an economic system with two features: (1) **specialization**, in which each of us concentrates on a limited number of productive activities, and

Specialization A method of production in which each person concentrates on a limited number of activities.

Exchange The act of trading with others to obtain what we desire.

(2) **exchange,** in which we obtain most of what we desire by trading with others rather than producing for ourselves.

> *Specialization and exchange enable us to enjoy greater production and higher living standards than would otherwise be possible. As a result, all economies exhibit high degrees of specialization and exchange.*

Where do the gains from specialization and exchange come from?

Development of Expertise. Each of us can learn only so much in a lifetime. By limiting ourselves to a narrow set of tasks—fixing plumbing, managing workers, writing music, or designing Web pages—we can hone our skills. We can become experts at one or two things, instead of remaining amateurs at a lot of things. An economy of experts will produce more than an economy of amateurs.

Minimizing Downtime. When people specialize, and thus spend their time doing one type of task, there is less unproductive "downtime" from switching activities. On a smaller scale, we see this in most households every night, when it's time to wash the dishes. "I'll wash, you dry" enables both members of a couple to keep doing their part nonstop, and the dishes get done faster.

Comparative Advantage. We would gain from developing expertise and minimizing downtime even if everyone, initially, had identical capabilities. But a third gain arises because of our *differences:* We are not all equally suited to different tasks. This idea applies not just to labor, but to the other resources as well. Not all plots of land are equally suited for all crops, nor are all types of capital equipment equally suited for all types of production. When we allocate our resources according to their *suitability* for different types of production, we get further gains from specialization. The principle behind this gain—*comparative advantage*—is such a central idea in economics that it gets its own section.

Comparative Advantage

Imagine a shipwreck in which there are only two survivors—let's call them Maryanne and Gilligan—who are washed ashore on opposite ends of a deserted island. Initially they are unaware of each other, so each is forced to become completely self-sufficient. And there are only two kinds of food on the island: fish and berries.

Table 2 shows how much time it takes for each castaway to pick a cup of berries or catch one fish. For simplicity, we'll assume that the time requirement remains constant, no matter how much time is devoted to these activities.

On one side of the island, Maryanne finds that it takes her 1 hour to catch a fish and 1 hour to pick a cup of berries, as shown in the first row of the table. On the other

TABLE 2

Labor Requirements for Fish and Berries

	Labor Required For:	
	I Fish	**I Cup of Berries**
Maryanne	I hour	I hour
Gilligan	3 hours	I½ hours

side of the island, Gilligan—who is less adept at both tasks—requires 3 hours to catch a fish and 1½ hours to pick a cup of berries, as listed in the second row of the table. Since both castaways would want some variety in their diets, we can assume that each would spend part of their time catching fish and part picking berries.

Suppose that, one day, Maryanne and Gilligan discover each other. After rejoicing at the prospect of human companionship, they decide to develop a system of production that will work to their mutual benefit. Let's rule out two of the gains from specialization that we discussed earlier (minimizing downtime and developing expertise). Will it still make sense for these two to specialize? The answer is yes, as you will see after a small detour.

Absolute Advantage: A Detour

When Gilligan and Maryanne sit down to figure out who should do what, they might fall victim to a common mistake: basing their decision on *absolute advantage*.

> *An individual has an **absolute advantage** in the production of some good when he or she can produce it using fewer resources than another individual can.*

Absolute advantage The ability to produce a good or service, using fewer resources than other producers use.

On the island, labor is the only resource. The castaways might (mistakenly) reason as follows: Maryanne can catch a fish more quickly than Gilligan (see Table 2), so she has an *absolute advantage* in fishing. Therefore, Maryanne should be the one to catch fish.

But wait! Maryanne can also pick berries more quickly than Gilligan, so she has an absolute advantage in that as well. If absolute advantage is the criterion for assigning work, then Maryanne should do *both* tasks. This, however, would leave Gilligan doing nothing, which is certainly *not* in the pair's best interests.

What can we conclude from this example? That absolute advantage is an unreliable guide for allocating tasks to different workers.

Comparative Advantage

The correct principle to guide the division of labor on the island is comparative advantage:

> *A person has a **comparative advantage** in producing some good if he or she can produce it with a smaller opportunity cost than some other person can.*

Comparative advantage The ability to produce a good or service at a lower opportunity cost than other producers.

Notice the important difference between absolute advantage and comparative advantage: You have an *absolute* advantage in producing a good if you can produce it using fewer *resources* than someone else can. But you have a *comparative* advantage if you can produce it with a smaller *opportunity cost*. As you'll see, these are not necessarily the same thing.

Who Has a Comparative Advantage in What?

Let's first see who has a comparative advantage in fishing. To do this, we need to calculate the opportunity cost—for each castaway—of catching one more fish.

For Maryanne, catching one more fish takes one more hour. That requires one hour less picking berries, and that, in turn, means sacrificing 1 cup of berries. We can summarize it this way:

Maryanne: 1 more fish ⇒ 1 more hour fishing
⇒ 1 less hour picking berries ⇒ 1 less cup berries

Even castaways do better when they specialize and exchange with each other, instead of trying to be self-sufficient.

Therefore, for Maryanne: *the opportunity cost of one more fish is 1 cup of berries.* Because we've assumed that the time requirements for each activity don't change, this opportunity cost of 1 more fish remains constant, no matter how many fish Maryanne catches.

Doing the same analysis for Gilligan, who needs three hours to catch a fish, we find:

<u>Gilligan</u>: 1 more fish ⇒ 3 more hours fishing
⇒ 3 fewer hours picking berries ⇒ 2 fewer cups berries

So for Gilligan, the *opportunity cost of one more fish is 2 cups of berries.* Because Maryanne has the lower opportunity cost for one more fish (1 cup of berries rather than 2 cups), *Maryanne has the comparative advantage in fishing.*

Now let's see who has the comparative advantage in picking berries. We can summarize the steps as follows:

<u>Maryanne</u>: 1 more cup berries ⇒ 1 more hour picking berries
⇒ 1 less hour fishing ⇒ 1 less fish

<u>Gilligan</u>: 1 more cup berries ⇒ 1½ more hours picking berries
⇒ 1½ fewer hours fishing ⇒ ½ less fish

You can see that the opportunity cost of one more cup of berries is 1 fish for Maryanne, and ½ fish for Gilligan.[3] When it comes to berries, Gilligan has the lower opportunity cost. So Gilligan—who has an *absolute* advantage in nothing—has a *comparative* advantage in berry picking.

Gains from Comparative Advantage

What happens when each castaway produces more of their comparative advantage good? The results are shown in Table 3. In the first row, we have Maryanne catching one more fish each day (+1) at an opportunity cost of one cup of berries (−1). In the second row, we have Gilligan producing one fewer fish (−1), which enables him to produce two more cups of berries (+2).

Now look at the last row. It shows what has happened to the production of both goods on the island as a result of this little shift between the two. While fish production remains unchanged, berry production rises by one cup. If the castaways specialize and trade with each other, they can both come out ahead: consuming the same quantity of fish as before, but more berries.

As you can see in Table 3, when each castaway moves toward producing more of the good in which he or she has a *comparative advantage*, total production rises. Now, let's think about this. If they gain by making this small shift toward their comparative advantage goods, why not make the change again? And again after that? In fact, why not keep repeating it until the opportunities for increasing total island production are exhausted, which occurs when one or both of them is devoting all of their time to producing just their comparative advantage good, and none of the other? In the end, specializing according to comparative advantage and exchanging with each other gives the castaways a higher standard of living than they each could achieve on their own.

---

[3] Of course, no one would ever catch half a fish unless they were using a machete. The number just tells us the rate of trade-off of one good for the other.

© CENGAGE LEARNING 2013

TABLE 3

A Beneficial Change in Production

	Change in Fish Production	Change in Berry Production
Maryanne	+1	−1
Gilligan	−1	+2
Total Island	+0	+1

Beyond the Island

What is true for our shipwrecked island dwellers is also true for the entire economy:

> *Total production of every good or service will be greatest when individuals specialize according to their comparative advantage.*

When we turn from our fictional island to the real world, is production, in fact, consistent with the principle of comparative advantage? Indeed it is. A journalist may be able to paint her house more quickly than a house painter, giving her an *absolute* advantage in painting her home. Will she paint her own home? Except in unusual circumstances, no, because the journalist has a *comparative* advantage in writing news articles. Indeed, most journalists—like most college professors, attorneys, architects, and other professionals—hire house painters, leaving them more time to practice the professions in which they have a comparative advantage.

Even fictional superheroes seem to behave consistently with comparative advantage. Superman can no doubt cook a meal, fix a car, chop wood, and do virtually *anything* faster than anyone else on earth. Using our new vocabulary, we'd say that Superman has an absolute advantage in everything. But he has a clear *comparative* advantage in catching criminals and saving the universe from destruction, which is exactly what he spends his time doing.

International Comparative Advantage

You've seen that comparative advantage is one reason people *within* a country can benefit from specializing and trading with each other. The same is true for trading among *nations*. We say that

> *A nation has a comparative advantage in producing a good if it can produce it at a lower opportunity cost than some other nation.*

To illustrate this, let's consider a hypothetical world that has only two countries: the United States and China. Both are producing only two goods: soybeans and T-shirts. And—to keep our model simple—we'll assume that these goods are being produced with just one resource: labor.

Table 4 shows the amount of labor, in hours, required to produce one bushel of soybeans or one T-shirt in each country. We'll assume that hours per unit remain *constant*, no matter how much of a good is produced. For example, the entry "5 hours" tells us that it takes 5 hours of labor to produce one bushel of soybeans in China. This will be true no matter how many bushels China produces.

TABLE 4

Labor Requirements for Soybeans and T-Shirts

	Labor Required For:	
	I Bushel of Soybeans	**I T-Shirt**
United States	½ hour	¼ hour
China	5 hours	I hour

In the table, the United States has an *absolute advantage* in producing both goods. That is, it takes fewer resources (less labor time) to produce either soybeans or T-shirts in the United States than in China. But—as you are about to see—China has a *comparative* advantage in one of these goods.

Determining a Nation's Comparative Advantage

Just as we did for our mythical island, we can determine comparative advantage for a country by looking at opportunity cost.

Let's first look at the opportunity cost of producing, say, 10 more bushels of soybeans. (Using 10 bushels rather than just one bushel enables us to use round numbers in this example.) For the United States, these 10 bushels would require 5 hours. That means 5 fewer hours spent producing T-shirts. Since each T-shirt requires ¼ hour, 5 fewer hours means sacrificing 20 T-shirts. We can summarize it this way:

United States: 10 more bshls soybeans ⇒ 5 more hours producing soybeans
⇒ 5 fewer hours producing T-shirts
⇒ 20 fewer T-shirts

Therefore, for the U.S. the opportunity cost of 10 more bushels of soybeans is 20 T-shirts.

Doing the same analysis for China, where it takes 5 hours to produce each bushel of soybeans, we find:

China: 10 more bshls soybeans ⇒ 50 more hours producing soybeans
⇒ 50 fewer hours producing T-shirts
⇒ 50 fewer T-shirts

So for China, the opportunity cost of 10 bushels of soybeans is 50 T-shirts. Since the U.S. has the lower opportunity cost for soybeans (20 T-shirts rather than 50), the *U.S. has the comparative advantage in soybeans.*

Now let's see who has the comparative advantage in T-shirts. We can choose any number of T-shirts to start off our analysis, so let's (arbitrarily) consider the opportunity cost of producing 40 more T-shirts:

United States: 40 more T-shirts ⇒ 10 more hours producing T-shirts
⇒ 10 fewer hours producing soybeans
⇒ 20 fewer bshls soybeans

China: 40 more T-shirts ⇒ 40 more hours producing T-shirts
⇒ 40 fewer hours producing soybeans
⇒ 8 fewer bshls soybeans

TABLE 5

A Beneficial Change in
World Production

© CENGAGE LEARNING 2013

	Soybeans (Bushels)	T-Shirts
United States	+10	−20
China	−8	+40
Total World Production	+2	+20

The opportunity cost of 40 more T-shirts is 20 bushels of soybeans for the U.S., but only 8 bushels for China. So China, with the lower opportunity cost, has a *comparative* advantage in T-shirts.

Global Gains from Comparative Advantage

What happens when each nation produces more of its comparative advantage good? The results, for our example, are shown in Table 5. In the first row, we have the U.S. producing 10 more bushels of soybeans (+10) at an opportunity cost of 20 T-shirts (−20). In the second row, China produces 8 fewer bushels of soybeans (−8), and 40 more T-shirts (+40).

As you see in our example, world production of *both* goods increases: 2 more bushels of soybeans and 20 more T-shirts. With greater world production, each country can enjoy a higher standard of living. How will the potential gains in living standards be shared among the two countries? That depends on how many T-shirts trade for a bushel of soybeans in the international market where these goods are traded. You'll learn more about this and other aspects of international trade—in a later chapter. But you can already see how this example illustrates a general point:

Total production of every good or service is greatest when nations shift production toward their comparative advantage goods and trade with each other.

Resource Allocation

Specialization and exchange permit a society to sustain higher levels of production than would otherwise be possible. But an economic system must do more than just increase production. It must also solve the thorny problem of *resource allocation*—deciding how society's scarce resources will be divided among competing claims and desires.

More specifically, resource allocation means coming up with answers to three important questions:

1. **Which goods and services should be produced with society's resources?**
   Should we produce more consumer goods for enjoyment now or more capital goods to increase future production? Should we produce more health care, and if so, what should we produce less of? In other words, where on the production possibilities frontier should the economy operate?

2. *How* should they be produced?
   Most goods and services can be produced in a variety of different ways, with each method using more of some resources and less of others. For example, there

are many ways to dig a ditch. We could use *no capital at all* and have dozens of workers digging with their bare hands. We could use *a small amount of capital* by giving each worker a shovel and thereby use less labor, since each worker would now be more productive. Or we could use *even more capital*—a power trencher—and dig the ditch with just one or two workers. Every economic system has some mechanism to select *how* goods and services will be produced from the many options available.

3. ***Who* should get them?**

This is where economics interacts most strongly with politics. There are so many ways to divide ourselves into groups: men and women, rich and poor, skilled and unskilled, workers and owners, families and single people, young and old . . . the list is almost endless. How should the products of our economy be distributed among these different groups and among individuals within each group? Determining *who* gets the economy's output is always the most controversial aspect of resource allocation. Over the last half-century, our society has become more sensitized to the way goods and services are distributed, and we increasingly ask whether that distribution is fair.

How do societies determine the answers to these questions about resources? Historically, three main methods have evolved: *tradition*, *command*, and *the market*. We can label an economic system based on which of the three methods is dominant. Let's consider each type of economic system in turn.

The Traditional Economy

Traditional economy An economy in which resources are allocated according to long-lived practices from the past.

In a **traditional economy,** resources are allocated according to the long-lived practices of the past. Tradition was the dominant method of resource allocation for most of human history and remains strong in many tribal societies and small villages in parts of Africa, South America, Asia, and the Pacific. Typically, traditional methods of production are handed down by the village elders, and traditional principles of fairness govern the distribution of goods and services.

Economies in which resources are allocated mostly by tradition tend to be stable and predictable. But these economies have one serious drawback: They don't grow. With everyone locked into the traditional patterns of production, there is little room for innovation and technological change. Traditional economies are therefore likely to be stagnant economies.

The Command Economy

Command or centrally planned economy An economic system in which resources are allocated according to explicit instructions from a central authority.

In a **command economy,** resources are allocated mostly by explicit instructions from some higher authority. Because the government must plan these instructions in advance, command economies are also called **centrally planned economies.**

But command economies are disappearing fast. Until about 25 years ago, examples would have included the former Soviet Union, Poland, Romania, Bulgaria, Albania, China, and many others. Beginning in the late 1980s, all of these nations began abandoning central planning because the system had so many problems.

To be fair, command economies did have some major achievements too. In their early years, production in China and the former Soviet Union grew rapidly, enabling these countries to provide everyone with a job and basic consumer goods like food, clothing, and shelter. But their governments often enforced commands through brute force, and millions who were suspected of opposing the government were imprisoned or killed. In their final decades, command economies were unable to keep up with the rising expectations of their populations. Living standards stagnated, and popular dissatisfaction—both political and economic—eventually led to the abandonment of strict central planning. The only command economies left today are North Korea and Cuba, although Cuba began taking major steps away from central planning in 2011.

The Market Economy

The third method of allocating resources—and the one with which you are no doubt most familiar—is "the market." In a **market economy,** instead of following long-held traditions or commands from above, people are largely free to do what they want with the resources at their disposal. In the end, resources are allocated as a result of individual decision making. *Which* goods and services are produced? The ones that producers *choose* to produce. *How* are they produced? However producers *choose* to produce them. *Who* gets these goods and services? Anyone who *chooses* to buy them.

> **Market economy** An economic system in which resources are allocated through individual decision making.

Of course, in a market economy, freedom of choice is constrained by the resources one controls. And in this respect, we do not all start in the same place in the economic race. Some of us have inherited great financial wealth, intelligence, talent, or beauty; and some, such as the children of successful professionals, are born into a world of helpful personal contacts. Others, unfortunately, will inherit none of these advantages. In a market system, those who control more resources will have more choices available to them than those who control fewer resources. Nevertheless, given these different starting points, individual choice plays the major role in allocating resources in a market economy.

But wait . . . isn't there a problem here? People acting according to their own desires, without command or tradition to control them? This sounds like a recipe for chaos! How, in such a free-for-all, could resources possibly be *allocated*?

The answer is contained in two words: *markets* and *prices.*

UNDERSTANDING THE MARKET

The market economy gets its name from something that nearly always happens when people are free to do what they want with the resources they possess. Inevitably, people decide to specialize in the production of one or a few things—often organizing themselves into business firms—and then sellers and buyers *come together to trade*. A **market** is a collection of buyers and sellers who have the potential to trade with one another.

> **Market** A group of buyers and sellers with the potential to trade with each other.

In some cases, the market is *global*; that is, the market consists of buyers and sellers who are spread across the globe. The market for oil is an example of a global market, since buyers in any country can buy from sellers in any country. In other cases, the market is local. Markets for restaurant meals, haircuts, and taxi service are examples of local markets.

Markets play a major role in allocating resources by forcing individual decision makers to consider very carefully their decisions about buying and selling. They do so because of an important feature of every market: the *price* at which a good is bought and sold.

The Importance of Prices

A **price** is *the amount of money a buyer must pay to a seller for a good or service*. Price is not always the same as *cost*. In economics, as you've learned in this chapter, cost means *opportunity cost*—the *total* sacrifice needed to buy the good. While the money price of a good is a *part* of its opportunity cost, it is not the only cost. For example, the price does not include the value of the time sacrificed to buy something. Buying a new jacket will require you to spend time traveling to and from the store, trying on different styles and sizes, and waiting in line at the cash register.

> **Price** The amount of money that must be paid to a seller to obtain a good or service.

Still, in most cases, the price of a good is a significant part of its opportunity cost. For large purchases, such as a home or automobile, the price will be *most* of the opportunity cost. And this is why prices are so important to the overall working of the economy: They confront individual decision makers with the costs of their choices.

Consider the example of purchasing a car. Because you must pay the price, you know that buying a new car will require you to cut back on purchases of other things. In this way, the opportunity cost to *society* of making another car is converted to an opportunity cost *for you*. If you value a new car more highly than the other things you must sacrifice for it, you will buy it. If not, you won't buy it.

Why is it so important that people face the opportunity costs of their actions? The following thought experiment can answer this question.

A Thought Experiment: Free Cars

Imagine that the government passes a new law: When anyone buys a new car, the government will reimburse that person for it immediately. The consequences would be easy to predict.

First, on the day the law was passed, everyone would rush out to buy new cars. Why not, if cars are free? The entire stock of existing automobiles would be gone within days—maybe even hours. Many people who didn't value cars much at all, and who seldom used them, would find themselves owning several—one for each day of the week or to match the different colors in their wardrobe. Others who weren't able to act in time—including some who desperately needed a new car for their work or to run their households—would be unable to find one at all.

Over time, automobile companies would drastically increase production to meet the surge in demand for cars. So much of our available labor, capital, land, and entrepreneurial talent would be diverted to making cars that we'd have to sacrifice huge quantities of all other goods and services. Thus, we'd end up *paying* for those additional cars in the end, by having less education, less medical care, perhaps even less food—all to support the widespread, frivolous use of cars. Almost everyone would conclude that society had been made worse off with the new "free-car" policy. By eliminating a price for automobiles, we would sever the connection between society's opportunity cost of producing cars and individuals' decisions to buy them. And we would create quite a mess for ourselves.

> *When resources are allocated by the market, and people must pay for their purchases, they are forced to consider the opportunity cost to society of the goods that they consume. In this way, markets help to create a sensible allocation of resources.*

Markets, Ownership, and the Invisible Hand

The complete label for market economies is *market capitalism*. While the market describes how resources are allocated, capitalism refers to one way that resources are *owned*. Under **capitalism**, most resources are owned by private citizens, who are mostly free to sell or rent them to others as they wish. The alternative mode of ownership is **socialism**, a system in which most resources are owned by the state, as in the former Soviet Union.

The market and capitalism go hand in hand, and for good reason. If individuals are left free to make decisions about resources, we want them to make their decisions carefully, in a socially useful way, and not waste society's scarce resources or use them frivolously. Private ownership of resources provides incentives for people to make careful, socially beneficial decisions.

This insight was best expressed by Adam Smith (1723–1790), the Scottish social philosopher who is often regarded as the first economist. In *The Wealth of Nations*, published in 1776, Smith argued that private resource owners are guided as if by an *invisible hand* to benefit society as a whole. As Smith put it, a private resource owner in a market economy

> . . . neither intends to promote the public interest, nor knows how much he is promoting it . . . he intends only his own gain, and he is in this, as in many other cases, led by an invisible hand to promote an end which was no part of his intention. Nor is it always the worse for the society that it was no part of it. By pursuing his own interest he frequently promotes that of the society more effectually than when he really intends to promote it.[4]

The key to this insight is that trade in a market economy is *voluntary*. No trade can take place unless both sides believe they will benefit from it. So in order to enjoy gains from trading, you must find a way to use your resources that will make someone else better off if they trade with you. For example, if you own land or a factory, or you have a skill, you will earn income only if you make your resources available for production. And those who buy or rent your resources will earn the most income for themselves by using your resources in the most productive way possible. In this way, our self-serving desires push the economy to be *productively efficient* (to operate on, rather than inside, the PPF). Moreover, business owners will earn income only if they produce goods that people actually want to buy (like chocolate ice cream), rather than goods that no one wants (broccoli-flavored ice cream). By producing and selling the most desirable goods, resource owners, business owners, and consumers all gain. Even though our motives may be selfish, our decisions benefit others in the economy too.

The U.S. Market System in Perspective

The United States has always been considered a leading example of a market economy. Each day, millions of distinct items are produced and sold in markets. Our grocery stores are always stocked with broccoli and tomato soup, and the drugstore always has tissues and aspirin—all due to the choices of individual producers and consumers. The goods that are traded, the way they are traded, and the price at which they trade are determined by the traders themselves.

But even in the United States, there are numerous cases of resource allocation *outside* the market. Many economic decisions are made within families, where tradition often dominates. For example, even when children get an allowance or have other earnings, they don't have to pay for goods consumed within the home. Other decisions within the family are based on command ("No TV until you finish your homework!").

In the broader economy, we find many examples of resource allocation by command. Various levels of government collect, in total, about one-third of our incomes as taxes. We are *told* how much tax we must pay, and those who don't comply suffer serious penalties, including imprisonment. Government—rather than individual decision makers—spends the tax revenue. In this way, the government plays a major role in allocating resources—especially in determining which goods are produced and who gets them.

[4] Adam Smith, *The Wealth of Nations* (Modern Library Classics Edition, 2000), p. 423

Mixed Economy A market economy in which the government also plays an important role in allocating resources.

There are also other ways, aside from strict commands, that the government limits our market freedoms. Regulations designed to protect the environment, maintain safe workplaces, and ensure the safety of our food supply are just a few examples of government-imposed constraints on our individual choice. Thus, the U.S. economy—like every other market economy today—uses both command and the market to allocate resources. For this reason, modern market economies are sometimes called **mixed economies**.

Changing the Mix

Many of the most controversial political debates in the United States are about the right mix between command and the market for allocating resources—a normative issue about which people can disagree. For example, consider the 2010 health care legislation mentioned at the beginning of this chapter. Opponents argued that the new law tilted the mix too far toward command and away from the market. After all, the law *requires* people to purchase health insurance, and it imposes stricter limits on the behavior of private decision makers (e.g., health insurance companies). But supporters argued that making health care available to more Americans was an important social goal that could best be accomplished by increasing the government's role. They felt this tilt away from the market was appropriate and necessary.

In countries that formerly used central planning—such as Russia and China—government's role in allocating resources has shrunk dramatically. But in market economies such as the United States, government has become more involved in resource allocation over the years. This is especially true of many Western European countries, such as France, Germany, and Sweden. Compared to the United States, citizens in these countries pay a higher percentage of their income in taxes, businesses face more restrictions on their activities, and *social safety nets* (government-run programs to assist the poor and the unemployed) are more generous.

Still, in Europe—as in the United States—the market remains dominant. For each example of resource allocation by command or a serious restriction of some market freedom, we can find hundreds of examples where individuals make choices according to their own desires. The goods and services that we buy, the jobs at which we work, the homes in which we live—in almost all cases, these result from market choices.

A Look Ahead …

The market is simultaneously the most simple and the most complex way to allocate resources. For each buyer and seller, the market is simple. There are no traditions or commands to be memorized and obeyed. Instead, we enter the markets we *wish* to trade in, and we respond to prices there as we *wish* to, unconcerned about the overall process of resource allocation.

But from the economist's point of view, the market is quite complex. Resources are allocated indirectly, as a by-product of individual decision making, rather than through easily identified traditions or commands. As a result, it often takes some skillful economic detective work to determine just how individuals are behaving and how resources are being allocated as a consequence.

How can we make sense of all of this apparent chaos and complexity? That is what economics is all about. You will begin your detective work in Chapter 3, where you will learn about the most widely used model in economics: supply and demand.

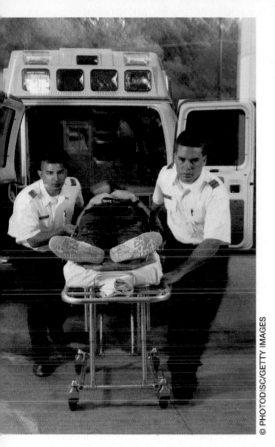

ARE WE SAVING LIVES EFFICIENTLY?

Earlier in this chapter, you learned that instances of gross productive inefficiency are not as easy to find in our economy as one might imagine. But many economists argue that our allocation of resources to lifesaving efforts is a glaring exception. In this section, we'll use some of the tools and concepts you've learned in this chapter to ask whether we are saving lives efficiently.

Lifesaving and the PPF

Let's view "saving lives" as the output—a service—produced by the "lifesaving industry." This industry consists of private firms (such as medical practices and hospitals), as well as government agencies (such as the Department of Health and Human Services or the Environmental Protection Agency). In a productively efficient economy, we must pay an opportunity cost whenever we choose to save additional lives. That's because saving more lives—by building another emergency surgery center, running an advertising campaign to encourage healthier living, or requiring the use of costly but safe materials instead of cheaper but toxic ones—requires resources. And these resources could be used to produce other goods and services instead.

Figure 7 illustrates this opportunity cost with a production-possibilities frontier. The number of lives saved per year is measured along the horizontal axis, and the quantity of all other goods

FIGURE 7   Efficiency and Inefficiency in Saving Lives

This PPF shows society's choice between saving lives (measured along the horizontal axis) and all other production (on the vertical axis). Operating on the curve (at points like A, A', or A″) would be productively efficient. But if the life-saving industry is not efficient, then society is operating inside the PPF (at a point like B). Eliminating the inefficiency would enable us to save more lives, or have more of other goods, or both.

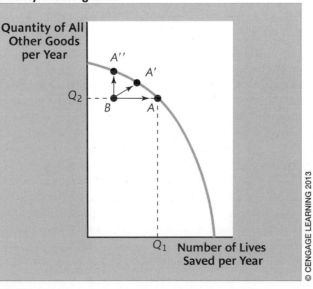

(lumped together into a single category) is measured on the vertical axis. A productively efficient economy would be *on* the frontier. Point *A* on the PPF is one such productively efficient point, where we would save Q_1 lives per year, and produce the quantity Q_2 of all other goods. Once we are on the frontier, we can only save more lives by pulling resources away from producing other goods and paying an opportunity cost in other goods forgone.

But what if there is productive *in*efficiency in the economy? And what if the source of the inefficiency is in lifesaving itself? More specifically, what if the "lifesaving industry" could save more lives using the current quantity of resources, simply by reallocating those resources among different types of lifesaving activities? In that case, we would be currently operating at a point like *B*, *inside* the PPF. By eliminating the inefficiency, we could move *to* the frontier. For example, we could save more lives with no sacrifice of other goods (a move from point *B* to point *A*) or have more of other goods while saving the same number of lives (a move to point *A″*) or have more of both (point *A′*).

Lifesaving in the United States

Economists argue that the United States and many other countries do, in fact, suffer from productive inefficiency in saving lives. How have they come to such a conclusion?

The first step in the analysis is to remember that, in a market economy, resources sell at a price. We can use the dollar cost of a lifesaving method to measure the value of the resources used up by that method. Moreover, we can compare the "cost per year of life saved" of different methods.

For example, one study showed that in the United States, we spend roughly $382 million on heart transplants each year, and thereby add about 1,600 years to the lives of heart patients. Thus, the cost per year of life saved from heart transplants is $381,000,000/1,600 = $238,000 (rounded to the nearest thousand).

The upper part of Table 6 lists this cost per life-year saved for heart transplants and several other methods we currently use to save lives in the United States. Some of these methods reflect legal or regulatory decisions (such as the ban on chlorobenzilate pesticides), while others are common or often-used medical care practices (such as flu shots and heart transplants).

You can see that the cost per life-year saved ranges widely. It costs just a few hundred dollars to save a year of life by giving flu shots or having doctors warn patients to quit smoking. But it costs millions of dollars for each life-year saved with certain regulations, such as workplace arsenic exposure.

Our society has largely exhausted the potential to save lives from some of the examples listed in the upper part of the table. For example, most doctors *do* warn their smoking patients to quit. But some methods—though common—are not fully exploited. Millions of people do *not* currently get flu shots, for example. Moreover, some methods of saving lives that are *not* common practice (shown in the bottom half of the table) are relatively low-cost. Whenever we use up resources for less cost-effective methods before fully exploiting more cost-effective methods, we are being productively *in*efficient in life saving.

To see why, let's do some thought experiments. First, let's imagine that we shift resources from heart transplants to *intensive* antismoking efforts. Then for each year of life we decided not to save with heart transplants, we would free up $238,000 in medical resources. If we applied those resources toward intensive antismoking efforts, at a cost of $3,518 per year of life saved, we could then save $238,000/$3,518 = 67 life-years instead of just one. In other words, we could increase the number of

TABLE 6

The Cost of Saving Lives

Method	Cost per Life-Year Saved (2010 dollars)
Common Practice or Regulation	
Flu vaccinations	$210
Brief physician antismoking intervention (Single personal warning from Physician to stop smoking)	$215
Chlorination of drinking water	$4,700
Trihalomethane limits for drinking water	$16,600
Benzene emissions regulations	$155,000
Heart transplants	$238,000
Reflective devices on heavy trucks	$287,000
Applying chlorobenzilate pesticide ban to citrus fruit	$1,812,000
Limits on workplace arsenic exposure	$2,452,000
Proposed or Possible	
Increase random motor vehicle inspections	$2,300
Replace ambulances with helicopters for medical emergencies	$3,337
Intensive antismoking intervention (Physician identification of smokers; three physician counseling sessions; two sessions with smoking cessation specialists; provision of nicotine patch or gum)	$3,500
Install more automated external defibrillators in workplaces	$7,500
Build additional trauma centers	$36,000
Intensive blood pressure counseling (2 years of monitoring and counseling for normal-weight patients with high blood-pressure)	$65,000
Change in cigarette warning labels (2010 FDA proposal to add color-coded graphics)	$110,000
Meningococcal vaccine for adolescents	$134,000
Triple the wind resistance of new buildings	$3,900,000
Seat belts on school buses	$4,300,000

Note: Author calculations used to adjust results to 2010 dollars, and (for a few studies) from cost per life saved to cost per life-year saved.

Sources: Tammy O. Tengs et al. (1995) "Five hundred life-saving interventions and their cost effectiveness," *Risk Analysis* 15 (3); Malcolm Law and Jin Ling Tan (October 1995) "An analysis of the effectiveness of interventions intended to help people stop smoking," *Archives of Internal Medicine* 155 (18); Jerry Cromwell et al. (1997) "Cost-effectiveness of the clinical practice recommendations in the AHCPR guideline for smoking cessation," *Journal of the American Medical Association* 278 (21); P.A. Gearhart and A. R. Wuerz (October 1997) "Cost-effectiveness analysis of helicopter EMS for trauma patients," *Annals of Emergency Medicine* 30 (4); W. Kip Viscusi (February 2006) "Regulation of health, safety and environmental risks," *Harvard John M. Olin Discussion Paper Series*, Discussion Paper No. 544; Ellen J. McKenzie et al. (July 2010) "The value of trauma center care," *Journal of Trauma-Injury Infection & Critical Care* 69(1):1–10; S. K. Datta et al. (August 2010) "Economic analysis of a tailored behavioral intervention to improve blood pressure control for primary care patients," *American Heart Journal* 160 (2) (results for men and women have been averaged); Colin W. Shephard et al. (May 2005) "Cost-effectiveness of conjugate meningococcal vaccination strategies in the United States," *Pediatrics* 115 (5); "Proposed rules: Required warnings for cigarette packages and advertisements," *Federal Register*, Nov 12, 2010.

life-years saved without any increase in the total value of resources used, and without any sacrifice in other goods and services.

But why pick on heart transplants? We use hundreds of millions of dollars worth of resources limiting arsenic exposure in the workplace, costing us about $2.5 million per life-year saved. Suppose these resources were used instead to install automated external defibrillators in more workplaces, which cost $7,500 per life-year saved. Then, for each life-year lost to arsenic exposure, we'd save $2.5 million/$7,500 = 333 life-years through defibrillators.

How much does this productive inefficiency in life saving cost us? One study looked at 185 actual and potential life-saving methods, and found that merely shifting resources around so that the most cost-effective methods were fully exploited would more than double the number of life-years saved.[5] All without any sacrifice in other goods and services.

Of course, allocating lifesaving resources is much more complicated than our discussion so far has implied. For one thing, the benefits of lifesaving efforts are not fully captured by "life-years saved" (or even by an alternative measure, which accounts for improvement in *quality* of life). The cost per life-year saved from mandating seat belts on school buses is extremely high—more than $4 million. This is mostly because very few children die in school bus accidents—about 11 per year in the entire United States—and, according to the National Traffic Safety Board, few of these deaths would have been prevented with seat belts. But mandatory seat belts—rightly or wrongly—might decrease the anxiety of millions of parents as they send their children off to school. How should we value such a reduction in anxiety? Hard to say. But it may be reasonable to include it as a benefit—at least in some way—when deciding about resources.

[5] Tammy O. Tengs, "Dying Too Soon: How Cost-Effectiveness Analysis Can Save Lives," *National Center for Policy Analysis Report*, No. 204, May 1997.

SUMMARY

The *production possibilities frontier* (PPF) is a simple model to illustrate the opportunity cost of society's choices. When we are *productively efficient* (operating *on* the PPF), producing more of one thing requires producing less of something else. The *law of increasing opportunity cost* tells us that the more of something we produce, the greater the opportunity cost of producing still more. Even when we are operating inside the PPF—say because of productive inefficiency or a recession—it is not necessarily easy or costless to move to the PPF and avoid opportunity cost.

In a world of scarce resources, each society must have an *economic system*: its way of organizing economic activity. All economic systems feature *specialization,* in which each person and firm concentrates on a limited number of productive activities, and exchange, through which we obtain most of what we desire by trading with others. Specialization and exchange enable us to enjoy higher living standards than would be possible under self-sufficiency.

One way that specialization increases living standards is by allowing each of us to concentrate on tasks in which we have a *comparative advantage.* When individuals within a country produce more of their comparative advantage goods and exchange with others, living standards in that country are higher. Similarly, when individual nations specialize in their comparative advantage goods and trade with other nations, global living standards rise.

Every economic system determines how resources are allocated. Resources can be allocated by *tradition, command,* or *the market.* In a *market economy,* resources are allocated primarily through individual choice. Prices play an important role in markets by forcing decision makers to take account of society's opportunity cost when they make choices. Another feature of market economies—*capitalism* (private ownership of resources)—helps to direct resources in ways that create benefits for others.

PROBLEM SET

Answers to even-numbered Problems can be found on the text Web site through www.cengagebrain.com

1. Redraw Figure 1, but this time identify a different set of points along the frontier. Starting at point *F* (5,000 tanks, zero production of wheat), have each point you select show equal increments in the quantity of wheat produced. For example, a new point *H* should correspond to 200,000 bushels of wheat, point *J* to 400,000 bushels, point *K* to 600,000 bushels, and so on. Now observe what happens to the opportunity cost of "200,000 more bushels of wheat" as you move leftward and upward along this PPF. Does the law of increasing opportunity cost apply to the production of wheat? Explain briefly.

2. How would a technological innovation in lifesaving— say, the discovery of a cure for cancer—affect the PPF in Figure 7?

3. How would a technological innovation in the production of *other* goods—say, the invention of a new kind of robot that speeds up assembly-line manufacturing— affect the PPF in Figure 7?

4. Suppose the Internet enables more production of other goods *and* helps to save lives (for simplicity, assume proportional increases). Show how the PPF in Figure 7 would be affected.

5. Suppose that one day, Gilligan (the castaway) eats a magical island plant that turns him into an expert at everything. In particular, it now takes him just half an hour to pick a cup of berries, and 15 minutes to catch a fish.
   a. Redo Table 2 in the chapter.
   b. Who—Gilligan or Maryanne—has a comparative advantage in picking berries? In fishing?
   c. Suppose that Gilligan reallocates his time to produce *two more units* of his comparative advantage good and that Maryanne does the same. Construct a new version of Table 3 in the chapter, showing how production changes for each castaway and for the island as a whole.

6. Suppose that two different castaways, Mr. and Mrs. Howell, end up on a different island. Mr. Howell can pick 1 pineapple per hour, or 1 coconut. Mrs. Howell can pick 2 pineapples per hour, but it takes her 2 hours to pick a coconut.
   a. Construct a table like Table 2 showing Mr. and Mrs. Howell's labor requirements.
   b. Who—Mr. or Mrs. Howell—has a comparative advantage in picking pineapples? In picking coconuts? Which of the two should specialize in which tasks?
   c. [Harder] Assume that Mr. and Mrs. Howell had originally washed ashore on different parts of the island, and that they originally each spent 12 hours per day working, spending 6 hours picking pineapples and 6 hours picking coconuts. How will their total production change if they find each other and begin to specialize?

7. You and a friend have decided to work jointly on a course project. Frankly, your friend is a less-than-ideal partner. His skills as a researcher are such that he can review and outline only two articles a day. Moreover, his hunt-and-peck style limits him to only 10 pages of typing a day. On the other hand, in a day you can produce six outlines or type 20 pages.
   a. Who has an absolute advantage in outlining, you or your friend? What about typing?
   b. Who has a comparative advantage in outlining? In typing?
   c. According to the principle of comparative advantage, who should specialize in which task?

8. Suppose that an economy's PPF is a straight line, rather than a bowed out, concave curve. What would this say about the nature of opportunity cost as production is shifted from one good to the other?

More Challenging

9. Go back to Table 5 in the chapter, which is based on the hours requirements in Table 4. Suppose that when trade opens up between the U.S. and China, the U.S. increases its production of soybeans by 100 bushels (instead of 10 as in the table). China increases its production of T-shirts by 400 (instead of 40). Assume that when the two countries trade with each other, each bushel of soybeans is exchanged for 3 T-shirts. Finally, suppose that the U.S. trades (exports) 90 bushels of soybeans to China.
   a. How many T-shirts from China will the U.S. receive in exchange for its soybean exports to China?
   b. After trading with China, how many more bushels of soybeans will be available for Americans to consume (compared to the situation before trade)? How many more T-shirts?
   c. After trading with the U.S., how many more bushels of soybeans will be available for the Chinese to consume? How many more T-shirts?
   d. Based on this example, consider the following statement: "When two countries trade with each other, one country's gain will always be the other country's loss." Is this statement true or false? Explain briefly.

10. Evaluate the following statement: "If the dollar values in Table 6 are accurate, it follows that providing meningococcal vaccines to all adolescents would be cheaper than installing seat belts on all school buses." True or false? Explain.

CHAPTER 3

Supply and Demand

F ather Guido Sarducci, a character on the early episodes of the TV show *Saturday Night Live*, once observed that the average person remembers only about five minutes worth of material from college. He therefore proposed the "Five Minute University," in which you'd learn only the five minutes of material you'd actually remember. The economics course would last only 10 seconds, just enough time for students to learn to memorize three words: "supply and demand."

Of course, there is much more to economics than these three words. But supply and demand does play a central role in economics. What, exactly, does this familiar phrase really mean?

First, supply and demand is an economic *model*, designed to explain *how prices are determined in certain types of markets.*

But it's an important model because prices themselves play such an important role in the economy. Once the price of something has been determined, only those willing to pay that price will get it. Thus, prices determine which households will get which goods and services and which firms will get which resources. If you want to know why the cell phone industry is expanding while the video rental industry is shrinking, or why homelessness is a more pervasive problem in the United States than hunger, you need to understand how prices are determined. In this chapter, you will learn how the model of supply and demand works and how to use it.

MARKETS

Put any compound in front of a chemist, ask him what it is and what it can be used for, and he will immediately think of the basic elements—carbon, hydrogen, oxygen, and so on. Ask an economist almost any question about the economy, and he will immediately think about *markets*.

When you hear the word "market," you probably think of a specific location where buying and selling take place: a supermarket, a flea market, and so on. In economics, "market" has a broader meaning:

> *A market is a group of buyers and sellers with the potential to trade with each other.*

The buyers and sellers in a market don't have to be in the same location, or even in the same country. For example, a seafood company in Vietnam might sell frozen shrimp to an import company in New York, without anyone from either company meeting face to face. Both the seller in Vietnam and the buyer in New York are part of the frozen-shrimp market. Economists think of the economy as a collection of markets. There is a market for oranges, another for automobiles, another for real estate, and still others for corporate stocks, plumbers' services, land, euros, and anything else that is bought and sold.

Characterizing a Market

The first step in analyzing a market is to figure out *which* market you are analyzing. This might seem easy. But we can choose to define a market in different ways, depending on our purpose.

Broad versus Narrow Definition

Suppose we want to study the personal computer industry in the United States. Should we define the market very broadly ("the market for computers"), or very narrowly ("the market for ultra-light laptops"), or something in between ("the market for laptops")? The right choice depends on the problem we're trying to analyze.

For example, if we're interested in why computers *in general* have come down in price over the past decade, we'd treat all types of computers as if they were the same good. Economists call this process **aggregation**—combining a group of distinct things into a single whole.

But suppose we're asking a different question: Why do laptops always cost more than desktops with similar computing power? Then we'd aggregate all laptops together as one good, and all desktops as another, and look at each of these more narrowly defined markets.

We can also choose to define the *geography* of a market more broadly or more narrowly, depending on our purpose. We'd analyze the *national* market for gasoline if we're explaining general nationwide trends in gas prices. But we'd define it more locally to explain, say, why gas prices are rising more rapidly in Los Angeles than in other areas of the country.

> In economics, **markets** *can be defined broadly or narrowly, depending on our purpose.*

Aggregation The process of combining distinct things into a single whole.

Markets A group of buyers and sellers with the potential to trade with each other.

How markets are defined is one of the most important differences between *macro*economics and *micro*economics. In macroeconomics, goods and services are aggregated to the highest levels. Macro models even lump all consumer goods—breakfast cereals, smart phones, denim jeans, and so forth—into the single category "consumption goods" and view them as if they are traded in a single, national "market for consumption goods." Defining markets this broadly allows macroeconomists to take an overall view of the economy without getting bogged down in the details.

In microeconomics, by contrast, markets are defined more narrowly. Instead of asking how much we'll spend on *consumer goods,* a microeconomist might ask how much we'll spend on *health care* or *video games.* Even in microeconomics, there is always some aggregation, but not as much as in macroeconomics.

Product and Resource Markets

Figure 1, often called the simple **circular flow** model of the economy, illustrates two different types of markets and how they relate to each other. The upper half illustrates **product markets,** where goods and services are bought and sold. The blue arrows show the flow of products from the business firms who supply them to the

Circular flow A simple model that shows how goods, resources, and dollar payments flow between households and firms.

Product markets Markets in which firms sell goods and services to households.

FIGURE I   The Circular Flow Model

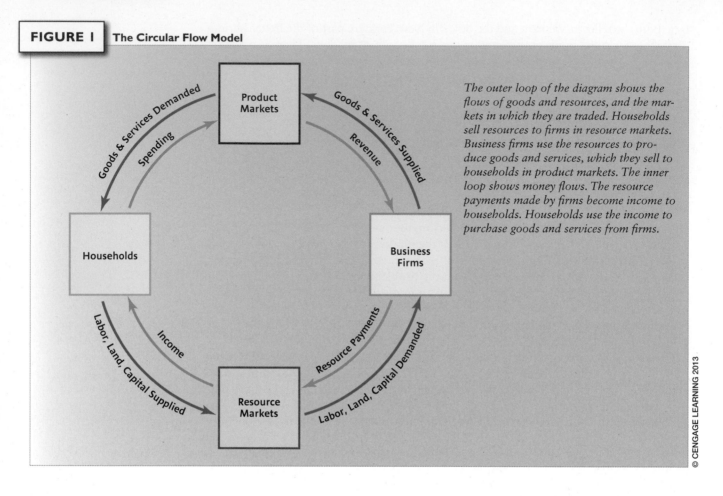

Product Markets

Households

Business Firms

Resource Markets

Goods & Services Demanded

Spending

Goods & Services Supplied

Revenue

Labor, Land, Capital Supplied

Income

Resource Payments

Labor, Land, Capital Demanded

The outer loop of the diagram shows the flows of goods and resources, and the markets in which they are traded. Households sell resources to firms in resource markets. Business firms use the resources to produce goods and services, which they sell to households in product markets. The inner loop shows money flows. The resource payments made by firms become income to households. Households use the income to purchase goods and services from firms.

© CENGAGE LEARNING 2013

Resource markets Markets in which households that own resources sell them to firms.

households who ultimately buy them. The green arrows show the associated flow of dollars from the households who spend the dollars, to the business firms who receive these dollars as revenue. (In the real world, businesses also sell products to the government and to other businesses, but this simple version leaves out these details.)

The lower half depicts a different set of markets: **resource markets,** where labor, land, and capital are bought and sold. Here, the roles of households and firms are reversed. The blue arrows show resources flowing from the households (who own and supply them) to the business firms (who demand them). The associated flow of dollars is indicated by the green arrows: Business firms pay for the resources they use, and households receive these payments as income.

In this chapter, we'll be using supply and demand to analyze product markets—particularly those where business firms supply goods and services that are bought by households. In later chapters, we'll look at resource markets, as well as some other types of markets that are not included in the circular flow depicted here. These include markets for existing homes, and markets for financial assets such as stocks and bonds.

Competition in Markets

A final issue in defining a market is how prices are determined. In one type of market, individual buyers or sellers have some *control* over the price of the product. Microsoft—a major seller of operating systems and other software—operates in this kind of market. Microsoft can raise the price of its Windows operating system and sell fewer units, or lower its price and sell more. Markets like these—in which individual buyers or sellers can control or influence the price—are called *imperfectly competitive markets*.

In the other type of market, each buyer and seller is *confronted* with a market price that they can do little or nothing about. Consider the market for wheat. On any given day, there is a going price for wheat—say, $5.80 per bushel. If a farmer tries to charge more than that—say, $5.85 per bushel—he won't sell any wheat at all! His customers will instead go to one of his many competitors and buy the identical product from them for less. Each wheat farmer must take the price of wheat as a "given."

The same is true of a single wheat *buyer:* If he tries to negotiate a lower price from a seller, he'd be laughed off the farm. "Why should I sell my wheat to you for $5.75 per bushel, when there are others who will pay me $5.80?" Accordingly, each buyer must take the market price as a given.

The market for wheat is an example of a *perfectly competitive market*.

> *In **perfectly competitive markets** (or just **competitive markets**), each buyer and seller takes the market price as a given.*

Perfectly competitive market (informal definition) A market in which no buyer or seller has the power to influence the price.

But wait. If no individual buyer or seller can influence the price, then who decides what the price of wheat will be? The answer is: The "market" decides. If that sounds a bit mysterious or circular right now, don't worry. Explaining how prices are determined in competitive markets is exactly what supply and demand is all about.

> *The supply and demand model is designed to show how prices are determined in perfectly competitive markets.*

Applying Supply and Demand in the Real World

You'll learn more about what makes some markets perfectly competitive and others not when you are further into your study of *micro*economics. But here's a hint: In perfectly competitive markets, there are many buyers and sellers that are each very small relative to the total market, and the product is standardized, like wheat. In imperfectly competitive markets, by contrast, individual buyers or sellers can be a relatively large part of the market, or else the product of each seller is unique in some way.

But don't worry too much about perfect competition in this chapter, because the supply and demand model is often useful even when markets are *not* perfectly competitive. For example, in the market for hamburgers, there are high-priced restaurants and low-priced restaurants, so there is no single price for hamburgers in the market. Moreover, each restaurant (or restaurant chain) has some control over its own hamburger price. So the market for hamburgers is *not* strictly perfectly competitive.

But it is not too far from competitive. Most restaurants do regard the *range* of possible prices they can charge as given. The supply and demand model can help us see how this range of prices is determined, and what makes the average price of hamburgers rise or fall. In fact, if you ask an economist to explain or predict changes in the price of hamburgers, books, automobiles, or almost any other good or service, he or she will reach for the supply-and-demand model first. Supply and demand is the most versatile and widely used model in the economist's toolkit.

© JEFF GREENBERG/ALAMY

In the rest of this chapter, we will build the supply-and-demand model. As the name implies, the model has two major parts: *supply* and *demand*. Let's start by analyzing the demand side of the market.

DEMAND

It's tempting to think of the "demand" for a product as psychological—a pure "want" or "desire." But that kind of thinking can lead us astray. For example, you *want* all kinds of things: a bigger apartment, a better car, nicer clothes, more and better vacations. The list is endless. But you don't always *buy* them. Why not?

Because in addition to your wants—which you'd very much like to satisfy—you also face *constraints*. First, you have to *pay* for the products you want. Second, your spending power is limited, so every decision to buy one thing is also a decision *not* to buy something else (or a decision to save less, and have less buying power in the future). As a result, every purchase confronts you with an opportunity cost. Your "wants," together with the real-world constraints that you face, determine what you will choose to buy in any market. Hence, the following definition:

> The **quantity demanded** of a good or service is the number of units that all buyers in a market would choose to buy over a given time period, given the constraints that they face.

Quantity demanded The quantity of a good that all buyers in a market would choose to buy during a period of time, given their constraints.

Since this definition plays a key role in any supply and demand analysis, it's worth taking a closer look at it.

Quantity Demanded Implies a Choice. Quantity demanded doesn't tell us the amount of a good that households feel they "need" or "desire" in order to be happy. Instead, it tells us how much households would choose to buy *when they take into account the opportunity cost* of their decisions. The opportunity cost arises from the constraints households face, such as having to pay a given price for the good, limits on spendable funds, and so on.

Quantity Demanded Is Hypothetical. Will households actually be *able* to purchase the amount they want to purchase? As you'll soon see, usually yes. But there are special situations—analyzed in microeconomics—in which households are frustrated in buying all that they would like to buy. Quantity demanded makes no assumptions about the availability of the good. Instead, it's the answer to a hypothetical question: How much would households buy, given the constraints that they face, if the units they wanted to buy were available?

Quantity Demanded Depends on Price. The price of the good is just one variable among many that influences quantity demanded. But because the price is a key variable that our model will ultimately determine, we try to keep that variable front-and-center in our thinking. This is why for the next few pages we'll assume that all other influences on demand are held constant, so we can explore the relationship between price and quantity demanded.

The Law of Demand

How does a change in price affect quantity demanded? You probably know the answer to this already: When something is more expensive, people tend to buy less of it. This common observation applies to air travel, magazines, guitars, and virtually everything else that people buy. For all of these goods and services, price and quantity are *negatively related*: That is, when price rises, quantity demanded falls; when price falls, quantity demanded rises. This negative relationship is observed so regularly in markets that economists call it the *law of demand*.

> The **law of demand** states that when the price of a good rises and everything else remains the same, the quantity of the good demanded will fall.

Law of demand As the price of a good increases, the quantity demanded decreases.

Read that definition again, and notice the very important words, "everything else remains the same." The law of demand tells us what would happen *if* all the other influences on buyers' choices remained unchanged, and only one influence—the price of the good—changed.

This is an example of a common practice in economics. In the real world, many variables change *simultaneously*. But to understand changes in the economy, we must first understand the effect of each variable *separately*. So we conduct a series of mental experiments in which we ask: "What would happen if this one influence— and only this one—were to change?" The law of demand is the result of one such mental experiment, in which we imagine that the price of the good changes, but all other influences on quantity demanded remain constant.

Mental experiments like this are used so often in economics that we sometimes use a shorthand Latin expression to remind us that we are holding all but one influence constant: ***ceteris paribus*** (formally pronounced KAY-ter-is PAR-ih-bus, although it's acceptable to pronounce the first word as SEH-ter-is). This is Latin for "all else the same," or "all else remaining unchanged." Even when it is not explicitly stated, the *ceteris paribus* assumption is virtually always implied. The exceptions are cases where we consider two or more influences on a variable that change simultaneously, as we will do toward the end of this chapter.

Ceteris paribus Latin for "all else remaining the same."

The Demand Schedule and the Demand Curve

To make our discussion more concrete, let's look at a specific market: the market for real maple syrup in the United States. In this market, we'll view the buyers as U.S. households, whereas the sellers (to be considered later) are maple syrup producers in the United States or Canada.

Table 1 shows a hypothetical **demand schedule** for maple syrup in this market. This is *a list of different quantities demanded at different prices, with all other*

Demand schedule A list showing the quantities of a good that consumers would choose to purchase at different prices, with all other variables held constant.

TABLE 1

Demand Schedule for Maple Syrup in the United States

Price (per bottle)	Quantity Demanded (bottles per month)
$1.00	75,000
$2.00	60,000
$3.00	50,000
$4.00	40,000
$5.00	35,000

© CENGAGE LEARNING 2013

FIGURE 2   The Demand Curve

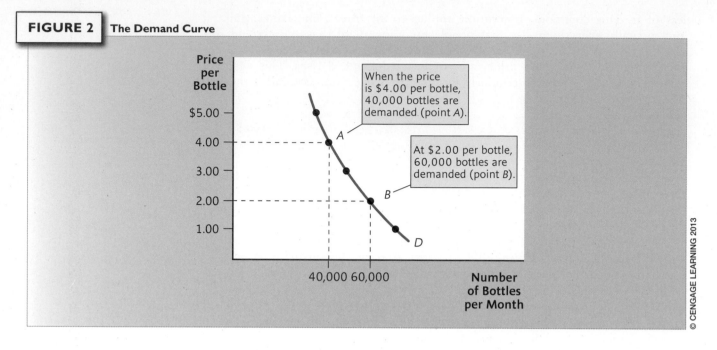

When the price is $4.00 per bottle, 40,000 bottles are demanded (point A).

At $2.00 per bottle, 60,000 bottles are demanded (point B).

© CENGAGE LEARNING 2013

variables that affect the demand decision assumed constant. For example, the demand schedule tells us that when the price of maple syrup is $2.00 per bottle, the quantity demanded will be 60,000 bottles per month. Notice that the demand schedule obeys the law of demand: As the price of maple syrup increases, *ceteris paribus,* the quantity demanded falls.

Now look at Figure 2. It shows a diagram that will appear repeatedly in your study of economics. In the figure, each price-and-quantity combination in Table 1 is represented by a point. For example, point *A* represents the price $4.00 and quantity 40,000, while point *B* represents the pair $2.00 and 60,000. When we connect all of these points with a line, we obtain the famous *demand curve,* labeled with a *D* in the figure.

Demand curve A graph of a demand schedule; a curve showing the quantity of a good or service demanded at various prices, with all other variables held constant.

> The **demand curve** shows the relationship between the price of a good and the quantity demanded in the market, holding constant all other variables that influence demand. Each point on the curve shows the total quantity that buyers would choose to buy at a specific price.

Notice that the demand curve in Figure 2—like virtually all demand curves—*slopes downward.* This is just a graphical representation of the law of demand.

Shifts versus Movements Along the Demand Curve

Markets are affected by a variety of events. Some events will cause us to *move along* the demand curve; others will cause the entire demand curve to *shift.* It is crucial to distinguish between these two very different types of effects.

Let's go back to Figure 2. There, you can see that when the price of maple syrup rises from $2.00 to $4.00 per bottle, the number of bottles demanded falls from 60,000 to 40,000. This is a movement *along* the demand curve, from point *B* to point *A.* In general,

> *a change in the price of a good causes a movement along the demand curve.*

TABLE 2

Increase in Demand for Maple Syrup in the United States

Price (per bottle)	Original Quantity Demanded (average income = $40,000)	New Quantity Demanded (average income = $50,000)
$1.00	75,000	95,000
$2.00	60,000	80,000
$3.00	50,000	70,000
$4.00	40,000	60,000
$5.00	35,000	55,000

In Figure 2, a *fall* in price would cause us to move *rightward* along the demand curve (from point *A* to point *B*), and a *rise* in price would cause us to move *leftward* along the demand curve (from *B* to *A*).

Remember, though, that when we draw a demand curve, we assume all other variables that might influence demand are *held constant* at some particular value. For example, the demand curve in Figure 2 might have been drawn to give us quantity demanded at each price when average household income in the United States remains constant at, say, $40,000 per year.

But suppose average income increases to $50,000. With more income, we'd expect households to buy more of *most* things, including maple syrup. This is illustrated in Table 2. At the original income level, households would choose to buy 60,000 bottles of maple syrup at $2.00 per bottle. But after income rises, they would choose to buy more at that price—80,000 bottles, according to Table 2. A similar change would occur at any other price for maple syrup: After income rises, households would choose to buy more than before. In other words, the rise in income *changes the entire relationship between price and quantity demanded.* We now have a *new* demand curve.

Figure 3 plots the new demand curve from the quantities in the third column of Table 2. The new demand curve lies to the *right* of the old curve. For example, at a price of $2.00, quantity demanded increases from 60,000 bottles on the old curve

FIGURE 3   **A Shift of the Demand Curve**

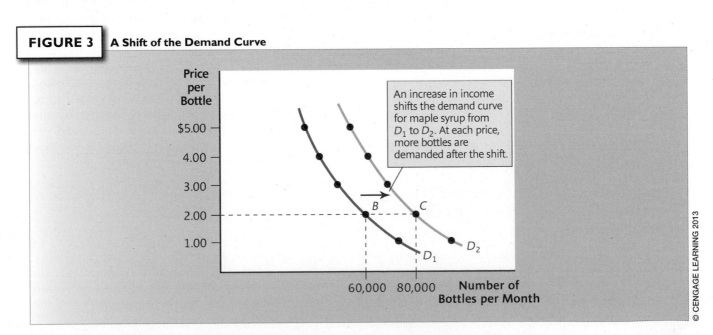

An increase in income shifts the demand curve for maple syrup from D_1 to D_2. At each price, more bottles are demanded after the shift.

(point *B*) to 80,000 bottles on the *new* demand curve (point *C*). As you can see, the rise in household income has *shifted* the demand curve to the right.

More generally,

> *a change in any variable that affects demand—except for the good's price— causes the demand curve to shift.*

When buyers would choose to buy a greater quantity at any price, the demand curve shifts *rightward*. If they would decide to buy less at any price, the demand curve shifts *leftward*.

"Change in Quantity Demanded" versus "Change in Demand"

Language is important when discussing demand. The term *quantity demanded* means a *particular amount* that buyers would choose to buy at a specific price, represented by a single point on a demand curve. *Demand*, by contrast, means the *entire relationship* between price and quantity demanded, represented by the entire demand curve.

Change in quantity demanded A movement along a demand curve in response to a change in price.

For this reason, when a change in the price of a good moves us *along* a demand curve, we call it a **change in quantity demanded**. For example, in Figure 2, the movement from point *A* to point *B* is an *increase* in quantity demanded. This is a change from one number (40,000 bottles) to another (60,000 bottles).

Change in demand A shift of a demand curve in response to a change in some variable other than price.

When something *other* than the price changes, causing the entire demand curve to shift, we call it a **change in demand**. In Figure 3, for example, the shift in the curve would be called an *increase in demand*.

Factors That Shift the Demand Curve

Let's take a closer look at what might cause a change in demand (a shift of the demand curve). Keep in mind that for now, we're exploring *one factor at a time*, always keeping *all other determinants of demand constant*.

Income The amount that a person or firm earns over a particular period.

Income. In Figure 3, an increase in **income** shifted the demand for maple syrup to the right. In fact, a rise in income increases demand for *most* goods. We call these **normal goods.** Housing, automobiles, health club memberships, and real maple syrup are all examples of normal goods.

Normal good A good that people demand more of as their income rises.

But not all goods are normal. For some goods—called **inferior goods**—a rise in income would *decrease* demand—shifting the demand curve *leftward*. Regular-grade ground chuck is a good example. It's a cheap source of protein, but not as high in quality as sirloin. With higher income, households could more easily afford better types of meat—ground sirloin or steak, for example. As a result, higher incomes for buyers might cause the demand for ground chuck to *decrease*. For similar reasons, we might expect that Greyhound bus tickets (in contrast to airline tickets) and single-ply paper towels (in contrast to two-ply) are inferior goods.

Inferior good A good that people demand less of as their income rises.

> *A rise in income will* increase *the demand for a* normal *good, and* decrease *the demand for an* inferior *good.*

Wealth The total value of everything a person or firm owns, at a point in time, minus the total amount owed.

Wealth. Your **wealth** at any point in time is the total value of everything you *own* (cash, bank accounts, stocks, bonds, real estate or any other valuable property) minus the total dollar amount you *owe* (home mortgage, credit card debt, auto loan, student loan, and so on). Although income and wealth are different (see the nearby Dangerous Curves box), they have similar effects on demand. When people have more wealth—because of an increase in the value of their stocks or bonds, for example—they have more funds with which to purchase goods and services. As you might expect,

> *an increase in wealth will* increase *demand (shift the curve rightward) for a normal good, and* decrease *demand (shift the curve leftward) for an inferior good.*

Prices of Related Goods. A **substitute** is a good that can be used in place of another good and that fulfills more or less the same purpose. For example, many people use real maple syrup to sweeten their pancakes, but they could use a number of other things instead: honey, sugar, jam, or *artificial* maple syrup. Each of these can be considered a substitute for real maple syrup.

When the price of a substitute rises, people will choose to buy *more* maple syrup. For example, when the price of jam rises, some jam users will switch to maple syrup, and the demand for maple syrup will increase. In general,

> *a rise in the price of a substitute increases the demand for a good, shifting the demand curve to the right.*

Of course, if the price of a substitute falls, we have the opposite result: Demand for the original good decreases, shifting its demand curve to the left.

A **complement** is the opposite of a substitute: It's used *together with* the good we are interested in. Pancake mix is a complement to maple syrup, since these two goods are used frequently in combination. If the price of pancake mix rises, some consumers will switch to other breakfasts—bacon and eggs, for—example—that *don't* include maple syrup. The demand for maple syrup will decrease.

> *A rise in the price of a complement decreases the demand for a good, shifting the demand curve to the left.*

To test yourself: How would a higher price for cashmere sweaters affect the demand for dry-cleaning services? How would it affect the demand for cotton or polyester sweaters?

Population. As the population increases in an area, the number of buyers will ordinarily increase as well, and the demand for a good will increase. The growth of the U.S. population over the last 50 years has been an important reason (but not the only reason) for rightward shifts in the demand curves for food, housing, automobiles, and many other goods and services.

Expected Price. If buyers expect the price of maple syrup to rise next month, they may choose to purchase more *now* to stock up before the price hike. If people expect the price to drop, they may postpone buying, hoping to take advantage of the lower price later.

> *In many markets, an expectation that price will rise in the future shifts the current demand curve rightward, while an expectation that price will fall shifts the current demand curve leftward.*

DANGEROUS CURVES

Income versus wealth It's easy to confuse *income* with *wealth,* because both are measured in dollars and both are sources of funds that can be spent on goods and services. But they are not the same thing. Your income is how much you earn *per period of time* (such as $20 *per hour;* $3,500 *per month;* or $40,000 *per year*). Your wealth, by contrast, is the value of what you own minus the value of what you owe at a particular *moment in time.* (For example, if on December 31, 2012, the value of what you own is $12,000, and you owe $9,000, then you have $3,000 in wealth on that date.)

Someone can have a high income and low or even negative wealth (such as college students who get good jobs after graduation but still owe a lot on their student loans). And a person with great wealth could have little or no income (for example, if they make especially bad investment choices and earn little or no income from their wealth).

© AXL/SHUTTERSTOCK.COM

Substitute A good that can be used in place of some other good and that fulfills more or less the same purpose.

Complement A good that is used together with some other good.

Expected price changes for goods are especially important for goods that can be purchased and stored until needed later. Expected price changes are also important in the markets for financial assets such as stocks and bonds and in the market for housing, as you'll see in the next chapter.

Tastes. Not everyone likes maple syrup. And among those who do, some *really* like it, and some like it just a little. Buyers' basic attitudes toward a good are based on their *tastes* or *preferences*. Economists are sometimes interested in where these tastes come from or what makes them change. But for the most part, economics deals with the *consequences* of a change in tastes, whatever the reason for its occurrence.

When tastes change *toward* a good (people favor it more), demand increases, and the demand curve shifts to the right. When tastes change *away* from a good, demand decreases, and the demand curve shifts to the left. An example of this is the change in tastes away from cigarettes over the past several decades. The cause

FIGURE 4   **The Demand Curve—A Summary**

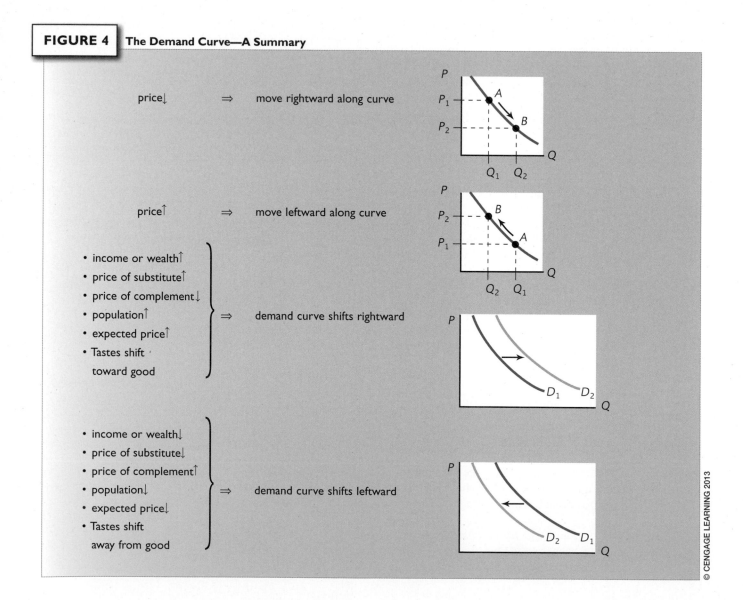

© CENGAGE LEARNING 2013

may have been an aging population, a greater concern about health among people of *all* ages, or successful antismoking advertising. But regardless of the cause, the effect has been to decrease the demand for cigarettes, shifting the demand curve to the left.

Other Shift Variables. Many other things, besides those we've discussed, can shift the demand curve. For example, if the government began to offer subsidies to households who buy maple syrup, demand would shift rightward. Also, if business firms (rather than just households) are among the buyers, then changes in the demand for their own products will influence their demand for maple syrup. We'll discuss additional shift variables in later chapters, as they become relevant.

Demand: A Summary

Figure 4 summarizes the key variables we've discussed that affect the demand side of the market and how their effects are represented with a demand curve. Notice the important distinction between events that move us *along* the curve (changes in price) and events that *shift* the curve.

SUPPLY

When most people hear the word *supply,* their first thought is that it's the amount of something "available," as if this amount were fixed in stone. For example, someone might say, "We can only drill so much oil from the ground," or "There are only so many apartments for rent in this town." And yet, the world's known oil reserves—as well as yearly production of oil—have increased dramatically over the last half century, as oil companies have found it worth their while to look harder for oil. Similarly, in many cities, low buildings have been replaced with high ones, and the number of apartments has increased. Supply, like demand, can change, and the amount of a good supplied in a market depends on the *choices* made by those who produce it.

Quantity supplied The specific amount of a good that all sellers in a market would choose to sell over some time period, given their constraints.

What governs these choices? We assume that those who supply goods and services have a goal: to earn the highest profit possible. But suppliers also face constraints. First, in a competitive market, the price they can charge for their product is a *given*—the market price. Second, suppliers have to pay the *costs* of producing and selling their product. These costs will depend on the production process they use, the prices they must pay for their inputs, and more. Business firms' desire for profit, together with the real-world constraints that they face, determines how much they will choose to sell in any market. Hence, the following definition:

> *Quantity supplied is the number of units of a good that all sellers in the market would choose to sell over some time period, given the constraints that they face.*

Let's briefly go over the notion of quantity supplied to clarify what it means and doesn't mean.

© AXL/SHUTTERSTOCK.COM

DANGEROUS CURVES ⚠

"Availability" and demand A common mistake is thinking that the amount of a good "available" should be a factor that influences demand. The reasoning might go like this: "If less maple syrup is available, people will have to buy less, so demand decreases." What's wrong with this? The most basic error involves forgetting that the demand curve comes from the answers to *hypothetical* questions, about how much people *would like* to buy at each price. A change in the amount available would not change how much people would *like* to buy at each price, and so it wouldn't affect the demand curve itself. As you'll see later in this chapter, changes in the amount of a good available *will* affect the price of the good and the amount ultimately bought. But this is represented by a movement along—not a shift of—the demand curve.

Quantity Supplied Implies a **Choice.** Quantity supplied doesn't tell us the amount of, say, maple syrup that sellers would like to sell *if* they could charge a thousand dollars for each bottle, and *if* they could produce it at zero cost. Instead, it's the quantity that firms *choose* to sell—the quantity that gives them the highest profit given the constraints they face.

Quantity Supplied Is **Hypothetical.** Will firms actually be *able* to sell the amount they want to sell at the going price? You'll soon see that they usually can. But the definition of quantity supplied makes no assumptions about firms' ability to sell the good. Quantity supplied answers the hypothetical question: How much *would* suppliers sell, given their constraints, if they were able to sell all that they wanted to?

Quantity Supplied Depends on **Price.**   The price of the good is just one variable among many that influences quantity supplied. But—as with demand—we want to keep that variable foremost in our thinking. This is why for the next couple of pages we'll assume that all other influences on supply are held constant, so we can explore the relationship between price and quantity supplied.

The Law of Supply

How does a change in price affect quantity supplied? When a seller can get a higher price for a good, producing and selling it become more profitable. Producers will devote more resources toward its production—perhaps even pulling resources from other goods they produce—so they can sell more of the good in question. For example, a rise in the price of laptop (but not desktop) computers will encourage computer makers to shift resources out of the production of other things (such as desktop computers) and toward the production of laptops.

In general, price and quantity supplied are *positively related:* When the price of a good rises, the quantity supplied will rise as well. This relationship between price and quantity supplied is called the law of supply, the counterpart to the law of demand we discussed earlier.

Law of supply As the price of a good increases, the quantity supplied increases.

> The **law of supply** *states that when the price of a good rises, and everything else remains the same, the quantity of the good supplied will rise.*

Once again, notice the very important words "everything else remains the same"—*ceteris paribus*. Although many variables influence the quantity of a good supplied, the law of supply tells us what would happen if all of them remained unchanged and only one—the price of the good—changed.

The Supply Schedule and the Supply Curve

Let's continue with our example of the market for maple syrup in the United States. Who are the suppliers in this market? Maple-syrup producers are located mostly in the forests of Vermont, upstate New York, and Canada. The market quantity supplied is the amount of syrup all of these producers together would offer for sale at each price for maple syrup in the United States.

Supply schedule A list showing the quantities of a good or service that firms would choose to produce and sell at different prices, with all other variables held constant.

Table 3 shows the **supply schedule** for maple syrup—a *list of different quantities supplied at different prices, with all other variables held constant.* As you can see, the supply schedule obeys the law of supply: As the price of maple syrup rises, the

TABLE 3

Supply Schedule for Maple Syrup in the United States

Price (per bottle)	Quantity Supplied (bottles per month)
$1.00	25,000
$2.00	40,000
$3.00	50,000
$4.00	60,000
$5.00	65,000

quantity supplied rises along with it. But how can this be? After all, maple trees must be about 40 years old before they can be tapped for syrup, so any rise in quantity supplied now or in the near future cannot come from an increase in planting. What, then, causes quantity supplied to rise as price rises?

Many things. With higher prices, firms will find it profitable to tap existing trees more intensively. Evaporating and bottling can be done more carefully, so that less maple syrup is spilled and more is available for shipping. Or syrup normally sold in other markets can be diverted and shipped to the U.S. market instead. For example, if the price of maple syrup rises in the United States (but not in Canada), producers would shift deliveries away from Canada so they could sell more in the United States, increasing supply to the U.S. market.

Now look at Figure 5, which shows a very important curve—the counterpart to the demand curve we drew earlier. In Figure 5, each point represents a price-quantity pair taken from Table 3. For example, point F in the figure corresponds to a price of $2.00 per bottle and a quantity of 40,000 bottles per month, while point G represents the price-quantity pair $4.00 and 60,000 bottles. Connecting all of these points with a solid line gives us the *supply curve* for maple syrup, labeled with an S in the figure.

FIGURE 5 **The Supply Curve**

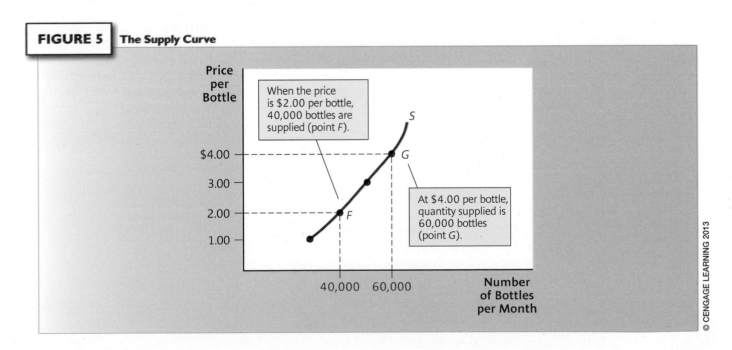

> *The **supply curve** shows the relationship between the price of a good and the quantity supplied in the market, holding constant the values of all other variables that affect supply. Each point on the curve shows the quantity that sellers would choose to sell at a specific price.*

Notice that the supply curve in Figure 5—like all supply curves for goods and services—is *upward sloping*. This is the graphical representation of the law of supply.

Shifts versus Movements Along the Supply Curve

As with the demand curve, it's important to distinguish those events that will cause us to *move along* a given supply curve for the good, and those that will cause the entire supply curve to *shift*.

If you look once again at Figure 5, you'll see that if the price of maple syrup rises from $2.00 to $4.00 per bottle, the number of bottles supplied rises from 40,000 to 60,000. This is a movement *along* the supply curve, from point *F* to point *G*. In general,

> *a change in the price of a good causes a movement* along *the supply curve.*

In the figure, a *rise* in price would cause us to move *rightward* along the supply curve (from point *F* to point *G*) and a *fall* in price would move us *leftward* along the curve (from point *G* to point *F*).

But remember that when we draw a supply curve, we assume that all other variables that might influence supply are *held constant* at some particular values. For example, the supply curve in Figure 5 might tell us the quantity supplied at each price when the cost of an important input—transportation from the farm to the point of sale—remains constant.

But suppose the cost of transportation drops. Then, at any given price for maple syrup, firms would find it more profitable to produce and sell it. This is illustrated in Table 4. With the original transportation cost, and a selling price of $4.00 per bottle, firms would choose to sell 60,000 bottles. But after transportation cost falls, they would choose to produce and sell more—80,000 bottles in our example—assuming they could still charge $4.00 per bottle. A similar change would occur for any other price of maple syrup we might imagine: After transportation costs fall, firms would choose to sell more than before. In other words, *the entire relationship between price and quantity supplied has changed,* so we have a *new* supply curve.

Figure 6 plots the new supply curve from the quantities in the third column of Table 4. The new supply curve lies to the *right* of the old one. For example, at a price

---

TABLE 4

Increase in Supply of Maple Syrup in the United States

Price (per bottle)	Original Quantity Supplied	Quantity Supplied After Decrease in Transportation Cost
$1.00	25,000	45,000
$2.00	40,000	60,000
$3.00	50,000	70,000
$4.00	60,000	80,000
$5.00	65,000	90,000

FIGURE 6 | A Shift of the Supply Curve

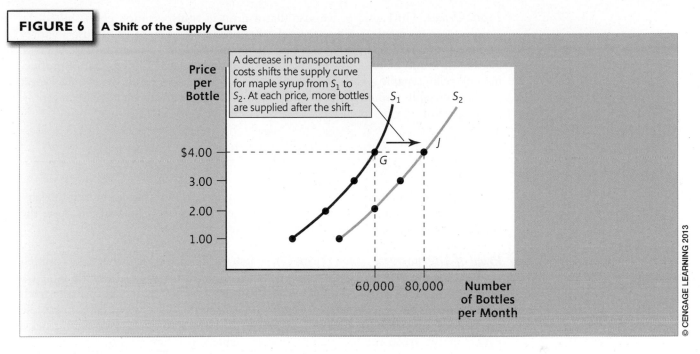

A decrease in transportation costs shifts the supply curve for maple syrup from S_1 to S_2. At each price, more bottles are supplied after the shift.

of $4.00, quantity supplied increases from 60,000 bottles on the old curve (point G) to 80,000 bottles on the *new* supply curve (point J). The drop in the transportation costs has *shifted* the supply curve to the right.

In general,

> *a change in any variable that affects supply—except for the good's price— causes the supply curve to shift.*

If sellers want to sell a greater quantity at any price, the supply curve shifts *rightward*. If sellers would prefer to sell a smaller quantity at any price, the supply curve shifts *leftward*.

Change in Quantity Supplied versus Change in Supply

As we stressed in our discussion of the demand side of the market, be careful about language when thinking about supply. The term *quantity supplied* means a *particular amount* that sellers would choose to sell at a *particular* price, represented by a single point on the supply curve. The term *supply,* however, means the *entire relationship* between price and quantity supplied, as represented by the entire supply curve.

For this reason, when the price of the good changes, and we move *along* the supply curve, we have a **change in quantity supplied.** For example, in Figure 5, the movement from point F to point G is an *increase* in quantity supplied.

When something *other* than the price changes, causing the entire supply curve to shift, we call it a **change in supply.** The shift in Figure 6, for example, would be called an *increase in supply*.

Change in quantity supplied A movement along a supply curve in response to a change in price.

Change in supply A shift of a supply curve in response to a change in some variable other than price.

Factors That Shift the Supply Curve

Let's look at some of the *causes* of a change in supply (a shift of the supply curve). As always, we're considering *one* variable at a time, keeping all other determinants of supply constant.

© CENGAGE LEARNING 2013

Input Prices.   In Figure 6, we saw that a drop in transportation costs shifted the supply curve for maple syrup to the right. But producers of maple syrup use a variety of other inputs besides transportation: land, maple trees, sap pans, evaporators, labor, glass bottles, and more. A lower price for any of these means a lower cost of producing and selling maple syrup, making it more profitable. As a result, we would expect producers to shift resources into maple syrup production, causing an increase in supply.

In general,

> *a fall in the price of an input causes an increase in supply, shifting the supply curve to the right.*

Similarly, a rise in the price of an input causes a decrease in supply, shifting the supply curve to the left. If, for example, the wages of maple syrup workers rose, the supply curve in Figure 6 would shift to the left.

Price of Alternatives.   Many firms can switch their production rather easily among several different goods or services, each of which requires more or less the same inputs. For example, a dermatology practice can rather easily switch its specialty from acne treatments for the young to wrinkle treatments for the elderly. An automobile producer can—without too much adjustment—switch to producing light trucks. And a maple syrup producer could dry its maple syrup and produce maple *sugar* instead. Or it could even cut down its maple trees and sell maple wood as lumber. These other goods that firms *could* produce are called **alternate goods** and their prices influence the supply curve.

Alternate goods Other goods that firms in a market could produce instead of the good in question.

For example, if the price of maple *sugar* rose, then at any given price for maple *syrup,* producers would shift some production from syrup to sugar. This would be a decrease in the supply of maple syrup.

Another alternative for the firm is to sell the *same* good in a *different* market, which we'll call an **alternate market.** For example, since we are considering the market for maple syrup in the United States, the maple syrup market in Canada is a different market for producers. For any given price in the United States, a rise in the price of maple syrup in Canada will cause producers to shift some sales from the United States to Canada. In the U.S. market, this will cause the supply curve to shift leftward.

Alternate market A market other than the one being analyzed in which the same good could be sold.

> *When the price for an alternative rises—either an alternate good or the same good in an alternate market—the supply curve shifts leftward.*

Similarly, a decrease in the price of an alternate good (or a lower price in an alternate market) will shift the supply curve rightward.

Technology.   A *technological advance* in production occurs whenever a firm can produce a given level of output in a new and cheaper way than before.

Examples would include a new, more efficient tap that draws more maple syrup from each tree, or a new bottling method that reduces spillage. Advances like these would reduce the cost of producing maple syrup, making it more profitable, and producers would want to make and sell more of it at any price.

In general,

> *cost-saving technological advances increase the supply of a good, shifting the supply curve to the right.*

Number of Firms.   A change in the number of firms in a market will change the quantity that all sellers together would want to sell at any given price. For example, if—over time—more people decided to open up maple syrup farms because it was a profitable business, the supply of maple syrup would increase. And if maple syrup farms began closing down, their number would be reduced and supply would decrease.

> *An increase in the number of sellers—with no other change—shifts the supply curve rightward.*

Expected Price.   Imagine you're the president of Sticky's Maple Syrup, Inc., and you expect the market price of maple syrup—over which you, as an individual seller, have no influence—to rise next month. What would you do? You might want to postpone selling some of your maple syrup until later, when the price and your profit would be higher. Therefore, at any given price *now,* you might slow down production, or just slow down sales by warehousing more of what you produce. If other firms have similar expectations of a price hike, they'll do the same. Thus, an expectation of a *future* price hike will decrease supply *in the present.*

Suppose instead you expect the market price to *drop* next month. Then—at any given price—you'd want to sell more *now,* by stepping up production and even selling out of your inventories. So an expected future drop in the price would cause an increase in supply in the present.

Expected price is especially important when suppliers can hold inventories of goods for later sale, or when they can easily shift production from one time period to another.

> *In many markets, an expectation of a* future price rise *shifts the current supply curve* leftward. *Similarly, an expectation of a* future price drop *shifts the current supply curve* rightward.

Changes in Weather and Other Natural Events.   Weather conditions are an especially important determinant of the supply of agricultural goods.

> Favorable weather *increases crop yields, and causes a* rightward *shift of the supply curve for that crop.* Unfavorable weather *destroys crops and shrinks yields, and shifts the supply curve* leftward.

In addition to bad weather, natural disasters such as fires, hurricanes, and earthquakes can destroy or disrupt the productive capacity of *all* firms in a region. If many sellers of a particular good are located in the affected area, the supply curve for that good will shift leftward.

For example, companies in the industrial northeast of Japan are major global suppliers of many goods, including semiconductors, solar panels, automobiles and auto parts, steel, beer, paper, and more. When a powerful earthquake and tsunami struck Japan in 2011, it destroyed or disabled many factories and much of the transportation network in the area. Supply curves in global markets for those goods shifted leftward for weeks, and, in some cases, months, until production was restored.

Other Shift Variables.   Many other things besides those listed earlier can shift the supply curve. For example, a government tax imposed on maple syrup producers

would raise the cost of making and selling maple syrup. To suppliers, this would have the same effect as a higher price for transportation: It would shift the supply curve leftward. We'll discuss other shift variables for supply as they become relevant in this and later chapters.

Supply—A Summary

Figure 7 summarizes the various factors we've discussed that affect the supply side of the market, and how we illustrate them using a supply curve. As with demand, notice which events move us along the supply curve (changes in price) and which shift the curve. To test yourself, you might want to create a list of the shift variables in Figure 4 and Figure 7, in random order. Then explain, for each item, which curve shifts and in which direction.

FIGURE 7   **The Supply Curve—A Summary**

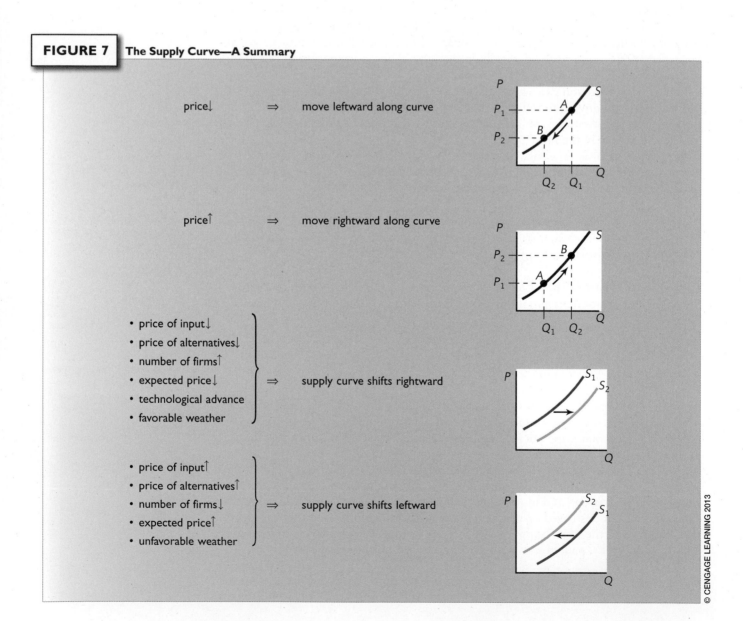

price↓   ⇒   move leftward along curve

price↑   ⇒   move rightward along curve

- price of input↓
- price of alternatives↓
- number of firms↑
- expected price↓
- technological advance
- favorable weather

⇒   supply curve shifts rightward

- price of input↑
- price of alternatives↑
- number of firms↓
- expected price↑
- unfavorable weather

⇒   supply curve shifts leftward

PUTTING SUPPLY AND DEMAND TOGETHER

Now that we've considered the demand and supply sides of the market separately, it's time to put the two sides together. As you are about to see, combining demand and supply will tell us how a market's price is determined.

Let's start by asking: What happens when buyers and sellers, each having the desire to trade, come together in a market? The two sides of the market certainly have different agendas. Buyers would like to pay the lowest possible price, while sellers would like to charge the highest possible price. Is there chaos when they meet, with each trade taking place at a wildly different price than the others? A casual look at the real world suggests not. In most markets, most of the time, there is order and stability in the encounters between buyers and sellers. In most cases, prices do not fluctuate wildly from moment to moment but seem to hover around a stable value. Even when this stability is short-lived—lasting only a day, an hour, or even a few minutes in some markets—for this brief time the market seems to be at rest. Whenever we study a market, therefore, we look for this state of rest—a price at which the market seems to settle, at least for a while.

Economists use the word *equilibrium* when referring to a state of rest. When a market is in equilibrium, both the price of the good and the quantity bought and sold each period have settled into a state of rest. More formally,

> the **equilibrium price** and **equilibrium quantity** are values for price and quantity in the market that, once achieved, will remain constant—unless and until the supply curve or the demand curve shifts.

Equilibrium price The market price that, once achieved, remains constant until either the demand curve or supply curve shifts.

Equilibrium quantity The market quantity bought and sold per period that, once achieved, remains constant until either the demand curve or supply curve shifts.

Finding the Equilibrium Price and Quantity

Look at Table 5, which combines the supply and demand schedules for maple syrup from Tables 1 and 3. We'll use Table 5 to find the equilibrium price in this market through the process of elimination.

Prices below the Equilibrium Price

Let's first ask what would happen if the price were less than $3.00 per bottle— say, $1.00. At this price, Table 5 tells us that buyers would want to buy 75,000 bottles each month, while sellers would offer to sell only 25,000. There would be an **excess demand** of 50,000 bottles. What would happen in this case? Buyers would

Excess demand At a given price, the amount by which quantity demanded exceeds quantity supplied.

						TABLE 5

Finding the Market Equilibrium

Price (per bottle)	Original Demanded (bottles per month)	Quantity Supplied (bottles per month)	Excess Demand or Supply?	Consequence
$1.00	75,000	25,000	Excess Demand	Price will Rise
$2.00	60,000	40,000	Excess Demand	Price will Rise
$3.00	**50,000**	**50,000**	**Neither**	**No Change in price**
$4.00	40,000	60,000	Excess Supply	Price will Fall
$5.00	35,000	65,000	Excess Supply	Price will Fall

FIGURE 8   Excess Demand Causes Price to Rise

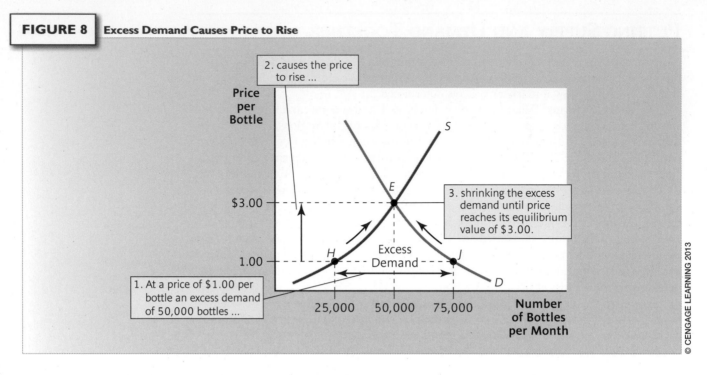

compete with each other to get more maple syrup than was available, and they would offer to pay a higher price rather than do without. The price would then rise. The same would occur if the price were $2.00 or any other price below $3.00.

We conclude that any price less than $3.00 cannot be an equilibrium price. If the price starts below $3.00, it would start rising—*not* because the supply curve or the demand curve had shifted, but from natural forces within the market itself. This directly contradicts our definition of equilibrium price.

Figure 8 illustrates the same process by putting the supply and demand curves together on the same graph. As you can see, at a price of $1.00, quantity supplied of 25,000 bottles is found at point *H* on the supply curve, while quantity demanded is at point *J* on the demand curve. The horizontal difference between the two curves at $1.00 is a graphical representation of the excess demand at that price. This excess demand would cause the price to rise.

How far will the price rise? Since excess demand is the only reason for the price to rise, it will stop rising when the excess demand is gone. And as you can see in Figure 8, the rise in price *shrinks* the excess demand in two ways. First, as price rises, buyers demand a smaller quantity—a leftward movement along the demand curve (from point *J* to point *E*). Second, sellers increase supply to a larger quantity—a rightward movement along the supply curve (from point *H* to point *E*). Finally, when the price reaches $3.00 per bottle, the excess demand is gone and the price stops rising.

This logic tells us that $3.00 is an *equilibrium* price in this market—a value that won't change as long as the supply and demand curves stay put.

Prices above the Equilibrium Price

We've shown that any price *below* $3.00 is not an equilibrium in our example. But could some price *above* $3.00—say, $5.00—be an equilibrium? Let's see.

Look again at Table 5. If the price were $5.00, quantity supplied would be 65,000 bottles per month, while quantity demanded would be only 35,000 bottles. There would be an **excess supply** of 30,000 bottles. Sellers would compete with each

Excess supply At a given price, the amount by which quantity supplied exceeds quantity demanded.

FIGURE 9   Excess Supply Causes Price to Fall

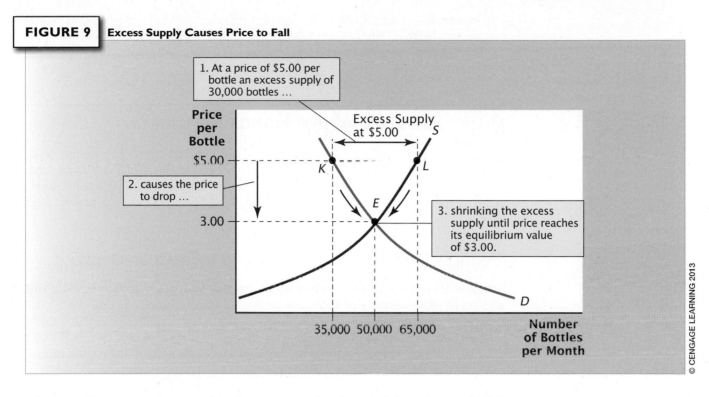

other to sell more maple syrup than buyers wanted to buy, and the price would fall. Thus, $5.00 cannot be the equilibrium price.

Figure 9 provides a graphical view of the market in this situation. With a price of $5.00, the excess supply is the horizontal distance between points K (on the demand curve) and L (on the supply curve). In the figure, the resulting drop in price would move us along both the supply curve (leftward) and the demand curve (rightward). As these movements continued, the excess supply of maple syrup would shrink until it disappeared, once again, at a price of $3.00 per bottle. Our conclusion: If the price happens to be above $3.00, it will fall to $3.00 and then stop changing.

You can see that $3.00 is the equilibrium price—and the *only* equilibrium price—in this market. Moreover, at this price, sellers would want to sell 50,000 bottles—the same quantity that households would want to buy. So, when price comes to rest at $3.00, quantity comes to rest at 50,000 per month—the *equilibrium quantity*.

Equilibrium on a Graph

No doubt, you have noticed that $3.00 happens to be the price at which the supply and demand curves cross. This leads us to an easy, graphical technique for locating our equilibrium:

> *To find the equilibrium in a competitive market, draw the supply and demand curves. Market equilibrium occurs where the two curves cross. At this crossing point, the equilibrium price is found on the vertical axis, and the equilibrium quantity on the horizontal axis.*

Notice that, in equilibrium, the market is operating on *both* the supply curve *and* the demand curve so that—at a price of $3.00—quantity demanded and quantity supplied are equal. There are no dissatisfied buyers unable to find goods they want to purchase, nor are there any frustrated sellers unable to sell goods they want to sell. Indeed, this is why $3.00 is the equilibrium price. It's the only price that creates consistency between what buyers choose to buy and sellers choose to sell.

But we don't expect a market to stay at any particular equilibrium forever, as you're about to see.

WHAT HAPPENS WHEN THINGS CHANGE?

Remember that in order to draw the supply and demand curves in the first place, we had to assume particular values for all the other variables—besides price—that affect demand and supply. If one of these variables changes, then either the supply curve or the demand curve will shift, and our equilibrium will change as well. Let's look at some examples.

Example: Income Rises, Causing an Increase in Demand

In Figure 10, point E shows an initial equilibrium in the U.S. market for maple syrup, with an equilibrium price of $3.00 per bottle and an equilibrium quantity of 50,000 bottles per month. Suppose that the incomes of buyers rise. We know that income is one of the shift variables in the demand curve (but not the supply curve). We also can reason that real maple syrup is a *normal good* (people want more as their income rises), so the demand curve will shift rightward. What happens then?

The old price—$3.00—is no longer the equilibrium price. How do we know? Because if the price *did* remain at $3.00 after the demand curve shifted, there would be an excess demand that would drive the price upward. The new equilibrium—at

FIGURE 10   **A Shift in Demand and a New Equilibrium**

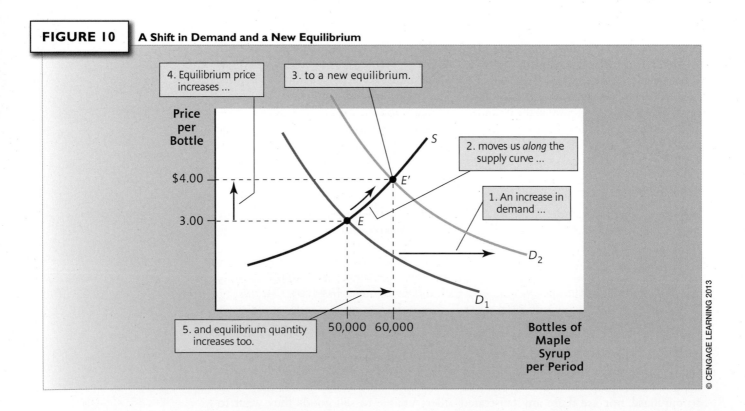

© CENGAGE LEARNING 2013

point E'—is the new intersection point of the curves *after* the shift in the demand curve. Comparing the original equilibrium at point E with the new one at point E', we find that the shift in demand has caused the equilibrium price to rise (from $3.00 to $4.00) and the equilibrium quantity to rise as well (from 50,000 to 60,000 bottles per month).

Notice, too, that in moving from point E to point E', we move *along* the supply curve. That is, a shift of the demand curve has caused a movement along the supply curve. Why is this? The demand shift causes the *price* to rise, and a rise in price always causes a movement *along* the supply curve. But the supply curve itself does not shift because none of the variables that affect sellers—other than the price of the good—has changed.

In this example, income rose. But *any* event that shifted the demand curve rightward would have the same effect on price and quantity. For example, if tastes changed in favor of maple syrup, or a substitute good like jam rose in price, or a complementary good like pancake mix became cheaper, the demand curve for maple syrup would shift rightward, just as it did in Figure 10. So, we can summarize our findings as follows:

> *A rightward shift in the demand curve causes a rightward movement* along *the supply curve. Equilibrium price and equilibrium quantity both rise.*

Example: Bad Weather, Supply Decreases

Unfavorable weather can affect supply for most agricultural goods, including maple syrup. An example occurred in 2007 and 2008, when abnormal weather patterns in Quebec and the northeastern U.S. slowed the flow of sap from maple trees. How did this affect the market for maple syrup?

As you've learned, weather can be a shift variable for the supply curve. Look at Figure 11. Initially, the supply curve for maple syrup is S_1, with the market in equilibrium at Point E. When bad weather hits, the supply curve shifts leftward—say, to S_2. The result: a rise in the equilibrium price of maple syrup (from $3.00 to $5.00 in the figure) and a fall in the equilibrium quantity (from 50,000 to 35,000 bottles).

Any event that shifts the supply curve leftward would have similar effects. For example, if the wages of maple syrup workers increase, or some maple syrup producers go out of business and sell their farms to housing developers, the supply curve for maple syrup would shift leftward, just as in Figure 11.

More generally,

> *A leftward shift of the supply curve causes a leftward movement* along *the demand curve. Equilibrium price rises, but equilibrium quantity falls.*

DANGEROUS CURVES ⚠

The Endless Loop of Erroneous Logic In trying to work out what happens after, say, a rise in income, you might find yourself caught in an endless loop. It goes something like this: "A rise in income causes an increase in demand. An increase in demand causes the price to rise. A higher price causes supply to increase. Greater supply causes the price to fall. A lower price increases demand ..." and so on, without end. The price keeps bobbing up and down, forever.

What's the mistake here? The first two statements ("a rise in income causes an increase in demand" and "an increase in demand causes price to rise") are entirely correct. But the next statement ("a higher price causes an increase in supply") is wrong, and so is everything that follows. A higher price does *not*, by itself, cause an "increase in supply" (a shift of the supply curve). It causes an increase in *quantity supplied* (a movement *along* the supply curve).

Here's the correct sequence of events: "A rise in income causes an increase in demand. An increase in demand causes price to rise. A higher price causes an increase in *quantity supplied*, moving us along the supply curve until we reach the new equilibrium, with a higher price and greater quantity."

FIGURE 11   **A Shift of Supply and a New Equilibrium**

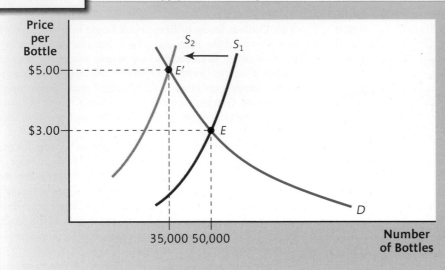

Unfavorable weather causes supply to decrease from S_1 to S_2. At the old equilibrium price of $3.00, there is now an excess demand. As a result, the price increases until excess demand is eliminated at point E'. In the new equilibrium, quantity demanded again equals quantity supplied. The price is higher, and fewer bottles are produced and sold.

Example: Higher Income and Bad Weather Together

So far, we've considered examples in which just one curve shifts due to a change in a single variable that influences *either* demand or supply. But what would happen if two changes affected the market simultaneously? Then both curves would shift.

Figure 12 shows what happens when we take the two factors we've just explored separately (a rise in income and bad weather) and combine them together. The rise in income causes the demand curve to shift rightward, from D_1 to D_2. The bad weather causes the supply curve to shift leftward, from S_1 to S_2. The result of all this is a change in equilibrium from point E to point E', where the new demand curve D_2 intersects the new supply curve S_2.

Notice that the equilibrium price rises from $3.00 to $6.00 in our example. This should come as no surprise. A rightward shift in the demand curve, with no other change, causes price to rise. And a leftward shift in the supply curve, with no other change, causes price to rise. So when we combine the two shifts together, the price must rise. In fact, the increase in the price will be greater than would be caused by either shift alone.

But what about equilibrium quantity? Here, the two shifts work in *opposite* directions. The rightward shift in demand works to increase quantity, while the leftward shift in supply works to decrease quantity. We can't say what will happen to equilibrium quantity until we know which shift is greater and thus has the greater influence. Quantity could rise, fall, or remain unchanged.

In Figure 12, it just so happens that the supply curve shifts more than the demand curve, so equilibrium quantity falls. But you can easily prove to yourself that the other outcomes are possible. First, draw a graph where the demand curve shifts rightward by more than the supply curve shifts leftward. In your graph, you'll see that equilibrium quantity rises. Then,

⚠ DANGEROUS CURVES

Do Curves Shift Up and Down? Or Right and Left?
When describing an increase in demand or supply, it's tempting to say "upward" instead of "rightward." Similarly, for a decrease, it's tempting to say "downward." But be careful! While this interchangeable language works for the demand curve, it does *not* work for the supply curve.

To prove this to yourself, look at Figure 6. There you can see that a rightward shift of the supply curve (an increase in supply) is also a *downward* shift. In later chapters, it will sometimes make sense to describe shifts as upward or downward. For now, it's best to avoid these terms and stick with *rightward* and *leftward*.

FIGURE 12   A Shift in Both Curves and a New Equilibrium

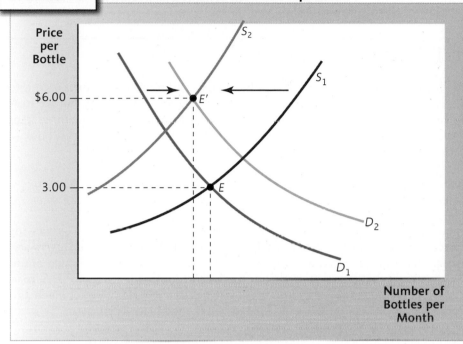

An increase in income shifts the demand curve rightward from D_1 to D_2. At the same time, bad weather shifts the supply curve leftward from S_1 to S_2. The equilibrium moves from point E to point E'. While the price must rise after these shifts, quantity could rise or fall or remain the same, depending on the relative sizes of the shifts. In the figure, quantity happens to fall.

draw one where both curves shift (in opposite directions) by equal amounts, and you'll see that equilibrium quantity remains unchanged.

We can also imagine other combinations of shifts. A rightward or leftward shift in either curve can be combined with a rightward or leftward shift in the other.

Table 6 lists all the possible combinations. It also shows what happens to equilibrium price and quantity in each case, and when the result is ambiguous (a question mark). For example, the top left entry tells us that when both the supply and demand curves shift rightward, the equilibrium *quantity* will always rise, but the equilibrium price could rise, fall, or remain unchanged, depending on the relative *size* of the shifts.

Do *not* try to memorize the entries in Table 6. Instead, remember the advice in Chapter 1: to study economics actively, rather than passively. This would be a good time to put down the book, pick up a pencil and paper, and see whether you can

TABLE 6

Effect of Simultaneous Shifts in Supply and Demand

	Increase in Demand (Rightward Shift)	No Change in Demand	Decrease in Demand (Leftward Shift)
• **Increase in Supply (Rightward Shift)**	$P?\,Q\uparrow$	$P\downarrow Q\uparrow$	$P\downarrow Q?$
• **No change in Supply**	$P\uparrow Q\uparrow$	No change in P or Q	$P\downarrow Q\downarrow$
• **Decrease in Supply (Leftward Shift)**	$P\uparrow Q?$	$P\uparrow Q\downarrow$	$P?\,Q\downarrow$

draw a graph to illustrate each of the nine possible results in the table. When you see a question mark for an ambiguous result, determine which shift would have to be greater for the variable to rise or to fall.

THE THREE-STEP PROCESS

In this chapter, we built a model—a supply and demand model—and then used it to analyze price changes in several markets. You may not have noticed it, but we took three distinct steps as the chapter proceeded. Economists take these same three steps to answer many questions about the economy, as you'll see throughout this book.

Let's review these steps:

> **Step 1—Characterize the Market:** *Decide which market or markets best suit the problem being analyzed, and identify how trading occurs in that market.*

In economics, we make sense of the very complex, real-world economy by viewing it as a collection of *markets*. Each of these markets involves a group of buyers and sellers who have the potential to trade with each other. At the very beginning of our analysis, we must decide which market or markets to look at (such as the U.S. market for maple syrup), and specify how trading takes place in that market (such as a competitive market with buyers and sellers who take the price as given).

> **Step 2—Find the Equilibrium:** *Describe the conditions necessary for equilibrium in the market, and a method for determining that equilibrium.*

Once we've defined a market, and put buyers and sellers together, we look for the point at which the market will come to rest—the equilibrium. In this chapter, we used supply and demand to find the equilibrium price and quantity in a competitive market, but this is just one example of how economists apply Step 2.

> **Step 3—What Happens When Things Change:** *Explore how events or government policies change the market equilibrium.*

Once you've found the equilibrium, the next step is to ask how different events will *change* it. In this chapter, for example, we explored how rising income or bad weather (or both together) would affect the equilibrium price and quantity for maple syrup.

Economists follow this same three-step procedure to analyze important questions in both microeconomics and macroeconomics. In this book, we'll be taking these three steps again and again, and we'll often call them to your attention. In fact, we're about to use them again, in the Using the Theory section that follows.

THE PRICE OF OIL

© PETER JORDAN/ALAMY

Every day, the world produces about 90 million barrels of oil and uses up the same amount making and delivering almost all the products we consume. So when the price of oil changes, every part of the economy is affected. Rapid rises in oil prices have contributed to economic downturns in the U.S. and other countries. And because oil consumption contributes to greenhouse gas emissions, the quantity of oil produced and consumed has important implications for climate change. Not surprisingly, economists are often asked to explain the past behavior of oil's price and quantity and to predict how they might change in the future.

Figure 13 provides data on price and quantity in what is called the oil *spot market*—where actual barrels of crude oil are bought and sold. (There is also a *futures* market for oil, where people buy and sell contracts promising future delivery of oil. Futures contracts amount to "side bets" on the future price and normally have little direct impact on the current price in the spot market.)

The upper panel plots the average monthly spot price of oil (dollars per barrel) from January 2005 through mid-2011. We'll be analyzing three periods—labeled with arrows—during which the price of oil changed rapidly. The slopes of the arrows tell us the direction that oil prices changed during each period.

The lower panel shows world oil *production* (millions of barrels per day) over the same time frame, with the same three episodes labeled. But this time, the slopes of the arrows indicate the direction of change for production, rather than price.

Why did oil prices change so rapidly during these episodes? The three-step process—along with the supply and demand model you learned in this chapter—can help us answer. Let's go through each step carefully.

Characterize the Market

We'll view the market for oil as a *global* market. It costs just a couple of dollars to ship a barrel of oil halfway around the world, so oil sellers and oil buyers around the globe can easily trade with each other. And our goal is to explain why oil prices changed worldwide, rather than in any particular country or region.

We'll also view the market for oil as *competitive*, and use supply and demand in our analysis. Is this realistic? Yes… and no. Virtually all oil buyers, and many of the world's oil sellers, do take the market price as a given. When the price rises, these sellers want to produce and sell more, while the buyers want to purchase less.

But about a third of the world's oil is produced by the large, government-run companies that belong to OPEC (Organization of Petroleum Exporting Countries). OPEC producers often behave like private producers—viewing the price of oil as a given and changing their quantity supplied when the price changes. But sometimes, OPEC members act in concert to *influence* the market price by intentionally changing their total production. Because OPEC produces so much of the world's oil, an artificial change in OPEC's total production can shift the market supply curve significantly rightward or leftward, and thereby change the market price. (One of the OPEC countries—Saudi Arabia—is such a large producer that it can artificially shift the market supply curve all by itself.)

However, while OPEC can shift the supply curve, it cannot change one important fact about the oil market: The price rapidly adjusts to the *equilibrium* price, which is where the supply and demand curves intersect. So in the market for oil—as in the market for maple syrup—the model of supply and demand will help us explain why prices change.

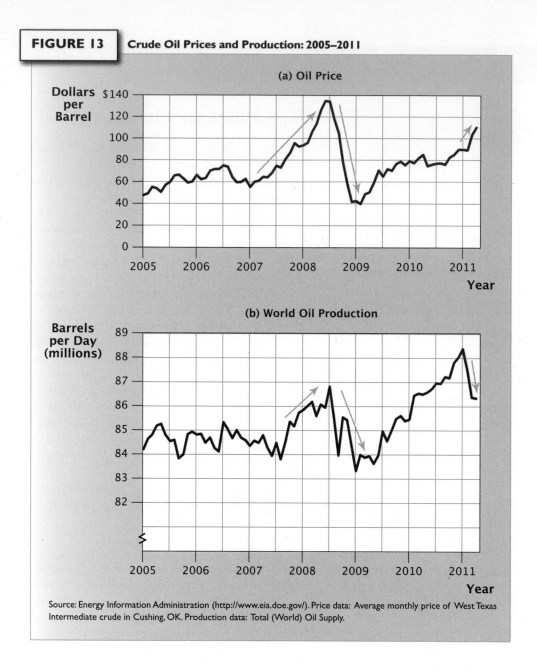

FIGURE 13 | **Crude Oil Prices and Production: 2005–2011**

Source: Energy Information Administration (http://www.eia.doe.gov/). Price data: Average monthly price of West Texas Intermediate crude in Cushing, OK. Production data: Total (World) Oil Supply.

Find the Equilibrium

Figure 14 shows market supply and demand curves for oil. The demand curve slopes downward, telling us that a rise in price, *ceteris paribus*, decreases the total quantity demanded in the market.[1] The supply curve slopes upward, telling us that a rise in price, *ceteris paribus*, increases the total quantity supplied to the market. The equilibrium price occurs where quantity supplied and demanded are equal. The curves in Figure 14

[1] Note that while ordinary households don't buy crude oil, they buy many goods and services—gasoline, motor oil, heating oil, electricity, plastic garbage bags, and more—that are made from oil. It is the manufacturers of these products—the actual buyers of oil—that want to purchase less oil when its price rises.

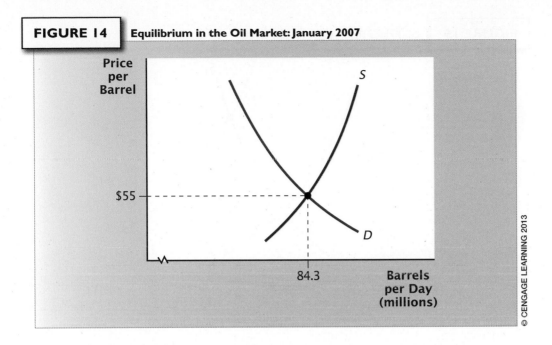

FIGURE 14   **Equilibrium in the Oil Market: January 2007**

Price per Barrel

S

$55

D

84.3   Barrels per Day (millions)

© CENGAGE LEARNING 2013

have been drawn to illustrate the equilibrium in January 2007, when the price averaged $55 per barrel, and world production averaged 84.3 million barrels per day.

What Happens When Things Change?

When we looked at the market for maple syrup, you saw how an event (such as bad weather) changed the equilibrium price and quantity. Now let's do the same for oil, focusing on each of the three episodes marked in Figure 13.

January 2007 to July 2008: Oil Prices Spike Upward

From January 2007 to July 2008, oil prices rose from $55 to $133 per barrel. As a result, gasoline prices shot up around the globe (and rose from $2.27 to $4.11 per gallon in the United States). Some commentators on cable news shows and blogs argued that the price spike could *not* be explained by supply and demand, because total oil production was rising, not falling. Since more oil was being produced than ever before, they argued, supply and demand would predict a *lower* price, not the higher price we observed. The pundits suggested that some other explanation—such as a conspiracy among oil traders—must have been at fault.

While these commentators were right that oil production was rapidly rising (see the lower panel of Figure 13), their belief that the price should have been falling is *not* correct. As you've learned, price and quantity can rise together when the demand curve shifts rightward. And in 2007 and early 2008, all the evidence pointed to a significant, rapid rightward shift in demand. As Figure 15 shows, a rightward shift in demand—with no shift in supply—causes both price *and* quantity to rise.

But why did demand increase so rapidly?

Let's go back a bit. Even before 2007, the world's total production of goods and services—and the incomes of those who produced them—were growing at a rapid pace. And in 2007 and early 2008, growth accelerated. Not only were the advanced

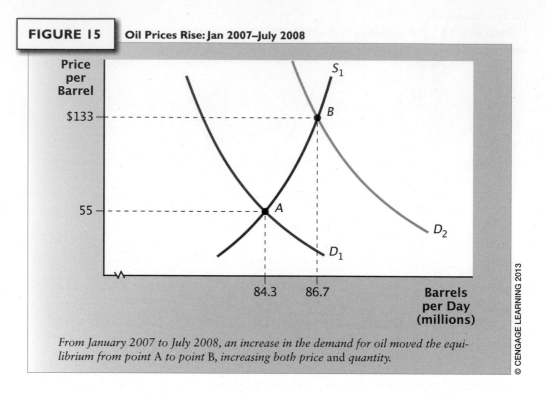

| FIGURE 15 | Oil Prices Rise: Jan 2007–July 2008 |

From January 2007 to July 2008, an increase in the demand for oil moved the equilibrium from point A to point B, increasing both price and quantity.

economies continuing to recover from earlier slowdowns, but several emerging economies grew especially fast. For example, incomes in China—which had been growing at 8 or 9 percent per year (already high)—grew by 12% in 2007. India's growth rate increased as well, from just under 6% to more than 9% per year. Moreover, these higher incomes enabled millions of people in emerging economies to afford cars for the first time, leading to a huge increase in demand for gasoline (and the crude oil from which gasoline is made). These changes caused the demand curve for oil to shift rightward.

If increases in supply had kept pace with the increases in demand, the price of oil would not have risen. (You can see this by drawing your own graph, in which both curves shift rightward by the same amount.) But during this period, no major new oil field was brought into production, and no new cost-saving technology was discovered. Nothing happened that might have shifted the supply curve significantly rightward. (Note that oil *production* rose, but this was a *movement along*—not a shift—of the supply curve.) So we had a rightward shift in demand, with no significant shift in supply, causing the price of oil to rise.

July 2008 to February 2009: Oil Prices Collapse

Look again at Figure 13, for the period from July 2008 to February 2009. In the upper panel, the price of oil plunged from $133 to $39 per barrel, while in the lower panel, oil production fell sharply, from 86.7 million to 83.8 million barrels per day. This change in price and quantity—the opposite of the one we just discussed—was caused by a *leftward* shift of demand, as shown in Figure 16.

Why did the demand curve shift leftward? In 2008, many of the world's economies suffered severe recessions. In the United States, total production fell by more than 4 percent, and millions of workers lost their jobs. In Europe and Japan, production fell even more sharply. Even in China and India, where production continued to increase,

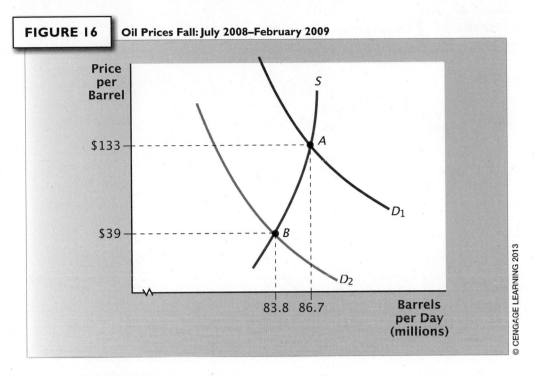

FIGURE 16 **Oil Prices Fall: July 2008–February 2009**

growth rates fell by one third or more. Worldwide demand for gasoline, jet fuel, and many other oil-based products plunged. As a result, the demand for oil itself decreased.

March and April 2011: Oil Prices Spike Again

Now take one more look at Figure 13. You can see in the figure that both price and quantity were steadily rising in the two years leading up to February 2011. In Europe, the U.S., and Japan, production was increasing. And in emerging economies like China and India, growth returned to its former rapid pace. These changes caused the demand curve to shift rightward during those two years, much as it had a few years earlier (depicted in Figure 15).

But in March and April, prices began shooting up suddenly. This time, both supply and demand played important roles.

Let's start with demand. With worldwide production and income continuing to rise, the demand curve continued shifting rightward. By some estimates, the demand curve for oil was increasing by about 500,000 barrels per day *every month*. So over this two-month period, the demand curve might have shifted rightward by $2 \times 500,000 = 1$ million barrels per day.

Second, the supply curve shifted sharply leftward, for two reasons. The first was internal conflict in Libya, which—in March and April—shut down most of that country's oil production. This alone removed about 1.3 million barrels per day from the market. Second, Saudi Arabia—which had often made up for past supply disruptions in the Middle East—did the opposite this time: It decreased production by about 200,000 barrels per day. In total, these two events caused the supply curve to shift leftward by about 1.5 million barrels per day.

The result is shown in Figure 17. Both the rightward shift in demand and the leftward shift in supply each contributed to the higher price of oil. But they had opposite effects on quantity. A rightward shift in demand tends to raise quantity, while a leftward shift in supply tends to lower it. Which effect dominated? If you

| FIGURE 17 | Oil Prices Rise: February 2011–April 2011 |

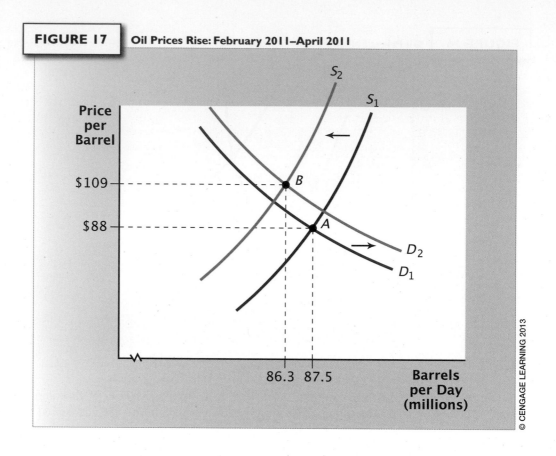

© CENGAGE LEARNING 2013

look back at Figure 13, you'll see that oil production fell during these two months. This tells us that the supply shift had the dominant effect on quantity, and that is what we've illustrated in Figure 17.

We'll be returning to oil prices later in this book. If you are studying microeconomics, you'll learn about some special features of oil and other commodities that explain why their prices can swing so widely and rapidly. If you are studying macroeconomics, you'll learn how sudden spikes in oil prices can cause (and have caused) recessions in the United States and other countries.

SUMMARY

In a market economy, prices are determined through the interaction of buyers and sellers in *markets*. In perfectly *competitive* markets, each buyer and seller regards the market price as given. If an individual buyer or seller has the power to influence the price of a product, the market is *imperfectly competitive*.

The model of *supply and demand* is designed to explain how prices are determined in perfectly competitive markets. The *quantity demanded* of any good is the total amount

buyers would choose to purchase given the constraints that they face. The *law of demand* states that quantity demanded is negatively related to price; it tells us that the *demand curve* slopes downward. The demand curve is drawn for given levels of income, wealth, tastes, prices of substitute and complementary goods, population, and expected future price. If any of those factors changes, the demand curve will shift (a *change in demand*). A change in price, however, moves us *along* the demand curve (a *change in quantity demanded*).

The *quantity supplied* of a good is the total amount sellers would choose to produce and sell given the constraints that they face. According to the *law of supply,* supply curves slope upward. The supply curve will shift (a *change in supply*) if there is a change in the price of an input, the price of an alternate good, the price in an alternate market, the number of firms, expectations of future prices, or (for some goods) a change in weather. A change in the price of the good, by contrast, moves us *along* the supply curve (a *change in quantity supplied*).

Equilibrium price and quantity in a market are found where the supply and demand curves intersect. If either or both of these curves shift, price and quantity will change as the market moves to a new equilibrium.

Economists frequently use a three-step process to answer questions about the economy. The three steps—taken several times in this chapter—are to (1) characterize the market or markets involved in the question; (2) find the equilibrium in the market; and (3) ask what happens when something changes.

PROBLEM SET

Answers to even-numbered Problems can be found on the text Web site through www.cengagebrain.com

1. Consider the following statement: "In late 2008, as at other times in history, oil prices came down at the same time that the quantity of oil produced fell. Therefore, one way for us to bring down oil prices is to slow down oil production." True or false? Explain.

2. Discuss, and illustrate with a graph, how each of the following events, *ceteris paribus*, will affect the market for coffee:
    a. A blight on coffee plants kills off much of the Brazilian crop.
    b. The price of tea declines.
    c. Coffee workers organize themselves into a union and gain higher wages.
    d. Coffee is shown to cause cancer in laboratory rats.
    e. Coffee prices are expected to rise rapidly in the near future.

3. Consider the following passage from an article in the *New York Times* on March 9, 2011, "In the last few years, coffee yields have plummeted here [Colombia] and in many of Latin America's other premier coffee regions as a result of rising temperatures and more intense and unpredictable rains, phenomena that many scientists link partly to global warming... [while] global demand is soaring as the rising middle classes of emerging economies like Brazil, India and China develop the coffee habit." Illustrate the impact of these events in a supply and demand diagram of the global market for coffee. *Ceteris paribus*, can we determine the direction of change in equilibrium quantity? Of equilibrium price? Explain briefly.

4. In the late 1990s and through 2000, the British public became increasingly concerned about "Mad Cow Disease," which could be deadly to humans if they ate beef from these cattle. Fearing the disease, many consumers switched to other meats, like chicken, pork, or lamb. At the same time, the British government ordered the destruction of thousands of head of cattle. Illustrate the effects of these events on the equilibrium price and quantity in the market for British beef. Can we determine with certainty the direction of change for the quantity? For the price? Explain briefly.

5. The following table gives hypothetical data for the quantity of two-bedroom rental apartments demanded and supplied in Peoria, Illinois:

Monthly Rent	Quantity Demanded (thousands)	Quantity Supplied (thousands)
$ 800	30	10
$1,000	25	14
$1,200	22	17
$1,400	19	19
$1,600	17	21
$1,800	15	22

a. Graph the demand and supply curves.
b. Find the equilibrium price and quantity.
c. Explain briefly why a rent of $1,000 cannot be the equilibrium in this market.
d. Suppose a tornado destroys a significant number of apartment buildings in Peoria but doesn't affect people's desire to live there. Illustrate on your graph the effects on equilibrium price and quantity.

6. How would each of the following affect the market for denim jeans in the United States? Illustrate each answer with a supply-and-demand diagram.
    a. The price of denim cloth increases.
    b. An economic slowdown in the United States causes household incomes to decrease.

7. The following table gives hypothetical data for the quantity of gasoline demanded and supplied in Los Angeles per month.

Price per Gallon	Quantity Demanded (millions of gallons)	Quantity Supplied (millions of gallons)
$1.20	170	80
$1.30	156	105
$1.40	140	140
$1.50	123	175
$1.60	100	210
$1.70	95	238

a. Graph the demand and supply curves.
b. Find the equilibrium price and quantity.
c. Illustrate on your graph how a rise in the price of automobiles would affect the gasoline market.

8. The table at the end of this problem gives hypothetical data for the quantity of electric scooters demanded and supplied per month.
a. Graph the demand and supply curves.
b. Find the equilibrium price and quantity.
c. Illustrate on your graph how an increase in the wage rate paid to scooter assemblers would affect the market for electric scooters.
d. What would happen if there was an increase in the wage rate paid to scooter assemblers at the same time that tastes for electric scooters increased?

Price per Electric Scooter	Quantity Demanded	Quantity Supplied
$150	500	250
$175	475	350
$200	450	450
$225	425	550
$250	400	650
$275	375	750

9. Indicate which curve shifted—and in which direction—for each of the following. Assume that only one curve shifts.
a. The price of furniture rises as the quantity bought and sold falls.
b. Apartment vacancy rates increase while average monthly rent on apartments declines.
c. The price of personal computers continues to decline as sales skyrocket.

10. Consider the following forecast: "Next month, we predict that the demand for oranges will continue to increase, which will tend to raise the price of oranges. However, the higher price will increase supply, and a greater supply tends to lower prices. Accordingly, even though we predict that demand will increase next month, we cannot predict whether the price of oranges will rise or fall." There is a serious mistake of logic in this forecast. Can you find it? Explain.

11. A couple of months after Hurricane Katrina in 2005, an article in *The New York Times* contained the following passage: "Gasoline prices—the national average is now $2.15, according to the Energy Information Administration—have fallen because higher prices held down demand and Gulf Coast supplies have been slowly restored."[2] The statement about supply is entirely correct and explains why gas prices came down. But the statement about demand confuses two concepts you learned about in this chapter.
a. What two concepts does the statement about demand seem to confuse? Explain briefly.
b. On a supply-and-demand diagram, show what most likely caused gasoline prices to rise when Hurricane Katrina shut down gasoline refineries on the Gulf Coast.
c. On another supply-and-demand diagram, show what most likely happened in the market for gasoline as Gulf Coast refineries were repaired—and began operating again—after the hurricane.
d. What role did the *demand* side of the market play in explaining the rise and fall of gas prices?

12. Draw supply-and-demand diagrams for market *A* for each of the following. Then use your diagrams to illustrate the impact of the following events. In each case, determine what happens to price and quantity in each market.
a. *A* and *B* are substitutes, and the price of good *B* rises.
b. *A* and *B* satisfy the same kinds of desires, and there is a shift in tastes away from *A* and toward *B*.
c. *A* is a normal good, and incomes in the community increase.
d. There is a technological advance in the production of good *A*.
e. *B* is an input used to produce good *A*, and the price of *B* rises.

13. When we observe an increase in both price and quantity, we know that the demand curve must have shifted rightward. However, we cannot rule a shift in the supply curve as well. Prove this by drawing a supply-and-demand diagram for each of the following cases:
a. Demand curve shifts rightward, supply curve shifts leftward, equilibrium price and quantity both rise.
b. Demand and supply curves both shift rightward, equilibrium price and quantity both rise.
c. Evaluate the following statement: "During the oil price spike from 2007 to mid-2008, we know the supply curve could not have shifted leftward, because quantity supplied rose." True or False? Explain.

[2] "Economic Memo: Upbeat Signs Hold Cautions for the Future," *The New York Times*, November 30, 2005.

14. In early 2011, even though cotton prices were high, cotton farmers in China began to hoard (rather than sell) most of the crop they had harvested, filling spare rooms and even living areas of their homes with cotton. Given the cost and inconvenience of storing large amounts of cotton rather than selling it, what could explain this behavior? [Hint: Review the section of this chapter on factors that shift the supply curve.] Could this behavior explain why cotton prices were high during this period? Explain, using the concepts of supply and demand.

More Challenging

15. Suppose that demand is given by the equation $Q^D = 500 - 50P$, where Q^D is quantity demanded, and P is the price of the good. Supply is described by the equation $Q^S = 50 + 25P$, where Q^S is quantity supplied. What is the equilibrium price and quantity? (See Appendix.)

16. While crime rates fell across the country over the past few decades, they fell especially rapidly in Manhattan. At the same time, there were some neighborhoods in the New York metropolitan area in which the crime rate remained constant. Using supply-and-demand diagrams for rental housing, explain how a falling crime rate in Manhattan could make the residents in *other* neighborhoods *worse off*. (Hint: As people from around the country move to Manhattan, what happens to rents there? If people already living in Manhattan cannot afford to pay higher rent, what might they do?)

17. An analyst observes the following equilibrium price-quantity combinations in the market for restaurant meals in a city over a four-year period:

Year	P	Q (thousands of meals per month)
1	$12	20
2	$15	30
3	$17	40
4	$20	50

He concludes that the market defies the law of demand. Is he correct? Why or why not?

In the body of this chapter, notice that the supply and demand curves for maple syrup were *not* graphed as straight lines. This is because the data they were based on (as shown in the tables) were not consistent with a straight-line graph. You can verify this if you look back at Table 1: When the price rises from $1.00 to $2.00, quantity demanded drops by 15,000 (from 75,000 to 60,000). But when the price rises from $2.00 to $3.00, quantity demanded drops by 10,000 (from 60,000 to 50,000). Since the change in the independent variable (price) is $1.00 in both cases, but the change in the dependent variable (quantity demanded) is different, we know that when the relationship between quantity demanded and price is graphed, it will not be a straight line.

We have no reason to expect demand or supply curves in the real world to be straight lines (to be *linear*). However, it's often useful to approximate a curve with a straight line that is reasonably close to the original curve. One advantage of doing this is that we can then express both supply and demand as simple equations, and solve for the equilibrium using basic algebra.

For example, suppose the demand for take-out pizzas in a modest-size city is represented by the following equation:

$$Q^D = 64,000 - 3,000\ P$$

where Q^D stands for the quantity of pizzas demanded per week. This equation tells us that every time the price of pizza rises by $1.00, the number of pizzas demanded each week *falls* by 3,000. As we'd expect, there is a negative relationship between price and quantity demanded. Moreover, since quantity demanded always falls at the same rate (3,000 fewer pizzas for every $1.00 rise in price), the equation is linear.[3]

Now we'll add an equation for the supply curve:

$$Q^S = -20,000 + 4,000\ P$$

where Q^S stands for the quantity of pizzas supplied per week. This equation tells us that when the price of pizza rises by $1.00, the number of pizzas supplied per week *rises* by 4,000—the positive relationship we expect of a supply curve.[4] And like the demand curve, it's linear:

Quantity supplied continues to rise at the same rate (4,000 more pizzas for every $1.00 increase in price).

We know that if this market is in equilibrium, quantity demanded (Q^D) will equal quantity supplied (Q^S). So let's *impose* that condition on these curves. That is, let's require $Q^D = Q^S$. This allows us to use the definitions for Q^D and Q^S that have price as a variable, and set those equal to each other in equilibrium:

$$64,000 - 3,000\ P = -20,000 + 4,000\ P$$

This is one equation with a single unknown—*P*—so we can use the rules of algebra to isolate *P* on one side of the equation. We do this by adding 3,000 *P* to both sides, which isolates *P* on the right, and adding 20,000 to both sides, which moves everything that *doesn't* involve *P* to the left, giving us:

$$84,000 = 7,000\ P$$

Finally, dividing both sides by 7,000 gives us

$$84,000/7,000 = P$$

or

$$P = 12$$

We've found our equilibrium price: $12.

What about equilibrium quantity? In equilibrium, we know quantity demanded and quantity supplied are equal, so we can *either* solve for Q^D using the demand equation, or solve for Q^S using the supply equation, and we should get the same answer. For example, using the demand equation, and using the equilibrium price of $12:

$$Q^D = 64,000 - 3,000\ (12)$$

or

$$Q^D = 28,000$$

To confirm that we didn't make any errors, we can also use the supply equation.

$$Q^S = -20,000 + 4,000\ (12)$$

or

$$Q^S = 28,000$$

We've now confirmed that the equilibrium quantity is 28,000.

[3] If you try to graph the demand curve, don't forget that supply and demand graphs reverse the usual custom of where the independent and dependent variables are plotted. Quantity demanded is the dependent variable (it *depends* on price), and yet it's graphed on the *horizontal* axis.

[4] Don't be troubled by the negative sign ($-20,000$) in this equation. It helps determine a minimum price that suppliers must get in order

to supply any pizza at all. Using the entire equation, we find that if price were $5.00, quantity supplied would be zero, and that price has to rise *above* $5.00 for any pizzas to be supplied in this market. But since a "negative supply" doesn't make sense, this equation is valid only for prices of $5.00 or greater.

CHAPTER **4**

Working with Supply and Demand

© MARK STOUT PHOTOGRAPHY/ SHUTTERSTOCK.COM

In the last chapter, we used supply and demand to explain how prices are determined in competitive markets, and what causes prices to change. In this chapter, you'll learn to work with supply and demand in new ways and in new contexts. We'll first analyze the different ways that governments intervene in markets to *change* the price of a good or service. Then we'll see how supply and demand—with some modifications—can be applied to a market with some special features: the market for residential housing. At the end of the chapter, you'll learn about the causes of the housing bubble from the late 1990s to 2006, why the bubble burst, and why housing prices have remained so low in the years following.

GOVERNMENT INTERVENTION IN MARKETS

The forces of supply and demand deserve some credit. They cause the market price to adjust until something remarkable happens: The quantity that sellers want to sell is also the quantity that buyers want to buy. Thus, every buyer and seller can turn their intentions into actual market trades.

So, three cheers for supply and demand! Or better make that *two* cheers. Because while everyone wants markets to function smoothly, not everyone is happy with the prices that supply and demand give us. Apartment dwellers often complain that their rents are too high, and farmers complain that the prices of their crops are too low.

We can also be dissatisfied with market *quantities*. We might ask the government to help increase the number of people attending college or to help decrease the quantity of gasoline that we use.

Responding to these dissatisfactions and desires, governments sometimes intervene to change the market outcome. And government can do so in a variety of ways.

We will first look at two policies in which the government tries to *fight* the market—that is, to prevent the price from reaching its equilibrium value. Economists are generally skeptical about the effectiveness and efficiency of these policies. Then we'll turn to methods government uses to *manipulate* markets—changing the equilibrium itself.

Fighting the Market: Price Ceilings

Figure 1 shows our familiar market for maple syrup, with an equilibrium price of $3.00 per bottle. Suppose that maple-syrup buyers complain to the government that this price is too high. And suppose the government responds by imposing a **price ceiling** in this market—a regulation preventing the price from rising above, say, $2.00 per bottle.

Price ceiling A government-imposed maximum price in a market.

89

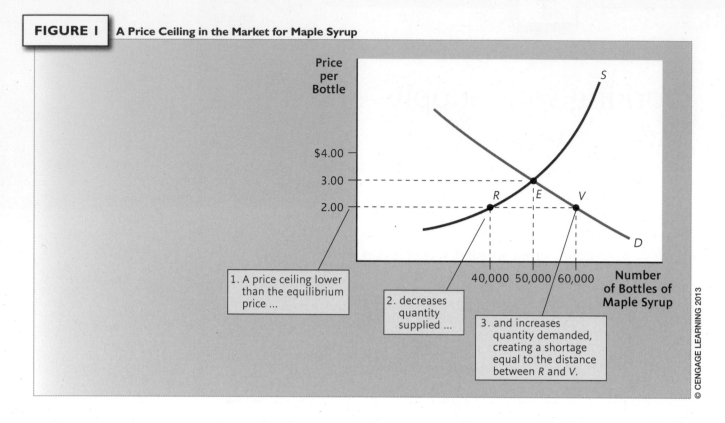

FIGURE 1   A Price Ceiling in the Market for Maple Syrup

1. A price ceiling lower than the equilibrium price ...

2. decreases quantity supplied ...

3. and increases quantity demanded, creating a shortage equal to the distance between *R* and *V*.

© CENGAGE LEARNING 2013

If the ceiling is enforced, then producers will no longer be able to charge $3.00 for maple syrup but will have to content themselves with $2.00 instead. In Figure 1, we will move down along the supply curve, from point *E* to point *R*, decreasing quantity supplied from 50,000 bottles to 40,000. At the same time, the decrease in price will move us along the demand curve, from point *E* to point *V*, increasing quantity demanded from 50,000 to 60,000. Together, these changes in quantities supplied and demanded create an *excess demand* for maple syrup of 60,000 − 40,000 = 20,000 bottles each month. Ordinarily, the excess demand would force the price back up to $3.00. But now the price ceiling prevents this from occurring. What will happen?

A practical observation about markets can help us arrive at an answer:

> *When quantity supplied and quantity demanded differ, the **short side of the market**—whichever of the two quantities is smaller—will prevail.*

Short side of the market The smaller of quantity supplied and quantity demanded at a particular price.

This simple rule follows from the voluntary nature of exchange in a market system: No one can be forced to buy or sell more than they want to. With an excess demand quantity supplied is less than quantity demanded, so *sellers* are on the short side of the market. Since we cannot force them to sell any more than they want to (40,000 units) the result is a **shortage** of maple syrup—not enough available to satisfy demand at the going price.

Shortage An excess demand not eliminated by a rise in price, so that quantity demanded continues to exceed quantity supplied.

But this is not the end of the story. Because of the shortage, all 40,000 bottles produced each month will quickly disappear from store shelves, and many buyers will be disappointed. The next time people hear that maple syrup has become available, everyone will try to get there first, and we can expect long lines at stores. Those who really crave maple syrup may have to go from store to store, searching for that rare bottle. When we include the *opportunity cost* of the time spent waiting in line or shopping around, the ultimate effect of the price ceiling may be a *higher* cost of maple syrup for many consumers.

> *A price ceiling creates a shortage and increases the time and trouble required to buy the good. While the price decreases, the opportunity cost may rise.*

And there is still more. The government may be able to prevent maple syrup *producers* from selling above the price ceiling. But it may not be able to prevent a **black market,** where goods are sold illegally at prices higher than the legal ceiling.

Ironically, the black market price will typically exceed the original, freely determined equilibrium price ($3.00 per bottle in our example). To see why, look at Figure 2. With a price ceiling of $2.00, sellers supply only 40,000 bottles per month. Suppose all 40,000 bottles are bought by lawbreakers—maple-syrup scalpers, if you will—who then sell them at the highest price they can get. What price will be charged in the black market?

To find out, let's use the demand curve. For any given quantity, the demand curve tells us the highest price consumers will pay and still buy that quantity. The highest price at which consumers would buy all 40,000 bottles offered on the black market is $4 per bottle (point T). And with a little reasoning, we can prove that the black-market price will, in fact, settle at $4.

Suppose the going price in the black market were initially less than $4 (say, $3). Then (according to the demand curve) buyers would want to buy *more* than the 40,000 bottles available each month. Maple syrup scalpers would quickly run out of maple syrup, and they'd raise their price. On the other hand, if the going black-market price were greater than $4, buyers would want to buy less than the 40,000 available each month. The maple-syrup scalpers would then lower their price. Only at a price of $4 is quantity demanded equal to the 40,000 bottles available in the black market each month.

Black market A market in which goods are sold illegally at a price above the legal ceiling.

FIGURE 2   **A Price Ceiling with a Black Market**

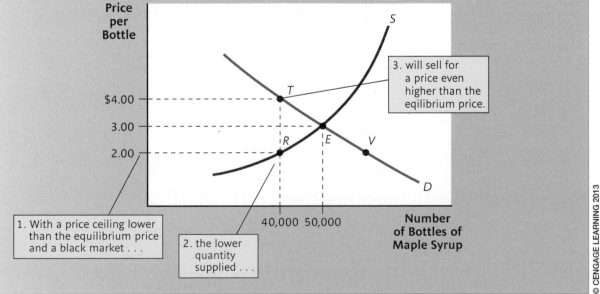

The unintended consequences of price ceilings—long lines, black markets, and, often, higher prices—explain why they are generally a poor way to bring down prices. Experience with price ceilings has generally confirmed this judgment. In the U.S., many states do have laws to limit price hikes during declared emergencies, thereby creating temporary price ceilings. But permanent or semipermanent price ceilings are exceedingly rare.

There is, however, one type of market in which several cities have imposed long-lasting price ceilings: the market for apartment rentals.

An Example: Rent Controls

Rent controls Government-imposed maximum rents on apartments and homes.

A price ceiling imposed in a rental housing market is called **rent control**. Most states have laws *prohibiting* rent control. But more than a dozen states do allow it. And in four of these states (New York, California, Maryland, and New Jersey), some form of rent control has existed in several cities and towns for decades.

In theory, rent control is designed to keep housing affordable, especially for those with low incomes. But for this purpose, it's a very blunt instrument because it doesn't target those with low incomes. Rather, *anyone* who was lucky enough to be living in one of the affected units when rent control was first imposed gets to pay less than market rent, as long as he or she continues to hold the lease on the unit. Many renters in cities such as New York and Santa Monica have higher incomes and living standards than do the owners from whom they rent.

Second, rent control causes the same sorts of problems as did our hypothetical price ceiling on maple syrup. It creates a persistent excess demand for rental units, so renters must spend more time and trouble finding an apartment. Typically, something akin to the black market develops: Real estate brokers quickly snap up the rent-controlled apartments (either because of their superior knowledge of the market, or their ability to negotiate exclusive contracts with the owners). Apartment seekers, who don't want to spend months searching on their own, will hire one of these brokers. Alternatively, one can sublet from a leaseholder, who will then charge market rent for the sublet and pocket the difference. Either way, many renters end up paying a higher cost for their apartments than the rent-controlled price.

Finally, rent controls cause a decrease in the quantity of apartments supplied (a movement along the supply curve). This is because lower rents reduce the incentives for owners to maintain existing apartments in rentable condition, and also reduce incentives to build new ones.

In our example of the market for maple syrup, the decrease in quantity supplied—combined with a black market—caused the average buyer to end up paying a higher price than before the ceiling was imposed (see point T in Figure 2). The same thing can happen in the apartment rental market. As supply decreases, the total money price of renting an apartment can rise above the original equilibrium price—if we include real estate commissions or the unofficial, higher rents paid by those who sublet.

Fighting the Market: Price Floors

Price floor A government-imposed minimum price in a market.

Sometimes, governments try to help sellers of a good by establishing a **price floor**—a minimum amount below which the price is not permitted to fall. The most common use of price floors around the world has been to raise prices (or prevent prices from falling) in agricultural markets. Price floors for agricultural goods are commonly called *price support programs*.

In the United States, price support programs began during the Great Depression, after farm prices fell by more than 50 percent between 1929 and 1932. The Agricultural Adjustment Act of 1933, and an amendment in 1935, gave the president the authority to intervene in markets for a variety of agricultural goods. Over the next 60 years, the United States Department of Agriculture (USDA) put in place programs to maintain high prices for cotton, wheat, rice, corn, tobacco, honey, milk, cheese, butter, and many other farm goods. Although some of these supports were removed in recent years, many remain. For example, government policy still maintains price floors for peanuts, sugar, and dairy products.

Let's consider dairy products, where the government has separate price floors for butter, cheese, and nonfat dry milk. These three price floors help to boost prices for *all* dairy products—even those without their own price floors. The price of fresh whole milk, for example, can only fall so far before the dairy industry would start producing less whole milk, and shifting production to butter, cheese, or nonfat dry milk, which have guaranteed minimum prices.

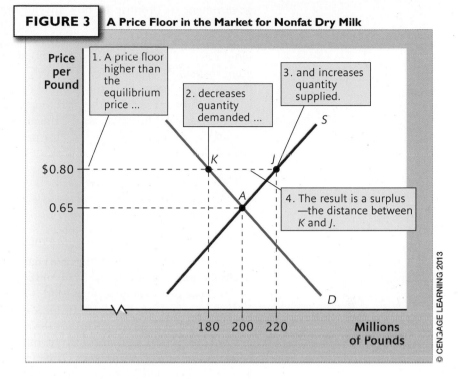

FIGURE 3   A Price Floor in the Market for Nonfat Dry Milk

© CENGAGE LEARNING 2013

But how does the government maintain its price floors for these three products? Let's narrow our focus to the market for nonfat dry milk—a market in which the USDA has been supporting prices for decades. In Figure 3—before any price floor is imposed—the market is in equilibrium at point *A*, with an equilibrium price of 65 cents per pound and an equilibrium quantity of 200 million pounds per month.

Now let's examine the impact of the price floor, which in recent years has been set at $0.80 per pound. At this price, producers want to sell 220 million pounds, while consumers want to purchase only 180 million pounds. There is an excess supply of 220 million − 180 million = 40 million pounds. Our short-side rule tells us that buyers determine the amount actually traded. They purchase 180 million of the 220 million pounds produced, and producers are unable to sell the remainder.

The excess supply of 40 million pounds would ordinarily push the market price down to its equilibrium value: $0.65. But now the price floor prevents this from happening. The result is a **surplus**—continuing extra production of nonfat dry milk that no one wants to buy at the going price.

Surplus An excess supply not eliminated by a fall in price, so that quantity supplied continues to exceed quantity demanded.

Maintaining a Price Floor

If the government merely *declared* a price floor of $0.80 per pound, many farmers who are unable to sell all of their product would be tempted to sell some illegally at a price below the floor. This would take sales away from other farmers trying to sell at the higher price, so they, too, would feel pressure to violate the floor. Soon, the price floor would collapse.

To prevent this, governments around the world have developed a variety of policies designed to prevent surplus goods from forcing down the price. One method, frequently used in the United States, is for the

© AXL/SHUTTERSTOCK.COM

DANGEROUS CURVES ⚠

Floor Above, Ceiling Below! It's tempting to think that a price floor should be set *under* the equilibrium price, or a price ceiling should be *above* the equilibrium price. After all, a floor is usually on the bottom of something, and a ceiling is on the top. Right? In this case, wrong! A price floor *below* the equilibrium price would have no impact, because the market price would *already* satisfy the requirement that it be higher than the floor. Similarly, a price ceiling set *above* the equilibrium price would have no impact (make sure you understand why). So remember: Always draw an effective price floor *above* the equilibrium price and an effective price ceiling *below* the equilibrium price.

government to promise to buy any unsold product at a guaranteed price. In the market for nonfat dry milk, for example, the government agrees to buy any unsold supplies from sellers at a price of $0.80 per pound. With this policy, no supplier would ever sell at any price *below* $0.80, since it could always sell to the government instead. With the price effectively stuck at $0.80, private buyers buy 180 million pounds—point *K* on the demand curve in Figure 3. But since quantity supplied is 220 million, at point *J*, the government must buy the excess supply of 40 million pounds per year. In other words, the government maintains the price floor by *buying up* the entire excess supply. This prevents the excess supply from doing what it would ordinarily do: drive the price down to its equilibrium value.

> *A price floor creates a surplus of a good. In order to maintain the price floor, the government must prevent the surplus from driving down the market price. In practice, the government often accomplishes this goal by purchasing the surplus itself.*

In 2009, for example, the USDA purchased more than 200 million pounds of non-fat dry milk, at a cost of almost $160 million.

Because purchasing surplus food is so expensive, price floors are usually accompanied by government efforts to *limit* any excess supplies. In the dairy market, for example, the U.S. government has developed a complicated management system to control the production and sale of milk to manufacturers and processors, which helps to limit the government's costs. In other agricultural markets, the government has ordered or paid farmers *not* to grow crops on portions of their land and has imposed strict limits on imports of food from abroad. As you can see, price floors often get the government deeply involved in production decisions, rather than leaving them to the market.

Price floors have certainly benefited farmers and helped them in times of need. But this market intervention has many critics—including most economists. They have argued that the government spends too much money buying surplus agricultural products, and the resulting higher prices distort the public's buying and eating habits—often to their nutritional detriment. For example, the General Accounting Office estimated that from 1986 to 2001, American consumers paid an extra $10.4 billion because of higher-than-equilibrium prices on dairy products. And this does not include the cost of the health effects—such as calcium and protein deficiencies among poor children—due to decreased milk consumption. The irony is that many of the farmers who benefit from price floors are wealthy individuals or large, powerful corporations that do not need the assistance. Economists argue that assistance to farmers would be more cost-effective if given directly to those truly in need, rather than supporting all farmers—rich and poor alike—with artificially high prices.

* * *

With price floors and price ceilings, the government tries to *prevent* the market price from reaching its equilibrium value. As you've seen, these efforts often backfire or have serious unintended consequences. But government can also intervene in a different way: It can try to influence the market outcome using *taxes* or *subsidies*—then stand out of the way and let the market help to achieve the desired outcome.

Manipulating the Market: Taxes

Taxes are imposed on markets to give the government revenue so it can provide public goods and services, to correct inequities in the distribution of income and wealth, or—our focus in this chapter—to change the price or quantity in a market.

A tax on a specific good or service is called an **excise tax**, which can be collected from either sellers or buyers. As you're about to see, the impact of a tax is the same, regardless of which side of the market (buyers or sellers) the tax is collected from.

An Excise Tax on Sellers

Let's explore the impact of an excise tax imposed on sellers with an example: Gasoline taxes. In the United States, the gasoline tax—collected from gasoline sellers—originated to fund the building and maintenance of the national highway system. But in recent years, many economists and others have wanted to increase this tax, for both geopolitical goals (to decrease U.S. imports of foreign oil) as well as environmental goals (to help fight pollution, traffic congestion, and climate change). Those who advocate a higher tax point out that gasoline taxes are much higher in Europe (approaching $5 per gallon in several European countries), while federal and state taxes on gasoline in the U.S. average only 48 cents per gallon.

In our example, we'll assume that initially there is no gas tax at all, and then we'll impose a tax of 60 cents per gallon on *sellers*. How would such a tax affect the market for gasoline?

Suppose that before the tax is imposed, the supply curve for gasoline is S_1 in Figure 4. (Ignore the curve above it for now.) Point A on this curve tells us that 400 million gallons will be supplied if the price is $3 per gallon. Let's state this another way: *In order for the gasoline industry to supply 400 million gallons they must get $3 per gallon.*

What happens when sellers must pay a tax of $0.60 on each gallon sold? What price must the industry charge now to supply the same 400 million gallons? The answer is $3.60, at point A'. Only by charging $0.60 more for each gallon could they continue to get the amount ($3) that makes it just worth their while to supply 400 million gallons. The same is true at any other quantity we might imagine: The price would have to be $0.60 more than before to get the industry to supply that same quantity. So imposing a $0.60 tax on gas suppliers shifts the entire supply curve *upward* by $0.60, to $S_{\text{After Tax}}$.

> *A tax collected from sellers shifts the supply curve upward by the amount of the tax.*

Now look at Figure 5, which shows the market for gasoline. Before the tax is imposed, with supply curve S_1 and demand curve D, the equilibrium is at point A, with price at $3 and quantity at 400 million. After the $0.60 tax is imposed and the supply curve shifts up to $S_{\text{After Tax}}$, the new equilibrium price is $3.40, with 300 million gallons sold.

Who is paying this tax? Let's take a step back and think about it. The tax is *collected* from gas sellers. But who really *pays*—that is, who sacrifices funds they would otherwise have if not for the tax—is an entirely different question. The distribution of this sacrifice on each unit sold is called the **tax incidence**.

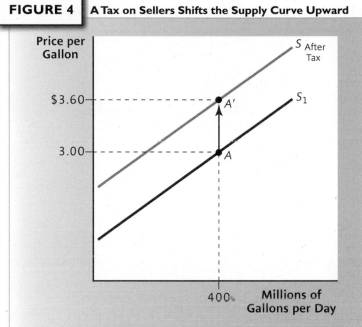

FIGURE 4 | **A Tax on Sellers Shifts the Supply Curve Upward**

After a $0.60 per gallon tax is imposed on sellers, the price at which any given quantity would be supplied is $0.60 greater than before, so the supply curve shifts upward. For example, before the tax, 400 million gallons would be supplied at $3 per gallon (point A); after the tax, to get that same quantity supplied requires a price of $3.60 (point A').

Excise tax A tax on a specific good or service.

Tax incidence The division of a tax payment between buyers and sellers, determined by comparing the new (after tax) and old (pretax) market equilibriums.

FIGURE 5 | The Effect of an Excise Tax Imposed on Sellers

After a $0.60 excise tax is imposed on sellers, the market equilibrium moves from point A to point B, with buyers paying sellers $3.40 per gallon. But sellers get only $3.40 − $0.60 = $2.80 after paying the tax. Thus, the tax causes buyers to pay $0.40 more per gallon, and sellers to get $0.20 less than before.

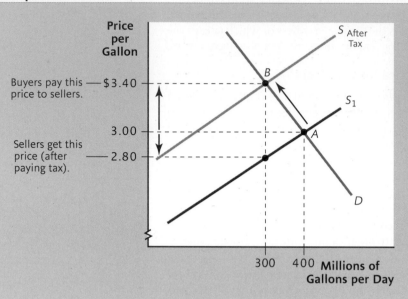

In our example, buyers paid $3.00 for each gallon before the tax, and $3.40 after. So buyers are really paying $0.40 of this tax each time they buy a gallon of gas in the form of a higher price.

What about sellers? Before the tax, they got $3.00 per gallon. After the tax, they collect $3.40 from drivers but $0.60 of that goes to the government. If we want to know how much sellers get after taxes, we have to go back to the old supply curve S_1, which lies below the new supply curve by exactly $0.60. In effect, the old supply curve deducts the tax and shows us what the sellers really receive. When the sellers charge $3.40, the original supply curve S_1 shows us that they receive only $2.80. This is $0.20 less than they received before, so sellers end up paying $0.20 of the tax.

Considering the impact on both buyers and sellers, we see that:

> *The incidence of a tax that is collected from sellers generally falls on both sides of the market. Buyers pay more, and sellers receive less, for each unit sold.*

An Excise Tax on Buyers

Suppose that, instead of collecting the $0.60 tax from the sellers, the tax was collected directly from buyers. Before the tax is imposed, the demand curve for gasoline is D_1 in Figure 6. Point A on this curve tells us that 400 million gallons will be demanded by buyers each day if the price they have to pay is $3.00. Or, rephrased, *in order for buyers to demand 400 million gallons, each gallon must cost them $3.00.* If the cost per gallon is any more than that, buyers will not buy all 400 million gallons.

Now let's impose the $0.60 tax on buyers. (Imagine a government tax collector standing at the pump, requiring each buyer to hand over $0.60 for every gallon they buy.) What price would buyers now be willing to pay and still buy all 400 million gallons? The answer is $2.40, at point A′. We know this because only if they paid

$2.40 would gasoline continue to cost them the $3.00 per gallon which makes it just worth their while to demand all 400 million gallons. The same is true at any other quantity we might imagine: The price would have to be $0.60 less than before to induce buyers to demand that same quantity. So imposing a $0.60 tax on buyers shifts the entire demand curve *downward* by $0.60, to $D_{\text{After Tax}}$.

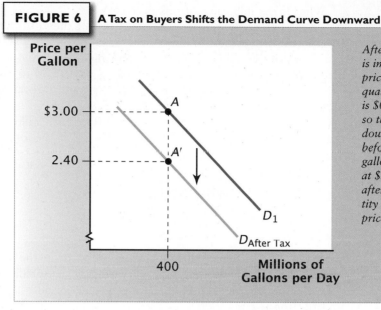

FIGURE 6   **A Tax on Buyers Shifts the Demand Curve Downward**

After a $0.60 per gallon tax is imposed on buyers, the price at which any given quantity would be demanded is $0.60 less than before, so the demand curve shifts downward. For example, before the tax, 400 million gallons would be demanded at $3 per gallon (point A); after the tax, that same quantity would be demanded at a price of $2.40 (point A′).

© CENGAGE LEARNING 2013

A tax collected from buyers shifts the demand curve downward by the amount of the tax.

Figure 7 shows the impact on the market. Before the tax is imposed, with demand curve D_1 and supply curve S, the equilibrium is at point A, with price at $3.00 and quantity at 400 million. After the $0.60 tax is imposed, and the demand curve shifts down to $D_{\text{After Tax}}$, the new equilibrium price is $2.80, with 300 million gallons sold. With the tax imposed on buyers this time, the supply curve is not affected.

FIGURE 7   **The Effect of an Excise Tax Imposed on Buyers**

After a $0.60 excise tax is imposed on buyers, the market equilibrium moves from point A to point C, with buyers paying sellers $2.80 per gallon. But buyers pay a total of $2.80 + $0.60 = $3.40 per gallon when the tax is included. Thus, the tax causes buyers to pay $0.40 more, and sellers to get $0.20 less, just as when the tax is imposed on sellers.

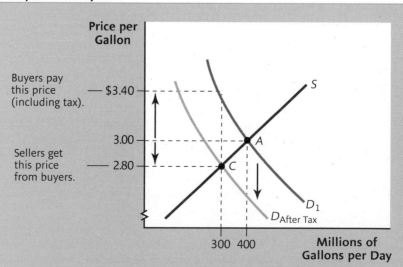

© CENGAGE LEARNING 2013

What is the incidence of this tax? Let's see . . . Buyers paid $3.00 for each gallon of gas before the tax, and $2.80 after. But they also have to pay $0.60 to the government. If we want to know how much buyers pay *including* the tax, we have to go back to the old demand curve D_1, which lies above the new demand curve by exactly $0.60. As you can see, when buyers pay $2.80 to the gas station they pay a total of $3.40. This is $0.40 more than they paid in total before, so buyers end up paying $0.40 of the tax.

What about sellers? Sellers received $3.00 for each gallon before the tax and $2.80 after. So sellers are really paying $0.20 of this tax, in the form of a lower price.

> *The incidence of a tax that is collected from buyers falls on both sides of the market. Buyers pay more, and sellers receive less, for each unit sold.*

Tax Incidence versus Tax Collection

The numerical incidence of any tax will depend on the shapes of the supply and demand curves. But you may have noticed that the incidence in our example is the same whether the tax is collected from buyers or sellers. In both cases, buyers pay $0.40 of the tax per gallon and sellers pay $0.20. If you'll excuse the rhyme, this identical incidence is no coincidence.

> *The incidence of a tax (the distribution of the burden between buyers and sellers) is the same whether the tax is collected from buyers or sellers.*

Why? Because the two methods of collecting taxes are not really different in any important economic sense. Whether the tax collector takes the $0.60 from the gas station owner when the gas is sold, or takes $0.60 from the driver when the gas is sold, one fact remains: Buyers will pay $0.60 more than the sellers receive. The market finds a new equilibrium reflecting this. In our example, this new equilibrium occurs where each gallon costs drivers $3.40 in total, and the gas suppliers receive $2.80 of this, because that is the only incidence at which quantity demanded and supplied are equal.

Manipulating the Market: Subsidies

Subsidy A government payment to buyers or sellers on each unit purchased or sold.

A **subsidy** is the opposite of a tax. Instead of the government demanding a payment *from* the buyer or seller, the government makes a payment *to* the seller or buyer. And whereas a tax raises the price to the buyer and decreases purchases of the product, a subsidy does the reverse: It lowers prices to buyers and *encourages* people to buy it. In the United States, federal, state, and local governments subsidize a variety of goods and services, including medical care for the poor and elderly, energy-saving equipment, smoking-cessation programs, and college education.

A Subsidy to Buyers

Let's explore the impact of a subsidy given to buyers with an example: Tuition assistance to college students.

Every year in the United States, federal and state governments provide more than $100 billion in subsidies—scholarships and other assistance—to help students pay the cost of a college education. The reasons for these policies are clear: We want to

FIGURE 8   A Subsidy for Students Attending College

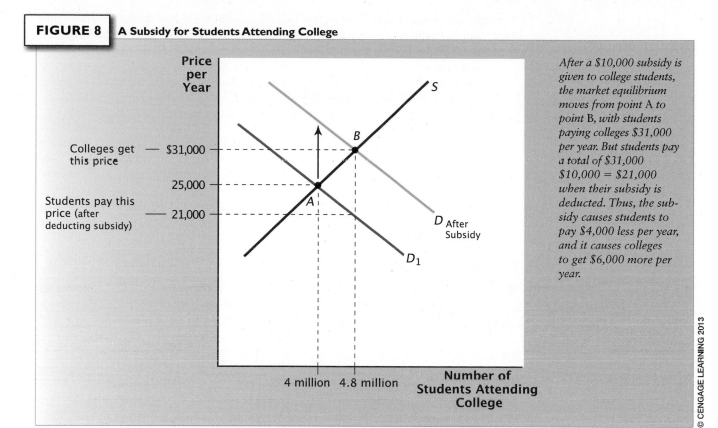

After a $10,000 subsidy is given to college students, the market equilibrium moves from point A to point B, with students paying colleges $31,000 per year. But students pay a total of $31,000 $10,000 = $21,000 when their subsidy is deducted. Thus, the subsidy causes students to pay $4,000 less per year, and it causes colleges to get $6,000 more per year.

© CENGAGE LEARNING 2013

encourage more people to get college degrees. A college education gives substantial benefits to the degree-holders themselves, in the form of higher future incomes. And a more educated population creates benefits for society as a whole. There are also important equity considerations: Financial assistance increases the number of students from poor households, many of whom might otherwise have to forgo the benefits of college.

Figure 8 shows the market for attending college. Initially, without any government involvement, demand curve D_1 intersects supply curve S at point A. Four million students attend college each year, with each paying a total of $25,000 in tuition.

Now, let's introduce financial assistance: a subsidy of $10,000 per year for each student. And we'll assume here that the subsidy is paid out to buyers—college students—to help them pay tuition.

The subsidy shifts the demand curve *upward* by $10,000, to $D_{\text{After Subsidy}}$. Why? Before the subsidy, 4 million students would attend college when the price was $25,000. So *after* the subsidy, those same 4 million would attend at a price of $35,000 (indicated by the tip of the vertical arrow in Figure 8). After all, paying $35,000 with a $10,000 subsidy is the same as paying $25,000 with no subsidy. This reasoning applies to any other number of students we might imagine: After the subsidy, that same number of students would attend college if the price were $10,000 higher than before.

A subsidy paid to buyers shifts the demand curve upward by the amount of the subsidy.

After the demand curve shifts upward, the market equilibrium moves from point A to point B. In the new equilibrium, 4.8 million students decide to attend college. But notice that the price is higher as well: Colleges are now charging $31,000 per year.

In general,

> *A subsidy paid to buyers benefits both sides of a market. Buyers pay less and sellers receive more for each unit sold.*

In the end, who benefits from the subsidy? Colleges benefit: They get more for each student who attends ($31,000 instead of $25,000). Students benefit as well: They pay $31,000 to the colleges, but the government pays $10,000 of that, so the cost to students has dropped to $21,000.

However, notice that the $10,000 subsidy has *not* reduced the cost of college by a full $10,000. In our example, only $4,000 of the subsidy ends up as a direct benefit to the student, while the other $6,000 goes to the college.

A Subsidy to Sellers

As you learned earlier, the burden (incidence) of a tax is the same, regardless of whether it is collected from sellers or buyers. What about a subsidy? Is the benefit to each side of the market the same, regardless of which side the payment is given to? Indeed it is.

We leave it to you to do the analysis, but here's a hint: If the subsidy in our example had been paid to colleges (the sellers) instead of students (the buyers), the supply curve would shift *downward* by the amount of the subsidy. If you draw the graph, using the same initial supply and demand curves as in Figure 8 and the same $10,000 subsidy, you'll see that students will pay $21,000 (and not receive anything from the government), while colleges will collect $31,000 when we include the subsidy they receive. What buyers end up paying, and what sellers end up receiving, is the same as in Figure 8.

In general,

> *The distribution of benefits from a subsidy is the same, regardless of whether the subsidy is paid to buyers or sellers.*

* * *

In this chapter, we've considered only one impact of taxes and subsidies: How they change the market price. But taxes and subsidies also change the market *quantity* and they affect taxpayers (through their impact on the government budget). If you are studying microeconomics, you'll learn how economists take account of all these effects in a later chapter. You'll also learn which types of taxes and subsidies can help the economy function more effectively.

SUPPLY AND DEMAND IN HOUSING MARKETS

So far in this text book, we've used supply and demand to analyze a variety of markets—for maple syrup, crude oil, higher education, and more. All of these markets have one thing in common: they are markets in which business firms sell currently produced goods or services.

But the supply-and-demand model is a versatile tool. With a bit of modification, we can use it to analyze almost any market in which something is traded at a price, including markets for labor, foreign currencies, stocks, bonds, and more. Our only requirement is that there are many buyers and sellers, and each regards the market price (or a narrow range of prices) as given. In the remainder of this chapter, we'll use supply and demand to understand a type of market that has been at the center of recent economic events: the market for residential housing.

What's Different about Housing Markets

Housing markets differ in an important way from others we've considered so far. When people buy maple syrup, they buy newly produced bottles, not previously owned ones. But when people shop for a home, they generally consider newly constructed homes and previously owned homes to be very close substitutes. After all, a house is a house. If properly maintained, it can last for decades or even centuries. Indeed, most of the homes that people own, and most that change hands each year, were originally built and sold long before.

This key difference—that housing markets are dominated by previously owned homes—means we'll need to think about supply and demand in a somewhat different way. To understand this new approach, we first need to take a short detour.

A Detour: Stock and Flow Variables

Many economic variables fall into one of two categories: *stocks* or *flows*.

> A **stock variable** *measures a quantity at a moment in time. A* **flow variable** *measures a process that takes place over a period of time.*

Stock variable A variable representing a quantity at a moment in time.

Flow variable A variable representing a process that takes place over some time period.

To understand the difference, think of a bathtub being filled with water. At any given moment, there are a certain number of gallons actually *in* the tub. This volume of water is a *stock variable*: a quantity that exists at that moment in time (such as 15 gallons). But each minute, a certain volume of water flows *into* the tub. This rate of flow is a *flow variable*: a process that takes place over a *period* of time (such as 2 gallons per minute).

In this book, you've encountered both types of variables. In Chapter 3, for example, the quantity of maple syrup demanded or supplied was a flow: a certain number of bottles bought or sold *per month*. Similarly, household income is a flow: so many dollars earned *per month* or *per year*. But household *wealth*—the total value of what someone owns minus the total owed—is a stock variable. Wealth is a certain number of dollars measured at a particular point in time.

Stocks versus Flows in the Housing Market

Now back to housing. Which of these two concepts—stock or flow—should we use in our supply-and-demand model for housing? Let's see.

If we use the now-familiar flow approach to supply and demand, then the "supply of housing" would be the number of homes everyone wants to sell per period, and the "demand for housing" would be the number that people want to buy per period. Both supply and demand would refer to a process (selling and buying) that takes place over a period of time.

If we use the stock approach, then the "supply of housing" would be the number of homes *available*—say, 100 million U.S. homes on January 1, 2013. This would be the total number of homes *in existence* at that time (often called the *housing stock*). The "demand for housing" would be the total number that people want to *own*. Both supply and demand would refer to quantities at a moment in time.

For some purposes, the two approaches would work equally well. But in many situations, the flow approach to the housing market creates confusion. For example, suppose that in a particular month, the number of homes people want to *sell* at any price decreases, because more homeowners want to continue living in their current homes rather than sell them. Using the flow approach, we'd have to say that the "supply of homes" is decreasing, because supply in the flow approach measures desired home *selling* during the month. But the total number of homes in *existence* and available for ownership would *not* be falling. In fact, if new homes are being built during the month (as usually happens), the number of homes available would actually be *rising*. Thus, the flow approach suggests something counter-intuitive: that "supply" is falling, even when the number of homes in existence is unchanged or rising.

To help us avoid this and other confusions, we'll use the stock approach to housing in this chapter. In the stock approach, the "supply of homes" is the number of homes available for ownership, and it rises if and only if the total number of homes in existence rises.

When we view demand and supply as stocks (rather than flows), equilibrium occurs when the total number of homes people *want to own* (demand) is equal to the total number *available* (supply). To see how this works, let's take a closer look at supply and demand as stock variables, and illustrate them graphically.

The Supply Curve for Housing

In Figure 9, panel (a) shows a supply curve for a local housing market in a small city. The average price of a home in this market is measured along the vertical axis, and the number of homes is on the horizontal axis. Remember that we are viewing housing supply as a stock variable. Accordingly,

Supply curve for housing A vertical line showing the total number of homes in a market that are available for ownership.

> the **supply curve for housing** tells us the number of homes in a market that are available for ownership—the housing stock.

It's a vertical line because, no matter what the price, the housing stock at any point in time is fixed, determined by the number of homes that were built in the past and

---

FIGURE 9   The Supply Curve in a Housing Market

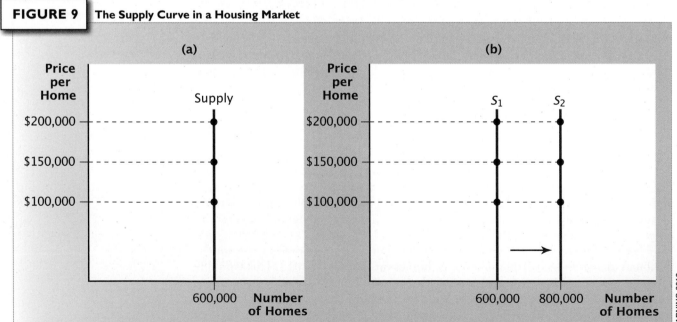

In panel (a), the supply curve tells us the number of homes (600,000) that exist at a particular time. It is a vertical line because the housing stock at any time does not depend on the price. Panel (b) shows the impact of building 200,000 new homes over the year. The housing stock rises to 800,000 so the supply curve shifts rightward, from S_1 to S_2.

still suitable for ownership. In the figure, we've assumed that the housing stock is currently 600,000, so the supply curve is a vertical line at 600,000.

Shifts versus Movements Along the Supply Curve

When the price of homes changes, we move *along* (up or down) the vertical supply curve for housing. Note that a change in the average price will not affect the current housing stock. A drop in the price from $200,000 to $100,000 will not cause existing houses to self-destruct, and a rise in the price from $100,000 to $200,000 will not cause more homes to suddenly appear.

Over time, however, the housing stock can change, causing the supply curve to *shift*. For example, if new homes are being built, the housing stock will rise over time. A year from now, more homes will be available for ownership than there are today. So the supply curve one year from now will lie further to the right than the current supply curve. Panel (b) of Figure 9 shows the rightward shift in the supply curve from its current position (S_1) to its position one year later (S_2) when 200,000 new homes are built over the year.

Could the supply curve ever shift *leftward*? Yes, if the housing stock *decreased*. This could occur if an earthquake or other natural disaster destroyed existing homes. After the disaster, fewer homes would be available at any price, so the supply curve would shift leftward.

The Demand Curve for Housing

As we did with supply, we will view the demand for homes as a stock variable. Specifically,

> the **demand curve for housing** *tells us, at each price, the total number of homes that everyone in the market would like to own, given the constraints that they face.*

Demand curve for housing A curve showing, at each price, the total number of homes that everyone in the market would like to own, given the constraints that they face.

Note the last phrase in that definition. As always, "demand" in a market takes into account the real-world constraints that people face. Home ownership is costly. So in deciding whether they want to own a home, people consider the cost, as well as their limited income and the alternatives to owning that are available to them.

Figure 10(a) shows the demand curve for housing in the small city that we've been considering. To keep things simple, we'll assume for now that households or families in this city can own just one home each. In that case, the demand curve tells us the number of families who want to be home owners at each price. (Later in the chapter, we'll discuss the role of owning multiple homes in the recent housing boom.)

As you can see in the figure, the demand curve slopes downward: As the average price of a home in this city falls, more people want to own them. To see why, let's take a closer look at the cost of home ownership.

Behind the Demand Curve: Ownership Costs

People deciding whether they want to own a home will compare the costs and benefits of owning a home with the costs and benefits of the next best alternative: renting. There are several advantages to owning rather than renting, including greater control over your living environment and the possibility that the home will increase in value. For many decades, owning a home was thought to be one of the most stable and profitable investments a family could make.

© AXL/SHUTTERSTOCK.COM

DANGEROUS CURVES

Misinterpreting the Supply and Demand Curves for Homes It's very easy to slip into thinking that the supply and demand curves for housing have the "flow" interpretation of the previous chapter, instead of the proper "stock" interpretation here. So remember: the supply curve does *not* represent the number of homes people want to sell each period. Rather, it represents the number of homes that *exist* at a point in time. Similarly, the demand curve does *not* tell us how many homes people would like to buy each period. Rather, it tells us how many homes people want to *own* at a point in time.

FIGURE 10   The Demand Curve in a Housing Market

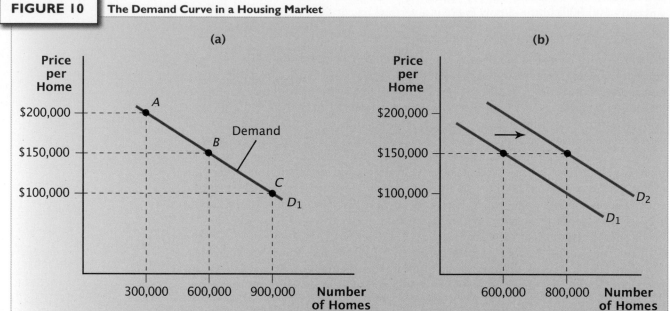

In panel (a), the demand curve tells us—at each price—the number of people who would like to own homes. It slopes downward because a decrease in the average selling price of a home lowers the ongoing interest cost of home ownership, increasing the number of people who want to own. In panel (b), tastes change in favor of home ownership. More people would like to own at each price, so the demand curve shifts rightward from D_1 to D_2.

But owning a home also entails costs, including maintenance, property taxes, and—the largest component—interest. As you are about to see, the interest cost of owning a home depends on the current price of the house—the price that it *could* be sold for. This is true for prospective owners (those thinking of *becoming* home owners by buying a home) and also for those who already own a home, even if they bought it long ago.

Costs for Prospective Home Owners. Let's first consider those thinking of *becoming* owners by buying a home. Suppose that a buyer pays entirely with his or her own funds. Then those funds can no longer be invested elsewhere, so the buyer will be forgoing interest. The greater the price of the home, the more the buyer will have to pay, and the more interest the buyer will forgo each year.

Most prospective home owners, however, do *not* pay the entire purchase price themselves. Instead, they pay for a small part of the purchase with their own funds—called the *down payment*—and *borrow* the rest, getting a housing loan called a **mortgage**. The mortgage is paid back monthly over many years. For most of that time, the monthly payments will consist largely of interest charges. So, once again, the owner has an interest cost. For a given down payment, the greater the price of the home, the more the buyer will have to borrow, and the higher the monthly interest payments on the mortgage.

Summing up so far, we've seen that for *prospective* home owners, higher home prices lead to greater interest costs, and therefore a greater cost of owning. But what about ownership costs for those who *already* own their home?

Costs for Current Owners. You might think that, once someone has already purchased a home, the interest cost is based on the price paid earlier, at the time of purchase, and is not affected if the price of the home changes later. But in fact, any change in the home's price—even after it was purchased—will change the owner's costs.

Mortgage A loan given to a home-buyer for part of the purchase price of the home.

To see why, remember that anyone who already owns a home could always choose to sell it. The owner could then pay back any amount remaining on the mortgage and also get some cash back (since the selling price is usually greater than the amount owed on the mortgage). That cash could earn interest. Continued ownership, therefore, means *continued forgone interest*.

Of course, the higher the price at which a house *could* be sold, the more interest the owner sacrifices by *not* selling. So once again, higher home prices mean more forgone interest, and therefore higher ownership costs.

Let's summarize what we've found about ownership costs:

> *Both current and prospective homeowners face an interest cost of ownership. This cost rises when current home prices rise, and falls when current home prices fall.*

Now you can understand why the demand curve in Figure 10(a) slopes downward. When housing prices fall and nothing else changes, the ongoing interest cost of owning a home declines as well. With lower costs, more people than before will prefer to own homes, so the quantity of homes demanded increases.

Shifts versus Movements Along the Demand Curve

As with any demand curve, when we change the price and move along the curve, we hold constant all other influences on demand. For example, in Figure 10(a), if the price of a home falls from $150,000 to $100,000, *ceteris paribus*, we move along the demand curve from point *B* to point *C*. The number of families who want to own rises from 600,000 to 900,000.

But as we make this movement, we hold constant all other influences on demand, such as the cost of the main alternative (*renting* a home), interest rates in the economy, tastes for home ownership, expectations about future home prices, average income, population—anything that might affect the number of homes demanded *other* than the current price of a home. If any of these other factors change, the demand curve will shift.

Suppose, for example, that tastes in this city shift away from renting apartments toward owning homes. Then at each price, more people would want to be homeowners than before. This is illustrated in Figure 10(b), where the demand curve shifts rightward from D_1 to D_2.

Housing Market Equilibrium

Figure 11 combines the supply and demand curves from Figures 9(a) and 10(a). The equilibrium, as always, occurs where the two curves intersect, at point *B*, with the average price of a house in this city at $150,000. But because this is a new type of market, it's worth spending a little time understanding *why* equilibrium occurs at this price.

Suppose the price of homes in this area were $100,000, which is less than the equilibrium price. Point *C* on the demand curve tells us that 900,000 people want to own homes at this price. But the supply curve tells us that only 600,000 homes are available—that is, only 600,000 homes *can* be owned. So with a price of $100,000, there is an excess demand for homes. What will happen?

People who want homes, but don't yet have them, will try to buy them from the current owners, bidding up prices. Because the housing stock is constant (at least for now), the rise in price will *not* change the quantity of homes available. But it *will* move us along the demand curve (upward and leftward from point *C*), as higher home prices drive up ownership cost and reduce the number of people who want to

FIGURE 11 Equilibrium in a Housing Market

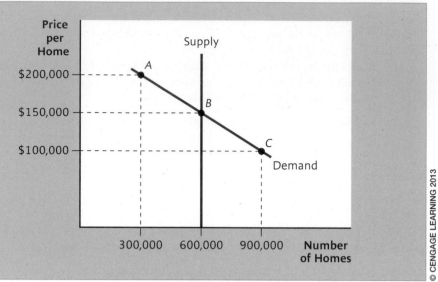

The equilibrium in this market is at point B, where the price of homes is $150,000. If the price were higher—say $200,000—the number of homes people want to own (300,000 at point A) would be less than the number in existence and currently owned (600,000). Owners would try to sell, and the price would fall until all 600,000 homes were demanded. If the price were lower than the equilibrium price—say $100,000—the number of homes people want to own (900,000 at point C) would be greater than the number in existence and currently owned (600,000). People would try to buy homes, and the price would rise until only 600,000 were demanded.

own. The price will continue rising until the number of people who *want* to own a home is equal to the number of homes that *can* be owned: the 600,000 that exist. This occurs when the price reaches $150,000, at point *B*.

What if the price started *higher* than $150,000—say, $200,000? Then only 300,000 people would want to own homes, at point *A*. But remember: 600,000 homes exist, and at any time, every one of them must be owned by *someone*. So at a price of $200,000, half of the current homeowners prefer *not* to own. They will try to sell, and home prices will fall. As home prices drop, and we move rightward along the demand curve, more people decide they want to own. The price continues dropping until it reaches $150,000, at point *B*, where people are content to own all 600,000 homes in existence.

The equilibrium price in a housing market is the price at which the quantity of homes demanded (the number that people want to own) and quantity supplied (the housing stock) are equal.

What Happens When Things Change

So far, in Figure 11, we've identified the equilibrium at a particular point in time. We did so by assuming that the housing stock was fixed at 600,000, and all influences on demand other than the price of homes were held constant.

But *over time*, in most housing markets, both the supply and demand curves will shift rightward. The supply curve shifts rightward as the housing stock rises (new homes are built). And the demand curve shifts rightward for a variety of reasons, including population growth and rising incomes. As a result, the market equilibrium will move rightward over time as well. But what happens to home *prices* depends on the *relative* shifts in the supply and demand curves. Let's look at three possibilities.

Equal Changes in Supply and Demand: A Stable Housing Market

Figure 12 illustrates a stable housing market, in which increases in the housing stock just keep pace with increases in demand over time. Let's start with the initial situation, at point *B*, with a housing stock of 600,000 homes and a price of $150,000. Over the

FIGURE 12   A Stable Housing Market

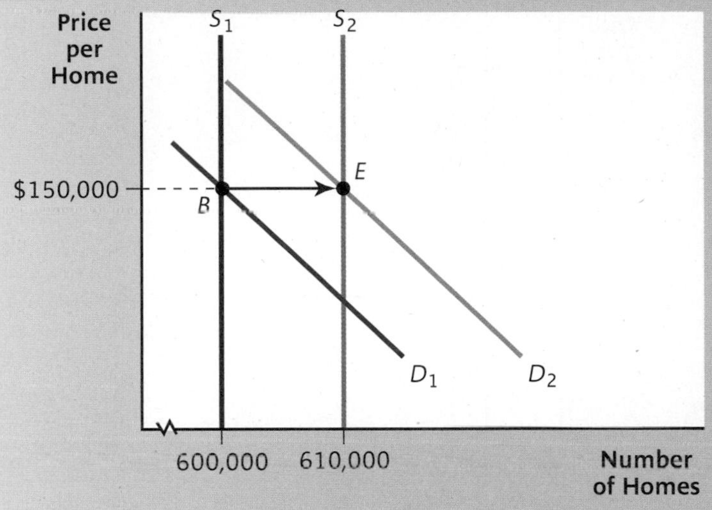

When the supply of homes increases at the same rate as demand for them, the equilibrium price remains unchanged. In the figure, the rightward shift in the supply curve (from S_1 to S_2) is equal to the rightward shift in the demand curve (from D_1 to D_2). Equilibrium moves from point B to point E, but the price remains at $150,000.

© CENGAGE LEARNING 2013

next year, population and income growth shifts the demand curve rightward to D_2. At each price, the demand for homes is 10,000 more than before. New construction increases the housing stock by 10,000 as well, shifting the supply curve to S_2. The equilibrium moves to point E, with a new, higher housing stock of 610,000, and an unchanged equilibrium price of $150,000.

> *When the housing stock grows at the same rate as housing demand, housing prices remain unchanged.*

We should note that Figure 12 is not entirely realistic. In most housing markets, construction costs for labor and raw materials tend to rise over time, as more homes are built. In order to cover these rising costs and continue increasing the housing stock, average home prices must rise, at least modestly. You'll learn more about these types of market adjustments when you study perfectly competitive markets in more detail, in microeconomics. In the figure, we've ignored rising construction costs.

But in some cases, we observe home prices rising *much* faster than can be explained by rising construction costs alone. When home prices rise especially rapidly, we know that increases in demand must be outpacing increases in supply. Let's consider two possible ways this could happen.

Restrictions on New Building: Rapidly Rising Prices

In some housing markets, local restrictions on new building can prevent the housing stock from keeping up with ongoing increases in demand. This is illustrated in Figure 13. As in our previous example, the initial market equilibrium is at point B, with price equal to $150,000. And once again, the demand curve shifts rightward over the year by 10,000 units, due to population and income growth. But now, we assume that restrictions allow construction of only 3,000 new homes, so the supply curve shifts by less than in the previous figure: to S_2'. After the demand shift, people want to own 610,000 homes (at point F) at a price of $150,000, but only 603,000 exist. The excess demand of 7,000 homes drives up home prices, and we move

FIGURE 13   A Housing Market with Restricted Supply Growth

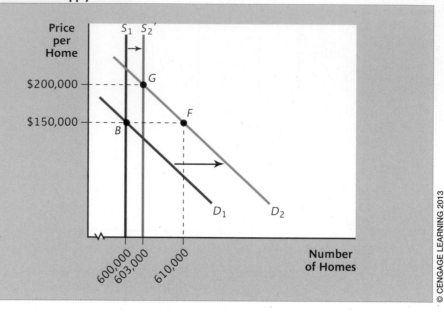

When supply is restricted, and cannot increase as fast as demand, housing prices rise. In the figure, the rightward shift in the supply curve (from S_1 to S_2') is less than the rightward shift in the demand curve (from D_1 to D_2). Equilibrium moves from point B to point G, and the price rises from $150,000 to $200,000.

leftward along the demand curve, until only 603,000 homes are demanded. At the new equilibrium (point G), the price is $200,000.

> *When restrictions on new building prevent the housing stock from growing as fast as demand, housing prices rise.*

Restrictions on new building explain why housing prices have risen rapidly for decades in cities like New York and in many areas of California. The *demand* for housing in these areas increases in most years, but various restrictions on new building or the limited supply of coastal land prevent the housing stock from keeping up.

Faster Demand Growth: Rapidly Rising Prices

Several factors could cause the demand curve for housing to begin shifting rightward more rapidly than in the past: population shifts (a sudden influx of new residents), rapid income growth (because of a booming industry in the area), or a change in expectations about future prices. Let's take a closer look at this last factor: expectations.

So far, we've considered home ownership as an alternative to renting. That is, whether you own or rent, you get valuable services—a roof over your head and a place to watch TV. And we've discussed these alternatives in terms of their relative ongoing costs.

But a house is more than just a place to live. It is also an example of an **asset**—something of value that someone owns. An asset can be sold in the future at whatever price prevails in the market at that time. If the asset is sold at a higher price than the purchase price, the seller enjoys a **capital gain**. If the asset is sold for *less* than the purchase price, the seller suffers a **capital loss**.

Anticipated capital gains are one of the reasons that people hold assets, including homes. In fact, the potential for capital gains are especially important in the housing market, for one reason: A home is one of the most *leveraged* financial investments that most people ever make.

The appendix to this chapter discusses leverage in more detail, as well as some special features of leverage in the housing market. But the takeaway from the appendix is this: Leverage *magnifies* the impact of a price change on the rate of return you will

Capital gain The gain to the owner of an asset when it is sold for a price higher than its original purchase price.

Capital loss The loss to the owner of an asset when it is sold for a price lower than its original purchase price.

| FIGURE 14 | Accelerating Demand Growth |

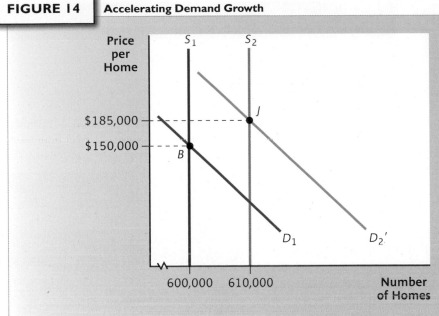

When demand begins to increase faster than previously, increases in supply usually lag behind. In the figure, the rightward shift in the supply curve (from S₁ to S₂) is less than the rightward shift in the demand curve (from D₁ to D₂′). Equilibrium moves from point B to point J, with the price rising from $150,000 to $185,000.

get from an asset. When home prices rise, your rate of return from investing in a home can be *several times* the percentage growth in housing prices. This makes the demand for housing particularly sensitive to changing expectations about future home prices.

Let's suppose that people begin to think housing prices will increase more rapidly over the next few years than they've risen in the past. With housing seen as an even more profitable investment than before, more people want to be homeowners at any given price for homes. The demand curve will shift rightward by more than it otherwise would.

Figure 14 illustrates the result. The demand curve—instead of shifting to D_2 as in Figure 12, now shifts further, to D_2'. But notice that the supply curve continues to shift only to S_2 (the housing stock rises by only 10,000 units), just as in Figure 12. Why doesn't the housing stock keep up with the suddenly higher demand?

Because it takes *time* for new construction to be planned and completed. The change in the housing stock over the *current* year is based on how many construction projects were initiated in the *previous* year. And the number of projects started in the previous year was based on prices *then*—before the surge in demand. With the demand curve shifting to D_2', and the supply curve to S_2, the equilibrium moves to point *J*, with a new equilibrium price of $185,000.

Note that, with higher housing prices, construction firms will have an incentive to increase building. Unless restrictions prevent them from doing so, the housing stock will rise at a faster rate—in *future* years. Eventually, the housing stock can catch up to the higher demand, but that will happen much later. In the meantime, the main impact of the rapid increase in demand is higher home prices.

In summary:

When the demand for housing begins rising faster than previously, the housing stock typically lags behind, and housing prices rise.

Changes in expectations—and rapidly shifting demand curves—were a major cause of the housing bubble from the late 1990s through 2006, as well as the housing bust that immediately followed, as you are about to see.

USING THE THEORY

THE HOUSING BOOM AND BUST: 1997–2011

Figure 15 shows an index measure of inflation-adjusted U.S. housing prices. (The inflation adjustment removes the effects of general inflation from the change in home prices, making comparisons over time more meaningful.) The index begins with a value of 100 in early 1987. In any other year, its value tells us the

percentage by which the median inflation-adjusted home price exceeded the median price in 1987. For example, in early 1999, the index's value was 105.5, telling us that the median home in 1999, after adjusting for inflation, cost about 5.5% more than the median home in 1987.

The most glaring feature of this graph is the startling price increase from 1997 to 2006. During that period, the housing price index almost doubled. (Remember—this is the rise in the index *after* we remove any increase due to general inflation.) Something special must have been happening with housing.

The rapid rise in housing prices—especially after 2001—has been described as a housing "bubble." The term *bubble* suggests something that is destined to burst.

FIGURE 15   **Index of Home Prices, Adjusted for Inflation**

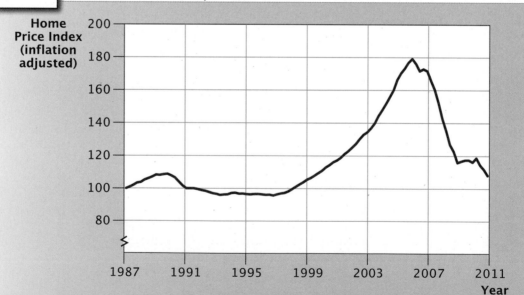

After adjusting for price changes from general inflation, the housing boom began in 1997, and home prices increased ever more rapidly until 2006. That marked the beginning of the housing bust, with prices dropping dramatically for several years.

Source: S&P/Case-Shiller Home Price Index

And Figure 15 shows this is just what happened: In mid-2006, U.S. housing prices began falling. And as the months went by, they continued to fall—faster. A similar pattern of bubble and burst occurred in many other countries. In some of them, such as Ireland, the boom and bust were even more extreme than in the United States.

What caused housing prices to behave this way? A complete answer requires some additional tools and concepts that you will learn later in microeconomics and macroeconomics. But at the center of this economic storm were the familiar forces of supply and demand.

The Housing Boom: Rapidly Rising Demand

As you've learned, rapid increases in home prices can occur when demand begins increasing faster than supply. From 1997 to 2006, several factors accelerated demand growth. While supply increased as well, it lagged behind—more and more each year—because of the ever-more-rapid increases in demand. The result of faster demand growth and lagging supply growth—as you've learned—is a surge in housing prices.

What caused demand to increase so rapidly during this period?

Economic Growth

In the United States and many other countries, the 1990s were a period of prosperity and rising incomes. Higher incomes increase the demand for most goods, including housing. In addition, after years of high employment, people felt increasingly confident about the future, and more willing to take on the long-term financial obligations associated with home ownership.

Interest Rates

Beginning in 2001, interest rates on many types of loans trended downward, including the interest rate on mortgage loans. The reasons for this general decline in interest rates are somewhat controversial. The policy of the U.S. Federal Reserve played a key role. But global financial forces may have contributed as well. Indeed, the decline in interest rates was observed in many other countries, not just the United States.

Recall that interest costs (interest foregone or interest actually paid) are the main component of ownership costs. So when interest rates drop, owning a home is less costly. By reducing the cost of home ownership, the drop in interest rates increased the total number of homes people wanted to own *at any given price*. Thus, the general drop in interest rates contributed to the rightward shift in the demand for housing.

Government Policy

In the United States (more so than most other countries), owning a home has been viewed as a desirable way to promote financial security for individuals and responsible citizenship for local communities. For this reason, the government has long encouraged home ownership in two major ways.

First, it allows homeowners to deduct mortgage interest payments from their taxable income. The government in effect says, "If you shift some of your spending from other things to mortgage payments, we will give you some of your tax dollars back." This amounts to a subsidy: a payment from the government to the borrower for each dollar of interest paid on a mortgage loan, lowering monthly home ownership costs.

Second, government agencies[1] have increased the funds available for mortgage lending by purchasing mortgages from banks and other financial institutions, giving

[1] The two main agencies are the Federal National Mortgage Association, informally known as "Fannie Mae" and the Federal Home Loan Mortgage Corporation, known as "Freddie Mac."

them fresh cash to lend out again for another mortgage. The resulting increase in funding for mortgages has helped to keep mortgage interest rates—and monthly home ownership costs—low.

These government policies have caused the demand for housing to be greater than it would otherwise be. But they had been in place for decades, so their mere existence cannot explain the housing boom. However, at the start of the boom, policy became even more pro-housing. Government agencies expanded their purchases of mortgage loans, helping to push mortgage interest rates even lower. And in 1997, the government added another tax benefit for homeowners: It raised the "capital gains exclusion" on home sales from $125,000 to $500,000, and made it easier to apply the exclusion to a second home. This meant that the first $500,000 of capital gains from selling a home would be entirely tax free. Thus, owning one or more homes with a mortgage—already an attractive, highly leveraged investment—became even more attractive.

Financial Innovations

Two types of financial innovation—both of which had existed prior to the boom—became more prevalent as the boom developed. The first type of innovation involved more-attractive terms for borrowers. The adjustable rate mortgage (ARM), for example, offered a very low interest rate and low monthly payments—*initially*. The interest rate and monthly payments would leap upward later, usually after two years. But during the initial low-payment period, ARMs lowered monthly home ownership costs and increased the demand for housing.

A second type of innovation made mortgage *lending* more attractive. Traditionally, a mortgage lender, such as a bank, would hold onto a mortgage and collect the monthly payments from the homeowner for the life of the loan, typically 30 years. But a technique called *securitization* pooled many mortgages together, and then divided them into smaller financial assets called *mortgage-backed securities*. These mortgage-backed securities were then sold to investors who received monthly payments from the entire pool of mortgages.

Though mortgage-backed securities had been around for decades, they became more popular during the housing boom because of *other* financial innovations. One innovation was a new way for lenders to quantify the risks of an individual mortgage (called "credit scoring"), so they could then quantify the risk of a mortgage-backed security. Also, new ways of combining and re-dividing the securities themselves were developed, which seemed to reduce their risks further.

Financial institutions in the United States and around the world—hungry for new, low-risk opportunities to lend—purchased hundreds of billions of dollars of these new securities each year. In this way, an entirely new group of global investors—and an entirely new source of funds—became available for mortgage lending. Mortgage interest rates—and therefore ownership costs for new home buyers—fell further. The demand curve for homes shifted further rightward.

Lending Standards

Banks and other financial institutions that make mortgage loans take a risk: If housing prices decline, and an owner owes more on the mortgage than the home is worth, the owner might *default* (stop making payments).

When a family defaults, it ultimately moves out of the home—either by walking away or because they are forced out by *foreclosure*. This process is costly, and when the home is resold, it is usually a distress sale, at a bargain price. All in all, 50% or more of the remaining value of the loan can be lost in a default. These losses are then transmitted to the lender or anyone currently holding the mortgage-backed security that contains that mortgage as part of its larger pool.

Traditionally, lenders have guarded against homeowner defaults in two ways (1) lending only to those whose incomes and credit histories suggest a small probability of default; and (2) requiring the borrower to make a sizeable down payment—traditionally 20% of the home's value. The down payment gives the borrower something at stake—and a reason to continue making payments—even if the price of the home declines modestly.

However, as the boom proceeded, with huge amount of funds flowing into the mortgage market and lenders competing with each other to find borrowers, lending standards deteriorated. Lenders made more and more so-called *subprime loans:* loans to borrowers who previously would not have qualified due to low or unstable incomes or bad credit histories. In 2006 alone, more than $600 billion in subprime mortgage loans were made—about one-fifth of all mortgage lending. Down payments began to shrink as well. From 2005 to 2007, more than half of the subprime mortgage loans in the U.S. actually had no down payment at all.

The decline in lending standards contributed to the housing boom by opening up the prospect of home ownership to millions of people who would not otherwise have qualified. This caused a further rightward shift in the demand curve for housing.

Speculation

Once housing prices had increased rapidly for several years, and people began expecting them to *keep* rising at those rates, speculation took over. Remember that—even with a 20% down payment—housing is a highly leveraged investment (see the appendix for full details). If the housing market gives you a way to turn a $40,000 investment into $100,000 or more in a few years, why *not* buy a home? And why just one? Why not buy two, three, or as many as you can obtain mortgages for? Your ARMs will have low monthly payments for a couple of years, and when the interest rates reset to higher, unaffordable levels, you can always sell your houses for a capital gain.

Once this kind of thinking takes over a market, it feeds on itself. People want to speculate in housing because they expect the price to keep rising, and the price keeps rising because more and more people are speculating and shifting the demand for housing ever rightward.

An Example: The Boom in Las Vegas

Figure 16 shows an example of how all of these forces drove up housing prices in one particular city—Las Vegas—where a full-force bubble began in mid-2003 (a bit later than in some other cities). Initially, with demand curve D_{2003} and supply curve S_{2003}, the market was in equilibrium at Point A, with the median home worth $179,000. Then, for all of the reasons we've discussed, the demand

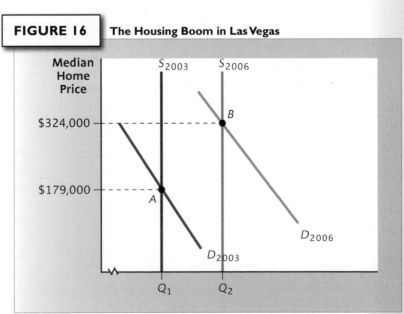

FIGURE 16   **The Housing Boom in Las Vegas**

curve for homes in Las Vegas shifted rapidly rightward, reaching D_{2006} in mid-2006. As housing prices rose, new construction picked up as well, increasing the housing stock and shifting the supply curve rightward, ultimately to S_{2006}. But, as discussed in this chapter, when demand increases rapidly, the housing stock often lags behind. That is what happened in Las Vegas. As shown in the figure, demand increased substantially more than supply, so home prices soared—rising to $324,000 in June 2006.

Unfortunately, what happened in Vegas didn't stay in Vegas. The same bubbles developed in many areas of the country—especially in towns and cities in California, Arizona, and Florida.

The Housing Bust: A Sudden Drop in Demand

Every bubble bursts at some point. If nothing else, there are natural limits to its growth. If home prices had continued to rise at such a rapid pace, eventually new buyers would not be able to make monthly mortgage payments, even with low interest rates. The speculation would ultimately slow, and then reverse direction when people realized that prices were no longer rising.

But a bubble can burst before it reaches a natural limit. And in U.S. housing markets, problems began to occur in mid-2006, largely due to two simultaneous events: (1) oil and gasoline prices spiked, so many new homeowners were having difficulty making their monthly mortgage payments; and (2) interest rates on a large group of adjustable rate mortgages reset to higher levels. Suddenly, people noticed a disturbing rise in defaults—especially on subprime mortgages with no down payments. Around the world, lenders to the U.S. mortgage market began to take a closer look at the housing market, and they did not like what they saw: more ARMs resetting to higher levels over the next several years, and more defaults down the road. Everyone suddenly took notice of how high home prices had risen, and how far they could fall.

For the first time, it seemed, investors began to ask questions about the statistical analysis used by financial institutions to measure the risk of ARMs and subprime mortgages, and the risks of their associated mortgage-backed securities. And it turned out that every financial institution had made the same assumption: That housing prices would continue rising or, at worst, fall only modestly. No one seemed to consider what would happen if home prices fell more dramatically.

Now, with the prospect of higher default rates, and the possibility of falling home prices, the former flood of funding for new mortgages turned into a drought. Interest rates on new mortgages—to the extent they were available at all—rose. The demand curve for housing shifted leftward. And the fears of mortgage lenders became self-fulfilling: Housing prices fell.

Moreover, once housing prices began to fall, speculative fever worked in reverse. By 2007, what had been a near-certain, highly leveraged gain for home buyers turned into the prospect of a highly leveraged loss. Anyone buying a home with a traditional down payment risked losing the entire investment in a few years or less. And many of those who already owned homes suddenly wished they didn't. The demand curve for housing shifted further leftward, and housing prices fell even more rapidly.

An Example: The Bust in Las Vegas

Figure 17 illustrates how these events affected the housing market in Las Vegas. Initially, at the peak of the bubble in mid-2006, with demand curve D_{2006} and supply curve S_{2006}, the market was at point B, with the average price of a home at $324,000.

FIGURE 17   The Housing Bust in Las Vegas

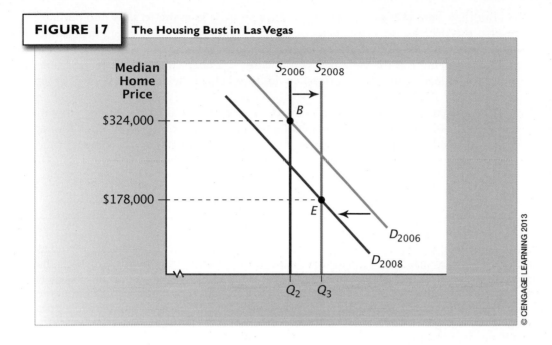

But then the demand curve shifted leftward, and by late 2008, it reached a location like that of D_{2008}.

The supply curve, of course, did *not* shift leftward. Houses generally last a long time, and the homes built during the bubble had now become permanent additions to the housing stock. In fact, the supply curve continued to shift *rightward* for a few years, as construction projects initiated during the boom years were finished and added to the housing stock. Due to the leftward shift in demand and the rightward shift in supply, the average price of a Las Vegas home fell from $324,000 to $178,000.

The Long Housing Slump

From the end of 2008 through 2011, the U.S. economy suffered the aftermath of an unusually severe recession. High unemployment and declining incomes left millions of homeowners struggling to pay their monthly mortgage bills, leading to further defaults. Defaults rose even among those who *could* afford the monthly payments, but whose homes were now worth less than the amount they owed on their mortgages. In 2008, 2009, and 2010, financial institutions foreclosed on close to 3 million homes, and several million additional homes had received legal notices and remained in the foreclosure pipeline. Each foreclosure meant another homeowner who was no longer willing or able to own a home, shifting the demand curve for housing further to the left.

If you flip back to Figure 15, however, you'll see that U.S. home prices stabilized a bit in 2009 and early 2010. In part, this may reflect efforts by the Obama administration and Congress. The Making Home Affordable Program, begun in early 2009, provided incentives for banks and homeowners to renegotiate mortgage agreements and prevent foreclosures. Other programs offered additional tax benefits to new home buyers. These programs were meant to offer some financial relief to struggling families.

But they were also designed with another purpose in mind: to slow and perhaps reverse the decrease in demand for housing. If successful, these programs would cause housing prices to bottom out sooner, and at a higher price, than otherwise. If you are studying macroeconomics, you'll learn in a later chapter that rising home prices (or at least stable home prices) could have helped the economy recover from recession.

Unfortunately, the government's efforts were too small in scope and too slow in execution. As Figure 15 shows, they had a temporary effect at best. In 2010, home prices resumed their downward trajectory. And by mid-2011, the average U.S. home price (adjusted for inflation) had fallen to 40% of its peak five years earlier.

SUMMARY

The model of supply and demand is a powerful tool for understanding all sorts of economic events. For example, governments often intervene in markets through *price ceilings* or *price floors,* designed to prevent the market from reaching equilibrium. Economic analysis shows that these policies are often ineffective in achieving their goal of helping one side of the market, and they often create additional problems.

Governments also intervene to change the market equilibrium itself, using taxes and subsidies. Taxes raise the full price consumers pay and lower the net price that sellers receive, regardless of which side of the market (buyers or sellers) the tax is collected from. Subsidies have the opposite effect: lowering the net price that buyers pay and raising the full price that sellers receive, regardless of which side of the market (buyers or sellers) receive the subsidy.

Supply and demand can also be used to understand markets other than those for currently produced goods and services. One important example is the market for residential housing, which can be usefully analyzed as a *stock variable* (a quantity that exists at a particular point in time), rather than a *flow variable* (a process that takes place over a period of time). In the housing market, the supply curve tells us the quantity of homes in existence, and the demand curve tells us the number of homes that the population would like to own. The demand curve slopes downward because housing entails an ongoing ownership cost, with interest cost (paid or foregone) one of its major components. The lower the price of a home, the lower the monthly ownership cost, and the more attractive owning is compared to renting.

In a stable housing market, the housing stock keeps pace with demand growth, so prices remain stable. But restrictions on new building, or a sudden acceleration of demand, can cause housing prices to soar. Because people usually buy homes with *mortgage loans,* housing is a highly *leveraged* financial investment: The value of the home is a multiple of the funds invested. As a result, the demand for housing is especially sensitive to changes in expected prices. This played a role in the most recent housing boom and the housing bust that followed.

PROBLEM SET

Answers to even-numbered Problems can be found on the text Web site through www.cengagebrain.com

1. Suppose the market for rice has the following supply and demand schedules:

P (per ton)	Q^D (tons)	Q^S (tons)
$10	100	0
$20	80	30
$30	60	40
$40	50	50
$50	40	60

To support rice producers, the government imposes a price floor of $50 per ton.
a. What quantity will be traded in the market? Why?
b. What steps might the government have to take to enforce the price floor?

2. In Figure 2, a price ceiling for maple syrup caused a shortage, which led to a black market price ($4) higher than the initial equilibrium price ($3). Suppose that the price ceiling remains in place for years. Over time, some maple syrup firms go out of business. With fewer firms, the supply curve in the figure shifts leftward by 10,000 bottles per month. After the shift in the supply curve:
a. What is the shortage caused by the $2 price ceiling? (Provide a numerical answer.)
b. If all of the maple syrup is once again purchased for sale on the black market, will the black market price be greater, less than, or the same as that in Figure 2? Explain briefly.

3. In the chapter, you learned that one way the government enforces agricultural price floors is to buy up the excess supply itself. If the government wanted to follow a similar kind of policy to enforce a price *ceiling* (such as rent control), and thereby prevent black-market-type activity, what would it have to do? Is this a sensible solution for enforcing rent control? Briefly, why or why not?

4. In Figure 5, explain why the incidence of a $0.60 tax imposed on sellers could not be split equally between buyers and sellers, given the specific supply and demand curves as drawn. [Hint: What price would gasoline sellers have to charge after the tax if there were an even split? What would happen in the market if sellers charged this price?]

5. Figure 8 shows the impact of a $10,000 subsidy on the market for college education when the subsidy is paid to college students. Starting with the same initial supply and demand curves, show what happens when the same $10,000 subsidy per student is paid to the *colleges* they attend. Suggestion: Trace the relevant curves from the figure on your own sheet of paper. [Hint: If a subsidy is paid directly to the colleges, which curve will shift? In what direction?]

6. State whether each of the following is a stock variable or a flow variable, and explain your answer briefly.
   a. Total farm acreage in the U.S.
   b. Total spending on food in China
   c. The total value of U.S. imports from Europe
   d. Worldwide iPhone sales
   e. The total number of parking spaces in Los Angeles
   f. The total value of human capital in India
   g. Investment in new human capital in India

7. In a study session, one of your fellow students says, "I think our econ text book has a mistake: It shows the supply curve for housing as a vertical line, which implies that a rise in price causes no change in quantity supplied. But everyone knows that if home prices rise, construction firms will build more homes and supply them to the market. So the supply curve should be drawn with an upward slope: higher price, greater quantity supplied." Explain briefly the mistake this student is making.

8. Suppose you buy a home for $200,000, using your own funds. The annual interest rate you could earn by investing your funds elsewhere is 5%. (Ignore any sales commissions or fees associated with buying or selling a home.)
   a. If the price at which you could sell the home remains at $200,000, what is your annual interest cost of home ownership?

   b. Suppose that, after a few years of owning, home prices rise dramatically, and you can now sell your home for $300,000. If you continue to own, what is your annual interest cost now?
   c. Suppose once again that, after a few years of owning, you can now sell your home for $300,000. But the interest rate you could earn by investing your funds elsewhere has risen to 7%. If you continue to own, what is your annual interest cost now?

9. Suppose you buy a home for $200,000, making a $40,000 down payment and taking out a mortgage for the rest. The annual interest rate on your mortgage is 5%, which is also the interest rate you can earn when you invest your funds elsewhere. (Ignore any possible tax benefits from your mortgage, as well as commissions or fees from buying or selling a home.)
   a. If the price at which you could sell the home remains at $200,000, what is your annual interest cost of home ownership? [Hint: Be sure to include both actual interest payments and foregone interest.]
   b. Suppose that, after a few years of owning, you still owe the same amount on your mortgage, but you could now sell your home for $300,000. If you continue to own, what is your annual interest cost now? [Hint: When calculating the foregone interest component, note that if you sell your home, you'll have to pay off the mortgage.]

10. Every year, the housing market in Monotone, Arizona, has the same experience: The demand curve for housing shifts rightward by 500 homes, 500 new homes are built, and the price of the average home doesn't change. Using supply and demand diagrams, illustrate how each of the following new events, *ceteris paribus*, would affect the price of homes in Monotone over the current year, and state whether the price rises or falls.
   a. Because of special tax breaks offered to Monotone home builders, 800 new housing units are built during the current year.
   b. Because of events in the overall economy, interest rates fall.
   c. The Monotone city council passes a new zoning law that prevents *any* new home construction in Monotone during the year.
   d. Because of the new zoning law, and the resulting change in home prices, people begin to think that homes in Monotone are a better investment than they had thought before.
   e. Five hundred new homes are built in Monotone during the year. But that same year, an earthquake destroys 2,000 preexisting homes. As a result of the earthquake, 3,000 homeowners decide they no longer want to live in or own homes in Monotone.

11. Every year in Houseville, California, builders construct 2,000 new homes—the most the city council will allow them to build. And every year, the demand curve for housing shifts rightward by 2,000 homes as well. Using supply and demand diagrams, illustrate how each of the following new events, *ceteris paribus*, would affect the price of homes in Houseville over the current year, and state whether home prices would rise or fall.
    a. Houseville has just won an award for the most livable city in the United States. The publicity causes the demand curve for housing to shift rightward by 5,000 this year.
    b. Houseville's city council relaxes its restrictions, allowing the housing stock to rise by 3,000 during the year.
    c. An earthquake destroys 1,000 homes in Houseville. There is no effect on the demand for housing, and the city council continues to allow only 2,000 new homes to be built during the year.
    d. The events in a., b., and c. all happen at the same time.

12. [Requires appendix.] Suppose you buy a home for $400,000 with a $100,000 down payment and finance the rest with a home mortgage.
    a. Immediately after purchasing your home, before any change in price, what is the value of your *equity* in the home?
    b. Immediately after purchasing your home, before any change in price, what is your simple leverage ratio on your investment in the home?
    c. Now suppose that over the next three years, the price of your home has increased to $500,000. Assuming you have not borrowed any additional funds using the home as collateral, but you still owe the entire mortgage amount, what is the new value of your equity in the home? Your new simple leverage ratio?
    d. Evaluate the following statement: "An increase in the value of a home, with no additional borrowing, increases the degree of leverage on the investment in the home." True or false? Explain.

13. [Requires appendix.] Suppose, as in the previous problem, you buy a home for $400,000 with a down payment of $100,000 and take out a mortgage for the remainder. Over the next three years, the price of the home rises to $500,000. However, during those three years, you also borrow $50,000 in *additional* funds using the home as collateral (called a "home equity loan"). Assume that, at the end of the three years, you still owe the $50,000, as well as your original mortgage.
    a. What is your equity in the home at the end of the three years?

    b. How many times are you leveraged on your investment in the home at the end of the three years?
    c. By what percentage could your home's price fall (after it reaches $500,000) before your equity in the home is wiped out?

14. [Requires appendix.] A homeowner is said to be "under water" if he or she owes more on the mortgage than the home is worth. Suppose someone bought a home for $300,000 with a $60,000 down payment, and took out a mortgage loan for the rest. A few years later, the value of the home has fallen by 15%, but the amount owed on the home has not changed.
    a. In this example, how much was borrowed to buy the home?
    b. What was the leverage ratio when the home was first purchased?
    c. After the home drops in value, is the homeowner under water?
    d. Answer the three questions above again, this time assuming that the down payment was only $30,000.
    e. Based on your answers above, when home prices are falling, what is the general relationship between the degree of leverage on a home and the likelihood that the owner will end up "under water" on the home?

More Challenging

15. [Requires appendix.] Suppose, as in a previous problem, you buy a home for $400,000 with a down payment of $100,000 and take out a mortgage for the remainder. Over the next three years, the price of the home rises to $500,000. However, during those three years, you borrow the *maximum* amount you can borrow without changing the value of your home equity. Assume that, at the end of the three years, you still owe all that you have borrowed, including your original mortgage.
    a. How much do you borrow (beyond the mortgage) over the three years?
    b. What is your simple leverage ratio at the end of the three years?
    c. By what percentage could your home's price fall (from $500,000) before your equity in the home is wiped out?

16. [Requires appendix.] Could any combination of home price, mortgage, or further borrowing on a home result in a simple leverage ratio of 1/2? If yes, provide an example. If no, briefly explain why.

This appendix discusses the concept of *leverage*: what it means, how it can be measured, and its implications for owning an asset. Our focus here is on the housing market. But leverage can be applied to many other markets, as you will see later in this text book.

Let's start by exploring how the housing market would operate *without* leverage. Imagine that you had to pay for a home in full, using only your own funds. In that case, if you have $100,000 available for buying a home, you could buy a home worth $100,000 and no more.

Suppose you bought a home for $100,000, and, over the year, housing prices rose 10%. The home would then be worth $110,000. If you then sold it (and if we ignore selling costs and maintenance), your $100,000 investment would have turned into $110,000—a capital gain of $10,000. This gives you a 10% rate of return on your financial investment of $100,000. We'll also note that, if the price of the home *fell* by 10%, down to $90,000, you would have a capital *loss* of $10,000—again, 10% of your financial investment. Notice that, when you use only your own funds, your rate of return on your investment ($+10\%$ or -10%) is the same as the rate of change for the home's price.

But as discussed in the chapter, most people do not buy a home using only their own funds. In the United States and many other countries, you will use your own funds for just *part* of the purchase—called the *down payment*—and borrow the remainder. This allows you to buy a home worth substantially more than you are investing yourself. Using borrowed money to buy a home is an example of a *leveraged* financial investment.

To see how this works in practice, let's once again assume you have $100,000 of your own funds available to invest in a home. But now, you'll use it as a down payment, equal to 20% of the home's purchase price. You'll buy a home for $500,000, and take out a mortgage loan for the amount not covered by your down payment: $400,000.

Panel (a) of Figure A.1 illustrates how this works: You use your own $100,000, plus $400,000 from the mortgage lender, to purchase a home worth $500,000. In return, you sign a mortgage contract, promising to pay back $400,000 in monthly payments over a few decades.

Now let's suppose, once again, that housing prices rise by 10% over the year. Because you own a $500,000 home, its price has risen to $550,000. Panel (b) shows what happens when you sell this home. You sell the house for $550,000, pay back what you owe the bank ($400,000),

and the mortgage contract is paid in full. You now have $150,000 left over. Remember: Your original investment was $100,000, and you now have $150,000, for a capital gain of $50,000. Thus, a 10% rise in housing prices has given you a 50% annual rate of return on your investment.

Of course, if the price *fell* by 10%, your home would be worth only $450,000. If you sold it at that price, and paid off the $400,000 loan, you'd be left with only $50,000 of the $100,000 you started with. In that case, you'd have *lost* 50% of your initial investment.

As you can see, when you borrow to buy a home, the potential capital gains and losses on your original investment are magnified. This magnification of gains and losses through borrowing is called leverage.

Measuring Leverage

For many purposes, it's useful to calculate the *degree* of leverage associated with an investment, such as a home purchase. There are various ways of measuring leverage, but all of them rely on the concept of *equity*:

> An owner's equity *in an asset is the difference between the asset's value and any unpaid debts on the asset (that is, debts for which the asset was used as collateral):*

Equity in Asset = Value of Asset − Debt Associated
with Asset

Notice that an owner's equity depends on the asset's *value.* For assets owned by individuals or families, we use the *current market value* of the asset—the price at which it could be sold.[2] So, for example, a homeowner's equity is the price at which the home could be sold, minus any debts for which the home was used as collateral. The equity represents the part of the asset's value that truly belongs to its owner. It is what the owner would get if the asset were sold, after paying back the associated debt.

The concept of equity leads directly to one way of measuring leverage, which we'll call the *simple leverage ratio*:

> The **simple leverage ratio** *is the ratio of an asset's value to the owner's equity in the asset:*

[2] Owner's equity for a business firm is defined very much like equity for a household: The total value of its assets minus what it owes to others. But for firms, asset values are typically based on historical prices paid, rather than current market value.

FIGURE A.1 Leveraged Buying and Selling

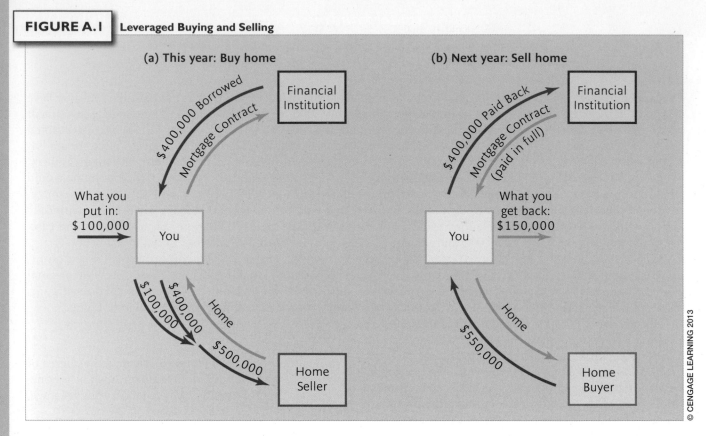

(a) This year: Buy home

$400,000 Borrowed

Mortgage Contract

Financial Institution

What you put in: $100,000

You

$100,000

$400,000

Home

$500,000

Home Seller

(b) Next year: Sell home

$400,000 Paid Back

Mortgage Contract (paid in full)

Financial Institution

What you get back: $150,000

You

$550,000

Home

Home Buyer

© CENGAGE LEARNING 2013

$$\text{Simple Leverage Ratio} = \frac{\text{Value of Asset}}{\text{Equity in Asset}}$$

Now, let's apply these concepts to home ownership. Suppose, as in our first example, you use only your own funds to buy a $100,000 home, and you never use the home as collateral for a loan. Using the definitions above, your equity in the home is $100,000 − $0 = $100,000. Your simple leverage ratio is $100,000/$100,000 = 1. A leverage ratio of 1 means no leverage at all: There is no borrowing to magnify capital gains and losses.

Now let's calculate the leverage ratio in our second example, in which you make a $100,000 down payment on a $500,000 home and borrow the remaining $400,000. Your equity in the home is $500,000 − $400,000 = $100,000. And your simple leverage ratio is $500,000/$100,000 = 5. In words, we'd say you are "leveraged five times."

Leverage and Rate of Return

The simple leverage ratio serves as a "rate-of-return multiplier." That is, we can multiply the rate of change in a home's price by the leverage ratio to get the rate of return on the (leveraged) investment. For example, we found earlier that, when you invest $100,000 to buy a $500,000 home and are leveraged 5 times, a 10% rise in housing prices over the year gives you a 50% annual rate of return on your investment. Your rate of return is five times the percentage increase in the home's price.[3]

As you can see, when asset prices rise, leverage can increase your rate of return dramatically. But when asset prices fall, leverage increases the chance of wiping out your entire investment. With no leverage, your home's price would have to fall by 100% before your owner's equity would disappear. If you are leveraged 5 times, a drop of 20% eliminates your equity. And if you're leveraged 20 times, it takes only a 5% drop in prices to wipe out your entire investment.

One last word. In this appendix, we've been applying the concept of leverage, and the simple leverage ratio, to a single asset. But leverage can also refer to the *combined* assets of a household or business firm, or even to an entire sector of the economy. As you'll see in later chapters, high leverage played a crucial role in creating the financial crisis of 2008.

[3] More accurately, the leverage ratio is a multiplier for your *gross* rate of return, which ignores the annual cost of the borrowed funds. Your net rate of return (accounting for the cost of borrowing) will be lower. In our example, suppose that—based on the interest rate and tax benefits on your mortgage—your annual interest cost is 3% of the amount borrowed. Then borrowing costs for the year would be 0.03 × $400,000 = $12,000. Deducting this cost from your $50,000 capital gain leaves you with a $38,000 net gain for the year. So the *net* rate of return on your $100,000 investment would be $38,000/$100,000 = 38%.

CHAPTER 5

IOFOTO/SHUTTERSTOCK.COM

What Macroeconomics Tries to Explain

You have no doubt seen photographs of the earth taken from satellites thousands of miles away. Viewed from that great distance, the world's vast oceans look like puddles, and its mountain ranges look like wrinkles on a bedspread. In contrast to our customary close-up perspective, this is a view of the big picture.

The two different ways of viewing the earth—from up close or from thousands of miles away—are analogous to two different ways of viewing the economy. When we look through the *microeconomic* lens—from up close—we see the behavior of individual decision makers and individual markets. When we look through the *macroeconomic* lens—from a distance—these smaller features fade away, and we see only the broad outlines of the economy.

Which view is better? That depends on what we're trying to do. If we want to know why computers are getting better and cheaper each year, or why the earnings of physician assistants are surging while those of factory workers are lagging, we need the close-up view of microeconomics. But to answer questions about the entire economy—about the overall level of economic activity, our standard of living, or the percentage of our potential workforce that is unemployed—we need the more comprehensive view of *macroeconomics*.

MACROECONOMIC GOALS

While there is some disagreement among economists about *how* to make the macroeconomy perform well, there is widespread agreement about the goals we are trying to achieve:

> *Economists—and society at large—agree on three important macroeconomic goals: economic growth, full employment, and stable prices.*

Why is there such universal agreement on these three goals? Because achieving them gives us the opportunity to make *all* of our citizens better off. Let's take a closer look at each of these goals and see why they are so important.

Economic Growth

Imagine that you were a typical American worker living at the beginning of the 20th century. You would work about 60 hours every week, and your yearly salary—about $450—would buy a bit less than $9,000 would buy today. You could expect to die at the age of 47. If you fell seriously ill before then, your doctor wouldn't be able to help much: There were no X-ray machines or blood tests, and little effective medicine for the few diseases that could be diagnosed. You would probably never hear the sounds produced by the best musicians of the day, or see the performances of the best actors, dancers, or singers. And the most exotic travel you'd enjoy would likely be a trip to a nearby state.

Today, the typical full-time worker has it considerably better. He or she works about 35 hours per week and is paid about $40,000 per year, not to mention fringe benefits such as health insurance, retirement benefits, and paid vacation. Thanks to advances in medicine, nutrition, and hygiene, the average worker can expect to live into his or her late 70s. And more of a worker's free time today is really free: There are machines to do laundry and dishes, cars to get to and from work, smart phones and the Internet for quick communication and to help us keep track of finances, appointments, and correspondence. Finally, during their lifetimes, most Americans will have traveled—for enjoyment—to many locations in the United States or abroad.

Economic growth The increase in our production of goods and services that occurs over long periods of time.

What is responsible for these dramatic changes in economic well-being? The answer is: **economic growth**—the increase in our production of goods and services that occurs over long periods of time. In the United States, as in most developed economies, the annual output of goods and services has risen over time, and risen faster than the population. As a result, the average person can consume much more today—more food, clothing, housing, medical care, entertainment, and travel—than in the year 1900.

Economists monitor economic growth by keeping track of *real gross domestic product* (*real GDP*): the total quantity of goods and services produced in a country over a year. When real GDP rises faster than the population, output per person rises, and so does the average standard of living.

Figure 1(a) shows real GDP in the United States from 1929 to mid-2011, measured in dollars of output at 2005 prices. As you can see, real GDP has increased dramatically. Part of the reason for the rise is an increase in population: More workers can produce more goods and services.

However, real GDP has actually increased *faster* than the population: In 2011, the population was about two-and-a-half times greater than in 1929, but annual production of goods and services was more than *13 times* greater. Hence, the remarkable rise in the average American's living standard.

Panel (b) shows the behavior of *real GDP per capita* (real GDP divided by the population) over the same period. This is closely related to the value of goods and services the average person in the U.S. can *consume* each year. Real GDP per capita grew from $8,000 in 1929 to about $45,000—a more than fivefold increase.

When we look more closely at the data, we discover something important: Although output has grown, the *rate* of growth has varied over the decades. For example, from 1959 to 1973, real GDP grew, on average, by 4.2 percent per year. But from 1973 to 2007, average annual growth slowed to 3.0 percent. This difference of 1.2 percentage points in annual growth may seem trivial. But over long periods of time, small differences in growth rates can cause huge differences in living standards.

For example, suppose that in each of the years between 1997 and 2007, real GDP had grown by just 1.2 percentage points more each year than its actual rate. Then, over that entire ten-year period, the United States would have produced a total of about $8 trillion *more* in goods and services than we *actually* produced

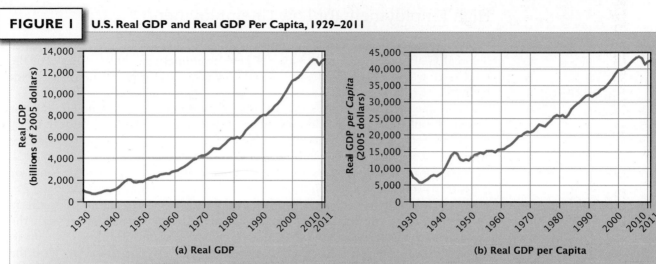

FIGURE 1 | **U.S. Real GDP and Real GDP Per Capita, 1929–2011**

(a) Real GDP

(b) Real GDP per Capita

Panel (a) shows real GDP—total annual U.S. production of goods and services (valued at 2005 prices) from 1929 through the first half of 2011. Real GDP has grown dramatically, much faster than the population. As a result, real GDP per capita in panel (b) has grown rapidly as well.

Source: Bureau of Economic Analysis. Real GDP for 2011 is based on first half of year only.

© CENGAGE LEARNING 2013

(valuing these goods and services at 2005 prices). That amounts to more than $25,000 for each person in the population.

Growth increases the size of the economic pie, so it becomes possible—at least in principle—for every citizen to have a larger slice. But in practice, growth does *not* benefit everyone. Living standards will always rise more rapidly for some groups than for others, and some may even find their slice of the pie shrinking.

For example, since the late 1970s, economic growth has improved the living standards of the highly skilled, while less-skilled workers have benefited very little. Partly, this is due to improvements in technology that have lowered the earnings of workers whose roles can be taken by computers and machines. But very few economists would advocate a halt to growth as a solution to the problems of unskilled workers. Some believe that, in the long run, everyone will indeed benefit from growth. Others see a role for the government in taxing successful people and providing benefits to those left behind by growth. But in either case, economic growth, by increasing the size of the overall pie, is seen as an important part of the solution.

As you study macroeconomics, you'll learn about a variety of issues related to economic growth. What makes real GDP grow in the first place? Why does it grow more rapidly in some decades than in others? Why do some countries experience very rapid growth—some much faster than the United States— while others seem unable to grow at all? Can government policy do anything to alter the growth rate? And are there any downsides to such policies?

© AXL/SHUTTERSTOCK.COM

DANGEROUS CURVES ⚠️

Growth rates from graphs In Figure 1, it looks like real GDP has not only been growing, but growing at a faster and faster rate, since the line becomes steeper over time. But the real GDP line would get steeper even if the growth rate were *constant* over the entire period. That's because as real GDP rises from an increasingly higher and higher level, the same *percentage* growth rate causes an increasingly greater *absolute* increase in GDP. Since the slope of the line depends on the *absolute* rise rather than the *percentage* rise, the line gets steeper when the growth rate remains constant.

In fact, the line can become steeper even if the percentage growth rate *decreases* over time. As you've read, real GDP actually grew at a faster rate from 1959 to 1973 (where the line is flatter) than during any subsequent lengthy period (where the line is steeper).

High Employment (or Low Unemployment)

Economic growth is one of our most important goals, but not the only one. Suppose our real GDP were growing at, say, a 4 percent annual rate, but a quarter of the workforce was unable to find work. Would the economy be performing well? Not really, for two reasons.

First, unemployment affects the distribution of economic well-being among our citizens. People who cannot find jobs suffer a loss of income. And even though many of the jobless receive some unemployment benefits and other assistance from the government, the unemployed typically have lower living standards than the employed. Concern for those without jobs is one reason that consistently high employment—or consistently low *unemployment*—is an important macroeconomic goal.

But in addition to the impact on the unemployed themselves, joblessness affects *all* of us—even those who *have* jobs. A high unemployment rate means that the economy is not achieving its full economic potential: Many people who *want* to work and produce additional goods and services are not able to do so. With the same number of people—but fewer goods and services to distribute among that population—the average standard of living will be lower. This general effect on living standards gives us another reason to strive for consistently high rates of employment and low rates of unemployment.

One measure economists use to keep track of employment is the *unemployment rate*—the percentage of the workforce that is searching for a job but hasn't found one. Figure 2 shows the average unemployment rate during each year since

| FIGURE 2 | U.S. Unemployment Rate, 1920–2011 |

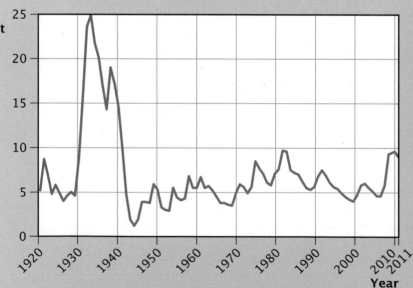

The unemployment rate fluctuates over time. During the Great Depression of the 1930s, unemployment was extremely high, reaching 25 percent in 1933, and plunged as the United States entered World War II. From the end of the war through the first half of 2011, it averaged 5.7 percent, with dramatic spikes upward during recessions, such as the mid-1970s, the early 1980s, and 2008 to 2011.

Source: Unemployment Rates: 1920–1930 from Christina D. Romer, "Spurious Volatility in Historical Unemployment Data," *Journal of Political Economy*, 1986, vol. 94, issue 1, pages 1–37; 1931–1939 from Stanley Lebergott, *Manpower in Economic Growth* (New York: McGraw-Hill, 1964); 1940–2011 from Bureau of Labor Statistics.

1920. Notice that the unemployment rate is never zero; there are always *some* people looking for work, even when the economy is doing well. But in some years, unemployment is unusually high. The worst example occurred during the Great Depression of the 1930s, when millions of workers lost their jobs, and the unemployment rate reached 25 percent. One in four potential workers could not find a job. More recently, in 2009, 2010, and 2011, the average unemployment rate was above 9 percent.

© AP PHOTO/RICK BOWMER

The nation's commitment to high employment has twice been written into law. With the memory of the Great Depression still fresh, Congress passed the *Employment Act of 1946,* which required the federal government to "promote maximum employment, production, and purchasing power." It did not, however, dictate a target rate of unemployment the government should aim for. A numerical target was added in 1978, when Congress passed the *Full Employment and Balanced Growth Act,* which called for an unemployment rate of 4 percent.

A glance at Figure 2 shows how seldom we have hit this target over the last few decades. In fact, since the 1970s, the unemployment rate averaged 4 percent in only one year: 2000. And as you can see in the figure, it did not stay there long.

Why has the unemployment rate been above its target so often? Why were we able to have 4 percent unemployment in 2000, but not keep it there? And what causes the average unemployment rate to fluctuate from year to year, as shown in Figure 2? These are all questions that relate to the *business cycle.*

Employment and the Business Cycle

When firms produce more goods and services, they hire more workers; when production drops, they tend to lay off workers. We would thus expect real GDP and employment to be closely related, and indeed they are. In recent years, each 1 percent drop in real GDP has been associated with the loss of more than half a million jobs. Consistently high employment, then, requires a high, stable level of output.

Unfortunately, output has *not* been very stable. If you look back at Figure 1(a), you will see that while real GDP has climbed upward over time, it has been a bumpy ride. The periodic fluctuations in GDP—the bumps in the figure—are called **business cycles.**

Figure 3 shows a close-up view of a hypothetical business cycle. First, notice the thin upward-sloping line. This shows the long-run upward trend of real GDP, which we refer to as *economic growth.* The thicker line shows the business cycle that occurs *around* the long-run trend. When output rises, we are in the **expansion** phase of the cycle; when output falls, we are in the *contraction* or **recession** phase. (Officially, a recession is a contraction considered significant in terms of depth, breadth, and duration.)

Of course, real-world business cycles never look quite like the smooth, symmetrical cycle in Figure 3, but rather like the jagged, irregular cycles of Figure 1. Recessions can be severe or mild, and they can last several years or less than a single year. When a recession is particularly severe and long lasting, it is called a **depression.** In the 20th century, the United States experienced just one decline in output serious enough to be considered a depression—the worldwide *Great Depression* of the 1930s. From 1929 to 1933, the first four years of the Great Depression, U.S. output dropped by more than 25 percent.

Business cycles Fluctuations in real GDP around its long-term growth trend.

Expansion A period of increasing real GDP.

Recession A period of significant decline in real GDP.

Depression An unusually severe recession.

FIGURE 3	The Business Cycle

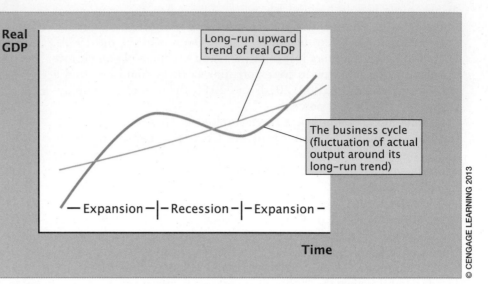

Over time, real GDP fluctuates around an overall upward trend. Such fluctuations are called business cycles. When output rises, we are in the expansion phase of the cycle; when output falls, we are in a recession.

Real GDP

Long-run upward trend of real GDP

The business cycle (fluctuation of actual output around its long-run trend)

— Expansion —|— Recession —|— Expansion —

Time

© CENGAGE LEARNING 2013

But even during more normal times, the economy has gone through many recessions. Since 1959, we have suffered through three severe recessions (in 1974–75, 1981–82, and 2008–2009) and several more mild ones.

Why are there business cycles? Is there anything we can do to prevent recessions from occurring, or at least make them milder and shorter? And why—after a serious recession—does it take so long for the economy to return to normal? These are all questions that macroeconomics helps us answer.

Stable Prices

Figure 4 shows the annual inflation rate—the percentage increase in the average level of prices—from 1920 through mid-2011.[1] With very few exceptions, the inflation rate has been positive: On average, prices have risen in each of those years. But notice the wide variations in inflation. From 1979 through 1981, we had double-digit inflation: Prices rose by more than 10 percent in each of those years. During that time, polls showed that people were more concerned about inflation than any other national problem—more than unemployment, crime, poverty, pollution, or anything else. During the 1990s and the first decade of the 2000s, the inflation rate averaged less than 3 percent per year. As a result, we hardly seem to notice it at all. Pollsters no longer include "rising prices" as a category when asking about the most important problems facing the country.

⚠ **DANGEROUS CURVES**

Expansion versus economic growth Although the terms *expansion* and *economic growth* both refer to increases in real GDP, they are not the same. *Economic growth* refers to the long-run upward trend in output over a long period of time, usually more than a decade. It is measured as the *average* annual change in output over the entire period. An *expansion* refers to a rise in real GDP over the business cycle—usually a shorter period of time.

© AXL/SHUTTERSTOCK.COM

[1] Figure 4 is based on the Consumer Price Index, the most popular measure of the price level, as well as historical estimates of what this index *would* have been in the early part of the 20th century, before the index existed. We'll discuss the Consumer Price Index and other measures of inflation in more detail in later chapters.

FIGURE 4 U.S. Annual Inflation Rate, 1920–2011

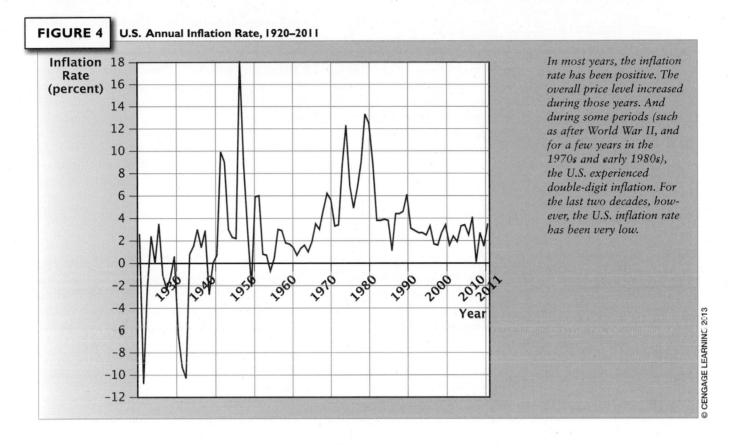

In most years, the inflation rate has been positive. The overall price level increased during those years. And during some periods (such as after World War II, and for a few years in the 1970s and early 1980s), the U.S. experienced double-digit inflation. For the last two decades, however, the U.S. inflation rate has been very low.

© CENGAGE LEARNING 2013

Other countries have not been so lucky. In the 1980s, several Latin American nations experienced inflation rates of thousands of percent per year. In the early 1990s, some of the newly emerging nations of Central Europe and the former Soviet Union suffered annual inflation rates in the triple digits.

An extreme case is Zimbabwe, where—from mid-November 2007 to mid-November 2008—price roses by 89,700,000,000,000,000,000,000 percent. (If you're wondering, the name for that number is 89.7 sextillion.) During the last few weeks of that period, prices were doubling every *day*. To get a sense of what this means: Imagine that a cup of coffee costs one dollar at the beginning of the month. With the price doubling every day, by the end of the month, the price would be $1 billion.

Of course, when prices are rising that rapidly, wages are rising rapidly too. You'd have billions of dollars of income each day, so you could still afford to buy that coffee.

Given that fact, why are stable prices—a low inflation rate—an important macroeconomic goal? Because inflation, itself, is *costly* to society. With annual inflation rates in the thousands of percent or higher, the costs are easy to see: The purchasing power of the currency declines so rapidly that people are no longer willing to hold it or accept it from others. This breakdown of the monetary system forces people to waste valuable time and resources bartering with each other—for example, trading plumbing services for dentistry services. With so much time spent trying to find trading partners, there is little time left for producing goods and services. As a result, the average standard of living falls.

With inflation rates of 12 or 13 percent—such as the United States experienced in the late 1970s—the costs to society are less obvious and less severe. But they are still significant. And when it comes time to bring down the inflation rate, painful corrective actions by government are sometimes required. These actions can cause output to decline and unemployment to rise. For example, in order to bring the inflation rate down from the high levels of the late 1970s (see Figure 4), government policy purposely caused a severe recession in 1981–82, reducing output and increasing unemployment.

Economists regard *some* inflation as good for the economy. In fact, in late 2008 and early 2009, as the general price level *fell* during several months, policy makers worried that we might be heading for a prolonged and harmful *deflation* (a negative rate of inflation). Price stabilization requires not only preventing the inflation rate from rising too high, but also preventing it from falling too *low*, where it could more easily turn negative.

The previous paragraphs may have raised a number of questions in your mind. What causes inflation or deflation? How would a *moderately* high inflation rate (say, 7 or 8 percent) harm society? How does a recession bring down the inflation rate, and how does the government actually *create* a recession? And why might a period of decreasing prices—which sounds so wonderful—be a threat to the economy? Your study of macroeconomics will help you answer all of these questions.

THE MACROECONOMIC APPROACH

If you have already studied microeconomics, you will notice much that is familiar in macroeconomics. The *three-step process* introduced in Chapter 3 plays an important role in both branches of the field. But the macroeconomic approach differs from the microeconomic approach in significant ways.

Most importantly, in *microeconomics,* we typically apply our three steps to *one market at a time*—the market for soybeans, for neurosurgeons, or for car washes. In *macroeconomics,* by contrast, we want to understand how the entire economy behaves. Thus, we apply the steps to *all markets simultaneously*. This includes not only markets for goods and services, but also markets for labor and for financial assets like stocks and bonds.

How can we possibly hope to deal with all of these markets at the same time? One way would be to build a gigantic model that included every individual market in the economy. The model would have tens of thousands of supply and demand curves, which could be used to determine tens of thousands of prices and quantities. With today's fast, powerful computers, we could, in principle, build this kind of model.

But the model would not be very useful. For one thing, we would not learn much about the economy from it: With so many individual trees, we would not be able to see the forest.

Moreover, the model's predictions would be highly suspect: With so much information and so many moving parts, high standards of accuracy would be difficult to maintain. Even the government of the former Soviet Union, which directed production throughout the economy until the 1990s, was unable to keep track of all the markets under its control. In a market economy, where production decisions are made by individual firms, the task would be even harder.

What, then, is a macroeconomist to do? The answer is a word that you will become very familiar with in the chapters to come: *aggregation*.

Aggregation in Macroeconomics

Aggregation is the process of combining different things into a single category, and treating them as a whole. It is a basic tool of reasoning, one that you often use without being aware of it. If you say, "I applied for five jobs last month," you are aggregating five very different workplaces into the single category, *jobs*. Whenever you say, "I'm going out with my friends," you are combining several different people into a single category: people you consider *friends*.

Aggregation plays a key role in both micro- and macroeconomics. Microeconomists will speak of the market for automobiles, lumping Toyotas, Fords, BMWs, and other types of cars into a single category. But in macroeconomics, we take aggregation to the extreme. Because we want to consider the entire economy at once, and yet keep our model as simple as possible, we must aggregate all markets into the broadest possible categories. For example, we lump together all the goods and services that households buy—pizza, couches, haircuts, medical care—into the single category *consumption goods*. We combine all the different types of capital purchased by business firms—forklifts, factory buildings, office computers, and trucks—into the single category *investment goods*. Often we go even further, lumping consumption, investment, and all other types of goods into the single category *output* or *real GDP*. And in macroeconomics, we typically combine the thousands of different types of workers in the economy—doctors, construction workers, teachers, truck drivers—into the category *labor*. By aggregating in this way, we can create workable and helpful models that teach us a great deal about how the overall economy operates.

Aggregation The process of combining different things into a single category.

MACROECONOMIC CONTROVERSIES

Macroeconomics is full of disputes and disagreements. Indeed, modern macroeconomics, which began with the publication of *The General Theory of Employment, Interest, and Money* by British economist John Maynard Keynes in 1936, originated in controversy. Keynes was arguing against the conventional wisdom of his time, *classical economics*. According to the classical view, the macroeconomy worked reasonably well on its own, and the best policy for the government to follow was *laissez-faire*—"leave it alone." As he was working on *The General Theory,* Keynes wrote to his friend, the playwright George Bernard Shaw, "I believe myself to be writing a book on economic theory which will largely revolutionize—not, I suppose, at once but in the course of the next ten years—the way the world thinks about economic problems."

Keynes's prediction was on the money. After the publication of his book, economists argued about its merits, but 10 years later, the majority of the profession had been won over: They had become Keynesians. This new school of thought held that the economy does *not* do well on its own (one needed only to look at the Great Depression for evidence) and requires continual guidance from an activist and well-intentioned government.

DANGEROUS CURVES

"Micro" versus "macro" In many English words, the prefix *macro* means "large" and *micro* means "small." As a result, you might think that in microeconomics, we study economic units in which small sums of money are involved, while in macroeconomics we study units involving greater sums. But this is not correct.

The annual production of some large corporations, such as Google or Microsoft, is considerably greater than the total annual production of some small countries, such as Albania or Kyrgystan. Yet when we study the behavior of Microsoft, we are practicing *microeconomics*, and when we study changes in total output in Albania, we are practicing *macroeconomics*. Microeconomics is concerned with the behavior and interaction of *individual* firms and markets, even if they are very large; macroeconomics is concerned with the behavior of *entire economies*, even if they are very small.

From the late 1940s until the early 1960s, events seemed to prove the Keynesians correct. Then, beginning in the 1960s, several distinguished economists began to challenge Keynesian ideas. Their counterrevolutionary views, which in many ways mirrored those of the classical economists, were strengthened by events in the 1970s, when the economy's behavior began to contradict some Keynesian ideas. But in 2008 and 2009, as the economy sank into the most serious worldwide recession since the Great Depression, Keynesian ideas were once again at the center of a heated debate about the causes of the problem and the appropriate remedies.

Consider the controversy that erupted in August 2011. The U.S. economy—already mired deep in a slump from the financial crises three years earlier—suffered further negative shocks. Public and media attention was focused on the possibility of a "double dip"—another recession hitting the economy before it had recovered from the prior one. One possible policy response was an increase in federal government spending: The government could borrow funds to spend on a variety of programs and projects—a policy of *fiscal stimulus*. Two very prominent economists took sharply opposing positions in the debate:

> *The only thing that can be done is fiscal stimulus, spending more money. And, the United States is in a sense in a good position, because we can borrow at very low interest rates.*
> — Joseph Stiglitz, Nobel-prize winner and professor at Columbia University.[2]

> *We have had a gigantic increase in government spending over the last three years... That is not the answer. That has been tried and it has not worked.*
> — John B. Taylor, former economic advisor to two presidents and a professor at Stanford University.[3]

What are we to make of disagreements like this, which occur so often?

Remember the distinction between *positive (what is)* and *normative (what should be)*? A disagreement like this one can be entirely positive in nature. That is, economists may disagree about the facts themselves: about the economy's current direction or momentum, or the relative effectiveness and risks of different policies that might alter the economy's course. Indeed, the economists quoted above framed their disagreement in terms of a key fact: the likely *impact* a fiscal stimulus would have on the macroeconomy.

But sometimes, what seems like an entirely positive disagreement actually has *normative* roots. For example, an increase in government spending is likely to have different effects in the short run and the long run. Two economists—even if they agreed completely on the policy's impacts—might disagree about its wisdom, based on the relative importance they attach to the short-run or long-run consequences.

Moreover, economists—like politicians and citizens—may have deeper, ideological differences involving the proper role of government. In the competitive and confrontational arena of politics—with each side trying to muster all the arguments it can—positive economics often becomes a weapon. In the heat of battle, economists in their public role may stress positive conclusions that correspond most closely with their political beliefs. In August 2011, for example, economists

[2] Joseph Stiglitz interview at http://www.americablog.com/2011/08/stiglitz-only-thing-that-can-be-done-to.html, August 30, 2011.

[3] John B. Taylor interview at http://www.pbs.org/newshour/bb/politics/july-dec11/debt_08-02.html, August 2, 2011.

who favored a greater role for government *in general* were also likely to argue that increased government spending would help to simulate the macroeconomy. And economists who favored a smaller role for government *in general* were also likely to argue that increased government spending would *not* stimulate the macroeconomy.

Because of such political battles, people who follow the news often think that there is little agreement among economists about how the macroeconomy works. But in fact, the profession has come to a consensus on many basic principles, and we will stress these as we go. And even when there are positive disagreements, there is often a consensus on the approach that should be taken to resolve them. You won't find this consensus expressed in a hot political debate. But you will find it in academic journals and conferences, and in reports issued by certain nonpartisan research organizations or government agencies. And—we hope—you will find it in the chapters to come.

AS YOU STUDY MACROECONOMICS . . .

Macroeconomics is a fascinating and wide-ranging subject. You will find that each piece of the macroeconomic puzzle connects to all of the other pieces in many different ways. Each time one of your questions is answered, ten more will spring up in your mind, each demanding immediate attention. This presents a problem for textbook writers, and for your instructor as well: What is the best order in which to present the principles of macroeconomics?

One way is to follow the order of questions as they would occur to a curious student. For example, learning about unemployment raises questions about imports and exports, so we could then skip to that topic. But it also raises questions about government spending, economic growth, wages, banking, and much more. And each of these topics raises questions about still others. Bouncing from topic to topic like this is the approach taken by the media when reporting on the economy. If you have ever tried to learn economics from a newspaper or a Web site, you know how frustrating this approach can be.

In our study of macroeconomics, we will follow a different approach: presenting material as it is *needed* for what follows. In this way, what you learn in one chapter will form the foundation for the material in the next, and your understanding of macroeconomics will deepen as you go.

But be forewarned: This approach requires *patience* on your part. Many of the questions that will pop into your head will have to be postponed until the proper foundations for answering them have been established. It might help, though, to give you a *brief* indication of what is to come.

In the next two chapters, we will discuss several of the most important aggregates in macroeconomics: GDP, employment (and unemployment), the price level, and the inflation rate. You will see how each of these aggregates affects our lives, how we keep track of them with government statistics, and how to interpret these statistics with a critical eye.

Then, in the remainder of the book, we study how the macroeconomy operates. We'll start with the long run: What makes an economy grow over long periods of time, and which government policies are likely to help or hinder that growth.

Then, we turn our attention to the short run. You will learn why the economy behaves differently in the short run than in the long run, why we have business cycles, and how these cycles may be affected by government policies. We'll also expand our analysis to include the banking system and the money supply, and the special challenges they pose for government policy makers.

Finally, we'll turn our attention to the special problems of a global economy. You'll learn how trade with other nations constrains and expands our macro policy options at home and how economic events abroad influence our own economy. You will also learn why the United States has run persistent trade deficits with the rest of the world and what that means for our citizens.

This sounds like quite a lot of ground to cover, and, indeed, it is. But it's not as daunting as it might sound. As you go from chapter to chapter, each principle you learn is a stepping-stone to the next one. Little by little, your knowledge and understanding will accumulate and deepen. Most students are genuinely surprised at how well they understand the macroeconomy after a single introductory course, and they find the reward well worth the effort.

SUMMARY

Macroeconomics is the study of the economy as a whole. Economists generally agree about the importance of three main macroeconomic goals. The first of these is economic growth. If output (real gross domestic product) grows faster than population, the average person can enjoy an improved standard of living.

High employment is another important goal. When employment is low (that is, unemployment is high), it harms not only the unemployed themselves, but also society in general: Society loses output that could have been produced.

The third macroeconomic goal is stable prices. This goal is important because inflation—especially very high

inflation—imposes costs on society and can lower living standards.

Because an economy like that of the United States is so large and complex, the models we use to analyze the economy must be highly aggregated. For example, we lump together millions of different goods to create an aggregate called "output."

Macroeconomics is often controversial. It may seem that macroeconomists agree on very little, but there is actually broad consensus on many positive economic issues.

PROBLEM SET

Answers to even-numbered Problems can be found on the text Web site through www.cengagebrain.com

1. "In 2010, in the aftermath of our most recent recession, the yearly average U.S. unemployment rate rose to its highest level in over 90 years." Is this statement true or false? Explain briefly.

2. "Over the past 90 years, the U.S., unlike some other countries, has not experienced 'double digit' inflation." Is this statement true or false? Explain briefly.

3. In 2004, real GDP (at 2005 prices) was $12,247 billion. In 2007, it was $13,206 billion. During the same period, the U.S. population rose from 292.9 million to 301.4 million.
   a. What was the total percentage increase in real GDP from 2004 to 2007?
   b. What was the total percentage increase in the U.S. population over this period?
   c. Calculate real GDP per capita in 2004 and 2007. By what percentage did output per person grow over this period?

4. Suppose that real GDP had grown by 3 percent each year from 2004 to 2007. Using some of the data in problem 3:
   a. What would real GDP have been in 2007?
   b. Based on your answer in (a) above, what would output per person have been in 2007?

5. Use the information in the table below to calculate the percentage change in real GDP from 2007 to 2008, from 2008 to 2009, and from 2009 to 2010.

Year	Real GDP (Billions of 2005 dollars)
2007	$13,206
2008	$13,162
2009	$12,703
2010	$13,088

6. Assume that the country of Ziponia produced real GDP equal to $5,000 (in billions) in the year 2000.

   a. Calculate Ziponia's output for each year from 2000 to 2006, assuming that it experienced a constant growth rate of 6 percent per year over this period. Use your answers to construct a graph similar to the one in Figure 1. Is the slope of this graph constant? Explain.

   b. Calculate Ziponia's output from 2000 to 2006, but this time assume that its growth rate was 6 percent from 2000 to 2001, and then the growth rate fell by 1 percentage point each year. Plot these points onto your graph from part (a). Is the slope of this graph constant? Explain.

APDESIGN /SHUTTERSTOCK.COM

CHAPTER 6

Production, Income, and Employment

I n 1931, a couple of years into the Great Depression, Congress summoned economists from government agencies, from academia, and from the private sector to testify about the state of the economy. Everyone knew that U.S. production and employment were plummeting. But Congress wanted a more accurate picture.

The economists were asked the most basic questions: How much output was the nation producing, and how much had production fallen since 1929? How much income were Americans earning, and how much were they spending? How much profit were businesses earning, and what were they doing with their profits? To the surprise of the members of Congress, no one could answer any of these questions, because *no one was keeping track of our national income and output!* The most recent measurement at the time, which was rather incomplete, had been made in 1929. Thus began the U.S. system of national income accounts, a system whose value was recognized around the world and rapidly copied by other countries.

Today, a variety of government agencies and related institutions collect information about production, employment, spending, income, wages, prices, lending, and more. And economists have even estimated what the measures *would* have been in earlier periods, before the government was actually tracking them. Although some measurement problems remain, we now have a more accurate and timely picture of how the economy is changing than was available to previous generations.

In this chapter, we will take our first look at how the government tracks the performance of the national economy, with a special focus on two key variables: *gross domestic product* and the *unemployment rate*. The purpose here is not to explain what causes these variables to rise or fall, or what government might do about it. That will come a few chapters later, when we begin to study macroeconomic models. Here, we focus on the reality behind the numbers: what they tell us about the economy, how the government obtains them, and how they are sometimes misused.

PRODUCTION AND GROSS DOMESTIC PRODUCT

You have probably heard the phrase *gross domestic product*—or the more familiar abbreviation GDP—many times. As our measure of production in the economy, it is one of those economic terms that is frequently used by the media and by politicians.

You might think that GDP is an easy number to calculate, at least in theory: Simply add up the output of every firm in the country during the year. Unfortunately, measuring total production is not so straightforward, and there are many conceptual traps and pitfalls. This is why economists have come up with a very precise definition of GDP.

GDP: A Definition

The definition of GDP is quite a mouthful:

> The nation's **gross domestic product** (GDP) *is the total value of all final goods and services produced for the marketplace during a given period, within the nation's borders.*

Gross domestic product (GDP) The total value of all final goods and services produced for the marketplace during a given year, within the nation's borders.

Every phrase in this definition helps to solve a potential problem with measuring our nation's total production. Let's look more closely at each part of the definition in more detail.

The total value . . .

An old expression tells us that "you can't add apples and oranges." But that is just what government statisticians must do when they measure our total output. In a typical day, American firms produce millions of *loaves* of bread, thousands of *pounds* of peanut butter, hundreds of *hours* of television programming, and so on. These are different products, and each is measured in its own type of units. Yet, somehow, we must combine all of them into a single number. But how?

The approach of GDP is to add up the *dollar value* of every good or service—the number of dollars each product is sold for. As a result, GDP is measured in dollar units. For example, in 2010, the GDP of the United States was about $14,526,500,000,000—give or take a few billion dollars. (That's about $14 1/2 trillion.)

Using dollar values to calculate GDP has two important advantages. First, it gives us a common unit of measurement for very different things, thus allowing us to add up "apples and oranges." Second, it ensures that producing a good that uses more resources (a computer chip) will count more in GDP than a good that uses fewer resources (a tortilla chip).

However, using the dollar prices at which goods and services actually sell also creates a problem: If prices rise, then GDP will rise, even if we are not actually *producing* more. For this reason, when tracking changes in production over time, GDP must be adjusted to take away the effects of inflation. We'll come back to this issue again a bit later in the chapter.

. . . of all final . . .

When measuring production, we do not count *every* good or service produced in the economy, but only those that are sold to their *final users*. An example will illustrate why.

Figure 1 shows a simplified version of the stages of production for a ream (500 sheets) of notebook paper: A lumber company cuts down trees and produces $1.00 worth of wood chips. These are sold to a paper mill for $1.00. The mill cooks, bleaches, and refines the wood chips, turning them into paper rolls.

FIGURE 1   **Stages of Production**

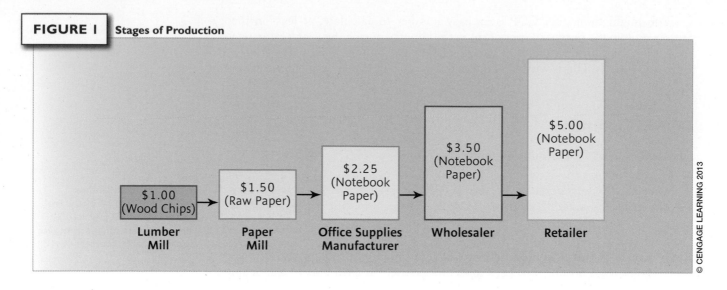

These are sold to an office supplies manufacturer for $1.50. This manufacturer cuts the paper, prints lines and margins on it, and sells it to a wholesaler for $2.25. The wholesaler sells it to a retail store for $3.50, and then, finally, it is sold to a consumer—perhaps you—for $5.00.

Should we add the value of *all* this production, and include $1.00 + $1.50 + $2.25 + $3.50 + $5.00 = $13.25 in GDP each time a ream of notebook paper is produced? No; this would clearly be a mistake, because all of this production ends up creating a good worth only $5 in the end. In fact, the $5 you pay for this good already *includes* the value of all the other production in the process.

In our example, the goods sold by the lumber company, paper mill, office supplies manufacturer, and wholesaler are all **intermediate goods**—goods used up in the process of producing something else. But the retailer (say, your local office supply store) sells a **final good**—a product sold to its *final user* (you). If we separately added in the production of intermediate goods when calculating GDP, we would be counting them more than once, since they are already included in the value of the final good.

Intermediate goods Goods used up in producing final goods.

Final good A good sold to its final user.

> To *avoid overcounting intermediate products* when measuring GDP, we add up the value of final goods and services only. The value of intermediate products is already included in the value of the final products.

...goods and services ...

We all know a good when we see one: We can look at it, feel it, weigh it, and, in some cases, eat it, sit on it, or swing a bat at it. Not so with a service: When you get a medical checkup, a haircut, or a car wash, the *effects* of the service may linger, but the service itself is used up the moment it is produced. Nonetheless, final services count in GDP in the same way as final goods.

Services have become an increasingly important part of our total output in recent decades. The service sector has grown from about a third of U.S. output in 1950 to about two-thirds today. These include the services produced by Internet providers, health care providers, the banking industry, the retail sector, the educational system, the entertainment industry and more.

...produced...

GDP counts only things that are *produced*. This may sound obvious, but it is easy to forget. Every day, Americans buy billions of dollars worth of things that are *not* produced, or at least not produced during the period being considered. These are not counted in that period's GDP. For example, people may buy land, or they may buy financial assets such as stocks or bonds. While these things cost money, they are not counted in GDP because they are not "goods and services *produced*." Land, for example, is not produced at all. Stocks and bonds represent a claim to ownership or to receive future payments, but they are not themselves produced goods or services.

...for the marketplace...

GDP does not include *all* final goods and services produced in the economy. Rather, with a few exceptions, it includes only those produced for the marketplace, that is, with the intention of being *sold*. Because of this restriction, we exclude many important goods and services from our measure. For example, when you clean your own home, you have produced a final service—housecleaning—but it is *not* counted in GDP because you are doing it for yourself, not for the marketplace. If you hire a housecleaner to clean your home, however, this final service *is* included in GDP; it has become a market transaction.

...during a given period...

GDP measures production during some specific period of time. Only goods produced during that period are counted. But people and businesses spend billions of dollars each year on *used* goods, such as secondhand cars, previously occupied homes, used furniture, or an old signed photo of Elvis. These goods were all *produced*, but not necessarily in the current period. And even if they *were* produced in the current period, they would only count when sold the *first* time, as new goods. If we counted them again each time they were resold, we would overestimate total production for the period.

...within the nation's borders.

U.S. GDP measures output produced *within U.S. borders*, regardless of whether it was produced by Americans. This means we *include* output produced by foreign-owned resources and foreign citizens located in the United States, and we *exclude* output produced by Americans located in other countries. For example, when the rock band U2, whose members reside in Ireland, gives a concert tour in the United States, the value of their services is counted in U.S. GDP but not in Ireland's GDP. Similarly, the services of an American nurse working in a South African hospital are part of South Africa's GDP and not U.S. GDP.

Tracking and Reporting GDP

If you read a news article about recent changes in GDP, it is easy to get confused. That's because some major conceptual adjustments are made to those numbers

© AXL/SHUTTERSTOCK.COM

DANGEROUS CURVES ⚠️

The services of dealers, brokers, and other sellers You've learned that GDP excludes the value of many things that are bought and sold—such as land, financial assets, and used goods—because they are not *currently produced goods and services*. But all of this buying and selling *can* contribute to GDP indirectly. How? If a dealer or broker is involved in the transaction, then that dealer or broker is producing a current service: bringing buyer and seller together. The value of this service is part of current GDP.

For example, suppose you bought a secondhand book at your college bookstore for $50. Suppose, too, that the store had bought the book from another student for $30. Then the purchase of the used book will contribute $20 to this year's GDP. Why? Because $20 is the value of the bookstore's services; it's the premium you pay to buy the book in the store, rather than going through the trouble to find the original seller yourself. The remainder of your purchase—$30—represents the value of the used book itself, and is *not* counted in GDP. The book was already counted when it was newly produced, in this or a previous year.

Quarters	GDP (billions of dollars)	Real GDP (billions of 2005 dollars)	Real GDP Growth Rate
2010–I	$14,277.9	$12,937.7	3.9%
2010–II	$14,467.8	$13,058.5	3.8%
2010–III	$14,605.5	$13,139.6	2.5%
2010–IV	$14,755.0	$13,216.1	2.3%
2011–I	$14,867.8	$13,227.9	0.4%
2011–II	$15,012.8	$13,271.8	1.3%
2011–III	$15,180.9	$13,337.8	2.0%

Source: Bureau of Economic Analysis (*www.bea.gov*), November 22, 2011 revision.

before you see them. Reporters aren't always careful in handling or explaining these adjustments, and, on occasion, they get confused themselves.

Annualization

GDP is a flow variable: It measures a rate of production. In theory, we could measure it over any time period we choose. In 2010, for example, the United States produced an average of $40 billion worth of output each *day*, $1.2 trillion each *month*, and $14.5 trillion for the year. Thus, we could measure GDP as a daily rate, a monthly rate, and so on. In practice, the government reports GDP as an *annual* rate. But it is measured and reported that way *each quarter*.

To understand this, look at Table 1, which shows how GDP was measured and reported by the government during 2010 and the first three quarters of 2011. Look at the row for 2010—I, which is the first quarter (January through March of 2010), and find the entry for GDP in that quarter ($14,277.9).

That number is *not* how much the U.S. economy actually produced during that quarter. The actual amount was about $3,569.5 billion. But you won't see that number in the table or anywhere in the government's report. What you see instead is what we *would* have produced during an entire year if we produced at that quarter's rate for four full quarters (4 × $3,569.48 billion = $14,277.9 billion).[1] That is, we take actual production during the three month period and *annualize* it. Once the fourth-quarter figures are in, the government also reports the official GDP figure for the entire year—what we *actually* produced during that year. For 2010, that was $14,526.5 billion (not shown in the table).

Real versus Nominal GDP

Because GDP is measured in dollars, we have a serious problem when we want to track the change in output over time. The problem is that the value of the dollar—its purchasing power—is itself changing. As prices have risen over the years, the value of the dollar has steadily fallen. Trying to keep track of GDP using dollars is like

---

[1] There is one other twist to the government's reporting: Each quarter's production is *seasonally adjusted*—raised or lowered to eliminate any changes that usually occur during that time of year. We'll discuss seasonal adjustment later in the chapter.

trying to keep track of a child's height using a ruler whose length changes each year: We cannot know how much the child has grown, if at all, until we adjust for the effects of a changing ruler. The same is true for GDP and for any other economic variable measured in dollars: We need to adjust our measurements to reflect changes in the value of the dollar.

> *When a variable is measured in dollars, with no adjustment for the dollar's changing value, it is called a **nominal variable**. When a variable is adjusted for the dollar's changing value, it is called a **real variable**.*

Nominal variable A variable measured without adjustment for the dollar's changing value.

Real variable A variable adjusted for changes in the dollar's value.

Most government statistics, including GDP, are reported in both nominal and real terms. In Table 1, the third column shows *real* GDP for each quarter, reported in "2005 dollars." Roughly speaking, this measure values GDP in each quarter at the prices that the goods and services would have sold for in 2005. (The selection of the year 2005 for this purpose is entirely arbitrary; what matters is that we use the same year's dollars to measure real GDP in different years.) There are a host of technical problems to be solved when converting a nominal variable (such as nominal GDP) into a real variable (such as real GDP). In the next chapter, you'll learn about some of these problems. But the goal is to measure something going on in the economy (such as production) using a consistent "ruler."

Economists focus almost exclusively on real variables in tracking the economy. This is because changes in nominal variables don't really tell us much. For example, when nominal GDP rises, some of the rise could be due to a rise in prices, rather than a rise in actual production. It is even possible for nominal GDP to rise while real GDP falls. The change in *real* GDP, which removes the effect of rising prices, tells us what is happening to total production.

The distinction between nominal and real values is crucial in macroeconomics. Whenever we want to track significant changes in key macroeconomic variables— such as the average wage rate, wealth, income, and GDP or any of its components— we always use real variables.

> *When comparing variables measured in dollars over time, it is important to translate nominal values (which are measured in current dollars) to real values (which adjust for the dollar's changing value as prices change).*

Growth Rates

When GDP is actually reported, the value of GDP itself does not get a lot of attention. Rather, the focus is on the *annual growth rate* of real GDP from one quarter to the next. These growth rates are indicated in the last column of Table 1. For example, from the first to the second quarter of 2010, real GDP actually grew by 0.9 percent. But if real GDP *continued* to grow at that same rate for four full quarters, it would grow by 3.8 percent over the entire year. This is the growth rate (3.8 percent) reported in the table.

The Expenditure Approach to GDP

The Commerce Department's Bureau of Economic Analysis (BEA), the agency responsible for measuring the nation's production, calculates GDP in several different ways. The most important of these is the *expenditure approach*. Because this method of measuring GDP tells us so much about the structure of our economy, we'll spend the next several pages on it.

In the expenditure approach, we divide output into four categories according to which group in the economy purchases it as the final user. The four categories are:

1. *Consumption goods and services (C),* purchased by households;
2. *Private investment goods and services (I),* purchased by businesses;
3. *Government goods and services (G),* purchased by government agencies;
4. *Net exports (NX),* purchased by foreigners.

This is an exhaustive list: Everyone who purchases a good or service included in U.S. GDP must be either a U.S. household, U.S. business, U.S. government agency (including state and local government), or a foreign buyer. Thus, when we add up the purchases of all four groups, we must get GDP:

Expenditure approach Measuring GDP by adding the value of goods and services purchased by each type of final user.

> In the **expenditure approach** to measuring GDP, *we add up the value of the goods and services purchased by each type of final user:*
>
> $$GDP = C + I + G + NX$$

Table 2 shows the part of GDP purchased by each sector during 2010. Ignore the finer details for now and just concentrate on the last number in each column. Applying the expenditure approach to GDP in 2010 gives us GDP = *C* + *I* + *G* + *NX* = $10,246 + $1,795 + $3,003 + (−$517) = $14,527 billion.

Now let's take a closer look at each of the four components of GDP.

TABLE 2 **GDP in 2010: The Expenditure Approach**

Consumption Purchases ($ billion)		Private Investment Purchases ($ billion)		Government Purchases ($ billion)		Net Exports ($ billion)	
Services	$6,859	Plant, Equipment, and Software	$1,390	Government Consumption	$2,498	Exports	$1,840
Nondurable Goods	$2,302	New-Home Construction	$338	Government Investment	$505	Imports	$2,357
Durable Goods	$1,085	Changes in Business Inventories	$67				
Consumption =	**$10,246**	**Private Investment =**	**$1,795**	**Government Purchases =**	**$3,003**	**Net Exports =**	**−$517**

GDP = *C* + *I* + *G* + *NX*
    = $10,246 + $1,795 + $3,003 + (−$517)
    = $14,527 billion

Source: Bureau of Economic Analysis, "National Income and Product Account Tables" (*www.bea.gov*), November 22, 2011 revision.

Consumption Spending

Consumption (C) is the largest component of GDP—making up about 70 percent of total production in recent years—and the easiest to understand:

> In general, **consumption** is the part of GDP purchased by households as final users.

Consumption (C) The part of GDP purchased by households as final users.

In general, if something is part of U.S. GDP and it is purchased by U.S. households during the year, it is considered consumption spending.

But notice the words *in general*. Some important exceptions to this general rule are:

- *Imported Consumption Goods and Components*. Some of the final goods purchased by households are either imported from abroad or have imported components. For example, suppose you buy an automobile for $20,000 that was assembled in the U.S., and the U.S. firm purchased $15,000 worth of imported components to make it. Then only the remaining $5,000 of the car's value was actually produced in the U.S. When measuring consumption spending, however, we include the entire $20,000 you pay for the car. (If you're concerned this will lead to an overestimate of U.S. GDP, don't worry: The government corrects for this overcount, as you'll see in a few pages.)
- *Imputed Items*. Two items are included in consumption spending even though they are not actually *purchased*. These are: (1) the total value of food products produced on farms and consumed by the farmers and their families themselves; and (2) the total value of housing *services* provided by owner-occupied homes. The government estimates how much the food consumed on farms *could* have been sold for, and how much owner-occupied homes *could* have been rented for to determine the value households are getting from these items. The estimates are included as part of consumption spending, and they are included as part of GDP as well.
- *New home construction*. Even though newly constructed homes are part of GDP, and ultimately purchased by households, they are included as investment.

Private Investment

The next category of GDP in the expenditure approach is private investment (typically called investment for short).

> In general, investment is the part of GDP purchased by business firms as final users.

The investment category can seem quirky when you first learn about it. So let's start by discussing the three categories of investment spending in GDP, and why they are included.

1. Business Purchases of Plant, Equipment, and Software. This category might seem confusing at first glance. Why aren't plant, equipment, and software considered intermediate goods? After all,

© MORENO SOPPELSA/SHUTTERSTOCK.COM

business firms buy these things in order to produce other things. Doesn't the value of their final goods include the value of their plant, equipment, and software as well?

Actually, no, and if you go back to the definition of intermediate goods, you will see why. Intermediate goods are *used up* in producing the current year's GDP. But a firm's plant, equipment, and software are intended to last for many years; only a small part of them is used up to make the current year's output. Thus, we regard new plant, equipment, and software as final goods, and we regard the firms that buy them as the final users of those goods.

For example, suppose our paper mill—the firm that turns wood chips into raw paper—builds a new factory building that is expected to last for 50 years. Then only a small fraction of that factory building—one-fiftieth—is used up in any one year's production of raw paper, and only this small part of the factory building's value will be reflected in the value of the firm's paper production. But since the entire factory is produced during the year, we must include its full value *somewhere* in our measure of production. We therefore count the whole factory building as investment in GDP.

Plant, equipment, and software purchases are always the largest component of private investment. And 2010 was no exception, as you can see in the second column of Table 2. That year, businesses purchased and installed $1,390 billion worth of plant, equipment, and software, which was more than three-quarters of total private investment.

2. Changes in Inventories. Inventories are goods that have been produced but not yet sold. They include goods on store shelves, goods making their way through the production process in factories, and raw materials waiting to be used. We count the *change* in firms' inventories as part of investment in measuring GDP. Why? When goods are produced but not sold during the year, they end up in some firm's inventory stocks. If we did *not* count changes in inventories, we would be missing this important part of current production. Remember that GDP is designed to measure total *production,* not just the part of production that is sold during the year.

To understand this more clearly, suppose that in some year, the automobile industry produced $100 billion worth of automobiles, and that $80 billion worth was sold to consumers. Then the other $20 billion remained unsold and was added to the auto companies' and dealers' inventories. If we counted consumption spending alone ($80 billion), we would underestimate automobile production in GDP. To ensure a proper measure, we must include not only the $80 billion in cars sold (consumption), but also the $20 billion *change* in inventories (private investment). In the end, the contribution to GDP is $80 billion (consumption) + $20 billion (private investment) = $100 billion, which is, indeed, the total value of automobile production during the year.

What if inventory stocks *decline* during the year, so that the change in inventories is negative? Our rule still holds: We include the change in inventories in our measure of GDP. But in this case, we add a *negative* number. For example, if the automobile industry produced $100 billion worth of cars this year, but consumers bought $120 billion, then $20 billion worth must have come from inventory stocks. This $20 billion worth of cars was produced (and counted) in previous years, so it should not be counted in this year's GDP. In this case, the consumption spending of $120 billion *overestimates* automobile production during the year, so subtracting $20 billion corrects for this overcount. In the end, GDP would rise by $120 billion (consumption) + [−$20 billion (private investment)] = $100 billion.

Note that our treatment of inventories as investment spending applies even to goods that would otherwise be considered intermediate goods. If an automobile company purchases $10 million of flat-rolled steel that it does *not* use during the year, the $10 million change in its steel inventories would be considered investment spending. After all, the steel was produced that year, so we have to count it somewhere. Because it was not counted in a final good purchased by anyone else that year, we treat the automobile company itself as the final user of the steel.

3. New-Home Construction. As we discussed earlier, even though new homes are ultimately purchased by households, they are counted as private investment spending, rather than consumption. One reason is that a household's decision to buy a home shares much in common with a business firm's decision to purchase a new plant or equipment. In both cases, the good is purchased in large part because of the benefits it will provide for many years in the future.

But another reason to include home construction as investment is because investment has an important relationship to the nation's capital stock. Let's explore this further.

Private Investment and the Capital Stock

In Chapter 1, you learned that one of the four resources is capital, a long-lasting tool used in production, and which is *itself* produced. Examples are oil drilling rigs, wireless phone towers, roads, and airports. When we sum the value of all capital goods like these in the country, we get our *capital stock*.

Private investment spending—in addition to representing business purchases in GDP—also has an important relationship to the capital stock.

> *Private investment spending adds to the nation's capital stock.*

This is easiest to see in the first category of investment spending: Purchases of plant, equipment, and software. When a business firm builds a factory or purchases a new computer, it becomes part of the nation's capital stock. Software, too, can be regarded as part of the capital stock. After all, when software is purchased, it usually provides benefits for several years, just like a factory or a computer. New homes, too, add to the capital stock. A newly constructed home provides benefits for many years into the future.

What about changes in inventories? Loosely speaking, the unsold goods that are added to inventory stocks during the year add to the nation's capital stock too. These goods can be consumed at some future date. An analogy might help make this clear. Imagine that your family decided to purchase, right now, all of the canned food, toothpaste, soap, and similar storable goods it was likely to need over the next 40 years. These stored goods would be counted as part of your family's wealth; they would provide benefits to your family for many years in the future. As the goods were used up over the years, your family's wealth (assuming no other change) would decline. In the same way, goods that our nation produces and doesn't consume now, but instead holds as inventories for future consumption, add to our "national wealth"—our nation's capital stock. And if, in a given year, the change in inventories is *negative* (i.e., we use up more of our inventories than we are adding), our capital stock declines.

Some Important Provisos. Changes in the nation's capital stock are somewhat more complicated than we are able to capture with private investment alone. First, private investment *excludes* some production that adds to the nation's capital stock. Specifically, private investment does not include:

- *Government investment.* An important part of the nation's capital stock is owned and operated not by businesses, but by government—federal, state, and local. Courthouses, police cars, fire stations, schools, weather satellites, military aircraft, highways, and bridges are all examples of government capital. If you look at the third column of Table 2, for example, you'll see that the BEA estimated government investment to be $505 billion in 2010; that was the part of government spending that was devoted to capital formation in 2010.

- *Consumer durables.* Goods such as furniture, automobiles, washing machines, and personal computers for home use can be considered capital goods because they will continue to provide services for many years. In 2010, households purchased $1,085 billion worth of consumer durables (see Table 2, first column).

- *Human capital.* Think about a surgeon's skills in performing a heart bypass operation, or a police detective's ability to find clues and solve a murder, or an electrician's ability to wire a home. These types of knowledge will continue to provide valuable services well into the future, just like plant and equipment or new housing. To measure the increase in the capital stock most broadly, then, we *should* include the additional skills and training acquired by the workforce during the year.

In addition to excluding some types of capital formation, private investment also errs in the other direction: It ignores *depreciation*—the capital that is used up during the year. Fortunately, the BEA estimates depreciation of the private and public capital stock, allowing us to calculate **net investment** (total investment minus depreciation) for these sectors. For example, for 2010, the BEA estimates that $1,541 billion of the private capital stock depreciated during the year (not shown in Table 2). So *net* private investment that year was only $1,795 billion − $1,541 billion = $254 billion. Similarly, the BEA estimates that $334 billion in government capital depreciated in 2010, so net government investment that year was $505 billion − $334 billion = $171 billion.

Net investment Investment minus depreciation.

Government Purchases

In 2010, the government bought $3,003 billion worth of goods and services that were part of GDP—about a fifth of the total. This component of GDP is typically called **government purchases**, although its technical name is *government consumption and investment purchases.* Government *investment,* as discussed earlier, refers to capital goods purchased by government agencies. The rest of government purchases is considered government *consumption:* spending on goods and services that are used up during the period. This includes the salaries of government workers and military personnel, and raw materials such as computer paper for government offices, gasoline for government vehicles, and the electricity used in government buildings.

There are a few things to keep in mind about government purchases in GDP. First, we include purchases by state and local governments as well as the

Government purchases (G) Spending by federal, state, and local governments on goods and services.

federal government. In macroeconomics, it makes little difference whether the purchases are made by a local government agency, like the parks department of Kalamazoo, Michigan, or a huge federal agency, such as the U.S. Department of Defense.

Second, government purchases include *goods*—like fighter jets, police cars, school buildings, and spy satellites—and *services*—such as those performed by police, legislators, and military personnel. The government is considered to be the final purchaser of these things even if it uses them to make other goods or services. For example, if you are taking economics at a public college or university that produces educational services, then your professor is selling teaching services to a state or city government. His or her salary enters into GDP as part of government purchases.

Finally, it's important to distinguish between government *purchases*—which are counted in GDP—and government *outlays* as measured by local, state, and federal budgets and reported in the media. Outlays include not just purchases, but also **transfer payments**. These are funds *given* to people or organizations—*not* to buy goods or services from them, but rather to fulfill some social obligation or goal. For example, Social Security payments by the federal government, unemployment insurance and welfare payments by state governments, and money disbursed to homeless shelters and soup kitchens by city governments are all examples of transfer payments. They are not included in government purchases, because the government itself has not actually purchased any goods and services with these funds.

The important thing to remember about transfer payments is this:

> *Transfer payments represent money redistributed from one group of citizens (taxpayers) to another (the poor, the unemployed, the elderly). While transfers are included in government budgets as outlays, they are not included in the government purchases component of GDP.*

Transfer payment Any payment that is not compensation for supplying goods, services, or resources.

Net Exports

There is one more category of buyers of output produced in the United States: *the foreign sector.* Looking back at Table 2, the fourth column tells us that in 2010, purchasers *outside* the nation bought approximately $1,840 billion of U.S. goods and services—about 14 percent of our GDP. These exports are part of U.S. production of goods and services and so are included in GDP.

However, in recognizing dealings with the rest of the world, we must correct an inaccuracy in our measure of GDP the way we've reported it so far. Recall that when we measure consumption spending, we include the value of imports in the goods that consumers buy. The same is true when we measure private investment and government purchases: the value of any imported goods or imported components is included. Thus, when we add up the final purchases of households, businesses, and government agencies, we *overcount* U.S. production because we include goods and services produced abroad. But these are *not* part of U.S. output. To correct for this overcount, we deduct all U.S. *imports* during the year, leaving us with just the output produced in the United States. In 2010, these imports amounted to $2,357 billion, an amount equal to about 18 percent of our GDP.

Let's recap: To obtain an accurate measure of GDP, we must include U.S. production that is purchased by foreigners: total exports. But to correct for including goods produced abroad, we must subtract Americans' purchases of goods produced outside of the United States: total imports. In practice, we take both of these steps together by adding **net exports** (*NX*), which are total exports minus total imports.

Net exports (NX) Total exports minus total imports.

> *To properly account for output sold to, and bought from, foreigners, we must include net exports—the difference between exports and imports—as part of expenditure in GDP.*

In 2010, when total exports were $1,840 billion and total imports were $2,357 billion, net exports (as you can see in Table 2) were $1,840 − $2,357 = −$517 billion. The negative number indicates that the imports we're subtracting from GDP are greater than the exports we're adding.

Other Approaches to GDP

Aside from the expenditure approach, in which we calculate GDP as $C + I + G + NX$, there are other ways of measuring GDP. You may be wondering: Why bother? Why not just use one method—whichever is best—and stick to it?

Actually, there are two good reasons for measuring GDP in different ways. The first is practical. Each method of measuring GDP is subject to measurement errors. By calculating total output in several different ways and then trying to resolve the differences, the BEA gets a more accurate measure than would be possible with one method alone.

The second reason is that the different ways of measuring total output give us different insights into the structure of our economy. Let's take a look at two more ways of measuring—and thinking about—GDP.

The Value-Added Approach

In the expenditure approach, we record goods and services only when they are sold to their final users—at the end of the production process. But we can also measure GDP by adding up each *firm's* contribution to the product *as it is produced*.

A firm's contribution to a product is called its *value added*. More formally,

Value added The revenue a firm receives minus the cost of the intermediate goods it buys.

> *a firm's **value added** is the revenue it receives for its output, minus the cost of all the intermediate goods that it buys.*

Look back at Figure 1, which traces the production of a ream of notebook paper. The paper mill, for example, buys $1.00 worth of wood chips (an intermediate good) from the lumber company. It turns wood chips into raw paper, which it sells for $1.50. The value added by the paper mill is $1.50 − $1.00 = $0.50. Similarly, the office supplies maker buys $1.50 worth of paper (an intermediate good) from the paper mill and sells it for $2.25. Its value added is $2.25 − $1.50 = $0.75. If we total the value added by each firm, we should get the final value of the notebook paper, as shown in Table 3. (Notice that we assume the first producer in this process—the lumber company—uses no intermediate goods.)

TABLE 3

Firm	Cost of Intermediate Goods	Revenue	Value Added
Lumber Company	$ 0	$1.00	$1.00
Paper Mill	$1.00	$1.50	$0.50
Office Supplies Manufacturer	$1.50	$2.25	$0.75
Wholesaler	$2.25	$3.50	$1.25
Retailer	$3.50	$5.00	$1.50
			Total: $5.00

Value Added at Different Stages of Production

© CENGAGE LEARNING 2013

The total value added is $1.00 + $0.50 + $0.75 + $1.25 + $1.50 = $5.00, which is equal to the final sales price of the ream of paper. For any good or service, it will always be the case that the sum of the values added by all firms equals the final sales price. This leads to our second method of measuring GDP:

> *In the **value-added approach**, GDP is the sum of the values added by all firms in the economy.*

Value-added approach Measuring GDP by summing the values added by all firms in the economy.

The Factor Payments Approach

If a bakery sells $200,000 worth of bread during the year and buys $25,000 in intermediate goods (flour, eggs, yeast), then its value added is $200,000 − $25,000 = $175,000. This is also the sum that will be *left over* from its revenue after the bakery pays for its intermediate goods.

Where does this $175,000 go? Since we've already deducted the payment for intermediate goods, the rest must go to pay for the *resources* used by the bakery during the year: the land, labor, capital, and entrepreneurship that it used to add value to its intermediate goods.

Payments to owners of resources are called **factor payments,** because resources are also called the factors of production. Owners of capital (such as those who lend funds to the firm so that it can buy its buildings and machinery) receive *interest payments*. Owners of land and natural resources receive *rent*. And those who provide labor to the firm receive *wages and salaries*.

Factor payments Payments to the owners of resources that are used in production.

Finally, there is one additional resource used by the firm: *entrepreneurship*. In every capitalist economy, the entrepreneurs are those who visualize society's needs, mobilize and coordinate the other resources so that production can take place, and/or risk their funds on the enterprise. The people who provide this entrepreneurship (often the owners of the firms) receive a fourth type of factor payment: *profit*.

For our bakery, or any other firm in the economy:

> *in any year, the value added by a firm is equal to the total factor payments made by that firm.*

TABLE 4

The Factor Payments Approach

Firm	Value Added (from Table 3)	Distribution of Value Added:			
		Wages & Salaries	Rent	Interest	Profit
Lumber Company	$1.00	$0.65	$0.15	$0.05	$0.15
Paper Mill	$0.50	$0.35	$0.02	$0.08	$0.05
Office Supplies Manufacturer	$0.75	$0.45	$0.05	$0.15	$0.10
Wholesaler	$1.25	$0.85	$0.10	$0.15	$0.15
Retailer	$1.50	$1.00	$0.20	$0.10	$0.20
Totals	$5.00	$3.30	$0.52	$0.53	$0.65

Wages + Rent + Interest + Profit = $3.30 + $0.52 + $0.53 + $0.65 = $5.00

© CENGAGE LEARNING 2013

To see how this helps us measure GDP, let's go back to our example of a ream of paper that sells for $5.00. We already know—using the expenditure or value added approaches—that the paper's contribution to GDP is $5.00. Table 4 shows how we can obtain the same $5.00 contribution to GDP using the factor payments approach.

Look at the row for the lumber company, whose value added (from Table 3) is $1.00. Where does this $1.00 go? In Table 4, we assume that $0.65 is paid out for wages and salaries, $0.15 for rent, $0.05 for interest. That leaves $0.15, which is the profit of the owners. The rest of the rows show the other firms' value added is distributed among the four factor payments. Now look at the last row, which adds the factor payments for each type of resource. We find that labor at all firms involved in producing the paper earned, in total, $3.30 in wages and salaries. And those who provided capital, land, and entrepreneurship earned (respectively) $0.52, $0.53, and $0.65. When payments to all four types of resources are totaled, we end up with $5.00—the paper's contribution to GDP.

We could repeat this procedure for every ream of paper or any other good produced in the economy over the year. In each case, if we total the wages and salaries, rent, interest, and profit earned in producing the good, we will get the value of the final product itself. So now we have our *third* method of measuring GDP:

Factor payments approach Measuring GDP by summing the factor payments earned by all households in the economy.

> In the **factor payments approach**, GDP is measured by adding up all of the income—wages and salaries, rent, interest, and profit—earned by all households in the economy.[2]

As stated earlier, having alternative methods to get GDP helps deal with measurement errors. But the factor payments approach, in particular, also gives us a key insight about the macroeconomy. On the one hand, total factor payments are just

---

[2] Actually, this is just an approximation. Before a firm pays its factors of production, it first deducts a small amount for depreciation of its plant and equipment, and another small amount for the sales taxes it must pay to the government. There are also adjustments made for income earned by U.S.-owned resources for production outside the U.S., and income paid to foreign-owned resources for production in the U.S. Thus, GDP and total factor payments are slightly different. We ignore this difference in the text.

another way of measuring GDP. On the other hand, total factor payments are equal to total household income. Therefore,

> *the total output of the economy (GDP) is equal to the total income earned in the economy.*

This simple idea—output equals income—follows directly from the factor payments approach to GDP. It explains why macroeconomists use the terms *output* and *income* interchangeably. They are one and the same. If output rises, income rises by the same amount; if output falls, income falls by an equal amount. We'll be using this very important insight in several chapters to come.

Measuring GDP: A Summary

You've now learned three different ways to calculate GDP:

Expenditure Approach: $GDP = C + I + G + NX$

Value-Added Approach: $GDP =$ Sum of value added by all firms

Factor Payments Approach: $GDP =$ Sum of factor payments earned by all households

$=$ Wages and salaries + interest + rent + profit

$=$ Total household income

We will use these three approaches to GDP again and again as we study what makes the economy tick. But for now, make sure you understand why each one of them should, in theory, give us the same number for GDP.

How GDP Is Used

Keeping track of the nation's production using GDP helps us in several important ways. In the short run, sudden changes in real GDP can alert us to the onset of a recession or a too-rapid expansion that can overheat the economy. Many (but not all) economists believe that, if alerted in time, policies can be designed to help keep the economy on a more balanced course.

GDP is also used to measure the long-run growth rate of the economy's output. Indeed, we typically define the average *standard of living* as *output per capita*: real GDP divided by the population. In order for output per capita to rise, real GDP must grow faster than the population. Since the U.S. population tends to grow by about 1 percent per year, a real GDP growth rate of 1 percent per year is needed just to *maintain* our output per capita; higher growth rates are needed to increase it.

Look at Figure 2, which shows the annual percentage change in real GDP from 1970 through the first half of 2011. The lower horizontal line indicates the 1 percent growth needed to just maintain output per capita. You can see that, on average, real GDP has grown by more than this. This tells us that output per capita has steadily increased over time.

But growth in real GDP is also important for another reason: to ensure that the economy generates sufficient new *jobs* for a workforce that is not only growing

| FIGURE 2 | Real GDP Growth Rate, 1970–2011 |

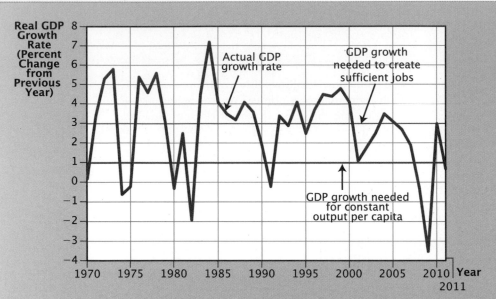

Although the growth rate of real GDP has fluctuated over time, it has on average been well above the 1 percent rate needed to maintain output per person, so real GDP per capita has risen over time. And for most of the period, the average growth rate was high enough to create the jobs needed by a growing and more productive workforce. During some years (e.g., 2008–2011), growth slowed, and an insufficient number of jobs were created.

Source: Bureau of Economic Analysis, *National Economic Accounts*, Table 1.1.1.

in number, but also becoming more productive. Each year, the average worker is capable of producing more output, due to advances in technology, increases in the capital stock, and the greater skills of workers themselves. But if each worker can produce more output, then output must increase even *faster* than the population to create enough jobs for everyone who wants to work.

During the years shown in Figure 2, real GDP needed to grow by about 3% per year to provide enough jobs for a workforce that was growing in number and becoming more productive every year. You can see that in most years, real GDP rose rapidly enough to satisfy this goal.

But you can also see that growth has fluctuated considerably, sometimes falling below the level needed to create a sufficient number of jobs. A painful example occurred during the recession of 2008–2009, and the period of slow growth that followed.

Most economists are confident that, over the long run, real GDP will rise fast enough to generate the jobs needed by a growing and more productive workforce, just as it has in the past. Later, you'll learn the reasons for this confidence. You'll also learn why, for sometimes years at a time, GDP can grow more slowly (or fall), causing unemployment to rise.

Problems with GDP

You have seen that GDP is an extremely useful concept. But the measurement of GDP is plagued by some serious problems.

Quality Changes

Suppose a new ballpoint pen comes out that lasts four times as long as previous versions. What *should* happen to GDP? Ideally, each new pen should count the same as four old pens, since one new pen offers the same *writing services* as four old ones. But the analysts at the Bureau of Economic Analysis would most likely treat this new pen the same as an old pen and record an increase in GDP only if the total number of pens increased. Why? Because the BEA has a limited budget. While it does include the impact of quality changes for many goods and services (such as automobiles, buildings, and computers), the BEA simply does not have the resources to estimate quality changes for millions of different goods and services. These include many consumer goods (such as razor blades that shave closer and last longer), medical services (increased surgery success rates and shorter recovery periods), and retail services (faster checkout times due to optical scanners). Ignoring these quality improvements causes GDP to understate the true growth in output from year to year.

The Underground Economy

Some production is hidden from government authorities, either because it is illegal (drugs, prostitution, most gambling) or because those engaged in it are avoiding taxes. Production in these hidden markets, which comprise the *underground economy*, cannot be measured accurately. The BEA does attempt to estimate production of legal but unreported activity. But it does *not* attempt to estimate the production of illegal goods. As a result, the official estimate of GDP understates our total output.

However, because the *relative* importance of the underground economy does not change rapidly, the BEA's estimates of *changes* in GDP from year to year should not be seriously affected.

Nonmarket Production

With a few exceptions, GDP excludes **nonmarket production:** goods and services that are produced but not sold in the marketplace. All of the housecleaning, typing, sewing, lawn mowing, and child rearing that people do themselves, rather than hiring someone else, is excluded from GDP. Whenever a nonmarket transaction (say, cleaning your apartment) becomes a market transaction (hiring a housecleaner to do it for you), GDP will rise, even though total production (cleaning one apartment) has remained the same.

Nonmarket production Goods and services that are produced but not sold in a market.

Over the last half-century, much production has shifted away from the home and into the market. Parenting, which was not counted in past years' GDP, has become day care, which *does* count—currently contributing several billion dollars annually to GDP. Similarly, home-cooked food has been replaced by takeout, talking to a friend has been replaced by therapy, and the neighbor who watches your house while you're away has been replaced by a store-bought alarm system or an increase in police protection. In all of these cases, real GDP increases, even though production has not. This can exaggerate the growth in GDP over long periods of time.

Other Aspects of Economic Well-Being

Earlier we mentioned that output per capita (real GDP divided by the population) is often referred to as a country's standard of living. And for good reason: Our economic well-being depends to a large extent on the quantity of goods and services available per person. Food, clothing, transportation, and health care are all examples of things that contribute to our economic satisfaction, and all are included in our measure of GDP.

But output per capita is an imperfect measure of living standards. First, many things that contribute to our economic welfare are not captured by GDP at all: leisure time, fairness, a sense of community, and more. GDP also ignores economic "bads"—crime, pollution, traffic congestion, and more—which make us worse off.

Finally, GDP does not distinguish between production that makes us better off and production that only prevents us from becoming worse off. For example, every year hundreds of thousands of automobile accidents result in billions of dollars spent on car repair, medical expenses, insurance, and legal services—production that counts in GDP as much as any other production. But we'd be better off if we had fewer accidents and the same total output of goods and services was devoted to doing things that we enjoy, rather than to coping with things that harm us.

Using GDP Properly

The previous discussion suggests that, for certain purposes, GDP must be used with caution. One example is interpreting changes in GDP growth over the long run. Suppose, for example, that over the next 10 or 15 years, growth in real GDP per capita slows down a bit. It might mean that something is going wrong, and we should change course. But it *could* be partly a measurement problem: the underground economy or unrecorded quality changes may be becoming more important. Or it could be a willing tradeoff: less output growth in exchange for more leisure time.

Caution is also required for some comparisons of economic well-being across countries. Everyone agrees that economic welfare is substantially greater in the United States than in Cambodia. Real GDP per capita—which is almost more than 20 times greater in the United States—captures most of this difference.

But what about the United States versus, say, Germany? Output per capita is about 23 percent greater in the United States. But during most years, a greater fraction of Americans work, and the average American worker spends about 25 percent more hours on the job each year than the average German. So Americans have more goods, but Germans have more leisure. Who is economically better off? And by how much? There is no objective answer, but using output per capita as the sole criterion would be misleading.

> *Due to measurement problems, small changes in long-run growth rates, or modest differences in real GDP per capita between one country and another, may not tell us much about the economy.*

GDP works very well, however, as a guide to the short-run performance of the economy. Look back at the list of problems with GDP. The distortion in GDP measurement caused by each problem is likely to remain fairly constant from quarter to quarter. If GDP suddenly drops, it is extremely unlikely that the underground economy has suddenly become more important, or that there has been a sudden shift from market to nonmarket activities, or that we are suddenly missing more quality changes than usual. Rather, we can be reasonably certain that output and economic activity are slowing down.

> *Short-term changes in real GDP are fairly accurate reflections of the state of the economy. A significant quarter-to-quarter change in real GDP very likely indicates a change in actual production, rather than a measurement problem.*

This is why policy makers, businesspeople, and the media pay such close attention to GDP as a guide to the economy from quarter to quarter.

EMPLOYMENT AND UNEMPLOYMENT

When you think of unemployment, you may have an image in your mind that goes something like this: As the economy slides into recession, an anxious employee is called into an office and handed a pink slip by a grim-faced manager. "Sorry," the manager says, "I wish there were some other way. . . ." The worker spends the next few months checking the classified ads, pounding the pavement, and sending out résumés in a desperate search for work. And perhaps, after months of trying, the laid-off worker gives up and sinks ever lower into despair and inertia.

For some people, joblessness begins and ends very much like this—a human tragedy, and a needless one. On one side, we have people who want to work and support themselves by producing something; on the other side is the rest of society, which could certainly use more goods and services. Yet somehow, the system isn't working, and the jobless cannot find work. The result is often hardship for the unemployed and their families, and a loss to society in general.

But this is just one face of unemployment, and there are others. During normal times, most unemployment has little to do with macroeconomic conditions. And in some cases, unemployment causes a lot less suffering than in our grim story.

Types of Unemployment

In the United States, people are considered unemployed if they are: (1) not working and (2) actively seeking a job. But unemployment can arise for a variety of reasons, each with its own policy implications. This is why economists have found it useful to classify unemployment into four different categories.

Frictional Unemployment

Short-term joblessness experienced by people who are between jobs or who are entering the labor market for the first time or after an absence is called **frictional unemployment.** In the real world, it takes time to find a job—time to prepare your résumé, to decide where to send it, to wait for responses, and then to investigate job offers so you can make a wise choice. It also takes time for different employers to consider your skills and qualifications and to decide whether you are right for their firms. If you are not working during that time, you will be unemployed: searching for work but not working.

Frictional unemployment
Joblessness experienced by people who are between jobs or who are just entering or reentering the labor market.

Because frictional unemployment is, by definition, short term, it causes little hardship to those affected by it. In most cases, people have enough savings to support themselves through a short spell of joblessness, or else they can borrow on their credit cards or from friends or family to tide them over. Moreover, this kind of unemployment has important benefits: By spending time searching rather than jumping at the first opening that comes their way, people find jobs for which they are better suited and in which they will ultimately be more productive. As a result, workers earn higher incomes, firms have more productive employees, and society has more goods and services.

Seasonal Unemployment

Joblessness related to changes in weather, tourist patterns, or other seasonal factors is called **seasonal unemployment.** For example, most ski instructors lose their jobs every April or May, and many construction workers are laid off each winter.

Seasonal unemployment
Joblessness related to changes in weather, tourist patterns, or other seasonal factors.

ETHAN MILLER/GETTY IMAGES FOR OPPORTUNITY VILLAGE

Seasonal unemployment, like frictional unemployment, is rather benign: It is short term, and, because it is entirely predictable, workers are often compensated in advance for the unemployment they experience in the off-season. Construction workers, for example, are paid higher-than-average hourly wages, in part to compensate them for their high probability of joblessness in the winter.

However, seasonal unemployment complicates the interpretation of unemployment data. Seasonal factors push the unemployment rate up in certain months of the year and pull it down in others, even when overall conditions in the economy remain unchanged. For example, each June, unemployment rises as millions of high school and college students—who do not want to work during the school year—begin looking for summer jobs. If the government reported the actual rise in unemployment in June, it would *seem* as if labor market conditions were deteriorating. In fact, the rise is just a predictable and temporary seasonal change.

Seasonal adjustment Adjusting an economic variable to remove the effects of changes predicted to occur at that time of year.

To prevent any misunderstandings, each month's unemployment rate undergoes **seasonal adjustment**—a process that removes from the rate any change that usually occurs during that month. For example, if the unemployment rate in June is typically one percentage point higher than during the rest of the year, then the seasonally adjusted rate for June will be the actual rate minus one percentage point. Many other types of macroeconomic data are seasonally adjusted in a similar way, including quarterly GDP, the monthly inflation rate, and more.

Structural Unemployment

Sometimes, there are jobs available and workers who would be delighted to have them, but job seekers and employers are mismatched in some way. For example, in late 2007, before our most recent recession began, the U.S. unemployment rate stood at 4.7 percent. At that time, there were plenty of jobs for nurses and nurse practitioners; for chemists and engineers; and for high school math and science teachers. Many of those unemployed, however, had been laid off from the automobile industry or other manufacturing jobs. They did not have the skills and training to work at the jobs that were available. This is a *skill* mismatch.

The mismatch can also be *geographic,* as when manufacturing jobs in the solar panel industry are available in Massachusetts, but unemployed factory workers live in other states.

Structural unemployment Joblessness arising from mismatches between workers' skills and employers' requirements or between workers' locations and employers' locations.

Unemployment that results from these kinds of mismatches is called **structural unemployment**, because it arises from *structural change* in the economy: when old, dying industries are replaced with new ones that require different skills and are located in different areas of the country. Structural unemployment is generally a stubborn, *long-term* problem, often lasting several years or more. It can take considerable time for the structurally unemployed to find jobs—time to relocate to another part of the country or time to acquire new skills. To make matters worse, the structurally unemployed—who could benefit from financial assistance for job training or relocation—usually cannot get loans because they don't have jobs.

TABLE 5

Average Unemployment Rates in Several Countries, 1995–2005 and 2007

Country	Average Unemployment Rate, 1995–2005	Average Unemployment Rate, 2007
France	10.2 %	8.6 %
Italy	9.9 %	6.2 %
Canada	7.2 %	5.3 %
United Kingdom	6.2 %	5.4 %
Germany	8.9 %	8.7 %
Sweden	7.2 %	6.1 %
United States	5.2 %	4.6 %

Source: Bureau of Labor Statistics, "Comparative Unemployment Rates in Nine Countries, 1995–2006," and Bureau of Labor Statistics, "International Comparisons of Annual Labor Force Statistics: 10 Countries, 1960–2007," Division of Foreign Labor Statistics, October 21, 2008. European rates have been adjusted by the BLS for comparability to U.S. rates. Ten-year averages were calculated by authors from the BLS data.

In recent decades, structural unemployment has been a much bigger problem in other countries, especially in Europe, than it is in the United States. Table 5 shows average unemployment rates in the United States and several European countries from 1995 to 2005 as well as 2007, just before the recession of 2008-2009 caused a different type of unemployment (cyclical) to spike upward. Unemployment rates were consistently higher in continental Europe than in the United States during this decade and, in most of these countries, were still high in 2007. This difference is mostly structural unemployment. Unemployment benefits tend to be higher in Europe and are offered for longer periods than in the United States. While this has provided a generous safety net for those without work, it has also reduced incentives for the unemployed to accept alternative jobs or acquire new training. At the same time, legal obstacles to laying off workers make firms more reticent to hire when the economic future is uncertain.

However, as you can see in Table 5, the difference in unemployment between Europe and the United States has been narrowing. Part of the reason is a change in labor market policies. For example, several nations—including Sweden, Denmark, and Germany—have reduced the duration of unemployment benefits and toughened eligibility requirements.

Our fourth and last type of unemployment, however, has an entirely *macroeconomic* cause and requires macroeconomic solutions.

Cyclical Unemployment

The types of unemployment we've considered so far—frictional, structural, and seasonal—arise largely from *microeconomic* causes; that is, they are attributable to changes in specific industries and specific labor markets, rather than to the overall level of production in the country. But our fourth and last type of unemployment has an entirely *macroeconomic* cause.

When the economy goes into a recession and total output falls, the unemployment rate rises. Many previously employed workers lose their jobs and have difficulty finding new ones. At the same time, there are fewer openings, so new entrants to the labor force must spend more than the usual time searching before they are

| FIGURE 3 | U.S. Quarterly Unemployment Rate, 1970–2011 |

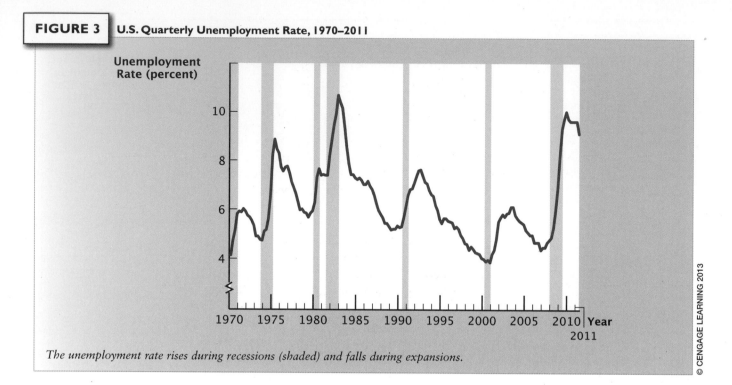

The unemployment rate rises during recessions (shaded) and falls during expansions.

© CENGAGE LEARNING 2013

Cyclical unemployment
Joblessness arising from changes in production over the business cycle.

hired. This type of unemployment—because it is caused by the business cycle—is called **cyclical unemployment.**

Look at Figure 3, which shows the average unemployment rate in the United States for each quarter from 1970 to mid 2011. Notice how unemployment rises during periods of recession (shaded), and how it continues to rise or remains elevated for several years after recessions end. In our most recent recession, for example, the unemployment rate rose from 4.7 percent at the end of 2007 to 10 percent by the end of 2009. It remained above 9 percent through mid 2011, and is expected to take another few years before falling back to more normal levels.

Since it arises from conditions in the overall economy, cyclical unemployment is a problem for *macroeconomic* policy. This is why macroeconomists focus almost exclusively on cyclical unemployment, rather than the other types of joblessness. Reflecting this emphasis, macroeconomists say we have reached **full employment** when *cyclical unemployment is reduced to zero,* even though substantial amounts of frictional, seasonal, and structural unemployment may remain:

Full employment A situation in which there is no cyclical unemployment.

> *In macroeconomics, full employment means zero cyclical unemployment. But the overall unemployment rate at full employment is greater than zero because there are still positive levels of frictional, seasonal, and structural unemployment.*

How do we tell how much of our unemployment is cyclical? Many economists believe that today, normal amounts of frictional, seasonal, and structural unemployment account for an unemployment rate of between 5 and 5.5 percent in the United States, and the Congressional Budget Office (the non-partisan research arm of Congress) puts the number at 5.2 percent. Any unemployment beyond this is considered cyclical unemployment.

For example (using the 5.2 percent value), when the actual unemployment rate was 9.1% in mid-2011, we might measure cyclical unemployment as 9.1% − 5.2% = 3.9% of the labor force. However, as we'll discuss in a few pages, this simple calculation seriously underestimates the problem of cyclical joblessness, due to problems in the way the unemployment rate is measured.

The Costs of Unemployment

Why are we so concerned about achieving a low rate of unemployment? What are the *costs* of unemployment to our society? We can identify two different types of costs: economic costs (those that can be readily measured in dollar terms) and broader costs (which are difficult to measure in dollars, but still affect us in important ways).

Economic Costs

The chief economic cost of unemployment is the *opportunity cost* of lost output: the goods and services the jobless *would* produce if they were working but do not produce because they cannot find work. This cost is borne by our society in general, although the burden may fall more on one group than another. If, for example, the unemployed were simply left to fend for themselves, then *they* would bear most of the cost. In fact, many who are unemployed are given government assistance—at least temporarily—so that the costs are spread somewhat among citizens in general. But there is no escaping this central fact:

> When there is cyclical unemployment, the nation produces *less output, and therefore some group or groups within society must ultimately* consume *less output.*

One way of viewing the economic cost of cyclical unemployment is illustrated in Figure 4. The green line shows quarterly real GDP over time, while the orange line shows the path of our **potential output**—the output we *could* have produced if the economy were operating at full employment.

Potential output The level of output the economy could produce if operating at full employment.

Notice that actual output is sometimes *above* potential output. At these times, unemployment is *below* its normal rate, so employment is higher than full employment. For example, during the expansion in the late 1990s and into 2000, cyclical unemployment was eliminated, and the sum of frictional, seasonal, and structural unemployment dropped well below their normal levels. At other times, real GDP is *below* potential output. At these times, unemployment rises above its normal rate, and employment falls below its normal, full-employment rate. This usually occurs during and following a recession.

The general public often uses the term "recession" to mean any period when real GDP falls below potential, and unemployment is high. But, as you've learned, recession has a more specific meaning to economists: it refers only to the *contraction* phase of the business cycle, when the economy is turning downward. But even after a recession ends and we begin the expansion phase of the cycle, real GDP can remain below potential for several quarters or years. In this text, we'll use the term **slump** to mean the entire period in which real GDP is below its potential and/or the rate of employment is below normal.

Slump A period during which real GDP is below potential and/or the employment rate is below normal.

In Figure 4, you can see that over the past several decades we have spent more time in slumps than we have producing above our potential. The cyclical ups and downs of the economy have, on balance, led to lower living standards than we would have had if the economy had always operated just at potential output.

Figure 5 shows potential and actual real GDP for the most recent two decades only, so it is easier to see the gaps between them. During the 2001 recession, the unemployment

FIGURE 4   Actual and Potential Real GDP, 1970–2011

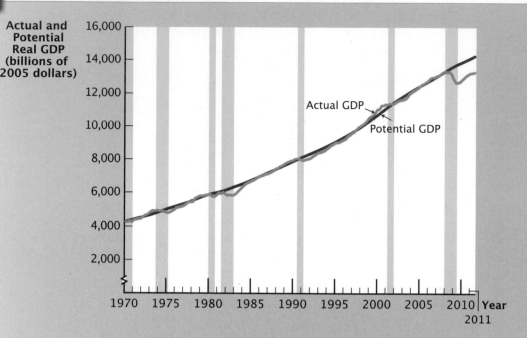

Sources: Real GDP from Bureau of Economic Analysis (*www.bea.gov*), Potential Real GDP from Congressional Budget Office, *The Budget and Economic Outlook: Fiscal Years 2009–2019*, January 2009 (*www.cbo.gov*).

rate (not shown) rose from 4.2 percent to 5.6 percent, then hovered near or above 6 percent for the next two years before coming down slowly. During this time, real GDP remained below potential. And as you can see in the figure, our most recent recession was especially severe. Output began falling rapidly below potential at the end of 2007. And even though the recession (contraction) officially ended in June 2009, the slump continued. In all, from 2008 through the first half of 2011, real GDP averaged about 6 percent below its potential, an unusually long and severe slump. During this time, the U.S. sacrificed about $3 trillion dollars in output—more than $25,000 per household—and the losses are forecast to continue for at least a few more years.

⚠ DANGEROUS CURVES

What makes it a recession? In Figures 3, 4, and 5, we've shaded the periods of recession. How are those periods determined? Newspapers and television commentators often state that a recession occurs when real GDP declines for two consecutive quarters. But that is not officially correct. During the recession of 2001, for example, real GDP never declined in two consecutive quarters. Our most recent recession began in December 2007, even though a two-quarter decline in real GDP did not begin until the third quarter of 2008.

Actually, *when* a U.S. recession begins and ends is determined by a committee within the National Bureau of Economic Research, an entirely private, nonprofit research organization headquartered in Boston. (For the past few decades, the NBER's Business Cycle Dating Committee has been chaired by Robert E. Hall, coauthor of this textbook.) The committee makes its decisions by looking at a variety of factors, including employment, industrial production, sales, and personal income, all of which are reported *monthly*. Each of these measures tends to move closely with real GDP. But real GDP is measured only quarterly and plays only a supporting role in dating recessions.

Broader Costs

There are also costs of unemployment that go beyond lost output. Unemployment—especially when it lasts for many months or years—can have serious psychological and physical effects. Some studies have found that increases in unemployment cause noticeable rises in the number of suicides and admissions to state prisons and psychiatric hospitals. And, tragically, most of those who lose their job and remain unemployed for long periods also lose their health insurance.

Unemployment also causes setbacks in achieving important social goals. For example, most of us want a fair and just society where all people have an equal

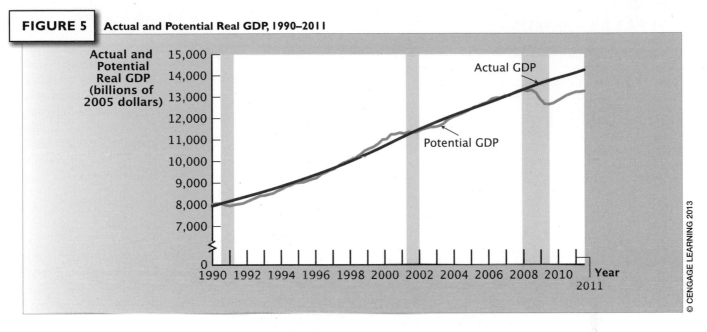

FIGURE 5   Actual and Potential Real GDP, 1990–2011

© CENGAGE LEARNING 2013

chance to better themselves. But our citizens do not bear the burden of unemployment equally. In a recession, we do not all suffer a reduction in our work hours; instead, some people are laid off entirely, while others continue to work roughly the same hours.

Moreover, the burden of unemployment is not shared equally among different groups in the population, but tends to fall most heavily on minorities, especially minority youth. This contributes to a vicious cycle of poverty and discrimination: When minority youths are deprived of that all-important first job, they remain at a disadvantage in the labor market for years to come.

Table 6 shows unemployment rates for various groups during August 2007 (when the economy was roughly at full employment) and four years later, in the midst of

TABLE 6

Unemployment Rate for Various Groups

	Unemployment Rate	
	Aug 2007 (Economy at Full Employment)	**Aug 2011** (Severe Slump)
Overall	4.6%	9.1%
Whites	4.2%	8.0%
Hispanics	5.5%	11.3%
Blacks	7.7%	16.7%
White Teenagers	14.1%	23.0%
Black Teenagers	32.1%	46.5%
Less than High School Diploma	6.6%	14.3%
High School Graduates, no College	4.4%	9.6%
Bachelor's or Higher Degree	2.1%	4.3%

© CENGAGE LEARNING 2013

FIGURE 6   **How the BLS Measures Employment Status**

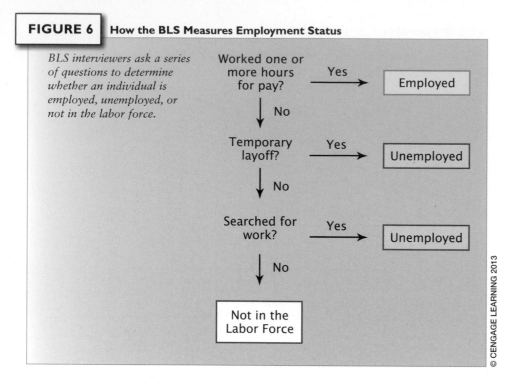

BLS interviewers ask a series of questions to determine whether an individual is employed, unemployed, or not in the labor force.

© CENGAGE LEARNING 2013

our recent deep slump. Notice that even when the economy is doing well, unemployment rates are considerably higher for some groups, including blacks and those with less than a high school diploma. Especially disturbing is the unemployment rate for black teenagers: 32.1% in August 2007—a relatively good period for the economy overall.

Notice, too, what happens after the economy turns down: Unemployment rates rise for *all* groups. But the rise is worse for minorities and those with less than a high school education. These groups have the highest unemployment rates in good times, and they bear a disproportionate share of the burden when the macroeconomy turns bad.

How Unemployment Is Measured

In August 2011, about 172 million Americans were not employed, according to official government statistics. Were all of these people unemployed? Absolutely not. In theory, the unemployed are those who are *willing and able* to work but do not have jobs. Most of the 172 million nonworking Americans were either *unable* or *unwilling* to work. For example, the very old, the very young, and the very ill were unable to work, as were those serving prison terms. Others were able to work, but preferred not to, including millions of college students, homemakers, and retired people. Still others were in the military and are counted in the population, but not counted when calculating civilian employment statistics.

But how, in practice, can we determine who is willing and able to work? This is a thorny problem, and there is no perfect solution to it. In many European countries, where virtually all potential workers are eligible for unemployment benefits, the approach is relatively simple: Just count up the number of people collecting unemployment benefits. In the United States, where eligibility for benefits is limited, this approach won't work. Instead, we determine whether a person is willing and able to work by his or her *behavior*. More specifically, to be counted as unemployed, you must have recently *searched* for work. But how can we tell who has, and who has not, recently searched for work?

The Census Bureau's Household Survey

Every month, thousands of interviewers from the United States Census Bureau—acting on behalf of the U.S. Bureau of Labor Statistics—conduct a survey of 60,000 households across America. This sample of households is carefully selected to give information about the entire population. Household members who are under

16, in the military, or currently residing in an institution like a prison or hospital are excluded from the survey. The interviewer will then ask questions about the remaining household members' activities during the *previous week*.

Figure 6 shows roughly how this works. First, the interviewer asks whether the household member has worked one or more hours for pay or profit. If the answer is yes, the person is considered employed; if no, another question is asked: Has she been *temporarily* laid off from a job from which she is waiting to be recalled? A yes means the person is unemployed whether or not the person searched for a new job; a no leads to one more question: Did the person actively *search* for work during the previous four weeks? If yes, the person is unemployed; if no, she is not in the labor force.

Figure 7 illustrates how the BLS, extrapolating from its 60,000-household sample, classified the U.S. population in August 2011. First, note that about 72 million people were ruled out from consideration because they were under 16 years of age, living in institutions, or in the military. The remaining 240 million people made up the civilian, noninstitutional population, and of these, 139.6 million were employed and 14.0 million were unemployed. Adding the employed and unemployed together gives us the **labor force**, equal to 139.6 million + 14.0 million = 153.6 million.

Finally, we come to the official **unemployment rate**, which is defined as the percentage of the labor force that is unemployed:

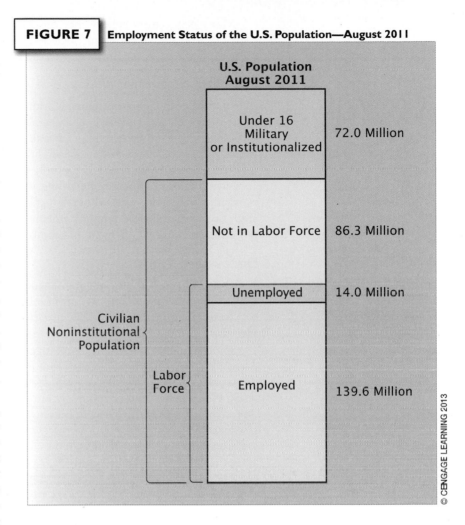

FIGURE 7 Employment Status of the U.S. Population—August 2011

© CENGAGE LEARNING 2013

Labor force Those people who have a job or who are looking for one.

Unemployment rate The fraction of the labor force that is without a job.

$$\text{Unemployment rate} = \frac{\text{Unemployed}}{\text{Labor force}} = \frac{\text{Unemployed}}{(\text{Unemployed} + \text{Employed})}$$

Using the numbers in Figure 7, the U.S. unemployment rate in August 2011 was calculated as 14.0/153.6 = .091 or 9.1 percent.

Problems in Measuring Unemployment

The Census Bureau earns very high marks from economists for both its sample size—60,000 households—and the characteristics of its sample, which very closely match the characteristics of the U.S. population. Still, the official unemployment rate suffers from some important measurement problems.

Many economists believe that our official measure seriously underestimates the extent of unemployment in our society. There are two reasons for this belief: the treatment of *involuntary part-time workers* and the treatment of *discouraged workers*.

Involuntary Part-Time Workers

Involuntary part-time workers Individuals who would like a full-time job, but who are working only part time.

As you can see in Figure 6, anyone working one hour or more for pay during the survey week is treated as employed. This includes many people who would like a full-time job—and may even be searching for one—but who worked only part-time during the week. Some economists have suggested that these people, called **involuntary part-time workers**, should be regarded as partially employed and partially unemployed.

How many involuntary part-time workers are there? In August 2011, the BLS estimated that there were about 8.8 million. If each of these workers were considered, say, half-employed and half-unemployed, the unemployment rate in that month would have been 12.0 percent, instead of the officially reported 9.1 percent.

Discouraged Workers

Discouraged workers Individuals who would like a job, but have given up searching for one.

Another problem with the unemployment rate is the treatment of **discouraged workers**. These are individuals who would like to work but feel little hope of finding a job and have given up searching. Because they are not taking active steps to find work, they are considered "not in the labor force" (see Figure 6).

Some economists feel that discouraged workers should be counted as unemployed. After all, these people are telling us that they are willing and able to work, but they are not working. It seems wrong to exclude them just because they are not actively seeking work. Others argue that counting discouraged workers as unemployed would reduce the objectivity of our unemployment measure. Talk is cheap, they believe, and people may *say* anything when asked whether they would like a job; the real test is what people *do*. Yet even the staunchest defenders of the current method of measuring employment would agree that *many* discouraged workers are, in fact, willing and able to work and should be considered unemployed. The problem, in their view, is determining which ones.

How many discouraged workers are there? No one knows for sure. The BLS tries to count them, but defining who genuinely belongs in this category is yet another thorny problem. The BLS policy is to count someone as a discouraged worker if (1) they are not working; (2) they searched for a job at some point in the last 12 months; (3) they currently want a job; and (4) they state that the *only* reason they are not currently searching for work is their belief that no job is available for them. Using this rather strict definition, there were 977,000 discouraged workers in August 2011.

But the BLS also reports a more loosely defined measure: *marginally attached to the labor force*. These are people who meet the first three requirements of discouraged workers, but not necessarily the fourth: They can give *any* reason for not currently searching for work. Using this broader measure, 2.6 million people were marginally attached to the labor force in August 2011. Counting some or all of them as unemployed would have significantly raised the reported unemployment rate in that month.

Alternative Measures of Employment Conditions

The official unemployment rate gets more attention than any other measure relating to employment. Within minutes of its release (at 8:30 AM on the first Friday of every month), it becomes the lead story on cable news networks and news Web sites. But changes in the unemployment rate can be a misleading indicator of changes in joblessness.

To see why, remember that to be counted as unemployed, someone must be searching for work. But when the economy is in a slump and it becomes harder to find a job, many people just give up looking. They become "discouraged workers" or "marginally attached to the labor force"—which means they are no longer considered unemployed. Their decision to stop searching for work in hard times tends to pull the unemployment rate artificially downward. If the effect is strong enough, the unemployment rate could actually fall as the economy and joblessness worsen. For this reason, economists tend to rely more on other measures to monitor the employment situation from month to month.

The Six "U"s

The BLS actually reports six different unemployment rates (the official unemployment rate and five other "unofficial" rates), each labeled with a "U" followed by a number. They are listed in Table 7 along with their reported rates in August 2007 and August 2011. The official unemployment rate—the one favored by the media—is "U 3." The other measures are obtained by starting with those officially counted as unemployed, and then removing or adding other groups of people without jobs. For example, U-1 is obtained by subtracting from the unemployed all those who have been jobless for less than 15 weeks, leaving just those unemployed for several months and most likely to be suffering labor market hardship.

All of these measures deteriorated significantly as the economy went into recession at the end of 2007 and then entered its long slump. But while the (official) unemployment rate rose by 4½ percentage points, the U-5 measure rose by more than 5 percentage points, and the U-6 measure rose by almost 8 percentage points. These two measures (U-5 and U-6) are immune to the distortion caused by people who stop looking for work, because they continue to be included after they stop looking.

TABLE 7

Alternative Unemployment Measures

	"Unemployment" Rate	
	Aug 2007 (Economy at Full Employment)	Aug 2011 (Severe Slump)
U-1: Unemployed for 15 weeks or longer as % of labor force	1.5%	5.4%
U-2: Unemployed due to loss of a job or completion of temporary work as % of labor force	2.4%	5.3%
U-3: Official Unemployment Rate	4.6%	9.1%
U-4: [Unemployed + discouraged workers] as % of [labor force + discouraged workers]	4.9%	9.7%
U-5: [Unemployed + marginally attached to labor force] as % of [labor force + marginally attached to labor force]	5.5%	10.6%
U-6: [Unemployed + marginally attached to labor force + involuntary part-time workers] as % of [labor force + marginally attached to labor force] Note: Involuntary part-time workers are already included as part of the labor force.	8.5%	16.2%

© CENGAGE LEARNING 2013

The Establishment Survey

Each month, in addition to its survey of households used to determine the unemployment rate, the BLS surveys business establishments to track the number of jobs that have been added and lost. The establishment survey (sometimes also called the "payroll survey") has one major advantage over the unemployment rate: It provides an objective measure of the jobs created and destroyed by employers, unaffected by individuals' decisions or memories about job-seeking.

But the establishment survey has some weaknesses too. For example, unlike the household survey, the establishment survey excludes the self-employed, agricultural workers, and private household workers. And it must rely on statistical techniques to estimate jobs at newly-created business firms, which are introduced into the survey sample only after a lag. As a result, the employment figures in the establishment survey are revised more than a month after they are first reported, and the revised numbers can be dramatically different from the initial reports.

The Employment-Population Ratio

employment-population ratio Total employment (from the household survey) divided by the total population over age 16.

One final measure—often favored by economists who want an accurate short-term picture of the employment picture—is the **employment-population ratio**. It is defined as the total number employed (from the household survey) divided by the *entire* population over the age of 16. Simply put, it tracks the fraction of the adult population that is working.

Because it counts employment rather than unemployment, and its denominator is the entire population rather than just the labor force, the employment-population ratio is not affected by job-searching behavior. After all, someone without a job is not considered employed (the numerator) and is still part of the population (the denominator) regardless of whether he or she is looking for work or not.

As you can see in Figure 8, the employment-population ratio began to nose-dive during the recession that began at the end of 2007, and continued to drop in the aftermath. To many economists, this rapid drop in the ratio provides the most direct and objective evidence of the long slump's devastating impact on people who want to work but cannot find a job.

FIGURE 8   The Employment Population Ratio: 1996–2011

The employment-population ratio often measures labor market conditions more accurately than the unemployment rate. The ratio falls during recessions, such as the deep recession of 2008 and 2009.

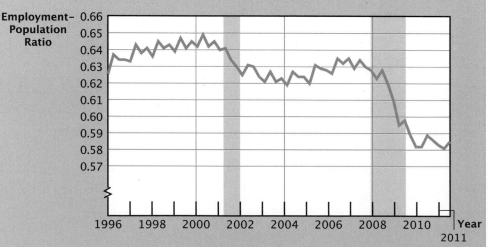

© CENGAGE LEARNING 2013

USING THE THEORY

SUDDEN DISASTERS AND GDP

The world's attention is often riveted by a sudden natural or man-made disaster. Recent examples have included severe earthquakes in Haiti and Chile in 2010, and the earthquake, tsunami, and nuclear meltdown that struck Japan in 2011. These events are human tragedies, sometimes on a huge scale, with hundreds, thousands, or (in the case of Haiti) even hundreds of thousands of deaths, and even more displaced from their homes.

The purely economic effects, too, can be devastating, at least in the local area of the disaster, where homes, factories, and jobs are destroyed. Yet in many cases, even the most horrific disasters have relatively little impact on a country's GDP in the short run (say, a few months to a year), and virtually no impact in the long run (more than a year later).

For example, look at Figure 9, which shows quarterly GDP from 1998 through early 2006. Two major U.S. disasters occurred within this period. The first was the terrorist attack of September 11, 2001, which killed more than 3,000 people, destroyed one of the largest office complexes in the United States, and led to major disruptions of production in lower Manhattan for weeks. If you search for the impact in Figure 9, you may think you've found it in the widening gap between actual and potential real GDP around that time. But look closely. GDP began to flatten in mid-2000, more than a year *before* the attack, due to a slowdown from other causes. Even though the attack may have worsened or prolonged that slowdown, any separate impact it might have had on production is hardly discernible.

Now consider Hurricanes Katrina and Rita, which hit the Gulf Coast in August and September of 2005. The hurricanes devastated huge areas of Louisiana and Mississippi, destroyed hundreds of thousands of homes, and left most of the city of New Orleans uninhabitable for months. About 250,000 people

---

AP PHOTO/JOHN BAZEMORE

FIGURE 9   Quarterly GDP during Two Recent Disasters

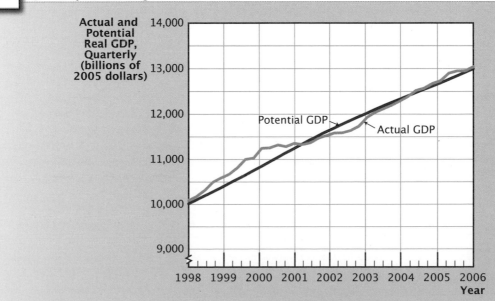

in the area lost their jobs—many of them for months or longer. But once again, the impact on GDP is so small that we cannot see it in the graph.

Why was GDP so *unaffected* by these events? We can start to answer by taking a closer look at the hurricanes of 2005.

Hurricanes Katrina and Rita: A Case Study

Natural or man-made disasters—such as the U.S. hurricanes in 2005—generally have two types of effects on real GDP. One is the direct impact of the event itself. The other is the indirect effects that follow as economic decision makers respond to the event. Let's consider each of these effects in turn.

Direct Effects: Destruction and Disruption

Table 8 shows a range of estimates for the physical destruction caused by Hurricanes Katrina and Rita in 2005. The total loss—between $69 billion and $130 billion—included about 287,000 homes destroyed or damaged (about half of them in New Orleans), as well as severe damage to oil and natural gas platforms and pipelines. Even though much of this property destruction was insured, the insurance merely redistributes the financial burden; it does not change the central fact that the country's *capital stock* declined.

But GDP dropped by much less than the decline in the capital stock. Remember that GDP does not measure the resources at our disposal, but rather the production we get from those resources.[3] The impact on GDP is therefore limited to the loss of *output* that the destroyed resources would otherwise have produced. Fewer factory buildings, oil rigs, and office buildings mean less production of manufactured goods, energy, and services. And every destroyed home is one that is no longer producing housing services (which are also part of GDP). This is the direct effect of a disaster on GDP.

How much *production* did we lose from the loss of capital in the hurricanes? Table 9 shows how the U.S. Congressional Budget Office (CBO) answered this question. The first three rows list the direct effect on production. Notice that the CBO uses the value-added approach (rather than the expenditure approach) to estimate this impact. That is, the direct effects on GDP are calculated as the decreases in value added in different industries, as well as the lost value of housing services. This is for practical reasons. It's easier to identify the decrease in production if we measure at the source—the sectors of the economy where the capital was destroyed—rather than try to track down the decreased purchases by final users.

TABLE 8		
Property Destruction from Hurricanes Katrina and Rita, 2005	**Type of Property**	**Estimated Loss**
	Residential housing	$17 billion to $33 billion
	Consumer durables (autos, furniture, appliances)	$5 billion to $9 billion
	Energy infrastructure	$18 billion to $31 billion
	Nonenergy business property	$16 billion to $32 billion
	Public infrastructure	$13 billion to $25 billion
	Total	**$69 billion to $130 billion**

Source: Based on Douglas Holtz-Eakin, "The Macroeconomic and Budgetary Effects of Hurricanes Katrina and Rita," *CBO Testimony before the Committee on the Budget, U.S. House of Representatives*, October 6, 2005.

---

[3] Destruction of capital does, however, directly affect *net national product*, which is defined as GDP minus depreciation of the capital stock during the period. Destruction of capital from a disaster is considered depreciation, and it is therefore deducted when calculating net national product.

If you subtotal the decrease in value added for the second half of 2005, you'll find the direct impact of the hurricanes on GDP: a decrease of between $20 billion and $32 billion. While this is a large number, it is very small compared to the size of the economy. In the second half of 2005, GDP was running at an annual rate of $12.7 trillion. Thus, the direct impact on production was at most 0.25 percent (a quarter of 1 percent) of GDP during that period.[4]

Indirect Effects: Government and Private Responses

We've seen that the direct effect of the hurricanes on GDP was relatively small. But what about the *indirect effects*—those that result from decisions made afterward? These are listed in the second three rows of numbers in Table 9. Notice that these effects are estimated using the expenditure approach to GDP, because they arise from decisions about spending made by households, businesses, and government agencies. As you'll learn a few chapters from now, changes in spending can cause changes in production—at least in the short run.

Of the three indirect effects based on spending, only one is negative: the decrease in consumption spending. Why did consumption spending fall after the hurricane? First, those who lived in the affected region and lost jobs and property saw significant reductions in their income and wealth, so their spending declined. Second, the hurricanes knocked out large chunks of the nation's oil refining infrastructure, causing gas prices to rise around the country. Because people had to spend more for gasoline, they had less to spend on other goods and services.

But working against the drop in consumption spending was *increased* spending by other sources. Government and businesses spent to rebuild and repair damage, and the government purchased food, housing, and medical care to distribute to those in need. In Table 9, you can see that the total indirect effects of the hurricanes were only slightly negative in the second half of 2005, and were projected to turn positive in 2006.

The Total Impact on GDP

The last row of Table 9 traces the total impact of the hurricanes on GDP over time. In the second half of 2005, GDP drops by $22 billion to $32 billion—a reduction of

	Second Half, 2005	First Half, 2006	Second Half, 2006
Direct effects			
Energy production	−18 to −28	−8 to −10	−5 to −7
Housing services	−1 to −2	−2 to −4	−1 to −3
Agricultural production	−1 to −2	0	0
Indirect effects			
Reduced consumption spending (beyond direct effects)	−14 to −22	−7 to −11	−3 to −8
Replacement investment	+6 to +12	+16 to +34	+16 to +35
Increased government spending on goods and services	+6 to +10	+12 to +18	+14 to +20
Total impact on real GDP	**−22 to −32**	**+11 to +27**	**+21 to +37**

TABLE 9

Estimated and Projected Effects of Hurricanes Katrina and Rita on GDP (billions of 2005 dollars at annual rates)

Source: Based on Douglas Holtz-Eakin, "The Macroeconomic and Budgetary Effects of Hurricanes Katrina and Rita," *CBO Testimony before the Committee on the Budget, U.S. House of Representatives*, October 6, 2005.

[4] Another way to understand why the effect is relatively small is to compare the total destruction of capital in Table 8—$69 billion to $130 billion—to the nation's total physical capital stock in 2005, which was $38 trillion. Thus, the hurricanes destroyed at most 0.34 percent of the nation's capital.

0.25 percent. But in 2006, the total impact turns positive: production in both halves of 2006 is greater than if there had been no hurricane. As you can see, this happens because the negative *direct* effects (through destruction) gradually weaken, while the positive *indirect* effects (through spending) gradually grow and ultimately dominate.

Does this mean that, economically speaking, the U.S. was better off because of the hurricanes? Not at all. Remember that GDP measures total output, regardless of what the output is used for. After a large disaster, virtually all of the increased production, and more, is used to bring the capital stock back to its prior level. If not for the disaster, we could be producing more of the goods and services that people enjoy, or increasing (rather than just restoring) our capital stock. Although the disaster may cause a country to *produce* more for a while, that does not mean the country is better off.

Drawing Conclusions

The impact of hurricanes Katrina and Rita on U.S. GDP helps us understand why some disasters have such a small effect on GDP. Is this experience typical of these types of events? A growing body of research[5] suggests that the impact of a disaster on GDP depends on the type of disaster, as well as the type of country in which it occurs.

Limited Local and Regional Disasters

The most obvious conclusion emerging from the research is that purely local disasters within a country typically have little impact on its GDP, because they affect such a small percentage of the country's total production. The total production of Louisiana and Mississippi—the two states most affected by the hurricanes—is only about 2 percent of U.S. GDP. And the total production of Manhattan—the area most profoundly affected by the attacks of September 11—is about 1.5 percent of GDP.

Larger Disasters in Developed Countries

In a developed country, even large disasters that destroy a significant share of a nation's capital stock have surprisingly short-lived effects. Japan's 2011 earthquake and tsunami, for example, hit a major industrial area, destroying about $200 billion in property. This was significantly more damage than the U.S. hurricanes, in an economy less than one-third as large as the U.S. economy. Supply chains across Japan were disrupted, and production declined sharply.

But the effects on GDP were short-lived. Japan is a highly developed country. Almost immediately after the disaster struck, its financial institutions and government agencies began channeling funds toward repair and rebuilding (the indirect effects via spending, discussed above). The manufacturing sector quickly found alternative sources for inputs, and alternative modes of transportation to deliver them. A month after the disaster, production was recovering, and Japan's GDP was expected to return to normal levels within a few quarters.

Larger Disasters in Poorer Countries

While rich countries typically recover rapidly and completely from even large disasters, poor countries fare much worse. The capital stock in a poor country is more easily destroyed, because of weak or unenforced building codes. Repairs are hindered by poorly-functioning financial and government institutions. Bad roads and transportation networks make it difficult to distribute aid, and diseases that would be quickly controlled in a wealthier country instead become health crises. For all of these reasons, the effects on GDP are likely to be much more severe, and much longer lasting, in a poor country.

---

[5] Much of this research is summarized in Eduardo Cavallo, Sebastián Galiani, Ilan Noyand Juan Pantano, "Catastrophic Natural Disasters and Economic Growth," Inter-American Development Bank, June 2010.

A horrific example occurred in January 2010, when Haiti (with a GDP per capita of about $600) was struck by a strong earthquake in a densely populated area. Estimates of the number of deaths range from 50,000 to more than 200,000. And property destruction was estimated at about 100% of Haiti's annual GDP. In spite of international assistance, production was not expected to recover for years.

By contrast, Chile's GDP per capita is about 12 times greater than Haiti's. Just one month after Haiti's earthquake, Chile was hit by an even stronger one, also in a densely populated area. But due to better quality buildings, better transportation, and a more advanced health care system, the death toll was much smaller (about 500). And although Chile's real GDP fell by 2 percent during the quarter of the earthquake, production was back to normal within a few months.

SUMMARY

This chapter discusses how two key macroeconomic aggregates are measured and reported. One is *gross domestic product*—the total value of all final goods and services produced for the marketplace during a given period, within a nation's borders. GDP is a measure of an economy's total production.

Since nominal GDP is measured in current dollars, it changes when either production or prices change. *Real GDP* is nominal GDP adjusted for price changes; it rises only when production rises.

Nominal and real GDP are all reported quarterly, but the numbers are *annualized* (expressed as annual rates of production).

In the *expenditure approach*, GDP is calculated as the sum of spending by households, businesses, government agencies, and foreigners on domestically produced goods and services. The *value-added approach* computes GDP by adding up each firm's contributions to the total product as it is being produced. Value added at each stage of production is the revenue a firm receives minus the cost of the intermediate inputs it uses. The *factor payments approach* sums the wages and salaries, rent, interest, and profit earned by all households. The three approaches reflect three different ways of viewing and measuring GDP.

Real GDP is most useful in the short run, for giving warnings about impending recessions. For other uses, it is plagued by important inaccuracies. It does not fully reflect quality changes or production in the underground economy, and it does not include many types of nonmarket production. GDP is only a very rough measure of economic welfare because it excludes many aspects of the economy that add to or detract from economic well-being.

When real GDP grows, employment tends to rise and—if real GDP grows fast enough—the unemployment rate falls. In the United States, a person is considered unemployed if he or she does not have a job but is actively seeking one. Economists have found it useful to classify unemployment into four different categories. *Frictional unemployment* is short-term unemployment experienced by people between jobs or by those who are just entering the job market. *Seasonal unemployment* is related to changes in the weather, tourist patterns, or other predictable seasonal changes. *Structural unemployment* results from mismatches, in skills or location, between jobs and workers. Finally, *cyclical unemployment* occurs because of the business cycle. Seasonal and frictional unemployment can be beneficial to the economy. Structural and cyclical unemployment, however, create harm to the individuals involved, and the economy as a whole suffers the loss of output that the unemployed could have produced. From a macroeconomic perspective, we say the economy is at *full employment* when there is no cyclical unemployment, even though normal amounts of frictional, seasonal, and structural unemployment remain. At full employment, the economy would be producing its *potential GDP*. When the economy is in a *slump*, we are producing less than our potential output, and unemployment is higher than normal.

Because of measurement problems, economists often prefer to monitor labor market conditions using measures other than the unemployment rate. These include data on employment from the *establishment survey*, and the *employment-population ratio*.

PROBLEM SET

Answers to even-numbered Problems can be found on the text Web site through www.cengagebrain.com

1. Using the expenditure approach, which of the following would be directly counted as part of U.S. GDP? For those that count, state whether the action causes an increase in *C*, *I*, *G*, or *NX*. (If you need to make any special assumptions, state them.)
   a. A new personal computer produced by IBM, which remained unsold at the year's end
   b. A physician's services to a household
   c. Produce bought by a restaurant to serve to customers
   d. The purchase of 1,000 shares of Disney stock
   e. The sale of 50 acres of commercial property
   f. A real estate agent's commission from the sale of property
   g. A transaction in which you clean your roommate's apartment in exchange for his working on your car

h. An Apple iMac computer produced in the United States and purchased by a French citizen
i. The government's Social Security payments to retired people

2. Calculate the total change in a year's U.S. GDP for each of the following scenarios. (Assume that all production takes place in the U.S., unless otherwise stated.)
    a. A family sells a home, without using a broker, for $150,000. They could have rented it on the open market for $700 per month. They buy a 10-year-old condominium for $200,000; the broker's fee on the transaction is 6 percent of the selling price. The condo's owner was formerly renting the unit at $500 per month.
    b. General Electric uses $10 million worth of steel, glass, and plastic to produce its dishwashers. Wages and salaries in the dishwasher division are $40 million; the division's only other expense is $15 million in interest that it pays on its bonds. The division's revenue for the year is $75 million.
    c. On March 31, you decide to stop throwing away $50 a month on convenience store nachos. You buy $200 worth of equipment, cornmeal, and cheese and make your own nachos for the rest of the year. (Include both of your decisions about nachos in determining the impact on GDP.)
    d. You win $25,000 in your state's lottery. Ever the entrepreneur, you decide to open a Ping-Pong ball washing service, buying $15,000 worth of equipment from SpiffyBall Ltd. of Hong Kong and $10,000 from Ball-B-Kleen of Toledo, Ohio.
    e. Tone-Deaf Artists, Inc., produces 100,000 new CDs that it prices at $15 apiece. Ten thousand CDs are sold abroad, but, alas, the rest remain unsold on warehouse shelves.

3. The country of Freedonia uses the same method to calculate the unemployment rate as the U.S. Bureau of Labor Statistics uses. From the following data, compute Freedonia's unemployment rate.

Population	10,000,000
Under 16	3,000,000
Over 16	
In military service	500,000
In hospitals	200,000
In prison	100,000
Worked one hour or more in previous week	4,000,000
Searched for work during previous four weeks	1,000,000

4. Toward the end of this chapter, it was stated that if half of the 8.8 million involuntary part-time workers in August 2011 were counted as unemployed, then the unemployment rate that month would have been 12.0 percent instead of 9.1 percent. Do the necessary calculations to confirm this statement, using the information in Figure 7. (Hint: The size of the labor force will not be affected.)

5. In December 2005, the BLS estimated there were 7.4 million unemployed, 142.8 million employed, 451,000 discouraged workers, and 4.8 million people (including discouraged workers) who were marginally attached to the labor force. What would the unemployment rate have been in December 2005 if it had included among the unemployed:
    a. All officially discouraged workers?
    b. All those who were marginally attached to the labor force? (Hint: Don't forget about how these inclusions would affect the labor force.)

6. Ginny asks, "If I buy a sweater that was produced in Malaysia, why is its purchase price subtracted from GDP?" How should you answer her question? (You may assume, for simplicity, that there was no value added to the sweater in the United States.)

7. Suppose that in one year household consumption falls by $20 billion (compared to the year before), but business firms continue to produce consumer goods at an unchanged rate. If there is no other change affecting real GDP that year, what will happen to total real GDP? What will happen to each of its components?

8. a. The country of Ziponia uses the same method to calculate the unemployment rate as the U.S. Bureau of Labor Statistics uses. From the data below, compute Ziponia's unemployment rate.

Population	60,000
Under 16	9,000
Over 16	
In military service	600
In hospitals	60
In prison	200
Worked one hour or more in previous week	46,000
Searched for work during previous four weeks	2,140
Did not work in previous week but would have taken a job if one were offered	200

    b. How large is Ziponia's labor force?
    c. How many discouraged workers (loosely defined) live in Ziponia?
    d. Not all of Ziponia's citizens are accounted for in part (a). How are the missing citizens classified? Give some examples of what they may be doing.
    e. How many of Ziponia's citizens are not in the labor force?

9. Refer to question 8. The 2,140 Ziponians who searched for work during the previous four weeks included: 54 ski resort employees who lost their winter jobs but expect to get them back in late fall; 200 recent high school graduates; 258 former textile workers who lost their jobs when their employers moved their operations overseas; 143 mothers and 19 fathers who had stayed at home to raise their children but who recently decided to reenter the workforce; 394 high school and college students who want summer jobs; 127 people who live in West Ziponia and lost their jobs when their employers moved operations to East Ziponia, but who are not qualified for the remaining jobs in the west; 110 recent college graduates; and 32 retirees who decided to return to the workforce. The remaining job seekers lost their jobs due to a recession. Use this information to:
   a. Classify the job seekers by their type of unemployment, and calculate how many fell into each category.
   b. Find the frictional, seasonal, structural, and cyclical unemployment rates.

10. The following table shows an estimate of the destruction caused by the terrorist attacks of September 11:

Type of Property	Estimated Loss
World Trade Center Complex buildings	$ 6.7 billion
Contents of buildings in World Trade Center Complex	$ 5.2 billion
Buildings nearby	$ 4.5 billion
Public infrastructure (subway, commuter rail, and utilities)	$ 3.7 billion
Total	**$20.1 billion**

Source: Modified from Jason Bram, James Orr, and Carol Rapaport, "Measuring the Effects of the September 11 Attack on New York City," *Federal Reserve Bank of New York Policy Review,* November 2002.

Use the following two facts (from the Bureau of Economic Analysis) as needed to answer the questions below:

Fact #1: GDP in 2001 was $10 trillion.
Fact #2: Manhattan produces 1.5 percent of the nation's GDP.

   a. Assume that each dollar of destroyed property reduces annual production by 10 cents (a rough estimate of the general impact of capital destruction on GDP), and that none of the destroyed property was replaced over the following 12 months. Estimate the percentage impact on GDP during the 12 months after the attacks due to the physical destruction alone.
   b. Suppose that, in addition to the property destruction, the attack created disruption of economic activity, and that Manhattan's production was cut in half for 2 weeks. Estimate the percentage impact on GDP for the *quarter* due to this disruption alone.
   c. Again, suppose Manhattan's production was cut in half for 2 weeks. Estimate the percentage impact on GDP for the *year* due to this disruption alone.

11. The Bureau of Economic Analysis (BEA) currently treats research and development (R&D) expenses as an *intermediate* good. That is, R&D expenses are assumed to be already included in other goods sold by firms that pay for the R&D. Beginning in 2013, however, the BEA will begin counting R&D spending as investment spending—a final good purchased by the business firms that pay for it. In effect, the BEA will begin treating R&D spending (which creates long-lasting productive knowledge) just like spending on plant and equipment (the purchase of long-lasting physical capital).

   Suppose that in 2013, the BEA decides to *retroactively* revise nominal GDP in 2010 to reflect the new treatment of R&D, and that in 2010, U.S. businesses spent $400 billion on R&D.
   a. By what percentage would private investment spending be greater in 2010 (compared to its official reported number given in the chapter)?
   b. By what percentage would GDP be greater in 2010 (compared to its official reported number given in the chapter)?

More Challenging

12. Suppose, in a given year, someone buys a Ford automobile for $30,000. That same year, Ford produced the car in Michigan, using $10,000 in parts imported from Japan. However, the parts imported from Japan themselves contained $3,000 in components produced in the United States.
   a. By how much does U.S. GDP rise?
   b. Using the expenditure approach, what is the change in each component (C, I, G, and NX) of U.S. GDP?
   c. What is the change in Japan's GDP and each of its components?

13. After the attacks of September 11, 2001, U.S. businesses began to spend more on security, and they continue to do so today. For example, airlines and package delivery services run more background checks on their employees, and office buildings employ more security guards than they did before the attack. What impact have these decisions had on real GDP? (Hint: Is the new spending considered to be purchases of final goods?)

The Price Level and Inflation

About a hundred years ago, you could buy a pound of coffee for 15 cents, see a Broadway play for 40 cents, buy a new suit for $6, and attend a private college for $200 in yearly tuition.[1] Needless to say, the price of each of these items has gone up considerably since then. Microeconomic causes—changes in individual markets—can explain only a tiny fraction of these price changes. For the most part, these price rises came about because of a continually rising **price level**—the average level of prices in the economy.

Price level The average level of prices in the economy.

When the price level rises, the value of the dollar—its purchasing power—falls. And this presents a problem. We measure many economic variables—such as income, production, or the wage rate—in dollars. But over time, how can we keep track of them when our unit of measurement—the dollar—has a changing value? To make sensible comparisons of variables measured in dollars, we must know how the dollar's purchasing power changes from period to period. And this requires us to know how the price level is changing.

In this chapter, we'll discuss how the price level and its rate of change are measured, and some of the difficulties and controversies involved. We'll postpone until later chapters the question of *why* prices change from year to year.

MEASURING THE PRICE LEVEL AND INFLATION

Economists use several different measures of the price level, depending on their purpose. But all of them have one thing in common: They are all calculated and reported as *index numbers*. Because index numbers have some special features, it's worth discussing them more generally before we look specifically at price indexes.

Index Numbers in General

Index A series of numbers used to track a variable's rise or fall over time.

Most measures of the price level are reported in the form of an **index**—a series of numbers, each one representing a different period. Index numbers are meaningful only in a *relative* sense: We compare one period's index number with that of another period and can quickly see which one is larger and by what percentage. But the actual value of an index number for a particular period has no meaning in and of itself.

[1] Scott Derks, ed., *The Value of the Dollar: Prices and Incomes in the United States: 1860–1989* (Detroit, MI: Gale Research Inc., 1994), various pages.

In general, an index number for any measure is calculated as

$$\frac{\text{Value of measure in current period}}{\text{Value of measure in base period}} \times 100.$$

Let's see how index numbers work with a simple example. Suppose we want to measure how violence on TV has changed over time, and we have data on the number of violent acts shown in each of several years. We could then construct a TV-violence index. Our first step would be to choose a *base period*—a period to be used as a benchmark. Let's choose 2000 as our base period, and let's suppose that there were 10,433 violent acts on television in that year. Then our violence index in any current year would be calculated as

$$\frac{\text{Number of violent acts in current year}}{10,433} \times 100.$$

In 2000, the base year, the index will have the value (10,433/10,433) × 100 = 100. Look again at the general formula for index numbers, and you will see that this is always true: *An index will always equal 100 in the base period*.

Now let's calculate the value of our index in another year. If there were 14,534 violent acts in 2009, then the index that year would have the value

$$\frac{14,534}{10,433} \times 100 = 139.3.$$

Index numbers compress and simplify information so that we can see how things are changing at a glance. Our media violence index, for example, tells us at a glance that the number of violent acts in 2009 was 139.3 percent of the number in 2000. Or, more simply, TV violence grew by 39.3 percent between 2000 and 2009.

The Consumer Price Index

The most widely used measure of the price level in the United States is the **Consumer Price Index (CPI)**. This index, which is designed to track the prices paid by the typical consumer, is compiled and reported by the Bureau of Labor Statistics (BLS).

Measuring the prices paid by the typical consumer is not easy. The BLS must solve a number of conceptual problems before it begins (such as deciding which items to include and what weight to give to each item). Then there are a host of practical problems. Let's discuss how all these problems are dealt with in the CPI.

Which Items to Include?

The goal of the CPI is to track the prices paid by *consumers*, and no one else. So, as a start, the CPI includes the part of GDP that consumers purchase as final users (new clothes, new furniture, new cars, haircuts, or restaurant meals). But it also includes two types of goods and services that consumers buy, even though they are *not* part of GDP: (1) household purchases of used goods such as used cars or used computers and (2) household purchases of imports from other countries—French cheese, Japanese cars, and Mexican tomatoes.

The CPI does *not* include goods and services purchased by anyone other than consumers. It leaves out purchases by businesses (for capital equipment, raw materials, or wholesale goods). It leaves out goods and services purchased by government agencies (military equipment and the services of police officers and public school teachers). And it leaves out goods and services that are purchased by other countries (U.S. exports).

Consumer Price Index An index of the cost, through time, of a market basket of goods purchased by a typical household.

Finally, remember that the CPI tracks the prices of goods and services only. Consumers also buy assets, such as stocks, bonds, and homes. The prices paid for these assets are *not* included in the CPI. For housing, the CPI (like GDP) includes the price of housing *services* rather than the value of the home or apartment itself. So for rental units, the CPI tracks the average rent people pay; for owner-occupied units, the CPI uses the rent that owners *would* pay if they had to rent their homes instead of owning them.

How Much Weight for Each Item?

In any given month, different prices will change by different amounts. The average price of doctors' visits might rise by 1 percent, the price of jeans might rise by a tenth of a percent, the price of milk might fall by half a percent, and so on. When prices change at different rates, and when some are rising while others are falling, how can we track the change in the *average* price level? It would be a mistake to use a simple average of all prices, adding them up and dividing by the number of goods. A proper measure must recognize that we spend very little of our incomes on some goods—such as Tabasco sauce—and much more on others—like gasoline or rent.

The CPI's approach is to track the cost of the *CPI market basket*—the collection of goods and services that the typical consumer buys. If the market basket's cost rises by 10 percent over some period, then the price level, as reported by the CPI, will rise by 10 percent. This way, goods and services that are relatively unimportant in the typical consumer's budget will have little weight in the CPI. Tabasco sauce could triple in price and have no noticeable impact on the cost of the complete market basket. Goods that are more important—such as gas or rent—will have more weight.

To determine the CPI market basket, the BLS surveys thousands of families every couple of years, and records their spending in detail. It uses these spending patterns to construct a market basket containing thousands of different goods and services, with each one weighted according to its relative importance in the average family's budget.[2]

Figure 1 shows the broadest categories of the CPI market basket, and the proportion of total spending on each one in December 2010. For example, all the items in the category "food and beverages" together made up 14.8 percent of the typical consumer's spending, while all of the items included in "housing" amounted to 41.5 percent. The communication category—amounting to 3.3 percent—includes phone and Internet service, as well as computer hardware and software.

Tracking and Reporting the Price Level

Each month, hundreds of BLS employees visit thousands of stores, gas stations, medical offices, and apartments across the country. Their job is to record the prices of specific goods and services in the market basket—about 80,000 price quotes in all. All this information is fed into a central database, and used to determine the new cost of the CPI market basket for that month.

---

[2] More specifically, the Bureau of Labor Statistics compiles two different types of market baskets to reflect the spending habits of two different types of people: (1) "All Urban Workers," resulting in the CPI-U; and (2) "Urban Wage Earners and Clerical Workers," resulting in the CPI-W. The CPI-U is the index most commonly reported and followed in the media, and unless otherwise noted, it is used throughout this chapter.

FIGURE 1	Broad Categories and Relative Importance in the CPI, December 2010

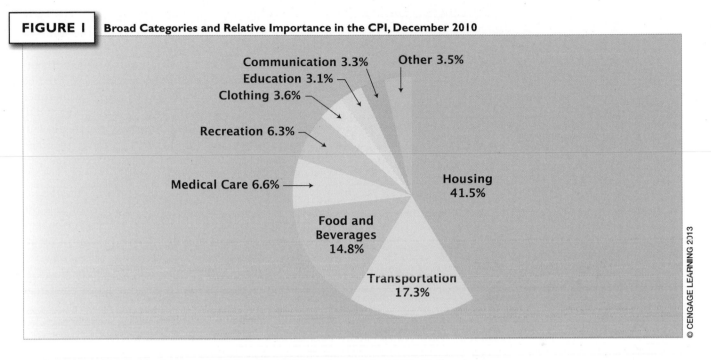

© CENGAGE LEARNING 2013

In recent years, the base period for the CPI has been July 1983. Following our general formula for price indexes, the CPI is calculated as follows:

$$\text{CPI} = \frac{\text{Cost of market basket in current period}}{\text{Cost of market basket in July 1983}} \times 100.$$

This simple formula shows us what the CPI tracks: the changing cost of a basket of goods.[3] In July 1983, the value of the CPI is 100. In any month in which the basket cost more than July 1983, the CPI's value is greater than 100. For periods (before July 1983) in which the basket's cost was lower, the CPI is less than 100. The appendix to this chapter provides a more detailed example of how the CPI is calculated.

Table 1 shows the actual value of the CPI for December of selected years. Because it is reported in index-number form, we can easily see how much the price level has changed over different time intervals. In December 2000, for example, the CPI had a value of 174.0, telling us that the typical market basket in that year cost 74 percent more than it would have cost in the July 1983 base period. In December 1970, the CPI was 39.8, so the cost of the market basket in that year was only 39.8 percent of its cost in July 1983.

From Price Index to Inflation Rate

The Consumer Price Index is a measure of the price *level* in the economy. The **inflation rate** measures how fast the price level is changing. More specifically, it tells us the percentage change in the price level from one period to the next. For example, let's calculate the inflation rate for the year 2010. Table 1 tells us that, from December 2009 to December 2010, the CPI rose from 215.9 to 219.2. Therefore, the annual inflation rate for 2010 was $(219.2 - 215.9)/215.9 = 0.0153$, or 1.5 percent.

Inflation rate The percentage change in the price level from one period to the next.

[3] The formula, however, ignores another feature of the CPI: the periodic updating of items and their relative importance in the CPI market basket. Each time the market basket is updated, the BLS splices a new CPI series onto the old one. But it retains July 1983 as the base period for setting the index numbers, so that the CPI in July 1983 continues to be 100.

TABLE 1

Consumer Price Index, December, Selected Years, 1970–2010

Year	Consumer Price Index (December)
1970	39.8
1980	86.3
1990	133.8
2000	174.0
2005	196.8
2006	201.8
2007	210.0
2008	210.2
2009	215.9
2010	219.2

Source: Bureau of Labor Statistics, Consumer Price Index—All Urban Consumers (*www.bls.gov*). Rounded to nearest tenth of a percent.

Deflation A *decrease* in the price level from one period to the next.

The CPI is reported each month, seasonally adjusted. The CPI's *growth rate*—the rate of inflation—is reported each month as well. Sometimes the growth rate is stated in simple percentage terms for that month. When it is reported as an annual rate, the one-month rate is sometimes *annualized* (as is done with the quarterly GDP growth rate). But more commonly, the media will report the annual inflation rate as the percentage change in that month's CPI from its value *one year earlier*.

Figure 2 shows the annual rate of inflation, as measured by the CPI, since 1950. For each year, the inflation rate is calculated as the percentage change in the CPI from December of the previous year to December of that year. Whenever the price level rises, as it usually does, the inflation rate will be positive. When the price level falls, as it did during the Great Depression (not shown) and in 1954 (shown in Figure 2), we have negative inflation, which is called **deflation.** As you can see in the figure, the U.S. inflation rate was low in the 1950s, began to creep up in the 1960s, then spiked upward in the 1970s and early 1980s, and has been low ever since. In later chapters, you will learn what causes the inflation rate to rise and fall, and some of the reasons it has behaved as it has over the past several decades.

FIGURE 2 **The Rate of Inflation Using the Consumer Price Index, 1950–2010**

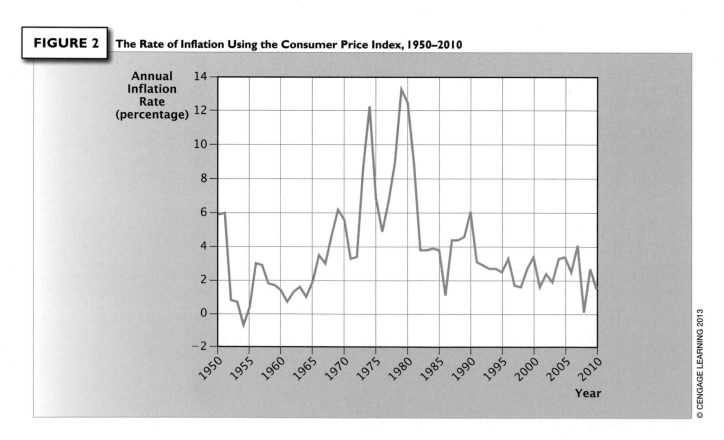

© CENGAGE LEARNING 2013

How the CPI Is Used

The CPI is the most important and widely used measure of prices in the United States. It is used in three ways:

1. *As a Policy Target.* In the introductory macroeconomics chapter, we saw that price stability—or a low inflation rate—is one of the nation's important macroeconomic goals. One of the measures used to gauge our success in achieving low inflation is the CPI.

2. *To Index Payments.* An **indexed payment** is one that is periodically adjusted so that it rises and falls by the same percentage as a price index. Indexing a payment makes up for any loss of purchasing power caused by inflation. Ideally, indexing would adjust a nominal payment by just enough to keep its purchasing power unchanged. In the United States, more than 60 million Social Security recipients and another 5 million government and military retirees have their benefit or pension payments indexed to the CPI. More than 2 million workers have labor contracts that index their wages to the CPI. The U.S. income tax is indexed as well: The threshold income levels—at which people move into higher tax brackets—rise along with the CPI. And the government sells bonds that are indexed to the CPI. The owner of an indexed bond receives a payment each year to make up for the loss of purchasing power when the CPI rises.

   > **Indexed payment** A payment that is periodically adjusted in proportion with a price index.

3. *To Translate from Nominal to Real Values.* In order to compare economic values from different periods, we must translate *nominal variables,* measured in the number of dollars, into *real variables,* which are adjusted for the change in the dollar's purchasing power. The CPI is often used for this translation. Since calculating real variables is one of the most important uses of the CPI, let's discuss this in more detail.

Real Variables and Adjustment for Inflation

Suppose that from December 2010 to December 2015, your nominal wage—what you are paid in dollars—rises from $15 to $30 per hour. Will you be better off? That depends. You will be earning twice as many dollars. But you should care not about how many green pieces of paper you earn, but how many goods and services you can buy with that paper. How, then, can we tell what happens to your purchasing power? By focusing not on the *nominal wage* (the number of *dollars* you earn) but on the *real wage* (the *purchasing power* of your wage). To track your real wage, we need to look at the number of dollars you earn *relative to the price level.*

In government reports, the CPI is usually the price index used to calculate the real hourly wage rate. The real-wage formula is as follows:

$$\text{Real wage in any year} = \frac{\text{Nominal wage in that year}}{\text{CPI in that year}} \times 100.$$

To see that this formula makes sense, let's go back to our fictional example: From 2010 to 2015, your nominal wage doubles from $15 to $30 per hour. Now, suppose the price of everything that you buy doubles at the same time. It is easy to see that in this case, your purchasing power would remain unchanged. And that is just what

⚠ DANGEROUS CURVES

Rising prices versus rising inflation People often confuse the statement "prices are rising" with the statement "inflation is rising," but they do not mean the same thing. Remember that the inflation rate is the *rate of change* of the price level. To have rising inflation, the price level must be rising by a greater and greater percentage each period. But we can also have rising prices and *falling* inflation. For example, in 2010, the CPI rose: "Prices were rising." But they rose by a smaller percentage over 2010 than they rose in 2009, so "inflation was falling"—from 2.7 percent in 2009 to 1.5 percent in 2010.

our formula tells us: If prices double, the CPI doubles as well. With 2010 as our base year, the CPI would increase from 100 in 2010, to 200 in the year 2015. The *real* wage would be ($15/100) × 100 = $15 in 2010, and ($30/200) × 100 = $15 in 2015. The real wage would remain unchanged.

Now suppose that prices doubled over this period but your nominal wage remains unchanged at $15. In this case, your purchasing power would be cut in half. You'd have the same number of dollars, but each one would buy half as much as it did before. Our formula gives us a real wage of ($15/100) × 100 = $15 in 2010 and ($15/200) × 100 = $7.50 in 2015. The real wage falls by half.

Now look at Table 2, which shows the median weekly earnings of wage and salary workers over the past three decades. In the first two columns you can see that the average worker earned $269 per week in 1980, and almost three times as much—$751—in 2010. Does this mean the average worker was almost three times better off in 2010 than in 1980? In *dollars*, the answer is clearly yes. But what about in *purchasing power*? Or, using the new terminology you've learned: What happened to *real earnings* over this period?

Let's see. From 1980 to 2010, the CPI rose from 86.3 to 219.2. Using our formula, we find that:

$$\text{Real earnings in 1980} = \frac{\$269}{86.3} \times 100 = \$312.$$

$$\text{Real earnings in 2010} = \frac{\$751}{219.2} \times 100 = \$343$$

Thus, although the average worker earned almost three times more *dollars* in 2010 than in 1980, when we use the CPI as our measure of prices, his or her purchasing power rose by much less. Specifically, the percentage increase in *real* weekly earnings was ($343 − $312) / $312 = .099 or 9.9 percent.

TABLE 2

Nominal and Real Weekly Earnings (December of Each Year)

Year	Nominal Weekly Earnings	CPI	Real Weekly Earnings (1983 dollars)
1980	$269	86.3	$312
1985	$348	109.3	$318
1990	$417	133.8	$312
1995	$482	153.5	$314
2000	$581	174.0	$334
2005	$658	196.8	$334
2010	$751	219.2	$343

Source: Bureau of Labor Statistics, Statistical Tables, *http://www.bls.gov*. Earnings and CPI data for 4th quarter and December of each year, respectively. Earnings: Median usual weekly earnings of wage and salary workers employed full-time. CPI: CPI-U (All Urban Consumers).

© AXL/SHUTTERSTOCK.COM

Important Provisos about Real Earnings

Our calculations just showed that real earnings increased by only about 10 percent over 30 years—not much at all. But this is an *underestimate* of how much pay rose over this period, for two reasons.

First, over the past three decades, an increasing share of worker compensation has been nonwage benefits, such as employer contributions to retirement accounts and health insurance. By 2008, these benefits reached more than 30 percent of total compensation, but they are not included in the earnings in Table 2. If benefits were included, earnings would have risen by more over the three decades.

Second, as we'll discuss later in this chapter, changes in the CPI *overestimate inflation*. Over a long time period such as three decades, this can make a big difference. A more accurate measure of the price level would show a rise in real earnings (even excluding benefits) over this period.

Still, while the adjustment for inflation in Table 2 is imperfect, no one would argue that we would get a clearer picture of worker pay by leaving the adjustment out. Using nominal earnings, we would erroneously conclude that pay (excluding benefits) almost tripled during this period. This is *not* a meaningful description of what happened. The important point to remember here is that

when comparing dollar values over time, we care not about the number of dollars, but about their purchasing power. Thus, we translate nominal values into real values using the formula

$$\text{Real value} = \frac{\text{Nominal value}}{\text{Price index}} \times 100.$$

This formula, often using the CPI as the price index, is how most real values are calculated in government reports. But there is one important exception: To calculate real GDP, the government uses a different procedure, to which we now turn.

Real GDP and the GDP Price Index

In the previous chapter, we discussed the difference between nominal GDP and real GDP. After reading this chapter, you might think that real GDP is calculated just like the real hourly wage rate or real earnings: dividing nominal GDP by the Consumer Price Index. But the Consumer Price Index is *not* used to calculate real GDP. Instead, the Bureau of Economic Analysis (BEA) calculates real GDP directly, by choosing a base year (currently 2005) and valuing the quantities of each good produced at the prices it would sell for in the base year. The BEA also reports (separately) a price index—called the **GDP price index**—that helps economists track the average price of goods and services included in GDP.

GDP price index An index of the price level for all final goods and services included in GDP.

The most important differences between the CPI and the GDP price index are in the types of goods and services covered by each index. First, the GDP price index *includes* some prices that the CPI ignores. In particular, while the CPI tracks only the prices of goods bought by American *consumers,* the GDP price index must also include the prices of goods purchased by the government, investment goods purchased by businesses, and exports, which are purchased by those in other countries.

Second, the GDP price index *excludes* some prices that are part of the CPI. In particular, the GDP price index leaves out used goods and imports, both of which are included in the CPI. This makes sense, because while used goods and imports are part of the typical consumer's market basket, they do not contribute to current U.S. GDP.

We can summarize the chief difference between the CPI and the GDP price index this way:

> *The GDP price index measures the prices of all goods and services that are included in U.S. GDP, while the CPI measures the prices of all goods and services bought by U.S. households.*

THE COSTS OF INFLATION

A high rate of inflation—whether it is measured by the CPI or the GDP price index—is never welcome news. What's so bad about inflation? As we've seen, it certainly makes your task as an economics student more difficult: Rather than taking nominal variables at face value, you must do those troublesome calculations to convert them into real variables.

But inflation causes much more trouble than this. It can impose costs on society and on each of us individually. Yet when most people are asked *what* the cost of inflation is, they come up with an incorrect answer.

The Inflation Myth

Most people think that inflation, merely by making goods and services more expensive, erodes the purchasing power of our incomes. The reason for this belief is easy to see: The higher the price level, the fewer goods and services a given number of dollars will buy. It stands to reason, then, that inflation—which raises prices—must be destroying our purchasing power. Right?

Actually, this statement is mostly wrong.

To see why, remember that every market transaction involves *two* parties—a buyer and a seller. When a price rises, buyers of that good must pay more, but sellers get more revenue when they sell it. The loss in buyers' purchasing power is matched by the rise in sellers' purchasing power. Inflation may *redistribute* purchasing power, but it does not directly change the *average* purchasing power in the economy, when we include both buyers and sellers in the average.

In fact, most people in the economy participate on both sides of the market. On the one hand, they are consumers—as when they shop for food or clothing or furniture. On the other hand, they work in business firms that *sell* products and may benefit (in the form of higher wages or higher profits) when their firms' revenues rise. Thus, when prices rise, a particular person may find that her purchasing power has either risen or fallen, depending on whether she is affected more as a seller or as a buyer. But regardless of the outcome for individuals, our conclusion remains the same:

> *Inflation can redistribute purchasing power from one group to another, but it does not directly decrease the average real income in the economy.*

Why, then, do people continue to believe that inflation robs the average citizen of real income? Largely because real incomes sometimes do decline—for *other* reasons. Inflation—while not the *cause* of the decline—will often be the *mechanism* that brings it about. Just as we often blame the messenger for bringing bad news, so too we often blame inflation for lowering our purchasing power when the real cause lies elsewhere.

An Example: Purchasing Power and Inflation in the 1970s

Let's consider an example. During the late 1970s, the typical American worker—as well as many small-business owners and corporate shareholders—saw their real incomes decline. What was the cause?

There were several reasons, but one of the most important was the dramatic rise in the price of imported oil—from $3 per barrel in 1973 to $34 in 1981, an increase of more than 1,000 percent. The higher price for oil meant that oil-exporting countries, like Saudi Arabia, Kuwait, and Iraq, got more goods and services for each barrel of oil they supplied to the rest of the world, including the United States. But with these countries claiming more of the output of the United States, less remained for the typical American. That is, the typical American family had to suffer a decline in real income. As always, a rise in price shifted income from buyers to sellers. But in this case, the sellers (of oil) were in other countries, while the buyers were Americans. Thus, the rise in the price of foreign oil caused average purchasing power in the United States to decline.

But what was the mechanism that brought about the decline? Since real income is equal to (Nominal income/Price index) × 100, it can decrease through a fall in the numerator (nominal income) or a rise in the denominator (the price index). The decline in real income in the 1970s came entirely from an increase in the denominator.

Look back at Figure 2. You can see that this period of declining real income in the United States was also a period of unusually high inflation; at its peak in 1979, the inflation rate exceeded 13 percent. As a result, most people blamed *inflation* for their loss of purchasing power. But inflation was not the cause; it was just the *mechanism*. The cause was a change in the terms of trade between the United States and the oil-exporting countries—a change that resulted in higher oil prices and lower real incomes in the United States.

To summarize, the common idea that inflation imposes a cost on society by directly decreasing average purchasing power is incorrect. But inflation *does* impose costs on society, as the next section shows.

The Redistributive Cost of Inflation

One cost of inflation is that it often redistributes purchasing power *within* society. But because the winners and losers are chosen haphazardly—rather than by conscious social policy—the redistribution of purchasing power is not generally desirable. In some cases, the shift in purchasing power is downright perverse—harming the needy and helping those who are already well off.

How does inflation sometimes redistribute real income? An increase in the price level reduces the purchasing power of any payment that is specified in *nominal* terms. For example, some workers have contracts that set their nominal wage for two or three years, regardless of any future inflation. The nationally set minimum wage, too, is set for several years and specified in nominal dollars. Under these circumstances, inflation can harm ordinary workers, since it erodes the purchasing power of their prespecified nominal wage. Real income is redistributed from these workers to their employers, who benefit by paying a lower real wage.

But the effect can also work the other way: benefiting ordinary households and harming businesses. For example, many homeowners sign fixed-dollar mortgage agreements with a bank. These are promises to pay the bank the same nominal sum each month. Inflation can reduce the *real* value of these payments, thus redistributing purchasing power away from the bank and toward the average homeowner.

In general,

inflation can shift purchasing power away from those who are awaiting future payments specified in dollars, and toward those who are obligated to make such payments.

But does inflation *always* redistribute income from one party in a contract to another? Actually, no; if the inflation is *expected* by both parties, it should not redistribute income. The next section explains why.

Expected Inflation Does *Not* Shift Purchasing Power

Suppose a labor union is negotiating a 3-year contract with an employer, and both sides agree that each year, workers should get a 3 percent increase in their *real wage*. Labor contracts, like most other contracts, are usually specified in nominal terms: The firm will agree to give workers so many additional *dollars per hour* each year. If neither side anticipates any inflation, they should simply negotiate a 3 percent *nominal* wage hike. With an unchanged price level, the *real* wage would then also rise by the desired 3 percent.

But suppose instead that both sides anticipate 10 percent inflation each year for the next three years. Then, they must agree to *more* than a 3 percent nominal wage increase in order to raise the real wage by 3 percent. How much more?

We can answer this question with a simple mathematical rule, which we'll call the *approximation rule*:

Over any period, the percentage change in a real value (%ΔReal) is approximately equal to the percentage change in the associated nominal value (%ΔNominal) minus the percentage change in the price level (%ΔP):

$$\%\Delta Real = \%\Delta Nominal - \%\Delta P$$

Over each year, if the inflation rate is 10 percent and the real wage is to rise by 3 percent, then the change in the nominal wage must (approximately) satisfy the equation

$$3 \text{ percent} = \%\ \Delta\ \text{Nominal} - 10 \text{ percent}$$
$$\%\ \Delta\ \text{Nominal} = 13 \text{ percent.}$$

The required nominal wage hike is 13 percent.

You can see that as long as both sides correctly anticipate the inflation, and no one stops them from negotiating a 13 percent nominal wage hike, inflation will *not* affect either party in real terms:

If inflation is correctly anticipated, and if both parties take it into account, then inflation will not redistribute purchasing power.

We come to a similar conclusion about contracts between lenders and borrowers. When you lend someone money, you receive a reward—an interest payment—for letting that person use your money instead of spending it yourself. The annual *interest rate* is the interest payment divided by the amount of money you have lent. For example, if you lend someone $1,000 and receive back $1,040 one year later, then your interest is $40, and the annual interest *rate* on the loan is $40/$1,000 = 0.04, or 4 percent.

But there are actually *two* interest rates associated with every loan. One is the **nominal interest rate**—the percentage increase in the lender's *dollars* each year from making the loan. The other is the **real interest rate**—the percentage increase in the lender's *purchasing power* each year from making the loan. It is the *real* rate—the change in purchasing power—that lenders and borrowers should care about.

In the absence of inflation, real and nominal interest rates would always be equal. A 4 percent increase in the lender's *dollars* would always imply a 4 percent increase in her purchasing power. But if there is inflation, it will reduce the purchasing power of the money paid back. Does this mean that inflation redistributes purchasing

Nominal interest rate The annual percent increase in a lender's dollars from making a loan.

Real interest rate The annual percent increase in a lender's purchasing power from making a loan.

power? Not if the inflation is correctly anticipated, and if both parties can take it into account when the loan is negotiated.

For example, suppose both parties anticipate annual inflation of 5 percent and want to arrange a contract whereby the lender will be paid a 4 percent *real* interest rate each year. What *nominal* interest rate should they choose? Since the annual interest rate is the *percentage change* in the lender's funds over the year, we can use our approximation rule,

$$\%\Delta \text{ Real} = \%\Delta \text{ Nominal} - \%\Delta \ P.$$

For each year of the loan, this becomes

$\%\Delta$ in lender's purchasing power = $\%\Delta$ in lender's dollars − Rate of inflation

or

Real interest rate = Nominal interest rate − Rate of inflation.

In our example, where we want the real interest rate to equal 4 percent per year when the inflation rate is 5 percent per year, we must solve the following equation:

$$4 \text{ percent} = \text{Nominal interest rate} - 5 \text{ percent}$$

giving us:

$$\text{Nominal interest rate} = 9 \text{ percent}.$$

Once again, we see that as long as both parties correctly anticipate the inflation rate, and face no restrictions on contracts (that is, they are free to set the nominal interest rate at 9 percent), then no one gains or loses.

When inflation is *not* correctly anticipated, however, our conclusion is very different.

Unexpected Inflation *Does* Shift Purchasing Power

Suppose that, expecting no inflation, you agree to lend money at a 4 percent nominal interest rate for one year. You and the borrower think that this will translate into a 4 percent real rate. But it turns out you are both wrong: The price level actually rises by 3 percent, so the *real* interest rate ends up being 4 percent − 3 percent = 1 percent. As a lender, you have given up the use of your money for the year, expecting to be rewarded with a 4 percent increase in purchasing power. But you get only a 1 percent increase. *Unexpected* inflation has led to a better deal for your borrower and a worse deal for you, the lender.

That will not make you, as lender, happy. But it could be even worse. Suppose the inflation rate is higher—say, 6 percent. Then your real interest rate ends up at 4 percent − 6 percent = −2 percent, a negative real interest rate. You get back *less* in purchasing power than you lend out. You are *paying* (in purchasing power) for the privilege of lending out your money. The borrower is *rewarded* (in purchasing power) for borrowing!

Negative real interest rates like this are not just a theoretical possibility. In the late 1970s, when inflation was higher than expected for several years in a row, many borrowers ending up "paying" negative real interest rates to lenders.

Now, let's consider one more possibility: Expected inflation is 6 percent, so you negotiate a 10 percent nominal rate, thinking this will translate to a 4 percent real rate. But the actual inflation rate turns out to be zero, so the real interest rate is 10 percent − 0 percent = 10 percent. In this case, inflation turns out to be *less* than expected, so the *real* interest rate is higher than either of you anticipated. The borrower is harmed and you (the lender) benefit.

These examples apply, more generally, to any agreement on future payments: to a worker waiting for a wage payment and the employer who has promised to pay it; to a doctor who has sent out a bill and the patient who has not yet paid it; or to a supplier who has delivered goods and his customer who hasn't yet paid for them.

> *When inflationary expectations are inaccurate, purchasing power is shifted between those obliged to make future payments and those waiting to be paid. An inflation rate higher than expected harms those awaiting payment and benefits the payers; an inflation rate lower than expected harms the payers and benefits those awaiting payment.*

The Resource Cost of Inflation

In addition to its possible redistribution of income, inflation imposes another cost upon society. To cope with inflation, we are forced to use up time and other resources as we go about our daily economic activities (shopping, selling, saving) that we could otherwise have devoted to productive activities. Thus, inflation imposes an *opportunity cost* on society as a whole and on each of its members:

> *When people must spend time and other resources coping with inflation, they pay an opportunity cost—they sacrifice the goods and services those resources could have produced instead.*

Resource Costs for Consumers

Let's first consider the resources used up by *consumers* to cope with inflation. Suppose you shop for clothes twice a year. You've discovered that both The Gap and J. Crew sell clothing of similar quality and have similar service, and you naturally want to shop at the one with the lower prices. If there is no inflation, your task is easy: You shop first at The Gap and then at J. Crew; thereafter, you rely on your memory to determine which is less expensive.

With inflation, however, things are more difficult. Suppose you find that prices at J. Crew are higher than you remember them to be at The Gap. It may be that J. Crew is the more expensive store, or it may be that prices have risen at *both* stores. How can you tell? Only a trip back to The Gap will answer the question—a trip that will cost you extra time and trouble. If prices are rising very rapidly, you may have to visit both stores on the same day to be sure which one is cheaper.

Now, multiply this time and trouble by all the different types of shopping you must do on a regular or occasional basis—for groceries, an apartment, a car, concert tickets, restaurant meals, and more. Inflation can make you use up valuable time—time you could have spent earning income or enjoying leisure activities. True, if you shop for some of these items on the Internet, you can compare prices in less time, but not zero time. And most shopping for food, clothing, and many other goods is *not* done over the Internet.

Resource Costs for Producers

Inflation also forces *producers* to use up resources. First, remember that producers of goods and services are also buyers of resources and intermediate goods. They, too, must do comparison shopping when there is inflation, which uses up hired labor time. Second, each time sellers raise prices, labor is used to enter the new prices into a computer scanning system, to update the information on a Web page, or to change the prices on advertising brochures or menus.

Resource Costs for Wealth Management

Finally, inflation can make people use up resources managing their financial affairs. When there is little or no inflation, we don't mind holding cash in our wallets or our funds in a zero interest-rate checking account. Our money will lose little or none of its purchasing power. But when the inflation rate is high, we'll try to keep our funds in accounts that pay high nominal interest rates, in order to preserve our purchasing power. And we'll try to keep as little as possible in cash or in low-interest checking accounts. Of course, this means more frequent trips to the ATM to get cash when we need it, or more time spent managing our funds online.

* * *

All of these additional activities—inspecting prices at several stores or Web sites, changing prices in stores, going back and forth to the automatic teller machine—use up time and other resources. From society's point of view, these resources could have been used to produce *other* goods and services that we'd enjoy.

You may not have thought much about the resource cost of inflation because in recent years, U.S. inflation has been so low—averaging about 2.4 percent per year from 2000 to 2010. Such a low rate of inflation is often called *creeping inflation;* from week to week or month to month, the price level creeps up so slowly that we hardly notice the change. The cost of coping with creeping inflation is negligible. And (as you'll see in a later chapter) low, creeping inflation may actually be good for the economy.

But it has not always been this way. Three times during the last 50 years, we have had double-digit inflation: about 14 percent during 1947–48, 12 percent in 1974, and 13 percent during 1979 and 1980. Going back further, the annual inflation rate reached almost 20 percent during World War I and rose above 25 percent during the Civil War.

And as serious as these episodes of American inflation have been, they pale in comparison to the experiences of other countries. In the 1980s, several South American countries experienced inflation greater than 1,000 percent per year. In Germany during the 1920s, the inflation rate reached thousands of percent per *month*. And a couple of chapters ago, we noted Zimbabwe's astounding inflation rate in late-2008, where prices were doubling every day, rising at an annual rate of 89.7 sextillion percent. (Flip back to the first macro chapter if you want to remind yourself how many zeros are in that number.)

When inflation reaches extremely high rates like these, normal economic life breaks down. No one wants to hold the national currency—or even accept it as payment—because it loses its value so rapidly. For some transactions, people will use a foreign currency, such as the U.S. dollar. But because there are insufficient quantities of foreign currency available in the country, most people are forced to barter—trading goods for goods rather than goods for money. Buying and selling becomes so inefficient and time consuming that production and living standards plummet.

IS THE CPI ACCURATE?

The Bureau of Labor Statistics spends millions of dollars each year gathering data to ensure that its measure of inflation is accurate. It is a highly professional agency, and deserves high praise for keeping its measurement honest and free of political manipulation. Nevertheless, conceptual problems and resource limitations make the CPI fall short of the ideal measure of inflation. Economists—even those who work in the BLS—widely agree that the CPI overstates the U.S. inflation rate. This is often called the *upward bias* of the CPI.

Sources of Bias in the CPI

There are several reasons for the upward bias in the CPI.

Substitution Bias

Until recently, the CPI almost completely ignored a general principle of consumer behavior: People tend to *substitute* goods that have become relatively cheaper in place of goods that have become relatively more expensive. For example, in the seven years from 1973 to 1980, the retail price of oil-related products—like gasoline and home heating oil—increased by more than 300 percent, while the prices of most other goods and services rose by less than 100 percent. As a result, people found ways to conserve on oil products. They joined car pools, used public transportation, insulated their homes, and in many cases moved closer to their workplaces to shorten their commutes. Yet throughout this period, the CPI basket—based on a survey of buying patterns in 1972–73—assumed that consumers were buying unchanged quantities of oil products.

The treatment of oil products is an example of a more general problem that has plagued the CPI for decades. Until recently, the CPI assumed that consumers bought unchanging *quantities* of each good or service for ten years—the same quantities they were purchasing during the once-every-ten-year household survey used to determine the typical consumer's market basket. So by the end of each 10-year period, the CPI's assumptions about spending habits could be far off the mark, as they were in the case of oil in the 1970s.

The BLS has *partially* fixed this problem, in two ways. First, beginning in 2002, it began updating the quantities in its market basket with a new household survey every *two* years instead of every ten years. This is widely considered an important improvement in CPI measurement.

Second, since 1999, the CPI has taken account of *some* changes in quantities when people substitute cheaper items for more expensive ones. For example, suppose that over a particular month, the price of McIntosh apples rises while the price of Red Delicious apples remains unchanged. The CPI assumes that people will buy fewer McIntosh and more Red Delicious apples, rather than waiting for the next survey of consumer spending habits to register the change.

However, this is only a partial fix. The CPI still only recognizes the possibility of such substitution *within* narrow categories of goods and not *among* them. So if, for example, the price of apples rises relative to the price of oranges, the quantities of apples and oranges in the market basket are assumed to remain fixed, even though in reality people will buy fewer apples and more oranges. Apples are then given too much weight (and oranges too little weight) in the CPI, at least until the next survey of spending habits, two years later.

> *Although the BLS has partially fixed the problem, the CPI still suffers from substitution bias. That is, categories of goods whose prices are rising most rapidly are overweighted in the CPI market basket and categories of goods whose prices are rising most slowly are underweighted.*

New Technologies

New technologies are another source of upward bias in the CPI. One problem is that goods using new technologies are introduced into the BLS market basket only after a lag. These goods often drop rapidly in price after they are introduced, helping to balance out price rises in other goods. By excluding a category of goods whose prices are dropping, the CPI overstates the overall rate of inflation. For example, even though many consumers were buying and using cell phones throughout the 1990s, they were not included in the BLS basket of goods until 1998. As a result, the CPI missed the rapid decline in the price of cell phones. Now that the market basket of the typical consumer is updated every 2 years instead of every 10, this source of bias has been reduced but not completely eliminated.

But there is another issue with new technologies: They often offer consumers a lower-cost alternative for obtaining the same service. For example, services such as Netflix have dramatically lowered the cost of entertainment, by offering new, cheaper alternatives to going out to see movies. This should have registered as a drop in the price of "seeing movies." But the CPI does not have any good way to measure this reduction in the cost of watching a movie. Instead, it treats Netflix as an entirely separate service.

> *The CPI excludes new products that tend to drop in price when they first come on the market. When those products are included, the CPI regards them as entirely separate from existing goods and services, instead of recognizing that they lower the cost of obtaining a given service.*

Changes in Quality

Many products are improving over time. Cars are much more reliable than they used to be and require much less routine maintenance. They have features like air bags and antilock brakes that were unknown in the early 1980s. The BLS struggles to deal with these changes. As far back as 1967, it has recognized that when the price of a car rises, some of that price hike is not really inflation, but instead the result of charging more because the consumer is *getting* more. In recent years, the BLS has adopted some routine statistical procedures to automatically adjust price changes for quality improvements for certain goods, such as personal computers, televisions, and clothing.

And in 1997, it introduced a major change in its treatment of health care costs. Before then, the CPI would track the price of individual health care components, such as "a night in the hospital" or "a post-surgery checkup." But after 1997, it began tracking the overall cost of treating specific diseases or conditions. Thus, the introduction of a new type of heart surgery that requires fewer days of hospitalization (and no change in other inputs) would be recorded as a *decrease* in the price of heart surgery.

But most goods and services do not get this special treatment. There is no explicit recognition that many medical treatments are more *effective* at prolonging life and health (aside from reducing hospital stays or doctor visits), that home power tools are safer, and so on.

Take the Internet. Every year, it offers more information and entertainment content, a greater number of retailers from which to buy things, and faster and more intelligent search engines to help you find it all. Yet, the Internet—which was introduced into the CPI in 1998—has been treated as a service whose quality has not changed. If the price of Internet service rises, the CPI considers this as pure inflation rather than paying more to *get* more. And if the price stays the same, the CPI ignores the *decrease* in the cost per unit of available content and treats the price as unchanged.

> *The CPI fails to fully account for quality improvements in the goods and services in its market basket and, therefore, overestimates how fast the price of the basket is rising.*

Growth in Discounting

When a Wal-Mart opens up, many people begin to shop there. And for good reason: Prices at Wal-Mart are substantially lower than at other stores. For example, identical food items cost between 15 and 25 percent less at a Wal-Mart than at the typical supermarket (unless the supermarket has to compete with a nearby Wal-Mart).

The BLS recognizes that people shop at Wal-Mart, and it tracks changes in the prices of items sold there. But it fails to register a drop in prices when a new Wal-Mart first opens, and people can suddenly buy the same goods for less. Wal-Mart and other discount chains have expanded rapidly in recent years, and continue to do so; the CPI systematically misses the price drop from the shift to these discounters.

The CPI does not recognize that a new discount outlet lowers the prices on many items for the people who begin shopping there. As a result, as discount outlets expand into new areas, the CPI overstates the inflation rate for food, electronic appliances, clothing, and other items sold there.

The Overall Bias

While the BLS has fixed some of the problems with the CPI, economists are in general agreement that it continues to overestimate inflation. By how much?

No one knows for sure, but many economists believe the remaining upward bias is between 0.5 and 1.0 percentage points. That is, if official inflation is reported at 3 percent, a more accurate measure might show inflation between 2.0 and 2.5 percent. The BLS itself has attempted to help measure the bias by creating other, unofficial measures of the price level that are believed to be more accurate.

One such measure is known as the *chained CPI*. This measure addresses the substitution bias by reestimating the consumer market basket each *month*, instead of every two years. In this way, it attempts to take account of virtually *all* shifts in spending due to changes in preferences or changes in relative prices. As you can see in Figure 3(a), in almost every year, the chained CPI gives us a lower inflation rate than the official CPI. The difference between the two measures gives us an idea of the size of the substitution bias still present in the official CPI.

Another question the BLS has tried to answer is how much the upward bias might have affected reported inflation rates in *past* years. For this purpose, it has created the *CPI-RS* (RS stands for "research series"). The CPI-RS takes the methods currently used to calculate the official CPI—including all the improvements made over the last several decades—and applies them retroactively, back to 1978. In effect, the CPI-RS tells us what the official CPI *would* have been in past years if it had been measured as accurately in the past as it is today.

In Figure 3(b), you can see the inflation rates based on the CPI-RS were considerably lower in several years, especially in the late 1970s. For example, in 1979, when the official inflation rate was 13.3 percent, it would have been 10.8 percent if current CPI methods had been used that year. Starting around 1999, the official CPI and the CPI-RS differ little or not at all, because most of the improvements reflected in the CPI-RS were by then being used in the official CPI itself.

Consequences of CPI Bias

What are the implications of the bias in the CPI? That depends on our purpose in using it. If we are trying to measure inflationary tendencies in the economy to help

FIGURE 3   Alternative Measures of Inflation

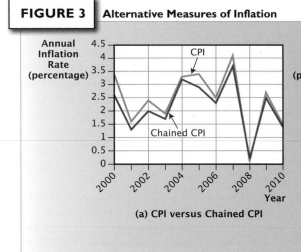

(a) CPI versus Chained CPI

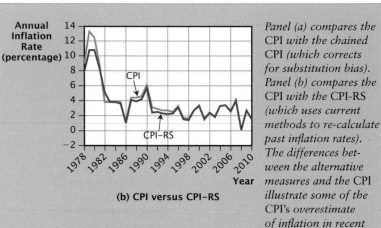

(b) CPI versus CPI-RS

Panel (a) compares the CPI with the chained CPI (which corrects for substitution bias). Panel (b) compares the CPI with the CPI-RS (which uses current methods to re-calculate past inflation rates). The differences between the alternative measures and the CPI illustrate some of the CPI's overestimate of inflation in recent history.

guide macroeconomic policy, then the measurement issues we've discussed so far are not much of a problem. As you can see in Figure 3, the CPI inflation rate does move in tandem with the experimental but more accurate measures. So the official CPI can be one of several useful tools to warn us when inflation threatens to rise.

But for two purposes, the upward bias in the CPI matters a great deal.

Calculating Real Income

Recall that the CPI is used to track the behavior of real income over long periods of time. Look back at Table 2, which shows the real weekly earnings (not including benefits) over the past few decades. Earlier, we used it to calculate that real earnings rose by only about 10 percent from 1980 to 2010. Can we have faith in this result?

Not really. Aside from the problem discussed earlier (the exclusion of increasingly important nonwage benefits), we have the problem of CPI bias. With the errors in each year's CPI accumulating over time, the total overstatement of the price level after a few decades is huge. For example, if we had used the CPI-RS (instead of the CPI) to calculate the change in the real wage from 1980 to 2010, we would have found that the real earnings grew by 18 percent, not the 10 percent we calculated earlier.

Indexing

Another purpose for which CPI bias matters is indexing. Millions of people have their retirement benefits, wages, interest payments, or federal tax brackets adjusted for inflation as determined by the CPI. Thus, any errors have important implications for the government budget, as well as the economy. Later, in the Using the Theory section, we'll look at one example of this issue: the controversy over indexing Social Security benefits to the CPI.

The Larger, Conceptual Problem

So far, we've looked at price indexes as a simple measure of the price level—a weighted average of the prices that consumers face. Our only questions have been:

(1) How accurate are the estimates of price changes? and (2) how accurate do the weights reflect the typical consumer's spending patterns?

But the CPI is widely viewed as measuring something else: *the cost of achieving a given standard of living*. Interpreted or used in this way, the CPI has an even greater upward bias than we've considered so far. This is because new goods and services—made possible by new discoveries—create entirely new ways to raise our economic well-being.

Although this problem is related to new technology, it is entirely different than the new-technology problem we discussed earlier (that the CPI fails to account for early price drops and that new goods provide lower-cost alternatives for existing goods). Here, we are considering a more serious problem: The increase in living standards from *introducing* the good in the first place—and from its continued availability—is never accounted for at all in the CPI.

For example, the CPI has *never* recognized how the Internet has provided us with new ways of enjoying life (think of news, online entertainment, online purchases, social networking, blogs, and more). The same is true for new medical procedures or prescription drugs that can treat or cure formerly untreatable diseases: The CPI ignores the longer and healthier lives that the new treatments often make possible. In this way, using the CPI misses a highly relevant fact: New goods raise the living standard we can achieve at any given dollar cost. Or, equivalently, they lower the dollar cost of achieving any given living standard.

How serious is this problem? No one knows for sure. But many economists believe that the error from ignoring the effect of new goods on living standards could be substantial—much larger than the combined effects of the other biases in the CPI discussed in this chapter.[4] And even alternative measures—such as the CPI-RS—do not begin to address this problem.

For example, if we use the CPI-RS to track the cost of achieving a given standard of living we'd conclude (based on a calculation mentioned earlier) that the typical worker's living standard rose by 18 percent from 1980 to 2010. But here's a simple mental experiment that might help you see that living standards must have risen by more than this.

Suppose you were the typical worker in 2010, and we gave you a choice: (1) We take away 18 percent of your 2010 purchasing power, thereby (supposedly) reducing your living standard to the typical worker in 1980; or (2) we once again take away 18 percent of your 2010 purchasing power, and add one other condition: *you can only buy goods and services that were available in 1980*. Choice (1) *supposedly* reduces your living standard to the typical worker in 1980 (if we think the CPI-RS tracks the cost of living), while choice (2) is a more direct approach to giving you that 1980 living standard. If the CPI-RS truly tracked the cost of achieving a given standard of living, you should be indifferent between choices (1) and (2). But would you be?

Before you answer, remember that choice (2) would mean giving up e-mail, online social networking, downloaded music, and everything else associated with the Internet; it would mean not having access to any medications or surgical procedures that were invented after 1980; it would mean your only telephone would be attached to the wall with a cord; and your computer would be 1,000 times slower than your current one, without most of the software you are used to, which wouldn't matter anyway because you wouldn't have room for it on your floppy disk. (If you don't know what a floppy disk is, Google it—which is another thing you couldn't do in 1980.) Would you really be indifferent between choices (1) and (2)?

---

[4] See, for example, the suggestions of Jerry Hausman, "Sources of Bias and Solutions to Bias in the CPI," *Journal of Economic Perspectives*, Vol. 17, No. 1, Winter 2003.

If you (as the typical worker) answer no, and have a strong preference for (1), then the typical worker's living standard must have risen by *more* than 18 percent over those three decades. That is, even when we use the more accurate CPI-RS to calculate real earnings over time, we *understate* the rise in our living standard, because our price index *overstates* the rise in the cost of achieving a given living standard.

> *The upward bias in the CPI depends on what we are trying to measure. If the target is the cost of the typical consumer's market basket, then the current upward bias is probably less than one percentage point per year. If the target is the cost of achieving a given standard of living, the upward bias is substantially greater.*

USING THE THEORY

© JEFF GREENBERG/THE IMAGE WORKS

THE CONTROVERSY OVER INDEXING SOCIAL SECURITY BENEFITS

In recent years, the Social Security system—which provides benefits to about 60 million former workers in the United States—has become embroiled in controversy. On the one hand, it has been of immense benefit to millions of people. For most recipients, social security payments are the largest component of their retirement income. This has made the program immensely popular.

On the other hand, Social Security is one of the largest and most expensive of all federal government programs, costing more than $700 billion in 2010. And as the baby-boom generation retires over the next decade or so, the costs of the system will balloon, adding to the government's projected budget deficits. This has led to calls to reduce the budgetary costs by changing the way that benefits are calculated.

Let's consider how someone's Social Security benefits are determined. First, the benefits of each year's *new* retirees are tied to the average wage rate in the economy at the time of retirement. As living standards and wages rise over time, each new group of retirees is granted a higher real benefit payment when they first retire.

Second, once a retiree's initial benefit is assigned, his payments in future years are indexed to the CPI. That is, his nominal (dollar) benefit automatically increases at the same percentage rate as the CPI. This is the issue that we'll focus on.

The justification for indexing is to preserve the purchasing power of the benefit payment for all retirees for as long as they live. But because changes in the CPI *overstate* inflation, benefits are *over*indexed. That is, the nominal payment rises by more than the actual rise in the price level. As a result, the real benefit payment rises over time.

Table 3 illustrates how this works, with a hypothetical example. We assume that someone retired in 2006 with an initial promise of $25,000 per year in benefits (about the maximum initial benefit payable that year). The benefit payment is then indexed to the CPI for the next 20 years. We also assume that an *accurate* price index would rise at 2 percent per year. Column (1) shows the value of this accurate price index in each year, using 2006 as our base year.

TABLE 3

Indexing and "Overindexing" Social Security Benefits

Year	(1) Accurate Price Index (2006 = 100)	Benefits Indexed to Accurate CPI (rising at 2%)		Benefits Indexed to Overstated CPI (rising at 3%)	
		(2) Nominal Annual Benefit (indexed at 2% per year)	(3) Real Annual Benefit, $[(2) \div (1)] \times 100$	(4) Nominal Annual Benefit (indexed at 3% per year)	(5) Real Annual Benefit, $[(4) \div (1)] \times 100$
2006	100.00	$25,000	$25,000	$25,000	$25,000
2007	102.00	$25,500	$25,000	$25,750	$25,245
2008	104.04	$26,010	$25,000	$26,523	$25,493
2009	106.12	$26,532	$25,000	$27,318	$25,742
...	...	...	...	...	...
2026	148.59	$37,149	$25,000	$45,153	$30,388

© CENGAGE LEARNING 2013

Column (2) shows nominal benefits starting at $25,000 and then growing by 2 percent per year with the accurate CPI. For example, in the second year, benefits rise to $25,000 × 1.02 = $25,500. In the third year, they rise by another 2 percent, to $25,500 × 1.02 = $26,010. Continuing in this way, the nominal payment in 2026 would reach $25,000 × $(1.02)^{20}$ = $37,149.

Column (3) shows the real benefit payment in each year. It is obtained using our formula:

$$\text{Real value} = \frac{\text{Nominal value}}{\text{Price index}} \times 100.$$

In our example, each value in column (2) is divided by the accurate price index in column (1) to obtain the real payment in column (3). For example, in the second year, with the price index equal to 102, the real payment is

$$\text{Real payment} = \frac{\$25,500}{102} \times 100 = \$25,000.$$

As you can see, when the benefit payment is indexed to an accurate CPI, the real payment remains unchanged at $25,000 (in 2006 dollars). This is not surprising. The purpose of indexing is to keep a real payment constant. With an *accurate* CPI, this is exactly what indexing does.

Now, let's see what happens when benefits are indexed to a CPI that *overestimates* inflation by one percentage point each year. That is, we'll continue to assume that inflation is actually 2 percent per year, but nominal benefit payments will now rise with the (erroneous) CPI at 3 percent per year. In column (4), nominal benefits start at $25,000. In the second year, benefits are $25,000 × 1.03 = $25,750; in the third year, they rise to $25,750 × 1.03 = $26,523, and so on.

Finally, we calculate the real benefit payment each year. But remember: The real benefit is its *actual* purchasing power. In this scenario, although the CPI reports inflation of 3 percent, prices are *actually* rising at only 2 percent per year. So, to determine the real benefit in any year, we must divide the overindexed nominal payment in column (4) by the actual price level in column (1). In the second year, the real payment is

$$\text{Real payment} = \frac{\$25,750}{102} \times 100 = \$25,245.$$

In the third year, the real payment is

$$\text{Real payment} = \frac{\$26,523}{104.04} \times 100 = \$25,493.$$

As you can see, rather than just maintaining the real benefit over time, indexing to an upward-biased CPI results in a *continually increasing real benefit payment*. By the last year of retirement, the real benefit payment rises to $30,388—an increase of more than 21 percent.

This will suit Social Security recipients just fine. And it may suit the rest of us too—when the economy is growing at a rapid pace. After all, why shouldn't retirees get a larger slice of the economic pie when the pie itself is growing rapidly and everyone else's slice is growing as well? But note that the increase in real benefits happens *automatically*, due to overindexing, *regardless* of the rate of economic growth. If real GDP growth slows down or disappears, the average Social Security recipient will *still* get a growing slice of the pie each year, even if everyone else's slice is shrinking. (Because Social Security is financed by tax payments from the rest of society, any increase in real benefits shrinks the after-tax real income of nonretirees.)

More generally,

> *when a payment is indexed and the price index overstates inflation, the real payment increases over time. Purchasing power is automatically shifted toward those who are indexed and away from the rest of society.*

This general principle applies whether the economy is growing rapidly or slowly, and it applies to anyone who is indexed: Social Security recipients, government pensioners, union workers with indexed wage contracts, or anyone else.

Because it is widely recognized that the CPI overstates inflation, there have been calls to adjust the indexing formula for Social Security. One proposal is to index to the CPI minus one-half of a percentage point, to correct for at least some of the measurement error. Other proposals are to substitute a more accurate measure of the price level, such as the chained CPI discussed earlier, which might decrease the reported annual inflation rate by a half percentage point or more.

But some economists have argued that the system should be left alone. For one thing, the elderly consume a different market basket than the "typical consumer." They spend a greater fraction of their income on health care (for which prices are rising rapidly) and much less on new technology goods like laptop computers or cell phones (for which prices are falling). According to this argument, any overstatement of inflation by the CPI helps to compensate for the higher inflation faced by the elderly.

The Bureau of Labor Statistics has been compiling an experimental index, the CPI-E ("E" for elderly), based on a market basket more representative for those receiving benefits. From 1997 to 2009, the CPI-E rose a bit faster than the CPI used for indexing Social Security, by about 0.15 percentage points each year. But this tells us that reasonable estimates of the upward bias of the CPI have *more* than compensated for the higher inflation faced by the elderly, suggesting that some change to indexing may still be appropriate.

Another argument used by advocates of the current system is that it helps to reduce a source of inequity among retirees. Remember that each group's initial benefit is determined by the average wage at their time of retirement. Thus, those who retired in earlier years were awarded a lower initial real benefit than those who retired in later years. Overindexing for inflation thus helps to reduce the difference in real benefits among retirees, because the longer someone has been retired, the more they have gained from the upward bias in the CPI.

SUMMARY

The value of a dollar is its purchasing power, and this changes as the prices of the things we buy change. The overall trend of prices is measured using a price index. Like any index number, a price index is calculated as: (Value in current period/Value in base period) × 100. The most widely used price index in the United States is the *Consumer Price Index (CPI)*, which tracks the prices paid for a typical consumer's "market basket." The percentage change in the CPI is the inflation rate.

The most common uses of the CPI are for indexing payments, as a policy target, and to translate from nominal to real variables. Many nominal variables, such as the nominal wage rate or nominal earnings, can be corrected for price changes by dividing by the CPI and then multiplying by 100. The result is a real variable, such as real earnings, that rises and falls only when its purchasing power rises and falls. Another price index in common use is the GDP price index. It tracks prices of all final goods and services included in GDP.

Inflation, a rise over time in a price index, is costly to our society. One of inflation's costs is an arbitrary redistribution of purchasing power. Unanticipated inflation shifts purchasing power away from those awaiting future dollar payments and toward those obligated to make such payments. Another cost of inflation is the resource cost: People use valuable time and other resources trying to cope with inflation.

It is widely agreed that the CPI has overstated inflation in recent decades. The CPI suffers from *substitution bias*, and it only partially accounts for new technologies, quality changes, and discounting. The Bureau of Labor Statistics has been improving the CPI over time, but some upward bias remains. The CPI is especially inaccurate as an index of the cost of achieving a given standard of living.

PROBLEM SET

Answers to even-numbered Problems can be found on the text Web site through www.cengagebrain.com

1. Calculate each of the following from the data in Table 1 in this chapter.
   a. The inflation rate for the year 2008
   b. *Total* inflation (the total percentage change in the price level) from December 1970 to December 2005

2. Using the data in Table 2, calculate the following for the period 2000–2005:
   a. The total percentage change in the nominal weekly earnings
   b. The total percentage change in the price level

3. Use your answers from problems 2(a) and 2(b) to obtain the total percentage change in real weekly earnings (excluding benefits) from 2000 to 2005. (Hint: Use the approximation rule.)

4. Calculate the total percentage change in real weekly earnings (excluding benefits) from 2000 to 2005 using the last column of Table 2. Compare your answer to the answer in problem 3. Which is the more accurate answer?

5. Given the following *year-end* data, calculate both the inflation rate and the real hourly wage rate for years 2, 3, and 4.

Year	CPI	Inflation Rate	Nominal Wage	Real Wage
1	100		$10.00	—
2	110	—	$12.00	—
3	120	—	$13.00	—
4	115	—	$12.75	—

6. If there is 5 percent inflation each year for 8 years, what is the *total* amount of inflation (i.e., the total percentage rise in the price level) over the entire 8-year period? (Hint: The answer is *not* 40 percent.)

7. Given the following data, calculate the approximate real interest rate for years 2, 3, and 4. (Assume that each CPI number tells us the price level at the *end* of each year.)

End of Year	CPI	Nominal Interest Rate	Real Interest Rate
1	100		
2	110	15%	—
3	120	13%	—
4	115	8%	—

If you lent $200 to a friend at the beginning of year 2 at the prevailing nominal interest rate of 15 percent, and your friend returned the money, with the interest, at the end of year 2, did you benefit from the deal?

8. (Requires appendix.) An economy has only two goods, whose prices and typical consumption quantities are as follows:

	Dec. 2010		Dec. 2011	
	Price	Quantity	Price	Quantity
Fruit (lbs)	$1.00	100	$1.00	150
Nuts (lbs)	$3.00	50	$4.00	25

a. Using December 2010 as the base period for calculations and also as the year for measuring the typical consumer's market basket, calculate the CPI in December 2010 and December 2011.

b. What is the annual inflation rate for 2011?

c. Do you think your answer in (b) would understate the actual inflation rate in 2011? Briefly, why or why not?

9. Complete the following table. (CPI numbers are for the end of each year.)

Year	CPI	Inflation Rate	Nominal Wage	Real Wage
1	37	—	$ 5.60	
2	48		$ 7	
3		10%	$11.26	
4		19%		$25
5	60		$15	

10. a. Jodie earned $25,000 at the end of year 1, when the CPI was 460. If the CPI at the end of year 2 is 504, what would Jodie have to earn at the end of year 2 to maintain a constant real wage?

b. What would she have to earn in year 2 to obtain a 5 percent increase in her real wage? [Use the approximation rule.]

11. During the late 19th and early 20th centuries, many U.S. farmers favored inflationary government policies. Why might this have been the case? (Hint: Do farmers typically pay for their land in full at the time of purchase?)

12. As in Table 3, consider someone who retired in 2006 with $25,000 in initial Social Security benefits per year, and that the actual inflation rate is 2 percent per year over the next 20 years. But now, suppose that the CPI overstates inflation by 2 full percentage points each year.

a. What would the *real* benefit payment be in 2026?

b. What would be the *total percentage increase* in the real benefit payment from 2006 to 2026?

13. In December 2008, some economists forecast *deflation* for the coming year—a decrease in the price level, and therefore a negative inflation rate. Suppose a lender at that time expected deflation over the next twelve months of −1.0 percent, and loaned out funds for one year at a nominal annual interest rate of 0.5 percent.

a. What real interest rate was the lender expecting to get on the loan? [Use the approximation rule.]

b. The inflation rate from December 2008 to December 2009 was *actually* 1.5 percent. What real interest rate did the lender *actually* earn on the loan?

More Challenging

14. Suppose we want to change the base period of the CPI from July 1983 to December 2000. Recalculate December's CPI for each of the years in Table 1, so that the table gives the same information about inflation, but the CPI in December 2000 now has the value 100 instead of 174.0.

15. In Table 2, you can see that the CPI rose from 174.0 in December 2000 to 219.2 in December 2010. The *average* annual inflation rate from 2000 to 2010 was 2.34 percent. That is, $174.0 \times (1.0234)^{10} = 219.2$. Suppose that this average annual rate of inflation overstates the actual annual inflation rate by one percentage point each year, starting in December 2000.

a. What would be the value of an *accurate* CPI in December 2010?

b. What would be an accurate value for real weekly earnings (excluding benefits) in December 2010? (Use information in Table 2.)

c. Determine the total percentage change in real weekly earnings (excluding benefits) from December 2000 to December 2010 using your answer in (b).

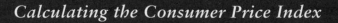
The Consumer Price Index (CPI) is the government's most popular measure of inflation. It tracks the cost of the collection of goods, called the *CPI market basket,* bought by a typical consumer in some *base period*. This appendix demonstrates how the Bureau of Labor Statistics calculates the CPI. To help you follow the steps clearly, we'll do the calculations for a very simple economy with just two goods: hamburger meat and oranges (not a pleasant world, but a manageable one). Table A.1 shows prices for each good, and the quantities produced and consumed, in two different periods: December 2011 (the base period) and December 2012. The market basket (measured in the base period) is given in the third column of the table: In December 2011, the typical consumer buys 30 pounds of hamburger and 50 pounds of oranges. Our formula for the CPI in any period t is

$$\text{CPI in period } t$$
$$= \frac{\text{Cost of market basket at prices in period } t}{\text{Cost of market basket at 2009 prices}} \times 100$$

where each year's prices are measured in December of that year.

Table A.2 shows the calculations we must do to determine the CPI in December 2011 and December 2012. In the table, you can see that the cost of the 2011 market basket at 2011 prices is $200. The cost of the *same* market basket at 2012's higher prices is $235.

To determine the CPI in December 2011—the base period—we use the formula with period t equal to 2011, giving us

$$\text{CPI in 2011}$$
$$= \frac{\text{Cost of 2011 basket at 2011 prices}}{\text{Cost of 2011 basket at 2011 prices}} \times 100$$
$$= \frac{\$200}{\$200} \times 100 = 100.$$

That is, the CPI in December 2011—the base period—is equal to 100. (The formula, as you can see, is set up so that the CPI will always equal 100 in the base period, regardless of which base period we choose.)

Now let's apply the formula again, to get the value of the CPI in December 2012:

$$\text{CPI in 2012}$$
$$= \frac{\text{Cost of 2011 basket at 2012 prices}}{\text{Cost of 2011 basket at 2012 prices}} \times 100$$
$$= \frac{\$235}{\$200} \times 100 = 117.5.$$

From December 2011 to December 2012, the CPI rises from 100 to 117.5. The rate of inflation over the year 2012 is therefore 17.5 percent.

TABLE A.1 — **Prices and Weekly Quantities in a Two-Good Economy**

	December 2011		December 2012	
	Price (per lb)	Quantity (lbs)	Price (per lb)	Quantity (lbs)
Hamburger Meat	$5.00	30	$6.00	10
Oranges	$1.00	50	$1.10	100

TABLE A.2 — **Calculations for the CPI**

	At December 2011 Prices	At December 2012 Prices
Cost of 30 lbs of Hamburger	$ 5.00 × 30 = $150	$ 6.00 × 30 = $180
Cost of 50 lbs of Oranges	$ 1.00 × 50 = $50	$ 1.10 × 50 = $55
Cost of Entire Market Basket	$150 + $50 = $200	$180 + $55 = $235

Notice that the CPI gives more weight to price changes of goods that are more important in the consumer's budget. In our example, the percentage rise in the CPI (17.5 percent) is closer to the percentage rise in the price of hamburger (20 percent) than it is to the percentage price rise of oranges (10 percent). This is because a greater percentage of the budget is *spent* on hamburger than on oranges, so hamburger carries more weight in the CPI.

But one of the CPI's problems, discussed in the body of the chapter, is *substitution bias*. The CPI recognizes that consumers substitute *within* categories of goods. For example, if we had a third good, steak, the CPI would recognize that consumers will buy more steak if the price of hamburger rises faster than the price of steak. But the CPI assumes there is no substitution *among* categories—between beef products and fruit, for example. No matter how much the relative price of beef products like hamburger rises, the CPI assumes that people will continue to buy the same quantity of it, rather than substitute goods in other categories like oranges. Therefore, as the price of hamburger rises, the

CPI assumes that we spend a greater and greater percentage of our budgets on it; hamburger gets *increasing weight* in the CPI. In our example, spending on hamburger is assumed to rise from 75 percent of the typical weekly budget ($150 out of $200), to 76.6 percent ($180 out of $235). In fact, however, the rapid rise in price would cause people to substitute *away* from hamburger toward other goods whose prices are rising more slowly.

This is what occurs in our two-good example, as you can see in the last column of Table A.1. In 2012, the quantity of hamburger purchased drops to 10, and the quantity of oranges rises to 100. In an ideal measure, the decrease in the quantity of hamburger would reduce its weight in determining the overall rate of inflation. But the CPI ignores the information in the last column of Table A.1, which shows the new quantities purchased in 2012. (In fact, that's the only reason we included that column in the table; to show the information *not* used in calculating the CPI.) This failure to correct for substitution bias across categories of goods is one of the reasons the CPI overstates inflation.

CHAPTER 8

The Classical Long-Run Model

© JOHN TERENCE TURNER/GETTY IMAGES

As we've discussed in previous chapters, economists often disagree with each other. In interviews, editorials, and blog posts, they make opposing recommendations about matters of great importance to the nation's economy. To the casual observer, it might seem that economists agree on very little about how the economy works. But looking closer, we often find that a seemingly positive disagreement is based on a hidden normative disagreement.

Consider the controversy surrounding the *American Recovery and Reinvestment Act* of 2009, the government's first major attempt to help the economy recover from the financial crisis and recession of 2008. The Act enabled the government to borrow an additional $787 billion so it could increase government spending and cut taxes by that amount.

Economists and politicians debated a number of positive and normative aspects of the policy: whether or not tax cuts and spending increases were properly proportioned, their timing, the microeconomic details, the wisdom of expanding government's role in the economy, and more. But one of the most heated arguments concerned whether or not government spending—if financed by government borrowing—*could* help the economy.

On one side were economists who argued that such policies would worsen the economy's performance and lower U.S. living standards. On the other side were those who argued the opposite: The policy would *improve* the economy's performance and *failing* to enact it would cause living standards to drop. (If you're a bit confused about the logic behind these arguments, don't worry; it will become clear over the next several chapters.) Which side was right?

Surprisingly, it's possible that *both* sides were right. But how can this be? Aren't the two arguments mutually exclusive? Not necessarily. Economists on each side might have been thinking about—and addressing—a different question. Many of those who opposed the policy were focusing on the expected long-run effects of government *borrowing*: the impact we'd begin to observe after several years had passed. Those in favor generally focused on the short-run effects of government *spending*: the impact expected over the next year or two. How to weigh the long run versus the short run is in large part a normative issue: a question of values. Yes, there were also positive disagreements about the impact over *each* of these time horizons. But even with complete agreement about the positive questions, there would still have been a major dispute over whether the short run or the long run should take priority in guiding the economy.

Ideally, we would like our economy to do well in both the long run and the short run. Unfortunately, there is often a tradeoff between these two goals: Doing better in the short run can require some sacrifice of long-run goals, and vice versa. The problem for policy makers is much like that of the captain of a ship sailing through the North Atlantic. On the one hand, he wants to reach his destination (his long-run goal); on the other hand, he must avoid icebergs along the way (his short-run goal). As you might imagine, avoiding icebergs may require the captain to deviate from an ideal long-run course. At the same time, reaching port might require risking the occasional iceberg.

The same is true of the macroeconomy. If you flip back to the chapter titled Production, Income, and Employment and look at Figure 4 (actual and potential real GDP), you will see the two types of movements in total output. The long-run trajectory shows the growth of potential output. The short-run movements around that trajectory we call economic fluctuations or business cycles. Macroeconomists are concerned with both types of movements. But, as you will see, policies that can help us smooth out economic fluctuations may prove harmful to growth in the long run, while policies that promise a high rate of growth might require us to put up with more severe fluctuations in the short run.

A few chapters from now, we'll be looking at the economy's behavior in the short run. But in this and the next chapter, we focus on the long run. We'll analyze how a nation's potential GDP is determined, what makes it grow over time, and how a variety of government policies affect the long-run path of the economy.

MACROECONOMIC MODELS: CLASSICAL VERSUS KEYNESIAN

The **classical model,** developed by economists in the 19th and early 20th centuries, was an attempt to explain a key observation about the economy: Over periods of several years or longer, the economy performs rather well. That is, if we step back from conditions in any one year and view the economy over a long stretch of time, we see that it operates reasonably close to its potential output. And even when it deviates, it does not do so forever. Business cycles may come and go, but the economy eventually returns to full employment. Indeed, if we think in terms of decades rather than years or quarters, the business cycle fades in significance.

Classical model A macroeconomic model that explains the long-run behavior of the economy.

This is illustrated in Figure 1, which shows estimates of U.S. real GDP (in 1990 dollars) from 1820 through 2010. In the figure, real GDP is plotted with a *logarithmic scale*, so that equal vertical distances represent equal *percentage* changes rather than equal absolute changes. If real GDP grew at a constant percentage rate, the graph would be a perfectly straight line.

The startling feature of Figure 1 is how real GDP hovers near its long-run trend, and how insignificant even the most severe departures from that trend appear in the graph. Even the Great Depression of the 1930s appears as just a ripple, with real GDP returning back to the trend. And the severe recession that began in 2008 appears as a hard-to-notice slight bend away from the trend.

In the classical view, this behavior is no accident: Powerful forces are at work that drive the economy toward full employment. Many of the classical economists went even further, arguing that these forces could operate within a reasonably short period of time. And even today, an important group of macroeconomists continues to believe that the classical model is the foundation for explaining the economy's short-run behavior.

Until the Great Depression of the 1930s, there was little reason to question these classical ideas. True, output fluctuated around its trend, and from time to time there were serious recessions, but output always returned to its potential, full-employment level within a few years or less, just as the classical economists predicted. But during the Great Depression, output was stuck far below its potential for many years. For some reason, the economy wasn't working the way the classical model said it should.

FIGURE 1   **U.S. Real GDP, 1820–2010 (Logarithmic Scale)**

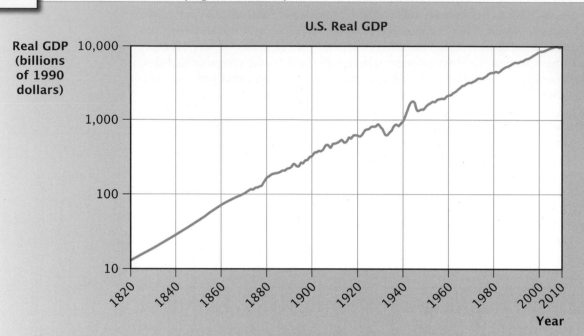

Source: Data for 1820–1990: Angus Maddison, *Contours of the World Economy*; Data for 1991–2010: The Conference Board, *Total Economy Database*.

Note: Data for 1820 to 1870 is interpolated between decades, hence the smoother appearance for those years.

In 1936, in the midst of the Great Depression, the British economist John Maynard Keynes offered an explanation for the economy's poor performance. His new model of the economy—soon dubbed the *Keynesian model*—changed many economists' thinking.[1] Keynes and his followers argued that, while the classical model might explain the economy's operation in the long run, the long run could be a very long time in arriving. In the meantime, production could be stuck below its potential, as it seemed to be during the Great Depression.

Keynesian ideas became increasingly popular in universities and government agencies during the 1940s and 1950s. By the mid-1960s, the entire profession had been won over: Macroeconomics *was* Keynesian economics, and the classical model was removed from virtually all introductory economics textbooks. You might be wondering, then, why we are bothering with the classical model here. After all, isn't it an older model of the economy, one that was largely discredited and replaced, just as the Ptolemaic view that the sun circled the earth was supplanted by the more modern, Copernican view? Not at all.

Why the Classical Model Is Important

The classical model retains its importance for two reasons. First, over the last several decades, there has been an active counterrevolution against Keynes's approach to

---

[1] Keynes's attack on the classical model was presented in his book *The General Theory of Employment, Interest and Money* (1936). Unfortunately, it's a very difficult book to read, though you may want to try. Keynes's assumptions were not always clear, and some of his text is open to multiple interpretations. As a result, economists have been arguing for decades about what Keynes really meant.

understanding the macroeconomy. Many of the counterrevolutionary new theories are based largely on classical ideas. By studying classical macroeconomics, you will be better prepared to understand the controversies centering on these newer schools of thought.

The second—and more important—reason for us to study the classical model is that it remains the best model for understanding the economy over the long run. Even the many economists who find the classical model inadequate for understanding the economy in the short run find it extremely useful in analyzing the economy in the long run.

> *Keynes's ideas and their further development help us understand economic fluctuations—movements in output around its long-run trend. But the classical model has proven more useful in explaining the long-run trend itself.*

This is why we will use the terms "classical view" and "long-run view" interchangeably in the rest of the book; in either case, we mean "the ideas of the classical model used to explain the economy's long-run behavior."

Assumptions of the Classical Model

Remember from Chapter 1 that all models begin with *assumptions* about the world. The classical model is no exception. Many of its assumptions are *simplifying;* they make the model more manageable, enabling us to see the broad outlines of economic behavior without getting lost in the details. Typically, these assumptions involve aggregation. We combine the many different interest rates in the economy and refer to a single interest rate. We combine the many different types of labor in the economy into a single aggregate labor market. These simplifications are usually harmless: Adding more detail would make our work more difficult, but it would not add much insight; nor would it change any of the central conclusions of the classical view.

There is, however, one assumption in the classical model that goes beyond mere simplification. This is an assumption about how the world works, and it is *critical* to the conclusions we will reach in this and the next chapter. We can state it in two words: *Markets clear.*

> *A critical assumption in the classical model is that **markets clear:** The price in every market will adjust until quantity supplied and quantity demanded are equal.*

Market clearing Adjustment of prices until quantities supplied and demanded are equal.

Does the market-clearing assumption sound familiar? It should: It was the basic idea behind our study of supply and demand. When we look at the economy through the classical lens, we assume that the forces of supply and demand work fairly well throughout the economy and that markets do reach equilibrium. An excess supply of anything traded will lead to a fall in its price; an excess demand will drive the price up.

The market-clearing assumption, which permeates classical thinking about the economy, provides an early hint about why the classical model does a better job over longer time periods (several years or more) than shorter ones. In some markets, prices might not fully adjust to their equilibrium values for many months or even years after some change in the economy. An excess supply or excess demand might persist for some time. Still, if we wait long enough, an excess supply in a market will eventually force the price down, and an excess demand will eventually drive the price up. That is, *eventually,* the market will clear. Therefore, when we are trying to explain the economy's behavior over the long run, market clearing seems to be a reasonable assumption.

In the remainder of the chapter, we'll use the classical model to answer a variety of important questions about the economy in the long run, such as:

- How is total employment determined?
- How much output will we produce?
- What role does total spending play in the economy?
- What happens when things change?

Keep in mind that many of the variables we will use in the classical model are expressed in dollars, such as the wage rate or total output. In all cases, these variables are real, rather than nominal: They are measured in dollars of constant purchasing power (such as "1990 dollars" or "2005 dollars").

HOW MUCH OUTPUT WILL WE PRODUCE?

Over the three years from 2005 through 2007 (just before our most recent recession began), the U.S. economy produced an average of about $13 trillion worth of goods and services per year (valued in 2005 dollars). How was this average level of output determined? Why didn't production average $18 trillion per year? Or just $6 trillion? There are so many things to consider when answering this question, variables you constantly hear about in the news: wages, interest rates, investment spending, government spending, taxes, and more. Each of these concepts plays an important role in determining total output, and our task in this chapter is to show how they all fit together.

But what a task! How can we disentangle the web of economic interactions we see around us? Our starting point will be the first step of our *three-step process*, introduced toward the end of Chapter 3. To review, that first step was to *characterize the market*—to decide which market or markets best suit the problem being analyzed, which means identifying the buyers and sellers and the type of environment in which they trade.

But which market should we start with?

The classical approach is to start at the beginning, with the *reason* for all this production in the first place: our desire for goods and services, and our need for income in order to buy them. In a market economy, people get their income from supplying labor and other resources to firms. Firms, in turn, use these resources to make the goods and services that people demand. Thus, a logical place to start our analysis is the markets for resources: labor, land, capital, and entrepreneurship.

For now we'll concentrate our attention on just one type of resource: labor. We'll assume that firms are already using the available quantities of the other resources. Moreover, because we are building a *macroeconomic* model, we'll aggregate all the different types of labor—office workers, construction workers, factory workers, teachers, waiters, writers, and more—into a single variable, simply called *labor*.

Our question is: How many workers will be employed in the economy?

The Labor Market

Consider the economy of a fictional country called Classica, in which all workers have the same skills. Classica's labor market is illustrated in Figure 2. The number of workers is measured on the horizontal axis, and the real hourly wage rate is measured on the vertical axis. Remember that the *real wage*—which is measured in the dollars of some base year—tells us the amount of goods that workers can buy with an hour's earnings.

FIGURE 2   The Labor Market

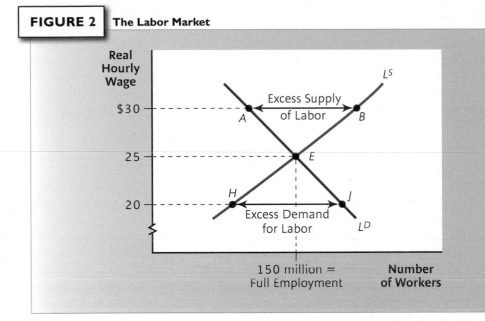

The equilibrium wage rate of $25 per hour is determined at point E, where the upward-sloping labor supply curve crosses the downward-sloping labor demand curve. At any other wage, an excess demand or excess supply of labor will cause an adjustment back to equilibrium.

Now look at the two curves in the figure. These are supply and demand curves, similar to the supply and demand curves for maple syrup, but there is one key difference: For a *good* such as maple syrup, households are the demanders and firms the suppliers. But for labor, the roles are reversed: Households supply labor and firms demand it. Let's take a closer look at each of these curves in Classica's labor market.

Labor Supply

The curve labeled L^S is Classica's aggregate **labor supply curve;** it tells us how many people in the country will want to work at each wage rate. The upward slope tells us that the greater the real wage, the greater the number of people who will want to work. Why does the labor supply curve slope upward?

Labor supply curve Indicates how many people will want to work at various real wage rates.

Think about yourself. To earn income, you must go to work and give up other activities such as going to school, exercising, or just hanging out with your friends. You will want to work only if the income you will earn *at least* compensates you for the other activities that you will give up.

Of course, people value their time differently. But for each of us, there is some critical wage rate above which we would decide that we're better off working. Below that wage, we would be better off not working. In Figure 2,

> *the labor supply curve slopes upward because, as the wage rate increases, more and more individuals decide they are better off working than not working. Thus, a rise in the wage rate increases the number of people in the economy who want to work—to supply their labor.*

Labor Demand

The curve labeled L^D is the **labor demand curve,** which shows the number of workers Classica's firms will want to hire at any real wage. Why does this curve slope downward?

Labor demand curve Indicates how many workers firms will want to hire at various real wage rates.

In deciding how much labor to hire, a firm's goal is to earn the greatest possible profit: the difference between sales revenue and costs. Each time a firm in Classica hires another worker, output rises, and the firm can get more revenue by selling that worker's output. But most types of production are characterized by *diminishing returns to labor*: the rise in output (and the revenue the firm gets from selling it) gets smaller and smaller with each successive worker.

Why are there diminishing returns to labor? For one thing, as we keep adding workers, further gains from specialization are harder to achieve. Moreover, as we continue to add workers, each one will have less and less of the other resources to work with. For example, each time more agricultural workers are added to a fixed amount of farmland, output might rise. But as we continue to add workers and there are more workers per acre, output will rise by less and less with each new worker. The same is true when more factory workers are added to a fixed amount of factory floor space and machinery, or more professors are added to a fixed number of classrooms: Output continues to rise, but by less and less with each added worker.

So let's recap: Each additional worker causes a firm's output and revenue to rise, but by less and less for each new worker. Also, each additional worker adds to the firm's costs. A firm will want to keep hiring additional workers as long as they add to the firm's profit, that is, as long as they add more to revenue than they add to cost.

Now think about what happens as the wage rate rises. Some workers that added more to revenue than to cost at the lower wage will now cost more than they add in revenue. Accordingly, the firm will not want to employ these workers at the higher wage.

> As the wage rate increases, each firm in the economy will find that, to maximize profit, it should employ fewer workers than before. When all firms behave this way together, a rise in the wage rate will decrease the quantity of labor demanded in the economy.

Equilibrium Total Employment

Remember that in the classical model, we assume that *all markets clear,* and that includes the market for labor. Specifically, the real wage adjusts until the quantities of labor supplied and demanded are equal. In the labor market in Figure 2, the market-clearing wage is $25 per hour because that is where the labor supply and labor demand curves intersect. While every worker would prefer to earn $30 rather than $25, at $30 there would be an excess supply of labor equal to the distance *AB*. With not enough jobs to go around, competition among workers would drive the wage downward. Similarly, firms might prefer to pay their workers $20 rather than $25, but at $20, the excess demand for labor (equal to the distance *HJ*) would drive the wage upward. When the wage is $25, however, there is neither an excess demand nor an excess supply of labor, so the wage will neither increase nor decrease. Thus, $25 is the equilibrium wage in the economy. Reading along the horizontal axis, we see that at this wage, 150 million people in Classica will be working.

Notice that, in the figure, labor is fully employed; that is, the number of workers that firms want to hire is equal to the number of people who want jobs. Therefore, everyone who wants a job at the market wage of $25 should be able to find one. Small amounts of frictional unemployment might exist, since it takes some time for new workers or job switchers to find jobs. And there might be structural unemployment, due to some mismatch between those who want jobs in the market and the types of jobs available. But there is no *cyclical* unemployment of the type we discussed two chapters ago.

Full employment of the labor force is an important feature of the classical model. As long as we can count on markets (including the labor market) to clear, government action is not needed to ensure full employment; it happens automatically:

> In the classical model, the economy achieves full employment on its own.

Automatic full employment may strike you as odd, since it contradicts the cyclical unemployment we sometimes see around us. For example, in our most recent recession and the slump that followed, millions of workers around the country, in all kinds of professions and labor markets, were unable to find jobs. Remember, though, that the classical model takes the long-run view, and over long periods of time (a period of many years), full employment is a fairly accurate description of the U.S. labor market. Cyclical unemployment, by definition, lasts only as long as the current business cycle itself; it is not a permanent, long-run problem.

From Employment to Output

So far, we've focused on Classica's labor market to determine its level of employment. In our example, 150 million people will have jobs. Now we ask: How much output (real GDP) will these 150 million workers produce? The answer depends on two things: (1) the amount of other resources available for labor to use; and (2) the state of *technology*, which determines how much output we can produce with those resources.

In this chapter, remember that we're focusing on only one resource—labor—and we're treating the quantities of all other resources firms use as fixed during the period we're analyzing. Now we'll go even further: We'll assume that technology does not change.

Why do we make these assumptions? After all, in the real world technology *does* change, the capital stock *does* grow, new natural resources *can* be discovered, and the number and quality of entrepreneurs *can* change. Isn't it unrealistic to hold all of these things constant?

Yes, but our assumption is only temporary. The most effective way to master a macroeconomic model is "divide and conquer": Start with a part of the model, understand it well, and then add in other parts. Accordingly, our classical analysis of the economy is divided into two separate questions: (1) What would be the long-run equilibrium of the economy *if* there were a constant state of technology and *if* quantities of all resources besides labor were fixed? And (2) What happens to this long-run equilibrium when technology and the quantities of other resources change? In this chapter, we focus on the first question. In the next chapter on economic growth, we'll address the second question.

The Production Function

With a constant technology, and given quantities of all resources other than labor, only one variable can affect total output: the quantity of labor. So it's time to explore the relationship between total employment and total production in the economy. This relationship is given by the economy's *aggregate production function*.

> The **aggregate production function** (or just **production function**) *shows the total output the economy can produce with different quantities of labor, given constant amounts of other resources and the current state of technology.*

Aggregate production function The relationship showing how much total output can be produced with different quantities of labor, when quantities of all other resources and technology are held constant.

The bottom panel of Figure 3 shows Classica's aggregate production function. The upward slope tells us that an increase in the number of people working will increase the quantity of output produced. But notice the shape of the production function: It flattens out as we move rightward along it.

The declining slope of the aggregate production function is the result of the *diminishing returns to labor* that we discussed earlier: At each firm in Classica—and in the country as a whole—output rises when another worker is added, but the rise is smaller with each successive worker.

FIGURE 3	Output Determination in the Classical Model

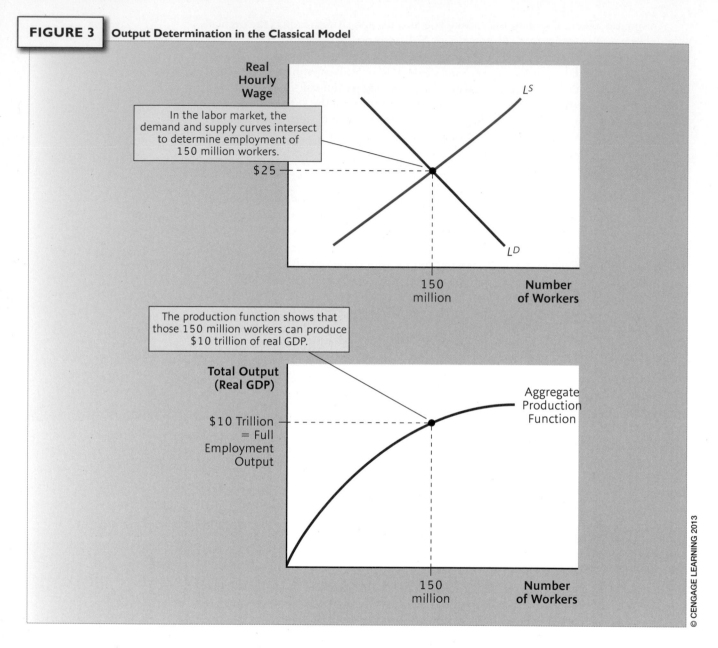

Equilibrium Real GDP

The two panels of Figure 3 illustrate how the aggregate production function, together with the labor market, determine Classica's total output or real GDP. The labor market (upper panel) automatically generates full employment of 150 million workers, and the production function (lower panel) tells us that 150 million workers—together with the available amounts of other resources and the current state of technology—can produce $10 trillion worth of output. Because $10 trillion is the output produced by a fully employed labor force, it is also the economy's potential output level.

In the classical, long-run view, the economy reaches its potential output automatically.

This last statement is an important conclusion of the classical model and an important characteristic of the economy in the long run: Output tends toward its potential, full-employment level *on its own,* with no need for government to steer the economy toward it. And we have arrived at this conclusion merely by assuming that the labor market clears and observing the relationship between employment and output.

THE ROLE OF SPENDING

Something may be bothering you about the classical view of output determination, an issue we have so far carefully avoided: What if business firms are unable to *sell* all the output that a fully employed labor force produces? Firms won't continue making goods they can't sell, so they would have to decrease production and employ fewer workers. The economy would not remain at full employment for very long.

Thus, if we are asserting that equilibrium total output is *potential* output, we had better be sure there is enough spending to buy all of the output produced. But can we be sure of this?

In the classical view, the answer is an unequivocal "yes." We'll demonstrate this in two stages: first, with some very simple (but unrealistic) assumptions, and then, under more realistic conditions.

Total Spending in a Very Simple Economy

Imagine an economy much simpler than our own, with just two types of economic units: domestic households and domestic business firms. Households spend all of their income (they do not save) and households are the only spenders in the economy. There is no government collecting taxes or purchasing goods; no business investment; and no imports from or exports to other countries.

Production, income, and spending in this economy are illustrated in Figure 4. During the year, firms produce the economy's potential output, assumed to be $10 trillion in the figure. This is represented by the size of the first rectangle.

Next we ask: how much income will households earn during the year? As you learned two chapters ago, the value of the economy's total output is equal to the total income (factor payments) of households. So with firms producing $10 trillion in output, they must also pay out $10 trillion to households in the form of wages, rent, interest, and profit. This total income is represented by the second rectangle.

Now, we ask our final question: What is total spending? Because we assume that households spend all of their income, and no sector other than households buys goods and services, we have an easy answer: Total spending is the same as total consumption spending, which must be the same as household income: $10 trillion. Total spending is represented by the third rectangle. As you can see, all three rectangles are the same size and represent the same value: $10 trillion. So total spending (the last rectangle) is equal to total output (the first rectangle).

> *In a simple economy with just domestic households and firms, in which households spend all of their income on domestic output, total spending must be equal to total output.*

FIGURE 4   Total Spending in a Simple Economy

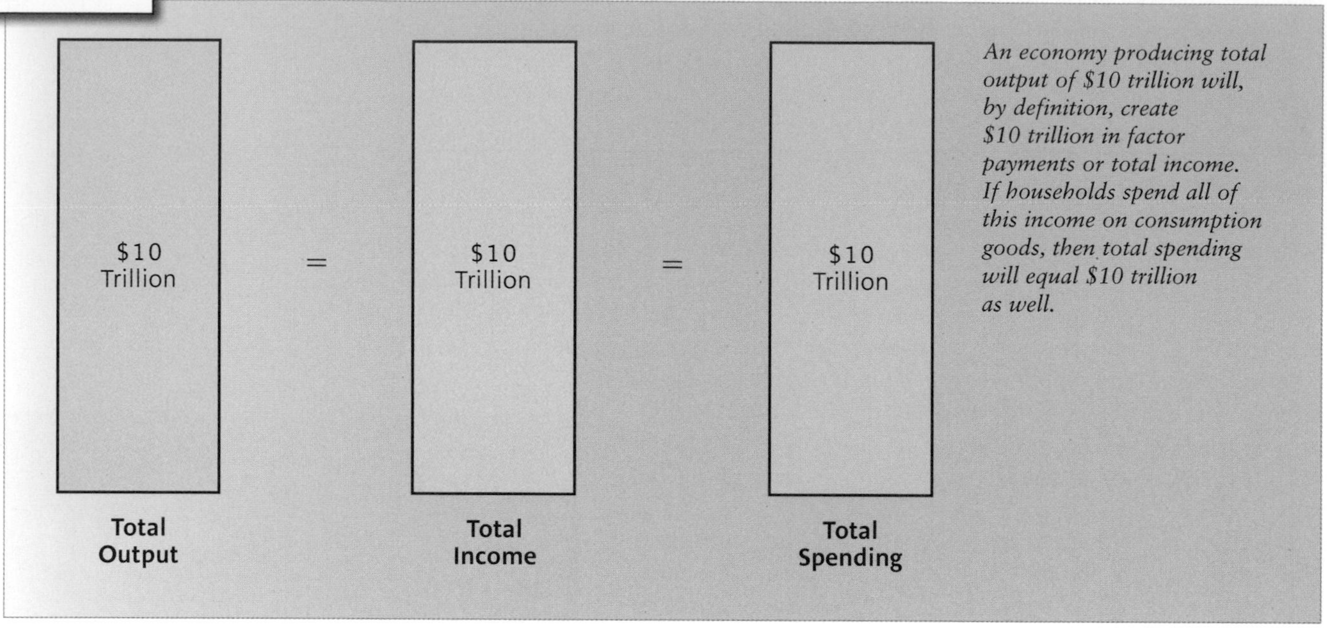

$10 Trillion	=	$10 Trillion	=	$10 Trillion
Total Output		Total Income		Total Spending

An economy producing total output of $10 trillion will, by definition, create $10 trillion in factor payments or total income. If households spend all of this income on consumption goods, then total spending will equal $10 trillion as well.

© CENGAGE LEARNING 2013

Say's Law

Say's law The idea that total spending will be sufficient to purchase the total output produced.

The idea that total spending will equal total output is called **Say's law,** after the early 19th-century economist Jean Baptiste Say, who popularized it. As you'll soon see, Say's law can apply not just to our overly simple economy, but to a more realistic one as well. For now, let's stay with the simple case.

Say noted that each time a good or service is produced, an equal amount of income is created. Thus, the act of producing a good creates the very income that is needed to purchase the good.

In Say's own words:

> *A product is no sooner created than it, from that instant, affords a market for other products to the full extent of its own value. . . . Thus, the mere circumstance of the creation of one product immediately opens a vent for other products.*[2]

For example, each time a shirt manufacturer produces a $25 shirt, it creates $25 in factor payments to households. (Forgot why? Go back two chapters and refresh your memory about the factor payments approach to GDP.) But in the simple economy we're analyzing, that $25 in factor payments will lead to $25 in total spending—just enough to buy the very shirt produced. Of course, the households who receive the $25 in factor payments won't necessarily buy a shirt with it; the shirt manufacturer must still worry about selling its own specific output. But in the *aggregate,* we needn't worry about there being sufficient demand for the total output produced. Business firms—by producing output—also create a demand for goods and services equal to the value of that output.

> *Say's law states that by producing goods and services, firms create a total demand for goods and services equal to what they have produced. Or, more simply, supply creates its own demand.*

[2] J. B. Say, *A Treatise on Political Economy,* 4th ed. (London: Longman, 1821), Vol. I, p. 167.

Say's law is crucial to the classical view of the economy. Why? Remember that because the labor market is assumed to clear, firms will hire all the workers who want jobs and produce our *potential* or *full-employment* output level. But firms will be able to *continue* producing this level of output only if they can *sell* it all. In the simple economy of Figure 4, Say's law assures us that, in the aggregate, spending will be just high enough for firms to sell all the output that a fully employed labor force can produce. As a result, full employment can be maintained.

But the economy in Figure 4 leaves out some important details of economies in the real world. Does Say's law also apply in a more realistic economy? Let's see.

Total Spending in a More Realistic Economy

The real-world economy is more complicated than the imaginary one we've just considered. One complication is trade with the rest of the world. We'll deal with the foreign sector and international trade in the appendix to this chapter. For now, we'll continue to assume that we're in a *closed economy*—one that does not have any economic dealings with the rest of the world. But here we'll add a few features that we ignored before.

In particular, we'll now assume:

- A *government* collects taxes and purchases goods and services.

- Households no longer spend their entire incomes on consumption. Instead, some is used to pay *taxes*, and some is *saved*.

- Business firms purchase capital goods (investment spending).

With these added details, will Say's law still apply? Can we have confidence that total spending will equal total output? To answer, let's go back to our fictional economy of Classica, which has the labor market and aggregate production function you saw earlier in Figure 2. But now we'll add the details we've just listed.

Data on Classica's economy in 2012 are given in Table 1. Classica's potential (full-employment) output is $10 trillion, and, because it behaves according to the classical model, that is what Classica actually produces during the year. Notice that total output and total income are each equal to $10 trillion in 2012.

Next come three entries that refer to spending by the final users who purchase Classica's GDP. Note that, unlike the households in Figure 4, Classica's households spend only *part* of their income, $7 trillion, on consumption goods (C). Skipping down to government purchases (G), we find that Classica's government sector buys $2 trillion in goods and services.

In addition to consumption and government purchases—with which you are already familiar—Table 1 includes some new variables. Because these will be used throughout the rest of this book, it's worth defining and discussing them here.

TABLE 1

Flows in the Economy of Classica, 2012

Actual and Potential Output (GDP)	$10 trillion
Total Income	$10 trillion
Consumption Spending (C)	$7 trillion
Planned Investment Spending (I^p)	$1 trillion
Government Purchases (G)	$2 trillion
Net Taxes (T)	$1.25 trillion
Disposable Income	$8.75 trillion
Household Saving (S)	$1.75 trillion

© CENGAGE LEARNING 2013

Planned Investment Spending (I^P)

Our ultimate goal is to find out if Say's law works in Classica—if total spending matches total output, so that firms in Classica will be able to sell all that they produce. Thus, when we measure total spending, we want to include only the spending that decision makers *want* to do, and will likely *continue* to do. Consumption spending, for example, is virtually always intentional. In *The Simpsons,* Homer would sometimes wake up and "discover" that he had purchased a new car or a lifetime supply of Slurpees. But in real life, that doesn't happen very often. The same is true of *most* investment spending. Businesses don't "discover" that they've purchased a new factory: they intend to purchase it, and usually plan to do so well in advance.

But inventory changes—a component of investment in GDP—are often *un*intentional, and can come as a surprise to firms. They occur when firms sell less than they've produced (an increase in inventories) or more than they've produced (a decrease in inventories). It would be a mistake to include unintended inventory changes—which represent the mismatch between sales and production—when we measure the economy's total spending. On the contrary, we want to *exclude* unintended inventory changes from our measure of spending.

To keep our discussion simple, we'll treat *all* inventory changes as if they are unintentional (even though, in reality, some inventory changes are intended). So when we calculate total spending, we'll exclude *all* inventory changes from the spending of business firms (investment). When we subtract inventory changes from investment, we're left with the economy's *planned investment spending*.

Planned investment spending Business purchases of plant and equipment.

> *Planned investment spending* (I^P) *over a period of time is total investment* (I) *minus the change in inventories over the period:*
>
> $$I^P = I - \Delta \text{ inventories.}$$

Here, we're using the Greek letter Δ ("delta") to indicate a change in a variable. In Table 1, you can see that Classica's planned investment spending—which excludes any changes in inventories—is $1 trillion.

Net Tax Revenue (T)

Recall (from two chapters ago) that *transfer payments* are government outlays that are *not* spent on goods and services. These transfers—which include unemployment insurance, welfare payments, and Social Security benefits—are just *given* to people, either out of social concern (welfare payments), to keep a promise (Social Security payments), or elements of both (unemployment insurance).

In the macroeconomy, government transfer payments are like negative taxes: They represent the part of tax revenue that the government gives right back to households (such as Social Security recipients). This revenue is not available for government purchases. Because transfer payments stay *within* the household sector, we can treat them as if they were never collected by the government at all. We do this by focusing on *net taxes:*

Net taxes Government tax revenues minus transfer payments.

> *Net taxes* (T) *are total government tax revenue minus government transfer payments:*
>
> $$T = \text{Total tax revenue} - \text{Transfers.}$$

From the table, Classica's net taxes in 2012 are $1.25 trillion. This number might result from total tax revenue of $2 trillion and $0.75 trillion in government transfer payments. It could also result from $3 trillion in tax revenue and

$1.75 trillion in transfers. From the macroeconomic perspective, it makes no difference: Net taxes are $1.25 trillion in either case.

Disposable Income

Disposable income is the income households have left after net taxes are taken away. We call it disposable income, because it represents the part of income that households are free to "dispose" of as they wish.

Disposable income Household income minus net taxes, which is either spent or saved.

> *Disposable Income = Total Income − Net Taxes*

In Classica, total income is $10 trillion and net taxes are $1.25 trillion, so disposable income is $10 trillion − $1.25 trillion = $8.75 trillion.

Household Saving (S)

Households can do only two things with their disposable income: spend it or save it. The part that is spent is the *consumption spending (C)* component of GDP. Therefore, the remainder of disposable income must be saved.

> *Household saving (S) = Disposable Income − C*

(Household) saving The portion of after-tax income that households do not spend on consumption.

In the table, Classica's household saving is listed as $1.75 trillion. But this number follows from the other numbers listed above it. In particular, because disposable income is $8.75 trillion, and consumptions spending is $7 trillion, our formula tells us that S = $8.75 trillion − $7 trillion = $1.75 trillion

Total Spending in Classica

In Classica, total spending is the sum of the purchases made by the household sector (C), the business sector (I^P), and the government sector (G):

$$\text{Total spending} = C + I^P + G.$$

Or, using the numbers in Table 1:

$$\text{Total spending} = \$7 \text{ trillion} + \$1 \text{ trillion} + \$2 \text{ trillion} = \$10 \text{ trillion}.$$

This may strike you as suspiciously convenient: Total spending is exactly equal to total output, just as we'd like it to be if we want Classica to continue producing its potential output of $10 trillion. And just what we needed to illustrate Say's law in this more realistic economy.

But we haven't yet proven anything; we've just cooked up an example that made the numbers come out this way. The question is, do we have any reason to *expect* the economy to give us numbers like these automatically, with total spending precisely equal to total output?

The rectangles in Figure 5 can help us answer this question. Total output (represented by the first rectangle) is, by definition, always equal in value to total income (the second rectangle). As we've seen in Figure 4, if households *spent* all of this income, then consumption spending would equal total output.

But in Classica, households do *not* spend all of their income. Some income goes to pay net taxes ($1.25 trillion), and some is saved ($1.75 trillion). We can think of saving and net taxes as **leakages** out of spending: income that households receive, but do not spend on Classica's output. Leakages reduce consumption spending below total income, as you can see in the third, lower rectangle. In Classica, total leakages = $1.75 trillion + $1.25 trillion = $3 trillion, and this must be subtracted

Leakages Income earned by households that they do *not* spend on the country's output during a given year.

FIGURE 5 | Leakages and Injections

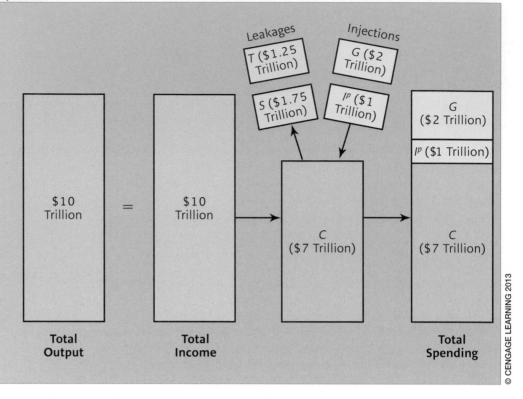

By definition, total output equals total income. Leakages—net taxes (T) and saving (S)—reduce consumption spending below total income. Injections—government purchases (G) plus planned investment spending (I^p)—contribute to total spending. When leakages equal injections, total spending equals total output.

from income of $10 trillion to get consumption spending of $7 trillion. Thus, if consumption spending were the only spending in the economy, business firms would be unable to sell their entire potential output of $10 trillion.

Fortunately, in addition to leakages, there are **injections**—spending from sources *other* than households. Injections boost total spending and enable firms to produce and sell a level of output greater than just consumption spending.

There are two types of injections in the economy. First is the government's purchases of goods and services. When government agencies—federal, state, or local—buy aircraft, cleaning supplies, cell phones, or computers, they are buying a part of the economy's output.

The other injection is planned investment spending (I^p). When business firms purchase new computers, trucks, or machinery, or they build new factories or office buildings, they are buying a part of the GDP along with consumers and the government.

Take another look at the rectangles in Figure 5. Notice that in going from total output to total spending, leakages are subtracted and injections are added. Clearly, total output and total spending will be equal only if leakages and injections are equal as well.

Injections Spending on a country's output from sources other than its households.

> *Total spending will equal total output if and only if total leakages in the economy are equal to total injections—that is, only if the sum of saving and net taxes (S + T) is equal to the sum of planned investment spending and government purchases (I^p + G).*

And here is a surprising result: In the classical model, this condition will automatically be satisfied. To see why, we must first take a detour through another important market. Then we'll come back to the equality of leakages and injections.

THE LOANABLE FUNDS MARKET

The **loanable funds market** is where the economy's saving is made available to those who need additional funds. In the complex real world, households, businesses, government, and the foreign sector can all supply funds to this market. And the funds can be provided to a variety of entities as well: other households (that need funds to buy a home or car), businesses (that need funds to buy capital equipment), government (which often spends more than it collects in taxes), or other countries.

To keep our discussion simple, we'll assume that just one sector of the economy saves and *supplies* funds to the loanable funds market: the household sector. And we'll assume that only two sectors *demand* loanable funds: business firms and the government.

Loanable funds market The market in which savers make their funds available to borrowers.

The Supply of Loanable Funds

Households can supply the funds they are saving in a variety of ways. They can put their funds in a bank, which will lend the funds for them. They can lend directly to corporations or the government by purchasing a *bond* (a contractual promise by the bond issuer to pay the funds back). Or they can purchase shares of corporate stock (shares of ownership in a corporation). In each of these cases, households supply funds to the market (rather than just stuffing cash into their mattress) because they receive a payment for doing so. We'll assume all the funds that households save are supplied to the loanable funds market, where they are loaned out. The payment households receive is called *interest*.

> *The total supply of loanable funds is equal to household saving. The funds supplied are loaned out, and households receive interest payments on these funds.*

The Supply of Funds Curve

Interest is the reward for saving and supplying funds to the loanable funds market. So a rise in the interest rate will *increase* the quantity of funds supplied (household saving), while a drop in the interest rate decreases it.[3] This relationship is illustrated by Classica's upward-sloping **supply of funds curve** in Figure 6. If the interest rate is 3 percent, households save $1.5 trillion, and if the interest rate rises to 5 percent, people save more and the quantity of funds supplied rises to $1.75 trillion.

Supply of funds curve Indicates the level of household saving at various interest rates.

> *The quantity of funds supplied to the financial market depends positively on the interest rate. This is why the saving or supply of funds curve slopes upward.*

Of course, other things can affect saving besides the interest rate: tax rates, expectations about the future, and the general willingness of households to postpone consumption, to name a few. In drawing the supply of funds curve, we assume each of these variables is constant. In the next chapter, we'll explore what happens when some of these variables change.

---

[3] In this chapter, we'll assume there is no inflation or expected inflation, so there is no need to distinguish between the real interest rate and the nominal interest rate. But if we wanted to bring inflation into our model, then saving would depend on the *real* interest rate that households expected to earn for supplying loanable funds. Similarly, business borrowing for investment (to be discussed next) would depend on the *real* interest rate that businesses expected to pay for borrowing.

| **FIGURE 6** | Household Supply of Loanable Funds |

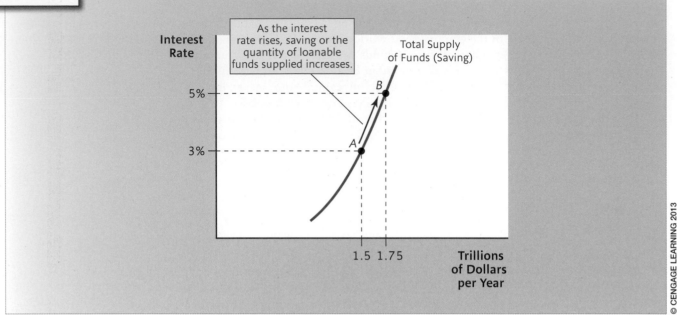

© CENGAGE LEARNING 2013

The Demand for Loanable Funds

On the demand side of the market are the business firms and government agencies who borrow. In our classical model, when Avis wants to add cars to its automobile rental fleet, when McDonald's wants to build a new beef-processing plant, or when the local dry cleaner wants to buy new dry-cleaning machines, it will raise the funds it needs in the loanable funds market. So each firm's planned investment spending is equal to its demand for funds in the loanable funds market. Combining all firms together:

> *Businesses' total demand for loanable funds is equal to their total planned investment spending. The funds obtained are borrowed, and firms pay interest on these funds.*

Budget deficit The excess of government purchases over net taxes.

The other major borrower in the loanable funds market is the government sector. When government purchases of goods and services (G) are greater than net taxes (T), the government runs a **budget deficit** equal to $G - T$. Because the government cannot spend funds that it does not have, it must cover its deficit by borrowing in the loanable funds market. Thus, in any year, the government's demand for funds is equal to its deficit.

In our example in Table 1, Classica's government is running a budget deficit: Government purchases are $2 trillion, while net taxes are $1.25 trillion, giving us a deficit of $2 trillion − $1.25 trillion = $0.75 trillion.

> *The government's demand for loanable funds is equal to its budget deficit. The funds are borrowed, and the government pays interest on its loans.*

Budget surplus The excess of net taxes over government purchases.

It is also possible for government purchases of goods and services (G) to be *less* than net taxes (T). In that case, the government runs a **budget surplus** equal to $T - G$. You'll be asked to to explore the classical model with a budget surplus in an end-of-chapter problem.

The Demand for Funds Curve

Businesses buy plant and equipment when the expected benefits exceed the costs. Since businesses obtain the funds for their investment spending from the loanable funds market, a key cost of any investment project is the interest rate that must be paid on borrowed funds. As the interest rate falls and investment costs decrease, more projects will look attractive, and planned investment spending will rise. This is the logic of the downward-sloping **business demand for funds curve** in Figure 7. At a 5 percent interest rate, firms would borrow $1 trillion and spend it on capital equipment; at an interest rate of 3 percent, business borrowing and investment spending would rise to $1.5 trillion.

Business demand for funds curve Indicates the level of investment spending firms plan at various interest rates.

> *When the interest rate falls, investment spending and the business borrowing needed to finance it rise.*

What about the government's demand for funds? Will it, too, be influenced by the interest rate? Probably not very much. Government seems to be cushioned from the cost–benefit considerations that haunt business decisions. For this reason, when government is running a budget deficit, our classical model treats government borrowing as independent of the interest rate: No matter what the interest rate, the government sector's deficit—and its borrowing—is the same. This is why we have graphed the **government's demand for funds curve** as a vertical line in panel (b) of Figure 8.

Government demand for funds curve Indicates the amount of government borrowing at various interest rates.

> *The government sector's deficit and, therefore, its demand for funds are independent of the interest rate.*

In Figure 8, the government deficit—and hence the government's demand for funds—is equal to $0.75 trillion at any interest rate.

Figure 8 also shows that the **total demand for funds curve** is found by horizontally summing the business demand curve [panel (a)] and the government demand curve

Total demand for funds curve Indicates the total amount of borrowing at various interest rates.

FIGURE 7   **Business Demand for Loanable Funds**

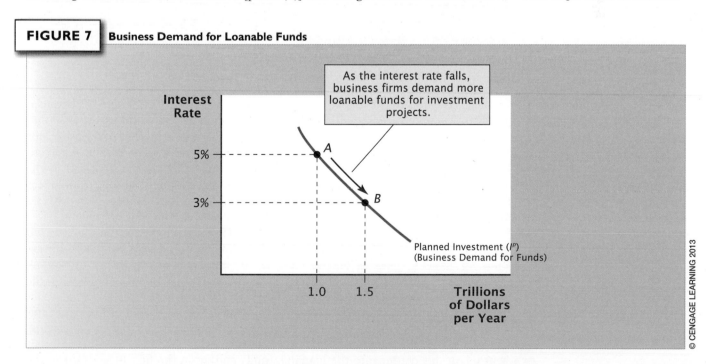

As the interest rate falls, business firms demand more loanable funds for investment projects.

Interest Rate

5% — A

3% — B

Planned Investment (I^P) (Business Demand for Funds)

1.0   1.5   **Trillions of Dollars per Year**

© CENGAGE LEARNING 2013

FIGURE 8 | **The Demand for Funds**

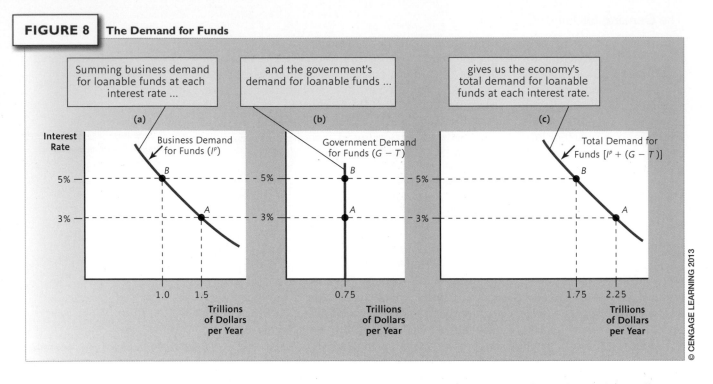

Summing business demand for loanable funds at each interest rate ...

and the government's demand for loanable funds ...

gives us the economy's total demand for loanable funds at each interest rate.

(a)   (b)   (c)

[panel (b)]. For example, if the interest rate is 5 percent, firms demand $1 trillion in funds and the government demands $0.75 trillion, so that the total quantity of loanable funds demanded is $1.75 trillion. A drop in the interest rate—to 3 percent—increases business borrowing to $1.5 trillion while the government's borrowing remains at $0.75 trillion, so the total quantity of funds demanded rises to $2.25 trillion.

> *As the interest rate decreases, the quantity of funds demanded by business firms increases, while the quantity demanded by the government remains unchanged. Therefore, the total quantity of funds demanded rises.*

Equilibrium in the Loanable Funds Market

In the classical view, the loanable funds market—like all other markets—is assumed to clear: The interest rate will rise or fall until the quantities of funds supplied and demanded are equal. Figure 9 illustrates the loanable funds market of Classica, our fictional economy. Equilibrium occurs at point *E*, with an interest rate of 5 percent and total saving equal to $1.75 trillion. (To convince yourself that 5 percent is the equilibrium interest rate, mark an interest rate of 4 percent on the graph. Would there be an excess demand or an excess supply of loanable funds at this rate? How would the interest rate change? Then do the same for an interest rate of 6 percent.)

Once we know the equilibrium interest rate (5 percent), we can use the first two panels of Figure 8 to tell us exactly where the total household saving of $1.75 billion ends up. Panel (a) tells us that at 5 percent interest, business firms are borrowing $1 trillion of the total, and panel (b) tells us that the government is borrowing the remaining $0.75 trillion to cover its deficit.

So far, our exploration of the loanable funds market has shown us how three important variables in the economy are determined: the interest rate, the level of saving, and the level of investment. But it really tells us more. Remember the question that sent us on this detour into the loanable funds market in the first place: Can we be

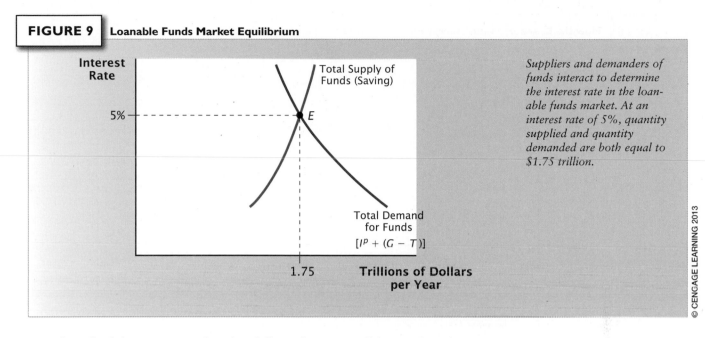

FIGURE 9 | Loanable Funds Market Equilibrium

Suppliers and demanders of funds interact to determine the interest rate in the loanable funds market. At an interest rate of 5%, quantity supplied and quantity demanded are both equal to $1.75 trillion.

sure that all of the output produced at full employment will be purchased? We now have the tools to answer this question.

The Loanable Funds Market and Say's Law

In Figure 5 of this chapter, you saw that total spending will equal total output if and only if *total leakages* in the economy (saving plus net taxes) are equal to *total injections* (planned investment plus government purchases). Now we can see why this requirement will be satisfied automatically in the classical model. Look at Figure 10, which duplicates the rectangles from Figure 5. But there is something added: arrows to indicate the flows between leakages and injections.

Let's follow the arrows to see what happens to all the leakages out of spending. One arrow shows that the entire leakage of net taxes ($1.25 trillion) flows to the government, which spends it. Now look at the other two arrows that show us what happens to the $1.75 trillion leakage of household saving. $0.75 trillion of this saving is borrowed by the government, while the rest—$1 trillion—is borrowed by business firms. Figure 10 shows us that net taxes and savings don't just disappear from the economy. Net taxes go to the government, which *spends them*. And any funds saved go either to the government—which spends them—or to business firms—which spend them.

But wait . . . how do we know that *all* funds that are saved will end up going to either the government or businesses? Because the loanable funds market clears: The interest rate adjusts until the quantity of loanable funds supplied (saving) is equal to the quantity of loanable funds demanded (government and business borrowing).

We can put all this together as follows: Every dollar of output creates a dollar of household income, by definition. And—as long as the loanable funds market clears—every dollar of income will either be spent by households themselves or passed along to some *other* sector of the economy that will spend it in their place.

Or, to put it even more simply,

as long as the loanable funds market clears, Say's law holds: Total spending equals total output. This is true even in a more realistic economy with saving, taxes, investment, and a government deficit.

FIGURE 10   How the Loanable Funds Market Ensures That Total Spending = Total Output

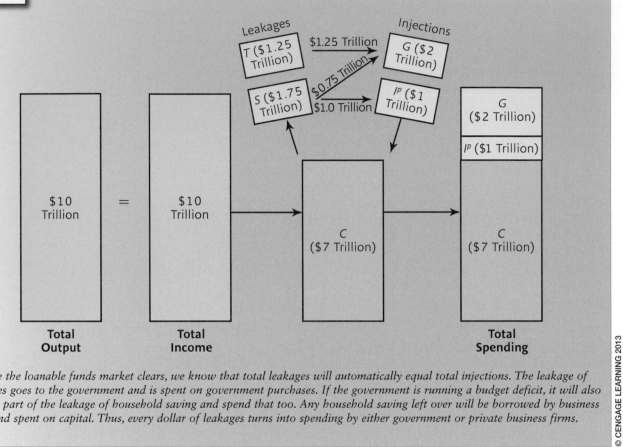

Because the loanable funds market clears, we know that total leakages will automatically equal total injections. The leakage of net taxes goes to the government and is spent on government purchases. If the government is running a budget deficit, it will also borrow part of the leakage of household saving and spend that too. Any household saving left over will be borrowed by business firms and spent on capital. Thus, every dollar of leakages turns into spending by either government or private business firms.

Say's Law with Equations

Here's another way to see the logic behind Say's law, with some simple equations. Because the loanable funds market clears, we know that the interest rate—the price in this market—will rise or fall until the quantity of funds supplied (savings, S) is equal to the quantity of funds demanded (planned investment plus the deficit, or $I^p + (G - T)$):

Loanable funds market clears $\Longrightarrow$ $\underset{\substack{\text{Quantity of} \\ \text{funds supplied}}}{\underline{S}}$ $=$ $\underset{\substack{\text{Quantity of} \\ \text{funds demanded}}}{\underline{I^p + (G - T)}}$

Rearranging this equation by moving T to the left side, we have:

Loanable funds market clears $\Longrightarrow$ $\underset{\text{Leakages}}{\underline{S + T}}$ $=$ $\underset{\text{Injections}}{\underline{I^p + G}}$

So now, we know that as long as the loanable funds market clears, leakages equal injections. Finally, remember that

Leakages = Injections $\Longrightarrow$ Total spending = Total output

In other words, market clearing in the loanable funds market *assures us* that total leakages in the economy will equal total injections, which in turn *assures us* that total spending will be just sufficient to purchase total output.

Say's Law in Perspective

Say's law is a powerful concept. But be careful not to overinterpret it. Say's law shows that the *total* value of spending in the economy will equal the *total* value of output, which rules out a *general* overproduction or underproduction of goods in the economy. It does not promise us that each firm in the economy will be able to sell all of the particular good it produces. It is perfectly consistent with Say's law that there be excess supplies in some markets, as long as they are balanced by excess demands in other markets.

But lest you begin to think that the classical economy might be a chaotic mess, with excess supplies and demands in lots of markets for different goods, don't forget about the *market-clearing* assumption. In each market for each good, the price adjusts until the quantities supplied and demanded are equal. For this reason, the classical, long-run view rules out over- or underproduction in individual markets, as well as the generalized overproduction ruled out by Say's law.

FISCAL POLICY IN THE CLASSICAL MODEL

When the government changes either net taxes or its own purchases in order to influence total output, it is engaging in **fiscal policy**. There are two different effects that fiscal policy, in theory, could have on total output.

The *supply-side* effects of fiscal policy on output come from changing the quantities of resources available in the economy. We'll discuss these supply-side effects in the next chapter. Here, we'll discuss only the potential **demand-side effects** of fiscal policy, which are entirely different. These effects arise from fiscal policy's impact on total *spending*.

At first glance, using fiscal policy to change total spending and thereby change the economy's real GDP seems workable. For example, if the government cuts taxes or increases transfer payments, households would have more income, so their consumption spending would increase. Or the government itself could purchase more goods and services. In either case, if total spending rises, and business firms *sell* more output, they should want to hire more workers and *produce* more output as well. The economy's real GDP would rise, and so would total employment.

It sounds reasonable. Does it work?

Not if the economy behaves according to the classical model. As you are about to see, in the classical model *fiscal policy has no demand-side effects at all*.

Fiscal policy A change in government purchases or net taxes designed to change total output.

Demand-side effects Macroeconomic policy effects on total output that work through changes in total spending.

© WON DAE-YEON/AFP/GETTY IMAGES

An Increase in Government Purchases

Let's first see what would happen if the government of Classica attempted to increase output and employment by increasing government purchases. More specifically, suppose the government raised its spending by $0.5 trillion, hiring people to fix roads and bridges, or hiring more teachers, or increasing its spending on goods and services for homeland security. What would happen?

To answer this, we must first answer another question: Where will Classica's government get the additional $0.5 trillion it spends? If the government raises taxes, it will lower households' disposable income,

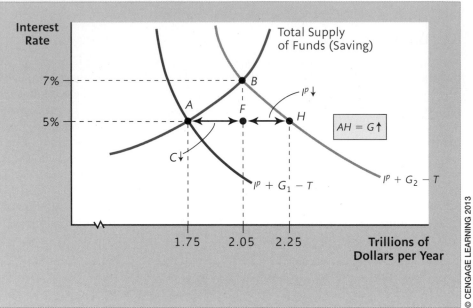

FIGURE 11   Crowding Out from an Increase in Government Purchases

Beginning from equilibrium at point A, an increase in the budget deficit caused by additional government purchases shifts the demand for funds curve from $I^p + G_1 - T$ to $I^p + G_2 - T$. At point H, the quantity of funds demanded exceeds the quantity supplied, so the interest rate begins to rise. As it rises, households are led to save more, and business firms invest less. In the new equilibrium at point B, both consumption and investment spending have been completely crowded out by the increased government spending.

and their consumption spending would decrease. In terms of spending, the government would be taking away with one hand what it is giving with the other. So let's assume the government does *not* raise taxes. In that case, with more government spending, the government's budget deficit $(G - T)$ will rise, so the government must dip into the loanable funds market to *borrow* the additional funds.

Figure 11 illustrates the effects. Initially, with government purchases equal to $2 trillion, the demand for funds curve is $I^p + G_1 - T$, where G_1 represents the initial level of government purchases. The equilibrium occurs at point A with the interest rate equal to 5 percent.

If government purchases increase by $0.5 trillion, with no change in taxes, the budget deficit increases by $0.5 trillion and so does the government's demand for funds. The demand for funds curve shifts rightward by $0.5 trillion to $I^p + G_2 - T$, where G_2 represents an amount $0.5 trillion greater than G_1. After the shift, there would be an excess demand for funds at the original interest rate of 5 percent. The total quantity of funds demanded would be $2.25 trillion (point H), while the quantity supplied would continue to be $1.75 trillion (point A). Thus, the excess demand for funds would be equal to the distance AH in the figure, or $0.5 trillion. This excess demand drives up the interest rate to 7 percent. As the interest rate rises, two things happen.

First, a higher interest rate chokes off some investment spending, as business firms decide that certain investment projects no longer make sense. For example, the local dry cleaner might wish to borrow funds for a new machine at an interest rate of 5 percent, but not at 7 percent. In the figure, we move along the new demand for funds curve from point H to point B. Planned investment drops by $0.2 trillion (because the total demand for funds falls from $2.25 trillion to $2.05 trillion). (Question: How do we know that only business borrowing, and not also government borrowing, adjusts as we move from point H to point B?) Thus, one consequence of the rise in government purchases is a *decrease in planned investment spending*.

But that's not all: The rise in the interest rate also causes saving to increase. Of course, when people save more of their incomes, they spend less, so another consequence of the rise in government purchases is a *decrease in consumption spending*. In the figure, we move from point A to point B along the saving curve. As saving increases from $1.75 trillion to $2.05 trillion—a rise of $0.3 trillion—consumption falls by $0.3 trillion.

Crowding Out and Complete Crowding Out

As you've just seen, the increase in government purchases causes both planned investment spending and consumption spending to decline. We say that the government's purchases have *crowded out* the spending of households (C) and businesses (I^p).

> *Crowding out is a decline in one sector's spending caused by an increase in some other sector's spending.*

But we are not quite finished. If we sum the drop in C and the drop in I^p, we find that total private sector spending has fallen by $0.3 trillion + $0.2 trillion = $0.5 trillion. That is, the drop in private sector spending is *precisely equal* to the rise in government purchases, G. Not only is there crowding out, there is **complete crowding out**: Each dollar of government purchases causes private sector spending to decline by a full dollar. The net effect is that total spending ($C + I^p + G$) does not change at all!

> *In the classical model, a rise in government purchases completely crowds out private sector spending, so total spending remains unchanged.*

The Logic of Complete Crowding Out

A closer look at Figure 11 shows why, in the classical model, an increase in government purchases will always cause complete crowding out, regardless of the particular numbers used or the shapes of the curves. When G increases, the demand for funds curve shifts rightward by the same amount that G rises, or the distance from point A to point H. Then the interest rate rises, moving us along the supply of funds curve from point A to point B. As a result, saving rises (and consumption falls) by the distance AF. But the rise in the interest rate *also* causes a movement along the demand for funds curve, from point H to point B. As a result, investment spending falls by the amount FH.

The final impact can be summarized as follows:

- $G\uparrow = AH$
- $C\downarrow = AF$
- $I^p\downarrow = FH$

And since *AF + FH = AH,* we know that the combined decrease in C and I^p is precisely equal to the increase in G.

Because there is complete crowding out in the classical model, a rise in government purchases cannot change total spending. If we step back from the graph and think about it, this result makes perfect sense. Each additional dollar the government spends is obtained from the loanable funds market, where *it would have been spent by someone else* if the government hadn't borrowed it. How do we

---

DANGEROUS CURVES ⚠️

G and T are separate variables It is common to think that a rise in government purchases (G) implies an equal rise in net taxes (T) to pay for it. But as you've seen in our discussion, economists treat G and T as two separate variables. Unless stated otherwise, we use the *ceteris paribus* assumption: When we change G, we assume T remains constant, and when we change T, we assume G remains constant. It is the budget deficit (or surplus) that changes when T or G changes.

© AXL/SHUTTERSTOCK.COM

Crowding out A decline in one sector's spending caused by an increase in some other sector's spending.

Complete crowding out A dollar-for-dollar decline in one sector's spending caused by an increase in some other sector's spending.

know this? Because the loanable funds market funnels every dollar of household saving—no more and no less—to either the government or business firms. If the government borrows more, it just removes funds that would have been spent by businesses (the drop in I^p) or by consumers (the drop in C).

Remember that the goal of this increase in government purchases was to increase output and employment *by increasing total spending*. But now we see that the policy fails to increase spending at all. Therefore,

> *in the classical model, an increase in government purchases has no demand-side effects on total output or total employment.*

Of course, the opposite sequence of events would happen if government purchases *decreased*: The drop in G would *shrink* the deficit. The interest rate would decline, and private sector spending (C and I^p) would rise by the same amount that government purchases had fallen. (See if you can draw the graphs to prove this to yourself.) Once again, total spending and total output would remain unchanged.

A Decrease in Net Taxes

Suppose that the government, instead of increasing its own purchases by $0.5 trillion, tried to increase total spending through a $0.5 trillion cut in net taxes. For example, the government of Classica could decrease income tax collections by $0.5 trillion, or increase transfer payments such as unemployment benefits by that amount. What would happen?

In general, households respond to a cut in net taxes by spending some of it and saving the rest. But let's give this policy every chance of working by making an extreme assumption in its favor: We'll assume that households *spend the entire $0.5 trillion tax cut* on consumption goods; they save none of it.

Figure 12 shows what will happen in the market for loanable funds. Initially, the demand for funds curve is $I^p + G - T_1$, where T_1 is the initial level of net taxes. The equilibrium is at point A, with an interest rate of 5 percent. If we cut net taxes (T) by $0.5 trillion, while holding government purchases constant, the budget deficit increases by $0.5 trillion, and so does the government's demand for funds. The demand for funds curve shifts rightward to $I^p + G - T_2$, where T_2 is an amount $0.5 trillion less than T_1.

The increase in the demand for funds drives the interest rate up to 7 percent, until we reach a new equilibrium at point B. As the interest rate rises, two things happen.

First, a higher interest rate will encourage more saving, which means a decrease in consumption spending. This is a movement along the supply of funds curve, from point A to point B, with saving rising (and consumption falling) by $0.3 trillion.

Second, a higher interest rate will decrease investment spending. This is shown by the movement from H to B along the new demand for funds curve. Planned investment decreases by $0.2 trillion.

What has happened to *total* spending? Only two components of spending have changed in this case: C and I^p. Let's first consider what's happened to consumption (C). First, we had a $0.5 trillion *rise* in consumption from the tax cut (remember: we assumed the entire tax cut was spent). This is equal to the horizontal distance AH. Then, because the interest rate rose, we had a $0.3 billion *decrease* in consumption. This decrease is equal to the horizontal distance AF. Taking both effects together,

| FIGURE 12 | Crowding Out from a Tax Cut |

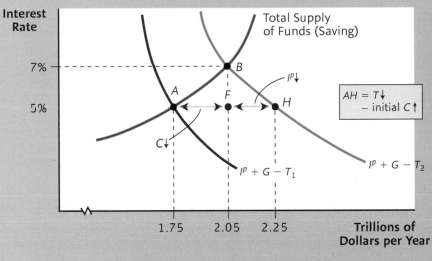

Beginning from equilibrium at point A, an increase in the budget deficit caused by a tax cut shifts the demand for funds curve from $I^P + G - T_1$ to $I^P + G - T_2$. If the tax cut is entirely spent, consumption initially rises by the distance AH.

At the original interest rate of 5 percent, the quantity of funds demanded now exceeds the quantity supplied. This causes the interest rate to rise.

As the interest rate rises, we move from A to B along the supply of funds curve. Saving rises (and consumption falls) by the distance AF. The final rise in consumption is FH. We also move along the demand for funds curve from H to B, so investment falls by the distance FH. In the new equilibrium at point B, consumption (which has risen by FH) has completely crowded out investment (which has dropped by FH).

© CENGAGE LEARNING 2013

the net effect is a rise of $0.5 trillion − $0.3 trillion = $0.2 trillion. This net rise in consumption is shown by the distance *FH*.

Now remember what has happened to planned investment spending: It fell by $0.2 billion (the distance *FH*)—the same amount that consumption spending rose. In other words, the tax cut increases consumption but decreases planned investment by the same amount. We can say that greater consumption spending *completely crowds out* planned investment spending, leaving total spending unchanged.

> In the classical model, a cut in net taxes raises consumption, which completely crowds out planned investment. Total spending remains unchanged, so the tax cut has no demand-side effects on total output or employment.

THE CLASSICAL MODEL: A SUMMARY

You've just completed a tour of the classical model, our framework for understanding the economy in the long run. Let's review what we've done, and what we've concluded.

We began with a critical assumption: All markets clear. We then applied the three-step process to organize our thinking of the economy. First, we focused on an important market—the labor market. We identified the buyers and sellers in that market (Step 1), and then found equilibrium employment (Step 2) by assuming that the labor market cleared. We went through a similar process with the loanable funds market, identifying the suppliers and demanders (Step 1) and finding the equilibrium in that market as well (Step 2). We then showed that total spending will be just sufficient to purchase our potential output, reinforcing our confidence in the full-employment equilibrium we found. Finally, we explored what happens when things change (Step 3). In particular, we saw that fiscal policy changes have no demand-side effects on total output and total employment.

Our explorations have considered just some of the possible scenarios under which the economy might operate. For example, we've assumed that the government runs a budget deficit. But we could also explore what happens when the government starts out with a budget *surplus*, collecting more in net taxes than it spends on its purchases. We also assumed that any tax cut was entirely spent by households on consumption goods. But we could also ask what happens when some or all of a tax cut is saved.

You'll be asked to explore some of these other scenarios in the end-of-chapter problems. When you do, you'll see that the graphs may look different, but the important conclusions still hold. These general conclusions are:

- In the classical model, the government needn't worry about employment. The economy—if left to itself—will achieve full employment on its own.

- In the classical model, the government needn't worry about total spending. The economy will generate just enough spending on its own to buy the output that a fully employed labor force produces.

- In the classical model, fiscal policy has no *demand-side effects* on output or employment.

* * *

This chapter does not end with the usual Using the Theory section. Instead, there is an (optional) appendix, extending the classical model to the global economy. And in the next chapter, we'll be using the theory to analyze *economic growth*, a topic for which the classical model is very well-suited.

SUMMARY

The classical model is an attempt to explain the behavior of the economy over long time periods. Its most critical assumption is that markets clear—that prices adjust in every market to equate quantities demanded and supplied. The labor market is the starting point of the classical model. When the labor market clears, we have full employment and the economy produces the potential level of output.

The *aggregate production function* shows the total output that can be produced with different quantities of labor and for given amounts of other resources and a given state of technology. When the labor market is at full employment, the production function can be used to determine the economy's potential level of output.

In the loanable funds market, the quantity of funds supplied equals household saving, which depends positively on the interest rate. The quantity of funds demanded equals planned investment, which depends negatively on the interest rate, and any government budget deficit, if there is one. The interest rate adjusts so that the quantity of funds supplied always equals the quantity demanded. Equivalently, it adjusts so that saving (S) equals the sum of planned investment spending (I^p) and the government budget deficit ($G - T$), where T represents *net taxes*.

According to *Say's law*, total spending in the economy will always be just sufficient to purchase the amount of total output produced. By producing and selling goods and services, firms create a total demand equal to what they have produced. Net taxes are channeled to the government, which spends them. If households do not spend their entire after-tax incomes, the excess is channeled, as saving, into the *loanable funds market*, where it is borrowed and spent by businesses and government.

Fiscal policy has no *demand-side effects* on output in the classical model. An increase in government purchases results in *complete crowding out* of planned investment and consumption spending. A tax cut causes greater consumption spending to completely crowd out investment spending. In both cases, fiscal policy leaves total spending unchanged.

PROBLEM SET

Answers to even-numbered Problems can be found on the text Web site through www.cengagebrain.com

1. Use a diagram similar to Figure 3 to illustrate the effect, on aggregate output and the real hourly wage, of (a) an increase in labor demand and (b) an increase in labor supply.

2. Draw a diagram (similar to Figure 11 in this chapter) illustrating the impact of a *decrease* in government purchases. Assume the government is running a budget deficit both before and after the change in government purchases. On your diagram, identify distances that represent:
   a. The decrease in government purchases
   b. The increase in consumption spending
   c. The increase in planned investment spending

3. Consider the following statement: "In the classical model, just as an *increase* in government purchases causes complete crowding *out*, so a *decrease* in government purchases causes complete crowding *in*."
   a. In this statement, explain what is meant by "crowding in" and "complete crowding in."
   b. Is the statement true? (Hint: Look at the diagram you drew in problem 2.)

4. The following data ($ millions) are for the island nation of Pacifica over a year.

Total output	$10
Total income	$10
Consumption	$ 6
Government spending	$ 3
Total tax revenue	$ 2.5
Transfer payments	$ 0.5

   a. Use this information to find Pacifica's net taxes, disposable income, and savings.
   b. Determine whether the government is running a budget surplus, budget deficit, or balanced budget.
   c. Find planned investment by calculating how much is available in the loanable funds market after the government has borrowed what it might need.
   d. Does total output equal total spending?
   e. Show your answers on a diagram similar to the one in Figure 10 in the chapter.

5. Return to problem 4. What will happen if consumption spending starts to rise? Assume no change in net taxes. Show the effect on the loanable funds market, and explain what will happen to C, I^p, and G. (Note: You won't be able to find specific numbers.)

6. As the baby boomers retire, spending on Social Security benefits is rising. Assume that (1) the government—which is already running a budget deficit—pays for the increased benefits with further *borrowing*;

(2) the additional Social Security benefits are *spent* by households; (3) there are no shifts in the labor supply or labor demand curves. With no other change in policy, what would you expect to happen to each of the following variables?
   a. the government's budget deficit
   b. the interest rate
   c. consumption spending
   d. planned investment spending
   e. total output

7. The following data give a complete picture of the household, business, and government sectors for 2011 in the small nation of Sylvania. (All dollar figures are in billions.)

Consumption spending	$ 50
Capital stock (end of 2010)	$100
Capital stock (end of 2011)	$103
Change in inventories	$ 0
Government welfare payments	$ 5
Government unemployment insurance payments	$ 2
Government payroll	$ 3
Government outlays for materials	$ 2
Depreciation	$ 7
Interest rate	6%

   Assuming the government budget for 2011 was in balance, (G = T), calculate each of the following (in order):
   a. Government purchases
   b. Net taxes
   c. Total planned investment
   d. Real GDP
   e. Total saving
   f. Total leakages
   g. Total injections

8. For the economy in problem 7, suppose that the government had purchased $2 billion more in goods and services than you found in that problem, with no change in taxes.
   a. Explain how each of the variables you calculated in problem 7 would be affected (i.e., state whether it would increase or decrease).
   b. Draw a graph illustrating the impact of the $2 billion increase in government purchases on the loanable funds market. Label the equilibrium interest rate, saving, and total quantity of funds demanded at both the original and the new level of government purchases. (Note: You won't be able to find specific numbers.)

More Challenging

9. When the government runs a budget surplus ($T > G$), it deposits any unspent tax revenue into the banking system, thus adding to the supply of loanable funds. In this case, the supply of loanable funds is household saving plus the budget surplus $[S + (T - G)]$, while the demand for funds is just planned investment (I^p).

   a. Draw a diagram of the loanable funds market with a budget surplus, showing the equilibrium interest rate and quantity of funds demanded and supplied.

   b. Prove that when the loanable funds market is in equilibrium, total leakages ($S + T$) are equal to total injections ($I^p + G$). (Hint: Use the same method as used in the chapter for the case of a budget deficit.)

   c. Show (on your graph) what happens when government purchases increase, identifying any decrease in consumption and planned investment on the graph (similar to what was done in Figure 11).

   d. When the government is running a budget surplus, does an increase in government purchases cause complete crowding out? Explain briefly.

10. Figure 12 shows the impact of a tax cut on the loanable funds market when the entire tax cut is spent. What if, instead, the entire tax cut had been *saved*?

    a. Draw a diagram of the loanable funds market showing the impact of a tax cut that is entirely saved. (Assume the government is already running a budget deficit.)

    b. What happens to the interest rate after the tax cut? Explain briefly.

    c. In Figure 12, the tax cut caused consumption spending to crowd out planned investment spending. How does a tax cut that is entirely saved affect the components of total spending?

11. [Requires appendix.] Suppose that the government budget is balanced ($G = T$), and household saving is $1 trillion.

    a. If this is a closed economy, what is the value of planned investment (I^p)?

    b. If this is an open economy with balanced trade ($IM = X$), will investment have the same value as you found in (a)? Briefly, why or why not?

    c. If this is an open economy with a trade deficit ($IM > X$), will planned investment have the same value as you found in (a)? Briefly, why or why not?

12. [Requires appendix.] Suppose that Classica has international trade, but it is running a trade surplus ($X > IM$) rather than a trade deficit as in the appendix. Suppose, too, that Classica's government is running a budget deficit.

    a. Draw a diagram for Classica's loanable funds market, being careful to include the trade surplus in the label for one of the curves. (Hint: When Classica runs a trade surplus equal to $X - IM$, foreigners spend more dollars on Classica's goods than they get by selling their goods to Classica. From where do you think foreigners get these dollars?)

    b. Label the initial equilibrium point A.

    c. Give an equation showing that, in equilibrium, the quantity of loanable funds demanded (on one side) is equal to the quantity of loanable funds supplied (on the other side).

    d. Rearrange your equation to show that, even when Classica runs a trade surplus, its leakages and injections are equal.

So far in this chapter, we've been working with a *closed economy*—one that has no trade with other nations. What is different in an *open economy* with imports and exports of goods and services? The most general answer is: not much. All of the conclusions of the classical model still hold. But there are a few added complications in showing that Say's law holds—that total spending equals total output.

Leakages and Injections in an Open Economy

Let's suppose that in Classica (the economy used in the chapter), households, business firms, and government agencies spend $1.5 trillion on *imports* from other countries. This $1.5 trillion is income received by households, but *not* spent on *Classica's* output. It is an additional *leakage* out of spending on Classica's output. Total leakages are now imports (*IM*) along with the other leakages of saving (*S*) and taxes (*T*).

But once we recognize international trade, we must also account for Classica's *exports* of goods and services. These are *injections* for Classica, because exports are spending on Classica's output that does not come from its households. Total injections are now exports (*X*) along with planned investment (*I*^{p}) and government purchases (*G*).

> *In an economy with international trade, imports (IM) are a leakage, along with saving and taxes. Exports (X) are an injection, along with planned investment (I^P) and government purchases (G).*

Total Spending in an Open Economy

International trade requires a change in the expression for total spending. In a closed economy, recall that total spending is $C + I^p + G$. But in an open economy, some of the spending included in consumption (*C*), planned investment (*I*^{p}), and government purchases (*G*) is spent on goods produced in other countries. Thus, $C + I^p + G$ *overstates* spending on domestic goods. To correct for this, we have to subtract imports (*IM*) from $C + I^p + G$.

On the other hand, in an open economy, goods and services can be *sold* to other countries as well. These are not included in *C*, *I*^{p}, or *G*. So we must add exports (*X*) to get total spending on domestic output. Combining these two changes together:

> *total spending in an open economy is* $C + I^P + G + (X - IM)$.

Say's Law in an Open Economy

In the chapter, you learned that—as long as the loanable funds market clears—Say's law holds: total spending equals total output, so there will always be just enough spending to buy what has been produced. Therefore, the economy can continue to produce its potential output, and spending will take care of itself. But does the same result hold in an open economy? Let's explore this under two different scenarios.

Balanced Trade: Exports = Imports

Balanced trade means that exports (*X*) and imports (*IM*) are equal, so the last term added in total spending $(X - IM)$ is zero. With balanced trade, total spending in Classica will be $C + I^p + G$, just as it was in a closed economy.

Will total spending of $C + I^p + G$ be equal to total output, even though there are exports and imports? The answer is yes, as we can see by thinking about leakages and injections. In the case of balanced trade, the $1.5 trillion that leaks out of Classica's spending to buy imports (*IM*) is equal to the $1.5 billion that comes back to Classica to buy its exports (*X*). Because total leakages and total injections were equal in the closed economy (before we included imports and exports), they must be equal now as well.

> *In the classical model, when a country has balanced trade (exports = imports), Say's law holds: total spending on the country's output will be equal in value to its total output.*

But what happens if trade is *not* balanced?

In the next section, we'll consider what happens to spending when a country imports more than it exports. You'll be invited to analyze the opposite case (exports exceed imports) in an end-of-chapter problem.

Unbalanced Trade: Imports > Exports

Suppose, as before, that Classica's households import $1.5 trillion in goods produced in other countries. But now, residents of these other countries want to purchase only $1 trillion in goods from Classica. Classica will then be running a *trade deficit* equal to the excess of its imports (*IM*) over its exports (*X*):

Trade deficit = *IM* − *X* = $1.5 trillion − $1 trillion

= $0.5 trillion.

Now, it seems we have a problem. With imports greater than exports, won't Classica's leakages (*S* + *T* + *IM*) be greater than injections (*I*^{p} + *G* + *X*)? And won't total spending therefore be less than total output?

The answer is no.

To see why, let's assume (as we've done all along in the chapter) that Classica's currency is the dollar. The 1.5 trillion in dollars that Classica's households spend on imports during the year does not just disappear. Rather, the dollars are passed along to the foreign countries producing the goods that Classica imports. In our current example, the residents of these foreign countries return $1 trillion of the $1.5 trillion back to Classica as spending on Classica's exports. But what about the other $0.5 trillion? If foreigners are rational, they will not want to just keep this money, because dollars by themselves pay no interest or other return. Foreigners will, instead, want to purchase Classica's stocks or bonds, or even just deposit funds in a bank in Classica. If they do any of these things, they *supply funds to Classica's loanable funds market* and make them available to Classica's borrowers.[4]

> *When a country runs a trade deficit (imports exceed exports), foreigners will supply loanable funds to that country equal to its trade deficit.*

With a trade deficit, the supply of loanable funds in Classica becomes household saving (*S*) *plus* the flow of funds coming from foreigners (*IM* − *X*):

Total supply of funds = *S* + (*IM* − *X*)

[4] There is another part of the story we are leaving out here: the foreign exchange market. When Classica's households import goods, they may pay in dollars, but the foreign firms are paid in their own local currencies. Someone must exchange Classica's dollars for foreign currency—a bank or a foreign government. It is these banks or foreign governments that return the excess dollars to Classica's loanable funds market. We'll deal more explicitly with foreign exchange markets in the last chapter of this book.

The total demand for funds is still business borrowing (*I*^{p}) plus the government's budget deficit (*G* − *T*):

Total demand for funds = *I*^{p} + (*G* − *T*)

Figure A.1 shows the loanable funds market in Classica, where we've added Classica's trade deficit to its supply of loanable funds. Equilibrium occurs at point *E*, with an interest rate of 5 percent and $2.25 trillion in loanable funds supplied and demanded. Of this $2.25 trillion, we know that foreigners are supplying $0.5 trillion of the total, so households must be supplying (saving) the other $1.75 trillion.

In equilibrium, the quantity of funds supplied and demanded are equal:

Loanable funds market clears ⟹

$$\underbrace{S + (IM - X)}_{\substack{\text{Quantity of} \\ \text{funds supplied}}} = \underbrace{I^p + (G - T)}_{\substack{\text{Quantity of} \\ \text{funds demanded}}}$$

Let's now rearrange this equation by moving *T* over to the left and *X* over to the right:

Loanable funds market clears ⟹

$$\underbrace{S + T + IM}_{\text{Leakages}} = \underbrace{I^p + G + X}_{\text{Injections}}$$

This last equation shows us that total leakages and total injections are equal in Classica, even when it runs a trade deficit. But if leakages and injections are equal, then total spending must equal total output. Even with a trade deficit, Say's law still holds.

> *In the classical model, even when a country runs a trade deficit (exports < imports), Say's law holds: total spending on the country's output will be equal in value to its total output.*

Let's take a step back and understand the reasoning behind this result about spending. Classica produces $10 trillion in output, and therefore creates $10 trillion in income. Even though Classica is running a trade deficit, every dollar of the $10 trillion that households earn will still be spent on Classica's production—either by households themselves or by some other sector that spends it in their place. The dollars spent on imports are either spent on Classica's exports or put into its loanable funds market, where they are borrowed and spent by business firms or the government. And, as before, taxes and saving are also spent by either the government or business firms.

FIGURE A.1	The Loanable Funds Market with a Trade Deficit

When Classica runs a trade deficit (its imports exceed its exports), foreigners earn more dollars (Classica's currency) selling goods to Classica than they spend on goods from Classica. The excess dollars are returned to Classica's loanable funds market, where they become part of the supply of loanable funds. When the loanable funds market clears, we have $S + IM - X = I^P + G - T$. This, in turn, means that total leakages $(S + T + IM)$ equal total injections $(I^P + G + X)$.

Crowding Out in an Open Economy

In the chapter, you learned that in a closed economy, a rise in government purchases completely crowds out domestic consumption and investment spending, leaving total spending unchanged. Does this result also hold in an open economy? Yes . . . and no. It depends on how broadly we interpret the concept of crowding out.

For example, suppose government purchases increase in Classica, with no change in net taxes. The budget deficit and the demand for loanable funds will increase. Classica's interest rate will rise, reducing its planned investment spending and increasing saving by Classica's households. But something else will happen too: With higher interest rates, foreigners will regard Classica's loanable funds market as a more attractive place to lend. The supply of funds to Classica's loanable funds market will increase *beyond* any rise in Classica's own household saving. Because of these additional foreign funds, Classica's interest rate will rise by *less* than it would in a closed economy. While there would be *some* crowding out of consumption and investment spending in Classica, it might not be *complete* crowding out. Indeed, if Classica is a very small country, the flood of foreign funds into its loanable funds market may be so great relative to the demand for funds that Classica's interest rate rises hardly at all. In that case, its own consumption and investment might fall by very little.

However, in the *world as a whole*, crowding out *will* be complete. If foreigners are supplying more funds to Classica's loanable funds market, they must be either *spending* less themselves (a decrease in the rest of the world's consumption) or else shifting loanable funds from the rest of the world's loanable funds markets. With a smaller pool of loanable funds available elsewhere, investment spending in the rest of the world will fall. Remember: all the funds that flow into Classica's loanable funds market *would* have been spent elsewhere, but are now spent in Classica instead. This is how we know that, in the world as a whole, crowding out will be complete, and Classica's increase in government purchases will leave total spending unchanged.

> In the classical model with an open economy, an increase in government purchases in one country may not cause complete crowding out in that country. But worldwide, crowding out will be complete: The rise in government purchases in one country will be matched by an equal drop in global consumption and investment spending.

Similar logic leads to the same conclusion about a tax cut. If Classica cuts its taxes and increases its budget deficit, its interest rate will rise, attracting more loanable funds from abroad. As a result, Classica's investment spending may not be completely crowded out as it was in a closed economy. But the foreign funds supplied to Classica's market reduce spending in the rest of the world. Worldwide, crowding out will be complete, and total world spending will remain unchanged.

© JENNIFER GRUBBA

CHAPTER 9

Economic Growth and Rising Living Standards

Economist Thomas Malthus, writing in 1798, came to a striking conclusion: "Population, when unchecked, goes on doubling itself every twenty-five years, or increases in a geometrical ratio. . . . The means of subsistence . . . could not possibly be made to increase faster than in an arithmetic ratio."[1] From this simple logic, Malthus forecast a horrible fate for the human race. There would be repeated famines and wars to keep the rapidly growing population in balance with the more slowly growing supply of food and other necessities.

But history has proven Malthus wrong . . . at least in part. In the industrialized nations, living standards have increased beyond the wildest dreams of anyone alive in Malthus's time. Over the past half century, several nations—such as South Korea, Hong Kong, and Singapore—have joined the club, transforming themselves from relatively poor countries to among the richest in the world. More recently, China and India have begun growing rapidly, and are on track to reach living standards close to those in the United States within a few decades. At the same time, living standards in many of the less developed countries have remained stubbornly close to survival level and, in some cases, have fallen below it.

What are we to make of this? Why have living standards steadily increased in some nations but not in others? And what, if anything, can governments do to speed the rise in living standards? These are questions about economic growth—the long run increase in an economy's output of goods and services.

In this chapter, you'll learn what makes economies grow. You'll see that economic growth can be understood in terms of *shifts* of the curves of the classical model. But what *causes* these curves to shift is more complex, involving government policy and the institutional setting in which the government and private businesses operate.

THE MEANING AND IMPORTANCE OF ECONOMIC GROWTH

Before we analyze the causes of economic growth, let's address some fundamental questions. The first is: What do we mean by economic growth? In general, economic growth refers to a rise in the *standard of living* in a country. But this raises another question: What do we mean by the standard of living? And how can it be measured?

[1] Thomas Robert Malthus, *An Essay on the Principle of Population.* John Murray, London. First published in 1798, 6th edition published in 1826.

Measuring Living Standards

A country's standard of living is the level of economic well-being its economy delivers to its citizens. The most straightforward way to measure a nation's standard of living—and the one used most often by economists—is *real gross domestic product per capita,* or real GDP divided by the population. At first glance, this measure may seem limiting. After all, as you saw three chapters ago, many important aspects of our economic well-being are *not* captured by GDP. Leisure time, workplace safety, good health, a clean environment—we care about all of these. Yet none of them are measured in GDP.

Moreover, GDP per capita is the ratio of one aggregate (real GDP) to another (the total population). So it does not take account of how goods and services are *distributed* within the country. Suppose a country had a GDP per capita of $50,000 per year. If almost all of this production was distributed to a few people, then living standards for almost everyone in the country would be much lower than our simple measure suggests. Because of these problems, GDP per capita is an imperfect measure of average living standards.

But in practice, it's not as bad as you might think. When real GDP per capita is high, countries have a greater desire and ability to improve other aspects of life, such as general health, fairness, and safety. This is why a high real GDP per capita is almost always associated with a higher quality of life for most people, while a very low GDP per capita is associated with a lower quality of life for most people.

Table 1 provides an illustration. It lists GDP per capita, mortality rates for children under age 5, life expectancies, adult literacy rates, and the percentage of people

TABLE 1

Some Indicators of Economic Well-Being in Rich and Poor Countries, 2010

Country	GDP per Capita (2008 Dollars)	Under-5 Mortality, (per 1,000 live births)	Life Expectancy at Birth	Adult Literacy Rate	Percent of Population living on < $1.25 per day
Rich Countries					
United States	$47,094	8	79.6	>99%	...
Germany	$35,308	4	80.2	>99%	...
United Kingdom	$35,087	6	79.8	>99%	...
France	$34,341	4	81.6	>99%	...
Japan	$34,692	3	83.2	>99%	...
Italy	$29,619	4	81.4	98.8%	...
Poor Countries					
Pakistan	$ 2,678	89	67.2	53.7%	22.6%
Cambodia	$ 1,868	90	62.2	77.0%	25.8%
Ghana	$ 1,385	76	57.1	65.8%	30.0%
Sierra Leone	$ 809	194	48.2	39.8%	53.4%
Niger	$ 675	167	52.5	28.7%	65.9%
DR-Congo	$ 291	199	48.0	66.6%	59.2%

Source: United Nations Development Programme, *Human Development Report,* 2010. Data on child mortality, literacy, and extreme poverty are for 2008; all others 2010.

living on less than $1.25 per day. The countries in the upper half of the table are among the richest (highest GDP per capita), while those in the lower half are among the poorest (lowest GDP per capita). For all countries, GDP per capita and the $1.25 per day poverty figures are expressed in U.S. dollars after adjusting for differences in local purchasing power, so the figures indicate amounts of goods and services that can be purchased in each country.

As you can see, the high quality of life in wealthy countries goes beyond just GDP per capita. Wealthy countries also do much better in terms of health care and literacy and eliminating extreme poverty. (In the rich countries, the percentage of people living on less than $1.25 per day—or even several times that amount—is too small to measure.) For the poorest countries, the data in the table—as grim as it is—captures only a small part of the story. Unsafe and unclean workplaces, inadequate housing, and other sources of misery are part of daily life for most people in the poorest countries.

The close connection in the table between real GDP per capita and other quality-of-life variables is no accident. In the poorest nations, almost all production goes toward food and primitive housing. Very little is left for health care, workplace safety, or education, other than for the small fraction of the population that is wealthy. For the vast majority in the poorest countries, other than emigration, economic growth is the only hope.

Even among the most prosperous countries, growth is a high priority. As we know, resources are scarce and we cannot produce enough of everything to satisfy all of our desires simultaneously. We want more and better medical care, education, vacations, entertainment . . . the list is endless. When output per capita is growing, it's at least *possible* for everyone to enjoy an increase in material well-being without anyone else having less. A growing economy can also accomplish important social goals—helping the poor, improving education, cleaning up the environment—by asking those who are doing well to sacrifice part of the *rise* in their living standard, rather than suffer a drop. When real GDP per capita stagnates, material gains become a fight over a fixed pie: The more purchasing power my neighbor has, the less is left for me. With everyone struggling for a large slice of this fixed pie, conflict replaces cooperation.

Small Differences and the Rule of 70

In most growing countries, real GDP per capita rises by just a few percent in an average year. Thus, improvements in living standards from one year to the next are hardly noticeable. Over many years, however, a growth rate of a few percentage points per year can make a big difference.

Consider the United States, where GDP per capita in 2011 (in current dollars) was about $48,000. In real terms, it has grown at an average rate of about 2 percent per year over the past century. If real growth continues at that rate, then in 2031, real GDP per capita would rise to about $71,000—a significant improvement in living standards over 20 years. In 50 years, when most of today's college students are thinking about retiring, it would reach $129,000. And in 100 years, with the grandchildren of today's college students still in their prime working years, real GDP per capita would be $348,000. This means the average American 100 years from now would be able to produce and consume about seven times more in goods and services than the average person today. If that seems unimaginable, remember that the average American today produces and consumes more than seven times the goods and services as our predecessors did 100 years ago. Clearly, small growth rates matter over time.

Small *differences* in growth rates matter too. One way to see this is to use the rule of 70.

> *The rule of 70 tells us that if a variable is growing by X percent per year, it will double in approximately 70/X years.*

Let's apply this rule to U.S. economic growth. If real GDP per capita continues to grow at 2 percent per year, living standards in the United States would double in about 70/2 = 35 years. But if the U.S. can increase its annual growth rate by just 1 percentage point—to 3 percent—the rule tells us that living standards would double in only 23 years—12 years sooner. Add one more percentage point (a 4 percent growth rate), and living standards would double about every 17 years.

Growth Prospects

Almost all of the countries that were relatively rich 50 years ago have continued to grow, and living standards have improved remarkably. But what about the poorest countries? Is growth a realistic prospect for them?

At first glance, it might seem not. Look, for example, at Figure 1. It shows the paths of real GDP per capita from 1950 to 2010 for a selection of rich and poor countries, including some of those in Table 1. The figure suggests that the most successful countries are not only rich, but steadily growing richer. And it suggests that the poorest countries—those near the bottom of the figure—are not growing much at all. This is the way the global economy is often portrayed in the media: The rich get richer and the poor stay poor—or get poorer. Indeed, some poor countries *are* getting poorer.

FIGURE 1 | **Real GDP per Capita in 1990 U.S. Dollars, Selected Countries**

Source: The Conference Board Total Economy Database™, September 2011, http://www.conference-board.org/data/economydatabase/.

To be sure, Figure 1 tells a deceptively bleak story about the poorest countries, and we'll discuss why in a moment. But before we leave Figure 1, notice the remarkable paths of South Korea and Singapore. They were once among the poorest nations. Then, starting in the late 1960s, they began growing rapidly, even surpassing countries that were much better off. In 1970, South Korea's real GDP per capita was less than half that of Mexico (not shown). By 1986, South Korea had surpassed Mexico, and today its standard of living is more than three times as high. Singapore began far below Italy but shot past it in the 1990s. These examples suggest that a country that was once poor can become rich. And so do other success stories that mirrored them, but not shown in the graph, such as Hong Kong and Taiwan.

Now let's discuss why Figure 1 is somewhat deceptive for the poorest countries. The first problem is the scale of the vertical axis. In order to show real GDP per capita in both rich and poor countries together, the vertical axis has to go from a few hundred dollars to $35,000. This causes the growth paths for the poorest countries to be scrunched up near the bottom, making it hard to distinguish one from the other. Second, in Figure 1, we've purposely left out some countries that—until recent decades—were among those at the bottom but have shot away from the pack and grown very rapidly.

Figure 2 addresses both of these issues. First, it leaves out the richest countries entirely, so that we can enlarge the vertical scale and zoom in a bit on the poorest (the ones graphed toward the bottom of Figure 1). Second, it adds in two countries that have had impressive recent success. The result is a more complex, and considerably less bleak, picture.

Look first at the growth paths of the two added countries: China and India. They began to break away from the poorest countries in the 1980s and have widened

FIGURE 2 Real GDP per Capita in 1990 U.S. Dollars: Another Perspective

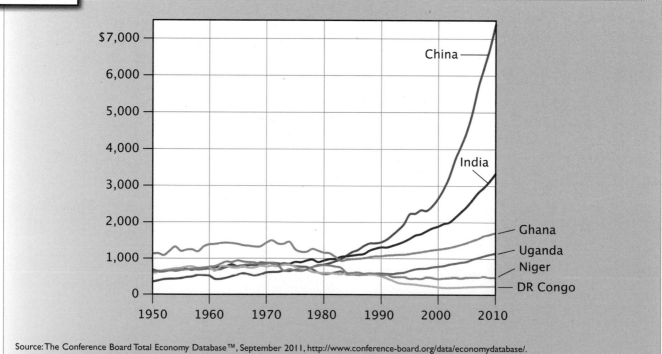

Source: The Conference Board Total Economy Database™, September 2011, http://www.conference-board.org/data/economydatabase/.

the gap ever since. Among all six countries shown in Figure 2, China was the very poorest until the mid-1970s. But by 2010, its real GDP per capita was about 7 times greater than any of the bottom three. The growth paths of China and India show that starting at the bottom does not necessarily mean staying there.

Now look more closely at the remaining countries. Two of them have not performed well over the past two decades. Niger has stagnated, and the Democratic Republic of Congo has deteriorated. But Ghana and Uganda began growing steadily in the 1990s and haven't stopped. Over the past decade, growth in Uganda and several other countries in Africa has averaged about 4 percent per year. If they continue to grow at this rate, the rule of 70 tells us that living standards will double every $17\frac{1}{2}$ years. Once again, we see that a poor country need not remain poor.

WHAT MAKES ECONOMIES GROW?

We'll begin our analysis of economic growth with some inescapable mathematical logic. Real GDP per capita is a fraction. In order for this fraction to grow, the numerator (real GDP) must grow faster than the denominator (population). For example, suppose real GDP rose by 10 percent over some period, while the population rose by 20 percent. With 10 percent more goods and services distributed among 20 percent more people, output *per person* would fall. However, if output rose by 25 percent while population rose only 20 percent, output per person would rise.

We'll come back to the role of population growth toward the end of this chapter. For now, let's focus a bit on the numerator: real GDP. What determines the size of a country's real GDP?

The Determinants of Real GDP

In any given year, we can view real GDP as being determined by four numbers:

1. The amount of output the average worker produces in an hour
2. The number of hours the average worker spends at the job
3. The fraction of the population that is working
4. The size of the population

If you spend a moment thinking about each of these variables, you'll see that—holding the others constant—an increase in any one of them will cause real GDP to rise. And to help us distinguish among them, economists have given the first three their own labels.

Productivity

The amount of output the average worker produces in an hour is called **labor productivity,** or just **productivity.** It is measured by taking the total output (real GDP) of the economy over a period of time and dividing by the total number of hours that *everyone* worked during that period.

Labor productivity The output produced by the average worker in an hour.

$$\text{Productivity} = \text{Output per hour} = \frac{\text{Total output}}{\text{Total hours worked}}$$

For example, if during a given year, all workers in the United States spent a total of 300 billion hours at their jobs and produced $15 trillion worth of output, then on average, labor productivity would be $15 trillion/300 billion hours = $50 per hour.

Or in words, the average worker would produce $50 worth of output in an hour. As you'll see later in this chapter, increases in productivity are one of the most important contributors to economic growth.

Average Hours

The average number of hours a worker spends on the job can be found by dividing the total hours worked by everyone by total employment (the *number* of people who worked during the period).

$$\text{Average Hours} = \frac{\text{Total hours}}{\text{Total employment}}$$

For example, if total employment is 150 million people and they work a total of 300 billion hours during the year, then average annual hours would be 300 billion hours/150 million workers = 2,000 hours.

The Employment-Population Ratio (EPR)

Now we turn to the fraction of the population that is working. This is the *employment–population ratio (EPR)* we discussed a couple of chapters ago. It is found by dividing total employment by the total population:[2]

$$\text{EPR} = \frac{\text{Total employment}}{\text{Population}}$$

So if the total population is 300 million, and 150 million of them are working, then the employment population ratio would be 0.5.

Combining the Determinants

Something interesting happens when we multiply the four determinants of real GDP and cancel out terms that appear in both a numerator and a denominator:

$$\frac{\text{Total output}}{\text{Total hours}} \times \frac{\text{Total hours}}{\text{Total employment}} \times \frac{\text{Total employment}}{\text{Population}} \times \text{Population}$$

$$= \frac{\text{Total output}}{\text{Total hours}} \times \frac{\text{Total hours}}{\text{Total employment}} \times \frac{\text{Total employment}}{\text{Population}} \times \text{Population}$$

= Total output (Real GDP)

Let's take a step back to think about what we've done. We've multiplied together four different terms, each of which describes a different feature of the economy, and the result is real GDP. This tells us that we can interpret real GDP in any given year as the product of the four determinants. Using the definitions you've learned for these determinants, we can express real GDP as follows:

$$\text{Real GDP} = \text{Productivity} \times \text{Average Hours} \times \text{EPR} \times \text{Population}$$

[2] In actual practice in the United States and many other countries, the population base for the EPR is more limited. In the United States, for example, the EPR is technically the fraction of the *civilian, non-institutional population over the age of 16* that is employed. We'll ignore this technical definition in our analysis and consider the EPR to be the fraction of the entire population that is working.

The Growth Equation

So far, we've broken real GDP down into four determinants. But we define economic growth as a rise in real GDP *per capita*. To change the real GDP equation into an equation for real GDP per capita, we divide both sides of the equation by the population:

$$\frac{\text{Real GDP}}{\text{Population}} = \text{Productivity} \times \text{Average Hours} \times \text{EPR} \times \text{~~Population~~}$$

or

$$\text{Real GDP per capita} = \text{Productivity} \times \text{Average Hours} \times \text{EPR}$$

Now we'll borrow a rule from mathematics that states that if two variables A and B are multiplied together, then the percentage change in their product is approximately equal to the sum of their percentage changes. In symbols:

$$\%\Delta\,(A \times B) \approx \%\Delta A + \%\Delta B$$

Applying this rule to all four variables in the right side of our equation, as well as to total output on the left, we find that the growth rate of total output over any period of time is

$$\%\Delta \text{ Real GDP per capita} \approx \%\Delta \text{ Productivity} + \%\Delta \text{ Average Hours} + \%\Delta \text{ EPR}$$

This last equation, which we'll call the economy's **growth equation**, shows how three different variables contribute to the growth rate of real GDP.

In theory, an increase in any of the terms on the right side of the growth equation—productivity, average hours, or the EPR—can create a rise in living standards. In practice, they are not equally important for growth. This is illustrated for the United States in Table 2, which shows how each of these variables has contributed to economic growth during different periods. For example, look at the column labeled 1973 to 1995. During this period, real GDP per capita grew at an average rate of 1.4 percent per year. Of that growth, 0.4 percentage points were due to a rise in the employment-population ratio. Average hours—which decreased during the period—contributed negatively to the growth rate, reducing it by about a third of a percentage point. Finally, growth in labor productivity contributed 1.3 percentage points—accounting for almost all of the economic growth in that period.

During all of the periods in the table, average hours declined. A similar pattern is seen in most of the industrialized countries of the world: Average hours have been trending *downward* over the last half century, tending to *reduce* any rise in real GDP

Growth equation An equation showing the percentage growth rate of real GDP per capita as the sum of the growth rates of productivity, average hours, and the employment-population ratio.

Annual Percentage Growth in Real GDP Per Capita Due to Growth in:	1953 to 1973	1973 to 1995	1995 to 2008
EPR	0.2	0.4	0.0
Average Hours	−0.3	−0.3	−0.2
Productivity	2.1	1.3	2.3
Total	**2.0**	**1.4**	**2.1**

Source: *Economic Report of the President*, 2009, Table 1–2, and author calculations to convert nonfarm business productivity growth to overall productivity growth.

TABLE 2

Factors Contributing to Growth in U.S. Real GDP Per Capita

per capita from the other determinants. This trend—driven by shorter workdays and longer vacations—is expected to continue in most wealthy countries. And in poorer countries as well, changes in average hours have not been, nor are they expected to be, an important driver of economic growth.

This leaves two potential determinants to explore: the EPR and productivity. As you are about to see, the classical model from the last chapter can help us understand how these factors contribute to economic growth.

GROWTH IN THE EMPLOYMENT-POPULATION RATIO (EPR)

Mathematically, the employment-population ratio increases only when total employment rises at a faster rate than the population. For example, if total employment is 100 million out of a total population of 200 million, the EPR is 0.5. If both total employment and population grow by 10 percent, the EPR will remain unchanged at 110 million/220 million = 0.5. If the population grows at 10 percent, total employment would have to rise by *more* than 10 percent for the EPR to rise, and thereby contribute to a rise in living standards. In the United States, Table 2 tells us that the EPR has grown in some periods, but not in others.

Understanding the impact of changes in the EPR is simpler if we treat the population for now as a given.

> With a given population, greater total employment means an increase in the EPR, and a rise in real GDP per capita.

But what causes total employment to rise? The classical model suggests two possibilities.

Changes in Labor Supply and Labor Demand

One cause of a rise in total employment is an increase in labor *supply*. This is illustrated in Figure 3, in which the labor supply curve shifts rightward. Before the shift, with labor supply curve L_1^S, the labor market clears at a wage of $25 per hour, with total employment at 150 million. The aggregate production function tells us that, with the given amounts of other resources in the economy and a given state of technology, 150 million workers produce $10 trillion in goods and services.

If more people want to work at any wage, so that the labor supply curve shifts to L_2^S, the market-clearing wage begins to drop. Business firms, finding labor cheaper, hire more workers, moving the market from point A to point B. The market clearing wage drops to $20, total employment rises to 180 million workers, and total output rises to $11.5 trillion. For a given population, the rise in total employment would increase the EPR, and the rise in total output would increase real GDP per capita.[3]

---

[3] You may be troubled by something: If labor supply increases and labor demand does not, the wage rate falls. How can real GDP per capita and living standards rise with a lower wage rate? Assuming no change in average hours or the population, there are two possible answers. First, remember that more people are working. So even with a lower wage rate, the *total* labor income of all workers in the economy *could* still rise. But even if total labor income falls, remember that wages are not the only factor payment that households earn. There is also rent, profit, and interest. As you learned a few chapters ago, total output must equal total income. Therefore, greater total output means greater total income. And with a constant population, income per capita rises as well.

FIGURE 3 | An Increase in Labor Supply

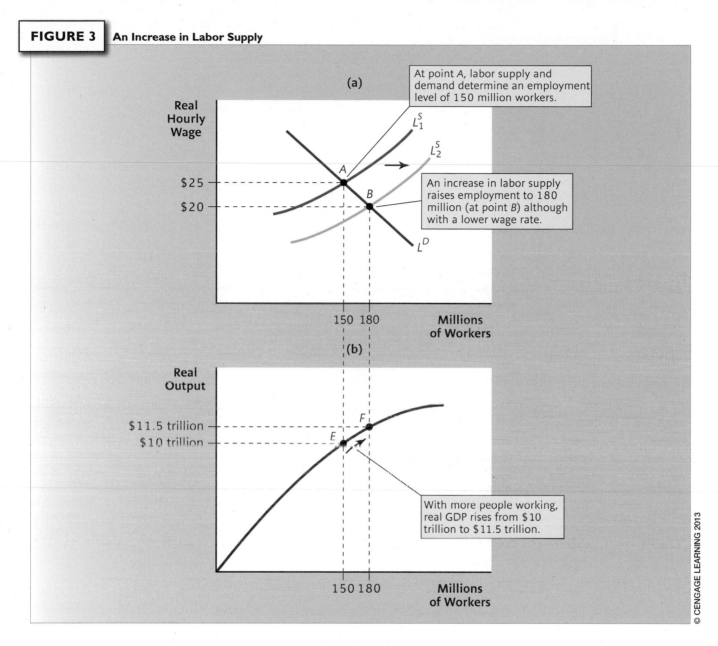

(a)

At point A, labor supply and demand determine an employment level of 150 million workers.

Real Hourly Wage

L_1^S

L_2^S

$25 ---- A

$20 ---- B

An increase in labor supply raises employment to 180 million (at point B) although with a lower wage rate.

L^D

150 180   Millions of Workers

(b)

Real Output

$11.5 trillion ---- F

$10 trillion ---- E

With more people working, real GDP rises from $10 trillion to $11.5 trillion.

150 180   Millions of Workers

Greater employment can also arise from an increase in labor *demand*. This is illustrated in Figure 4, where the labor demand curve shifts rightward. As the wage rate begins to rise, more people decide to work, moving the market from point A to point B. The new market-clearing wage rate rises from $25 to $28, and equilibrium employment rises from 150 million to 180 million workers.

Notice an important difference between the labor market outcomes in Figures 3 and 4: When labor *supply* increases, the wage rate falls. When labor *demand* increases, the wage rate rises. In countries that have experienced increases in the EPR, both shifts have usually taken place simultaneously, with labor demand increasing faster than labor supply. If you draw that situation on your own, you'll see that it causes both the wage rate and total employment to rise, which is the typical experience in growing economies.

FIGURE 4   **An Increase in Labor Demand**

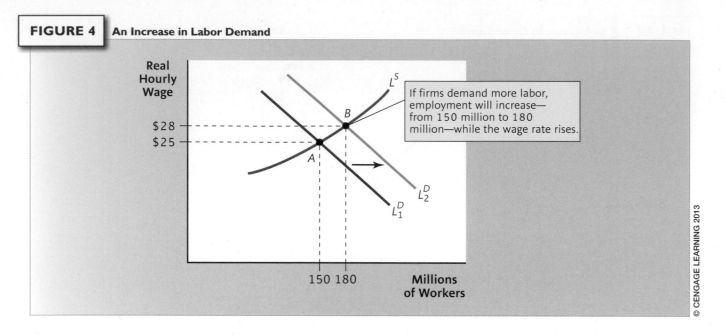

Government and the EPR

Over the next decade, the U.S. employment-population ratio is expected to shrink a bit, as the baby boom generation retires. This will have a negative influence on real GDP per capita. So, based on current forecasts, the EPR will not be contributing to economic growth. Nor is it expected to do so in other industrialized nations.

Could something be done about this? Can government policy cause an increase in the EPR, so it could contribute to growth? The answer is a qualified yes. But as we discuss some of these policies, keep one thing in mind: They are not necessarily socially desirable. Most likely, each of the policies we discuss would accomplish the goal. But they would also have costs—costs that a society may or may not be willing to pay.

Increasing the Growth of Labor Supply

Government can spur increases in labor supply through a variety of measures. One such measure is a decrease in income tax rates. Let's imagine that you do not *have* to work (say, you have the option of retiring or getting more education as alternatives to working). Further, let's imagine if you get a job right now, you would earn $30 per hour. If your average tax rate is 33 percent, then one-third of your income will be taxed away, so your take-home pay would be only $20 per hour. But if your tax rate were cut to 20 percent, you would take home $24 per hour. Because you care about your take-home pay, you will respond to a tax cut in the same way you would respond to a wage increase—even if the wage your potential employer pays does not change at all. If you would be willing to take a job that offers a take-home pay of $24, but not one that offers $20, then the tax cut would be just what was needed to get you to seek work.

When we apply this reaction to the population as a whole, we can see that a cut in the income tax rate can convince more people to seek jobs at any given wage, shifting the labor supply curve rightward. This is why economists and politicians who focus on the economy's long-run growth often recommend lower tax rates on labor income to encourage more rapid growth in employment. They also worry that significant *increases* in tax rates could *decrease* labor supply.

In addition to tax rate changes, some economists have advocated changes in government transfer programs to speed the growth in employment. They argue that the current structure of many government programs—such as welfare payments, food stamps, unemployment benefits, and social security retirement benefits—can create disincentives to work. These payments decrease the overall hardship suffered from *not* working, and because benefits are cut or taken away when someone begins working, they lower the reward for working.

This reasoning was an important motive behind the sweeping reforms in the U.S. welfare system during the Clinton administration. In recent years, many European governments have made their unemployment insurance and other social assistance less generous, in an effort to increase labor supply and the EPR, with some modest success.

Later in this chapter, we'll discuss some of the costs of potentially growth-enhancing measures such as these. Here, we only point out that changes in benefit programs have the potential to change labor supply.

> *A cut in tax rates increases the reward for working, while a cut in certain benefit programs increases the hardship of not working. All else equal, either policy can increase labor supply and employment, raising the EPR and real GDP per capita.*

Increasing the Growth of Labor Demand

The labor demand curve can also be affected by government policies. In recent decades, subsidies for education and training—such as government-guaranteed loans for college students or special training programs for the unemployed—have helped to increase the skills of the labor force and made workers more valuable to potential employers. Government also subsidizes employment more directly by contributing part of the wage when certain categories of workers are hired—the disabled, college work-study participants, and, in some experimental programs, inner-city youth. By enlarging these programs, government could increase the number of workers hired at any given wage and thus increase labor demand:

> *All else equal, government policies that help increase the skills of the workforce or that subsidize employment more directly increase labor demand and employment, raising the EPR and real GDP per capita.*

The Limits to the EPR as a Growth Strategy

You've seen that government policies could, in theory, create growth in the EPR and thereby foster economic growth. Indeed, a rising EPR has helped raise living standards in the past. For example, as women—especially married women—entered the U.S. labor force in large numbers during the 1960s, 1970s, and 1980s, the EPR rose dramatically.

But no nation today thinks of raising its EPR as a way to create sustained economic growth. The government policies we've been discussing would create, at best, a short-lived burst of growth.

To see why, look again at the growth equation a few pages back. Notice that it is not the EPR, but rather the *percentage change* in the EPR that creates economic growth. To create ongoing economic growth, the EPR must not only increase, but *continue* to increase, year after year. For example, if a nation's EPR rises from 0.60 to 0.65 over a few years, then real GDP per capita will rise *while the EPR is increasing.* But if, after rising, the EPR remains at 0.65, the percentage *change* in the EPR drops to zero. The new, higher EPR would mean a *higher* living standard than otherwise, but it would not contribute to any further *growth* in the standard of living.

Moreover, the EPR cannot continue rising forever. Its mathematical upper limit is 1.0 and its realistic social limit is well below 1.0, because some fraction of the population will always be retired, in school, or too young to work.

> *Government policy can raise the EPR and so create economic growth temporarily (while the EPR is rising). But significant, sustained economic growth would require significant, sustained growth in the EPR, which is not realistic.*

PRODUCTIVITY GROWTH: INCREASES IN THE CAPITAL STOCK

If you look back at Table 2, you'll see that increases in productivity—the amount of output the average worker can produce in an hour—have been responsible for most of the economic growth in the United States over the last 50 years. The same is true in Western Europe, Japan, South Korea, China, and India. Indeed, wherever living standards are continually rising, productivity growth is the driving force.

> *The most important determinant of long-run economic growth—and the one that economists and policy makers focus on—is rising productivity.*

Capital per worker The total capital stock divided by total employment.

But what causes productivity to increase? In this section, we'll explore one major reason: Increases in the capital stock. Or more precisely: An increase in the amount of capital available for the average worker in the economy.

> *All else equal, a rise in **capital per worker**—the total capital stock divided by total employment—causes labor productivity to rise.*

As business firms acquire more machinery and other capital equipment, the economy's production function shifts upward.

The reasoning behind this statement is straightforward. You can dig more ditches with a shovel than with your hands, and even more with a backhoe. And the economy can produce more automobiles, medical services, and education when the average employee in these industries has more machinery, technical equipment, and computers to work with.

Figure 5 shows this from the perspective of the classical model. Initially, the economy operates at point *A* on the lower aggregate production function, where 150 million workers produce $10 trillion in output. An increase in the capital stock shifts the production function upward, because any given number of workers can produce more output

FIGURE 5   Capital Accumulation and the Production Function

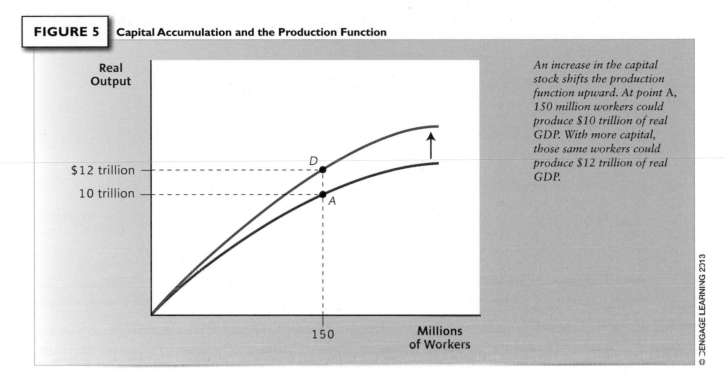

An increase in the capital stock shifts the production function upward. At point A, 150 million workers could produce $10 trillion of real GDP. With more capital, those same workers could produce $12 trillion of real GDP.

if they have more capital to work with. Assuming that total employment remains at 150 million, there will be more capital per worker, greater productivity, and the economy would move to point *D*. At this point, 150 million workers produce $12 trillion in output.

Investment and the Capital Stock

What determines how fast the capital stock rises? The answer is: the rate of planned investment spending in the economy. Investment spending and the capital stock are related to each other, but they are different kinds of variables. Specifically, capital is a *stock* variable while investment spending is a *flow* variable. You learned about the difference between these two types of variables in Chapter 4. An analogy we used in that chapter can help you see the relationship between the capital stock and investment. Think of the capital stock—the total amount of plant and equipment that exists in the economy—as the quantity of water in a bathtub at any given moment. And think of investment spending—the amount of *new* capital being installed over some time interval—as the water flowing *into* the tub. In the simplest terms, investment spending is how much we *add* to the capital stock over some period of time.

But there is one more flow involved in the capital–investment relationship: *depreciation*. Each year, some of the capital stock is used up. If a computer is expected to last only three years, for example, then the computer depreciates by about a third of its initial value each year. Depreciation tends to reduce the capital stock over time. (In our tub analogy, depreciation is like water draining out of the tub each period.) As long as investment is greater than depreciation (more water flows into the tub than drains out), the capital stock will rise. Moreover, for any rate of depreciation, the greater the flow of investment spending, the faster the rise in the capital stock.

Pulling all of this together leads us to an important conclusion about investment spending and the capital stock:

> *For a given rate of depreciation and given total employment, a higher rate of investment spending causes faster growth in capital per worker, faster growth in productivity, and faster growth in the average standard of living.*

This is why policy discussions about raising productivity via the capital stock focus on the flow of investment spending.

How to Increase Investment

A government seeking to spur investment has more than one weapon in its arsenal. It can direct its efforts toward businesses themselves, toward the household sector, or toward its own budget.

Targeting Businesses: Increasing the Incentive to Invest

One kind of policy to increase investment targets the business sector itself, with the goal of increasing planned investment spending. Figure 6 shows how this works. The figure shows a simplified view of the loanable funds market where—to focus on investment—we assume that there is no budget deficit, so there is no government demand for funds. The initial equilibrium in the market is at point *A*, where household saving (the supply of funds) and investment (the demand for funds) are both equal to $1.5 trillion and the interest rate is 3 percent.

Now suppose that the government takes steps to make investment more profitable so that—at any interest rate—firms will want to purchase $0.75 trillion more in capital equipment than before. Then the investment curve would shift rightward by $0.75 trillion and the interest rate would rise from 3 percent to 5 percent. Note that, as the interest rate rises, some—but not all—of the original increase in planned investment is choked off. In the end, investment rises from $1.5 trillion to

| **FIGURE 6** | **An Increase in Investment Spending** |

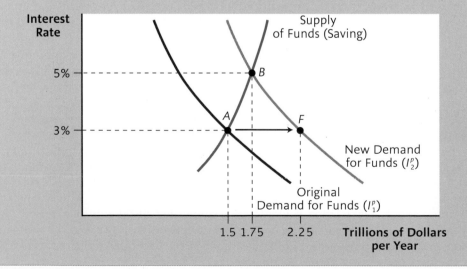

Government policies that make investment more profitable will increase investment spending at each interest rate. The resulting rightward shift of the investment demand curve (by the distance AF) leads to a higher level of investment spending, at point B.

$1.75 trillion; so each year $0.25 trillion more is added to the capital stock than would otherwise be added.

These are the mechanics of a rightward shift in the investment curve. But what government measures would *cause* such a shift in the first place? That is, how could the government help to make investment spending more profitable for firms?

One such measure would be a reduction in the **corporate profits tax**, which would allow firms and their owners to keep more of the profits they earn from investment projects. Another, even more direct, policy is an **investment tax credit**, which reduces firms' taxes when they invest in new capital equipment.

> **Corporate profits tax** A tax on the profits earned by corporations.
>
> **Investment tax credit** A reduction in taxes for firms that invest in new capital.

> *Reducing business taxes or providing specific investment incentives can shift the investment curve rightward, thereby creating faster growth in physical capital. This leads to faster growth in productivity and output per capita.*

Of course, the same reasoning applies in reverse: An *increase* in the corporate profits tax or the *elimination* of an investment tax credit would shift the investment curve to the left, slowing the rate of investment, the growth of the capital stock, and the rise in living standards.

Targeting Households: Increasing the Incentive to Save

An increase in investment spending can also originate in the household sector, through an increase in the desire to save. This is illustrated in Figure 7. If households decide to save more of their incomes at any given interest rate, the supply of funds curve will shift rightward. The increase in saving drives down the interest rate, from 5 percent to 3 percent, which, in turn, causes investment to increase. With a lower interest rate, NBC might decide to borrow funds to build another production studio, Google might purchase more servers, or the corner grocery store may decide to borrow the funds it needs for a new electronic scanner at the checkout stand. In this way, an increase in the desire to save is translated, via the loanable funds market, into an increase in investment and faster growth in the capital stock.

FIGURE 7 | **An Increase in Saving**

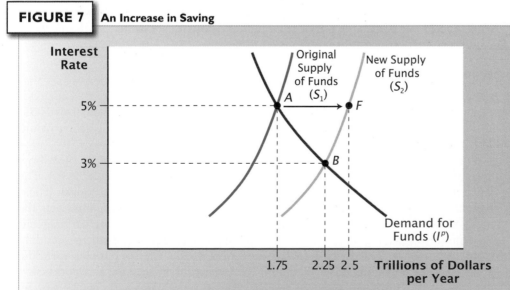

If households decide to save more of their incomes, the supply of funds curve will shift rightward (by the distance AF). With more funds available, the interest rate will fall. Businesses will respond by increasing their borrowing, and investment will increase from $1.75 trillion to $2.25 trillion.

© CENGAGE LEARNING 2013

Capital gains tax A tax on profits earned when a financial asset is sold at more than its acquisition price.

Consumption tax A tax on the part of their income that households spend.

A variety of government policies can—and have—been used to increase saving.

One is a decrease in the **capital gains tax** rate. Recall from Chapter 4 that a capital gain is the profit you earn when you sell an asset, such as a share of stock or a bond, at a higher price than you paid for it. The less tax owners have to pay on their capital gains, the more attractive it is to hold stocks and bonds. In the United States, capital gains on assets held more than a year are taxed at a lower rate than other forms of income. If the tax rate were lowered further, households could keep even more of the capital gains they earn, possibly encouraging them to reduce their current spending (increase their saving) in order to buy more of these assets.

Another frequently proposed measure is to switch from the current U.S. income tax—which taxes all income whether it is spent or saved—to a **consumption tax,** which would tax only the income that households spend. A consumption tax could work just like the current income tax, except that you would deduct your saving from your income and pay taxes on the remainder. This would increase the reward for saving. By saving, you would earn additional interest on the part of your income that would have been taxed away under an income tax.

Currently, individual retirement accounts (IRAs) and employer-sponsored 401(k) plans allow households to deduct limited amounts of saving from their incomes before paying taxes. A general consumption tax would go much further and allow *all* saving to be deducted.

Finally, the government could increase saving by modifying the government programs that form our social safety net. Social Security payments to the elderly, unemployment insurance payments for those who lose their jobs, and Medicaid for those too poor to afford health care—all help to guarantee a basic floor for living standards. But by reducing the fear and anxiety of possible adverse economic outcomes, these government transfer programs also reduce households' incentive to save.

> *Government can alter the tax and transfer system to increase incentives for saving. This would make more funds available for investment, speed growth in the capital stock, and speed the rise in living standards.*

(Do any of these methods of increasing saving disturb you? Remember, we are not advocating any measures here; rather, we are merely noting that such measures would increase saving and promote economic growth. We'll discuss the *costs* of growth-promoting measures later.)

Shrinking the Budget Deficit

A final pro-investment measure is directed at the government sector itself. The previous chapter showed that, in the long run, an increase in the budget deficit crowds out business investment spending. By the same reasoning, a *decrease* in the deficit would likely *increase* investment spending.

Figure 8 reintroduces the government to the loanable funds market to show how this works. Initially, the budget deficit is $0.75 trillion, equal to the distance *EA*. The total demand for funds is the sum of investment and the government's budget deficit, given by the curve labeled $I^p + (G - T)$. The demand for funds curve intersects the supply of funds curve at point *A,* creating an equilibrium interest rate of 5 percent and equilibrium saving of $1.75 trillion. At this interest rate, investment spending is only $1 trillion. The part of saving not going to finance investment spending ($1.75 trillion $-$1 trillion = $0.75 trillion) is being used to finance the budget deficit.

Now consider what happens if the government eliminates the deficit—say, by reducing its purchases by $0.75 trillion. The demand for funds would consist of

FIGURE 8   Deficit Reduction and Investment Spending

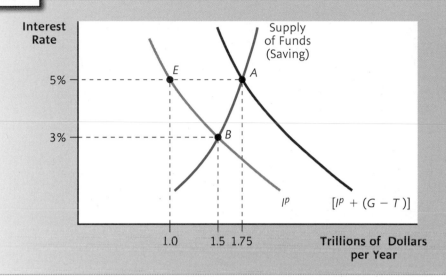

Eliminating the government's budget deficit will reduce government borrowing in the loanable funds market. As a result, the total demand for funds will fall, as will the interest rate. At a lower interest rate, businesses will increase their investment spending from $1.0 trillion (point E) to $1.5 trillion (point B).

investment spending only. Because there would be no other borrowing, the new equilibrium would be point B, with an interest rate of 3 percent and Investment equal to $1.5 trillion—greater than before. By balancing its budget, the government no longer needs to borrow in the loanable funds market, and it thus frees up funds to flow to the business sector instead.

> *All else equal, a decrease in the budget deficit tends to reduce interest rates and increase investment, thus speeding the growth in the capital stock.*

The link between the government budget, the interest rate, investment spending, and economic growth is one reason the U.S. government and governments around the world try to keep budget deficits low and worry when they rise.

An Important Proviso about the Budget Deficit

A reduction in the deficit—even if it stimulates private investment—is not *necessarily* a pro-growth measure. It depends on *how* the budget deficit shrinks. By an increase in taxes? A cut in government spending? And if the latter, which government programs will be cut? Welfare? National defense? Highway repair? The answers can make a big difference to the impact on growth.

For example, in our discussion so far, we've focused on the privately-owned capital stock. But the government provides capital as well—roads, communication lines, bridges, dams, and more. To understand the importance of government capital, just imagine what life would be like without it. How would factories obtain their raw materials or distribute their goods if no one repaired the roads? How would contracts between buyers and sellers be enforced if there were no public buildings to house courts and police departments?

It is clear that

> *government investment in new capital and the maintenance of existing capital make important contributions to economic growth.*

This important observation complicates our view of deficit reduction. It is still true that a decrease in government spending will lower the interest rate and increase private investment. But if the budget cutting falls largely on government investment, the negative effect of smaller *public* investment will offset some of the positive impact of greater *private* investment. Shrinking the deficit will then alter the *mix* of capital—more private and less public—and the effect on growth could go either way. A society rife with lawlessness, deteriorating roads and bridges, or an unreliable communications network would probably have slower economic growth if it increased private investment at the expense of government investment.

> *The impact of deficit reduction on economic growth depends on which government programs are cut. Shrinking the deficit by cutting government investment will not stimulate growth as much as would cutting other types of government spending.*

Human Capital and Economic Growth

So far, the only type of capital we've discussed is physical capital—the plant and equipment workers use to produce output. But when we think of the capital stock most broadly, we include *human capital* as well. Human capital—the skills and knowledge possessed by workers—is as central to economic growth as is physical capital. After all, most types of physical capital—computers, CAT scanners, and even shovels—will contribute little to output unless workers know how to use them. And when more workers gain skills or improve their existing skills, output rises just as it does when workers have more physical capital:

> *An increase in human capital works like an increase in physical capital to increase output: It causes the production function to shift upward, and can raise productivity and living standards.*

Can we do anything to increase our rate of investment in human capital?

In part, we've already answered this question: The same policies that increase investment in *physical* capital also work to raise investment in human capital. For example, growth policies that lower the interest rate (such as shrinking the budget deficit or increasing households' incentives to save) make it cheaper for households to borrow for college loans and training programs.

The Limits to Growth from More Capital

It might seem that growth in the capital stock (physical and/or human) can lead to never-ending economic growth. After all, the greater the capital per worker, the greater the productivity. So, it seems, a nation that continues to invest in new capital (and keep it growing faster than its population) should be able to generate never-ending economic growth.

But in fact, there are limits to growth from new capital. One limitation is caused by *diminishing returns*. When capital per worker is very low, providing more capital can create very large increases in productivity. For example, in a poor agrarian economy, where most farming is done without machinery, adding tractors and harvesting equipment can cause huge increases in output per farm worker.

But what happens as the economy grows, and most farmers have such equipment already? Adding more would still raise output per worker but not nearly as much as it did earlier. The richer the country becomes, the harder it is to grow by increasing capital per worker alone.

Another problem is caused by depreciation. As the capital stock grows, so does the amount of capital that depreciates each year. The physical capital stock simply wears out over time, and the human capital stock depreciates as workers retire and take their human capital out of the labor force. Thus, in a growing economy, a greater and greater share of investment spending must replace the capital that has been used up, with a smaller and smaller share left over to actually *add* to the capital stock. Eventually, if the capital stock keeps growing, it becomes so large—and so much of it would depreciate each year—that *all* investment would go toward preventing capital per worker from falling. Once that point is reached, capital per worker would remain constant and no longer contribute to rising living standards.

> As capital per worker grows, further increases in capital per worker suffer from diminishing returns, and rising depreciation makes it harder and harder to increase capital per worker out of ongoing investment spending. Thus, increases in the capital stock alone cannot create permanent high rates of economic growth.

This does not mean that capital is not important for growth. On the contrary, growth in the capital stock is crucial in two ways. First, in the poorest countries, where capital per worker is very low, more capital can still make a big difference. In the United States, Western Europe, and Japan, the value of physical capital per workers exceeds $75,000. In poor nations, it is typically less than $1,000. Poor countries have a lot of room to increase their capital and grow their living standards before running into the limits imposed by diminishing returns and depreciation.

Second, as we'll discuss in the next section, the capital stock often plays a supporting role for growth from another source, technology, to which we'll turn now.

PRODUCTIVITY GROWTH: TECHNOLOGICAL CHANGE

In Table 2, you saw that over the past half-century, U.S. productivity has continued to grow. And it does not show any signs of a significant slowdown. The same is true of other wealthy nations. This is not what we'd expect if productivity growth were driven by increases in capital per worker alone, given the limits that we discussed in the previous section. Something else must be driving productivity growth—and ultimately, economic growth—in rich countries. The something else is **technological change**—the invention and use of new inputs, new outputs, or new methods of production.

Technological change The invention and use of new inputs, new outputs, or new production methods.

Graphically, technological change affects the economy in a similar way as increases in the capital stock. Flip back to Figure 5 of this chapter. There, you saw that an increase in the capital stock shifts the production function upward. New technology, too, shifts the production function upward, because it enables any given number of workers to produce more output. New technology often requires the production of new capital in order to use it. But technology has an impact that goes beyond simple growth in the capital stock itself.

Capital Growth versus Technological Change

To understand the distinction between a rising capital stock and technological change, consider this simple example. Suppose that in 1970, a technically savvy individual was given a quarter-pound each of plastic, metal, and silica, and told to make the most productive communication equipment he or she could make with those ingredients. That person might have used the plastic and metal to make a landline telephone (and would have thrown out the silica). Using that phone, as well as a network of other phones, a business manager, doctor, farmer, or journalist could acquire information from others—information that would help him or her be productive.

Today, a technically savvy person could use that same amount of plastic, metal, and silica to make a smartphone, with access to the Internet. Information that required an hour of conversations using a phone can be obtained in less than a minute by searching the Web. Add some sunscreen, and that minute of work can take place at the beach. The smartphone uses pretty much the same ingredients as the landline phone but combines them in a new and different way—one that dramatically increases productivity. And the reason this can be done now, and not 40 years ago, is a slew of new ideas and discoveries that were made over the last 40 years.

In inflation-adjusted dollars, the cost of producing the phone of 40 years ago (and its sales price) were about the same as for the smartphone of today. So if we measure capital in constant (inflation-adjusted) dollars, both the regular phone and the smartphone would increase the capital stock by the same value. But with the smartphone, that same increase in the measured capital stock causes a greater upward shift in the production function. For this reason, we can think of two separate effects on the production function when a piece of capital embodying a new technology is produced: (1) the familiar increase in production from increasing the *amount* of capital, holding technology constant; and (2) the extra boost to production because of the new, productivity-enhancing technology that comes with that capital.

Every year, new discoveries in medicine, communications, logistics, and transportation are creating new ways of combining the same raw materials to make new productivity-enhancing tools for us to use. In the growth equation, the pace of these new discoveries and their implementation is a major determinant of the productivity growth rate.

> *The faster the rate of technological change, the greater the growth rate of productivity, and the faster the rise in living standards.*

In many cases—as in our example of the smartphone—making *use* of a new technology also requires the production of new physical capital. *Knowing* how to make a smartphone wouldn't do you much good until one was made, and you actually had it in your hand. Similarly, to make productive use of the discovery that jet engines could power planes, we had to set up manufacturing plants, and actually *make* jet aircraft.

But some technological changes can increase productivity by themselves, without any assist from new capital. These are often basic discoveries of better ways of doing things that no one had thought of before. Paul Romer, an economist at Stanford University and one of the leading economists studying economic growth, has provided a simple example:

> *In most coffee shops, you can now use the same size lid for small, medium, and large cups of coffee. That was not true as recently as 1995. That small change in the geometry of the cups means that a coffee shop can serve customers at lower cost. Store owners need to manage the inventory for only one type of lid. Employees can replenish supplies more quickly throughout the day. Customers can get their coffee just a bit faster. Although big discoveries such as the transistor, antibiotics, and the electric motor attract most of the attention, it takes millions of little discoveries like the new design for the cup and lid to double a nation's average income.*[4]

Economists believe that much, perhaps most, of the productivity growth in the world is due to technological change, whether simple (as in the coffee-cup example) or complex (Google's search engine and advertising algorithms). But there is a difference in the type of technological change that creates growth in rich and poor countries.

Discovery-Based Growth

If not for a steady supply of new discoveries, productivity growth—and economic growth—in rich countries would depend only on growth in the capital stock. But such economic growth would be limited. Without new ideas, newly produced physical capital would not do anything different than the old capital; there would just be more of it. More computers that are no faster than the old ones; more farm equipment that is no different than the old equipment. Newly produced human capital, too, would not include any previously unknown ideas. It would just spread the current state of knowledge to more people. There would be more doctors using the same medical techniques as current doctors, more chemists and engineers with the same knowledge as those already trained. As you've learned, due to diminishing returns and depreciation, such growth in capital could not increase productivity forever. Without new ideas and new discoveries, growth in living standards in the rich countries would soon slow and eventually stop.

> *In rich countries, sustained growth in productivity and living standards arises from **discovery-based growth**. Without a continual supply of new ideas, growth in rich-country living standards would soon slow and ultimately come to a halt.*

Discovery-based growth Economic growth, primarily in advanced countries, based on technological change from new discoveries.

Note that economic growth based on new discoveries does *not* suffer from diminishing returns as a country develops more of them. There is no logical reason to expect tomorrow's new ideas to be any less productivity-increasing than yesterday's ideas. And a new idea doesn't depreciate the way that capital does. True, the physical capital and human capital needed to *exploit* a new idea need to be replaced as they depreciate. But the new idea itself never wears out and never needs to be "replaced." For example, to continue exploiting the Internet, we must use some of our investment spending each year to replace computers (physical capital) and to provide new generations with the skills needed to make use of it (human capital). This capital

[4] Paul Romer, "Economic Growth," in *The Concise Encyclopedia of Economics* (www.econlib.org/library/CEE.html).

depreciates over time and must be replaced. But the *idea* of the Internet does not depreciate. We can keep taking advantage of this idea without ever having to use scarce resources to reinvent it.

> *There are no logical or mathematical limits to productivity growth from new discoveries. New ideas are not subject to diminishing returns, nor do they depreciate over time.*

Government and Discovery-Based Growth

It might seem that an invention or discovery just "happens." True, random luck may play a part in any particular discovery. But in the aggregate, the overall *pace* of technological change is not as haphazard as it seems. And government policy can affect this pace in two major ways: through policies that increase research and development spending; and by providing the institutional infrastructure for innovation.

Research and Development Spending. Many important inventions that have increased productivity and living standards were developed or substantially improved by large corporations. For example, the transistor was invented as part of a massive research and development effort by AT&T to improve the performance of communications electronics. Today, large corporations such as Apple, Microsoft, Pfizer, and Ford have huge research departments to develop new products. While not all innovations come from large corporations, many of the ones that matter do.

R&D programs, like other investments, require firms to spend now for the uncertain prospect of profits in the future. The funds for these projects—like the funds for building a new factory—are drawn from the loanable funds market. Therefore, almost any policy we've discussed that increases investment spending will also increase spending on R&D, such as lower tax rates for capital gains or corporate profits, or policies that encourage saving or shrink the budget deficit and thus lower interest rates.

Government also funds R&D spending more directly. The funding for the Internet initially came from the U.S. Department of Defense. The National Aeronautics Space Administration and the National Institutes of Health have their own research facilities, and they also fund outside activities. Most of the scientific research done at universities is funded by grants from government agencies, such as the National Science Foundation. An increase in the government's R&D spending can—like private spending—increase the pace of technological change.

Institutional Infrastructure and Innovation. A second way that government can influence the pace of technological change is by providing an institutional infrastructure that encourages innovation. Laws to protect property rights, honest government agencies to enforce the law, an impartial judicial system to settle disputes—these are all things that we take for granted in wealthy countries such as the United States. But they play a crucial role in the discovery process.

Among advanced countries, the United States has for years been the leader in global innovation. The Internet, the personal computer, the medical laser, the cell phone, and most of the important pharmaceuticals in recent years were invented and first implemented on a practical scale in the United States. The precise reasons that the United States leads other advanced countries, such as the U.K. or Germany, are not fully understood. But many economists believe that the special features of U.S. institutions and policies are the key.

Catch-Up Growth

Economic growth in poor countries differs in two ways from growth in rich countries. First, as we've discussed earlier, capital per worker in poor countries is very low. So merely adding more units of capital (even capital based on the same technology as that already in use) could create substantial growth before diminishing returns would get in the way.

Second, and more importantly, poor countries have not yet implemented much of the new technology that is commonplace in rich countries. Thus, poor countries can enjoy productivity gains just by catching up to these new technologies, without making new discoveries themselves. They need only copy and adapt technologies already used elsewhere. In fact, when a worker in a poor country is provided with new capital that *embodies* a new technology, the worker gets a productivity boost in two ways: capital per worker increases and the technology of production changes.

Here's an example: A few years ago, fishermen in India began using cell phones. Suddenly, they could discover the going price for their fish in different markets with a few quick phone calls. Before cell phones, they would have to visit several markets to check prices themselves, or else take their chances on selling at a low price when they could have earned much more at another location. With cell phones, there is less risk of losing money on the catch, which helps to keep more productive fishermen in business. And the saving in travel time enables them to catch more fish, with less spoilage—a significant rise in productivity. (Consumers benefit, too: The use of cell phones helps to equalize fish prices across markets; consumers don't have to waste time visiting several markets to find the best price.) Note that this productivity boost did not have to await any new discovery in India. The only requirement was the acquisition of new capital that used a technology already commonplace in rich countries.

© CHRISTOPHER AND SALLY GABLE/GETTY IMAGES

*In poor countries, sustained growth in productivity and living standards is largely **catch-up growth**. They start with very low capital per worker, so catching up to the higher levels of rich countries yields large productivity gains. And technological change can occur rapidly, by copying and adapting technologies already in use in richer countries.*

Catch-up growth Economic growth, primarily in less-advanced countries, based on increasing capital per worker from low levels, and adopting technologies already used in more advanced countries.

A country that creates the conditions necessary for catch-up growth (more on this later) can grow rapidly. Discovery-based technological changes that took decades to develop in rich countries can be copied and implemented by poor countries very quickly. You can learn to *use* the Internet in much less time than it took to *invent* the Internet.

If you look back at Figures 1 and 2, you can see that India and China have been growing much more rapidly than any of the rich countries. In recent years, growth in real GDP per capita has averaged about 10 percent per year in China and about 9 percent in India, compared to an average of about 2 percent per year in the United States. India and China are enjoying catch-up growth. And they are catching up fast.

Government and Catch-Up Growth

Given how productive additional capital can be in a poor country, and given the ease of copying technologies already in use elsewhere, economic incentives should be driving rapid catch-up growth in poor countries. In Figure 2, you can see that this has happened in some cases. But not all cases. Why have countries like South Korea and Singapore in the past, and China and India in the present, been able to experience catch-up growth, while other countries—such as the Democratic Republic of the Congo, Niger, and Sierra Leone—have not? A large part of the answer is government—specifically, the institutions that government helps to create and manage. These institutions include a stable legal system that protects property rights and settles disputes, honest government that enforces regulations, a stable financial system that encourages a flow of savings to growing businesses, international openness that encourages the flow of new ideas from abroad, and access to education so that those new ideas can be put to use.

We'll consider some of the problems of the poorly performing countries later, in the Using the Theory section. But here, let's discuss some of the things that governments in the rapidly-growing countries seem to be doing right. We'll illustrate with the case of China.

An Example: China Every country is different. And there are many facets of China's growth story that are specific to that country. But the principles behind China's remarkable growth, in the most general terms, apply to other countries that have experienced rapid catch-up growth in the past and those that aspire to it now.

Over the past few decades, China's government has transformed the way the country does business, both domestically and internationally. Domestically, the government switched from a system without private property to one of increasingly well-defined property rights. This has helped to reassure entrepreneurs that they can reap rewards for the risk and effort of setting up new businesses. The government has encouraged competition in the marketplace, which forces firms to rapidly adopt new technologies in order to survive. It has made efforts to root out corrupt bureaucrats and judges, so a firm's profitability has more and more to do with the value it creates than the personal connections of its owners or the bribes it pays. And it has invested in education, so that its workers have the human capital to work with new (to China) technologies.

Internationally, China has specialized in goods and services that it is especially well-suited to produce and export. It has encouraged multinational corporations to set up branches and factories in the country. Foreign firms bring in physical capital, and also bring new ideas. China has also enabled—and encouraged—its young people to study abroad and come back with new skills and ideas.

A few decades ago, most of China's economy was centrally planned, and there was little encouragement of individual entrepreneurship or innovation. Even today, China still retains tight centralized control in some

⚠ DANGEROUS CURVES

Will China beat the U.S.? In the media, you will often hear predictions that real GDP per capita in China will surpass that of the United States in a few decades. This is often portrayed as both inevitable and threatening. The threat—if there is one—relates to geopolitics and the projection of power, not U.S. living standards. A higher living standard in China does not imply a lower living standard in the U.S. On the contrary: As China becomes rich and switches from catch-up growth to discovery-based growth, the pace of worldwide discoveries will increase, helping to raise living standards in *all* countries, including the United States.

In any case, projections of China leaping ahead of U.S. living standards are based on a faulty assumption: that China's growth will continue at current high rates even as it becomes a rich country. But as you've learned, the *reason* China's recent growth has been so rapid is that it started so far behind. As China narrows the gap, it's catch-up growth will slow due to diminishing returns, greater depreciation, and dwindling opportunities to catch up to advanced-country discoveries. At that point, China's growth rate (like those of its fellow rich countries) will be determined by the global pace of new discoveries.

© AXL/SHUTTERSTOCK.COM

areas—such as its financial system and the flow of political information. Corruption remains a serious problem, and the regulatory and legal system have far to go before they offer the kinds of oversight and protection common in rich countries. But China is a radically different country today than it was in the 1980s. The result of these changes is vividly illustrated in Figure 2, in the rapid rise of China's real GDP per capita.

GROWTH POLICIES: A SUMMARY

In this chapter, you've learned about the forces that affect economic growth, as well as a host of government policies with the potential to make the economy grow faster. If you are having trouble keeping it all straight, Table 3—which summarizes all of this information—might help. The table also helps us see some additional aspects of economic growth.

Fiscal Policy and Economic Growth

If you look through the table, you'll notice that many of the policies that affect growth are *fiscal policies*—changes in government purchases or net taxes designed to affect total output. In the previous chapter, you learned that in the classical/long-run model, fiscal policy has no *demand-side* effects on output. But in this chapter, you've seen that fiscal policy *can* affect output in a different way—by changing the resources available in the economy. For example, a cut in income tax rates can influence the number of people who want to work, making more labor available in the economy. Fiscal changes can also change the rate of investment spending and therefore influence the amount of capital firms will have in the future. These effects of fiscal policy—changing total output by changing the resources available in the economy—are called **supply-side effects**.

> *In the long run, fiscal policy cannot change total output through a change in total spending (demand-side effects). But it can change total output by altering the quantity of resources available for production (supply-side effects).*

Supply-side effects Macroeconomic policy effects on total output that work by changing the quantities of resources available.

Multiple and Competing Effects

Table 3 also helps us see that some policy changes affect economic growth in more than one way. For example, any policy that increases productivity has a direct impact on the productivity component of the growth equation. But when workers are more productive, firms will want to hire more of them at any wage—an increase in labor demand. This can raise the EPR and—for a time—increase the economy's growth rate through that channel as well.

In some cases, a policy sets off *competing* effects on growth. For example, a decrease in corporate profits taxes might contribute to growth by increasing investment spending. But a tax cut, with no other change, will raise the budget deficit and drive up interest rates. That tends to *decrease* investment, working *against* economic growth.

The fact that a single policy can have competing effects on growth helps us understand one reason for controversy in macroeconomic policy. When a policy has competing effects on its target (in this case, economic growth), its ultimate impact depends on which effect dominates. Economists can and do disagree about the relative strengths of these effects. The Bush Administration's tax cuts in 2001

TABLE 3

A Summary of Policies That Affect Economic Growth

Growth Policies	Method of Impact	Impact in Classical Model	Possible Effect through Growth Equation	Possible Impact on Growth
• Decreases in tax rates or changes in benefit programs	Increase in Labor Supply	Total Employment ↑	EPR Growth Rate ↑	Temporary increase in economic growth rate (while EPR growth rate is rising)
• Policies that raise labor productivity (see entries below)	Increase in Labor Demand			
• Tax or direct incentives to increase investment ($\Rightarrow I^P \uparrow$) • Tax incentives to increase saving ($r \downarrow \Rightarrow I^P \uparrow$)	Greater investment in physical and human capital $\Rightarrow$ Faster rise in Capital Stock	Production function shifts ↑	Productivity Growth Rate ↑	Poor countries: Increase in catch-up growth rate (under right conditions); Rich countries: Limited impact (except for capital using new discoveries)
• Reduction in budget deficit (with provisos) ($r \downarrow \Rightarrow I^P \uparrow$)	More Investment in R&D $\Rightarrow$ More-rapid technological change	Production function shifts ↑	Productivity Growth Rate ↑	Rich countries: Increase in discovery-based growth rate
• Establish and maintain institutions that promote discovery & implementation of new technologies	More-rapid technological change (through catching up or new discoveries)	Production function shifts ↑	Productivity Growth Rate ↑	Poor countries: Increase in catch-up growth rate; Rich countries: Maintenance of or increase in discovery-based growth rate

and 2003, for example, were seen by some economists as growth-enhancing and by others as a threat to growth because of their different estimates of these competing effects.

And in 2011 and early 2012, when the Obama administration proposed increasing government spending on roads, bridges, and other infrastructure, part of the debate concerned the long-run effects on growth. The administration argued that government investment was needed to increase public capital and contribute to economic growth. Republican opponents argued that higher budget deficits and greater government debt would crowd out private investment spending and decrease economic growth—perhaps not right away, but at some point in the future.

THE COSTS OF ECONOMIC GROWTH

So far in this chapter, we've discussed a variety of policies that could increase the rate of economic growth and speed the rise in living standards. Why, then, don't growing nations pursue these policies to push their rates of economic growth even higher? For example, why did the U.S. standard of living (output per capita) grow by 2.1 percent per year between 1995 and 2008? Why not 4 percent per year? Or 6 percent? Or even more?

In this section, you will see that

> *promoting economic growth involves unavoidable tradeoffs: It requires some groups, or the nation as a whole, to give up something else that is valued.*

Economics is famous for making the public aware of policy tradeoffs. One of the most important things you will learn in your introductory economics course is that there are no costless solutions to society's problems and dilemmas. Just as individuals face an opportunity cost when they take an action (they must give up something else that they value), so, too, policy makers face an opportunity cost whenever they pursue a policy: They must often compromise on achieving some other social goal.

What are the costs of growth, and how do they come about?

Budgetary Costs

Many of the pro-growth policies we've analyzed involve some kind of tax cut. Cutting taxes on capital gains or corporate profits can increase investment directly. And cutting taxes on saving can increase the supply of funds to the loanable funds market, lower interest rates, and thus increase investment spending indirectly.

Unfortunately, implementing any of these tax cuts would force the government to choose among three unpleasant alternatives: increase some other tax to regain the lost revenue, cut government spending, or permit the budget deficit to rise.

Who will bear the burden of this budgetary cost? That depends on which alternative is chosen. Under the first option—increasing some other tax—the burden falls on those who pay the other tax. The second option—cutting government spending— imposes the burden on those who currently benefit from government programs. The third option—a larger budget deficit—is more complicated. For one thing, it will add to the government's debt, which means that future generations will face higher tax rates to cover the higher interest payments on that debt. In addition, in the long run (when the economy is producing its potential output), a greater budget deficit will drive up the interest rate. The higher interest rate will reduce investment in physical capital and R&D by businesses, as well as investment in human capital by households. These effects work to *decrease* economic growth. At best, the growth-enhancing effects of the tax cut will be weakened. That is why advocates of high growth rates usually propose one of the other options—a rise in some other tax or a cut in government spending—as part of a pro-growth tax cut.

In sum,

> *even though properly targeted tax cuts can increase the rate of economic growth, they will generally force us to either redistribute the tax burden or cut government programs.*

Consumption Costs

Any pro-growth policy that works by increasing investment—in physical capital, human capital, or R&D—requires a sacrifice of current consumption spending. We use resources to construct new oil rigs or factory buildings, or to build and staff new colleges, training facilities, and research laboratories. These resources could have been used instead to produce clothing, automobiles, video games, and other consumer goods. In other words, we face a tradeoff: The more capital goods we produce in any given year, the fewer consumption goods we can enjoy in that year.

This tradeoff can be clearly seen with a familiar tool from Chapter 2: the production possibilities frontier (PPF). Figure 9 shows the PPF for a nation with some given amount of land, labor, capital, and entrepreneurship that must be allocated to the production of two types of output: capital goods and consumption goods. At point K, the nation is using all of its resources to produce capital goods and none to produce consumption goods. Point C represents the opposite extreme: all resources used to produce consumption goods and none for capital goods. Ordinarily, a nation will operate at an intermediate point such as A, where it is producing both capital and consumption goods.

Now as long as capital production at point A is greater than the depreciation of existing capital, the capital stock will grow. In future periods, the economy—with more capital—can produce more output, as shown by the outward shift of the PPF in the figure. If a nation can produce more output, then it can produce more consumption goods and the same quantity of capital goods (moving from point A to point B), or more capital goods and the same quantity of consumption goods (from point A to point D), or more of both (from point A to point E).

FIGURE 9   **Consumption, Investment, and Economic Growth**

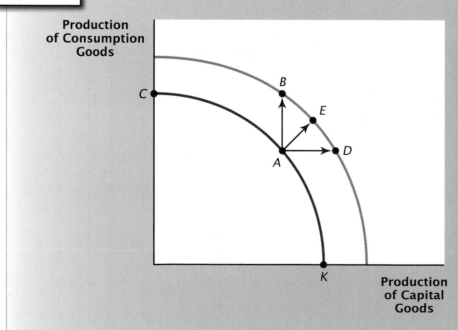

In the current period, a nation can choose to produce only consumer goods (point C), or it can produce some capital goods by sacrificing some current consumption, as at point A. If investment at point A exceeds capital depreciation, the capital stock will grow, and the production possibilities frontier will shift outward. After it does, the nation can produce more consumption goods (point B), more capital goods (point D), or more of both (point E).

© CENGAGE LEARNING 2013

Let's take a closer look at how this sacrifice of current consumption goods might come about. Suppose that some change in government policy—say, an investment tax credit (with some other tax increased and no change in the budget deficit)—increases investment spending. What will happen? A look back at Figure 6 provides the answer. Businesses—demanding more loanable funds—will drive up the interest rate, and households all over the country will find that saving has become more attractive. As families increase their saving, we move rightward along the economy's supply of funds curve. In this way, firms get the funds they need to purchase new capital. But a decision to *save more* is also a decision to *spend less*. As current saving rises, current consumption spending necessarily falls. By driving up the interest rate, *the increase in investment spending causes a voluntary decrease in consumption spending by households*. Resources are freed from producing consumption goods and diverted to producing capital goods instead.

Although this decrease in consumption spending is voluntary, it is still a cost that we pay. And in some cases, a painful cost: Some of the increase in the household sector's net saving results from a decrease in *borrowing* by households that—at higher interest rates—can no longer afford to finance purchases of homes, cars, or furniture.

In sum,

greater investment in physical capital, human capital, and R&D will lead to faster economic growth and higher living standards in the future, but we will have fewer consumer goods to enjoy in the present.

Sacrifice of Other Social Goals

Rapid economic growth is an important social goal, but it's not the only one. Some of the policies that quicken the pace of growth may require us to sacrifice other goals that we care about. For example, higher rates of economic growth (without other changes) would add to pollution and contribute to global warming. Weakening the social safety net would likely increase saving, leading to more investment and faster growth. But such a move would harm people who rely on the safety net and could force some citizens into levels of poverty that society may find unacceptable.

An example of the tradeoff between higher growth and an acceptable safety net is seen in China. One reason for China's rapid economic growth is that Chinese households save so much of their income. But they do so in large part because China's safety net is so primitive and, for many rural people, nonexistent. Without health insurance, unemployment benefits, or other social programs, households save large portions of their income each year to build up a cushion of funds in case calamity strikes.

Even growth that seems at first glance to require no sacrifice—say, from new, productivity-enhancing discoveries—proves to be costly upon closer examination. Technological change creates hardship for those whose livelihoods are tied to the old ways. In poor countries, technological change replaces traditional forms of agriculture with mechanized farming, and handicrafts with manufacturing. Rapid technological change can cause hardship in rich countries too. The Internet forced thousands of travel agents, telephone receptionists, newspaper delivery workers, music store clerks, and librarians to find new lines of work. While the overall benefits to society were huge, the cost was accepting some hardship and economic instability for a part of the population.

Of course, the argument cuts both ways: Just as economic growth often requires some sacrifice of other goals, so, too, can the pursuit of other goals impede economic growth. As in most matters of economic policy, we face a tradeoff:

> *Achieving social goals often requires the sacrifice of some economic growth along the way. Alternatively, achieving faster economic growth may require some compromise on other things we care about.*

When values differ, people will disagree on how much we should sacrifice other goals for greater economic growth, and vice versa.

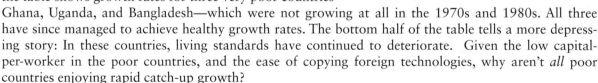

USING THE THEORY

BARRIERS TO CATCH-UP GROWTH IN THE POOREST COUNTRIES

© JENNY MATTHEWS/ ALAMY

As you've seen in this chapter, several nations that were poor just a half century ago—including South Korea, Hong Kong, and Singapore—have reached living standards on a par with the richest countries. India and China are growing so rapidly that they may achieve rich-country status in less than a generation. And even some of the very poorest nations—which had long seemed unable to grow—have begun to do so in recent years. But many countries—especially in Africa—continue to stagnate.

Table 4 provides some stark contrasts. The top half of the table shows growth rates for three very poor countries—Ghana, Uganda, and Bangladesh—which were not growing at all in the 1970s and 1980s. All three have since managed to achieve healthy growth rates. The bottom half of the table tells a more depressing story: In these countries, living standards have continued to deteriorate. Given the low capital-per-worker in the poor countries, and the ease of copying foreign technologies, why aren't *all* poor countries enjoying rapid catch-up growth?

There is considerable disagreement about this question among economists. One group argues that more assistance is needed and is optimistic about what it could achieve. Another group stresses the need for foreign investment rather than foreign assistance and argues that will not happen without serious institutional changes in the stagnating countries. But both groups agree that the poor countries are caught in a trap. And at the center of that trap is a problem involving *capital*.

Recall that catch-up growth involves *capital* in two ways. First, more capital—even with an unchanged technology—can raise productivity and living standards. Second, catching up to the advanced technologies of the richer countries typically requires new types of capital. A country that wants to improve communications does not have to invent wireless technology—the rich countries have already done that. But to make *use* of that invention requires physical capital (cell phone towers and cell phones) and human capital (the skills needed to operate, maintain and repair the system).

Just how does a nation acquire that capital? As you've learned, a country can produce more capital by shifting resources away from consumption spending. Some countries that were once very poor—such

		TABLE 4

Selected Poor Countries Where Living Standards Are:	Average Annual Growth Rate of Output per Capita	
	1970–1990	1990–2010
Growing		
Ghana	−1.5%	2.4%
Uganda	−2.0%	3.4%
Bangladesh	0.0%	3.6%
Stagnating or Deteriorating		
Niger	−2.1%	−0.7%
Zimbabwe	0.3%	−2.5%
DR-Congo	−2.0%	−3.8%

Growth in Selected Poor Countries

© CENGAGE LEARNING 2013

as Hong Kong, Singapore, and India—have done just that, using some of the growth policies discussed in this chapter: large subsidies for human and physical capital investments, pro-growth tax cuts to encourage saving and investment, and the willingness to sacrifice other social goals—including a clean environment—for growth. Some of these countries also had special advantages, like initially high levels of human capital, and growth-enhancing institutions inherited from their days as colonies.

But the countries in the bottom half of Table 4 have been unable to shift resources in this way. These countries seem to have three main problems in common:

1. *Extremely low output per capita.* Living standards are so low in some poor countries that—without assistance or draconian measures—they cannot reduce consumption further without threatening the very survival of many families. At the household level, the problem is an inability to save: Incomes are so low that households must spend all they earn on consumption.
2. *High population growth rates.* Low living standards and high population growth rates are linked together in a cruel circle of logic. On the one hand, rapid population growth by itself tends to reduce living standards. On the other hand, a low standard of living tends to increase population growth. Why? First, the poor are often uneducated in matters of family planning or don't have access to effective birth control. Second, high mortality rates among infants and children encourage families to have many offspring to ensure the survival of at least a few to care for parents in their old age. As a result, while the average woman in the United States will have fewer than two children in her lifetime, the average woman in Zimbabwe will have three children; in Niger, five children; and in DR-Congo, six.
3. *Poor institutions.* Political instability, poor law enforcement, corruption, and adverse government regulations make many poor countries unprofitable places for domestic residents to start businesses, or for foreigners to set up factories or manufacturing branches. Productivity is also affected when people must spend time guarding against thievery and trying to convince the government to let them operate businesses—time they could otherwise spend producing output.

These three problems—very low current production, high population growth, and poor infrastructure—interact to create a vicious circle of continuing poverty. Figure 10 illustrates this situation using the familiar PPF to show the tradeoff

FIGURE 10 | **Production Choices in a Very Poor Country**

In order to increase productivity when population is growing, yearly investment spending must exceed some minimum level N. But there is also a minimum level of consumption, S, needed to support the population. If output is currently at point H, capital per worker and living standards are stagnant. Movement to a point like J would increase productivity in the future, but require an unacceptably low level of consumption in the present.

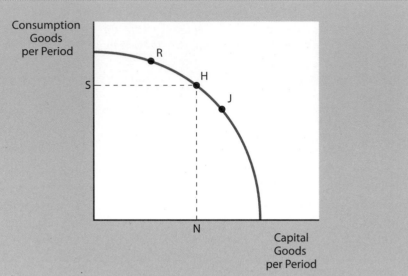

© CENGAGE LEARNING 2013

between capital and consumption goods, but with some added features. Point *N* on the horizontal axis represents the minimum amount of investment needed to maintain labor productivity and living standards, for a given rate of population growth. If investment *exceeds N*, then productivity and living standards rise.

The PPF in Figure 10 has another important feature: Point *S* on the vertical axis shows the minimum acceptable level of consumption: the consumer goods the economy *must* produce in a year. For example, *S* might represent the consumption goods needed to prevent starvation among the least well off, or to prevent unacceptable social consequences, such as violent revolution.

Now we can see the problem faced by a stagnating, poor country. Output is currently at a point like *H* in Figure 10, with annual investment just equal to *N*. The capital stock, along with any new technology that comes with it, is not growing fast enough to increase productivity, so living standards remain unchanged. In this situation, the PPF shifts outward each year but not quickly enough to improve people's lives. In the most desperate countries, the situation is worse: They operate at a point like *R*, with investment *below N*. Even though the capital stock is growing, it does not grow fast enough to maintain productivity, so living standards actually decline.

The solution to this problem appears to be an increase in capital production beyond point *N*—a movement *along* the PPF from point *H* to a point such as *J*. As investment rises beyond *N*, productivity rises, and the PPF shifts outward rapidly enough over time to raise living standards. In a wealthy country, such as the United States, such a move could be engineered by changes in taxes or other government policies. But in the very poor country depicted here, such a move would be intolerable: At point *H*, consumption is already equal to *S*, the lowest acceptable level. Moving to point *J* would require reducing consumption *below S*.

> *The poorest countries are too poor to increase living standards by exploiting the normal tradeoff between consumption and capital production. If they cannot reduce consumption below current levels, they cannot raise capital production enough to increase productivity over time.*

In recent history, a variety of methods have been attempted to break out of this vicious circle of poverty. They are not all pleasant.

Brute force. The most tragic way to break out of the cycle is to simply force the economy from a point like *H* to a point like *J*, even though consumption falls below the minimally acceptable level *S*. An example occurred during the 1930s, when the dictator Joseph Stalin moved the Soviet economy in this way by ordering farmers into the city to produce capital equipment rather than food. With fewer people working on farms, agricultural production declined, and there was not enough food to go around. Stalin's solution was to confiscate food from the remaining farmers and give it to the urban workforce. This meant starvation for millions of farmers.

Target the wealthy. Figure 11(a) illustrates the possibility of reducing consumption for just those who can afford it: the wealthy few. The minimally acceptable level of consumption is now lower (*S'* rather than *S*) because total consumption can be reduced to a lower level than before without threatening the survival of the poor. The economy can then more easily move from point *H* to point *J* (which is now acceptable), freeing up resources for investment. However, this solution is not as easy as it sounds. First, the wealthy often have the most influence with poor-country governments. And being more mobile, they can easily relocate to other countries, taking their wealth with them. That is why efforts to limit the consumption sacrifice to the wealthy are often combined with restrictions on personal liberties, such as the freedom to travel or to invest abroad. And these restrictions can backfire in the long run, because restrictions on personal and economic freedom are remembered long after they are removed and make the public—especially foreigners—hesitant to invest in that country.

Decrease population growth. Figure 11(b) illustrates what happens when a poor country is able to reduce its population growth rate. In that case, the level of capital production needed to just maintain productivity becomes *N'* instead of *N*. Once that happens, the economy can continue to operate at point *H*. But now—with the population growing more slowly—the same amount of capital production raises productivity and living standards.

Reducing population growth was an important part of China's growth strategy, bringing the number of births per woman down from six in 1970 to less than two by 1980, and maintaining that low rate through 2009. But this goal was achieved with severe restrictions on the rights of individual families to have children, including heavy fines and, in many cases, forced abortions and sterilizations. Although restrictions and enforcement have been loosened considerably, China's government continues to regulate childbearing as part of its growth policy.

Foreign assistance. Since the 1940s, assistance from wealthier countries—either individually or through international organizations such as the World Bank or the International Monetary Fund—has been viewed as a leading way to break the cycle of poverty in the poorest countries. If capital goods are *given* to the country—especially if they embody new technology—productivity can rise without a decrease in current consumption. This is illustrated in Figure 11(c), where the additional capital allows the country to operate *beyond* its PPF, moving from point *H* to point *F*. The country still *produces* at point *H*. But point *F* shows the new combination of consumption goods and new capital goods that are available for use each year.

Alternatively, foreign assistance could provide consumption goods, allowing the country to free up its own resources for capital production while maintaining

FIGURE 11   **Some Growth Options for Poor Countries**

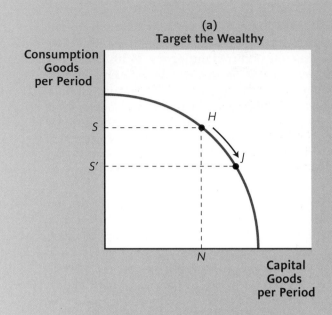

(a)
Target the Wealthy

Consumption Goods per Period

Capital Goods per Period

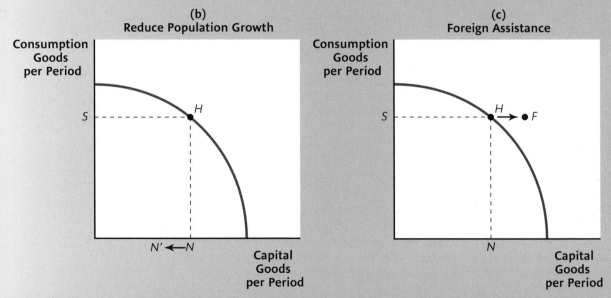

(b)
Reduce Population Growth

Consumption Goods per Period

Capital Goods per Period

(c)
Foreign Assistance

Consumption Goods per Period

Capital Goods per Period

In all three panels, a poor country is initially producing at point H, with consumption just equal to the amount needed for survival (S), and capital production just enough to maintain productivity with a rising population (N). In panel (a), resources are shifted from producing consumer goods to producing capital goods. But because the decrease in consumption is limited to the wealthy, the minimum survival level of total consumption is now from S' instead of S. At point J, the poor country can produce more capital—enough to raise productivity and living standards over time while still meeting survival needs for consumption.

In panel (b), the country reduces the population growth rate, so that the capital production needed to keep up with a rising population is now N' instead of N. Although capital production remains at point H, productivity now rises each year, raising living standards over time.

In panel (c), capital goods are obtained externally, through foreign investment or foreign assistance. The economy continues to produce at point H, but with the total amount of capital added each period greater than N (at point F), productivity and living standards rise over time.

minimal levels of consumption. Either form of assistance could, in theory, begin to raise capital per worker, productivity, and living standards. Once the country escapes from extreme poverty, it could then continue to grow on its own.

At least, that has long been the theory.

But the failure of so many poor countries to gain traction, despite trillions of dollars in foreign assistance over the past half-century, has made most economists skeptical. They put much of the blame on the poor institutions in these countries, where corrupt or undeveloped legal systems fail to protect property rights or enforce contracts. As a result, savers will not lend to domestic borrowers; entrepreneurs will not start productive businesses; and foreign firms will not bring much capital into the country. The country remains dependent on foreign assistance. And because corrupt governments siphon off most of the foreign aid dollars toward military spending or lavish lifestyles for the politically connected, little is left for improving the health and education of the population or increasing the stock of productive capital.

Some economists go even further, arguing that foreign assistance makes things *worse*, by preserving a corrupt bureaucracy, and slowing down institutional reform that might otherwise take place. They point out that much foreign aid also funds violent civil wars that, aside from the loss of life, suppress growth even further. In their view, the most effective assistance that rich countries can provide is pressure for institutional reform, and assistance with peace-keeping.

SUMMARY

Economic growth refers to the rise in living standards over time. Economists measure the average standard of living in a country as its *real GDP per capita*, which is a key determinant of economic well-being. If output grows faster than the population, then real GDP per capita rises. But in order for output per person to rise, *average working hours*, *the employment–population ratio (EPR)*, or *labor productivity* must increase. In developed countries, average hours have been decreasing and are unlikely to rise in the future.

Growth in the EPR has been responsible for considerable past growth in the United States and several other countries. It can be increased by policy changes that increase labor supply or labor demand. But increases in the EPR can't continue forever and are unlikely to be a significant source of growth in the future. This leaves increases in productivity—a major contributor to growth in the past—as the main source of growth in the future.

One determinant of productivity is *capital per worker*. The capital stock will rise when the flow of investment spending is greater than the flow of depreciation over some period of time. An increase in the capital stock shifts the production function upward, enabling any given number of workers to produce more output. If the capital stock rises at a faster rate than employment, then capital per worker rises, and so does productivity. Government policies can increase investment directly, by providing subsidies and incentives for business firms to invest. Government can also increase investment indirectly, through policies that lower interest rates, such as changes in tax policy to encourage more private saving or reductions in the government's budget deficit.

The other determinant of productivity is *technological change*—the discovery of new ways of combining inputs, including the creation of new types of capital. In rich countries, technological change from new discoveries is the main driver of economic growth. In poor countries, technological change is a major factor behind *catch-up growth*, because they can rapidly adopt discoveries already made in richer countries. The rate of technological change in rich countries depends partly on spending on R&D, either by government or private firms. Almost any government policy that increases investment spending in general will also increase spending on R&D, and therefore increase the pace of technological change. In addition, a country's institutions—such as its laws, regulations, and political system—are important in determining the pace of new discoveries.

Economic growth is not costless. Tax cuts that stimulate employment, capital formation, or technological progress require increases in other taxes, cuts in government spending, or an increase in the deficit that adds to the nation's total debt. Producing more capital or funding more R&D activities requires the sacrifice of current consumption. And growth often involves some tradeoff with other social goals, such as a clean environment or social stability.

PROBLEM SET

Answers to even-numbered Problems can be found on the text Web site through www.cengagebrain.com

1. For each of the following illustrate the immediate and long-run impact on real GDP using the classical model (labor market, production function, or loanable funds market) and state what happens to real GDP (increase, decrease, or remain unchanged).

   a. Increased immigration
   b. An aging of the population with an increasing proportion of retirees
   c. A decline in the tax rate on corporate profits
   d. A reduction of unemployment benefits
   e. The development of the Internet

2. Below are past GDP and growth data for the United States and four other countries:

	1950 Real GDP per Capita (in 1990 dollars)	1990 Real GDP per Capita (in 1990 dollars)	Average Yearly Growth Rate
United States	$9,573	$21,558	2.0%
France	$5,221	$17,959	3.0%
Japan	$1,873	$19,425	5.7%
Kenya	$ 609	$ 1,055	1.3%
India	$ 597	$ 1,348	2.0%

Source: Angus Maddison, *Monitoring the World Economy, 1820–1992* (Paris: OECD, 1995).

   a. For both years, calculate each country's per capita GDP as a percentage of U.S. per capita GDP. Which countries appeared to be catching up to the United States, and which were lagging behind?
   b. If all these countries had continued to grow (from 1990 onward) at the average growth rates given, in what year would France have caught up to the United States? In what years (respectively) would India and Kenya have caught up to the United States?

3. Below are hypothetical data for the country of Barrovia:

	Population (millions)	Employment (millions)	Average Yearly Hours	Labor Productivity (output per hour)	Total Yearly Output
2002	100	50	2,000	$4.75	—
2003	104	51	2,000	$4.75	—
2004	107	53	1,950	$5.00	—
2005	108	57	1,950	$5.00	—
2006	110	57	2,000	$5.00	—

   a. Fill in the entries for total output in each of the five years.
   b. Calculate the following for each year (except 2002):

      (1) Population growth rate (from previous year)
      (2) Growth rate of output (from previous year)
      (3) Growth rate of per capita output (from previous year)

4. In addition to shifting the production function upward, an increase in the capital stock will ordinarily make workers more productive and shift the labor demand curve rightward. Graphically illustrate the full impact of an increase in the nation's capital stock under this assumption.

5. Show what would happen to the production function if the capital stock *decreased*. Suppose, too, that the decrease in the capital stock—because it made workers less productive to firms—shifted the labor demand curve leftward. Graphically illustrate the full impact of a decrease in the nation's capital stock under this assumption. What government policies could cause a decrease in the capital stock?

6. State whether each of the following statements is true or false, and explain your reasoning briefly. Assume in each case that the population remains constant.
   a. "A permanent increase in employment from a lower to a higher level will cause an increase in real GDP per capita, but not continued growth in real GDP per capita."
   b. "A permanent increase in the nation's capital stock to a new, higher level will cause an increase in real GDP per capita, but not continued growth in real GDP per capita."
   c. "With constant average hours, EPR, and technology, as long as planned investment spending continues to be greater than depreciation, real GDP per capita can continue to grow at the same rate year after year."

7. On a diagram, draw an economy's aggregate production function. On the same diagram, add curves to illustrate where the production function would be in five years under each of the following assumptions. (Label your additional curves a, b, and c, and assume nothing else affecting economic growth changes.)
   a. Planned investment remains constant at its current level, which exceeds depreciation.
   b. Planned investment remains constant at its current level, which is less than depreciation.
   c. Planned investment rises above its current level, which exceeds depreciation.

8. Complete the table below, then find the growth rate of output per capita from Year 1 to Year 2, from Year 2 to Year 3, and from Year 3 to Year 4, in terms of the percentage change in each of its components.

	Year 1	Year 2	Year 3	Year 4
Total hours worked	192 million	200 million	285 million	368 million
Employment	1,200,000	1,400,000	1,900,000	2,100,000
Population	2,000,000	2,500,000	2,900,000	3,200,000
Productivity	$50 per hour	$52.50 per hour	$58 per hour	$60 per hour
Average hours per worker				
EPR				
Total output				
Real GDP per capita				

9. Redraw Figure 10 from the chapter, adding the new PPF the country would face in Year 2 if it produces at point *H* in Year 1. Explain your drawing. (Hint: Does a shifting PPF always mean a change in living standards?)

10. For each of the following scenarios, calculate the percentage change in real GDP per capita, assuming there is no change in technology:
    a. Average hours are constant; EPR, productivity, and population each increase by 2%.
    b. Average hours and EPR are constant; productivity increases by 2%.
    c. Average hours, productivity, and population each increase by 2%; EPR is constant.
    d. Average hours and EPR each decrease by 2%; productivity increases by 2%.

11. Evaluate the following statement: "Continual population growth, with no other change affecting economic growth, leads to continual growth in real GDP, but a continual drop in living standards." Briefly explain why you believe the statement is true or false.

More Challenging

12. Assume that average work hours, the employment–population ratio and technology all remain constant in a less developed country. The country initially has $100 billion in capital. For each of the following scenarios, describe what will happen over time to the country's (1) production possibilities frontier for capital and consumption goods; (2) capital per worker; and (3) average living standard.
    a. Population grows by 2% per year, depreciation of capital stock is 2% per year, and investment (new capital production) each year is equal to 4% of capital stock at the beginning of the year.
    b. Population grows by 1% per year, depreciation of capital stock is 2% per year, and investment (new capital production) each year is equal to 4% of capital stock at the beginning of the year.
    c. Population is constant, depreciation of capital stock is 2% per year, and investment (new capital production) each year is equal to 1% of capital stock at the beginning of the year.

13. Economist Amartya Sen has argued that famines in underdeveloped countries are not simply the result of crop failures or natural disasters. Instead, he suggests that wars, especially civil wars, are linked to most famine episodes in recent history. Using a framework similar to Figure 10, discuss the probable effect of war on a country's PPF. Explain what would happen if the country were initially operating at or near a point like *H*, producing the minimum acceptable level of consumption *S*.

CHAPTER 10

Economic Fluctuations

If you are like most college students, you will be looking for a job when you graduate, or you will already have one and want to keep it for a while. In either case, your fate is not entirely in your own hands. Your job prospects will depend, at least in part, on the overall level of economic activity in the country.

If the classical, long-run model of the previous two chapters described the economy at every point in time, you'd have nothing to worry about. Full employment would be achieved automatically, so you could be confident of getting a job at the going wage for someone with your skills and characteristics. Unfortunately, this is not always how the world works: Neither output nor employment grows as smoothly and steadily as the classical model predicts. Instead, as far back as we have data, the United States and similar countries have experienced *economic fluctuations*.

Look at panel (a) of Figure 1. (This is similar to a figure you saw four chapters ago that covered a longer time period.) The orange line shows estimated full-employment (or potential) output since 1979—the level of real GDP predicted by the classical model. As a result of economic growth (rising output per capita) and population growth, full-employment output rises steadily.

But now look at the green line, which shows *actual* output each quarter (at an annual rate). You can see that actual GDP fluctuates above and below the classical model's predictions. During *recessions,* which are shaded in the figure, output declines, occasionally sharply. During *expansions* (the unshaded periods) output rises quickly, usually faster than potential output is rising. Indeed, in the later stages of an expansion, output often *exceeds* potential output—a situation that economists call a **boom.**

Panel (b) shows another characteristic of expansions and recessions: fluctuations in employment. During expansions, such as almost all of the 1990s, employment grows rapidly. During recessions (shaded), such as our most recent one from December 2007 to June 2009, employment declines.

Figure 1 shows us that employment and output move very closely together. But the figure doesn't tell us anything about the *causal* relationship between them. However, as you'll see in this chapter, we have good reason to conclude that over the business cycle, it is changes in output that cause firms to change their employment levels. For example, in a recession, many business firms lay off workers. If asked why, they would answer that they are reducing employment *because* they are producing less output.

Now look at Figure 2, which gives us another perspective on fluctuations. It shows the employed percentage of the labor force aged 25–54, often called prime

Boom A period of time during which real GDP is above potential GDP.

FIGURE 1   Potential and Actual Real GDP and Employment, quarterly, 1979–2011

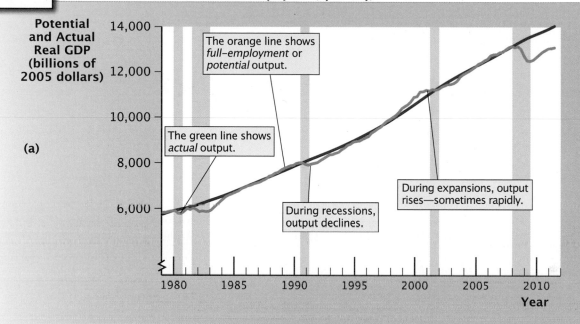

(a)

The orange line shows *full-employment* or *potential* output.

The green line shows *actual* output.

During recessions, output declines.

During expansions, output rises—sometimes rapidly.

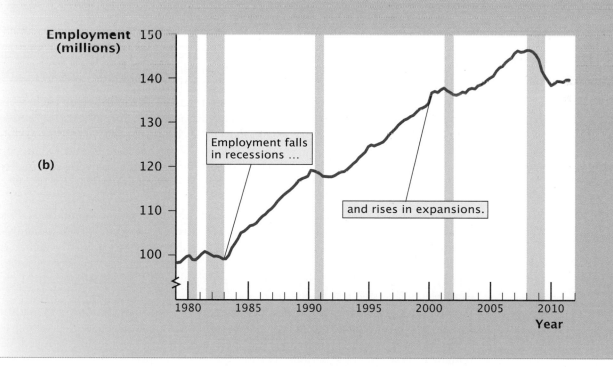

(b)

Employment falls in recessions ...

and rises in expansions.

© CENGAGE LEARNING 2013

FIGURE 2   U.S. Employment Rate for Workers Aged 25 to 54, 1979–2011

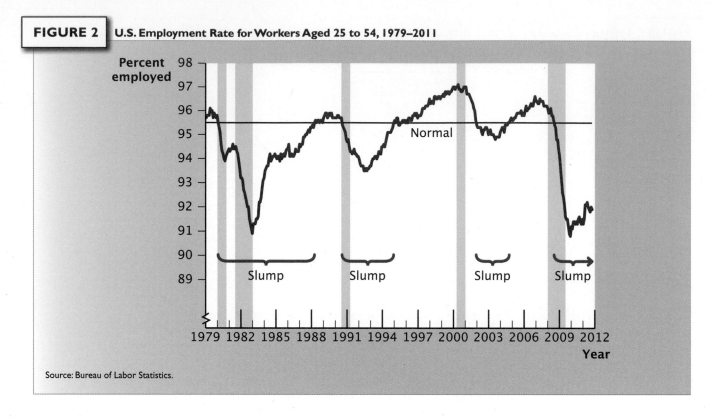

Source: Bureau of Labor Statistics.

slump A period during which real GDP is below potential and/or the employment rate is below normal.

age workers, from 1979 to mid-2011. When the economy is operating at potential output, 95.5% of these workers are typically employed (so 4.5% are *un*employed). So let's call 95.5% this group's *normal* rate of employment.

Notice how the employment rate begins to drop at the onset of each recession. As the recession proceeds, employment drops below normal. And it *remains* below normal even after the recession has ended. In this book, we're calling these periods of below-normal employment **slumps**. While recessions and expansions are official terms that define the turning points of the business cycle, slumps and booms are unofficial terms for periods when the employment rate is below or above normal.

Figures 1 and 2 show us some important facts about economic fluctuations. First, the shift from a strong expansion to a serious recession can occur rather suddenly—within a few quarters—as seen most easily by the sharp turning points in Figure 2.

Second, recessions and the resulting slumps don't last forever. The recession phase, in fact, can be relatively brief. The recessions of 1990–91 and 2001, for example, both lasted less than a year.

Finally, slumps—although they too eventually end—can be long and painful. During a typical slump, the number of people who are unemployed—looking for work but not working—is dramatically elevated. Many of the unemployed will remain jobless for long periods. During the Great Depression of the 1930s (not shown), it took more than a decade for the economy to return to normal. In the early 1980s—after back-to-back recessions—the slump lasted five years. And economists expect the slump caused by the recession of 2008–2009 to last four or five years, possibly longer, by the time the economy returns to normal.

The next several chapters deal with economic fluctuations. We have three things to explain: (1) *why* recessions and the resulting slumps occur in the first place, (2) why they sometimes last so long, and (3) why they do not last forever. But our first step is to ask whether the macroeconomic model you've already studied—the classical, long-run model—can explain why economic fluctuations occur.

CAN THE CLASSICAL MODEL EXPLAIN ECONOMIC FLUCTUATIONS?

The classical model does a good job of explaining why the economy tends to operate near its potential output level, on average, over long periods of time. But can it help us understand the facts of economic fluctuations, as shown in Figures 1 and 2? More specifically, can the classical model explain why GDP and employment typically fall *below* potential during a recession and often rise above it in an expansion? Let's see.

Shifts in Labor Supply

One way the classical model might explain a recession is through a shift in the labor supply curve. Figure 3 shows how this would work. If the labor supply curve shifted to the left, the equilibrium would move up and to the left along the labor demand curve, from point E to point G. The level of employment would fall, and output would fall with it.

This explanation of recessions has almost no support among economists. First, remember that the labor supply schedule tells us, at each real wage rate, the number of people who *would like to* work. This number reflects millions of families' preferences about working in the market rather than pursuing other activities, such as taking care of children, going to school, or enjoying leisure time. A leftward shift in labor supply would mean that fewer people want to work at any given wage—that preferences have changed toward these other, nonwork activities. But in reality, preferences tend to change very slowly, and certainly not rapidly enough to explain recessions.

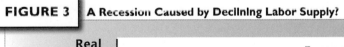

FIGURE 3   A Recession Caused by Declining Labor Supply?

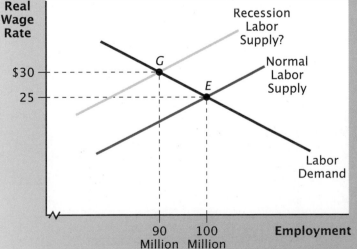

In theory, a recession could be caused by a sudden leftward shift in the labor supply curve, causing employment to fall. In fact, shifts in labor supply occur very slowly, so they cannot explain economic fluctuations.

© CENGAGE LEARNING 2013

Second, even if such a shift in preferences did occur, it could not explain the facts of real-world downturns. Recessions are times when unusually large numbers of people are looking for work. It would be hard to square that fact with a shift in preferences away from working.

The same arguments could be made about expansions: To explain them with labor supply shifts, we would have to believe that preferences suddenly change *toward* market work and away from other activities—an unlikely occurrence. And, in any case, expansions are periods when the unemployment rate typically falls to unusually low levels; *fewer*—not more—people are seeking work.

> *Because sudden shifts of the labor supply curve are unlikely to occur, and because they could not accurately describe the facts of the economic cycle, the classical model cannot explain fluctuations through shifts in the supply of labor.*

Shifts in Labor Demand

Another idea, studied by a number of economists, is that a recession might be caused by a leftward shift of the labor demand curve. This possibility is illustrated in panel (a) of Figure 4, in which a leftward shift in the labor demand curve would move us down and to the left along the labor supply curve. In the diagram, the labor market equilibrium would move from point E to point F, employment would fall, and so would the real wage rate (from \$25 to \$20). Is this a reasonable story that explains recessions? Most economists feel that the answer is no.

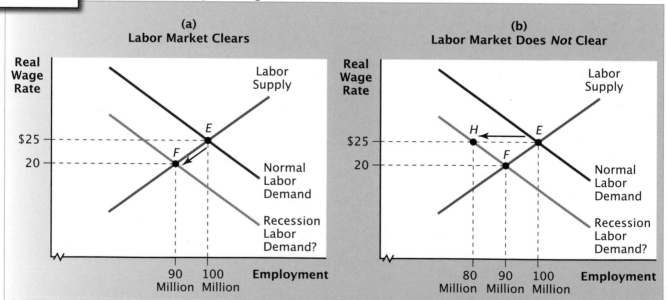

FIGURE 4 **A Recession Caused by Declining Labor Demand?**

Panel (a) shows how, in theory, a recession could be caused by a sudden leftward shift in the labor demand curve, causing employment to fall. But in panel (a), the labor market clears, so there would be no rise in unemployment, contradicting the facts of actual recessions.

In panel (b), downward wage rigidity prevents the labor market from clearing. This could, in theory, explain the rise in unemployment during a recession. But the classical model does not explain how such sudden leftward shifts in labor demand could realistically occur.

Does the Labor Market Clear?

The story told in panel (a) cannot explain the facts of recessions because it shows the labor market continuing to clear: the quantity of labor supplied and demanded at point *F* are equal. But as we've discussed, recessions are periods when millions of people who want to work cannot find jobs. This does not square with the story in panel (a).

Perhaps we can amend the model slightly. Suppose (as is the case during real-world recessions) that the real wage rate does not drop to the market-clearing level right away. Panel (b) shows an extreme case in which the labor demand curve shifts leftward but the real wage rate remains unchanged at $25. At that wage rate, the quantity of labor demanded falls to 80 million (at point *H* on the labor demand curve), while the quantity of labor supplied remains at 100 million (at point *E* on the labor supply curve). In the figure, 20 million people will be unemployed—although they *want* to work, they won't find jobs because their labor is not demanded.

This explanation for a recession raises a number of questions. First, why wouldn't the wage rate fall to the market clearing level right away, when so many unemployed workers are searching for jobs? Economists call this phenomenon *sticky wages* or *downward wage rigidity,* and they have long researched the reasons for it. Possible explanations include the reluctance of firms to decrease wages because of the negative effects on worker morale or worker productivity, and the complexities of the way workers search for jobs and the way firms fill job openings. But regardless of the reason, downward wage rigidity combined with a leftward shifting labor demand curve does seem to fit what happens in real world recessions.

But if this is our explanation for recessions, we still have an important question to answer: What causes the labor demand curve to shift leftward in the first place? The labor demand curve tells us the number of workers the nation's firms want to employ at each real wage rate. A leftward shift of this curve would mean that firms want to hire *fewer* workers at any given wage than they wanted to hire before. What could make them come to such a decision?

A Change in Productivity?

One possibility is that the labor demand curve shifts leftward because workers have become less *productive* and therefore less valuable to firms. This might happen if there were a sudden decrease in the capital stock, so that each worker had less equipment to work with. Or it might happen if workers suddenly forgot how to do things—how to operate a computer or use a screwdriver or fix an oil rig. Short of a major war that destroys plant and equipment, or an epidemic of amnesia, it is highly unlikely that workers would become less productive so suddenly. Thus, a sudden change in productivity is an unlikely explanation for recessions.

What about booms? Could they be explained by a sudden *increase* in productivity, causing the labor demand curve to shift *rightward*? Again, not likely. Even though it is true that the capital stock grows over time and workers continually gain new skills—and that both of these movements shift the labor demand curve to the right—such shifts take place at a glacial pace. Compared to the amount of machinery already in place, and to the knowledge and skills that the labor force already has, annual increments in physical capital or knowledge are simply too small to have much of an impact on labor demand.

> *While changes in labor productivity can shift the labor demand curve, they do not occur rapidly enough to explain real-world economic fluctuations.*

A Change in Total Spending?

Another possibility is that the labor demand curve shifts leftward because total *spending* declines, so firms are suddenly unable to sell all the output they produce, Therefore, the story would go, firms must cut back production and hire fewer workers than before at any given wage. This is a realistic story of what actually happens in a recession. So perhaps the classical model *can* explain recessions after all.

But hold on: We cannot use the classical model to tell this story. From the classical viewpoint, total spending is *never* deficient. On the contrary, Say's law—a central feature of the classical model—assures us that total spending will equal whatever level of output firms decide to produce. As you learned two chapters ago when we analyzed fiscal policy, a decrease in spending by one sector of the economy (such as the government) would cause an equal *increase* in spending by other sectors, with no change in total spending.

To be sure, *if* firms decide—for some reason—to produce less output, the classical model tells us that total income and total spending will fall too. But then we need to explain *why* firms would decide to produce less output in the first place. In the classical model, a change in spending cannot be the cause of a change in total output, because spending cannot change unless output changes first.

The same logic applies to booms. In the classical model, an increase in spending cannot explain why total output rises rapidly and sometimes goes beyond potential output. From the classical viewpoint, if one sector spontaneously increases its spending, some other sector's spending will be completely crowded out. Once again, total spending is always equal to total output; and spending cannot rise unless—for some other reason—output rises first.

> *While changes in spending play an important role in real-world economic fluctuations, the classical model rules them out as an initial cause.*

Verdict: The Classical Model Cannot Explain Economic Fluctuations

In earlier chapters, we stressed that the classical model works well in explaining the movements of the economy in the longer run. Now we see that it does a rather poor job of explaining the economy in the short run. Why is this?

Let's review. In the classical model, a change in output would have to come from a shift in either the labor supply curve or the labor demand curve. We ruled out several possible explanations for these shifts as unrealistic, and inconsistent with the facts of real-world fluctuations. The one promising explanation—a sudden change in spending combined with downward wage rigidity—is ruled out by the logic of the classical model, in which changes in total spending cannot arise on their own.

But once we step away from the classical model, we can begin to tell a realistic story about recessions, one in which spending—and expectations about future spending—play a central role.

WHAT TRIGGERS ECONOMIC FLUCTUATIONS?

Recessions that bring output below potential and expansions that drive output above potential are periods during which the economy is going a bit haywire. In a recession, millions of qualified people *want* to work, but firms won't hire them.

Managers would *like* to hire them, but they aren't selling enough output—in part because so many people are unemployed. The macroeconomy seems to be preventing opportunities for mutual gain.

In a boom, the economy is going haywire in a different way. The unemployment rate is so low that normal job-search activity—which accounts for frictional unemployment—is short-circuited. Firms, desperate to hire workers because production is so high, are less careful about whom they hire. The result is a poorer-than-normal match between workers and their jobs. Moreover, the overheating of the economy that occurs in a boom can lead to inflation. We'll discuss how this happens a few chapters from now. But the basic outline is this: Because qualified workers are so scarce, firms must compete fiercely with each other to hire them. This drives up wage rates in the economy, raises production costs for firms, and ultimately causes firms to raise their prices.

Booms and recessions are periods during which the economy deviates from the normal, full-employment equilibrium of the classical model. The question is: Why do such deviations occur? Let's start to answer this question by looking at a world that is much simpler than our own.

A Very Simple Economy

Imagine an economy with just two people: Yasmin and Pepe. Yasmin is especially good at making yogurt, but she eats only popcorn. Pepe, by contrast, is very good at making popcorn, but he eats only yogurt.

If things are going well, Yasmin and Pepe will make suitable amounts of yogurt and popcorn and trade with each other. Because of the gains from specialization, their trade will make them both better off than if they tried to function without trading. And under ordinary circumstances, Yasmin and Pepe will take advantage of all mutually beneficial opportunities for trading. Our two-person economy will thus operate at full employment, because both individuals will be fully engaged in making products for the other. You can think of their trading equilibrium as being like the labor market equilibrium in the classical model.

Now, suppose there is a breakdown in communication. For example, Yasmin may get the impression that Pepe is not going to want as much of her yogurt as before. She would then decide to *make* less yogurt for Pepe. At their next trading session, Pepe will be offered less yogurt, so he will decide to produce less popcorn. The result: Total production in the economy will decline, and our two traders will lose some of the benefits of trading. This corresponds to a recession.

Alternatively, suppose Yasmin thinks that Pepe will want *more* of her yogurt than before. This might lead her to *increase* her production, working more than she normally prefers to work so she can get more popcorn from Pepe before his demand for yogurt returns to normal. Yasmin's production of yogurt—and therefore, total output in the economy—rises even if Yasmin's expectations turn out to be wrong and Pepe does *not* want more yogurt. Production expands temporarily and might even lead to a boom.

In reading the previous paragraph, you might be thinking, "Wait a minute. If either Yasmin or Pepe got the impression that the other might want less or more of the other's product, wouldn't a simple conversation between them straighten things out?" If these are your thoughts, you are absolutely right. A breakdown in communication and a sudden change in production would be extremely unlikely . . . *in a simple economy with just two goods and two people*. And therein lies the problem: The real-world economy is much more complex than the world of Yasmin and Pepe.

The Real-World Economy

Think about the U.S. economy, with its millions of businesses producing goods and services for hundreds of millions of people. Production decisions made by any one firm, or spending decisions made by any one household, have virtually no impact on the economy as a whole. So in making decisions, each firm and each household considers only its own consequences. In this kind of environment, large numbers of people or firms, each doing the best for themselves, can create a macroeconomic change that makes everyone worse off. Let's consider some of the ways that the problem can arise.

A Change in Production

In many industries, production must be planned long before goods are actually sold. For example, from inception to final production, it takes nearly a year to build a house and two years to develop a new automobile model or produce a Hollywood film.

Suppose that Ford Motors believes, rightly or wrongly, that consumers will buy fewer of its cars next year. It cannot simply call a meeting of all potential customers and find out whether its fears are justified. Nor can it convince potential customers, as Yasmin can convince Pepe, that their *own* jobs depend on their buying a Ford car. Most potential car buyers do *not* work for Ford or any other car company, and don't perceive any connection between buying a car for themselves and keeping their own jobs.

Under the circumstances, it may be entirely logical for Ford to start producing fewer automobiles and lay off some of its workers. And Ford wouldn't be acting alone: The information that created worries at Ford would no doubt have the same effect on other automobile companies and their suppliers. They, too, would cut back production and lay off workers.

Of course, this would not be the end of the story. The automobile industry, by decreasing its workforce, would create further problems for the economy. The laid-off workers, who will earn less income or none at all, will cut back on *their* spending for a variety of consumer goods—restaurant meals, movies, vacation travel—anything not considered essential. And they will certainly postpone any large purchases they'd been planning, such as a new large-screen television or that family trip to Disney World. This will cause other firms—the firms producing these other consumer goods and services—to cut back on *their* production, to lay off *their* workers, and so on. In other words, what began as a production decrease in one sector of the economy—in this case, automobiles—can work its way through other sectors, causing a full-blown recession.

A rapid expansion—sometimes leading to a boom—can arise in much the same way as a recession. It might start because of an increase in production in one sector of the economy, say, the housing sector, as we discussed in Chapter 4. With more production and more workers earning higher incomes, spending increases in other sectors as well, until output rises above the classical, full-employment level.

A Change in Spending

In the previous example, a recession or rapid expansion was initiated by a large change in *production*. But the problem can also begin with a change in *spending*. Suppose, for example, that a large number of *consumers* begin to believe—rightly or wrongly—that a recession is likely in the near future. They know that if the recession occurs, their own jobs will be at risk. Quite logically, they start to save a larger proportion of their incomes so they'll be better able to weather any possible economic storm.

Of course, the only way to save more of your income is to spend less of it. So businesses, seeing their sales decline, will start to produce less and lay off some of their workers, who will in turn reduce *their* spending, and so on. Just as in our previous example, the decrease in spending can trigger a downward spiral of further declines in production, income, and spending.

When we step back and think about the situation, it seems absurd: People lose their jobs, because people were afraid of losing their jobs. Couldn't we prevent recessions if people just refused to give in to their fears and kept spending as they did in normal times? The answer is yes . . . in a simple economy with just a few people. In that case, each person would see a direct connection between their own lack of spending and the economy's problems.

But in the real-world economy, with hundreds of millions of consumers, each will reason as follows: "Whether or not *I* buy that car or *I* take that vacation won't make any difference to the economy. And if I *do* buy these things, and others don't, I'll be even worse off if I actually lose my job. So . . . better to hope that *others* spend, while I continue to save as much as I can, just in case."

Spending changes by *any* sector of the economy can have the same effect as a change in household consumption spending. If business firms—fearful of recession—cut their spending on new capital equipment, or government cuts back on purchases for defense or highway construction, or foreigners spend less on the economy's exports—any of these scenarios can trigger the same downward spiral.

Finally, note that spending changes can also trigger a boom. For example, if households begin to think that exceptionally good times are ahead, they may start spending more than normal—especially on big-ticket items that they were uncertain about buying before. As spending rises, firms produce more and hire more workers, creating still more spending, and so on.

Why Say's Law Doesn't Prevent Recessions

In this chapter, we've seen that changes in spending play a crucial role in recessions and expansions. For example, a decrease in consumption spending can, by itself, be the initial cause of a recession. Regardless of the cause, it is usually further drops in consumption spending that turn an initial disturbance into a full-blown recession.

But wait: a couple of chapters ago, as you studied the classical model, you learned about Say's law. It told us that total spending will equal total income. If one sector changes its spending, then other sectors should make up the difference, so that total spending remains unchanged. More specifically, if households spend less, they must be saving more. That additional saving will go into the loanable funds market, where it will be borrowed by business firms that will then spend it. Doesn't that eliminate the potential impact of changes in consumption spending?

The answer is yes—*if* a critical assumption of the classical model holds: *that the interest rate adjusts until saving is equal to business and government borrowing.* In that case, every dollar someone saves is borrowed (and spent) by someone else. If that's true, lower consumer spending—which is equivalent to greater saving—will not threaten the economy.

This assumption makes sense for the long run, which is why we used it in our presentation of the classical/long-run model. We also used this assumption in our discussion of economic growth: In the long run, greater saving leads to greater investment and faster growth of the capital stock. But over shorter periods of time, we cannot be sure that the loanable funds market will do its job. Let's discuss three possible ways that the loanable funds market could fail to turn one person's saving into someone else's spending.

"Saving" versus "Supply of Funds"

Not all saving is supplied to the loanable funds market. The piggy bank you may have had as a child is one example: Every coin you dropped into the slot was an example of saving (i.e., income or allowance not spent over some time period) that was *not* made available for someone else to spend. The coins just stayed in the piggy bank. A couple of chapters from now, when we discuss money and the banking system in more detail, you'll see other examples of saving that are not supplied to the loanable funds market.

To see why this matters, let's imagine that the economy is operating at full-employment output and firms are selling all the goods and services they produce. Then households become pessimistic about the future, and decide to cut their spending by $100 billion over the year, as shown in Figure 5(a). This means they are *saving*

FIGURE 5 | **Two Destinations for Additional Household Saving**

(a) Consumption Falls, Planned Investment Rises => Total Spending Unchanged

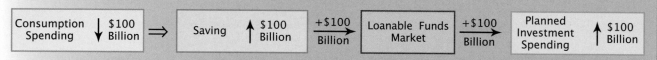

(b) Consumption Falls, Planned Investment Unchanged => Total Spending Falls

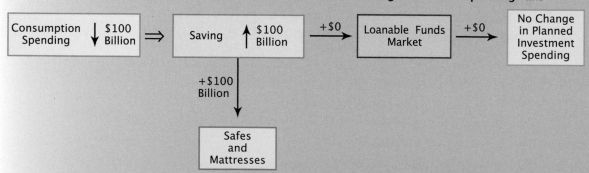

In panel (a), the loanable funds market behaves according to the classical model. Households cut their spending (increase their saving) by $100 billion per year, and supply it all to the loanable funds market. The funds are loaned out to business firms, and planned investment rises by $100 billion. Consumption falls by $100 billion and planned investment rises by $100 billion, so there is no change in total spending.

Panel (b) deviates from the classical model. As in panel (a), households cut their spending (increase their saving) by $100 billion per year, but now they supply none of it to the loanable funds market. The additional saving is not loaned out to business firms, and planned investment does not change. Consumption falls by $100 billion and planned investment does not change, so total spending drops by $100 billion.

an additional $100 billion. As long as they put the entire $100 billion of new saving into the loanable funds market, this need not cause any problem: The additional saving will flood into the market and drive down the interest rate, until investment spending increases by $100 billion. Notice that the $100 billion that households no longer spend is borrowed and spent by business firms. Thus, the decrease in spending by households has no effect on *total* spending.

Now look at Figure 5(b). Here we suppose, once again, that households decide to cut their spending by $100 billion over the year and must be saving this $100 billion. But this time, instead of putting this saving into the loanable funds market, they stuff $100 billion in cash into household safes and under their mattresses. Why would they do this? During recessions, bankruptcies rise, and people and companies default on loans. Savers may fear that funds they provide to the loanable funds market won't be paid back.

In Figure 5(b), the additional saving does *not* enter the loanable funds market, so the interest rate does *not* decrease, and planned investment does *not* increase. Households have decreased their consumption spending by $100 billion, but no one else's spending rises to make up for it. So *total* spending decreases—by $100 billion per year. The economy is violating Say's law: Total spending has fallen below total income.

More generally,

> *When households spend less (save more), but do not supply all of their additional saving to the loanable funds market, total spending will drop below total income, violating Say's law.*

This is one reason why, in theory, a decision by households to spend less (save more) can trigger a recession, or contribute to a downward recessionary spiral.

"Supply of Funds" versus "Lending"

Even if households *do* supply all of their savings to the loanable funds market, the funds may not be made available to others who want to borrow and spend it. Much of the saving and lending in the economy is done through *financial intermediaries* institutions that collect funds from savers and then lend them to borrowers. A bank is an example of a financial intermediary. By depositing funds into a savings account at a bank, you avoid the inconvenience, risk, and legal costs of finding a borrower and making the loan yourself. The bank can diversify its loans more easily than you can, and it has expertise and relatively inexpensive procedures to identify borrowers who are likely to repay their loans.

But banks, just like households and other business firms, can become pessimistic. If banks see economic trouble on the horizon, they may decide to hang on to some or all of the additional deposits until conditions look better.[1] This is illustrated in Figure 6, where—as in Figure 5(a)—households cut their spending by $100 billion and put the entire $100 billion of additional saving into the loanable funds market. But in Figure 6, we assume that pessimistic financial intermediaries do not increase their lending at all. As a result, the flow of borrowing and planned investment spending does not change. And once again, total spending falls below total income.

---

[1] Or the banks may only be willing to lend to the government, because that is considered safe. But unless the government changes its budget deficit, its demand for funds will not change, so new lending to the government won't be possible. Here, we are exploring what happens to total spending when households save more and there is no change in the deficit or any other government policy.

FIGURE 6   Additional Saving Supplied to the Market but Not Loaned Out

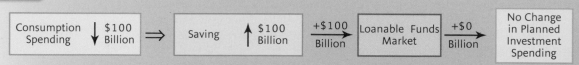

Households cut their spending (increase their saving) by $100 billion per year, and supply all of the additional funds to the loanable funds market. But if pessimistic financial intermediaries in the loanable funds market do not lend out the funds, there is no additional borrowing by business firms. Because consumption falls by $100 billion and planned investment does not change, total spending falls by $100 billion.

© CENGAGE LEARNING 2013

> *When households save more (spend less), but financial intermediaries do not lend out all of the additional saving, total spending will drop below total income, violating Say's law.*

Other Influences on the Interest Rate

In the classical model, the interest rate is entirely determined by saving (the supply of funds) and the sum of planned investment and the budget deficit (the demand for funds). A few chapters from now, you'll learn that—in the short run—interest rates can be influenced by other factors. For example, a nation's central bank (the Federal Reserve System in the United States) often manipulates the interest rate for reasons of economic policy. Interest rates can also change when firms and households that hold wealth—such as stocks, bonds, and bank accounts—decide to shift their holdings from one type of asset to another.

What does this imply about total spending during a recession? Normally, additional saving by households drives down the interest rate, causing investment spending to rise. But if households increase their saving and other forces *prevent* the interest rate from dropping, then planned investment spending will *not* rise. Once again, if households spend less and save more, total spending will decline.

> *When households save more (spend less), but other factors prevent the interest rate from falling to its market-clearing level, then some of the additional saving will not be borrowed and spent by others. Total spending will drop below total income, violating Say's law.*

The Interest Rate as a Cause of Booms and Recessions

The fact that the interest rate can be influenced by events outside the loanable funds market also suggests that interest-rate changes, by themselves, can cause economic fluctuations. If the interest rate rises, people will be encouraged to save more and spend less—especially on the most interest-sensitive purchases such as homes and automobiles. At the same time, the higher interest rate will decrease business spending on plant and equipment. Thus, the rise in the interest rate causes *both* household and business spending to drop—a decrease in total spending that can set off the downward spiral that we discussed earlier.

If events outside the loanable funds market drive the interest rate *lower,* the effect can be just the opposite. As the interest rate drops, households save less (spend more).

At the same time, planned investment rises. Once again, the effect is usually felt first in the most interest-sensitive sectors, as a rapid increase in spending on capital equipment, housing, and/or automobiles.

Examples of Recessions and Expansions

Table 1 lists some of the recessions and notable expansions of the last 50 years, along with the events and spending changes that are thought to have caused them or at least contributed heavily. You can see that each of these events first affected spending and output in one or more sectors of the economy. For example, several recessions have been set off by increases in oil prices. The initial impact of higher oil prices is often felt most strongly on energy-using goods and services, such as new cars and trucks, or vacation travel. Also, because consumers spend more on expensive gasoline and other products made from oil, they have less income left over to spend on a variety of other goods and services.

Other recessions were precipitated by military cutbacks. Still others came about when the Federal Reserve caused sudden increases in interest rates that led to decreased spending on new homes and other goods. (You'll learn more about the Federal Reserve and its policies a few chapters from now.) And our most recent recession had multiple causes, including oil prices, the bursting of the housing bubble, and Federal Reserve policy.

Strong expansions, on the other hand, have been caused by military buildups, by falling oil prices that stimulated consumption spending, and by bursts of planned investment spending. The expansion from 2002 to 2007, for example, began when a change in Federal Reserve policy and other global conditions caused interest rates to drop and stay low. This, in turn, prompted a rise in interest-sensitive spending, especially on housing, thereby prompting a spurt of investment in new home construction. Once the economy began expanding, it was further spurred by other factors, such as a rise in stock prices and consumer optimism, both of which led to an increase in consumption spending.

When a decrease in spending causes production cutbacks in one or more sectors of the economy, firms will lay off workers. The laid-off workers, suffering decreases in their incomes, cut back their own spending on other products, causing further lay-offs in other sectors. The economy can continue sliding downward for a year or longer. Even after the recession is over—and the economy is no longer worsening—it can remain in a slump for years. The forces that caused spending to decline in the first place often take time to reverse themselves, so spending, production, and employment remain at less than normal levels.

The same process works in reverse during an expansion: Higher spending leads to greater production, higher employment, and still greater spending, possibly leading to a boom in which the economy remains overheated for some time.

Booms and slumps do not last forever, however. The economy eventually adjusts back to full-employment output. Often, a change in government macroeconomic policy helps the adjustment process along, speeding the return to full employment. Other times, a policy mistake thwarts the adjustment process, prolonging or deepening a painful slump, or exacerbating a boom and overheating the economy even more.

© MAHAUX PHOTOGRAPHY/GETTY IMAGES

Half of our recessions since the early 1950s have been caused, at least in part, by rapid rises in oil prices.

TABLE I

Expansions and Recessions in the Last 50 Years

Period		Event	Initial Spending Changes
Late 1960s	Expansion	Vietnam War	Defense spending ↑
1970	Recession	Change in Federal Reserve policy	Spending on new homes ↓
1974	Recession	Dramatic increase in oil prices	Spending on cars and other energy-using products ↓
1980	Recession	Dramatic increase in oil prices	Spending on cars and other energy-using products ↓
1981–1982	Recession	Change in Federal Reserve policy	Spending on new homes, cars, and business investment ↓
1983–1990	Expansion	Military buildup, then dramatic decline in oil prices	Defense spending ↑; Spending on energy-using products ↑
1990	Recession	Large increase in oil prices; collapse of Soviet Union	Spending on cars and other energy-using products ↓; Defense spending ↓
1991–2000	Expansion	Technological advances in computers; development of the Internet; high wealth creation	Spending on capital equipment ↑; Consumption spending ↑
2001	Recession	Investment in new technology slows; technology-fueled bubble of optimism bursts; wealth destruction	Spending on capital equipment ↓
2002–2007	Expansion	Changes in fiscal and Federal Reserve policies; rapid rise in housing wealth	Consumption spending ↑
2008–2009	Recession	Oil prices rise; housing bubble bursts; financial crisis	Spending on cars, new homes, and capital equipment ↓

How does this adjustment process work? This is a question we'll be coming back to a few chapters from now, after you've learned some new tools for analyzing the economy's behavior over the short run.

WHERE DO WE GO FROM HERE?

The classical model that you've learned in previous chapters is certainly useful: It helps us understand economic growth over time, and how economic events and economic policies affect the economy over the long run. But in trying to understand economic fluctuations, we've had to depart from the strict framework of the classical model.

One theme of our discussion has been the central role of spending in understanding economic fluctuations. In the classical model, spending could be safely ignored. Say's law assured us that total spending would always be sufficient to buy the output produced at full employment. In the long run, we can have faith in the classical perspective on spending.

But in the short run, we've seen that actual or anticipated changes in spending—that begin in one or more specific sectors—will affect production. When employment changes in those sectors, the spending of workers *there* will change as well, affecting demand in still other sectors. Clearly, if we want to understand fluctuations, we need to take a close look at spending. This is what we will do in the next chapter, when we study the *short-run macro model*.

SUMMARY

The classical model does not always do a good job of describing the economy over short time periods. Over periods of a few years, national economies experience economic fluctuations in which output rises above or falls below potential. Significant periods of falling output are called *recessions*, while periods of rapidly rising output are *expansions*. A recession eventually causes employment to fall below its normal level, bringing the economy into a *slump*. An expansion often causes employment to rise above normal levels, causing a *boom*. When we try to explain economic fluctuations using the classical model, we come up short. Neither shifts in the labor demand curve, nor shifts in the labor supply curve, offer a realistic explanation for what happens during a recession or a boom.

In a simple economy with very few people, decisions about spending and production could be easily coordinated, so economic fluctuations would be easy to avoid. But in a market economy with millions of people and firms, decisions about spending and production cannot be coordinated, making the economy vulnerable to changes in production that are harmful to everyone involved.

Deviations from the full-employment level of output are often caused by changes in actual or expected spending that initially affect one or more sectors and then work their way through the entire economy. Decreases in spending can cause recessions that lead to slumps, while increases in spending can cause expansions that lead to booms. In the short run, we can't count on Say's law to ensure that total spending will always equal total production for several reasons: Households don't necessarily supply all of their saving to the loanable funds market, financial institutions don't necessarily lend out all of the funds supplied to them, and other forces can temporarily move the interest rate away from its normal equilibrium value. Moreover, these temporary movements in the interest rate can themselves trigger spending changes that, in turn, cause economic fluctuations.

When output deviates from its long-run potential, it eventually returns to potential output, but it does not do so immediately. The origins of economic fluctuations can be understood more fully with the short-run macro model, which we will study in the next chapter.

PROBLEM SET

Answers to even-numbered Problems can be found on the text Web site through www.cengagebrain.com

1. Using Figure 1 and/or Figure 2, identify a specific year during which the U.S. economy was clearly:
   a. in the midst of an expansion but *not* yet experiencing a boom.
   b. in the midst of an expansion and also in the midst of a boom.
   c. in the midst of an expansion and also in the midst of a slump.
   d. in the midst of a recession but not yet in a slump.

2. "Every U.S. recession over the last 5 decades has been caused by an increase in oil prices." True or false? Explain briefly.

3. "Immediately after a recession ends, the employment rate begins rising." Evaluate this statement, based on the historical record in Figure 2.

4. In Figure 5(b), we assumed that household saving rises by $100 billion per year, and none of this additional saving goes into the loanable funds market. Under this

assumption, would total lending during the year be zero? Explain. (Hint: Is *additional* saving the same as *total* saving?)

5. In Figure 5(b), we assumed that when saving rises, none of the additional saving enters the loanable funds market. Suppose, instead, that 40 percent of any additional saving is supplied to financial intermediaries, while the rest goes into safes and mattresses. Also assume that 30 cents out of every dollar provided to a financial intermediary is lent out. If there is no other deviation from the normal functioning of the loanable funds market, determine the impact of a $100 billion increase in annual saving on (a) planned investment per year and (b) total spending per year.

6. In the chapter, you learned that forces outside of the loanable funds market can influence the interest rate. Suppose the supply and demand curves in the loanable funds market are as depicted in Figure 7 of the previous chapter (Economic Growth and Rising Living Standards). Suppose that the saving curve shifts rightward by 0.75 trillion as shown in that figure, but that other influences on the interest rate prevent it from dropping at all. By how many trillions of dollars would total spending fall short of total income and total output?

© CHRIS HONDROS/NEWSMAKERS/ GETTY IMAGES

CHAPTER 11

The Short-Run Macro Model

Every December, newspapers and television news broadcasts focus their attention on spending. You might see a reporter standing in front of a shopping mall, warning that unless holiday shoppers loosen their wallets and spend big on computers, DVD players, vacation trips, toys, and new cars, the economy is in for trouble.

Of course, spending matters during the rest of the year, too. But holiday spending attracts our attention, because the normal forces at work during the rest of the year become more concentrated in late November and December. Factories churn out merchandise, and stores stock up at higher than normal rates. If consumers are in Scrooge-like moods, unsold goods will pile up in stores. In the months that follow, these stores will cut back on their orders for new goods. Factories will decrease production and lay off workers.

And the story will not end there. The laid-off workers—even those who collect some unemployment benefits—will see their incomes decline. As a consequence, they will spend less on a variety of consumer goods. This will cause other firms—the ones that produce those consumer goods—to cut back on *their* production.

This hypothetical example reinforces a conclusion we reached in the last chapter: Spending is very important in the short run. And it points out an interesting circularity: The less income households earn, the less they will spend. That is, *spending depends on income*. But the less households spend, the less income they will earn (because less spending means less production and employment, which lowers income). Thus, *income depends on spending*.

> *In the short run, spending depends on income, and income depends on spending.*

In this chapter, we will explore this circular connection between spending and income. We will do so with a very simple macroeconomic model, which we'll call the **short-run macro model**. Many of the ideas behind the model were originally developed by the economist John Maynard Keynes in the 1930s. The model's perspective on the economy is in many ways opposite to that of the classical model. When we take the short-run view, total spending determines the level of production, and changes in spending play the central role in explaining economic fluctuations.

To keep the model as simple as possible, we will—for the time being—ignore all influences on production *besides* spending. As a result, the short-run model may appear strange to you at first, like a drive along an unfamiliar highway. You may wonder: Where is all the scenery you are used to seeing along the classical road? Where are the labor market, the production function, the loanable funds market, and the

Short-run macro model
A macroeconomic model that explains how changes in spending can affect real GDP in the short run.

285

market-clearing assumption? Rest assured that many of these concepts are still with us, lurking in the background and waiting to be exposed, and we will come back to them in later chapters. But in this chapter, we assume that spending—and *only* spending—determines how much output the economy will produce.

As we proceed, remember that we are more interested in explaining real variables (adjusted for changes in the price level) than nominal variables (measured in current dollars). Therefore, whenever we discuss any dollar-denominated variable (such as consumption spending, income, or GDP) we will always mean the *real* variable—even when the word "real" is not included.

Consumption Spending

A natural place for us to begin our look at spending is with its largest component: *consumption spending*. In the United States, household spending on consumer goods—groceries, rent, car repairs, movies, telephone calls, and so on—is more than two-thirds of total spending in the economy.

Determinants of Consumption Spending

What determines the total amount of consumption spending? One way to answer is to start by thinking about yourself or your family. What determines your spending in any given month, quarter, or year?

Disposable Income. The first thing that comes to mind is your income: The more you earn, the more you spend. But in macroeconomics, small differences in language can be crucial. It's not exactly your *total income* per period that determines your spending, but rather what you get to *keep* from that income after deducting any taxes you have to pay. Moreover, some people receive a flow of transfer payments from the government—such as unemployment insurance benefits or Social Security payments—which they can spend in addition to any income they earn. If we start with the income households earn, deduct all tax payments, and then add in any transfer received, we get *disposable income*—a term introduced with the classical model. This is the income households are free to spend or save as they wish.

Disposable income = Income − Tax payments + Transfers received.

This can be rewritten as:

Disposable income = Income − (Taxes − Transfers).

Finally, remember that the term in parentheses, Taxes − Transfers, is defined as *net taxes*. So the easiest way to think of disposable income is:

Disposable income = Income − Net taxes.

All else equal, you'd certainly spend more on consumer goods with a disposable income of $50,000 per year than with $20,000 per year. And in the economy as a whole, *a rise in disposable income—with no other change—causes a rise in consumption spending.*

Wealth. Consumption spending is also influenced by *wealth*—the total value of household assets (home, stocks, bonds, bank accounts, and the like) minus outstanding liabilities (student loans, mortgage loans, credit card debt, and so on). Even if your disposable income stayed the same, an increase in your wealth—say, because you own stocks or bonds that have risen in value—would probably induce you to spend more. In general, *a rise in wealth, with no other change, causes a rise in consumption spending.*

The Interest Rate. The interest rate is the reward people get for saving, or what they have to pay when they borrow. You would probably save more each year if the interest rate was 10 percent than if it was 2 percent. But when you save more of your disposable income, you spend less. Even households with a negative net worth—who are not "savers" in the common sense of the term—are influenced by the interest rate. For example, people with credit card or other debts must decide each month how much of their debt balance to pay down. The higher the interest rate, the greater their incentive to pay back debt, and the less they will spend on consumption goods. *All else equal, a rise in the interest rate causes a decrease in consumption spending.*

Expectations. Expectations about the future can affect spending as well. If you become more optimistic about your job security or expect a big raise, you might spend more of your income *now.* Similarly, if you become more pessimistic—worried about losing your job or taking a pay cut—you'd probably spend less now. *All else equal, optimism about future income causes an increase in consumption spending.*

* * *

Other variables, too, can influence your consumption spending, including inheritances you expect to receive over your lifetime, and even how long you expect to live. But disposable income, wealth, the interest rate, and expectations are the key variables we'll be coming back to again and again in the short-run macroeconomic model. And just as these variables influence the consumption spending of each individual household, they also influence the consumption spending of the household sector as a whole.

> *All else equal, consumption spending increases when:*
>
> - *Disposable income rises*
> - *Wealth rises*
> - *The interest rate falls*
> - *Households become more optimistic about the future*

Consumption and Disposable Income

Of all the factors that influence consumption spending, the most important and stable determinant is disposable income. Figure 1 shows the relationship between (real) consumption spending and (real) disposable income in the United States from 2000 to 2011. Each point in the diagram represents a pair of values for a quarter: one value for disposable income and another for consumption, both expressed as annual rates. For example, the point labeled "2010–1" represents the first quarter of 2010, when the annual rate was $9,923 billion for disposable income, and $9,121 billion for consumption. Notice that as disposable income rises, consumption spending rises as well. Indeed, almost all of the variation in consumption spending from quarter to quarter and year to year can be explained by variations in disposable income. Although the other factors we've discussed do affect consumption spending, their impact is not as strong.

There is something even more interesting about Figure 1: The relationship between consumption and disposable income is roughly *linear;* the points lie reasonably close to a straight line. This almost-linear relationship between consumption and disposable income

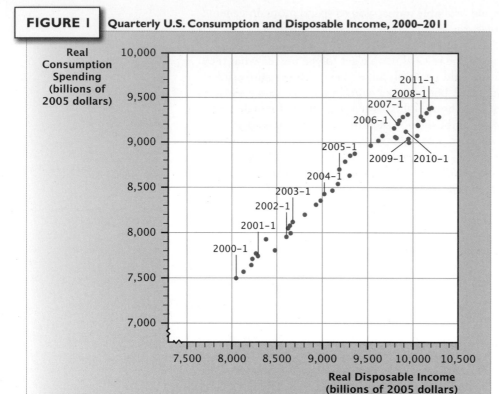

FIGURE 1 Quarterly U.S. Consumption and Disposable Income, 2000–2011

When real consumption expenditure is plotted against real disposable income, the resulting relationship is very close to linear: As real disposable income rises, so does real consumption spending.

Source: Bureau of Economic Analysis.

has been observed in a wide variety of historical periods and a wide variety of nations. This is why, when we represent the relationship between disposable income and consumption with a diagram or an equation, we use a straight line.

The Consumption Function

Let's now move from the actual data in Figure 1 to the hypothetical example in Table 1. Each row in the table represents a combination of (real) disposable income and (real) consumption we might observe in an economy. For example, the table shows us that if disposable income were equal to $7,000 billion in some year, consumption spending would equal $6,200 billion in that year. When we plot these data on a graph, we obtain the straight line in Figure 2. This line is called the **consumption function** because it illustrates the functional relationship between consumption and disposable income.

Like every straight line, the consumption function in Figure 2

Consumption function A positively sloped relationship between real consumption spending and real disposable income.

has two main features: a vertical intercept and a slope. Because these features will be important in our model, let's explore them a bit here.

Autonomous Consumption

Autonomous consumption spending The part of consumption spending that is independent of income; also the vertical intercept of the consumption function.

The vertical intercept of the consumption function—$2,000 billion in the figure—has a name: **autonomous consumption spending.** Mathematically, it also tells us how much consumption spending there would be in the economy if disposable income were zero. However, the real purpose of isolating autonomous consumption spending is not to identify consumption at zero disposable income, but rather to help us identify the particular line that represents consumption spending at other, positive income levels. After all, we could draw many lines that have the same slope as the one in the figure. But only one of them has a vertical intercept of $2,000.

Autonomous consumption represents the influence on consumption spending of everything *other than* disposable income. For example, if household wealth were to increase, consumption would be greater at any level of disposable income. In that case, the entire consumption function in the figure would shift upward, so its vertical intercept would increase. We would call this *an increase in autonomous consumption spending.* Similarly, a decrease in wealth would cause a *decrease in autonomous consumption spending,* and shift the consumption function downward.

Real Disposable Income (billions of dollars per year)	Real Consumption Spending (billions of dollars per year)
0	2,000
1,000	2,600
2,000	3,200
3,000	3,800
4,000	4,400
5,000	5,000
6,000	5,600
7,000	6,200
8,000	6,800

TABLE I

Hypothetical Data on Disposable Income and Consumption

© CENGAGE LEARNING 2013

FIGURE 2   The Consumption Function

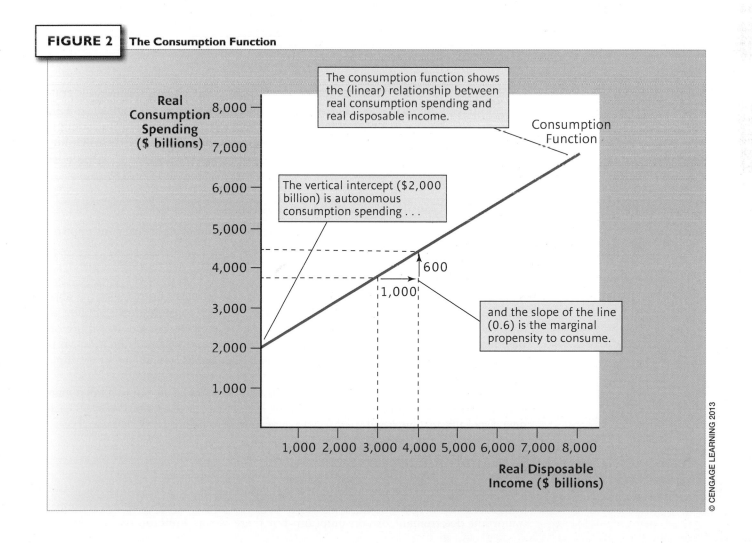

© CENGAGE LEARNING 2013

The Marginal Propensity to Consume

The second important feature of Figure 2 is the slope, which shows the change along the vertical axis divided by the change along the horizontal axis as we go from one point to another on the line:

$$\text{Slope} = \frac{\Delta \text{ Consumption}}{\Delta \text{ Disposable income}}$$

As you can see in the table, each time disposable income rises by \$1,000 billion, consumption spending rises by \$600 billion, so that the slope is

$$\frac{\$600 \text{ billion}}{\$1,000 \text{ billion}} = 0.6$$

The slope in Figure 2 is an important feature not just of the consumption function itself, but also of the macroeconomic analysis we will build from it. This is why economists have given this slope a special name, the *marginal propensity to consume,* abbreviated *MPC*. In our hypothetical economy, the *MPC* is 0.6.

We can think of the *MPC* in three different ways, but each of them has the same meaning:

Marginal propensity to consume The amount by which consumption spending rises when disposable income rises by one dollar.

> *The **marginal propensity to consume** (MPC) is (1) the slope of the consumption function; (2) the change in consumption divided by the change in disposable income; or (3) the amount by which consumption spending rises when disposable income rises by one dollar.*

Logic suggests that the *MPC* should be larger than zero (when income rises, consumption spending will *rise*), but less than one (the rise in consumption will be *smaller* than the rise in disposable income). This is certainly true in our example where *MPC* is 0.6 and each one-dollar rise in disposable income causes spending to rise by 60 cents. An *MPC* between zero and one is also observed in economies throughout the world. Accordingly, we will always assume that $0 < MPC < 1$.

Representing Consumption with an Equation

Sometimes, we'll want to use an equation to represent the straight-line consumption function. The most general form of the equation is

$$C = a + b \times (\text{Disposable income})$$

where C is consumption spending. The term a is the vertical intercept of the consumption function. It represents the theoretical level of consumption spending at disposable income = 0, which you've learned is called *autonomous consumption spending*. In the equation, you can see clearly that autonomous consumption (a) is the part of consumption that does *not* depend on disposable income. In our example in Figure 2, a is equal to \$2,000 billion.

The other term, b, is the slope of the consumption function. This is our familiar marginal propensity to consume (*MPC*), telling us how much consumption *increases* each time disposable income rises by a dollar. In our example in Figure 2, b is equal to 0.6.

Consumption and Income

The consumption function is an important building block of our analysis. Consumption is the largest component of spending, and disposable income is the most important determinant of consumption. But there is one limitation of the line as

TABLE 2

Income or GDP (billions of dollars per year)	Tax Collections (billions of dollars per year)	Disposable Income (billions of dollars per year)	Consumption Spending (billions of dollars per year)
2,000	2,000	0	2,000
3,000	2,000	1,000	2,600
4,000	2,000	2,000	3,200
5,000	2,000	3,000	3,800
6,000	2,000	4,000	4,400
7,000	2,000	5,000	5,000
8,000	2,000	6,000	5,600
9,000	2,000	7,000	6,200
10,000	2,000	8,000	6,800

The Relationship between Consumption and Income

© CENGAGE LEARNING 2013

we've drawn it in Figure 2: It shows us the value of consumption at each level of *disposable* income. But as you will soon see, we'll need to know the value of consumption spending at each level of *income*. Disposable income, you remember, is the income that the household sector has left after deducting net taxes. How can we convert the line in Figure 2 into a relationship between consumption and income?

Table 2 illustrates the consumption–income relationship when the household sector pays net taxes. In the table, we treat net taxes as a fixed amount—in this case, $2,000 billion. Some taxes are, indeed, fixed in this way, such as the taxes assessed on real estate by local governments. Other taxes, like the personal income tax and the sales tax, rise and fall with income in the economy. Still, treating net taxes as if they are independent of income, as in Table 2, will simplify our discussion without changing our results in any important way.

Notice that the last two columns of the table are identical to the columns in Table 1: In both tables, we assume that the relationship between consumption spending and *disposable* income is the same. For example, both tables show us that, when disposable income is $7,000 billion, consumption spending is $6,200 billion. But in Table 2, we see that disposable income of $7,000 billion is associated with *income* of $9,000 billion. Thus, when income is $9,000 billion, consumption spending is $6,200 billion. By comparing the first and last columns of Table 2, we can trace out the relationship between consumption and income. This relationship—which we call the **consumption–income line**—is graphed in Figure 3.

If you compare the consumption–income line in Figure 3 with the line in Figure 2, you will notice that both have the same slope of 0.6, but the consumption–income line is lower by $1,200 billion. Net taxes have lowered the consumption–income line. Why? Because at any level of income, taxes reduce disposable income and therefore reduce consumption spending.

More specifically, taxes cause disposable income to drop by T at any given income level, which in turn causes consumption spending to drop by $MPC \times T$. So taxes cause the consumption income line to shift down by $MPC \times T$. Another way to say this is: Because of taxes, the vertical intercept of the consumption–income line is no longer just autonomous consumption (a), but instead is $a - MPC \times T$.

In our example, when we impose taxes of $2,000 billion on the population, disposable income will drop by $2,000 billion at any level of income. With an *MPC* of 0.6,

Consumption–income line
A line showing aggregate consumption spending at each level of income or GDP.

FIGURE 3   The Consumption–Income Line

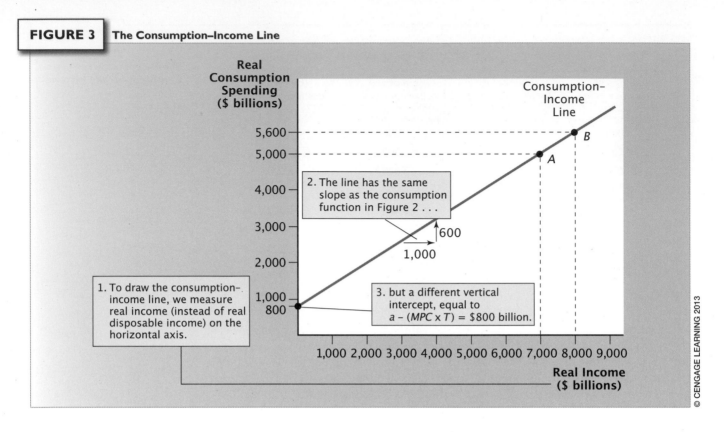

© CENGAGE LEARNING 2013

consumption at any level of income falls by $0.6 \times \$2,000$ billion $= \$1,200$ billion. So the new vertical intercept is $a - MPC \times T = \$2,000$ billion $- \$1,200$ billion $= \$800$ billion.

Finally, we noted earlier that the *slope* of the consumption–income line is unaffected by net taxes. This is because with net taxes held at a fixed amount, disposable income rises dollar-for-dollar with income. With an *MPC* of 0.6, consumption spending will rise by 60 cents each time income rises by a dollar, just as it rises by 60 cents each time *disposable* income rises by a dollar. You can see this in Table 2: Each time income rises by $1,000 billion, consumption spending rises by $600 billion, giving the consumption–income line a slope of $600 billion/$1,000 billion = 0.6, just as in the case with no taxes. More generally,

> *when the government collects a fixed amount of taxes from households, the line representing the relationship between consumption and income is shifted downward by the amount of the tax times the marginal propensity to consume (MPC). The slope of this line is unaffected by taxes and is equal to the MPC.*

Shifts in the Consumption–Income Line

As you've learned, consumption spending depends positively on income: If income increases and net taxes remain unchanged, disposable income will rise, and consumption spending will rise along with it. The chain of causation can be represented this way:

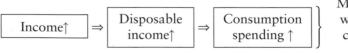

Income↑ $\Rightarrow$ Disposable income↑ $\Rightarrow$ Consumption spending ↑ } Movement rightward along the consumption–income line

In Figure 3, this change in consumption spending would be represented by a *movement along* the consumption–income line. For example, a rise in income from $7,000 billion to $8,000 billion would cause consumption spending to increase from $5,000 billion to $5,600 billion, moving us from point A to point B along the consumption–income line.

But consumption spending can also change for reasons other than a change in income, causing the consumption–income line itself to shift. For example, a decrease in net taxes will increase *disposable* income at each level of income. Consumption spending will then increase at any income level, shifting the entire line upward. The mechanism works like this:

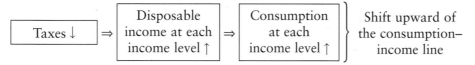

In Figure 4, a decrease in taxes from $2,000 billion to $500 billion increases spending income at each income level by $1,500 billion, and causes consumption at each income level to increase by $0.6 \times \$1,500$ billion = $900 billion. This means that the consumption line shifts upward, to the upper line in the figure.

In addition to net taxes, all the other influences on consumption spending, other than income, shift the consumption–income line as well. But these other shift-variables work by changing the value of *autonomous consumption*. For example, an increase in household wealth would increase autonomous consumption, and shift the consumption–income line upward, as in Figure 4. Increases in autonomous

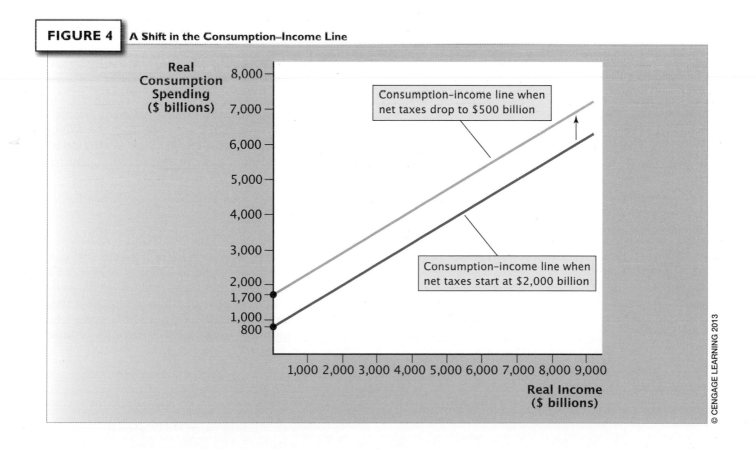

FIGURE 4 A Shift in the Consumption–Income Line

consumption could also occur if the interest rate decreased, or if households became more optimistic about the future. In general, increases in autonomous consumption work this way:

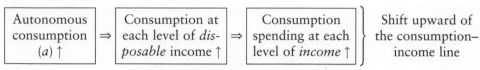

$$\left.\begin{array}{|c|}\hline \text{Autonomous} \\ \text{consumption} \\ (a) \uparrow \\\hline\end{array} \Rightarrow \begin{array}{|c|}\hline \text{Consumption at} \\ \text{each level of } dis\text{-} \\ posable \text{ income} \uparrow \\\hline\end{array} \Rightarrow \begin{array}{|c|}\hline \text{Consumption} \\ \text{spending at each} \\ \text{level of } income \uparrow \\\hline\end{array}\right\} \begin{array}{c} \text{Shift upward of} \\ \text{the consumption–} \\ \text{income line} \end{array}$$

We can summarize our discussion of changes in consumption spending as follows:

> *When a change in income causes consumption spending to change, we move along the consumption–income line. When a change in anything else besides income causes consumption spending to change, the line will shift.*

Table 3 provides a more specific summary of the various changes that cause the consumption–income line to shift.

TABLE 3

Shifts in the Consumption–Income Line

Consumption–Income Line Shifts Upward When:		Consumption–Income Line Shifts Downward When:	
Net taxes ↓	{ Transfers ↑ Taxes ↓	Net Taxes ↑	{ Transfers ↓ Taxes ↑
Autonomous consumption (a) ↑	{ Household wealth ↑ Interest rate ↓ Greater optimism	Autonomous Consumption (a) ↓	{ Household wealth ↓ Interest rate ↑ Greater pessimism

TOTAL SPENDING

While consumption is the largest component of aggregate expenditure in the economies of most countries, you'll see in a few pages that *total spending* is what determines production in the short run. So let's briefly discuss the other components of spending we need to consider.

Other Components of Total Spending

Besides consumption spending by households, the other types of spending on goods and services produced in a country are (planned) investment spending (I^p), government purchases (G) and net exports (NX). To keep the short-run model as simple as possible, we'll assume (in this chapter) that all three of these types of spending are determined outside of our analysis, and that all have fixed values. That is, unlike consumption spending, they do *not* automatically rise whenever income rises, or automatically fall when income falls. We will, however, discuss what happens when they change. Let's discuss each of these components briefly.

Investment Spending

Total spending by businesses, or planned investment (I^p), is *almost* like the investment component of GDP, with one important difference: it does not include changes in inventories. Remember that when business firms do not sell all of their goods, inventories rise (the change in inventories is positive). We include this change in inventories as part of GDP because these goods were *produced*, so we have to count them somewhere. But since no one purchased them, we do not include goods added to inventories as a source of spending.

Similarly, when inventories fall (the change in inventories is negative), we don't want to subtract this change from total spending. Inventories fall when spending is greater than production, so firms have to sell goods they produced in earlier periods. For example, if consumption spending on automobiles is greater than automobile production in one year, automobile companies will sell cars that they produced in earlier periods, thus taking them out of their existing inventories. While we deduct the value of these goods when calculating GDP for the current year (so as not to over-count that year's production), we should *not* deduct them when calculating the year's total spending, because these goods were, in fact, purchased during the year.

Government Purchases

Government purchases include all of the goods and services that government agencies—federal, state, and local—buy during the year. We treat government purchases in the same way as investment spending: as a given value, determined by forces outside of our analysis. Decisions about government purchases are most often determined by the political process; they don't change automatically when income or other economic conditions change. As with the other types of spending, we'll be exploring what happens when the "given value" of government purchases changes. But in this chapter, we will not try to explain what might motivate the change.

Net Exports

Some U.S.-produced goods and services are sold to other countries, so we must include exports as another component of spending on U.S.-produced output. At the same time, when we measure the other categories of spending, they include some imported goods and services, as well as the imported components used to make U.S. goods. Because we are interested in total spending on U.S. production only, we have to deduct imports; otherwise, we'd be over-counting total spending on U.S. goods and services. We include exports and deduct imports at the same time by including net exports (*NX*) in total spending. As you learned a few chapters ago, *net exports* are exports minus imports.

Note that when imports are greater than exports (as they have been for years in the U.S.), net exports are negative. In this case, when we add the net exports category, we are actually making total spending smaller than it would otherwise be. In the hypothetical economy we'll be considering in this chapter, we'll assume net exports are positive, because it will make our model easier to display graphically.

Summing Up: Aggregate Expenditure

In the short run model, where spending plays such an important role, total spending is given a special name: *aggregate expenditure*.

> *Aggregate expenditure is the sum of spending by households, businesses, the government, and the foreign sector on final goods and services produced in the United States.*

Aggregate expenditure (AE) The sum of spending by households, business firms, the government, and foreigners on final goods and services produced in the United States.

⚠ DANGEROUS CURVES

GDP versus aggregate expenditure The definition of aggregate expenditure looks very similar to the definition of GDP presented in the chapter entitled "Production, Income, and Employment." But they are not the same. GDP is defined as $C + I + G + NX$. Aggregate expenditure, by contrast, is defined as $C + I^p + G + NX$. The difference is that GDP adds actual investment (I), which includes business firms' inventory investment. That's because GDP must include all production, even if no one purchases it that year. Aggregate expenditure adds only planned investment (I^p), which *excludes* inventory investment. That's because aggregate expenditure includes only what is *purchased* during the year. The two numbers will not be equal unless inventory investment is zero. (We'll use this fact to help us find the equilibrium GDP in the next section.)

© AXL/SHUTTERSTOCK.COM

Using this special name for total spending helps us remember that it refers to the sum (aggregation) of different types of spending. Remembering that C stands for household consumption spending, I^p for investment spending, G for government purchases, and NX for net exports, we have

$$\text{Aggregate expenditure} = C + I^p + G + NX.$$

Aggregate expenditure plays a key role in explaining economic fluctuations, as you'll soon see.

Income and Aggregate Expenditure

As we discussed earlier, the relationship between income and spending is circular: Spending depends on income, and income depends on spending. In Table 4, we take up the first part of that circle: how total spending depends on income. In the table, column 1 lists some possible income levels, and column 2 shows the hypothetical level of consumption spending we might see at each income level. These two columns are just the consumption–income relationship we introduced earlier, in Table 2.

Column 3 shows that planned investment spending is $800 billion per year, regardless of the level of income. Government purchases are also fixed in value, as shown by column 4: At every level of income, the government buys $1,000 billion in goods and services. And net exports, in column 5, are assumed to be $600 billion at each level of income. Finally, if we add together the entries in columns 2, 3, 4, and 5, we get $C + I^p + G + NX$, or aggregate expenditure, shown in column 6. (For now, ignore column 7.)

TABLE 4

The Relationship between Income and Aggregate Expenditure

(1) Income or GDP (billions of dollars per year)	(2) Consumption Spending (billions of dollars per year)	(3) Investment Spending (billions of dollars per year)	(4) Government Purchases (billions of dollars per year)	(5) Net Exports (billions of dollars per year)	(6) Aggregate Expenditure (billions of dollars per year)	(7) Change in Inventories (billions of dollars per year)
4,000	3,200	800	1,000	600	5,600	−1,600
5,000	3,800	800	1,000	600	6,200	−1,200
6,000	4,400	800	1,000	600	6,800	−800
7,000	5,000	800	1,000	600	7,400	−400
8,000	**5,600**	**800**	**1,000**	**600**	**8,000**	**0**
9,000	6,200	800	1,000	600	8,600	400
10,000	6,800	800	1,000	600	9,200	800
11,000	7,400	800	1,000	600	9,800	1,200
12,000	8,000	800	1,000	600	10,400	1,600

© CENGAGE LEARNING 2013

Notice that aggregate expenditure increases as income rises. But notice also that the rise in aggregate expenditure is *smaller* than the rise in income. For example, you can see that when income rises from $4,000 billion to $5,000 billion (column 1), aggregate expenditure rises from $5,600 billion to $6,200 billion (column 6). Thus, a $1,000 billion increase in income is associated with a $600 billion increase in aggregate expenditure. This is because, in our analysis, consumption is the only component of spending that depends on income, and consumption spending always increases according to the marginal propensity to consume, here equal to 0.6.

> When income increases, aggregate expenditure (AE) *will rise by the* MPC *times the change in income:* $\Delta AE = MPC \times \Delta GDP$.

Notice that we've used ΔGDP to indicate the change in total income, because GDP and total income are always the same number.

EQUILIBRIUM GDP

Table 4 shows how aggregate expenditure depends on income. In this section, you will see how income depends on aggregate expenditure—that is, how spending determines the economy's *equilibrium income* or *equilibrium GDP*. We are about to use Step 2 of our three-step process: *Find the equilibrium*. As always, the equilibrium will be a point of rest for the economy: a value for GDP that remains the same until something we've been assuming constant begins to change. That part of Step 2 will be familiar to you.

However, be forewarned: Our method of *finding* equilibrium in the short run is very different from anything you've seen before in this text.

Finding the Equilibrium

Our starting point in finding the economy's short-run equilibrium is to ask ourselves what would happen, hypothetically, if the economy were operating at different levels of output. Let's start with a GDP of $12,000 billion. Could this be the equilibrium GDP we seek? That is, if firms were producing this level of output, would they keep doing so? Let's see.

Table 4 tells us that when GDP, and therefore income, is equal to $12,000 billion, aggregate expenditure is equal to $10,400 billion. Business firms are *producing* $1,600 billion more than they are *selling*. Since firms will certainly not be willing to continue producing output they cannot sell, we can infer that, in future periods, they will slow their production. Thus, if the economy finds itself at a GDP of $12,000 billion, it will not stay there. In other words, $12,000 billion is *not* where the economy will settle in the short run, so it is *not* our equilibrium GDP. More generally,

> when aggregate expenditure is less than GDP, output will decline in the future. Thus, any level of output at which aggregate expenditure is less than GDP cannot be the equilibrium GDP.

Now let's consider the opposite case: a level of GDP of $4,000 billion. At this level of output, Table 4 shows aggregate expenditure of $5,600 billion; spending is actually *greater* than output by $1,600 billion. What will business firms do in response? Since they are selling more output than they are currently producing, we can expect them to *increase* their production in future months. Thus, if GDP is $4,000 billion, it will tend to rise in the future. So $4,000 billion is *not* our equilibrium GDP.

> *When aggregate expenditure is greater than GDP, output will rise in the future. Thus, any level of output at which aggregate expenditure exceeds GDP cannot be the equilibrium GDP.*

Now consider a GDP of $8,000 billion. At this level of output, Table 4 shows that aggregate expenditure is precisely equal to $8,000 billion: Output and aggregate expenditure are equal. Since firms, on the whole, are selling just what they produce—no more and no less—they should be content to produce that same amount in the future. We have found our equilibrium GDP:

Equilibrium GDP In the short run, the level of output at which output and aggregate expenditure are equal.

> *In the short run, **equilibrium GDP** is the level of output at which output and aggregate expenditure are equal.*

Inventories and Equilibrium GDP

When firms *produce* more goods than they sell, what happens to the unsold output? It is added to their inventory stocks. When firms *sell* more goods than they produce, where do the additional goods come from? They come from firms' inventory stocks. You can see that the gap between output and spending determines what will happen to inventories during the year.

More specifically,

> *the change in inventories during any period will always equal output minus aggregate expenditure.*

For example, Table 4 tells us that if GDP is equal to $12,000 billion, aggregate expenditure is equal to $10,400 billion. In this case, we can find that the change in inventories is

$$\Delta\text{Inventories} = GDP - AE$$
$$= \$12,000 \text{ billion} - \$10,400 \text{ billion}$$
$$= \$1,600 \text{ billion}.$$

When GDP is equal to $4,000 billion, aggregate expenditure is equal to $5,600 billion, so that the change in inventories is

$$\Delta\text{Inventories} = GDP - AE$$
$$= \$4,000 \text{ billion} - \$5,600 \text{ billion}$$
$$= -\$1,600 \text{ billion}.$$

Notice the negative sign in front of the $1,600 billion; if output is $4,000 billion, then inventory stocks will *shrink* by $1,600 billion over the year.

Only when output and aggregate expenditure are equal—that is, when GDP is at its equilibrium value—will the change in inventories be zero. In our example, when GDP is at its equilibrium value of $8,000 billion, so that aggregate expenditure is also \$8,000 billion, the change in inventories is equal to zero. At this output level, we have

$$\Delta\text{Inventories} = GDP - AE$$

$$= \$8,000 \text{ billion} - \$8,000 \text{ billion}$$

$$= \$0.$$

What you have just learned about inventories suggests another way to find the equilibrium GDP in the economy: Find the output level at which the change in inventories is equal to zero. Firms cannot allow their inventories of unsold goods to keep growing for very long (they would go out of business), nor can they continue to sell goods out of inventory for very long (they would run out of goods). Instead, they will desire to keep their production in line with their sales, so that their inventories do not change.

To recap,

$$AE < GDP \Rightarrow \Delta\text{Inventories} > 0 \Rightarrow GDP \downarrow \text{ in future periods.}$$

$$AE > GDP \Rightarrow \Delta\text{Inventories} < 0 \Rightarrow GDP \uparrow \text{ in future periods.}$$

$$AE = GDP \Rightarrow \Delta\text{Inventories} = 0 \Rightarrow \text{No change in } GDP$$

Now look at the last column in Table 4, which lists the change in inventories at different levels of output. This column is obtained by subtracting column 6 from column 1. The equilibrium output level is the one at which the change in inventories equals zero, which, as we've already found, is \$8,000 billion.

Finding Equilibrium GDP with a Graph

To get an even clearer picture of how equilibrium GDP is determined, we'll illustrate it with a graph, although it will take us a few steps to get there. Figure 5 begins the process by showing how we can construct a graph of aggregate expenditure. The lowest line in the figure, labeled C, is our familiar consumption–income line, obtained from the data in the first two columns of Table 4.

The next line, labeled $C + I^p$, shows the *sum* of consumption and investment spending at each income level. Notice that this line is parallel to the C line, which means that the vertical distance between them—\$800 billion—is the same at any income level. This vertical difference is investment spending, which remains the same at all income levels.

The next line adds government purchases to consumption and investment spending, giving us $C + I^p + G$. The $C + I^p + G$ line is parallel to the $C + I^p$ line. The vertical distance between them—\$1,000 billion—is government purchases. Like investment spending, government purchases are the same at all income levels.

Finally, the top line adds net exports, giving us $C + I^p + G + NX$, or aggregate expenditure. The distance between the $C + I^p + G + NX$ line and the $C + I^p + G$ line—\$600 billion—represents net exports, which are assumed to be the same at any level of income.

Now look just at the aggregate expenditure line—the top line—in Figure 5. Notice that it slopes upward, telling us that as income increases, so does aggregate expenditure. And the slope of the aggregate expenditure line is less than 1: When income increases, the rise in aggregate expenditure is *smaller* than the rise in income. In fact, the slope of the aggregate expenditure line is equal to the MPC, or 0.6 in this example. This tells us that a one-dollar rise in income causes a 60-cent increase

FIGURE 5 Deriving the Aggregate Expenditure Line

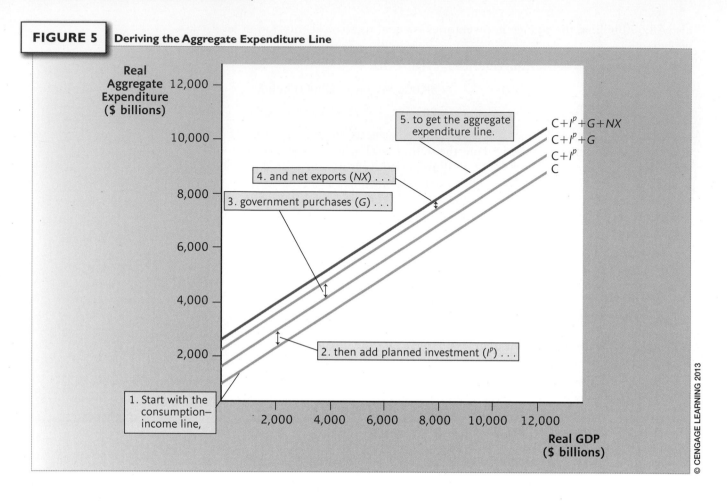

in aggregate expenditure. (Question: In the graph, which of the four components of aggregate expenditure rises when income rises? Which remain the same?)

Now we're almost ready to use a graph like the one in Figure 5 to locate equilibrium GDP, but first we must develop a little geometric trick.

The 45-Degree Line

Figure 6 shows a graph in which the horizontal and vertical axes are both measured in the same units, such as dollars. It also shows a line drawn at a 45° angle that begins at the origin. This 45° line has a useful property: Any point along it represents the same value along the vertical axis as it does along the horizontal axis. For example, look at point *A* on the line. Point *A* corresponds to the horizontal distance 0*B*, and it also corresponds to the vertical distance *BA*. But because the line is a 45° line, we know that these two distances are equal: 0*B* = *BA*. Now we have two choices for measuring the distance 0*B*: We can measure it horizontally, or we can measure it as the vertical distance *BA*. In fact, *any* horizontal distance can also be read vertically, merely by going from the horizontal value (point *B* in our example) up to the 45° line.

> *A 45° line is a translator line: It allows us to measure any horizontal distance as a vertical distance instead.*

FIGURE 6 | Using a 45° Line to Translate Distances

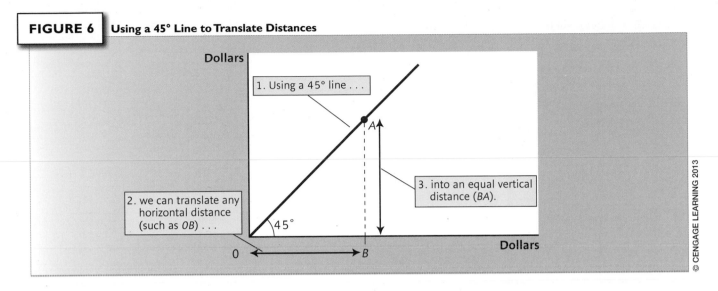

Let's use this translator line to help us find the equilibrium GDP. In our aggregate expenditure diagram, we want to compare output with aggregate expenditure. But output is measured horizontally, while aggregate expenditure is measured vertically. Our 45° line, however, enables us to translate output into a vertical distance, and thus permits us to compare output and aggregate expenditure as two vertical distances.

Figure 7 shows how this is done. The blue line is the aggregate expenditure line $(C + I^p + G + NX)$ from Figure 5. (We've dispensed with the other three lines that were drawn in Figure 5 because we no longer need them.) The black line is our 45° translator line. Now, let's search for the equilibrium GDP by considering a number of possibilities.

GDP Greater than Equilibrium

Let's first ask, could the output level $12,000 billion be our sought-after equilibrium? Let's see. We can measure output of $12,000 billion as the vertical distance from the horizontal axis up to point A on the 45° line. But when output is $12,000 billion, aggregate expenditure is the vertical distance from the horizontal axis to point H on the aggregate expenditure line. Notice that, since point H lies below point A, aggregate expenditure is less than output. If firms *did* produce $12,000 billion worth of output, they would accumulate inventories equal to the vertical distance HA (the excess of output over spending). We conclude graphically (as we did earlier, using our table) that if output is $12,000 billion, firms will accumulate inventories of unsold goods and reduce output in the future. Thus, $12,000 billion is not our equilibrium. In general,

> at any output level at which the aggregate expenditure line lies below the 45° line, aggregate expenditure is less than GDP. If firms produce any of these output levels, their inventories will grow, and they will reduce output in the future.

GDP Less than Equilibrium

Now let's see if an output of $4,000 billion could be our equilibrium. First, we read this output level as the vertical distance up to point J on the 45° line. Next, we note that when output is $4,000 billion, aggregate expenditure is the vertical distance up

FIGURE 7 Determining Equilibrium Real GDP

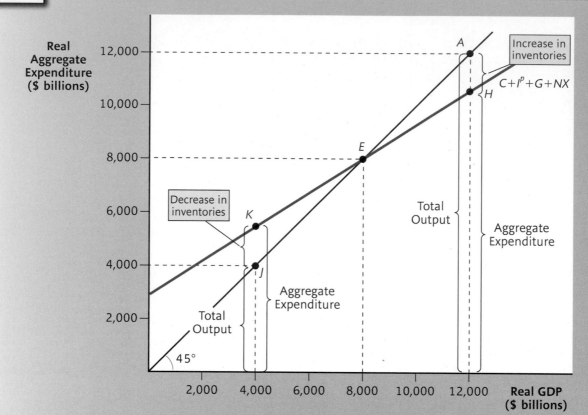

At point E, *where the aggregate expenditure line crosses the 45° line, the economy is in short-run equilibrium. With real GDP equal to $8,000 billion, aggregate expenditure equals real GDP. At higher levels of real GDP—such as $12,000 billion—total production exceeds aggregate expenditures, and firms will be unable to sell all they produce. Unplanned inventory increases equal to HA will lead them to reduce production. At lower levels of real GDP—such as $4,000 billion—aggregate expenditure exceeds total production. Firms find their inventories falling, and they will respond by increasing production.*

to point *K* on the aggregate expenditure line. Point *K* lies *above* point *J*, so aggregate expenditure is greater than output. If firms *did* produce $4,000 billion in output, inventories would *decrease* by the vertical distance *JK*. With declining inventories, firms would want to increase their output in the future, so $4,000 billion is not our equilibrium. More generally,

> *at any output level at which the aggregate expenditure line lies above the 45° line, aggregate expenditure exceeds GDP. If firms produce any of these output levels, their inventories will decline, and they will increase their output in the future.*

GDP at Equilibrium

Finally, consider an output of $8,000 billion. At this output level, the aggregate expenditure line and the 45° line cross. As a result, the vertical distance up to point *E* on the 45° line (representing output) is the same as the vertical distance up to point E on the aggregate expenditure line. If firms produce an output level of $8,000 billion, aggregate expenditure and output will be precisely equal, inventories will remain unchanged, and firms will have no incentive to increase or decrease output in the future. We have thus found our equilibrium on the graph: $8,000 billion.

> *Equilibrium GDP is the output level at which the aggregate expenditure line intersects the 45° line. If firms produce this output level, their inventories will not change, and they will be content to continue producing the same level of output in the future.*

© AXL/SHUTTERSTOCK.COM

DANGEROUS CURVES ⚠

What about prices? You may be wondering why, in the short-run macro model, a firm that produces more output than it sells wouldn't just lower the price of its goods. That way, it could sell more of them and not have to lower its output as much. Similarly, a firm whose sales exceeded its production could take advantage of the opportunity to raise its prices rather than increase production.

To some extent, firms *do* change prices when spending changes—even in the short run. But they change their output levels, too. To keep things as simple as possible, this first version of the short-run macro model assumes that firms adjust *only* their output to match aggregate expenditure. That is, we assume that *prices don't change at all.* In a later chapter, we'll make the model more realistic by assuming that firms adjust both prices and output.

Goods versus Services

Inventories have played a central role in our story about how the economy adjusts to equilibrium GDP. For example, when businesses produce more than they sell, unsold goods pile up in inventories, spurring firms to start producing less. This analysis makes sense for firms that produce goods, such as cars, food, or computers. But what about *services*, such as haircuts, doctor visits, babysitting, or music lessons? There is no such thing as an inventory of services. A haircut, for example, is not produced until the moment it is purchased; it cannot be produced first and then put on the shelf if no one buys it.

Dealing with services changes our analysis a bit, but not entirely. Just as an increase in income leads people to spend more on goods, it also leads them to spend more on *services*. So consumption spending and aggregate expenditure both still rise with income. Moreover, equilibrium still requires that aggregate expenditure is equal to total income. So equilibrium in an economy with both goods and services occurs just as was depicted in Figure 7.

However, with services, adjustment to equilibrium is a bit different because inventories are not involved. If you're interested in how service-producers help the economy adjust toward equilibrium, see the challenge question at the end of this chapter, which guides you through the process.

Equilibrium GDP and Employment

Now that you've learned how to find the economy's equilibrium GDP in the short run, a question may have occurred to you: When the economy operates at equilibrium, will it also be operating at full employment? The answer is: *not necessarily.* Let's see why.

If you look back over the two methods we've employed to find equilibrium GDP—using columns of numbers or using a graph—you will see that in both cases we've asked only one question: How much will households, businesses, the government, and foreigners *spend* on goods produced in the United States? We did not ask any questions about the number of people who want to work. Therefore, it would be quite a coincidence if our equilibrium GDP happened to be the output level at which the entire labor force were employed.

During the Great Depression of the 1930s, the economy's short-run equilibrium output fell far below potential, and at least a quarter of the labor force became unemployed.

© GEORGE W. ACKERMAN/CORBIS

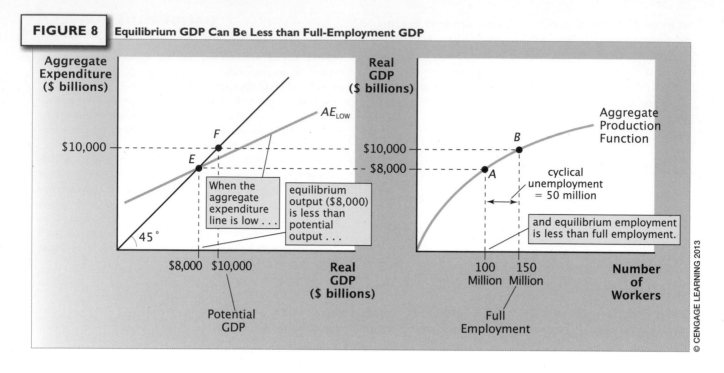

FIGURE 8   Equilibrium GDP Can Be Less than Full-Employment GDP

Figure 8 illustrates the connection between employment and equilibrium GDP. We'll be going back and forth between the panels, so it's good to make sure you understand each step before going on to the next. Let's start with the right-hand panel, which shows the economy's *aggregate production function,* introduced earlier as part of the classical model. This curve tells us the relationship between any given number of workers and the level of output, with the current state of technology and given quantities of other resources. In this economy, full employment is assumed to be 150 million workers, measured along the horizontal axis. Potential output—$10,000 billion on the vertical axis—is the amount of output a fully employed labor force of 150 million workers could produce. This is also the long-run equilibrium output level that the classical model would predict for the economy.

But will $10,000 billion be the economy's equilibrium in the *short run?* Not necessarily. One possible outcome is shown in the left panel. The short-run equilibrium occurs at point *E,* where the aggregate expenditure line crosses the 45° line. At this point, output (on the horizontal axis) is $8,000 billion.

How many people will have jobs? We can answer by using the 45° line to convert the $8,000 billion from a horizontal distance to a vertical distance, then (following the dashed line) carrying that vertical distance across to the right panel. The right panel's production function tells us that to produce $8,000 billion in output, only 100 million workers are needed. In short-run equilibrium, then, only 100 million workers will have jobs. The difference between *full* employment and *actual* employment is 150 million −100 million = 50 million, which is the amount of cyclical unemployment in the economy.

But why? What prevents firms from hiring the extra people who want jobs? After all, if more people were working, producing more output, wouldn't there be more income in the economy and therefore more spending? Indeed, there would. But not *enough* additional spending to justify the additional employment. To prove this, just look at what would happen if firms *did* hire 150 million workers. Output would rise to $10,000 billion, but at this output level, the aggregate expenditure line would lie below the 45° line so *firms would be unable to sell all their output.* Unsold goods would pile up in inventories, and firms would cut back on production until output reached $8,000 billion again, with employment back at 100 million.

In sum: Figure 8 shows that we can be in short-run equilibrium and yet have abnormally high unemployment. The reason: The aggregate expenditure line is *too low* to create an intersection at full-employment output.

> *In the short-run macro model, cyclical unemployment is caused by insufficient spending. As long as spending remains low, production will remain low, and unemployment will remain high.*

What about the opposite possibility? In the short run, is it possible for spending to be *too high,* causing unemployment to be *too low?* Absolutely. Figure 9 illustrates such a case. Here, the aggregate expenditure line and the 45° line intersect at point E', giving us a short-run equilibrium GDP at $12,000 billion. According to the aggregate production function, producing an output of $12,000 billion requires employment of 200 million workers. Since this is greater than the economy's full employment of 150 million, we will have abnormally high employment and abnormally low *un*employment.

> *In the short-run macro model, the economy can overheat because spending is too high. As long as spending remains high, production will exceed potential output, and unemployment will be unusually low.*

In the previous chapter, we concluded that the classical model could not explain economic fluctuations. The short-run macro model, on the other hand, does provide an explanation: The aggregate expenditure line may be low, so that in the short run, equilibrium GDP is below full employment. Or aggregate expenditure may be high, so that in the short run, equilibrium GDP is above the full-employment level.

FIGURE 9   **Equilibrium GDP Can Be Greater than Full-Employment GDP**

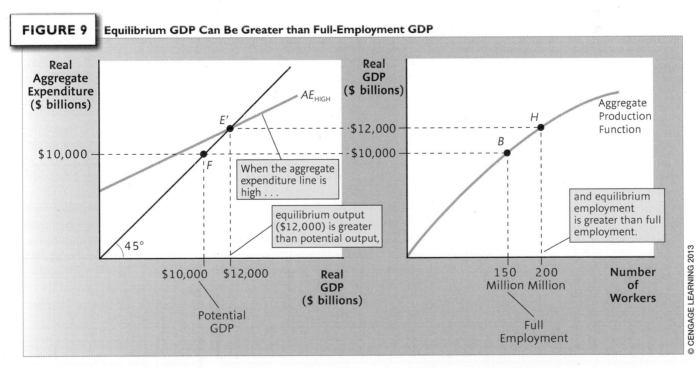

© CENGAGE LEARNING 2013

Either result—output that is too high or output that is too low—is undesirable. When output is too low, we suffer a costly slump. And as you'll learn a few chapters from now, output that is too high can create a high rate of inflation, which is also costly to society.

WHAT HAPPENS WHEN THINGS CHANGE?

So far, you've seen how the economy's equilibrium level of output is determined in the short run, and the important role played by spending in determining that equilibrium. But now it's time to use Step 3 and explore how a *change* in spending affects equilibrium output.

A Change in Investment Spending

Suppose the equilibrium GDP in an economy is $8,000 billion and then business firms increase their investment spending on plant and equipment. This might happen because business managers feel more optimistic about the economy's future, or because there is a new "must-have" technology (such as the Internet in the late 1990s). Whatever the cause, firms decide to permanently increase their yearly planned investment purchases by $1,000 billion above the original level. What will happen?

First, sales revenue at firms that manufacture investment goods—firms such as Dell Computer, Caterpillar, and Boeing—will increase by $1,000 billion. But remember, each time a dollar in output is produced, a dollar of income (factor payments) is created. Thus, the $1,000 billion in additional sales revenue will become $1,000 billion in additional income. This income will be paid out as wages, rent, interest, and profit to the households who own the resources used to produce the new investment goods.[1]

What will households do with their $1,000 billion in additional income? Remember that with net taxes fixed at some value, a $1,000 billion rise in income is also a $1,000 billion rise in *disposable* income. Households are free to spend or save this additional income as they desire. What they will do depends crucially on the *marginal propensity to consume (MPC) in the economy.* If the *MPC* is 0.6, then consumption spending will rise by 0.6 × $1,000 billion = $600 billion. Households will save the remaining $400 billion.

But that is not the end of the story. When households spend an additional $600 billion, firms that produce consumption goods and services—firms such as McDonald's, American Airlines, and Disney—will receive an additional $600 billion in sales revenue, which, in turn, will become income for the households that supply resources to these firms. And when *these* households see their annual incomes rise by $600 billion, they will spend part of it as well. With an *MPC* of 0.6, consumption spending will rise by 0.6 × $600 billion = $360 billion, creating still more sales revenue for firms, and so on and so on....

As you can see, an increase in investment spending will set off a chain reaction, leading to successive rounds of increased spending and income.

The process is illustrated in Table 5. The second column gives us the additional spending in each round of this chain reaction. The first entry shows the additional spending of $1,000 billion per year from the initial increase in investment. The next entry shows the $600 billion increase in annual consumption spending, then another $360 billion increase in consumption, and so on. Each successive round of additional spending is 60 percent of the round before. The third column adds up the additional spending created by all preceding rounds, to give the *total* additional

---

[1] Some of the sales revenue will also go to pay for intermediate goods, such as raw materials, electricity, and supplies. But the intermediate-goods suppliers will also pay wages, rent, interest, and profit for the resources *they* use, so that household income will still rise by the full $1,000 billion.

TABLE 5

Increases in Spending after Investment Spending Rises by $1,000 Billion per Year

Round	Additional Spending in Each Round (billions of dollars per year)	Total Additional Spending (billions of dollars per year)
Initial increase in investment spending	1,000	1,000
Round 2	600	1,600
Round 3	360	1,960
Round 4	216	2,176
Round 5	130	2,306
Round 6	78	2,384
Round 7	47	2,431
Round 8	28	2,459
Round 9	17	2,476
Round 10	10	2,486
...	...	...
Round 20	0.06	Very close to 2,500

© CENGAGE LEARNING 2013

spending as this chain reaction continues. For example, total additional spending after the first round is just $1,000 billion. In the second round, we add the $600 billion in additional consumption spending, to get $1,600 billion in additional spending per year. In the third round, additional spending rises to $1,960 billion per year.

Remember that each time spending rises, output rises to match it. Figure 10 illustrates what happens to GDP (at an annual rate) after each round of this chain reaction. When we analyze events like this in the U.S. economy, we find that the successive increases in spending and output occur quickly; the process is largely completed within a year. And at the end of the process, when the economy has reached its new equilibrium, total spending and total output are considerably higher.

But how much higher?

If you look at the second column of Table 5, you can see that each successive round adds less to total spending than the round before. And in Figure 10, you see that GDP rises by less and less with each round. Eventually, GDP rises by such a small amount, and the GDP will be so close to its new equilibrium value, that we can ignore any difference. In our example, when the chain reaction is virtually completed, equilibrium GDP will be $2,500 billion more than it was initially.

The Expenditure Multiplier

Let's go back and summarize what happened in our example: Business firms increased their investment spending by $1,000 billion, and as a result, spending and output rose by $2,500 billion. Equilibrium GDP increased by *more than* the initial increase in investment spending. In our example, the increase in equilibrium GDP ($2,500 billion) was 2.5 times the initial increase in investment spending ($1,000 billion). As you can verify, if investment spending had increased by half as much ($500 billion), GDP would have increased by 2.5 times *that* amount

FIGURE 10   The Effect of a Change in Investment Spending

An increase in investment spending sets off a chain reaction, leading to successive rounds of increased spending and income. As shown here, a $1,000 billion increase in investment spending first causes real GDP to increase by $1,000 billion. Then, with higher incomes, households increase consumption spending by the MPC times the change in disposable income. In round 2, spending and GDP increase by another $600 billion. In succeeding rounds, increases in income lead to further changes in spending, but in each round the increases in income and spending are smaller than in the preceding round.

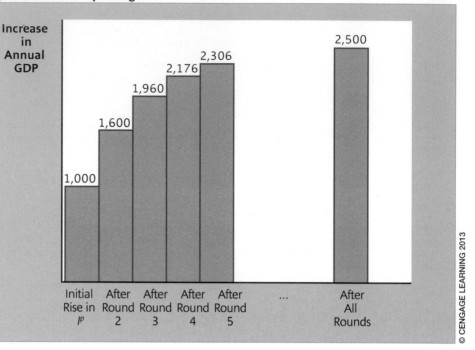

($1,250 billion). In fact, *whatever* the rise in investment spending, equilibrium GDP would increase by a factor of 2.5, so we can write

$$\Delta GDP = 2.5 \times \Delta I^p.$$

In our example, the change in investment spending was *multiplied by* the number 2.5 in order to get the change in GDP that it causes. For this reason, 2.5 is called the *expenditure multiplier* in this example.

> The **expenditure multiplier** is the number by which the change in investment spending must be multiplied to get the change in equilibrium GDP.

Expenditure multiplier The amount by which equilibrium real GDP changes as a result of a one-dollar change in autonomous consumption, investment spending, government purchases, or net exports.

The value of the expenditure multiplier depends on the value of the *MPC* in the economy. If you look back at Table 5, you will see that each round of additional spending would have been larger if the *MPC* had been larger. For example, with an *MPC* of 0.9 instead of 0.6, spending in round 2 would have risen by $900 billion, in round 3 by $810 billion, and so on. The result would have been a larger ultimate change in GDP, and a larger multiplier.

The Multiplier Formula

There is a very simple formula we can use to determine the multiplier for *any* value of the *MPC*.

> For any value of the MPC, *the formula for the expenditure multiplier is*
> $$\frac{1}{(1 - \text{MPC})}.$$

In our example, the *MPC* was equal to 0.6, so the expenditure multiplier had the value $1/(1 - 0.6) = 1/0.4 = 2.5$. If the *MPC* had been 0.9 instead, the expenditure multiplier would have been equal to $1/(1 - 0.9) = 1/0.1 = 10$. The formula $1/(1 - MPC)$ can be used to find the multiplier for any value of the MPC between zero and one. If you want to see how this formula is derived, see this footnote.[2]

Using the general formula for the expenditure multiplier, we can restate what happens when investment spending increases:

$$\Delta GDP = \left[\frac{1}{(1 - MPC)}\right] \times \Delta I^p.$$

The multiplier effect is a rather surprising phenomenon. It tells us that an increase in investment spending ultimately affects GDP by *more* than the initial increase in investment. Further, it tells us that as long as annual investment spending remains $1,000 billion greater than it was previously, yearly GDP will remain higher than previously—$2,500 billion higher in our example. That is, a sustained increase in investment spending will cause a sustained increase in GDP.

By contrast, a one-time increase in investment—followed by a drop in investment back to its original level—will cause only a temporary change in GDP. That's because the multiplier process works in *both* directions, as you're about to see.

The Multiplier in Reverse

Suppose that, in Table 5, investment spending had *decreased* instead of increased. Then the initial change in spending would be $-\$1,000$ billion. This would cause a $1,000 billion decrease in revenue for firms that produce investment goods, and they, in turn, would pay out $1,000 billion less in factor payments. In the next round, households, with $1,000 billion less in income, would spend $600 billion less on consumption goods, and so on. The final result would be a $2,500 billion *decrease* in equilibrium GDP.

> *Just as increases in investment spending cause equilibrium GDP to rise by a multiple of the change in spending, decreases in investment spending cause equilibrium GDP to fall by a multiple of the change in spending.*

The multiplier formula we've already established will work whether the initial change in spending is positive or negative.

---

[2] To derive the multiplier formula, let's start with our example, in which the change in GDP was:

$$\Delta GDP = (\$1,000 \text{ billion} + \$600 \text{ billion} + \$360 \text{ billion} \\ + \$216 \text{ billion} + \cdots).$$

Factoring out the $1,000 billion gives us:

$$\Delta GDP = \$1,000 \text{ billion} \times (1 + 0.6 + 0.36 + 0.216 + \cdots) \\ = \$1,000 \text{ billion} \times (1 + 0.6 + 0.6^2 + 0.6^3 + \cdots).$$

Now, in our example, $1,000 billion was the increase in investment spending and 0.6 was the MPC. Generalizing this for *any* change in investment or *any* MPC, we would have

$$\Delta GDP = \Delta I^p \times [1 + (MPC) + (MPC)^2 + (MPC)^3 + \cdots].$$

Next, we borrow a rule from the mathematics of infinite sums (such as the sum in brackets): For any value of H between 0 and 1, the infinite sum $1 + H + H^2 + H^3 + \cdots$ has the value $1/(1 - H)$. Replacing H with the MPC (which is between 0 and 1), we conclude:

$$\Delta GDP = \Delta I^p \times \left[\frac{1}{(1 - MPC)}\right].$$

Other Spending Changes

A change in *any* sector's spending will set off a chain of events similar to that in our investment example.

Suppose the government increased its purchases above previous levels. For example, the Department of Defense might raise its spending on new bombers, or state highway departments might hire more road-repair crews, or cities and towns might hire more teachers. If total government purchases rise by $1,000 billion, then, once again, household income will rise by $1,000 billion. As before, households will spend 60 percent of this increase, causing consumption, in the next round, to rise by $600 billion, and so on and so on. The chain of events is exactly like that of Table 5, with one exception: The first line in column 1 would read, "Initial increase in government purchases" instead of "Initial increase in investment spending." Once again, output would increase by $2,500 billion.

Besides planned investment and government purchases, there are two other components of spending that can set off the same process. One is an increase in net exports (*NX*). Since *NX* = Exports − Imports, either an increase in the economy's exports or a *decrease* in imports will cause *net* exports to rise.

Finally, a change in *autonomous consumption (a)* can set off the process. For example, after a $1,000 billion increase in autonomous consumption spending, we would see further increases in consumption spending of $600 billion, then $360 billion, and so on. This time, the first line in column 1 of Table 5 would read, "Initial increase in autonomous consumption," but every entry in the table would be the same.

> *Changes in planned investment, government purchases, net exports, or autonomous consumption lead to a multiplier effect on GDP. The expenditure multiplier, 1/(1 − MPC), is what we multiply the initial change in spending by in order to get the change in equilibrium GDP.*

The following four equations summarize how we use the expenditure multiplier to determine the effects of different spending changes in the short-run macro model. Keep in mind that these formulas work whether the initial change in spending is positive or negative.

$$\Delta GDP = \left[\frac{1}{(1-MPC)}\right] \times \Delta I^p$$

$$\Delta GDP = \left[\frac{1}{(1-MPC)}\right] \times \Delta G$$

$$\Delta GDP = \left[\frac{1}{(1-MPC)}\right] \times \Delta NX$$

$$\Delta GDP = \left[\frac{1}{(1-MPC)}\right] \times \Delta a$$

Changes in net taxes, too, have multiplier effects, although they work more indirectly on GDP than the spending changes we've been discussing. A tax cut—by allowing households to keep more of their income—raises disposable income. As a result, consumption spending rises, creating a multiplier effect that increases equilibrium GDP. Similarly, a tax increase lowers disposable income and consumption, creating a multiplier effect that decreases equilibrium GDP. But

⚠ DANGEROUS CURVES

The two kinds of consumption changes. The role of consumption spending in the multiplier process can be confusing. Does a change in consumption spending cause a multiplier effect? Or does the multiplier effect create a change in consumption spending? Actually, the causation runs in both directions. The key is to recognize that there are two kinds of changes in consumption spending.

One kind is caused by changes in income during each round of the multiplier process. This change is represented by a *movement along* the aggregate expenditure line.

But consumption can change when something *other than* income has changed. In this chapter, a change in autonomous consumption is an example. (In the next chapter, you'll see that tax changes are another example.) These kinds of changes *shift* the aggregate expenditure line up and down, *causing* a multiplier effect.

Whenever you discuss a change in consumption spending, make sure you know whether it is a change in autonomous consumption (which shifts the *AE* line) or a change in consumption caused by a change in income (a movement along the *AE* line).

there is a slightly different multiplier formula that applies to tax changes. We'll discuss the tax multiplier in more detail in the next chapter.

A Graphical View of the Multiplier

Figure 11 illustrates the multiplier using our aggregate expenditure diagram. The darker line is the aggregate expenditure line from Figure 7. The aggregate expenditure line intersects the 45° line at point E, giving us an equilibrium GDP of $8,000 billion.

Now, suppose that either autonomous consumption, investment spending, net exports, or government purchases rises by $1,000 billion. Regardless of which of these types of spending increases, the effect on our aggregate expenditure line is the same: It will *shift upward* by $1,000 billion, to the higher line in the figure. The new aggregate expenditure line intersects the 45° line at point F, showing that our new equilibrium GDP is equal to $10,500 billion.

What has happened? An initial spending increase of $1,000 billion has caused equilibrium GDP to increase from $8,000 billion to $10,500 billion, an increase of $2,500 billion. This is just what our multiplier of 2.5 tells us. In general,

$$\Delta GDP = \left[\frac{1}{(1 - MPC)} \right] \times \Delta\text{Spending}$$

FIGURE 11   **A Graphical View of the Multiplier**

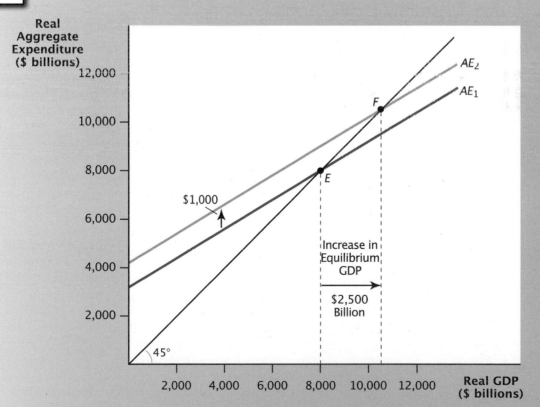

The economy starts off at point E with equilibrium real GDP of $8,000 billion. A $1,000 billion increase in spending shifts the aggregate expenditure line upward by $1,000 billion, triggering the multiplier process. Eventually, the economy will reach a new equilibrium at point F, where the new, higher aggregate expenditure line crosses the 45° line. At F, real GDP is $10,500 billion, an increase of $2,500 billion.

and in this case,

$$\$2,500 \text{ billion} = 2.5 \times \$1,000 \text{ billion.}$$

> *An increase in autonomous consumption spending, investment spending, government purchases, or net exports will shift the aggregate expenditure line upward by the initial increase in spending. Equilibrium GDP will rise by the initial increase in spending times the expenditure multiplier.*

THE MULTIPLIER PROCESS AND ECONOMIC STABILITY

Now that you understand how the expenditure multiplier works, let's discuss one of its important implications. The aggregate expenditure line can fluctuate up and down from quarter to quarter and year to year. For example, if business firms become pessimistic about the future and decrease orders for new capital equipment, investment spending can plummet. A rapid rise in household wealth (caused by, say, stock or home prices) can lead to a sudden rise in autonomous consumption spending. And—especially in smaller economies—events in *other* countries can cause major changes in their net exports. Because of the multiplier, these fluctuations in spending can cause even *larger* fluctuations in GDP. The larger the multiplier, the greater will be the changes in GDP caused by any given change in spending. Because employment depends on GDP, greater fluctuations in GDP also mean greater movements in employment.

Let's suppose that investment spending falls by $100 billion, and there is no other change. If the multiplier is 1.5, then real GDP would fall by $150 billion. But if the multiplier is 5, real GDP would fall by $500 billion. Production falls more with a larger multiplier, and more people lose their jobs, even though the initial decrease in investment spending is the same.

Putting all of this together, we see that

> *All else equal, the larger the multiplier, the more unstable the economy.*

In our simple model, the multiplier is easy to calculate. If the *MPC* is 0.6, as in the hypothetical economy we've been analyzing, the multiplier is $1/(1 - 0.6) = 2.5$. If the *MPC* is instead 0.8, the multiplier is $1/(1 - 0.8) = 5$. But in the real world, the multiplier is much more complex than our simple formula suggests. That's because during the multiplier process, a variety of influences on spending *other* than total income come into play. These influences—left out of our simple model—have important implications for the economy, as you're about to see.

Automatic Stabilizers and the Multiplier

Automatic stabilizer A feature of the economy that reduces the size of the expenditure multiplier and diminishes the impact of spending changes on real GDP.

An **automatic stabilizer** is any feature of the economy that automatically *reduces* changes in spending during the multiplier process, making the multiplier smaller. In Table 5, for example, as GDP increases, an automatic stabilizer would reduce the increases in spending in each round of the multiplier after the initial $1,000 billion, making the final increase in GDP less than the $2,500 billion shown in the table.

> *Automatic stabilizers reduce the size of the multiplier, and therefore reduce fluctuations in GDP and employment, making the economy more stable in the short run.*

The word "automatic" is important. Automatic stabilizers are *not* policy actions taken by Congress, the administration, or a country's central bank (such as the U.S. Federal Reserve). Rather, they occur on their own as part of the normal functioning of the economy. Let's discuss three important automatic stabilizers that were left out of our simple, short-run macro model.

Taxes and Transfers that Depend on Income

We've been assuming that the government collects a *given* amount of net taxes, which does not change as income rises or falls. Under this assumption, a rise in income causes an equal rise in *disposable* income. For example, in Table 5, when investment spending rises by $1,000 billion, income and disposable income each rise by the same $1,000 billion. This sets the stage for the next round of the multiplier process, in which households spend 60 percent of the rise in disposable income, or $600 billion. The process, as we've been viewing it so far, can be summarized this way:

$$
\begin{array}{ccccc}
\text{Income}\uparrow & & \text{Disposable income}\uparrow & & \text{Consumption }\uparrow & & \text{Further Rounds} \\
\$1{,}000\text{ billion} & \Rightarrow & \$1{,}000\text{ billion} & \Rightarrow & 0.6 \times \$1{,}000\text{ billion} & \Rightarrow & \text{of Multiplier} \\
& & & & = \$600\text{ billion} & & \text{Process}
\end{array}
$$

But in the real world, as income rises, many taxes (including the personal income and payroll taxes) automatically rise. And many government transfer payments automatically *fall*. For example, many laid-off workers receive unemployment benefits, which help support them for several months while they are unemployed. When output and employment rise, these newly hired workers give up their unemployment benefits, so transfers fall.

Let's suppose that as income rises by $1,000 billion, the government collects $200 billion in additional taxes, and also pays out $100 billion *less* in transfers such as unemployment insurance. Combining these changes, *net* taxes would rise by $300 billion. As a result, when *income* rises by $1,000 billion, *disposable* income rises by only $700 billion (that is, $1,000 billion − $300 billion). And in the next round of the multiplier process, consumption spending will rise by only 0.6 × $700 billion = $420 billion. So the initial steps of the multiplier process now look like this:

$$
\begin{array}{c}
\text{Taxes}\uparrow \\
\$200\text{ billion}
\end{array}
$$

$$
\begin{array}{ccccccc}
\text{Income}\uparrow & & \text{Net Taxes}\uparrow & & \text{Disposable income}\uparrow & & \text{Consumption }\uparrow & & \text{Further Rounds} \\
\$1{,}000\text{ billion} & & \$300\text{ billion} & \Rightarrow & \$700\text{ billion} & \Rightarrow & 0.6 \times \$700\text{ billion} & \Rightarrow & \text{of Multiplier} \\
& & & & & & = \$420\text{ billion} & & \text{Process}
\end{array}
$$

$$
\begin{array}{c}
\text{Transfers}\downarrow \\
\$100\text{ billion}
\end{array}
$$

Net taxes don't just affect the first round of the multiplier process; they affect every subsequent round as well. Each time income rises, the government collects some of the increase and also takes away some of the transfers it was paying previously. The result is less additional spending in each round, and a smaller multiplier.

An analogous effect occurs when income is falling. In that case, each drop in income is accompanied by *falling* taxes and *rising* transfer payments. As a result, in each round, disposable income falls by less than income falls, and spending falls by less than otherwise. Once again, the multiplier is smaller.

Imports

In our simple model, we've assumed that net exports remain constant as spending rises. In the real world, some additional spending is on goods and services from abroad. In the United States, for example, out of each additional dollar of spending, about 15 cents goes to imports. Even goods marked "Made in the USA" have imported components. This spending does *not* stimulate additional domestic production or domestic income to help power the next round of the multiplier.

What about exports? For the most part, they depend on events in *other* countries, and don't automatically change during the multiplier process. When we combine the stable behavior of exports with the automatic rise in imports as spending rises, each additional round of spending on *domestic* output will be smaller than in Table 5.

For example, let's suppose the *MPC* is 0.6, and that 15 cents out of each dollar that households spend goes to imports, while the other 85 cents is spent on U.S.-produced goods. Then each time income rises, consumption spending rises by 0.6 times the rise in income, but consumption spending on U.S.-produced goods rises by only $(0.6 \times 0.85) = 0.51$ times the rise in income. This makes the multiplier smaller.

The reverse happens when spending is falling: Some of the reduced spending comes out of imports, which doesn't directly affect production at domestic firms or the income they pay out. Thus, whether income is rising or falling, the behavior of imports—like taxes and transfers—works in the opposite direction of the multiplier process, and makes the multiplier smaller.

Forward-Looking Behavior

Although *current* disposable income is a strong influence on consumption spending, households also consider *future* disposable income—what they expect to earn in the future. Changes in disposable income regarded as *permanent* have more impact on spending than those seen as temporary—affecting your income in the current period only.

To see why, conduct this simple (and pleasant) mental experiment: First, imagine that you've just won a lottery that pays you $100,000 every year *for life*, tax free, and ask yourself how much your spending would rise during the current year. Let's suppose your answer is $90,000.

Now suppose that the lottery instead pays you $100,000 *one time only*. How much would your spending rise in the current year now? For most people, spending would rise by substantially less with the single payment, with most of it saved for spending in later years. Let's say that your current spending out of the single payment would be $30,000, with the other $70,000 saved for later.

Now think about what this means. In both scenarios, your disposable income rises by the same $100,000. But when we calculate the *MPC* for each of the two scenarios, we get two different answers. In the first scenario, when you expected the increase to be permanent (continuous), your spending rose by $90,000, so your *MPC* was $90,000/$100,000 = 0.9. In the second scenario, when the rise in income was temporary (one time only), your spending rose by $30,000, so your *MPC* was $30,000/$100,000 = 0.3. And remember that the smaller the *MPC*, the smaller the multipier.

Generalizing from this example:

> The MPC *(and the multiplier) will be smaller when income changes are regarded as temporary, and larger when income changes are regarded as permanent.*

This has an important implication: To the extent that people look ahead, and regard economic fluctuations as temporary, the *MPC* will be smaller as income changes over the business cycle. So forward-looking behavior can mean a smaller multiplier and a more stable economy.

Automatic Destabilizers and the Multiplier

You've just seen that some features of the economy make the multiple smaller. But other features have the opposite effect: They work to *increase* spending changes in each round of the multiplier process, and increase the final effect on equilibrium GDP. We call these features **automatic destabilizers.** In Table 5, for example, as GDP is increasing, an automatic destabilizer would make each rise in spending (after the initial $1,000 billion) larger, so that GDP would rise by *more* than $2,500 billion.

> *Automatic destabilizers increase the size of the multiplier, and therefore enlarge fluctuations in GDP and employment, making the economy less stable in the short run.*

Automatic destabilizers A feature of the economy that increases the size of the expenditure multiplier and enlarges the impact of spending changes on real GDP.

Let's discuss two important examples of automatic destabilizers.

Asset Prices, Wealth, and Consumption

In our short-run macro model, we've assumed until now that household wealth—one of the influences on autonomous consumption—remains constant during the multiplier process (except for a possible initial change in wealth that sets off the process itself). But in the real world, wealth often changes with income in a predictable way. As the economy expands, for example, corporate profits typically rise. People find stocks more attractive, and bid up their prices. Rising incomes increase the demand for homes, driving up housing prices. Homes, stocks, and other assets are part of household wealth. When the prices of these assets rise, household wealth rises.

Now let's put all this together and think about what happens as the multiplier increases GDP. As incomes rise in each round of the multiplier process, asset prices—and wealth—rise. The rise in wealth increases autonomous consumption spending.[3] This is an *additional* rise in consumption spending beyond the increases seen in Table 5. The final multiplier effect on GDP is larger.

The opposite happens when spending and income fall: Asset prices decline, wealth falls, creating further decreases in consumption spending. As you'll see in the Using the Theory section, this sequence of events played a major role in the recession of 2008–2009 and the long slump that followed.

Output and Investment Spending

In our model, we've assumed that planned investment spending is some given value, and doesn't change during the multiplier process (except for a possible initial change that sets off the multiplier in the first place). In fact, investment spending often changes *during* the multiplier process. As GDP rises, more firms approach the limits of their productive capacity; to increase production further, they purchase new plant and equipment. Also, as housing prices rise, construction companies build more new homes. Plant and equipment purchases and new home construction are components of investment spending. Thus, as income and consumption spending rise in each round of the multiplier, investment spending often rises as well. This increases the final rise in GDP.

On the way down, the process works in reverse. Declining output means that firms have *excess* capacity, decreasing their need for new capital. Housing prices fall,

---

[3] More specifically, a rise in *real* wealth causes a rise in *real* consumption spending. If the price level is rising, then in order for real wealth to rise, asset prices must rise faster than the price level.

so new home construction drops. As income and consumption spending fall, investment spending falls with them, causing a greater drop in GDP.

Real-World Multipliers

On the one hand, you've seen that automatic stabilizers reduce the size of the multiplier, tending to make it smaller than the simple formula $1/(1 - MPC)$. On the other, you've seen that automatic destabilizers increase the multiplier's value. So, what *is* the value?

Answering that question is not easy. For one thing, the multiplier can be different for different sized countries. And even within a single country, the multiplier's size can depend on economic conditions at the time. Still, most of the forecasting models used by economists in business and government predict that the multiplier effect, in large countries such as the United States, takes between 9 months and a year to work its way through the economy. And most of these models use a multiplier in the neighborhood of 1.5.

Although the exact number cannot be pinpointed, economists generally agree that the expenditure multiplier today is smaller than it was during the Great Depression. The main reason is today's higher taxes and transfers. In the U.S. economy of the early 1930s, income tax rates were very low and affected very few people, and there was no Social Security tax. There also was no unemployment insurance, no Social Security, and no food stamps to help maintain spending as income dropped. After stock prices plunged in 1929 and the banking system began to fail, both autonomous consumption and planned investment spending dropped. The larger multiplier at the time contributed to a huge drop in GDP during the years after 1929. Between 1929 and 1933, real GDP fell by about 30 percent, industrial production fell by more than 50 percent, and the unemployment rate neared 25 percent. Most European economies faced similar declines in output and similar rises in unemployment.

The Multiplier in the Long Run

When discussing the multiplier's value, remember that the impact of spending changes on output is mostly temporary. As time passes, the classical model—lurking in the background—stands ready to take over. If we wait long enough after a spending change—a couple of years or so—the economy will return to its potential output level—where it would have been *without* the spending change. True, some spending changes can have *supply*-side effects (changing the growth rate of potential GDP by changing the resources available for future production). In that case, our potential output level can be affected. But spending changes do *not* have permanent *demand*-side effects on the economy.

> *In the long run, given the growth of potential GDP, the value of the expenditure multiplier is zero: No matter what the change in spending, the economy will ultimately return to its potential GDP—just as it would have without the spending change.*

Of course, the few years we must wait can seem like an eternity to those who are jobless when the economy is operating below its potential. The short run is not to be overlooked. This is why, in the next several chapters, we'll continue with our exploration of the short run, refining and expanding the model we've developed in this chapter. But first, we'll see how the simple short-run model we've developed in this chapter can help us understand the recession of 2008–2009.

USING THE THEORY

2008 TO 2011: THE RECESSION AND THE LONG SLUMP

© PAUL J. RICHARDS/AFP/GETTY IMAGES

In 2008 and 2009, the United States and much of the rest of the world experienced a severe recession. (The official beginning in the United States was December 2007.) Output and employment fell sharply in many countries, followed by a deep slump. The concepts you've learned about in this chapter—the role of spending, the multiplier process, automatic stabilizers and destabilizers—can help us understand why the global recession occurred, and why the slump that followed lasted so long. We'll focus first on the downturn in the United States, and then turn to other countries.

The Recession in the United States

In the second half of 2007, two events were causing problems for the U.S. economy. One was a spike in oil prices (see Chapter 3), which caused a decrease in spending on automobiles, especially the larger vehicles with poor fuel economy that are most often produced in the United States. As automobile companies and auto parts makers laid off workers, the effects began to ripple through the economy—the start of the familiar multiplier process. The other event was the collapse of the housing bubble (see Chapter 4). As home prices fell, new home construction plunged. Remember that new home construction is part of investment spending. As investment spending fell, the aggregate expenditure line shifted downward.

The rapid fall in home prices had another important effect. Homes are a major component of household wealth. And—as you learned in this chapter—household wealth is an important determinant of consumption spending. When wealth declined, autonomous consumption spending declined with it. This, too, shifted the aggregate expenditure line downward.

As the economy faltered in 2008, it was hit by a third event: a serious financial crisis. As housing prices fell and income declined, hundreds of thousands—and then millions—of homeowners fell behind or defaulted on their mortgage payments. U.S. banks and other financial institutions that held mortgages and mortgage-backed securities (see Chapter 4) lost hundreds of billions of dollars. To make things worse, these securities were complex and difficult to value, creating great uncertainty about *which* financial institutions had suffered the biggest losses and which might go bankrupt. The result was a decrease in lending throughout the economy. We'll come back to the financial crisis in a few chapters, after you've learned more about the banking and financial system. Here, we'll note just two of its consequences.

First, the crisis contributed to fear and gloom about the economy's future, and caused households to cut back dramatically on spending. No one wanted to be caught short-handed in a financial emergency, such as the loss of a job, especially when the usual sources of credit couldn't be counted on. It was time to save.

Second, many firms were unable to raise funds, unless they were willing to pay extremely high interest rates. Corporate profits—which were already falling—now fell further. Owning corporate stock became less attractive, and share prices—already drifting downward—now began to plummet. In the six months starting September 2008, stock prices fell 45 percent—another major hit to household wealth.

The economy was in the grips of one of the automatic *de*stabilizers we discussed: falling output caused falling asset prices (homes and stocks), and falling asset prices led to further decreases in spending and

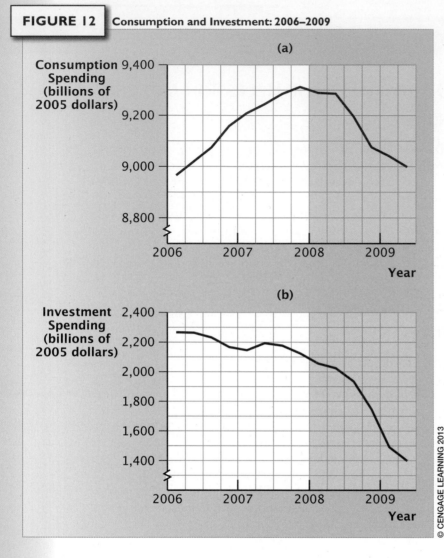

FIGURE 12   Consumption and Investment: 2006–2009

output. In late 2008 this destabilizer was especially powerful because of the financial crisis. By the end of the process, the wealth of U.S. households had declined by an astounding $14 trillion in a little over a year—an amount equivalent to an entire year's GDP.

Figure 12 shows how all of these events affect the components of aggregate expenditure. Look first at panel (a), which shows that consumption first drifted downward as the economy faltered, and then dropped rapidly as housing and stock prices tumbled. Keep in mind, though, that the graph combines *all* changes in consumption spending: the decline in *autonomous* consumption spending (caused by the decrease in wealth and pessimism), and the further drop in consumption as income fell.

Now look at panel (b), which shows a similar pattern for investment spending: an initial downward drift and then a steep decline. During the first year of the recession, only new home construction was dropping. As output declined further, businesses—faced with excess productive capacity and a very uncertain future—cut back on purchases of new plant and equipment as well. (This should sound familiar: It's another of the automatic destabilizers we discussed earlier.)

Of course, automatic *stabilizers* were working as well. As output declined, the government's tax revenues fell and transfer payments rose, helping to cushion the decline in disposable income and maintain spending. Imports, another automatic stabilizer, also declined, shifting some of the impact of lower spending to firms in other countries. Without these stabilizing forces, spending and output would have fallen even further.

Figure 13 illustrates how we can interpret these events in our short-run macro model. Start at panel (b), the upper right panel. It shows the economy's initial aggregate expenditure line for the fourth quarter of 2007, AE_{2007-4}. The equilibrium was at point A, with GDP at an annual rate of $13,326 billion, very close to potential. Then the aggregate expenditure line shifted downward, reaching AE_{2009-2} in the second quarter of 2009, with equilibrium GDP dropping to $12,641 billion (point B).

The behavior of GDP over time, as the AE line shifted downward, can be seen directly in panel (a). Notice the relationship between panels (a) and (b). In panel (b), GDP—measured horizontally—can also be measured on the vertical axis, using the 45-degree line. This allows us to see the correspondence with panel (a)'s vertical axis.

Finally, panel (c) shows total employment, which mirrored the behavior of GDP: falling slowly at first, and then more rapidly as the recession deepened. The

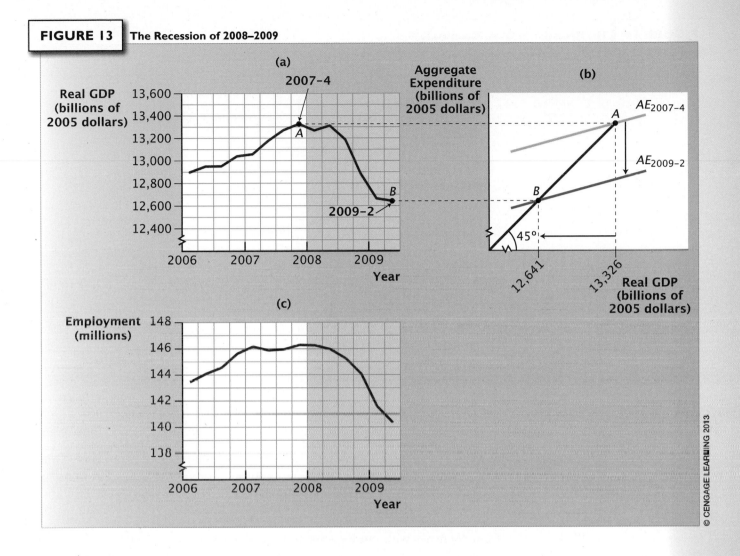

FIGURE 13 | The Recession of 2008–2009

© CENGAGE LEARNING 2013

unemployment rate (not shown) moved in the opposite direction—rising very slowly at first, then more rapidly, averaging 9.2 percent by the second quarter of 2009.

The Recession in Other Countries

Figure 14 tracks quarterly changes in GDP for the United States, United Kingdom, Japan, as well as the combined GDP of the 16 countries that were in the Eurozone throughout the period shown. The vertical axis measures the percentage difference between real GDP in each quarter and its value in the first quarter of 2007. For example, the line for Japan bottoms out near 9 percent, telling us that Japan's GDP in the first quarter of 2009 was about 9 percent below its value in the first quarter of 2007.

The most striking aspect of the figure is the similar timing of the recessions in all of these countries. What made this a *global* recession, and why was it so closely synchronized? First, many countries had their *own* housing boom and bust at roughly the same time as the United States. In the years leading up to the recession, at least a dozen countries (including Spain, the United Kingdom, and France) saw real housing prices rise even faster

FIGURE 14   **The Recession in Other Countries**

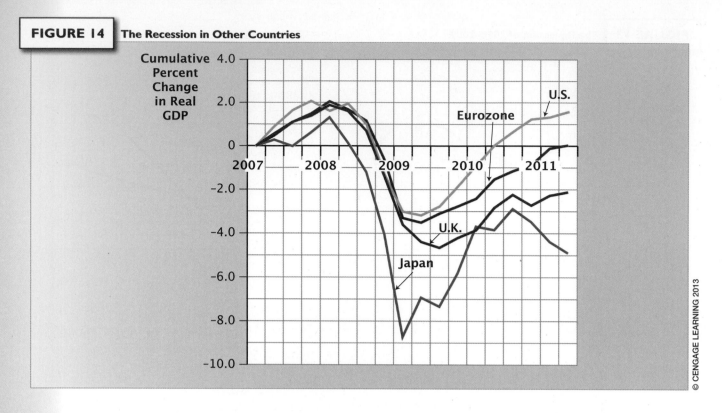

than in the United States. When these countries' housing bubbles burst, consumption and investment declined for the same reasons as they did in the United States.

But why did so many countries experience housing booms at the same time? One key cause was a lengthy period of low interest rates around the globe. The housing booms in some countries were further fed by leverage and speculation, just as in the United States. In the United Kingdom, for example, mortgage loans with little or no down payment were common.

Even countries with more conservative lending policies were infected by other countries' housing bubbles, because of the way real estate markets are interconnected. In Europe, for example, many people purchase second homes for vacations or investments. When prices rise in one market (say, England), demand increases in another, substitute market (say, France), and causes prices to rise there as well.

A second reason for the synchronized recessions was the financial crisis. Those mortgage-backed securities that created huge losses in the United States had also been purchased by financial institutions around the world. As the U.S. housing bubble burst, financial markets in other countries went through the same sequence of events as in the United States: huge losses on mortgage-backed securities, fear of bankruptcy at financial institutions, reluctance to lend, falling corporate profits, and plummeting stock markets. Worldwide, the decline in global wealth—from both falling housing prices and falling stock prices—has been estimated in the range of $50 trillion, with U.S. losses comprising about a third of that total. Consumption fell dramatically around the world, and so did investment, especially in new housing.

One ironic feature of the crash was that the two major economies that did *not* have housing bubbles—Germany and Japan—suffered especially severe downturns. In both cases, the reason was net exports. In the years before the recession, Germany and Japan had enjoyed very strong growth in exports. As global output and income declined, and country after country imported less, exports from Japan and Germany declined rapidly, reversing the growth of the previous several years.

The Long Slump

At first glance, Figure 14 seems to suggest that the U.S. economy had recovered by early 2010, and the Eurozone countries by late 2010. But the figure is misleading. In fact, all the economies pictured in the graph were still mired in deep slumps well into 2011. Why?

Think back about the 45-degree diagrams we've used to find equilibrium GDP in this chapter. In these diagrams, we assumed that our full-employment or potential GDP was a fixed value. But in fact, potential GDP *rises* each year, because of growth in both the labor force and labor productivity. Returning to 2007 levels of real GDP by 2010 would not end the slump in any country, because by 2010, potential GDP was higher than in 2007.

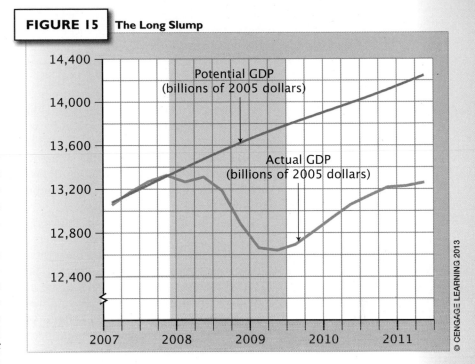

FIGURE 15 The Long Slump

© CENGAGE LEARNING 2013

Figure 15—which shows potential and actual real GDP for the U.S. from 2007 to mid-2011—illustrates the problem. In 2007, the U.S. economy was operating at potential output, about $13,050 billion. But in 2010, when we returned to this output level, *potential* GDP had risen to about $14,000 billion, leaving us short by almost $1 trillion.

The growth in potential GDP suggests one reason the economy can remain in a slump for many quarters or even a few years after a recession ends: Even when GDP starts to rise, it has a lot of catching up to do. But the recovery from our most recent slump has been unusually slow. As you can see in Figure 15, a full two years after the end of the recession, there had been almost *no* catching up to potential output. And in 2011, the gap was widening.

Why so little progress? Mainly, because the events that accompanied, and helped cause, the recession (the housing bust and the financial crisis) were themselves unusual. And they had the further effect of limiting the government's usual policy options to help speed the recovery. Before we consider government, let's look at some of the reasons why the private economy, on its own, was unable to work its way out of the slump.

Private Sector Solutions?

Recall that the recession was caused by big drops in autonomous consumption spending (due to a decline in real wealth) and investment spending (especially construction of new homes). These had set off a negative multiplier effect, propelling real GDP lower. To get out of the slump, we needed an *increase* in spending of sufficient magnitude that, with the multiplier effect, would drive GDP rapidly upward. But where would such a large increase in spending come from?

Consider investment. In most recoveries, construction of new homes leads the way out. But after the housing bust, home prices were unusually low. And they were likely to remain low well beyond 2011, because of mounting foreclosures that were adding to the already large number of homes being offered for sale (see Chapter 4). So there was little incentive to build new homes—a major component of investment spending. New home construction—which had averaged more than $700 billion annually before the housing bust—dropped below $350 billion by mid-2009, and remained at that low level well into 2011.

What about business investment in new capital equipment? Because production had slowed so much during the deep slump, most firms had *excess* productive capacity, and had no reason to expand by building new factories or stores. And many small businesses that might have wanted to purchase new capital had difficulty borrowing. Banks—which had made so many loans that went sour during the housing bust—had tightened lending standards. With investment in new housing depressed, and investment in new plant and equipment stagnating, no surge in investment spending could come to the rescue.

Next, consider consumption. Banks tightened lending standards for households too. So millions of unemployed workers—who in more normal times might borrow to maintain their spending until they found a job—were unable to get loans. One normally popular way to maintain spending while unemployed—a home equity loan, which uses the value of the home as collateral—was out of the question for millions of homeowners; they already owed more on their homes than the homes were worth. Thus, many of the unemployed—unable to borrow and with little or no wealth—had no alternative but to cut back spending.

People *with* jobs didn't want to spend much either. They had already lost considerable wealth during the housing bust. And now they had an additional fear: if they, too, lost their jobs, they, too, would be unable to borrow. Better to spend less and save more now, just in case. A surge in consumption spending seemed out of the question.

What about exports? As the slump continued, exports did increase, especially to countries such as Brazil, China, and India that had escaped the recession and were continuing to grow rapidly. But because so many of our other trading partners were mired in their own slumps (see Figure 14), exports could rise only modestly. They could not provide the needed surge in spending that would help trigger a rapid recovery.

As you can see, a quick end to the slump from the private sector was unlikely. This does not mean the slump would continue forever. At some point, private sector spending would rise again: Household saving would eventually reduce households' debts and replenish their wealth. People would eventually feel their cars were too old and want to buy new ones. Businesses would eventually need to replace worn out equipment. The population would grow and spending on new homes would revive. All of this would happen *eventually*. And gradually. But the costs of waiting were high. If private sector spending was unlikely to end the slump, could the government help?

Government Policy Solutions?

In *theory*, the government has several tools that might help the economy recover more rapidly. In the past, the Federal Reserve—a quasi-government agency—has used its policy instruments to trigger increases in private sector spending. We'll be discussing the Federal Reserve and its policies over several chapters—starting in the chapter after next. As you'll see, the Federal Reserve faced some special difficulties stimulating a recovery during the long slump.

Another option was for the government to increase its *own* purchases—by building or repairing roads and bridges, refurbishing schools, or other projects. This would increase the G component of $C + I^p + G + NX$ and—through the multiplier—increase equilibrium GDP. Or it could change net taxes (T), by altering its tax and transfer policies, in order to stimulate consumption spending. You might remember (from the chapter on the classical model) that changes in G and T designed to change output and employment are called *fiscal policy*. Because fiscal policy is so important and controversial, we devote the next entire chapter to this topic.

SUMMARY

In the short run, spending depends on income, and income depends on spending. The short-run macro model was developed to explore this circular connection between spending and income in the short run.

Total spending or *aggregate expenditure* is the sum of four other aggregates: consumption spending by households, investment spending by firms, government purchases of goods and services, and net exports. Consumption spending (C) depends primarily on *disposable income*—which is income minus net taxes. The *consumption function* is a linear relationship between disposable income and consumption spending. The slope of the consumption function is the *marginal propensity to consume,* a number between zero and one. It indicates the fraction of each additional dollar of disposable income that is consumed. The *consumption-income line* is the linear relationship between consumption and income. It has the same slope as the consumption function, but a different vertical intercept. The consumption-income line shifts as a result of changes in taxes, transfers, the interest rate, wealth, or expectations about the future.

In the simple model of this chapter, investment spending (I^p), government purchases (G), and net exports (NX) are taken as given values, determined by forces outside our analysis. Aggregate expenditure (AE) is the sum

$C + I^p + G + NX$; it varies with income because consumption spending varies with income.

Equilibrium GDP is the level of output at which aggregate expenditure is just equal to GDP. If AE exceeds GDP, then firms will experience unplanned decreases in inventories, and will increase production. If AE is less than GDP, firms will find their inventories increasing and will reduce production. Only when AE = GDP will there be no unplanned inventory changes and no reason for firms to change production. Graphically, this occurs at the point where the aggregate expenditure line intersects the 45-degree line.

Changes in spending will change the economy's short-run equilibrium. An increase in investment spending, for example, shifts the aggregate expenditure line upward and triggers the multiplier process. The economy reaches a new equilibrium with a change in GDP that is a multiple of the original increase in spending. Other spending changes have similar multiplier effects on GDP. In our simple model, the size of the *expenditure multiplier* is determined by the marginal propensity to consume.

In the real world, the size of the multiplier also depends on other features of the economy. *Automatic stabilizers* make the multiplier smaller and help to reduce fluctuations in GDP. *Automatic destabilizers* make the multiplier larger, and tend to enlarge fluctuations in GDP.

PROBLEM SET

Answers to even-numbered Problems can be found on the text Web site through www.cengagebrain.com

1.

Real GDP	C	I^p	G	NX
3,000	2,500	300	500	200
4,000	3,250	300	500	200
5,000	4,000	300	500	200
6,000	4,750	300	500	200
7,000	5,500	300	500	200
8,000	6,250	300	500	200

a. What is the marginal propensity to consume implicit in these data?
b. Plot a 45° line, and then use the data to draw an aggregate expenditure line.
c. What is the equilibrium level of real GDP? Illustrate it on your diagram.
d. Suppose that investment spending increased by 250 at each level of income. What would happen to equilibrium GDP?

2. a. Complete the following table when autonomous consumption is $30 billion, the marginal propensity to consume is 0.85, and net taxes are $0.

Real GDP ($ billions)	Autonomous Consumption	MPC × Disposable Income	Consumption − Autonomous Consumption + (MPC × Disposable Income)
$ 0			
$100			
$200			
$300			
$400			
$500			
$600			

b. Use your answers in part (a) and assume planned investment is $40 billion, government spending is $20 billion, exports are $20 billion, and imports are $35 billion. Complete the table at the bottom of the page.

c. Plot a 45° line, and then use your data to draw an aggregate expenditure line.

d. What is the equilibrium level of real GDP? Illustrate it on your diagram.

e. What will happen if the actual level of real GDP in this economy is $200 billion?

f. What will happen if the planned investment in this economy falls to $25 billion?

3.

Real GDP	C	I^p	G	NX
7,000	6,100	400	1,000	500
8,000	6,900	400	1,000	500
9,000	7,700	400	1,000	500
10,000	8,500	400	1,000	500
11,000	9,300	400	1,000	500
12,000	10,100	400	1,000	500
13,000	10,900	400	1,000	500

a. What is the marginal propensity to consume implicit in these data?

b. What is the numerical value of the expenditure multiplier for this economy?

c. What is the equilibrium level of real GDP?

d. Suppose that government purchases (G) decreased from 1,000 to 400 at each level of income. What would happen to equilibrium real GDP?

4. Draw a graph showing a 45° line and an aggregate expenditure line.

a. Choose a point where real GDP is less than aggregate expenditure and label it GDP^A. Explain what will happen to inventories if the economy is operating at this point. What signal does this send to firms? Is GDP^A sustainable?

b. Choose a point where real GDP is greater than aggregate expenditure and label it GDP^B. Explain what will happen to inventories if the economy is operating at this point. What signal does this send to firms? Is GDP^B sustainable?

5. Use an aggregate expenditure diagram to show the effect of each of the following changes:

a. An increase in autonomous consumption spending due, say, to optimism on the part of consumers

b. An increase in U.S. exports

c. An increase in U.S. imports

In each case, be sure to label the initial equilibrium and the new equilibrium.

6. What would be the effect on real GDP and total employment of each of the following changes?

a. As a result of restrictions on imports into the United States, net exports (NX) increase.

b. The federal government launches a new program to improve highways, bridges, and airports.

c. Banks are offering such high interest rates that consumers decide to save a larger proportion of their incomes.

7. Assuming the MPC is 0.8, construct a table similar to Table 5 in this chapter.

a. Show what would happen in the first five rounds following an increase in investment spending from $400 billion to $800 billion.

b. If investment spending stays at $800 billion, what would be the ultimate effect on real GDP?

c. How much would consumption spending rise as a result of the rise in investment spending?

8. Suppose that households become thriftier; that is, they now wish to save a larger proportion of their disposable income and spend a smaller proportion.

a. In the table in problem 1, which column of data would be affected?

b. Draw an aggregate expenditure diagram and show how the initial increase in saving can be measured in that diagram.

c. Use your aggregate expenditure diagram to show how an economy that is initially in short-run equilibrium will respond to an increase in thriftiness.

Table for 2(b)

Real GDP ($ billions)	Consumption Spending	Planned Investment	Government Spending	Net Exports	Aggregate Expenditure
$ 0					
$100					
$200					
$300					
$400					
$500					
$600					

9. Calculate the change in real GDP that would result in each of the following cases, assuming there are no automatic stabilizers or destabilizers.
   a. Planned investment spending rises by $100 billion, and the MPC is 0.9.
   b. Autonomous consumption spending decreases by $50 billion, and the MPC is 0.7.
   c. Government purchases rise by $40 billion, while at the same time investment spending falls by $10 billion. The MPC is 0.6.

10. Calculate the changes in real GDP that would result in each of the following cases:
    a. Government purchases rise by $7,500, and the MPC is 0.95.
    b. Planned investment spending falls by $300,000 and the MPC is 0.65.
    c. Export spending rises by $60 billion at the same time that import spending rises by $65 billion, and the MPC is 0.75.

11. Suppose that investment spending rises by $1,000 billion, and the MPC is 0.6, as in Table 5 in the chapter. But, unlike in the table, suppose that each time income rises by one dollar, taxes rise by 10 cents, and transfers fall by 10 cents. Precisely how would the numbers in both columns of the table differ, for each of the first four rounds of the multiplier? Would the final change in real GDP be larger or smaller than $2,500 billion?

12. Suppose that investment spending rises by $1,000 billion, and the MPC is 0.6, as in Table 5 in the chapter. But, unlike in the table, suppose that for each $100 rise in income and output, investment spending rises by $15. Precisely how would the numbers in both columns of the table differ, for each of the first four rounds of the multiplier? Would the final change in real GDP be larger or smaller than $2,500 billion?

13. "Saving is good for the economy; it increases GDP." Is this statement true, false, or sometimes true and sometimes false? Explain your reasoning. (Hint: You've now worked with two macroeconomic models: the classical/long-run model and the short-run model of this chapter.)

14. [Requires appendix.] Suppose that $a = 600$, $b = 0.75$, $T = 400$, $I^p = 600$, $G = 700$, and $NX = 200$. Calculate the equilibrium level of real GDP. Then check that the equilibrium value equals the sum $C + I^p + G + NX$.

15. [Requires appendix.] Suppose that $a = 1,000$, $b = 0.65$, $T = 700$, $I^p = 800$, $G = 600$, and $NX = -200$. Calculate the equilibrium level of real GDP. Then check that the equilibrium value equals aggregate expenditure.

More Challenging

16. Draw an aggregate expenditure line and 45-degree line for an imaginary economy that produces *only* services. Label the axes "Real GDP per day" and "Aggregate expenditure per day." Remember that with services, there can be no inventories.
    a. Assume that on day 1, the economy is in equilibrium, with total income and total spending on services both equal to $10 billion per day. Label this equilibrium (where the two lines in your diagram intersect) "E."
    b. Suppose that on the morning of Day 2, people want to save more than before. Show the shift in the aggregate expenditure line. (Make the shift a large one.)
    c. On day 2, each service worker goes to work *believing* his or her income will be the same as on day 1, but buying less in services that day. On your new aggregate expenditure line, label total spending on day 2 "H."
    d. On day 2, because fewer services are sold, fewer are produced, and actual income is lower than people expected it to be. On your 45-degree line, label total income on day 2 "K."
    e. On day 3, each service worker goes to work *believing* his or her income will be the same as on day 2. On your aggregate expenditure line, label total spending on day 3 "L."
    f. If the economy continues adjusting this way for several more days, where will it end up? Label the economy's final equilibrium point "J." Is the new equilibrium GDP the same as it would be if the economy produced only *goods*?

17. The equilibrium condition $Y = C + I^p + G + NX$ can be reinterpreted as follows. First, subtract C from both sides to get $Y - C = I^p + G + NX$. Then note that all income not spent on consumption goods is either taxed or saved, so that $Y - C = S + T$. Now combine the two equations to obtain $S + T = I^p + G + NX$.

    Construct a diagram with real GDP measured on the horizontal axis. Draw two lines, one for $S + T$ and the other for $I^p + G + NX$. How would you interpret the point where the two lines cross? What would happen if investment spending increased?

The chapter showed how we can find equilibrium GDP using tables and graphs. This appendix demonstrates an algebraic way of finding the equilibrium GDP.

Our starting point is the relationship between consumption and disposable income given in the chapter. Letting Y_D represent disposable income:

$$C = a + bY_D$$

where a represents autonomous consumption spending and b represents the marginal propensity to consume. Remember that disposable income (Y_D) is the income that the household sector has left after net taxes. Letting T represent net taxes and Y represent total income or GDP, we have

$$Y_D = Y - T.$$

If we now substitute $Y_D = Y - T$ into $C = a + bY_D$, we get an equation showing consumption at each level of income:

$$C = a + b(Y - T).$$

We can rearrange this equation algebraically to read

$$C = (a - bT) + bY.$$

This is the general equation for the consumption–income line. When graphed, the term in parentheses $(a - bT)$ is the vertical intercept, and b is the slope. (Figure 3 shows a specific example of this line in which $a = \$2,000$, $b = 0.6$, and $T = \$2,000$.)

As you've learned, total spending or aggregate expenditure (AE) is the sum of consumption spending (C), investment spending (I^p), government spending (G), and net exports (NX):

$$AE = C + I^p + G + NX.$$

If we substitute for C the expression $C = (a - bT) + bY$, we get

$$AE = a - bT + bY + I^p + G + NX.$$

Now we can use this expression to find the equilibrium GDP. Equilibrium occurs when output (Y) and aggregate expenditure (AE) are the same. That is,

$$Y = AE$$

or, substituting the equation for AE,

$$Y = a - bT + bY + I^p + G + NX.$$

This last equation will hold true only when Y is at its equilibrium value. We can solve for equilibrium Y by first bringing all terms involving Y to the left-hand side:

$$Y - bY = a - bT + I^p + G + NX.$$

Next, factoring out Y, we get

$$Y(1 - b) = a - bT + I^p + G + NX.$$

Finally, dividing both sides of this equation by $(1 - b)$ yields

$$Y = \frac{a - bT + I^p + G + NX}{1 - b}$$

This last equation shows how equilibrium GDP depends on a (autonomous consumption), b (the *MPC*), T (net taxes), I^p (investment spending), G (government purchases), and NX (net exports). These variables are all determined "outside our model." That is, in our simple model, they are given values that we use to determine equilibrium output, but they are not themselves affected by the level of output. If we use actual numbers for these given variables in the equation, we will find the same equilibrium GDP we would find using a table or a graph.

In the example we used throughout the chapter, the given values (found in Tables 1, 2, and 4) are, in billions of dollars, $a = 2,000$; $b = 0.6$; $T = 2,000$; $I^p = 800$; $G = 1,000$; and $NX = 600$. Plugging these values into the equation for equilibrium GDP, we get

$$Y = \frac{2,000 - (0.6 \times 2,000) + 800 + 1,000 + 600}{1 - 0.6}$$

$$= \frac{3,200}{0.4}$$

$$= 8,000$$

This is the same value we found in Table 4 and Figure 7.

CHAPTER 12

Fiscal Policy

© BLOOMBERG VIA GETTY IMAGES

In 2008 and 2009, as output declined in the United States and dozens of other countries around the world, governments tried to stop the downward spiral in any way they could. One tool used by almost all of these countries was fiscal policy—changes in government purchases, transfer payments, and taxes. The logic behind these moves was straightforward: If households and businesses are spending less, thus throwing the economy into a recession, why not have *government* purchase more goods and services? Or why not try to boost spending by households by cutting taxes or increasing transfer payments?

As country after country took these steps, politicians, pundits, and economists engaged in heated arguments. Many economists supported the idea of fiscal stimulus, but some were opposed—because they either believed it would not work or believed the long-run costs would be too high. And even among those who favored fiscal stimulus, there were disputes over the details. How large should the stimulus be? What would be the most effective mix of tax cuts, additional transfers, and new government purchases?

The arguments were especially heated in the United States where, in February 2009, the Obama administration won passage of a controversial fiscal stimulus: a combined change in government purchases and net taxes lasting a few years and totalling roughly $800 billion, or about 6 percent of annual GDP. This was the largest federal fiscal change since World War II.

In its aftermath, the U.S. economy performed worse than the Obama administration had predicted, and the long slump continued. By mid-2011, some prominent economists were calling for another round of fiscal stimulus—equal to or perhaps larger than the first. Other economists argued against this. When the Obama administration announced plans for a second stimulus in September 2011, it was only half the size of the first. And it was not even clear that this more modest proposal would get through Congress.

Fiscal changes—such as the two examples just discussed—often lead to disputes among both politicians and economists. But even when economists disagree about *using* fiscal policy, there is considerable agreement about how one should *think* about it, and about the concepts and principles that should guide the debate. In this chapter, you'll learn about some of these important concepts and principles.

THE SHORT RUN: COUNTERCYCLICAL FISCAL POLICY

We first discussed fiscal policy a few chapters ago, in the chapter on the long-run/classical model. In that model, fiscal policy had no demand-side effects: It could not influence total output by changing total spending, because it couldn't do the latter at all. For example, if the government purchased more goods and services, an equal amount of consumption and investment spending would be crowded out. This is a good description of how the economy operates in the long run.

But—as you've seen in the last couple of chapters—things work differently in the short run. An increase in government purchases *can*—for some period of time—cause an increase in total spending and, through the multiplier, raise equilibrium *GDP*. That is,

> *in the short run, fiscal policy can have demand-side effects on output and employment.*

This important observation suggests that an active fiscal policy could, in principle, improve the performance of the economy over time. By continually adjusting its own purchases or by changing net taxes, the government might be able to keep the economy closer to its potential output than it would otherwise be. It could avoid recessions that cause so many people to lose their jobs. And it could avoid booms that (as you'll see in a later chapter) can cause inflation and often set the stage for a recession. Government attempts to smooth out the business cycle in this way are called **countercyclical fiscal policy**—a change in government purchases or net taxes designed to reverse or prevent a recession or a boom.

countercyclical fiscal policy A change in government purchases or net taxes designed to reverse or prevent a recession or a boom.

The Mechanics of Countercyclical Fiscal Policy

Figure 1 illustrates the idea behind countercyclical fiscal policy. It shows the aggregate expenditure line for an economy that is initially operating at point *A*, producing its potential output of $10,000 billion. Then we suppose that some component of spending decreases—say, investment or autonomous consumption spending—so the aggregate expenditure line shifts downward. The new equilibrium output is now below potential at $9,000 billion—a recession.

FIGURE 1   **Countercyclical Fiscal Policy**

Initially, the economy's equilibrium is at full-employment output of $10,000 billion (Point A). Then a decrease in investment spending shifts the aggregate expenditure line down to AE₂, and the economy starts heading toward point B—a recession. The government could shift the AE line back to its original position by increasing its own purchases, or by decreasing net taxes with a change in tax or transfer policies. If the change were enacted quickly enough, the government could prevent the recession.

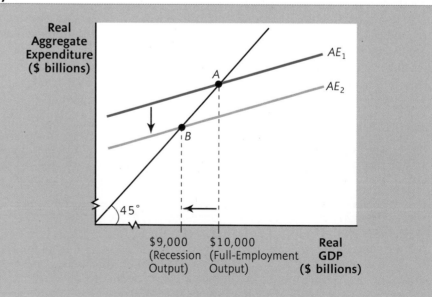

© CENGAGE LEARNING 2013

We could wait for a few years, knowing that recessions don't last forever. Eventually, the economy would operate according to the classical model, and we'd be back at our potential output. But why wait for the classical model to kick in when we have such a powerful tool—fiscal policy—at our disposal? Why not make things better right away, by either increasing government purchases or cutting net taxes?

A Change in Government Purchases

The most direct way to cure a recession with fiscal policy is to have the government buy things. Let's calculate how much government purchases (G) would have to rise in Figure 1 to bring us back to full employment. We'll start with the relationship between the change in government purchases (ΔG) and the change in GDP (ΔGDP) that you learned in the previous chapter:

$$\Delta GDP = \text{Multiplier} \times \Delta G$$

In Figure 1, equilibrium GDP is $9,000 billion, and we want it to be $10,000 billion, so the required ΔGDP is $1,000 billion. As for the multiplier, let's for now use the simplest formula, $1/(1 - MPC)$—which ignores automatic stabilizers and destabilizers—and assume that the MPC is 0.6. In that case, the multiplier for a change in government purchases will be $1/(1 - 0.6) = 2.5$. Substituting this value for the multiplier, and $1,000 billion for the required change in GDP, the equation becomes:

Greater defense spending is just one example of increasing government purchases.

$$\$1,000 \text{ billion} = 2.5 \times \Delta G$$

Finally, we can solve for ΔG:

$$\Delta G = \frac{\$1,000 \text{ billion}}{2.5} = \$400 \text{ billion}$$

This equation tells us that if government purchases rise by $400 billion, the aggregate expenditure line will shift upward just enough to bring the economy back to its potential output. Based on these simple multiplier mechanics, the change in government purchases can, in theory, cure the recession.

A Change in Net Taxes

A more indirect way to conduct fiscal policy is through net taxes (the difference between taxes and transfer payments). By cutting taxes or increasing transfers, the government can increase the spending of those directly affected, such as the households who get the tax cut or receive the transfers. However, the multiplier formula in this case is slightly different from the multiplier for government purchases.

Let's suppose that we *decrease* net taxes (T) collected from households by $1,000 billion. The immediate impact of the tax cut is to *increase* disposable income by $1,000 billion. A change in disposable income is not, in itself, a change in spending. But it should *cause* a change in spending. First, consumption spending will increase by $MPC \times \$1,000$ billion. Using, for example, an MPC of 0.6, consumption spending would increase by $0.6 \times \$1,000$ billion = $600 billion. *This is the initial rise in spending caused by the tax cut.* Once consumption spending rises by $600 billion, the multiplier works as with any other change in spending: Consumption rises by another $0.6 \times \$600$ billion = $360 billion in the next round and by another $0.6 \times \$360$ billion = $216 billion after that, and so on.

Now let's compare the full multiplier effects from a \$1,000 billion cut in net taxes and a \$1,000 billion increase in government purchases. Look back at Table 5 in the previous chapter, which showed the impact of an increase in investment spending, and note that the numbers would be exactly the same if a rise in government purchases had set off the process. From that table, we see that

$$G \uparrow \$1,000 \text{ billion} \Rightarrow \text{GDP} \uparrow \text{by } \$1,000 \text{ billion} + \$600 \text{ billion}$$
$$+ \$360 \text{ billion} + \ldots = \$2,500 \text{ billion}$$

But we've just determined that for a cut in net taxes,

$$T \downarrow \$1,000 \text{ billion} \Rightarrow \text{GDP} \uparrow \text{by } \$600 \text{ billion} + \$360 \text{ billion}$$
$$+ \$216 \text{ billion} + \ldots = ?$$

These two series of numbers are the same, but in the second series, every number is 60 percent of the value in the first series. Thus, the final rise in GDP from a \$1,000 billion tax cut must be 60 percent of the rise in GDP that we get from a \$1,000 billion rise in government purchases. And the **net tax multiplier**—the number a change in taxes is multiplied by in order to get the change in GDP—must be 60 percent of the value of the government purchases multiplier. More generally, for any value of the *MPC*, the multiplier for a change in net taxes will be *smaller* than the government purchases multiplier, by a factor equal to the *MPC*.

There is one more difference between the expenditure multiplier and the tax multiplier: While the government purchases multiplier is positive (because an increase in spending causes an increase in equilibrium GDP), the tax multiplier is *negative*, because a tax cut (a negative change in taxes) must be multiplied by a negative number to give us the positive change in GDP.

Putting all this together, we conclude that

> *In the short-run model, the tax multiplier is the marginal propensity to consume times the expenditure multiplier, and negative in sign.*
>
> $$\textit{Net tax multiplier} = -\text{MPC} \times \textit{Expenditure Multiplier} = \frac{-\text{MPC}}{(1 - \text{MPC})}$$

Net tax multiplier The amount by which real GDP changes for each one-dollar change in net taxes.

For example, with an *MPC* of 0.6, the net tax multiplier is $\frac{-\text{MPC}}{(1 - \text{MPC})} = \left(\frac{-0.6}{1 - 0.6}\right) = -1.5.$

⚠ DANGEROUS CURVES

Two kinds of changes in net taxes In our graphical and mathematical short-run model, we assume (for simplicity) that net taxes are a fixed value, independent of income, and determined by the government. Therefore, in our simple model, any change in the government's net tax revenue is considered a fiscal policy that shifts the aggregate expenditure line.

However, in the real world, net tax revenue also changes automatically whenever income changes. Such a change in net tax revenue is *not* considered a change in fiscal policy; rather, it is one of the economy's automatic stabilizers we discussed in the previous chapter. In the real world, a change in fiscal policy requires that the government change tax or transfer *policies*, e.g., a change in the tax rate applied to personal income, or a change in the eligibility rules for receiving transfer payments such as unemployment insurance.

Note that this is smaller (in absolute value) than the government purchases multiplier of 2.5.

Now let's go back to the economy in Figure 1, where GDP must rise by \$1,000 billion in order to reach full employment. What tax change will accomplish the same goal? We can use the following equation:

$$\Delta GDP = \text{Net tax multiplier} \times \Delta T$$

Substituting −1.5 for the net tax multiplier, and \$1,000 billion for the desired change in GDP, we find that

$$\$1,000 \text{ billion} = -1.5 \times \Delta T$$

Finally, we solve for ΔT:

$$\Delta T = \frac{\$1,000 \text{ billion}}{-1.5} = -\$666.7 \text{ billion}$$

This last equation tells us that, if net taxes *decrease* by $666.7 billion, the aggregate expenditure line in Figure 1 will shift upward just enough to bring the economy back to its potential output. A $666.7 billion tax cut, or an increase in transfer payments of that same amount, would accomplish the goal. So would any *combination* of tax cuts and additional transfers that totaled $666.7 billion.

Combining Fiscal Changes

Fiscal policy often changes on multiple fronts. To stimulate an economy, a government might decide to increase government purchases, cut taxes, and increase transfer payments—all at the same time. The final impact on equilibrium GDP can be found by adding up the separate multiplier effects of each policy change.

Let's try an example. With an $MPC = 0.6$, we found earlier that the expenditure multiplier for government purchases is 2.5, and the net tax multiplier is -1.5. Now suppose government purchases increase by $100 billion, transfers are raised by $100 billion, and taxes are cut by $100 billion, all at the same time. What is the total impact on GDP? Table 1 shows the calculations. Notice that each type of fiscal policy has its own multiplier. Also notice that an increase in transfer payments, like a tax cut, amounts to a *decrease* in net taxes, and works through the net tax multiplier. In the table you can see that the combined impact of all three policies is to increase equilibrium GDP by $550 billion—the sum of the separate impacts of each policy.

The Balanced Budget Multiplier

In Table 1, all three fiscal changes worked in the same direction, to increase equilibrium GDP. But what happens when fiscal policy changes *oppose* each other? One interesting example involves government purchases and net taxes increasing by *equal amounts*. In this case, the increase in government purchases is "paid for" by an increase in taxes, so there is no rise in the budget deficit.

What is the final effect of this fiscal change on equilibrium GDP? Your initial answer might be: No change. After all, the rise in G increases GDP, while the rise in T decreases GDP, so the two effects should cancel each other out. But this is not correct. Remember: The expenditure multiplier that applies to government purchases is larger (in absolute value) than the tax multiplier.

For example, suppose that both government purchases and net taxes rise by $100 billion, and we use the same multipliers as in Table 1. Then the rise in G will cause

---

TABLE 1

Combining Different Types of Fiscal Stimulus

Policy	Change in Fiscal Variable	Relevant Multiplier (with $MPC = 0.6$)	Impact on Equilibrium GDP
Increase government purchases by $100 billion	$\Delta G = \$100$ billion	Expenditure Multiplier = 2.5	2.5 × $100 billion = $250 billion
Cut taxes by $100 billion	$\Delta T = -\$100$ billion	Net tax multiplier = -1.5	-1.5 × ($-$100 billion) = $150 billion
Increase transfer payments by $100 billion	$\Delta T = -\$100$ billion	Net tax multiplier = -1.5	-1.5 × ($-$100 billion) = $150 billion
Combined Impact			**$550 billion**

$\Delta GDP = 2.5 \times \$100$ billion $= \$250$ billion, while the increase in T will cause $\Delta GDP = -1.5 \times \$100$ billion $= -\$150$ billion. Adding these two changes together, the final change in GDP is: $\Delta GDP = \$250$ billion $+ (-\$150$ billion$) = \$100$ billion. That is, GDP *rises* when taxes and government purchases are increased by equal amounts.

Balanced budget multiplier
The multiplier for a change in government purchases that is matched by an equal change in taxes.

The final multiplier effect of equal changes in G and T is called the **balanced budget multiplier**. In our example, G and T both rise by \$100 billion, and real GDP rises by \$100 billion, so the balanced budget multiplier has the value 1.0. In fact, in the simple model of this chapter, the balanced budget multiplier is always 1.0, no matter what the value of the *MPC*. (You'll be asked to prove this in an end-of-chapter problem.) This means that when both G and T change in the same direction and by equal amounts, equilibrium GDP will change in that same direction, and by that same amount.

Problems with Countercyclical Fiscal Policy

In the 1960s and early 1970s, many economists thought that fiscal policy could be used to fine-tune the economy. At the first sign of a contraction, the government could quickly increase its own purchases (say, hire more people to work with children in after-school programs) or cut taxes (offer everyone an immediate tax rebate). In theory, recessions and booms could be avoided.

Since the 1970s, economists have grown increasingly skeptical about the use of countercyclical fiscal policy. In fact, other than in unusual situations (such as the situation in our most recent slump), most economists would *not* advocate using it at all. Let's discuss four major reasons for this skepticism.

Timing Problems

In most countries, it usually takes many months—or even longer—for fiscal changes to be enacted. Consider, for example, a decision to decrease taxes in the United States. A tax bill originates in the House of Representatives and then goes to the Senate, where it is usually modified. Then a conference committee irons out the differences between the House and Senate versions, and the tax bill goes back to each chamber for a vote. Once the legislation has passed, the president must sign it. Even if all goes smoothly, this process can take many months.

But in most cases, it will *not* go smoothly. First, there is the thorny question of *distributing* the benefits of any total tax cut among different groups within the country—an issue about which Democrats and Republicans rarely agree. And some senators and representatives will see the bill as an opportunity to change the tax system in more fundamental ways, causing further political debate. Because of these problems, the tax cut may not take effect until long after it is needed—stimulating the economy after it has recovered from a slump, perhaps even when it is booming. The same type of problem occurs when a tax hike is needed to counteract a boom.

Increasing government purchases suffers from the same timing problems as tax cuts, plus one special one. To get the most value from a fiscal stimulus, government would ordinarily fund infrastructure projects, such as fixing roads and bridges, or building new schools or research centers. These can increase productivity long into the future and help the economy bear the burden of the increased debt it is taking on. (Remember: The government must borrow the funds it uses for a fiscal stimulus.) But there's the rub: Very few additional infrastructure projects will be "shovel ready" when the stimulus is needed. To avoid waste and corruption, the projects require careful planning, with spending and hiring phased in over time. As with taxes, it can take months, even years, before the bulk of the funds can be efficiently spent, by which time the economy may have recovered from recession.

Because of the long delays, regular use of countercyclical policy—via taxes or government purchases—could very well be a *destabilizing* force in the economy. It could cause us to step on the gas when we should be hitting the brakes, or vice versa.

Irreversibility

To be effective, countercyclical fiscal policy must be temporary. In our example in Figure 1, suppose the recession was caused by a drop in planned investment. After investment spending returned to more normal levels, the fiscal stimulation should be reversed as well, so as not to overheat the economy. But reversing a fiscal stimulus is difficult. When it is time to take back an increase in government purchases or transfer payments, or a decrease in taxes, those who benefited—and the politicians who represent them—will oppose the reversal.

Taxes and Forward-Looking Behavior

In the previous chapter, you learned that when changes in income are perceived as temporary, the *MPC* is likely to be smaller. This creates a special problem for countercyclical tax changes: They must, by definition, be *temporary* tax changes, designed to last only until the economy comes back to potential output. But a temporary tax cut is like winning a one-time lottery payment: Most of the increase in disposable income is likely to be saved, so it can be enjoyed over many years rather than all at once. As a result, the multiplier for a temporary tax change will be small. To engineer any given change in GDP would thus require a relatively large change in net taxes. Such frequent, large changes in tax policy can make economic decision-making and planning more difficult for households and businesses.

Policy makers are aware that forward-looking behavior can shrink the multiplier for countercyclical tax changes, and they have tried various ways to get around this problem. For example, a tax cut can be targeted at low-income workers, who are more likely to live from paycheck to paycheck and spend most or all of any increase in their disposable income. Or taxes can be targeted to encourage specific types of spending, such as on new cars or new capital equipment. But a tax change that requires difficult choices (such as selecting which types of households or which specific goods to be targeted) invites political debate, creating the potential for further delay.

The Reaction of the Federal Reserve

In the next chapter, you'll learn about the Federal Reserve—a quasi-governmental body responsible for another method of guiding the economy: monetary policy. In recent decades, the Federal Reserve has taken over the main role in reacting to and smoothing out economic fluctuations. And—for reasons you'll soon learn—the Federal Reserve can generally act more rapidly and flexibly than can Congress. In most circumstances, by the time any fiscal change would take place, the Federal Reserve would have *already* taken the steps it thought necessary to adjust aggregate expenditure. Any further changes in spending caused by fiscal policy would then be counteracted and effectively neutralized by the Federal Reserve.

* * *

Given all these problems with countercyclical fiscal policy, it is not surprising that economists turned away from it even as the economy went through the ups and downs of several business cycles. Based on the types of recessions and expansions we experienced over the last 70 years, this fiscal skepticism made sense. But in 2008–2009, when we experienced a recession with some unusual characteristics, economists took a fresh look at countercyclical fiscal policy. We'll come back to this in the Using the Theory section.

THE LONG RUN: DEFICITS AND THE NATIONAL DEBT

When we take a long-run perspective, the business cycle, fiscal multipliers, and other short-run considerations fade away to be replaced by other concerns. That's because in the long run, Say's law ensures us that total spending will equal total output, which in turn, will equal potential output. But fiscal policy can still have long-run consequences for the economy. In fact, trends in government spending, taxes, and transfers can influence potential output itself. To understand why, we'll need to focus on the long-run impact of budget deficits.

Recall that when government purchases exceed net tax revenue, the government runs a *budget deficit*. These deficits can have some immediate consequences: raising interest rates and crowding out consumption and investment spending. But another consequence of budget deficits is an increase in the government's debt. Simply put, each time the government spends more than it takes in, it must borrow the difference. And year after year, this borrowing adds up.

National debt The total amount the federal government still owes to the general public from past borrowing.

The amount that the federal government owes at any given point in time is called the **national debt**. It is equal to the total of all past years' deficits, minus whatever the government has paid back (in the years when it ran surpluses). Thus, decisions about government spending and taxing—because they determine current budget deficits—also determine the change in the national debt over time.

Numbers in Perspective

In discussing long-run fiscal trends, it's important to view the numbers in their proper perspective. To see why, let's start with some simple budget-related data. In 1959, the federal government's total spending—on goods and services, as well as transfer payments and interest on its debt—was $92 billion. In 2008—the year before the big fiscal stimulus—federal government outlays were more than 30 times as large, running at about $3,000 billion ($3 trillion). What does this tell us?

Before answering, let's consider another number: the U.S. national debt. It stood at $235 billion in 1959, but by the end of 2008, it had risen to $5,800 billion. What does *that* tell us?

Actually, the numbers we've just presented don't tell us much of anything. First, prices rose during that 50-year period, so *real* government outlays and the *real* national debt rose considerably less than these nominal figures suggest. In addition, from 1959 to 2008, the U.S. population grew, the labor force grew, and the average worker became more productive. As a result, real GDP and real income more than quadrupled during this period. Why does this matter? Because *the government's spending and its total debt should always be viewed in relation to the economy's total income.*

We automatically recognize this principle when we think about an individual family or business. Suppose you are told that a family is spending $50,000 each year, and has a total debt—a combination of mortgage debt, car loans, student loans, and credit card balances—of $200,000. Is this family acting responsibly? Or is its spending and borrowing out of control? That depends. If the income of the household is less than its spending—say, an income of $40,000—and is expected to remain so, then there is serious trouble. A family with unchanging income that continues to spend more than it earns would see its debt grow every year until it could not handle the monthly interest payments.

But what if the family's income is $800,000 per year? Then our conclusion would change dramatically: We'd wonder why this family spends so *little*. And if it owed $200,000, we would not think it irresponsible at all. After all, the family could pay the interest on its debt with a tiny fraction of its income.

What is true for an individual family is also true for the nation. Spending and debt are *relative* concepts. As a country's total income grows, it will want more of the things that government can provide—education, high environmental standards, domestic security, programs to help the needy, and more. Therefore, we expect government spending to rise as a nation becomes richer. Moreover, as its income grows, a country can *handle* higher interest payments on its debt. Government spending and the total national debt, considered in isolation, tell us nothing about how responsibly or irresponsibly the government is behaving.

> *Budget-related figures such as government purchases, tax revenues, or government debt should be considered relative to a nation's total income—as percentages of GDP.*

Viewing budget-related figures relative to GDP helps to put things in perspective. In 1959, the federal government's total outlays were 19 percent of GDP. In 2008, they were 21 percent—slightly higher, but far from out of control. And, relative to GDP, the national debt in the hands of the public was lower in 2008 (40 percent) than in 1959 (47 percent).

This doesn't suggest that everything is fine with the federal budget, and we'll discuss reasons for *very* serious concern later in this chapter. But our concerns should be based on, and expressed with, the proper perspective.

In the rest of this chapter, as we explore long-run trends in fiscal behavior and their effects on the economy, we'll do so with these lessons in mind. Accordingly, we'll look at fiscal variables as *percentages of GDP*. These percentages are typically measured and discussed as the ratio of a *nominal* variable (e.g., nominal national debt) to *nominal* GDP. But using real variables would give us the same percentages (e.g., *real* national debt as a percentage of *real* GDP). That's because when we adjust for inflation in both the numerator and denominator of a ratio, it leaves the ratio unchanged.

Outlays, Revenue, and the Deficit

You may have noticed that we've been careful in this book to use the term *government purchases* for the term *G* in GDP. But "G" is *not* the same as what the government pays out in any given year. In addition to purchasing goods and services, the government also disburses funds for transfer payments and to pay interest on its debt. While these represent government spending in the budgetary sense, they are not part of government purchases when we measure GDP.

However, transfer and interest payments do affect the *budget* in the same way government purchases do: They represent funds flowing out of the government. We'll use the term **government outlays** for the total outflow of funds for government purchases, transfer payments, and interest on the national debt.

Government outlays Total disbursements by the government for purchases, transfer payments, and interest on the debt.

Look at the upper panel of Figure 2. The blue line shows federal government outlays as a percentage of GDP for each fiscal year[1] from 1959 through 2010, along with a projection for 2011. The purple line shows federal tax revenue during those years. The difference between these two lines in any year is the federal budget deficit (when outlays exceed revenue) or surplus (when revenue exceeds outlays), also expressed as a percentage of GDP.[2]

$$\text{Budget surplus} = \text{Tax revenue} - \text{Outlays}$$

$$\text{Budget deficit} = \text{Outlays} - \text{Tax revenue}$$

The bottom panel shows the history of the budget in recent decades, with surpluses as positive values and deficits as negative values. You can see that there was a dramatic change in the behavior of the budget around 1975. Until that year, the government mostly ran deficits, but rarely more than 2 percent of GDP. But from 1975 until 1993 the deficit grew significantly. During that period, it was usually greater than 3 percent of GDP, and often more. Notice, for example, the especially large rise in the deficit that occurred in the early 1980s. This was the combined result of a severe recession, a buildup in military spending, and a large cut in income taxes during President Reagan's first term in office.

In the mid-1990s, during the Clinton Administration, the deficit began to come down, and in the late 1990s, the federal government even began running budget surpluses for a few years. Then, in 2002, during the Bush administration, the budget went back into deficit, with larger deficits each year. The reasons were a repeat of history: a recession, increased military spending, and a sizable, multiyear tax cut.

Finally, you can see that the deficit exploded in 2009. This was caused by a deep recession followed a very long slump, and the extraordinary fiscal measures taken by the government in response.

Deficits over Time

In the previous paragraphs, we noted that recessions are associated with budget deficits. You can also see this in the two panels of Figure 2, where recession periods are shaded. If you look carefully, you'll notice that the deficit tends to rise during recessions (the budget balance becomes more negative), and fall during expansions (the periods between the recessions). Why is this?

Economic fluctuations affect both transfer payments (which are part of government outlays) and tax revenues. These changes are automatic—they occur without any change in government policy. When many people lose their jobs during a recession, the federal government automatically contributes larger amounts to state-run unemployment insurance systems and pays more in transfers to the poor, because

---

[1] The fiscal year starts on October 1 of the year before and ends on September 30.

[2] If we consider interest payments as part of transfer payments, these are the same definitions for surplus $(T - G)$ and deficit $(G - T)$ used earlier, in the chapter on the classical/long-run model. To see this, start with our current definition of the deficit:

$$\begin{aligned}
\text{Budget deficit} &= \text{Outlays} - \text{Tax revenue} \\
&= (\text{Government purchases} + \text{Transfers}) - \text{Tax revenue} \\
&= \text{Government purchases} - (\text{Tax revenue} - \text{Transfers}) \\
&= \text{Government purchases} - \text{Net taxes} \\
&= G - T
\end{aligned}$$

The last line is the definition for the deficit given in the chapter on the classical model, where G is government purchases in GDP and T is net taxes.

© CENGAGE LEARNING 2013

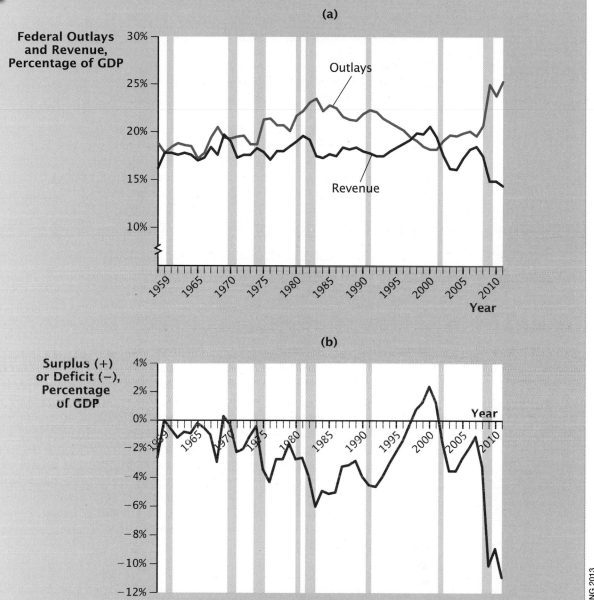

FIGURE 2 Federal Outlays, Revenue, and Surplus or Deficit, 1959–2011

In any given year, if federal revenue exceeds federal outlays [panel (a)], the government runs a surplus [(panel (b)]. If federal outlays exceed revenue, the government runs a deficit [a negative number in panel (b)]. During recessions (shaded), net taxes automatically fall, enlarging the deficit. The deficit becomes even greater if a change in fiscal policy is used to fight the recession, as in 2009 and 2010.

more families qualify for these types of assistance. Thus, a recession causes transfer payments to rise. Recessions also cause a drop in tax revenue, because household income and corporate profits—two important sources of tax revenue—decrease during recessions. The drop in tax revenue occurs even though there has been no change in tax rates.

In a recession, because transfers rise and tax revenue falls, the federal budget deficit automatically increases (or the surplus decreases).

An expansion has the opposite effect on the federal budget: With falling unemployment and higher levels of output and income, federal transfers decrease and tax revenues increase. Thus,

in an expansion, because transfers decrease and tax revenue rises, the budget deficit automatically decreases (or the surplus increases).

The term *automatic* might sound familiar to you. Recall that in the previous chapter changes in taxes and transfers over the business cycle were characterized as *automatic stabilizers,* making the short-run expenditure multiplier smaller. Now you can see that these same automatic stabilizers have automatic effects on the budget deficit as well—increasing the deficit in a recession, and decreasing it in an expansion.

The Deficit and the National Debt

The federal deficit and surplus are *flow* variables: They measure the difference between government spending and tax revenue *over a given period,* usually a year. The national debt, by contrast, is a *stock* variable: It measures the total amount that the federal government owes *at a given point in time.* (See Chapter 4 if you need a refresher on stocks and flows.) The deficit and the debt are, however, very closely related. Each year that the government runs a deficit, it must borrow funds equal to the deficit, *adding to the national debt.* The government borrows these funds by issuing federal government *bonds* (also called *treasury securities*), which are legal promises to pay back the funds at a certain date in the future. Government bonds are bought and sold in an active U.S. and world market. When the payment comes due, the current owner of the bond receives the payment. For example, in 2007, the federal government ran a deficit of $161 billion. During that year, it issued about $161 billion in new government bonds, adding about that much to the national debt.

On the other hand, if the government runs a surplus, it uses the surplus to *pay back* some of the national debt. For example, in 2000, the federal government ran a surplus of about $236 billion. That year, it purchased about that much in government bonds (bonds that it had issued in the past), thus reducing the national debt.[3]

We can thus measure the national debt as the total value of government bonds held by the public.

Budget deficits—which add to the public's holdings of federal government bonds—add to the national debt. Surpluses—which decrease the public's bond holdings—subtract from the national debt.

Because the economy tends to go back and forth between recessions and booms, the effects of the business cycle on the budget tend to balance out over time. Business cycles and the fiscal changes they cause are not responsible for most of the growth in the national debt. Indeed, it would *not* be advisable to eliminate deficits that arise during recessions. To do so would require raising taxes or reducing government outlays, making the recession worse.

But, as you can see in Figure 2, we don't just run budget deficits during recessions. We run deficits in both good times and bad, and rarely run budget surpluses.

---

[3] Because of accounting details, the increase or decrease in the national debt is never exactly the same as the annual deficit or surplus.

FIGURE 3 | The U.S. Debt Ratio (1940–2011)

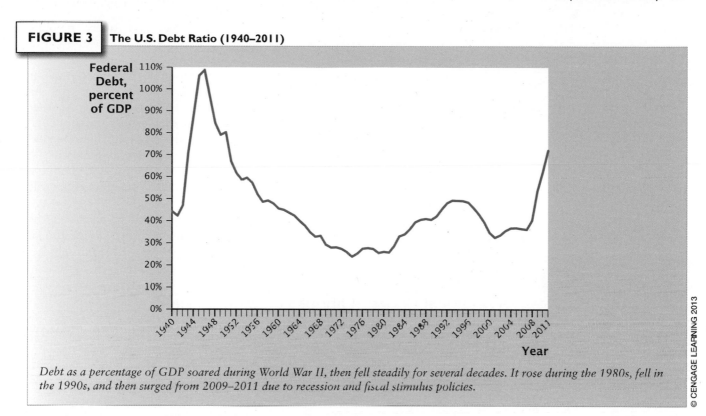

Debt as a percentage of GDP soared during World War II, then fell steadily for several decades. It rose during the 1980s, fell in the 1990s, and then surged from 2009–2011 due to recession and fiscal stimulus policies.

Because the cumulative total of the government's deficits has been greater than its surpluses, the national debt has grown over the past several decades.

Remember, though, that budget-related numbers, including the national debt, are meaningful only relative to GDP. Figure 3 shows the U.S. **debt ratio**, which is the nominal federal debt held by the public as a percentage of nominal GDP. (As discussed earlier, this is the same as *real* debt as a percentage of *real* GDP. However, for some of what follows, using nominal variables makes the discussion easier.) As you can see in Figure 3, the debt ratio ballooned relative to GDP during World War II, when the government financed most of its military spending by borrowing. The debt ratio came down steadily in the decades after the war, rose during the 1980s, fell during the 1990s, and then began rising again in 2002. During and after the recession of 2008 to 2009, the deficit spiked upward and the debt ratio rose especially rapidly. Part of the rise was automatic, caused by the effect of declining income on transfer payments and tax revenue. But part was caused by aggressive fiscal policy used to combat the recession. We'll come back to those policy changes a bit later, but first we need to take a closer look at the national debt and what it implies about our economic well-being.

Debt ratio Publicly held national debt as a percentage of GDP.

THE NATIONAL DEBT: MYTHS AND REALITIES

On a billboard in midtown Manhattan, a giant clocklike digital display tracks the U.S. national debt up to the second.[4] In 2011, as the clock headed toward $16 trillion (rising by about $50,000 per second), the last five digits on the display changed so rapidly that they appeared as a blur. The national debt clock is one of

[4] You can find similar debt clocks on the Web (google "national debt clock").

several public relations campaigns that have spread fear among the American public for years. How can we ever hope to repay all of this debt? How can we allow it to grow so rapidly?

For years, economists railed against gimmicks like national debt clocks. A major problem is that they show debt in dollars, rather than as a percentage of GDP. As a result, they can make even sensible budget behavior seem irresponsible. Another problem is that they exaggerate the burden by showing the "total national debt," rather than the "publicly held debt." The *total* debt includes amounts that one government agency owes to another, and these have no macroeconomic impact at all. At the end of 2011, when the *total* national debt was approaching $16 trillion, the relevant *publicly* held debt (what the government owed to everyone but itself) was about $10 trillion.

But the biggest problem with debt clocks and the often-heard statements in the media that are based on them is that they help to propagate myths about the national debt. Even though virtually all economists agree that projected growth in the debt is a serious problem, it is not for the reason that most people think.

A Mythical Concern about the National Debt

What bothers many people about a growing national debt is the belief that one day we will have to pay it all back. But although we might *choose* to repay the national debt, we do not have to. *Ever.* Moreover, there is nothing automatically wrong with a national debt that *grows* every year. That may sound surprising. How could a government keep borrowing funds without ever paying them back? Surely, no business could behave that way.

But actually, many successful businesses *do* behave that way. For example, the debt of many major corporations—like Pfizer and Verizon—continues to grow, year after year. While they continue to pay interest on their debt, they may have no plans to pay back the amount originally borrowed. As these companies' bonds become due, they simply *roll them over*; they issue new bonds to pay back the old ones.

Why don't these firms pay back their debt? Because they believe they have a better use for their funds: investing in new capital equipment and research and development to expand their businesses. This will lead to higher future profits.

Of course, this does not mean that *any* size debt would be prudent. A firm must pay interest on its debt each year. If a firm's income is growing by 5 percent each year, but its interest payments are growing by 10 percent per year, it would eventually find itself in trouble. Each year, its interest payments would take a larger and larger fraction of its income, and at some point interest payments would exceed total income.

But even *before* this occurred, the firm would encounter another problem. Lenders, anticipating the firm's eventual inability to pay interest, would cut the firm off. At that point, the firm would reach its *credit limit*—the maximum amount it can borrow based on lenders' willingness to lend. Since it could no longer roll over its existing debt with further borrowing, it would have to pay back any bonds coming due until its debt was comfortably below its credit limit.

All of these observations apply to the federal government as well. As long as the nation's total income (its GDP) is rising, the government can safely take on more debt. More specifically, if the nation's income is growing at least as fast as its total interest payments, the debt can continue to grow indefinitely, without putting the government in danger.

The federal government *could* pay back the national debt—by running budget surpluses for many years. But the government could also choose to behave like most corporations and *not* pay back its debt. In fact, the government would better serve the public by not paying down the debt if it has better uses for its revenue than debt repayment.

In fact, the government can even allow its debt to *grow* every year, forever, without imposing any added burden on the economy, as long as the debt does not rise too fast. But before we go any further, let's discuss what we mean by the burden of the debt.

The Burden of the National Debt

The burden of the debt arises from the interest payments the government must make every year on the total amount it owes, and the taxes it must collect to pay that interest. More specifically,

> the **burden of the debt** is annual interest on the national debt as a percentage of annual GDP. It can also be defined as the tax rate (taxes as a percentage of GDP) needed to pay interest on the debt.

Burden of the debt Interest payments on the national debt as a percentage of GDP.

If annual interest payments on the debt rise by 5 percent of GDP, then the government must either collect 5 percent of GDP more in taxes, or cut non-interest government outlays by 5 percent of GDP. (It can also borrow even more to cover the interest, but that only postpones the problem. Future interest payments would be even higher, and eventually they would have to be covered by higher tax rates or lower government outlays.)

But why are these interest payments, and the taxes needed to pay them, a burden for the country as a whole? After all, one party's interest *payment* is another party's interest *earnings*. Aren't we just paying interest to ourselves? And if so, considering both the payment and receipt of interest, doesn't the impact net out to zero for our citizens? The answer is no, for two reasons.

First, a portion of the national debt is owed to foreign residents, who have loaned funds to the U.S. government in the past by purchasing U.S. government bonds. In recent decades, the foreign-owned portion has been growing, and today almost half of the publicly held U.S. national debt is in the hands of foreign governments or foreign private investors. Table 2 shows the dollar amounts of debt, and the percentage of total public U.S. debt held by foreigners, in July 2011. China holds the largest share of the total, followed closely by Japan.

Interest payments on the foreign-owned portion of the debt are a transfer of purchasing power from U.S. residents to foreign residents. While these interest payments do not directly affect our potential output, they decrease the portion of that output that U.S. residents can purchase. In this way, they reduce U.S. living standards.

But what about the portion of debt held by Americans? It is true that on this part of the debt, we are paying the interest to *ourselves*. But to pay interest to those U.S. residents who hold government bonds, we must tax other U.S. residents. This redistribution of income requires the tax rate to be higher than it would otherwise be. You've already learned (in the chapter on economic growth) that lower tax rates can lead to faster economic growth. An obvious corollary is that the *higher* tax rates due to the higher debt burden can lead to *slower* economic growth.

> *Higher tax rates needed to pay interest on the national debt are a burden because they either (1) transfer purchasing power to other countries, or (2) lead to slower economic growth.*

TABLE 2

Major Foreign Holders of U.S. Federal Debt, July 2011

Country	Value of Holdings	Percent of All Publicly Held U.S. Federal Debt
China	$1,174 billion	11.6%
Japan	$ 915 billion	9.1%
United Kingdom	$ 353 billion	3.5%
Oil Exporters	$ 234 billion	2.3%
Brazil	$ 210 billion	2.1%
Caribbean Banking Centers	$ 125 billion	1.2%
Hong Kong	$ 112 billion	1.1%
Switzerland	$ 108 billion	1.1%
Russia	$ 100 billion	1.0%
All others	$1,147 billion	11.4%
Total	**$4,478 billion**	**44.4%**

Source: Department of the Treasury. Caribbean banking centers are Bahamas, Bermuda, Cayman Islands, Netherlands Antilles, Panama, and British Virgin Islands; Oil exporters are Ecuador, Venezuela, Indonesia, Bahrain, Iran, Iraq, Kuwait, Oman, Qatar, Saudi Arabia, the United Arab Emirates, Algeria, Gabon, Libya, and Nigeria

Preventing the Debt Burden from Rising

Our discussion so far seems to suggest that if a country's debt grows, the burden of its debt will grow too. But that is not necessarily the case. In fact, a country's debt can keep rising forever, without imposing any added burden, as long as the country follows what we'll call the *basic debt guideline*: *total nominal debt should grow no faster than nominal GDP.* For example, suppose a country's nominal GDP rises by 10% per year. Then the basic guideline says that its debt should rise by no more than 10% per year.

Table 3 shows what happens when a country with nominal GDP growing at 10% per year stays just barely within the guideline, allowing its debt to rise at the same 10% rate. In the table, nominal GDP in the first year is $10,000 billion, and the nominal debt starts out at $5,000 billion, so the debt ratio (debt as a percentage of GDP) starts out at 50%. We assume the nominal interest rate remains constant at 8 percent, so the government must pay $.08 \times \$5,000$ billion = $400 billion in interest during the year. This $400 billion amounts to 4% of GDP, so the government must collect taxes equal to 4% of total income to pay the interest on its debt.

In year 2 and each subsequent year, both nominal GDP and the debt grow at 10% per year. This keeps the debt ratio constant, at 50%. More important, interest payments as a *percentage* of GDP remain unchanged, so the same 4% tax rate completely covers the interest on the debt.

Notice that, in the table, the total debt grows every year in *dollars*, which means the country is continually running budget deficits that add to the debt. But the *burden* of the debt—measured by the 4% tax rate—remains unchanged. To prevent the burden of the debt from rising, we do *not* have to run budget surpluses and we do *not* have to reduce our total debt. We need only limit how fast the total debt grows.

> As long as the debt grows by the same percentage as nominal GDP, the debt ratio will remain constant. And with an unchanging interest rate, the burden of the debt will remain constant as well.

TABLE 3

A Growing National
Debt with a *Constant*
Debt Burden

	(1) Nominal GDP (growing at 10% per year)	(2) Nominal National Debt (growing at 10% per year)	(3) Debt Ratio Column (2) ÷ Column (1)	(4) Interest Payments (at 8% interest rate) 0.08 × Column (2)	(5) Debt Burden (Interest payments as % of GDP) Column (4) ÷ Column (1)
Year 1	$10,000 billion	$5,000 billion	50%	$400 billion	4%
Year 2	$11,000 billion	$5,500 billion	50%	$440 billion	4%
Year 3	$12,100 billion	$6,050 billion	50%	$484 billion	4%
Year 4	$13,310 billion	$6,655 billion	50%	$532.4 billion	4%

© CENGAGE LEARNING 2013

This last statement suggests when a country *should* become genuinely concerned about its national debt: when it violates the guideline by allowing its debt to rise faster than its nominal GDP. Violating this guideline causes the burden of the debt to rise, and could even bring about a debt disaster. Let's explore these genuine concerns more closely.

Genuine Concern #1: A Rising Debt Burden

Table 4 shows an example of a country that is allowing its debt to grow faster than its nominal GDP, in violation of the basic guideline. As in Table 3, we assume that nominal GDP rises by 10% each year. But now, we assume the debt grows faster, by 20% each year. This causes the debt ratio to rise. As you can see, the tax rate needed to cover interest payments rises each year as well, reaching 5.2% in year 4. This 5.2% tax rate would be *in addition* to the taxes used to pay for other, non-interest government functions, such as national defense, retirement benefits, health care, environmental protection, federal courts, and more.

The violation of the basic debt guideline (that debt grow no faster than GDP) cannot go on forever, because the tax rate has a mathematical upper limit of 100 percent of GDP. And even before that limit is reached, tax rates would become oppressive, harming growth and—if pushed too high—actually reducing potential GDP per capita. (Just ask yourself how much you would work if 70, 80, or 90 percent of your income was taxed, or how much you would invest in human capital if you anticipated a tax rate that high on your future income.)

What if the violation of the debt guideline is temporary? Then the *rise* in the burden of the debt will be temporary too. But the previous sentence needs to be interpreted with care, because even a temporary violation of the guideline can create a permanently *higher* burden. To see why, remember that during the time that debt grows faster than nominal GDP, tax rates must rise to cover the rising interest payments as a fraction of total income. Once the debt starts growing at the same rate as nominal GDP again, the tax rate can stop rising—but *the tax rate must remain at its new, higher level.* Thus,

TABLE 4					
A Growing National Debt with a *Rising* Debt Burden	**(1)** **Nominal GDP** (growing at 10% per year)	**(2)** **Nominal Debt** (growing at 20% per year)	**(3)** **Debt Ratio** Column (2) ÷ Column (1)	**(4)** **Interest Payments (at 8% interest rate)** 0.08 × Column (2)	**(5)** **Debt Burden (Interest payments as % of GDP)** Column (4) ÷ Column (1)
Year 1	$10,000 billion	$5,000 billion	50%	$400 billion	4%
Year 2	$11,000 billion	$6,000 billion	54.5%	$480 billion	4.4%
Year 3	$12,100 billion	$7,200 billion	59.5%	$576 billion	4.8%
Year 4	$13,310 billion	$8,640 billion	65.0%	$691.2 billion	5.2%

© CENGAGE LEARNING 2013

while a temporary violation of the guideline does not mean a disaster, it *does* leave us with a permanently elevated debt burden . . . at least, until we do something about it.

Reversing a Rise in the Debt Burden

How can the debt burden be brought back down after a temporary violation of the guideline? There are only two basic ways: (1) raise the growth rate of nominal GDP *above* the growth rate of the debt for some time; or (2) lower the growth rate of the debt below the growth rate of nominal GDP for some time. Either of these solutions could return the debt ratio back to its original level, so that the debt burden and the tax rate needed to pay interest could return to their original levels as well.

But these solutions are costly to society. Let's first consider raising the growth rate of nominal GDP. Because policy has only limited ability to influence the growth rate of *real* GDP over long periods, the only practical method to ensure a higher growth rate of *nominal* GDP is faster growth in the price level. This means allowing the inflation rate to rise for some time. But we've already seen that allowing the inflation rate to rise can be costly for society in numerous ways—including the buildup of inflationary expectations that would be difficult to reverse.

Moreover, inflation might not solve the problem. Much of the national debt must be "rolled over" on a continual basis: Government bonds that come due are repaid by issuing new bonds, which must pay the prevailing interest rate at the time. As soon as lenders suspect that inflation might be the chosen method for reducing the debt ratio, they will demand higher nominal interest rates to compensate for expected inflation. The government's ongoing interest payments will rise, enlarging the deficit, and possibly sabotaging the effort to slow the growth of the debt.

Now consider the second option: slowing down the growth rate of the debt itself, so it falls below the given growth rate of nominal GDP. The only way to do this is to run *smaller deficits* as a fraction of GDP than the deficits that would keep the debt ratio constant. Running smaller deficits for a time means higher tax rates or reduced government outlays during that period.

Thus,

a debt that rises too fast—faster than nominal GDP—for some period of time will impose an opportunity cost in the future. The cost will be either a permanently higher tax burden, a period of inflation (which may or may not work), or a period of reduced government outlays or higher taxes relative to GDP.

Genuine Concern #2: A Debt Disaster

If debt were to rise *too* rapidly relative to GDP, for *too* long, there is a danger of reaching the nation's credit limit—a debt ratio that would make lenders worry about the government's ability to continue paying interest. If this credit limit were approached, a nation would be truly flirting with disaster: A tiny increase in the debt ratio would lead to a cutoff of further lending, or lenders might require prohibitively high interest rates to compensate them for the added risk. Without the ability to borrow at affordable interest rates, the budget would have to be balanced immediately. There would have to be a significant and sudden drop in government outlays, and/or a significant rise in tax rates—a policy often called *fiscal austerity*, the opposite of fiscal stimulus. But sudden fiscal austerity can create even bigger problems for a country. First, any sudden cut in transfer payments or government purchases would be painful for those who had come to rely on government benefits or government jobs. The cuts would come without warning, so those affected would have no time to plan.

Moreover, fiscal austerity might not even succeed in restoring fiscal health, and could even make it worse for some time. That's because even if the country completely eliminates its deficit—so it is not *adding* to its debt—most or all of the debt it built up in past years remains. At the same time, by cutting government purchases or transfers, or raising taxes, the government is causing aggregate expenditure and equilibrium GDP to fall. With the debt remaining stubbornly high and equilibrium GDP falling, fiscal austerity would raise the debt ratio, putting the country even further over its credit limit.

Caught in this macroeconomic trap, a government may have only two choices left: (1) very high inflation; or (2) default. A very high rate of inflation can be extremely costly to society, as we discussed several chapters ago (The Price Level and Inflation). And as we discussed in *this* chapter, the inflation solution might not work: Once lenders catch on, they will demand higher nominal interest rates on any new lending to compensate them for *expected* inflation. These higher interest rates enlarge the budget deficit, add to the debt, and could end up *raising* the debt ratio.

In a *default*, the government would simply announce that bondholders would receive only part—or none—of the payments they are due. A default would immediately—and by definition—reduce the government's debt and its debt ratio. Short of war, no one can force a government to pay back debt that it refuses to pay.

But default would also create a great deal of economic pain. Government bonds would drop in value, devastating the wealth of households and businesses that held them. And a government default could collapse a country's own financial system, as well as the systems of other countries that hold its bonds. (You'll learn more about how default can affect the financial system in the next chapter.)

When a nation hits its credit limit, it is forced to choose among extremely unpleasant options. Each option is likely to impose more economic pain than the country would have faced if it had gradually reduced its debt ratio earlier and more gradually, and not reached its credit limit in the first place.

How high can a country's debt ratio go before it hits its credit limit? There is no hard and fast rule. A country's credit limit is determined not just by its current debt ratio, but also by its reputation for honoring its obligations in the past, and the likely change in its debt ratio in the near and distant future. Some guesswork is involved, including guesses about decisions that a country's politicians will make in the future. In 2011, several Eurozone countries seemed to be getting close to their credit limits. And most observers believed that one of them—Greece—was already over its limit, and dangerously close to default.

Greece: An Example

By the early 2000s, after years of spending more than it collected in taxes, the Greek government's debt was about equal to its annual GDP—a debt ratio of 100%. This can be seen in the upper panel of Figure 4, which shows both nominal GDP and nominal debt in Greece. But until 2008, Greece was not yet at its credit limit. This can be seen in the lower panel of Figure 4, which tracks the interest rate on 10-year government bonds in Greece and also Germany (for comparison). German bonds were considered free of any default risk. For most of the period shown, investors were willing to lend to the Greek government at annual interest rates very close to Germany's.

But in 2008, when Europe fell into recession, Greece was particularly hard hit. Greece's budget deficits rose and its GDP fell, causing Greece's debt ratio to rise rapidly from its already high level. Lenders began to worry about a Greek government default. They were still willing to lend to Greece, but only at sharply higher interest rates. Greece was now bumping up against its credit limit.

Then the vicious cycle began. The higher interest rates demanded by lenders (in the lower panel) added to Greece's deficit, causing its debt (in the upper panel) to rise even more rapidly. The rapidly rising debt escalated fears of default, causing the interest rate (the lower panel) to rise even higher. As you can see, deterioration in each of the panels of Figure 4 caused further deterioration in the other panel. Greece was in the midst of a debt disaster.

Was there a solution? It was too late for Greece to avoid the disaster with gradual fiscal austerity; its interest payments were rising fast, so its debt ratio—even if it cut government outlays or

FIGURE 4 **Greece's Debt Disaster**

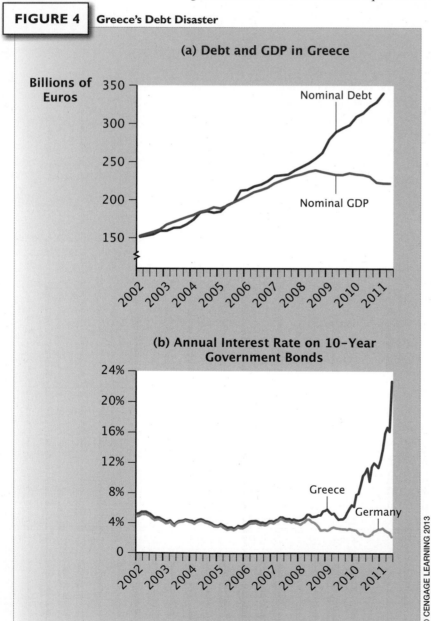

(a) Debt and GDP in Greece

Billions of Euros

Nominal Debt

Nominal GDP

(b) Annual Interest Rate on 10–Year Government Bonds

Greece

Germany

© CENGAGE LEARNING 2013

raised taxes—would continue to rise. Inflation was not an option either. Later in this book, you'll learn that a country generates higher inflation through *monetary policy*, which requires the country to control its own money supply. But Greece—like all Eurozone countries—had turned over control of its monetary policy to the European Central Bank, which chose not to create higher inflation in Europe. And if it left the Eurozone, Greece would have to give up important long-run benefits (as you'll see in the last chapter of this book).

That left default. If the default were too small (say, the government announced it would continue to make payments on only 80% of its debts), it wouldn't help much. But if the default were too large (say, a complete repudiation of all debt), Greece might be cut off from all further borrowing, and its government would have to bring its budget into immediate balance.

And there was another problem. A Greek default threatened financial systems throughout Europe. Large banks—which held hundreds of billions of euros worth of Greek bonds—might go bankrupt. Even worse, lenders would worry that *other* European countries with high and rising debt ratios—including Spain, Italy, Portugal, and Ireland—might default next. Interest rates on *their* government bonds—which were already rising—would rise further, putting these countries into the same trap that Greece was in.

In 2010 and 2011, European governments and international organizations were scrambling to prevent a Greek default. Against popular opinion in their own countries, they agreed to lend Greece billions of euros at interest rates lower than private lenders were demanding. But in exchange, Europe demanded fiscal austerity from Greece—higher taxes and government spending cuts. Greek citizens took to the streets in protests that sometimes turned violent. And, as many economists had predicted, austerity caused Greece's GDP to drop and its debt ratio to rise. By late 2011, a default was inevitable, and the only remaining questions were (1) what percentage of Greece's debt would be subject to the default; (2) how would the fallout for the rest of Europe be contained; and (3) how much more fiscal austerity would be imposed on Greece. Regardless of the outcome, Greece was in for hard times—a lesson about the dangers of getting too close to a national credit limit.

The U.S. Long-Term Debt Problem

If you flip back to Figure 3, you'll see that at the end of World War II, the U.S. debt ratio exceeded 100%. Yet even with the debt greater than a year's GDP, no one doubted the U.S. government would continue to honor its obligations.

In 2011, the U.S. debt ratio stood at about 72%—substantially less than in the mid-1940s. Yet the U.S. fiscal situation was substantially worse than in the 1940s. The problem was not the debt ratio itself, and the U.S. in 2011 was not Greece. The problem was the *projected rise* of the debt ratio over the next couple of decades, due to promises the U.S. government made to millions of people—to pay social security benefits when they retire, and to fund health care for the elderly and the poor (through Medicare, Medicaid, and related programs). And unfortunately, keeping these promises—especially those related to health care—is becoming ever more expensive. The population is aging, and older people use substantially more health care than younger people. More significantly, the discovery of new and ever-more expensive technologies and procedures is raising the costs of providing health care to each person treated. As a result, the government's social security and health care payments are rising faster than GDP. From 1971 to 2011, as a share of GDP, these payments rose from 4% to 10%. If current trends continue, they will increase to 17% of GDP (and still be rising) by 2037.

FIGURE 5   The U.S. Debt Ratio: Past and Projected

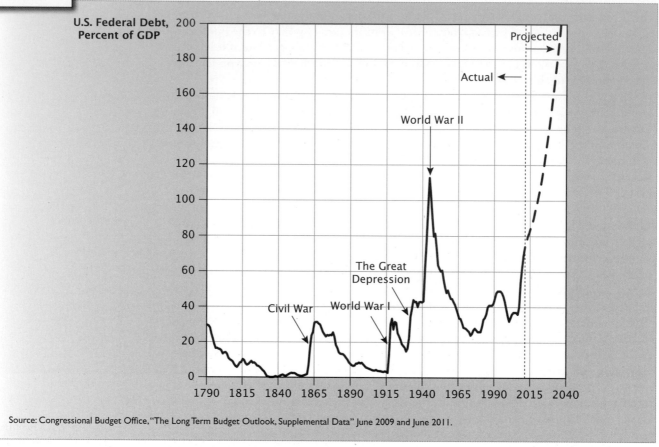

Source: Congressional Budget Office, "The Long Term Budget Outlook, Supplemental Data" June 2009 and June 2011.

Figure 5 puts the problem in perspective. It shows the debt ratio through U.S. history, and also shows projections of the ratio (made in June 2011) by the Congressional Budget Office (CBO), a non-partisan research organization for the U.S. Congress. The projection shown in the figure is the CBO's "Alternative Fiscal Scenario," which, contrary to its title, roughly translates to "Government as Usual." This scenario assumes that Congress will continue to adjust the federal tax code as it has in the past, so that federal taxes continue to be 18% of GDP—their long-run historical average. And it assumes that the government's health care and social security payments will continue to keep pace with the aging population and the expected rise in medical treatment costs. Any deviation from this projection would require unusual behavior from Congress—a tighter fiscal policy than it has been willing to deliver in the past.

As you can see, under this scenario, the debt ratio will skyrocket—shooting past World War II levels by 2023, and past "Greek levels" by 2031—less than two decades from now. And the longer we continue on this path, the more difficult will be our future choices. At some point, in order to avoid hitting our national credit limit, we would have to convince domestic and foreign lenders that we will change our fiscal habits, and stabilize the debt ratio to prevent it from rising further. Even if we succeeded, we would still be left with a much higher debt ratio than we have today, and higher tax rates to pay the interest.

But it could be worse. If lenders, looking ahead, begin to doubt our resolve to slow the growth of the debt, we could bump up against our national credit limit and face a debt disaster. It is extremely unlikely that the U.S. government would allow such doubts to arise. And if it did, the disaster would differ in important ways from Greece's. Unlike Greece in 2011, the U.S. controls its own monetary policy, and could—if it chose to—use higher inflation to bring down the debt ratio. But as we discussed earlier, higher inflation is costly to society, and it is not guaranteed to work: Once lenders catch on, they will demand higher interest rates. And higher inflation—while it would help to reduce the burden of past debt—would do nothing to erode the future rise in the debt ratio, because the government's future social security and health care payments would rise with inflation.

Of course, long-range forecasts like the one in Figure 5 are, at best, educated guesswork. But they do indicate where current trends are leading us, absent big surprises. A pleasant surprise—such as the high-tech boom that led to unexpectedly rapid growth in real GDP in the 1990s—would improve the picture. But an *un*pleasant surprise—such as the recession that hit the U.S. and other countries in 2008, or an unexpected rise in interest rates that adds to the burden of the debt—could hasten the debt disaster.

The Question of Timing

Virtually all economists agree that the U.S. debt ratio's rapid growth is a looming danger that must be solved by shrinking projected future budget deficits. But there is another danger: shrinking deficits *too soon*, before the economy has sufficiently recovered from its long slump. Significant cuts in government purchases or transfer payments, or across-the-board tax increases, would reduce aggregate expenditure. At best, a decline in spending would deepen and prolong the economic slump; at worst, it could propel the economy into another recession. In 2011, some prominent economists went even further, calling for large *increases* in government outlays in 2012 and 2013. They wanted another round of countercyclical fiscal policy, similar to the fiscal stimulus that began in 2009, even at the cost of temporarily higher budget deficits. We'll look at the 2009 fiscal stimulus—and the controversy it created—in the Using the Theory section.

USING THE THEORY

© NORMA JEAN GARGASZ/AGE FOTOSTOCK

THE AMERICAN REINVESTMENT AND RECOVERY ACT

As we discussed at the beginning of this chapter, when country after country descended into serious recessions in 2008, most of them, including the United States, used some form of countercyclical fiscal policy. In early 2009, the Obama administration requested, and Congress passed, the *American Reinvestment and Recovery Act* (ARRA), a roughly two-year fiscal stimulus originally estimated at $787 billion, and later revised to $862 billion. Of that total, roughly one-third was tax cuts, and one-third greater government purchases. The remaining third consisted of increased transfer payments to help those most directly affected by the recession, along with transfers to state and local governments (to help them avoid raising their own taxes or cutting their own outlays). While the tax cuts and aid to state and local governments took place relatively rapidly, the new government purchases were to be phased in over two years.

The fiscal stimulus, as mentioned earlier, was controversial, so let's take a closer look at why the government took this step, and what it may have done for the economy.

Why Fiscal Stimulus?

Why use countercyclical fiscal policy, given the skepticism we discussed earlier? To many economists, the conditions in 2009 were exceptional, and the usual objections didn't apply.

For example, one traditional objection relates to timing. Remember that legislating a fiscal change ordinarily takes months or longer. By the time it takes effect, we may already be close to potential output, and the economy will then overheat. In 2009, that risk was perceived as minimal. For one thing, the recession was expected to be long lasting, with full recovery taking several years. For another, the recession had focused the nation's attention, and there was substantial incentive in Congress to act. The President and a majority of Congress were from the same party, suggesting there might be less political delay than when government is divided. Indeed, the fiscal stimulus package was signed by the President just a few weeks after the Senate and House versions of the bills were first introduced.

Another traditional objection to countercyclical fiscal policy is the likely reaction of the Federal Reserve, which typically takes the lead in steering the economy, and acts to neutralize any stimulus from fiscal policy. In 2009, the Federal Reserve had already used all of its *traditional* tools to stimulate the economy, and these had proven insufficient. (You'll learn more about these tools in the next two chapters.) The Federal Reserve still had some unconventional tools, and was using them aggressively, but their effectiveness and timing were highly uncertain. So in this case, the Federal Reserve actually *welcomed* fiscal stimulus.

In light of these special considerations, many (but not all) prominent economists reversed their usual objections to countercyclical fiscal policy and endorsed the idea of fiscal stimulus.

Was the ARRA Effective?

How effective was the ARRA? It did not end the slump, nor did it meet the Obama administration's expectations. In early 2009, when the ARRA passed, the unemployment rate stood at 7.2%. The administration confidently predicted that its fiscal policy would prevent unemployment from rising above 8.0%. In fact, the unemployment rate reached 10.1% in late 2009 and remained stubbornly above 9% for another two years.

That does not, however, mean the stimulus had no effect. Policy changes are not controlled experiments, in which a single variable changes while all others are held constant. In the real world, many economic variables are always changing. The impact of any policy should be measured as the difference between what *did* happen and what *would* have happened without the policy. What would have happened is often called a *counterfactual*.

While a counterfactual can never be observed, it can be estimated. A straightforward approach to measure the counterfactual for the ARRA, and the approach taken by the Congressional Budget Office[5], is to assume that the ARRA had multiplier effects. Then, using values for the relevant multipliers, we can estimate what would have happened without the ARRA.

---

[5] Congressional Budget Office, "Estimated Impact of the American Recovery and Reinvestment Act on Employment and Economic Output," August 2011; CBO's potential output estimates from Federal Reserve Bank of St. Louis.

TABLE 5

Range of Estimates for
Multipliers in the ARRA

Type of Activity	Estimated Multiplier	
	Low Estimate	High Estimate
Federal Government Purchases	1.0	2.5
Transfer Payments to State and Local Government for Infrastructure	1.0	2.5
Transfer Payments to State and Local Governments for Other Purposes	0.7	1.8
Transfer Payments to Individuals	0.8	2.1
One-time Payments to Retirees	0.3	1.0
Two-year Tax Cut for Lower- and Middle-Income People	0.6	1.5
One-year Tax Cut for Higher Income People	0.2	0.6
Extension of First-Time Homebuyer Credit	0.3	0.8

As discussed in the chapter, estimates of fiscal multipliers can vary. They depend on initial conditions in the economy, expectations about the future, the size and type of fiscal change, the reaction of the Federal Reserve, and more. The CBO—in gauging the impact of the stimulus—relied on estimates by a variety of academic and government economists, and chose a range of multiplier values believed to correspond most closely to U.S. economic conditions at the time. Table 5 shows the range of multiplier estimates that the CBO used to gauge the impact of each part of the ARRA. For example, for government purchases, the multiplier range was 1.0 to 2.5. For low- and middle-income tax cuts, the range was 0.6 to 1.5.

Figure 6 puts the various pieces of the CBO analysis together. For comparison, we've included the path of potential real GDP (the top line) and actual real GDP (the next highest line). The other two lines are two counterfactuals for real GDP in the absence of the ARRA, based on the CBO's multiplier estimates. The line marked "best counterfactual" assumes each multiplier is at the low end of its range. That would make the impact of the ARRA relatively small. But even in that case, the hypothetical performance of the economy would have been considerably worse without the stimulus. Instead of real GDP falling 8% below potential output (as it did), it would have fallen 9.2% below. Translating the result for GDP to employment (not shown), the CBO estimates that without the stimulus, 2 million more jobs would have been lost and the unemployment rate would have risen to 10.6% at its peak (instead of the actual 10.1%).

The line marked "worst counterfactual" assumes that each fiscal multiplier is at the high end of its estimated range. With larger multipliers, the stimulus would have made a bigger difference in the economy, so the counterfactual without the stimulus is much worse. In this case, real GDP would have fallen 11.2% below potential without the ARRA, and an additional 5 million jobs would have been lost. The unemployment rate would have peaked at 11.8% and remained near that high for several quarters.

FIGURE 6 | Actual GDP (with ARRA) and Possible Counterfactuals (without ARRA)

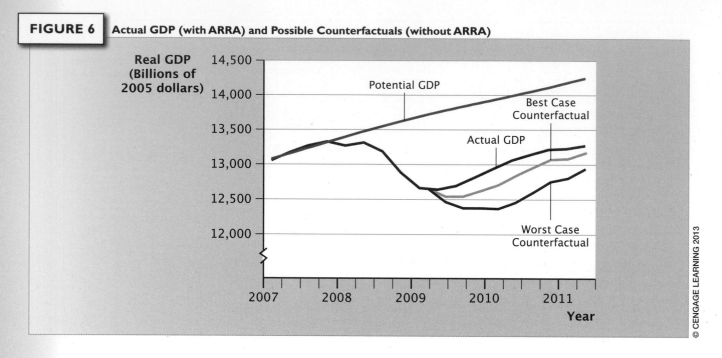

© CENGAGE LEARNING 2013

The CBO's conclusions about the impact of the ARRA are not necessarily correct. But they are respected by most economists, based on the CBO's decades-long reputation for non-partisanship and professionalism. Several private research organizations reached conclusions similar to those of the CBO.

Questions and Controversies about the ARRA

Figure 6 raises several important questions. First, why wasn't the ARRA designed to provide even more stimulus? Even by the administration's own forecasts, the ARRA would, at best, prevent an already deep recession from getting worse. Why not go all the way, and try to bring the economy more rapidly to full employment? One reason is that the administration did not believe that Congress would approve a larger stimulus. Concerns about the rising debt ratio, skepticism about the government's ability to rapidly increase spending, and skepticism about the size of the multipliers themselves made it difficult for even the administration's more modest proposal to win approval.

Second, why were the administration's forecasts wrong? Why did output fall and unemployment rise by so much more than anticipated? One reason was unrealistic expectations about how quickly the government could get infrastructure projects approved and started. Month after month, the increase in federal purchases lagged behind the administration's schedule.

But a more important reason was that the forces pulling the economy down were more powerful than the administration and many economists had suspected. The financial crisis had shattered consumer and business confidence more than had any recession in the previous 70 years, depressing both consumption and investment spending. Also, state and local governments decreased their own spending more than anticipated. In fact, the drop in state and local government purchases was about equal to the rise in federal purchases. So considering *all* levels of government together, government purchases did not change. This left only tax cuts and increased transfer payments—which had lower multipliers—to provide the stimulus.

A Second Stimulus?

Toward the end of 2011, as the slump continued and threatened to turn into another recession, some economists and politicians called for another fiscal stimulus. They pointed out that, in 2011, the impact of fiscal policy had turned *negative*. This is the natural cycle for any temporary change in fiscal policy. For example, a temporary increase in government purchases will have a positive multiplier effect as purchases are rising ($\Delta G > 0$). But as purchases return to their original level, the *change* in purchases is negative ($\Delta G < 0$), so the multiplier effect *decreases* GDP. Ideally, the negative multiplier impact will not occur until the economy is well on its way to recovery.

By 2011, the slump had outlasted almost all of the effects of the ARRA, and now G was decreasing: federal purchases were winding down, and state and local government purchases remained at depressed levels. So proponents of stimulus argued that more was needed if only to prevent the winding down of the ARRA from causing harm.

Second, advocates argued that another round of stimulus need not worsen, and could even improve, the long-run debt trajectory. Ending the slump sooner would at least raise nominal GDP (the denominator of the ratio), which would lessen, to some degree, the harmful impact of running a larger deficit. And this time, they argued, the stimulus could be focused entirely on infrastructure projects that improve productivity (such as repairing bridges and airports, modernizing the electrical grid, and fixing the nation's schools). These projects would raise the long-run growth rate of the economy, which, in turn, would help to *improve* the path of the debt ratio over time.

Economists and politicians opposed to another stimulus believed it would worsen the long-run debt trajectory while providing little benefit. They were skeptical of the government's ability to rapidly identify and set in motion infrastructure projects that would raise economic growth. And some believed there was a more effective and less costly tool that could pull the economy out of its slump: *monetary policy*. We'll be discussing monetary policy in the next several chapters.

SUMMARY

Government purchases and net taxes have multiplier effects. The multiplier for government purchases is larger, because it increases total spending directly, while the multiplier for net taxes is smaller in absolute value and negative in sign. The government can, in theory, use these multipliers in various combinations to conduct *countercyclical fiscal policy* in order to help stabilize the economy. However, economists have been skeptical of this tool because of numerous problems, including timing difficulties, irreversibility, small multipliers for temporary tax changes, and countermoves by the Federal Reserve.

Over the longer run, fiscal policy affects the economy primarily via ongoing budget deficits and the buildup of the national debt. To gauge these effects, fiscal variables should be viewed as percentages of GDP.

Federal government outlays consist of three broad categories: government purchases of goods and services, transfer payments, and interest on the national debt. When government outlays exceed tax revenue, the government runs a budget deficit. It finances that deficit by selling bonds, thereby adding to the national debt. When government outlays are less than tax revenue, the government runs a budget surplus. It uses that surplus to buy back bonds it has issued in the past, thus shrinking the national debt.

In recessions, government tax revenues fall and transfer payments rise. In this way, the tax and transfer system acts as an automatic stabilizer, helping to smooth out fluctuations in output.

A nation's *debt ratio* is its publicly held national debt as a percentage of its GDP. The national debt never has to be repaid, but it still imposes a *debt burden* on society, in the form of higher tax rates needed to pay continuing interest on the debt. The higher the debt ratio, the higher the burden of the debt. A basic *debt guideline*, which prevents the debt from rising, is that the nominal debt should grow no faster than nominal GDP. When that guideline is violated, the debt ratio rises, and so do interest payments as a percentage of GDP. This cannot continue indefinitely, because a nation would come up against its credit limit, inviting economic disaster and the requirement to immediately balance its budget. But even a temporary violation of the guideline imposes burdens on the economy: permanently higher taxes, a period of inflation, or greater fiscal tightening to bring the debt ratio back down.

The U.S. is projected to have a rapidly rising debt ratio over the next several decades, largely because of rising government payments for health care. The U.S. will have to change course at some point in the near future in order to avoid a debt disaster.

PROBLEM SET

Answers to even-numbered Problems can be found on the text Web site through www.cengagebrain.com

1. Calculate the changes in real GDP that would result in each of the following cases (assuming simple multipliers, with no automatic stabilizers or destabilizers):
   a. Government purchases rise by $7.5 billion and the *MPC* is 0.95.
   b. Taxes *fall* by $7.5 billion, and the *MPC* is 0.95.

2. Calculate the change in real GDP that would result in each of the following cases (assuming an *MPC* of 0.8, and simple multipliers, with no automatic stabilizers or destabilizers):
   a. Government purchases rise by $30 billion and taxes fall by $30 billion.
   b. Government purchases and taxes *both* rise by $30 billion.
   c. Government purchases and taxes *both fall* by $30 billion.

3. Suppose a country has the following statistics, in billions of units of currency, for the years shown.
   Nominal national debt in 1990:   1.2
   Nominal national debt in 2000:   13.8
   Nominal GDP in 1990:   101.7
   Nominal GDP in 2000:   552.2
   Price index in 1990:   35.2
   Price index in 2000:   113.3

   a. Calculate the country's real debt and real GDP in 1990 and 2000.
   b. Calculate real debt as a percentage of real GDP in 1990 and 2000.
   c. Calculate nominal debt as a percentage of nominal GDP in 1990 and 2000.

4. Some economists have argued that when the government cuts taxes in a way that increases the debt ratio, people recognize that tax rates will have to rise in order to pay higher interest on the debt. They may begin saving more now in order to pay those higher tax rates later. In the extreme case (called "Ricardian equivalence"), people would save *all* of their tax cut to pay the expected higher taxes in the future. If Ricardian equivalence holds, what would be the value of the tax multiplier? Why?

5. You are running for reelection as president of the nation of Utopia. Your opponents have criticized you for allowing the national debt to grow by almost 50 percent over the last 4 years. Use the following statistics, measured in millions of dollars, to defend yourself to Utopia's voters:

National debt in year 1 of your presidency:	$152
National debt in year 4 of your presidency:	$200
Nominal GDP in year 1 of your presidency:	$3,042
Nominal GDP in year 4 of your presidency:	$4,098
Price index in year 1 of your presidency:	45
Price index in year 4 of your presidency:	72

6. Suppose there is a country with 30 households divided into three categories (A, B, and C), with 10 households of each type. If a household earns 20,000 zips (the country's currency) or more in a year, it must pay 15 percent of its income in taxes. If the household earns less than 20,000 zips, it doesn't pay any tax. When the economy is operating at full employment, household income is 250,000 zips per year for each type A household, 50,000 zips for type B households, and 20,000 zips for type C households.
   a. If the economy is operating at full employment, how much revenue does the government collect in taxes for the year?
   b. Suppose a recession hits and household income falls for each type of household. Type A households now earn 150,000 zips, type B households earn 30,000 zips, and type C households earn 10,000 zips for the year. How much does the government collect in tax revenue for the year?
   c. Assume the government spends all of the revenue it would have collected if the economy had been operating at full employment. Under this assumption, what is the effect of the recession on the government budget deficit?
   d. Suppose instead that the economy expanded and household incomes rose to 400,000 zips, 75,000 zips, and 30,000 zips, respectively, for the year. How much tax would the government collect

for the year? What is the effect on the budget deficit (assume again that the government spends exactly the amount of revenue it collects when household income is at the values in part (a))?

e. What does this problem tell you about the relationship between shocks to the economy and the budget deficit?

7. Are either of the following countries violating the *basic debt guideline* as presented in the chapter?

Country A (Figures in Billions of $)

	Debt	GDP
1999	1	100
2000	2	110
2001	3	150

Country B (Figures in Billions of $)

	Debt	GDP
1999	1,236	1,400
2000	1,346	1,550
2001	1,406	1,707

8. Suppose a nation's government purchases are equal to $2 trillion, regardless of the state of the economy. However, its taxes and transfers depend on economic conditions. When the economy is at potential output, net taxes (taxes minus transfers) equal $2.2 trillion. However, for each 1 percent GDP falls below potential output, net taxes fall by 5 percent.

a. Suppose the economy was operating at potential output. What would be its budget deficit?

b. Suppose that real GDP was 5 percent below potential output. What would be its budget deficit?

9. Complete the table below for the small country of Microland. Assume all dollar values are nominal, and Microland started Year 1 with no federal debt.

a. Over which years does Microland's debt ratio rise?

b. Assuming that Microland always pays the same interest rate on its debt, over which years does the burden of Microland's debt rise?

c. During one of the years, Microland's nominal debt rises, yet the burden of its debt falls. Which year? Explain briefly how the debt can rise and yet its burden can fall?

10. Refer to Table 3 in the chapter, which assumes the country continues to pay an interest rate of 8% on its debt. Suppose, instead, that the interest rate were 10%, while each year's nominal GDP and nominal debt remain as specified in the table. Enter new numbers for the last two columns in the table. Briefly, what impact does a higher interest rate have on (a) the burden of the debt? (b) the *increase* in the burden of the debt over time?

11. Refer to Table 4 in the chapter, which assumes the country continues to pay an interest rate of 8% on its debt. Suppose, instead, that the interest rate were 10%, while each year's nominal GDP and nominal debt remain as specified in the table. Enter new numbers for the last two columns in the table. Briefly, what impact does a higher interest rate have on (a) the burden of the debt? (b) the *increase* in the burden of the debt over time?

More Challenging

12. In the example in the chapter, the balanced budget multiplier was equal to 1.0. Prove that this must always be the case in our model, regardless of the value of the *MPC* or the amount by which *G* and *T* change (as long as their changes are equal and in the same direction). Follow the following steps in your proof:

(1) Suppose that *G* rises by $X. Write a general expression for the change this will cause in equilibrium GDP, for any value of the *MPC*.

(2) Suppose that *T* rises by $X. Write a general expression for the change this will cause in equilibrium GDP, for any value of the *MPC*. (Don't forget to use the proper sign.)

(3) Add the two changes in GDP together. (Your expressions should have a common denominator, so you can add the numerators.)

(4) Divide the change in GDP by the change in *G* (or *T*) that caused GDP to change. What value do you get?

[Table for Problem 9]

	Year						
	1	2	3	4	5	6	7
GDP	$400	$500	$600	$700	$800	$900	$1,000
Outlays	$105	$126	$130	$135	$133	$130	$ 130
Tax revenue	$100	$120	$125	$133	$134	$138	$ 130
Deficit/Surplus							
National debt (end of year)							
Debt ratio (end of year)							

CHAPTER 13

Money, Banks, and the Federal Reserve

Everyone knows that money doesn't grow on trees. But where does it actually come from? You might think that the answer is simple: The government just prints it. Right?

Sort of. It is true that much of our money supply is, indeed, paper currency, provided by our national monetary authority. But most of our money is *not* paper currency at all.

Moreover, the monetary authority in the United States—the Federal Reserve System—is technically not a part of the executive, legislative, or judicial branch of government. Rather, it is a quasi-independent agency that operates *alongside* the government. And in order to create money, it must work with private banks.

In the next several chapters, we'll make our short-run macro model more realistic by discussing how money, interest rates, and the financial system affect the overall economy. But in this chapter, we'll focus on the financial system itself. We begin in the next section by taking a look at a key component of the financial system: money.

MONEY

What exactly *is* money? It might seem unimportant to define it, because we all use it all the time. But because it plays such a special role in macroeconomics, we have to be a bit more precise about it. So here's a formal definition:

> *Money is an asset that is widely accepted as a means of payment in the economy.*

Money An asset widely accepted as a means of payment.

Let's take a closer look at this definition. An *asset* is something of value that is owned by someone. Stocks and bonds, real estate, valuable paintings, cars—all of these are examples of assets. But money is an asset with a special property: It's a **means of payment**—we can use it to buy goods and services or other assets. Coins and paper currency (together called *cash*), *traveler's checks*, and funds held in *checking accounts* are all examples of assets that are widely accepted as a means of payment. So, all three of these are examples of money.

Means of payment Anything acceptable as payment for goods and services.

Debit cards and credit cards, however, are *not* money. A debit card—which draws on funds in your checking account—is indeed a means of payment. But it is the checking account funds themselves that are assets; the debit card is just a piece of plastic, giving you electronic access to those funds. A credit card gives you the right to borrow, up to your credit limit. But the right to borrow is not an asset. This is why the credit limit on your card, like your ability to go into a bank and borrow funds, is not considered money.

What about other assets, such as stocks and bonds or gold bars? These can *not* generally be used to pay for goods and services, and so they do not satisfy the means-of-payment requirement.

The Money Supply

Figure 1 shows the amounts of the different forms of money in the United States on September 12, 2011. The largest category is **cash in the hands of the public,** which is the total dollar value of all the coins and currency in circulation. On September 12, 2011, the public held $982 billion in cash. Next in line is a broad category called *checkable deposits,* which are accounts held by households and business firms at commercial banks, including huge ones like the Bank of America or Citibank, and smaller ones such as Simmons National Bank in Arkansas. The most basic checking accounts are called *demand deposits,* because when you write a check to someone on one of these accounts, the person can go into your bank and, on demand, be paid in cash. Demand deposits pay no interest. Other types of checking accounts work very much like demand deposits, but often pay interest. This includes *automatic transfers from savings accounts,* which are interest-paying savings accounts that automatically transfer funds into demand deposit accounts as you write checks. On September 12, 2011, the U.S. public held $1,120 billion of all types of checkable deposits.

Finally, *traveler's checks* are specially printed checks that you can buy from banks or other private companies, like American Express. Traveler's checks can be easily spent at almost any hotel or store. You can often cash them at a bank. You need only show an I.D. and countersign the check. On September 12, 2011, the public held about $4 billion in traveler's checks.

Cash in the hands of the public Currency and coins held by the non-bank public.

FIGURE 1 | **The U.S. Money Supply**

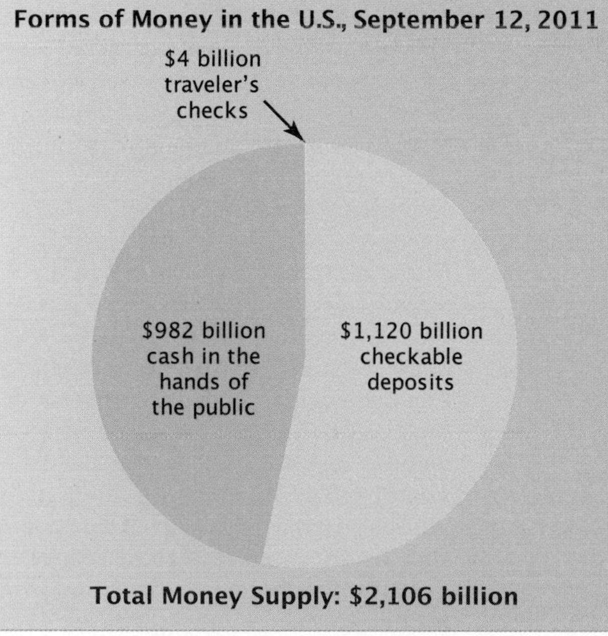

Forms of Money in the U.S., September 12, 2011

$4 billion traveler's checks

$982 billion cash in the hands of the public

$1,120 billion checkable deposits

Total Money Supply: $2,106 billion

The most basic definition of the U.S. money supply consists of cash in the hands of the public, checkable deposits, and travelers checks.

Source: Federal Reserve Statistical Release, Money Stock Measures, Table 5

Money supply The total amount of money (cash, checking deposits, and traveler's checks) held by the public.

When we add together the dollar value of cash in the hands of the public, checkable deposits, and traveler's checks, we get the total **money supply** in the United States:

> *Money supply = Cash in the hands of the public*
> *+ Checking account deposits*
> *+ Traveler's checks*

Thus, on September 12, 2011, the U.S. money supply was equal to $1,120 billion + $982 billion + $4 billion = $2,106 billion.

M1 versus M2

The money supply measure we've been discussing—comprised of cash, checkable deposits, and traveler's checks—is the most common measure of money, but not the only one. Technically, it is called *M1*. But another common measure—called *M2*—includes all of the components of M1, plus additional types of deposits that can fairly easily be turned into cash or checking deposits. For example, M2 includes savings deposits, from which funds can be *very* easily transferred into checking accounts. M2 also includes money market deposits (which work like checking accounts, but with some restrictions) and money market funds (which take investors' funds and lend them out for short periods). And it includes certificates of deposit under $100,000—which are often held by households and can be staggered to move funds into checking accounts at regular intervals. Because it includes these additional items, M2 is much larger than M1, with a value of more than $9 trillion dollars in September 2011.

When tracking what is happening to the "supply of money," economists have sometimes found it useful to look at M2, especially during periods when people are moving funds around from one kind of account to another. For example, suppose households were to move $100 billion out of money market funds and into checking accounts over a short period of time. Then M1 would balloon (because it includes checking accounts but not money market funds), while M2 would remain stable (because it includes both types of accounts). Using M1, we might think that the money supply is growing wildly, but a look at M2 would tell us otherwise.

In this and the next chapter, we won't be dealing with these sorts of movements from one type of easily accessible account to another. So when we refer to the "money supply," we'll continue to use the M1 measure. This measure fits most closely with the means-of-payment function of money, and it will help us keep our discussion simple.

⚠ DANGEROUS CURVES

Cash in banks or the Fed Money includes cash (coin and paper currency) only if it is *in the hands of the public*. The italicized words are important. Some of the nation's cash is stored in bank vaults and ATMs and is released only when the public withdraws cash from their accounts. Other cash is stored in the Federal Reserve or U.S. Treasury for future release. But until this cash is released from banks, the Fed, or the Treasury, it is not part of the money supply. Only the cash possessed by households, businesses, or government agencies (other than the Fed or Treasury) is considered part of the money supply.

Functions of Money

Money serves three functions in the economy. One—already discussed—is its use as a *means of payment*. Paying with money increases the efficiency of trading compared to the alternative: bartering. Without money, if you wanted to get a desk, you would have to offer a desk-maker something that he or she wanted in exchange. If you didn't have that item, you or the desk-maker would have to get it through another barter trade. The extra time spent arranging such trades could instead be spent producing things. Thus, without money, the economy would be less productive, and living standards would be lower.

Money also functions as a **store of value**. Because people have confidence they can use money as a means of payment in the future, they view money as one way to hold wealth. As you'll see in the next chapter, changes in the desire to hold wealth as money (rather than in other forms) can have important effects on the macroeconomy.

Store of value A form in which wealth can be held.

Finally, money serves as a **unit of account**—a common unit for measuring how much something is worth. A standard unit of account permits us to compare the costs of different goods and services and to communicate these costs when we trade. For example, the "dollar" is the unit of account in the United States. If a pair of running shoes costs $120, while a round-trip airline ticket from Phoenix to Minneapolis costs $360, we know immediately that the ticket has the same value in the marketplace as three pairs of running shoes.

Unit of account A common unit for measuring how much something is worth.

The unit-of-account and means-of-payment functions of money are closely related, but they are not the same. The unit-of-account function refers to the way we *think* about and record transactions; the means-of-payment function refers to how payment is actually made. The unit of account works in the same way as units of weight, volume, distance, and time.

In fact, the same sentence in Article I of the U.S. Constitution gives Congress the power to create a unit of value along with units of weights and measures. All of these units help us determine clearly and precisely what is being traded for what. Think about buying gas in the United States: You exchange dollars for gallons. The transaction will go smoothly and quickly only if there is clarity about both the unit of fluid volume (gallons) *and* the unit of purchasing power (dollars).

The means of payment can be different from the unit of account. For example, in some countries where local currency prices change very rapidly, it is common to specify prices in dollars or Euros—the unit-of-account function—while the local currency remains the means of payment. Even in the United States, if you write a check to pay for something, the unit of account is the dollar but the means of payment is a piece of paper with your signature on it.

In the United States, the "dollar" is the unit of account in every economic transaction, and dollar bills are very often the means of payment as well. How did the dollar come to play such an important role in the economy?

A Brief History of the Dollar

Prior to 1790, each colony had its own currency. It was named the "pound" in every colony, but it had a different purchasing power in each of them. In 1790, soon after the Constitution went into effect, Congress created a new currency called the dollar. Historical documents show that merchants and businesses switched immediately to the new dollar, thereby ending the chaos of the colonial monetary systems. Prices began to be quoted in dollars, and accounts were kept in dollars. The dollar rapidly became the standard unit of account.

But the primary means of payment in the United States until the Civil War was paper currency issued by private banks. Just as the government defined the length of the yard but did not sell yardsticks, the government defined the unit of account but let private organizations provide the means of payment.

During the Civil War, however, the government issued the first federal paper currency, the greenback. It functioned as both the unit of account and the major means of payment until 1879. Then the government got out of the business of money creation for a few decades. During that time, currency was once again issued by private banks. But in 1913, a new institution called the **Federal Reserve System** was created to be the national monetary authority in the United States. The Federal Reserve was charged with creating and regulating the nation's supply of money, and it continues to do so today.

Federal Reserve System The monetary authority of the United States, charged with creating and regulating the nation's supply of money.

Why Paper Currency Is Accepted as a Means of Payment

You may wonder why people are willing to accept paper dollars—or the promise of paper dollars—as a means of payment. Why should a farmer give up a chicken, or a manufacturer give up a new car, just to receive a bunch of green rectangles with words and numbers printed on them?

In fact, paper currency is a relatively recent development in the history of the means of payment. The earliest means of payment were precious metals and other valuable commodities such as furs or jewels. These were called *commodity money* because they had important uses other than as a means of payment. The nonmoney use is what gave commodity money its ultimate value. For example, people would accept furs as payment, because furs could be used to keep warm. Similarly, gold and silver had a variety of uses in industry, as religious artifacts, and for ornamentation.

Precious metals were an especially popular form of commodity money. Eventually, to make it easier to identify the value of precious metals, they were minted into coins whose weight was declared on their faces. Because gold and silver coins could be melted down into pure metal and used in other ways, they were still commodity money.

Commodity money eventually gave way to paper currency. Initially, paper currency was just a certificate representing a certain amount of gold or silver held by a bank. At any time, the holder of a certificate could go to the bank that issued it and trade the certificate for the stated amount of gold or silver. People were willing to accept paper money as a means of payment for two reasons. First, the currency could be exchanged for a valuable commodity such as gold or silver. Second, the issuer—either a government or a bank—could print new money only when it acquired additional gold or silver. This put strict limits on money printing, so people had faith that their paper money would retain its value in the marketplace.

But today, paper currency is no longer backed by gold or any other physical commodity. If you have a dollar handy, put this book down and take a close look at the bill. You will not find on it any promise that you can trade your dollar for gold, silver, furs, or anything else. Yet we all accept it as a means of payment. Why?

A clue is provided by the statement in the upper left-hand corner of every bill: *This note is legal tender for all debts, public and private.* The statement affirms that the piece of paper in your hands will be accepted as a means of payment (you can "tender" it to settle any "debt, public or private") by any American because the government says so. This type of currency is called **fiat money**. *Fiat,* in Latin, means "let there be," and fiat money serves as a means of payment by government declaration.

Fiat money Something that serves as a means of payment by government declaration.

The government need not worry about enforcing this declaration. The real force behind the dollar—and the reason that we are all willing to accept these green pieces of paper as payment—is its long-standing acceptability by *others*. As long as you have confidence that you can use your dollars to buy goods and services, you won't mind giving up goods and services for dollars. And because everyone else feels the same way, the circle of acceptability is completed. But while the government can declare that paper currency is to be accepted as a means of payment, it cannot declare the terms. Whether a gallon of gas will cost you 1 dollar, 4 dollars, or 10 dollars is up to the marketplace.

THE BANKING SYSTEM

Think about the last time you used the services of a bank. Perhaps you deposited a paycheck in the bank's ATM, or withdrew some cash. We make these kinds of transactions dozens of times every year without ever thinking about what a bank really is, or how our own actions at the bank—and the actions of millions of other bank customers—might contribute to a change in the money supply.

Financial Intermediaries in General

Let's start at the beginning: What are banks? They are important examples of **financial intermediaries:** business firms that specialize in assembling loanable funds from households and firms whose revenues exceed their expenditures, and channeling those funds to households and firms (and sometimes the government) whose expenditures exceed revenues. Financial intermediaries make the economy work much more efficiently than would be possible without them.

Financial intermediary A business firm that specializes in brokering between savers and borrowers.

To understand this more clearly, imagine that Boeing, the U.S. aircraft maker, wants to borrow a billion dollars for 3 years. If there were no financial intermediaries, Boeing would have to make individual arrangements to borrow small amounts of money from thousands—perhaps millions—of households, each of which wants to lend money for, say, 3 months at a time. Every 3 months, Boeing would have to renegotiate the loans, and it would find borrowing money in this way to be quite cumbersome. Each household, too, would find this arrangement troublesome. All of their funds would be loaned to one firm. If that firm encountered difficulties, the funds might not be returned at the end of 3 months.

An intermediary helps to solve these problems by combining a large number of small savers' funds and then lending them to larger borrowers. The intermediary can also reduce the risk to savers by spreading its loans among a number of different borrowers. If one borrower fails to repay its loan, that will have only a small effect on the intermediary and savers who have provided it with funds.

Of course, intermediaries must earn a profit for providing brokering services. They do so by charging a higher interest rate on the funds they lend than the rate they pay to savers. But when they are efficient at brokering, both the savers and the borrowers benefit. Savers earn higher interest rates, with lower risk and easier access to their funds on short notice, than if they had to deal directly with the ultimate users of funds. And borrowers end up paying lower interest rates on loans that are specially designed for their specific purposes.

The United States boasts a wide variety of financial intermediaries, including commercial banks, savings and loan associations, mutual savings banks, credit unions, insurance companies, and some government agencies. Some of these intermediaries—called *depository institutions*—accept deposits from the general public and lend the deposits to borrowers. *Commercial banks* are the largest group of depository institutions. They obtain funds mainly by accepting checkable deposits, savings deposits, and time deposits and use the funds to make business, mortgage, and consumer loans. Because commercial banks will play a central role in the rest of this chapter, let's take a closer look at how they operate.

Commercial Banks

A commercial bank (or just "bank" for short) is a private corporation, owned by its stockholders, that provides services to the public. For our purposes, the most important service is to provide checking accounts, which enable the bank's customers to pay bills and make purchases without holding large amounts of cash that could be lost or stolen. Checks are one of the most important means of payment in the economy. Every year, U.S. households and businesses write trillions of dollars' worth of checks to pay their bills, and many wage and salary earners have their pay deposited directly into their checking accounts. And as you saw in Figure 1, the public holds almost as much money in checking-type accounts as it holds in cash.

Banks provide checking account services in order to earn a profit. Where does a bank's profit come from? Mostly from lending out the funds that people deposit and

TABLE 1

The Balance Sheet of Mid-Size National Bank

Assets		Liabilities and Shareholders' Equity	
Property and Buildings	$ 40 million	Checking Account Deposits	$ 600 million
Government and Corporate Bonds	$ 100 million	Other Deposits	$ 200 million
Loans	$ 800 million	Bank Borrowing	$ 75 million
Cash in Vault and ATMs	$ 10 million		
In Accounts with Federal Reserve	$ 50 million	Shareholders' Equity	$ 125 million
Total Assets	**$1,000 million**	**Total Liabilities and Shareholders' Equity**	**$1,000 million**

charging interest on the loans, but also by charging for some services directly, such as check-printing or that annoying fee sometimes charged for using an ATM.

A Bank's Balance Sheet

Balance sheet A financial statement showing assets, liabilities, and shareholders' equity at a point in time.

We can understand more clearly how a bank works by looking at its *balance sheet*, a tool used by accountants. A **balance sheet** is a two-column list that provides information about the financial condition of a bank at a particular point in time. In one column, the bank's *assets* are listed—everything of value that it *owns*. On the other side, the bank's *liabilities* are listed—the amounts that the bank *owes*.

Table 1 shows a balance sheet for the (hypothetical) Mid-Size National Bank. Why does Mid-Size have these assets and liabilities? Let's start with the assets side.

A Bank's Assets

The first asset value listed in Table 1, $40 million, is the value of the bank's real estate—the buildings and the land underneath them. This is the easiest to explain, because a bank must have one or more branch offices in order to do business with the public.

Bond A promise to pay back borrowed funds, issued by a corporation or government agency.

Loan An agreement to pay back borrowed funds, signed by a household or noncorporate business.

Next comes $100 million in *bonds*, and $800 million in *loans*. A **bond** is a promise to pay funds to the holder of the bond, issued by a corporation or a government agency when it borrows money.[1] A bond promises to pay back the loan either gradually (e.g., each month), or all at once at some future date. **Loans** are promises, signed by households or noncorporate businesses, to pay back funds. Examples are auto loans, student loans, small-business loans, and home mortgages (where the funds lent out are used to buy a home). Both bonds and loans generate interest income for the bank.

Next come two categories that might seem curious: $10 million in "cash in vault and ATMs," and $50 million in "accounts with the Federal Reserve." The first of these is just like it sounds: the coin and currency that the bank has stored in its vault and in its automatic teller machines (ATMs), ready for withdrawal. In addition,

---

[1] We are using the term "bond" loosely to refer to *all* such promises issued by corporations and government agencies. Technically, a bond must be a long-term obligation to pay back money, 10 years or more from the time the money is first borrowed. Shorter-term obligations are called *notes* (between 1 and 10 years) or *bills* (1 year or less).

banks maintain their own accounts with the Federal Reserve, and they add to and subtract from these accounts when they make transactions with other banks.

The bank's cash does not pay any interest at all. And while the Federal Reserve began paying interest on reserve accounts in October 2008, the interest rate has—and will probably continue to be—lower than a bank could earn on many types of loans and bonds. Why, then, would a bank like Mid-Size hold cash and funds with the Federal Reserve? After all, every dollar Mid-Size holds as cash or with the Federal Reserve means the bank is foregoing some interest it could have earned.

There are several reasons that banks hold some of their assets in these forms. First, on any given day, some of the bank's customers might want to withdraw more cash than other customers are depositing. The bank must always be prepared to honor its obligations for withdrawals, so it must have some cash on hand to meet these requirements. This explains why it holds cash. And banks want to hold funds in accounts with the Federal Reserve to facilitate their transactions with other banks.

In any case, U.S. banks are required by law to hold **reserves,** which are defined as *the sum of cash in the vault and ATMs and in accounts with the Federal Reserve.* The amount of reserves a bank must hold is called **required reserves.** The more funds its customers hold in their checking accounts, the greater the amount of required reserves. The **required reserve ratio,** set by the Federal Reserve, tells banks the fraction of their checking accounts that they must hold as required reserves.

However, in the United States, many banks are able to reduce their reserve requirement by temporarily sweeping customer funds into other types of deposits where the requirements do not apply. And some countries have no reserve requirements at all, including England, Canada, and Australia. But banks in these countries—as well as U.S. banks that reduce their requirements through sweeps—still want to hold *some* fraction of their checking deposits as reserves. In these cases, the "required reserve ratio" can be interpreted more as a "*desired* reserve ratio"—the fraction of checking deposits that the bank *wants* to hold as reserves.

Mid-Size National Bank has $600 million in checking account deposits. If the required reserve ratio is 0.1, its required reserves are 0.1 × $600 million = $60 million in reserves. For now we'll assume that the required reserve ratio is strictly enforced, so that the bank must have *at least* this amount of its checking deposits as reserves. Because Mid-Size has $10 million in cash and $50 million in its reserve account with the Federal Reserve, it has a total of $60 million in reserves, the minimum required amount.

Sometimes, banks want to hold **excess reserves**—reserves *beyond* the minimum requirement. Why would a bank want to do this? It may want some flexibility to increase loans in the future, in case interest rates—the reward for lending—rise. Or, during a recession, it may want to hang on to reserves rather than lend them, because borrowers are more likely to declare bankruptcy and not repay their loans. The higher the interest rate the Fed pays on reserves, the lower is the bank's opportunity cost of holding excess reserves for these purposes. Thus, excess reserve holdings are influenced by a change in the interest rate the Fed pays on reserves.

Reserves Vault cash plus balances held at the Fed.

Required reserves The minimum amount of reserves a bank must hold, depending on the amount of its deposit liabilities.

Required reserve ratio The minimum fraction of checking account balances that banks must hold as reserves.

Excess reserves Reserves in excess of required reserves.

A Bank's Liabilities

Skipping to the right side of the balance sheet, we have several entries indicating what the bank *owes*. The first entry is *checking account deposits*. For a household or a business, checking account funds are assets. But for the bank, those same checking account funds are a liability. Why? Because the bank's customers have the right to withdraw funds from their checking accounts whenever they want. Until they do, the bank *owes* them these funds.

The same is true of the next entry on the right side of the balance sheet: *other deposits.* These are funds that households and firms hold at the bank in some form

⚠ DANGEROUS CURVES

Where are profit and loss on the balance sheet? If you are looking for profit or loss in Table 1, you've made the famous "stock versus flow" mistake. Take another look at the definition of a bank's balance sheet, and notice that it refers to assets, liabilities, and shareholders' equity at a *point in time*. Therefore, every entry on the balance sheet is a *stock* variable. By contrast, profit and loss are *flow* variables—they measure a process over a *period* of time. For example, when the bank's revenue *during a year* exceeds its costs *during that year*, the bank will earn a profit *for that year*. Flow variables such as cost, revenue, profit, and loss are included on a different financial statement, called an *income statement*.

Income statements and balance sheets, while not the same, are related. For example, suppose the bank in Table 1 earns $10 million in profit over some time period (which would appear on its income statement). And instead of paying the $10 million out to shareholders, it buys government bonds. Then, at the end of that period, its balance sheet entries for assets (government bonds) and shareholders' equity will both have increased by $10 million.

other than checking accounts, such as savings accounts or certificates of deposit (CDs). These funds are owed to the depositors, and are therefore on the liabilities side.

The next entry we've listed as *bank borrowing*. Banks themselves sometimes borrow funds by taking out loans from other banks, or by issuing their own bonds. For example, when someone purchases bonds newly issued by Citibank, they are lending funds to Citibank. The total amount that a bank has borrowed in the past and not yet paid back is a liability of the bank.

Shareholders' Equity

Finally, we come to the last entry on the balance sheet. When we total up the other entries on each side of the bank's balance sheet, we find that it has $1,000 million ($1 billion) in assets, but only $875 million in liabilities. If Mid-Size National Bank were to go out of business—selling all of its assets for their value on the balance sheet, and using the proceeds to pay off all of its liabilities (its deposits and loans)—it would have $125 million left over. Who would get this $125 million? Mid-Size's owners: its stockholders. The $125 million is called **shareholders' equity.**

More generally, for any corporation:

$$\text{Shareholders' equity} = \text{Total assets} - \text{Total liabilities.}$$

We include shareholders' equity on the same side of the balance sheet as liabilities, because it is, in a sense, what the bank would "owe" to its owners if it went out of business. Notice that because of the way shareholders' equity is defined, both sides of a balance sheet must always have the same total: *A balance sheet always balances*.

We'll come back to balance sheets—and how they can help us understand how money is created in a modern economy—a bit later. But first, we turn our attention to another key player in the financial system: The Federal Reserve.

Shareholders' equity The difference between total assets and total liabilities.

© AXL/SHUTTERSTOCK.COM

THE FEDERAL RESERVE SYSTEM

Central bank A nation's principal monetary authority responsible for controlling the money supply.

Every large nation controls its money supply with a **central bank**—the nation's principal monetary authority and the institution responsible for controlling its money supply. Most of the developed countries established their central banks long ago. For example, England's central bank—the Bank of England—was created in 1694. France was one of the latest in Europe, waiting until 1800 to establish the Banque de France. But the United States was even later. Although we experimented with central banks at various times in our history, we did not get serious about a central bank until 1913, when Congress established the *Federal Reserve System*.

Why did it take the United States so long to create a central bank? Part of the reason was the suspicion of central authority that has always been part of U.S. politics and culture. Another reason is the large size and extreme diversity of our country, and the fear that a powerful central bank might be dominated by the interests of one region

FIGURE 2   The Geography of the Federal Reserve System

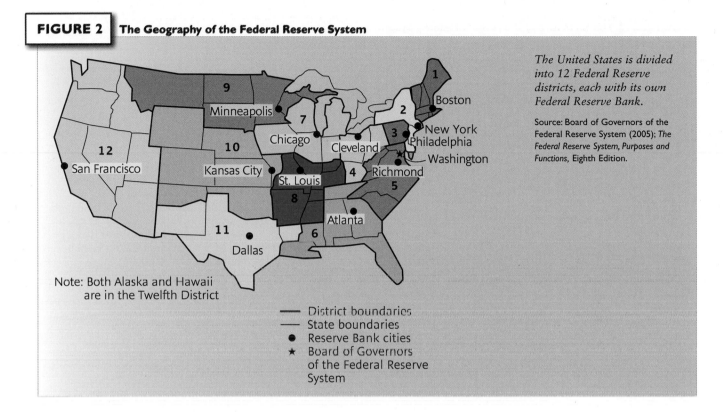

The United States is divided into 12 Federal Reserve districts, each with its own Federal Reserve Bank.

Source: Board of Governors of the Federal Reserve System (2005); *The Federal Reserve System, Purposes and Functions*, Eighth Edition.

Note: Both Alaska and Hawaii are in the Twelfth District

— District boundaries
— State boundaries
● Reserve Bank cities
★ Board of Governors of the Federal Reserve System

to the detriment of others. These special American characteristics help explain why our own central bank is different in form from most of its counterparts around the world.

One major difference is indicated in the very name of the institution: the Federal Reserve System. It does not have the word *central* or *bank* anywhere in its title, making it less suggestive of centralized power.

Another difference is the way the system is organized. Instead of a single central bank, the United States is divided into 12 Federal Reserve districts, each one served by its own Federal Reserve Bank. The 12 districts and the Federal Reserve Banks that serve them are shown in Figure 2. For example, the Federal Reserve Bank of Dallas serves a district consisting of Texas and parts of New Mexico and Louisiana, while the Federal Reserve Bank of Chicago serves a district including Iowa and parts of Illinois, Indiana, Wisconsin, and Michigan.

Another interesting feature of the Federal Reserve System is its peculiar status within the government. Strictly speaking, it is not even a *part* of any branch of government. But the *Fed* (as the system is commonly called) was created by Congress, and could be eliminated by Congress if it so desired. Second, both the president and Congress exert some influence on the Fed through their appointments of key officials in the system.

The Structure of the Fed

Figure 3 shows the organizational structure of the Federal Reserve System. Near the top is the Board of Governors, consisting of seven members who are appointed by the president and confirmed by the Senate for a 14-year term. The most powerful person at the Fed is the *chairman* of the Board of Governors—one of the seven governors who is appointed by the president, with Senate approval, to a 4-year term as chair.

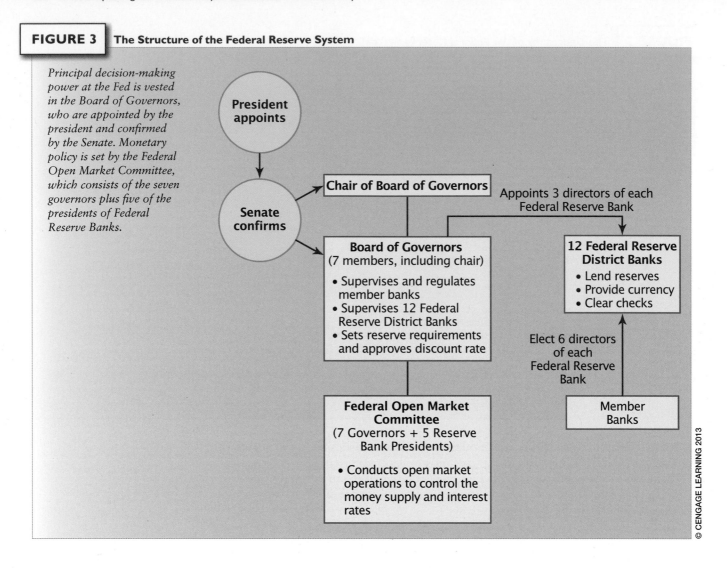

FIGURE 3   The Structure of the Federal Reserve System

Principal decision-making power at the Fed is vested in the Board of Governors, who are appointed by the president and confirmed by the Senate. Monetary policy is set by the Federal Open Market Committee, which consists of the seven governors plus five of the presidents of Federal Reserve Banks.

President appoints

Senate confirms

Chair of Board of Governors

Appoints 3 directors of each Federal Reserve Bank

Board of Governors
(7 members, including chair)

- Supervises and regulates member banks
- Supervises 12 Federal Reserve District Banks
- Sets reserve requirements and approves discount rate

12 Federal Reserve District Banks
- Lend reserves
- Provide currency
- Clear checks

Elect 6 directors of each Federal Reserve Bank

Federal Open Market Committee
(7 Governors + 5 Reserve Bank Presidents)

- Conducts open market operations to control the money supply and interest rates

Member Banks

© CENGAGE LEARNING 2013

In order to keep any president or Congress from having too much influence over the Fed, the 4-year term of the chair is *not* coterminous with the 4-year term of the president. As a result, every newly elected president inherits the Fed chair appointed by the previous president, and may have to wait several years before making an appointment of his own. For example, when President Obama took office in 2009, the chair of the Fed was Ben Bernanke—who had been appointed by President Bush in 2006. President Obama had to wait until January 2010 to appoint his "own" chair. (He decided to reappoint Ben Bernanke to another 4-year term ending January 2014.)

Each of the 12 Federal Reserve Banks is supervised by nine directors, three of whom are appointed by the Board of Governors. The other six are elected by private commercial banks, the official stockholders of the system. The directors of each Federal Reserve Bank choose a president of that bank, who manages its day-to-day operations.

Notice that Figure 3 refers to "member banks." Only about a third of the approximately 8,000 commercial banks in the United States are members of the Federal Reserve System. But they include all *national banks* (those chartered by the federal government) and about a thousand *state banks* (chartered by their state governments). All of the largest banks in the United States (e.g., Citibank, Bank of America, and Wells Fargo) are nationally chartered banks and therefore member banks as well.

The Federal Open Market Committee

Finally, we come to what most economists regard as the most important part of the Fed, the **Federal Open Market Committee (FOMC)**. As you can see in Figure 3, the FOMC consists of all seven governors of the Fed, along with five of the 12 district bank presidents.[2] The committee meets about eight times a year to discuss current trends in inflation, employment, GDP, interest rates, and more. After determining the current state of the economy, the FOMC decides if a change in course is needed. If so, it will take actions that—either by design or as a by-product of its actions—often change the nation's money supply.

The word "open" in the FOMC's name is ironic, because the committee's deliberations are private. Shortly after it reaches a decision, the FOMC releases a brief statement highlighting any major decisions and the reasoning behind them. But not even the president of the United States knows the details behind the decisions, or what the FOMC actually discussed at its meeting, until a full summary of the meeting is released three weeks later. And the FOMC waits several *years* before releasing a verbatim transcript of what was said at the meeting. The reason for the word "open" is that the committee exerts control over the nation's money supply and interest rates by buying and selling government bonds in the public ("open") bond market. Later, we will discuss how and why the FOMC does this.

Federal Open Market Committee (FOMC) A committee of Federal Reserve officials that establishes U.S. monetary policy.

The Functions of the Fed

The Federal Reserve has a variety of important responsibilities. Some of the most important are listed here.

Supervising and Regulating Banks. The Fed has long been one of the major regulatory agencies that oversees banks. For example, the Fed sets the required reserve ratio for all banks, not just member banks. And in 2010, new legislation expanded the Fed's role, giving it additional regulatory power over banks and extending its authority over many non-bank financial institutions as well. (See the Using the Theory section for more.) The Fed determines what sorts of loans and investments banks and other financial institutions are allowed to make, and it closely monitors their activities.

Acting as a "Bank for Banks." Commercial banks use the Fed in much the same way that ordinary citizens use commercial banks. For example, we've already seen that banks hold most of their reserves in reserve accounts with the Fed, and the Fed pays interest on these funds. In addition, banks can borrow from the Fed, just as we can borrow from our local bank. The Fed charges a special interest rate, called the **discount rate,** on loans that it makes to member banks.

Issuing Paper Currency. The Fed doesn't actually *print* currency; that is done by the government's Bureau of Engraving and Printing. But once printed, it is shipped to the Fed (under *very* heavy guard). The Fed, in turn, puts this currency into circulation. This is why every U.S. bill carries the label *Federal Reserve Note* on the top.

Check Clearing. Suppose you write a check for $1,000 to pay your rent. Your building's owner will deposit the check into his or her checking account, which is probably at a different bank than yours. Somehow, your rent payment must be

Discount rate The interest rate the Fed charges on loans to banks.

[2] Although all Reserve Bank presidents attend FOMC meetings, only 5 of the 12 presidents can vote on FOMC decisions. The president of the Federal Reserve Bank of New York has a permanent vote because New York is such an important financial center. But the remaining four votes rotate among the other district presidents.

transferred from your bank account to your landlord's account at the other bank, a process called *check clearing*. In some cases, the services are provided by private clearinghouses. But in many other cases—especially for clearing out-of-town checks—the Federal Reserve System performs the service by transferring funds from one bank's reserve account to another's.

Guiding the Macroeconomy: The Federal Reserve plays the lead role in guiding the macroeconomy. It uses a variety of tools to attempt to keep the economy as close to potential output as possible. The Fed tries to avoid not only painful recessions, but also booms that overheat the economy and lead to high inflation.

Dealing with Financial Crises: In times of financial crisis (as in 2008, when several large banks and other financial institutions collapsed), the Federal Reserve goes into overdrive. In addition to using its regular macroeconomic tools more aggressively, it also stands ready to act as the *lender of last resort*, to make sure that banks have enough reserves to meet their obligations to depositors. And it can use special emergency powers to intervene in financial markets more deeply, to prevent a crisis from spiraling out of control.

These tools the Fed uses to perform the last two functions—guiding the macroeconomy and dealing with financial crises—are often summarized by the phrase *monetary policy*. In the early 1980s, the Federal Reserve viewed the total *money supply* as its chief monetary policy tool. Today, the Fed and most other large central banks focus instead on *interest rates*. However, when the Fed tries to change interest rates, it often changes the money supply as well, as a by-product. In the next chapter, we'll look at how (and why) the Fed changes interest rates. But in the next section of this chapter, we'll discuss how various Fed actions—regardless of their goals—can change the money supply.

THE FED AND THE MONEY SUPPLY

The main type of Fed action that changes the money supply is called an open market operation.

Open market operations
Purchases or sales of government bonds by the Federal Reserve System.

> *In an* **open market operation,** *the Fed buys or sells government bonds in the bond market.*

When the Fed buys government bonds, it conducts an *open market purchase*. Selling government bonds is an *open market sale*. Let's consider open market purchases first.

How an Open Market Purchase Can Increase the Money Supply

How might an open market purchase cause the nation's money supply to increase? We'll make two special assumptions for now, to keep our analysis as simple as possible:

1. Banks never hold *excess reserves* (i.e., they never hold reserves beyond the minimum legal or necessary amounts).
2. Households and businesses do not withdraw or deposit *cash* (i.e., they remain satisfied holding the amount of cash they are initially holding).

We'll also assume, in our example, that the required reserve ratio is 0.1, so that for each $1,000 increase in deposits at a bank, its reserves must rise by $100.

With these assumptions, let's see what happens when the Fed purchases government bonds. Specifically, we'll suppose the Fed buys $100,000 worth of bonds from Acme Bond Company, a bond trading firm that has its own checking account with Mid-Size National Bank.

When the Fed buys the bonds from Acme, it will pay with a $100,000 check. Acme, in turn, will deposit this check into its account at Mid-Size National Bank. Mid-Size will immediately transmit an image of the check to the Fed, which will credit Mid-Size's reserve account for $100,000. Starting from the initial balance sheet you saw earlier in Table 1, Mid-Size's balance sheet will now undergo the following changes:

Changes in Mid-Size National Bank's Balance Sheet:

Action	Change in Assets	Change in Liabilities
Acme deposits $100,000 check from Fed	+ $100,000 in reserves	+ $100,000 in checking accts

Notice that in the table above, we show only *changes* in Mid-Size's balance sheet. Other balance sheet items—such as property and buildings, loans, government bonds, or shareholders' equity—do not change, so they are not listed here.

As you can see, Mid-Size has gained an asset—reserves—so we enter "+$100,000 in reserves" on the left side of the table. But Mid-Size also has a new liability: $100,000 in Acme's checking account. Because Mid-Size's balance sheet was in balance before Acme's deposit, and because assets and liabilities both grew by the same amount ($100,000), we know that the balance sheet still balances. As before, total assets are equal to total liabilities plus shareholders' equity.

Before we go further, let's take note of two important things that have happened. First, the Fed, by conducting an open market purchase, has *injected* $100,000 in *reserves* into the banking system. So far, these reserves are being held by Mid-Size Bank in its reserve account at the Fed.

The second thing to notice is easy to miss: The *money supply has already increased*. Why? Because checking accounts are part of the money supply, and they have increased by $100,000. As you are about to see, even more money will be created before our story ends.

To see what will happen next, let's take the point of view of Mid-Size's manager. She might reason as follows: "Our checking accounts have just increased by $100,000. So our reserves must rise by 10 percent of that amount, or $10,000. But our *actual* reserves have gone up by much more than that: $100,000. Therefore, we now have excess reserves equal to $100,000 − $10,000 = $90,000. Since the Fed is paying such a low interest rate on these excess reserves, it would be more profitable to lend them out." So Mid-Size will want to lend out $90,000.

Mid-Size could lend out $90,000 in cash from its vault. It would be more typical, however, for the bank to issue a $90,000 *check* to the borrower. Let's suppose the borrower is Paula, who wants a loan to buy new ovens for her restaurant, Paula's Pizza. When Paula deposits the $90,000 check from Mid-Size into her own bank account (at a bank we'll call "Second Bank"), the Federal Reserve—which keeps track of these transactions for the banking system—will transfer $90,000 from Mid-Size's reserve account to Second Bank's reserve account. The loan and the loss of reserves at Mid-Size will cause further changes in its balance sheet, as follows:

Changes in Mid-Size National Bank's Balance Sheet:

Action	Change in Assets	Change in Liabilities
Mid-Size Lends out Excess Reserves of $90,000	−$90,000 in reserves +$90,000 in loans	

By making the loan, Mid-Size has given up $90,000 in reserves in exchange for an asset of equal value—the $90,000 loan. (Remember: While loans are liabilities to the borrower, they are assets to banks.) Both changes are seen on the assets side of the balance sheet.

Let's now combine everything that has happened to Mid-Size's balance sheet, from the moment it got Acme's deposit to the lending out of its excess reserves. Reserves first rose by $100,000, then fell by $90,000, so their final change was +$10,000. Mid-Size also has $90,000 more in loans on the asset side, and $100,000 more in checking accounts on the liabilities side. From beginning to end, these are the net changes that have taken place on Mid-Size's balance sheet:

Changes in Mid-Size National Bank's Balance Sheet:

Action	Change in Assets	Change in Liabilities
Combined Effect of Acme's Deposit and Mid-Size's Loan	+$10,000 in reserves +$90,000 in loans	+$100,000 in checking accts

Notice that Mid-Size no longer has excess reserves: Compared to its initial situation, Mid-Size now has $100,000 more in checking accounts, and is holding $10,000 more in reserves. Its reserves rose by 10 percent of its checking accounts—just what a 10 percent required reserve ratio calls for. When a bank has no excess reserves, we say that it is "fully loaned up."

But there is still more to our story. Recall that when Mid-Size lent money to Paula and she deposited the loan proceeds into her checking account at Second Bank, the Fed added $90,000 to Second Bank's reserve account. So now *Second Bank* has excess reserves. Because its checking accounts rose by $90,000, it needs to hold 10 percent of that (or $9,000) as reserves, leaving it free to lend out the remaining $81,000. After making the loan, Second Bank will be left with a net increase of $9,000 in reserves ($90,000 minus the $81,000 loaned out), and its own balance sheet changes as follows:

Changes in Second Bank's Balance Sheet:

Action	Change in Assets	Change in Liabilities
Combined Effect of Paula's Deposit and Second Bank's Loan	+$9,000 in reserves +$81,000 in loans	+$90,000 in checking accts

But as you might have guessed, this isn't the end of the story either. Now some other bank (Third Bank) has just received the proceeds of the $81,000 loan made by Second Bank. Third Bank's reserves will rise by $81,000, it will hold onto $8,100 of those reserves, and lend out the excess ($72,900). And the process will continue. At each bank, more checking accounts are created, so the money supply increases at each stage. But each bank gets less in reserves, and creates less in new checking account funds, than the bank before. Eventually, the newly created checking accounts are so small that we can safely ignore them.

Table 2 summarizes the increases in checking accounts, reserves, and loans that will occur throughout the entire banking system. Notice that, at each bank, checking

TABLE 2

Bank	Checking Accounts	Reserves	Loans
Mid-Size National	+$100,000	+$10,000	+$90,000
Second Bank	+$90,000	+$9,000	+$81,000
Third Bank	+$81,000	+$8,100	+$72,900
Fourth Bank	+$72,900	+$7,290	+$65,610
…	…	…	…
Total Increase at All Banks	**+$1,000,000**	**+$100,000**	**+$900,000**

Effects of a $100,000 Open Market Purchase

© CENGAGE LEARNING 2013

accounts have increased by 10 times the increase in reserves, so no bank is holding excess reserves. Also note the *total* increase in checking accounts in the entire banking system: $1,000,000. How did we get this number? We know the $100,000 of reserves the Fed injected into the system are all being held by one bank or another, and all are required (there are no excess reserves). But with a required reserve ratio of 0.1, an additional $100,000 in total reserves will be required only if banks have, in total, an additional $1,000,000 in checking accounts.

The Money Multiplier

Let's go back and summarize what happened as a result of the Fed's open market purchase in our example. The Fed injected $100,000 in reserves into the banking system. As a result, checking deposits and the money supply rose by $1 million—10 times the injection in reserves. As you can verify, if the Fed had injected twice the amount of reserves ($200,000), the money supply would have increased by 10 times *that* amount ($2 million). In fact, *whatever* the injection of reserves, total checking deposits and the total money supply will increase by a factor of 10, so we can write:

Money multiplier The multiple by which the money supply changes after a change in reserves.

$$\Delta \text{Money Supply} = \Delta \text{Checking Deposits} = 10 \times \text{Reserve Injection}$$

The injection of reserves must be *multiplied* by the number 10 in order to get the change in the money supply that it causes. For this reason, we can say 10 is the *money multiplier* in this example.

> The **money multiplier** is the number by which we multiply the injection of reserves to get the total change in the money supply.

The size of the money multiplier depends on the value of the required reserve ratio (RRR). If the RRR had been 0.20 instead of 0.10, then each dollar of checking deposits would require 20 cents in reserves, or each dollar of additional reserves would support an additional $5 in deposits. In that case, our formula would be

$$\Delta \text{Money Supply} = 5 \times \text{Reserve Injection}$$

DANGEROUS CURVES

"Creating money" doesn't mean "creating wealth" Checking accounts are a means of payment, and banks create them. This is why we say that banks "create deposits" and "create money." But don't fall into the trap of thinking that money creation is the same as wealth creation.

To see why, think about what happened in our story when Acme Bond Dealers first deposited its $100,000 check from the Fed into Mid-Size National Bank. Acme was no wealthier: It gave up a $100,000 check from the Fed and ended up with $100,000 more in its checking account, for a net gain of zero. Similarly, the bank gained no additional wealth: It had $100,000 more in reserves, but it also owed Acme $100,000 more than before—once again, a net gain of zero.

And the same conclusion holds for every bank and every depositor in Table 2. When banks create new money, they do not create new wealth.

© AXL/SHUTTERSTOCK.COM

You may have already spotted the pattern here: In each case, the money multiplier is one divided by the required reserve ratio.

> *For any value of the required reserve ratio (RRR), the formula for the money multiplier is 1/RRR.*

In our example, the RRR was equal to 0.1, so the money multiplier had the value $1/0.1 = 10$.

Using our general formula for the money multiplier, we can state what happens when the Fed injects reserves into the banking system as follows:

$$\Delta \text{Money Supply} = \frac{1}{\text{RRR}} \times \Delta \text{Reserves}$$

How an Open Market Sale Can Decrease the Money Supply

Just as the Fed can increase the money supply by purchasing government bonds, it can also *decrease* the money supply by *selling* government bonds—an *open market sale*. Where does the Fed get the government bonds to sell? It has hundreds of billions of dollars worth of government bonds from open market purchases it has conducted in the past. On average, the Fed tends to increase the money supply each year, so it conducts more open market purchases than open market sales, and its supply of bonds keeps growing. So, except in unusual circumstances, we needn't worry that the Fed will run out of bonds to sell.

The effects of an open market sale are very similar to the effects of an open market purchase, but in the opposite direction. However, keeping track of what happens can be a bit tricky, so let's look at the first few steps. We'll suppose that the Fed now *sells* $100,000 in government bonds to Acme bond dealers. Acme will pay with a $100,000 check drawn on its account at Mid-Size. When the Fed gets the check, it will settle with Mid-Size by deducting $100,000 from the bank's reserve account. Mid-Size's balance sheet will thus change as follows:

Changes in Mid-Size National Bank's Balance Sheet:

Action	Change in Assets	Change in Liabilities
Acme writes a check for $100,000 to pay the Fed	−$100,000 in reserves	−$100,000 in checking accts

⚠ DANGEROUS CURVES

Selling bonds: Fed versus Treasury It's easy to confuse the Fed's open market sales with another type of government bond sale done by the U.S. Treasury.

The U.S. Treasury is the branch of government that collects taxes, pays for government purchases and transfers, and borrows to finance budget deficits. The Treasury borrows by issuing *new* government bonds and selling them to the public.

When the Fed conducts open market operations, however, it does not buy or sell *newly* issued bonds, but "secondhand bonds"—those already issued by the Treasury to finance past deficits. Thus, Fed bond sales are *not* government borrowing; they change the money supply, but have no direct effect on the government budget.

Now Mid-Size's manager reasons as follows: "Our checking accounts have just decreased by $100,000. So our required reserves are $10,000 less than before. But our actual reserves have dropped by much more than that: $100,000. Therefore, we now have *deficient reserves* equal to $100,000 − $10,000 = $90,000. We'll have to somehow get another $90,000 in reserves to meet our requirements." A bank that needs to acquire additional reserves has a few different options. But here, we'll explore just one of them: *calling in loans*.

In theory, calling in a loan means the bank would tell borrowers such as Paula's Pizza, "You know that new loan we gave you? Actually, we need it back." But in reality, bank loans are for specified time periods, and a bank cannot actually demand that a loan be repaid early. Our conclusion still holds, however. Most banks have a large volume of loans outstanding, with some being repaid each day. Typically, the funds will be lent out again the very same day they are repaid. A bank that needs to acquire reserves will simply reduce its rate of new lending on that day, thereby reducing its total amount of loans outstanding. This has the same effect as "calling in a loan."

The resulting changes for Mid-Size's balance sheet are as follows:

Changes in Mid-Size National Bank's Balance Sheet:

Action	Change in Assets	Change in Liabilities
Mid-Size "calls in" $90,000 in loans (reduces its outstanding loans volume by $90,000)	+$90,000 in reserves −$90,000 in loans	

© CENGAGE LEARNING 2013

What happens next? The $90,000 in loans paid back to Mid-Size came from checking accounts at some other bank, Second Bank. So now Second bank has lost $90,000 in reserves and checking accounts, and will have to "call in" loans equal to $81,000. And the process continues.

Keeping in mind that a withdrawal of reserves is a *negative change in reserves,* we can still use the money multiplier:

$$\Delta \text{Money Supply} = \frac{1}{\text{RRR}} \times \Delta \text{Reserves}$$

Applying it to our example, we have:

$$\Delta \text{Money Supply} = [1/0.1] \times (-\$100,000) = \quad \$1 \text{ million}$$

In other words, the Fed's $100,000 open market sale causes a $1 million decrease in the money supply.

Some Important Provisos about the Money Multiplier

The process of money creation and destruction as we've described it illustrates some basic ideas. But our formula for the money multiplier—$1/RRR$—is oversimplified. Among other things, it ignores changes in the behavior of the public and the banks that can reduce the value of the money multiplier.

Changes in the Public's Cash Holdings

In our simple story, we've assumed that the public does *not* change its cash holdings as the money supply changes. But as the money supply increases, the public will usually want to hold part of the increase in checking accounts, and part of the increase in cash. As a result, in each round of the money-creation process, some reserves will leak out of the banking system in the form of cash. This will lead to a smaller increase in lending and checking accounts than in our simple story.

Increased Reserve Holdings

Another assumption we've made in our simple story of money creation is that banks are always "fully loaned up"; that is, they hold the minimum required amount of reserves, and create the maximum amount of new checking deposits (the maximum amount of new loans). In reality, as we discussed earlier, banks sometimes hold *excess* reserves. If banks decide to *increase* their excess reserves as the Fed is injecting new reserves, each bank will lend out less than in our simple story, and the money supply will increase by less. This tends to make the money multiplier smaller than it would otherwise be.

It is even possible for the money multiplier to be zero. If, for example, interest rates dropped so low—say, down to the interest rate the Fed pays on reserves—then any new reserves injected into the system will be held by banks as excess reserves. Every bank manager would reason, "Why should we lend out funds if we can earn the same rate of return—with no risk—by holding the funds as reserves at the Fed?" Without new lending, the injection of reserves cannot create new money, so the money multiplier would be zero.

Other Fed Actions That Change the Money Supply

Open market purchases and sales are the most common way the Fed changes the money supply. But there are three additional Fed actions that can, at least in theory, change the money supply as well.

Changes in the Required Reserve Ratio

As long as banks are bound by legal reserve requirements, the Fed can set off the same process of deposit we've been describing by lowering the required reserve ratio. For example, suppose the Fed lowered the required reserve ratio from 0.10 to 0.05. Suddenly every bank in the system would find that its reserves—which used to support 10 times their value in checking deposits—could now support 20 times their value. To earn the highest profit possible, banks might then increase their lending, creating new checking deposits in the process. The money supply would increase.

On the other side, if the Fed *raised* the required reserve ratio, the process would work in reverse: All banks would suddenly find that—given their reserves—their checking accounts exceed the legal maximum. They would be forced to reduce their volume of outstanding loans, and the money supply would decrease.

For a variety of reasons, however, the Fed cannot count on the effectiveness of this tool. For example, suppose banks are already holding excess reserves. Then lowering the required reserve ratio will only make the bank regard more of its existing reserves as "excess," while raising the ratio will just make the bank regard less of its reserves as "excess." Neither action would change the amount of lending or total checking deposits.

Not surprisingly, changes in the required reserve ratio are rare in the United States. The most recent change was in April 1992, when the Fed lowered the ratio for most checking deposits from 12 percent to 10 percent. But in some countries—such as China—the ratio is changed much more often, and is one of the key tools of the central bank.

Changes in the Discount Rate

The discount rate, mentioned earlier, is the rate the Fed charges banks when it lends them reserves. In principle, a lower discount rate (which enables banks to borrow reserves from the Fed more cheaply) might encourage banks to borrow more reserves. Borrowed reserves works just like any other injection of reserves into the banking system: They increase the money supply.

On the other side, a *rise* in the discount rate would make it more expensive for banks to hang on to borrowed reserves, so they would pay back some reserves they had borrowed. This withdrawal of reserves from the banking system would lead to a decrease in the money supply.

So much for the theory. In reality, except during periods of great financial turmoil, banks have been hesitant to borrow from the Fed at all. They fear that potential investors will see such borrowing as a sign of weakness. After all, if the bank is turning to the Fed, it must be having trouble raising funds through customer deposits or other privately available means. Because of this hesitancy to borrow from the Fed, changes in the discount rate typically have little effect on bank borrowing, bank reserves, or the money supply. Although the Fed changes the discount rate often, it is usually combined with other, more powerful Fed actions (such as open market operations) to achieve the Fed's goals.

Changes in the Interest Rate on Reserves

Before the Fed began paying interest on reserves (IOR) in 2008, a bank's opportunity cost for holding reserves was the interest it could earn by lending them out. But once the Fed started paying IOR, the opportunity cost of holding reserves was reduced. If the Fed lowers the IOR rate, the opportunity cost of holding excess reserves rises. So lowering the IOR rate is another tool the Fed can use to encourage bank lending, and in the process, increase the money supply. Similarly, an *increase* in the IOR rate would reduce the opportunity cost of holding excess reserves; banks would decrease their volume of loans and hold more excess reserves instead. The money supply would shrink.

From 2008 to 2011, the Fed kept the IOR rate very low (0.25 percent), and did not use changes in the IOR rate as a policy tool. In the future, however, many economists believe that changes in IOR rate will become one of the Fed's major policy tools.

* * *

In the next chapter, we'll be combining what you've learned about banks, the Fed, and the money supply to explore how the Fed guides the macroeconomy. But what you've already learned about these topics can help you understand a potential threat to the financial system: bank failures and banking panics.

BANKING PANICS

In the 1946 film, *It's a Wonderful Life*, George Bailey (played by James Stewart) owns a bank-like financial institution, "Building and Loan." A rumor has started in the town that Building and Loan is in financial trouble and might close. The rumor is false. But townspeople—fearful of losing the funds in their accounts—begin arriving at the door, demanding cash. George Bailey tries to explain to them why they can't cash out their deposits . . . yet. Here's a passage of dialogue from the screenplay:

```
                    GEORGE
    No, but you . . . you . . . you're thinking
    of this place all wrong. As if I had the money
    back in a safe. The money's not here. Your
    money's in Joe's house . . . (to one of the
    men) . . . right next to yours. And in the
    Kennedy house, and Mrs. Macklin's house, and
    a hundred others. Why, you're lending them
    the money to build, and then, they're going
    to pay it back to you as best they can.
```

George is arguing (truthfully) that his institution is *not* in financial trouble. In the dry terminology of balance sheets, it has enough assets to cover all of its deposit liabilities. The assets are mostly the loans on its balance sheet—loans that people took out to buy the homes in the town. The problem is not the long-run financial health condition of the bank, but rather that the banking system is a

Fractional reserve system A system in which banks hold only a fraction of their deposit liabilities as reserves.

fractional reserve system—its reserves are only a fraction of its total deposits—so it cannot meet the claims of all of its depositors at once. It has invested their deposits in assets that pay back over the long run. But sometimes, many or all depositors become worried and want their cash *now*.

This, in a nutshell, has been the problem of banks and the banking system throughout most of financial history. It's a problem that—at least in the regular banking system—has been solved in the United States and many other countries. To understand the problem and how it was solved, let's take a step back and discuss how a bank can sometimes get into trouble.

Bank Insolvency and Bank Failure

Insolvent Condition of a firm (e.g., a bank) when total assets are less than total liabilities.

A bank becomes **insolvent** when its total assets are less than its total liabilities (or, equivalently, when its shareholders' equity becomes negative). When an insolvent bank goes out of business, we say that the bank has *failed*.

What causes a bank to become insolvent? The most frequent reason is the bankruptcies of businesses and households that have borrowed money from the bank. Table 3 shows how such bankruptcies would affect the balance sheet of Mid-Size National Bank. Ignore the red entries for now, and concentrate on the initial black entries that are taken from Mid-Size's balance sheet in Table 1. Initially, the bank has $800 million in loans (in black) that appear on the assets side. These loans—as long as the bank expects them to be repaid—are something of value that the bank owns. The bank could, in theory, sell them to another bank for $800 million. Alternatively, it can hang on to the loans and wait for repayment. In the latter case, the bank would get $800 million *plus* earn interest over time while it is waiting.

Notice that the bank begins with positive shareholders' equity, equal to $125 million. This tells us the bank could cease operations, sell off its $1,000 million in assets, and it would have more than enough to pay off all of its liabilities (including honoring all of its deposits). Moreover, it would have $125 million left over. That $125 million belongs to the bank's owners—its shareholders.

Now suppose that Mid-Size gets some bad news: $150 million of its loans will never be paid back, because the businesses and households that owed the money have declared bankruptcy. As a result, $150 million in loans must be "written off"

TABLE 3

Bad Loans Cause Mid-Size Bank to Become Insolvent

Assets		Liabilities and Shareholders' Equity	
Property and buildings	$ 40 million	Checking Account Deposits	$ 600 million
Government and Corporate Bonds	$ 100 million	Other Deposits	$ 200 million
Loans	$ 800 million $ 650 million	Bank Borrowing	$ 75 million
Cash in Vault and ATMs	$ 10 million		
In Accounts with Federal Reserve	$ 50 million	Shareholders' Equity	$ 125 million −$ 25 million
Total Assets	**$1,000 million** **$ 850 million**	**Total Liabilities and Shareholders' Equity**	**$1,000 million** **$ 850 million**

of the balance sheet; they are now worthless. The new (red-type) entries show how Mid-Size's balance sheet will change.

On the left side, outstanding loans are reduced from $800 million to $650 million, so total assets decrease from $1,000 million to $850 million. On the right side, the bank continues to owe the same amounts to various parties: $600 million to its checking account holders, $200 million to its other depositors (who hold savings accounts and CDs), and $75 million to its *creditors* (those who have lent the bank money and have not yet been repaid). These entries do *not* change. The only change on the right side is shareholders' equity. Subtracting the bank's liabilities ($875 million) from its assets (now $850 million), we find that shareholders' equity has become negative, equal to −$25 million. Now, even if the bank were to sell all of its assets to other banks, it would not have enough funds to honor all of its liabilities. The bank is *insolvent*.

> A bank is insolvent (it has "failed") when its total liabilities exceed its total assets, so that shareholders' equity is negative.

What will happen?

In the days before the banking system was regulated and strict financial reporting was enforced, an insolvent bank could continue to operate for some time. That's because on any given day only a small fraction of its checking account balances would be withdrawn. So as long as the bank had enough cash on hand to meet normal requests for withdrawals, its day of reckoning could be postponed.

Until, that is, word of the bank's insolvency leaked out.

How a Banking Panic Develops

Once depositors hear that their bank is insolvent, they will all try to be first in line to get their funds back. They would know that banks meet requests for withdrawals on a first-come, first-served basis, and those who wait might not get any cash at all. We call this situation—in which all depositors try to withdraw their funds at once—a **run on the bank.**

Ironically, even a bank in good financial health, with more than enough assets to cover its liabilities, could face a bank run if there is a rumor that it is insolvent. As you've seen in this chapter, even a solvent bank does not keep enough reserves on hand to cover all of its checking account liabilities. In the event of a run, it could not sell all of its loans and other assets quickly enough to get the cash needed to honor its withdrawals. It would have to close its doors and refuse (at least for a while) some of its customers' requests. This is not the same as a bank failure if the bank is solvent. But a temporary closure would create problems for a bank, because it would add fuel to the rumors that the bank was insolvent. This is what happened to George Bailey in *It's a Wonderful Life.*

A **banking panic** is when a run on many banks occurs simultaneously. In the past, a typical panic would begin with some unexpected event, such as the failure of a large bank. During recessions, for example, many businesses go bankrupt, so fewer bank loans are repaid. A bank that had an unusual number of "bad loans" would be in trouble, and if the public found out about this, there might be a run on that bank. The bank would fail, and many depositors would find that they had lost their deposits.

But that would not be the end of the story. Hearing that their neighbors' bank has failed might lead others to question the health of their own banks. Just to be sure, they might withdraw their own funds, preferring to ride out the storm and keep their cash at home. As we've seen, even healthy banks cannot withstand the pressure of a bank run. They, too, would have to close their doors, creating more worry about other banks' health, and so on.

Run on the bank An attempt by many of a bank's depositors to withdraw their funds.

Banking panic A situation in which fearful depositors attempt to withdraw funds from many banks simultaneously.

In the past, a banking panic would force many banks to "close their doors" (be unable to honor their depositors' requests for funds) even if they were solvent.

Banking panics can cause serious problems for a nation. First, there is the hardship suffered by people who lose their accounts when their bank fails. Second, the withdrawal of cash decreases the banking system's reserves which leads—through the money multiplier—to a decrease in the money supply. (The effect is the same as when the Fed drains reserves out of the system with an open market sale.) In the next chapter, you will learn that a decrease in the money supply can cause a recession. In a banking panic, the money supply can decrease suddenly and severely, causing a serious recession.

There were five major banking panics in the United States from 1863 to 1907. Indeed, it was the banking panic of 1907 that convinced Congress to establish the Federal Reserve System. From the beginning, one of the Fed's primary functions was to act as *a lender of last resort,* providing solvent banks with enough cash to meet their obligations in the event of a run on the bank.

But the creation of the Fed did not, in itself, solve the problem. Figure 4 shows the number of bank failures each year since 1921. As you can see, banking panics

| FIGURE 4 | Bank Failures in the United States, 1921–2011 |

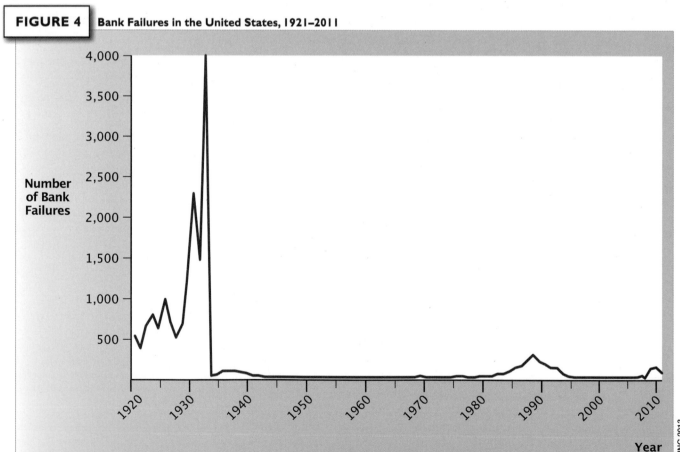

The bank failure rate was high even after the Fed was created in 1913. It peaked when a major banking panic struck during the Great Depression and a large number of banks failed. The creation of the Federal Deposit Insurance Corporation in 1933 strengthened faith in the stability of the banking system. Even during the financial crisis of 2008–2009, bank failures were far fewer than in the 1930s.

continued to plague the financial system even after the Fed was created. The Fed did not always act forcefully enough or quickly enough to prevent the panic from spreading.

The Great Depression is a good example of this problem. In late 1929 and 1930, many banks began to fail because of bad loans. Then, from October 1930 until March 1933, more than one-third of all banks shut down as frantic depositors stormed bank after bank, demanding to withdraw their funds—even from banks that were in reasonable financial health. Many economists believe that the banking panic of 1930–1933 turned what would have been just a serious recession into the Great Depression. Officials of the Federal Reserve System, not quite grasping the seriousness of the problem, stood by and let it happen.[3]

The End of Banking Panics

As you can see in Figure 4, banking panics were largely eliminated after 1933. There was a moderate increase in bank *failures* during the late 1980s and early 1990s, and another rise—including the failure of some very large banks—in 2008 and 2009 (more on that later). But even these periods of rising bank failures did *not* lead to system-wide banking panics and widespread failures of other banks. Why the dramatic improvement?

Largely, for two reasons. First, the Federal Reserve learned an important lesson from the Great Depression, and it now stands ready to inject reserves into the system more quickly in a crisis. Moreover, in 1933 Congress created the Federal Deposit Insurance Corporation (FDIC) to reimburse those who lose their deposits. If your bank is insured by the FDIC (today, accounts are covered in 99 percent of all banks) and cannot honor its obligations for any reason—bad loans, poor management, or even theft—the FDIC will reimburse you up to the first $250,000 you lose in each of your bank accounts.

The FDIC has had a major impact on the psychology of the banking public. Imagine that you hear your bank is about to go under. As long as you have less than $250,000 in your account, you will not care. Why? Because even if the rumor turns out to be true, you will be reimbursed in full. The resulting calmness on your part, and on the part of other depositors, will prevent a run on the bank. This makes it very unlikely that bank failures will spread throughout the system.

But FDIC protection comes with costs. First, banks must pay insurance premiums to the FDIC, and they pass this cost on to their depositors and borrowers by charging higher interest rates on loans and higher fees for their services.

And there is a more serious cost. The very same insurance system that prevents banking *panics* can make bank *failures* more likely. Why? With depositors protected in the event of a bank failure, bank managers have less incentive to develop a reputation for prudence in lending funds. After all, depositors will be happy to keep their money in the bank anyway.

This means that FDIC protection—with no other change in the banking system—would lead to more risky lending by banks, and more bank failures. The FDIC would have to pay out more to depositors, and FDIC insurance premiums would rise for all banks, even those that did not take excessive risks. Even worse, if the FDIC ever ran out of funds, it would have to get more from the U.S. Treasury—which means the losses would fall on taxpayers.

---

[3] The most exhaustive account of Fed actions during the Great Depression is the book by Milton Friedman and Anna Jacobson Schwartz, *A Monetary History of the United States, 1867–1960* (Princeton, NJ: Princeton University Press, 1963), especially p. 358.

But look again at Figure 4. Bank failures have actually become less likely after FDIC insurance was introduced in 1933. A major reason for this is another change in the banking system that accompanied insurance protection: increased government *regulation* of banks.

The Role of Regulation

The logic behind bank regulations is straightforward: *Someone* must watch over the banks to keep the failure rate low. If the public has no incentive to pay attention, then government must do the job. Most economists believe that if we want the freedom from banking panics provided by the FDIC, we must also accept the strict regulation and close monitoring of banks provided by the Fed and other agencies in the United States, and by various central banks and agencies in other advanced countries.

One of the key ways banks are regulated is through continuous monitoring of their financial condition, with a focus on the *shareholders' equity* entry in the balance sheet. This entry represents funds that the bank's owners (shareholders) have "put into" the bank. It includes any amounts paid for shares when they were first purchased, as well as any bank profits earned over the years that were reinvested in the bank (rather than distributed to the shareholders as dividends).

How do we know that shareholders' equity is what shareholders themselves have put into the bank? Because all of the bank's assets were obtained with funds that came from either (1) the shareholders or (2) others. Funds obtained from *others*—deposits or bank borrowing—are listed on the liabilities side of the balance sheet. Thus, when we subtract total liabilities from total assets, we are left with the funds contributed and left in the bank by the shareholders themselves.

Capital Requirements

Bank capital Another name for shareholders' equity in a bank.

When discussing the financial condition of a bank, shareholders' equity is often called **bank capital.** Over time, the monitoring and informal regulation of bank capital (shareholders' equity) has been strengthened with legal *capital requirements:* Banks must hold a significant percentage of their assets as bank capital. This encourages them to lend responsibly.

To see how this encouragement works, look back at Table 1, where Mid-Size National Bank has bank capital (shareholders' equity) of $125 million. Suppose that $50 million of Mid-Size's loans go bad, so their value goes to zero. Then total assets and bank capital will drop by $50 million. Now, if Mid-Size were to go out of business—selling all of its assets and paying off its liabilities—the shareholders would end up with $50 million less than they would get before. Thus, the shareholders take the full hit from defaults on loans the bank has made—as long as the "hit" is less than or equal to initial bank capital.

Capital Ratio A bank's capital (shareholders' equity) as a percentage of its total assets.

The greater is Mid-Size's capital, the more its shareholders—who ultimately control the bank—have to lose from bad loans. In Table 1, Mid-Size has total assets of $1,000 million, and bank capital of $125 million, so it has a **capital ratio** (capital as a percent of assets) equal to 12.5 percent. That means that the total value of its assets could fall by 12.5 percent (by $125 million) and the bank would still have enough assets to cover all of its liabilities. Losses up to 12.5 percent of assets would fall entirely on the bank's shareholders, rather than on the FDIC, the bank's creditors, or taxpayers.

In practice, capital requirements are complex. The percentage of total assets a bank must hold as capital depends on the riskiness of the bank's asset mix. That risk, in turn, is determined by government guidelines and private agencies that rate various assets. But when a bank's capital falls below its (risk-based) requirement, it must act quickly to meet the requirement again. It can do so by acquiring more capital (say, selling newly issued shares of stock), or reducing the risk of its asset mix (selling risky assets, such as subprime mortgages, and replacing them with safer assets, such as government bonds).

In setting bank capital requirements, the Fed and other regulatory agencies try to balance two opposing goals. Higher capital ratios provide greater incentives for banks to avoid risky loans. This reduces the likelihood of bank failures that pass losses onto non-owners. But higher capital ratios reduce the amount of interest-earning assets a bank can hold for each dollar of capital that the owners have invested. This reduces the rate of return to the bank's owners, and discourages people from forming or investing in banks.

A similar tradeoff exists with other bank regulations. For example, regulations that encourage banks to lend only to the most credit-worthy customers help to prevent bank failures. But they can also prevent some loans that, from society's point of view, would be beneficial (such as a loan to start a new, innovative business).

THE BANKING SYSTEM VERSUS THE SHADOW BANKING SYSTEM

Until the financial crisis of 2008, it appeared to most policy makers that banking regulations (including capital requirements) in the U.S. and around the world had struck the right balance. After all, banks were profitable, the banking industry and lending were growing, and the rate of bank failures was very low. But in a different part of the financial system—sometimes called the *shadow banking system*—trouble was brewing. In order to understand what was different about the shadow banking system, let's first look at the regular banking system from a broad perspective.

Another Look at the Banking System

When economists and government officials speak in general terms about "banks" and the "banking system," they mean not just commercial banks, but all institutions that take deposits and are closely regulated by government agencies. So, broadly speaking, the banking system includes savings and loan associations (S&Ls), credit unions, and other similar institutions. All of these entities share four characteristics:

1. Short-term liabilities
2. Long-term assets
3. Liabilities include government-insured deposits
4. Close regulation by government

The first characteristic—short-term liabilities—means that most of the funds that come into the bank can be demanded back on short notice. Checking deposits—which can be cashed out at any time—are an example. This promise of ready access to cash is what entices depositors to put their funds in the bank in the first place. By providing the convenience of ready access, depositors are willing to accept a relatively low interest rate—sometimes, no interest at all.

The second characteristic—long-term assets—means that the assets the bank acquires (when it lends) pay off over long periods of time. A home mortgage or mortgage-backed security, for example, typically earns revenue over 30 years, unless mortgage borrowers sell their homes early. Many corporate bonds mature in 10 years or longer. Borrowers will pay relatively high interest rates to borrow long term, and this is how the bank earns income: It earns more on its long-term assets than it pays on its short-term liabilities.

But how can the bank provide short-term access to its depositors while committing their funds to long-term loans? The answer is found in the law of large numbers. While each depositor is free to cash out on short notice, *total* outflows and inflows roughly balance out each day, and the bank's fractional reserves can take care of any small difference. A solvent bank can continue to keep lending out long-term while honoring requests to cash out deposits as long as it can avoid a bank run. And bank runs are avoided by the third characteristic of the banking system: much of their liabilities are *deposits,* insured by the government (or a government-backed organization). And as you've learned, deposit insurance is the reason banks must have the fourth characteristic: close regulation by government.

Non-Banks and the Shadow Banking System

Banks are not the only financial intermediaries in the economy. Other financial institutions that channel funds from savers to borrowers are known as *non-bank financial intermediaries.* Some economists have taken to calling them "non-banks" for short, and we'll use that term in this book. Collectively, non-bank financial intermediaries comprise what is sometimes called the **shadow banking system.**

Shadow banking system The entire collection of non-bank financial intermediaries.

Non-bank A financial intermediary less strictly regulated than a bank, and with no government-guaranteed deposits.

Non-banks in the shadow banking system share four characteristics:

1. Short-term liabilities
2. Long-term assets
3. Liabilities do *not* include government-insured deposits
4. *Not* closely regulated by government

Let's consider the four characteristics of these shadow-banking institutions in more detail.

Like banks, non-banks carry short-term liabilities on their balance sheets and invest in long-term assets. But these the short-term liabilities are not customer deposits. Instead they represent funds the non-bank has *borrowed*—from regular banks, pension funds, money market funds, individual households, and more. Much of this borrowing is very short-term—often just days or weeks—at relatively low interest rates. These borrowed funds are *not* insured by the government, so non-banks (until the financial crisis) faced few government regulations. The thinking was that you lend to a non-bank at your own risk. So if the non-bank fails and you lose what you've loaned to them, it's a private matter because taxpayers aren't guaranteeing your funds.

An example of a non-bank was the firm Lehman Brothers. Instead of depositing funds in a regular bank, you could provide the funds to Lehman by buying one of its corporate bonds—a promise from Lehman to return your funds, with interest, within days or weeks. Alternatively, you could put your savings in a regular bank, and the *bank* might lend to Lehman. Either way, Lehman would invest what it borrowed in a variety of assets that pay off over a long period, including mortgages, mortgage-backed securities, commercial real estate, or any financial asset or investment that Lehman's traders thought would earn the firm a profit.

How does a non-bank deal with the timing disparity between its long-term assets and short-term liabilities? In a way roughly similar to banks. But instead of balancing inflows and outflows of deposits like banks, non-banks rely on the ability to *roll over* their short-term debts: paying back what is due each day with new short-term borrowing, often from the same lender. As long as it can avoid a "bank run" and remain solvent, a non-bank can continue to borrow short-term and invest long-term indefinitely.

But what do we mean by a "run" on a non-bank? It has no deposits, so there is no angry mob demanding its money, as with a traditional bank run. Instead, a run on a non-bank occurs passively and quietly. It results from the simple word "no." Those that have been providing short-term loans to the non-bank in the past simply stop lending. Suddenly, the institution finds that it cannot get new loans to pay back the old ones coming due each day.

During the 1990s and 2000s, the shadow banking system grew larger, more complex, and more interconnected with the regular banking system. When the financial crisis hit, it became clear that bank regulations—including bank capital requirements—had not struck the right balance. Financial institutions around the world—including regular banks—failed. And governments had to come to the rescue. The result was a major overhaul of financial system regulations in the United States and many other countries. The Using the Theory section explains how the financial crisis happened, and how the new regulations might reduce the chance of it happening again.

The 1980s and Early 1990s: A Reminder

Before we get to the recent financial crisis, let's briefly consider an earlier episode. Look again at Figure 4, and notice the rise in bank failures of the late 1980s and the early 1990s. Most of these failures occurred in state-chartered banks. At the time, these banks were less closely regulated by the Fed, and were often insured by state agencies instead of the FDIC. When a few banks with insufficient capital went bankrupt because highly speculative loans turned sour, insurance funds in several states were drained. Citizens in those states began to fear that insufficient funds were left to insure their own deposits, and the psychology of banking panics took over. To many observers, the experience of the late 1980s and early 1990s was a reminder of the need for a sound insurance system, along with high capital requirements for banks, and close monitoring of the banking system.

AP PHOTO/DOUGLAS C. PIZAC

THE FINANCIAL CRISIS OF 2008

In 2008, the United States and dozens of other countries experienced a financial crisis—a major disruption of the financial system that seriously affected lending and other financial services. This is hard to see in Figure 4, where the rise in bank failures in the late 2000s looks rather modest, with just a few hundred (out of about 8,000) banks failing. While the figure does tells us that we managed to avoid a widespread banking panic, it does not begin to suggest the scope of the crisis, for several reasons.

First, the figure tells us nothing about the *size* of the banks that failed or the extent of losses suffered by their shareholders and creditors. Nor does it tell us anything about losses suffered by banks that survived. When the crisis ended, preliminary estimates of total losses in asset values at U.S. banks ranged well beyond $1 trillion, with at least another trillion lost in banks outside the U.S. Some respectable estimates were two or three times as high.

How did these losses come about? You've already learned about the event that initiated these losses: the collapse of housing prices beginning in 2007 (see Chapter 4) and the recession that followed (see the previous chapter). As housing prices fell and income declined, millions of homeowners began to default on their mortgages. Banks in the United States and around the world had invested heavily in these mortgages, especially through their purchases of *mortgage-backed securities*. Each mortgage-backed security paid its holder interest based, in turn, on the mortgage payments of hundreds or even thousands of individual homeowners. With default rates rising, no one wanted to buy these securities at prices even close to their previous value.

This presented banks with a serious problem. By law, these securities were supposed to be valued at the price they would sell for in the open market. But those prices were plummeting. In this chapter, you've learned how such a fall in asset values can affect a bank's balance sheet: Total assets and bank capital (shareholders' equity) declines. A big hit to bank capital—even if it remained positive—could bring a bank below its legal capital requirement. And if bank capital becomes negative, the bank would fail. The process we've described so far is summarized in Figure 5, in the boxes labeled 1, 2, and 3. (Ignore the other boxes for now.)

As bank capital declined, banks had three choices:

1. *Acquire more capital by issuing and selling new shares*. This option was unappealing, because bank share prices were plummeting. Selling shares would mean dividing the bank's future profits among more owners, even though the new shares were purchased at bargain prices.
2. *Reduce the risk of their assets*. By selling risky assets and replacing them with safer ones, a solvent bank could reduce its capital requirement and stay within the law. Banks tried to do this . . . all at the same time. But these "distress sales" of mortgage-backed securities and other risky assets caused their prices to fall even further. The drop in price was so severe that selling the assets—and recording the resulting huge losses on balance sheets—would deplete bank capital even more and might even expose the bank as insolvent. As a result, banks—for the most part—held on to these securities, which were soon labeled "toxic assets" by government officials and the media.

FIGURE 5   The Downward Spiral for Banks

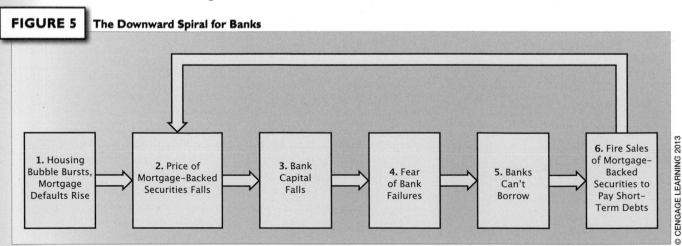

3. *Wait and hope.* If a bank could hold onto its "toxic assets," and adjust their values downward only gradually and partially, they could appear (for a while) to have more capital than a full adjustment would show. The bank could then hope that—after the crisis was over—the market price of the assets would rise, or that bank profits earned over time would add enough to bank capital to get them out of trouble.

Many banks in the U.S. and around the world chose this third, wait-and-hope strategy. They exploited existing leeway in accounting rules, won some changes in those rules, and found other ways to delay adjusting the asset values on their balance sheets.

This choice had an unfortunate side effect. The "toxic assets" were complex and difficult for outsiders to value. Because banks were known to be delaying balance sheet changes, no one was sure *which* banks had suffered the biggest losses and might be about to fail. The result was a reluctance to lend to banks *in general*—by anyone with funds to lend, including other banks and non-bank financial institutions. Unfortunately, most banks need to borrow funds every week—some every day—just to pay back debts coming due from earlier borrowing (such as the $75 million in bank borrowing on Mid-Size's balance sheets in our example). Without the ability to continue borrowing, banks would have to sell even more assets to pay back the debts coming due, causing the market value of the assets to fall further, and creating bigger problems for banks throughout the system. In Figure 5, this process is summarized in boxes 4, 5, and 6. Note that box 6 leads us back to box 2 (a further fall in asset prices) causing us to loop around again.

Still, banks had at least one thing going for them: Most of their liabilities were *deposits*, rather than short term debts. And thanks to the FDIC (and similar insurance in other countries), banks did *not* have to worry about bank runs. Depositors kept their funds in the banks, and a "banking panic" among depositors was avoided in the United States, as well as other advanced countries.

But the crisis *did* create a system-wide run—indeed, a panic—in the shadow banking system.

The Shadow Banking Panic

During the financial crisis of 2008, the sequence of events for non-banks began just as it did for banks: First, mortgage-backed securities declined in value, causing a drop in capital (shareholders' equity). Second, fearing these institutions might fail, lenders would only lend to them for very short periods and at very high interest rates. Third, the institutions had to continue paying off short-term debts as they came due, which meant they either had to pay very high interest rates to roll over their debt, or had to sell assets just as everyone else was selling them—at fire-sale prices. Either option reduced their capital further.

But for non-banks, the situation was even more dire than for banks, because they lacked two key advantages that banks had: insured deposits and government regulation. While a bank could count on its customers keeping its deposits in the bank, non-banks had no deposits; they had only short-term *debts*. And the debts had to be paid as they came due. Non-banks could not use the "wait-and-hope" strategy that banks used.

Also, because they were not closely regulated, non-banks held very little capital relative to their assets. For example, at the start of the crisis, commercial banks typically had capital ratios of about 10 percent; for many non-banks (such as Lehman Brothers and Bear Stearns), the figure was 3 percent or less. Another way to say this is: Non-banks were very highly *leveraged* (see the appendix to this chapter). Potential lenders knew that even a 3 percent loss in total asset value would make these institutions insolvent . . . which is precisely why they were hesitant to lend to them.

FIGURE 6   How Non-Banks Contributed to Problems for Banks

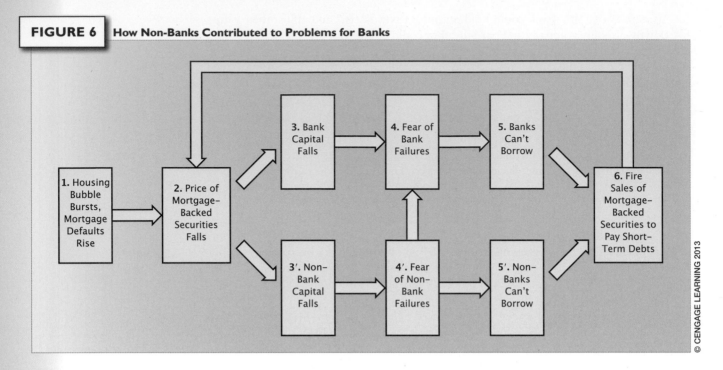

The crisis peaked in September 2008 when one of the largest of these institutions—Lehman Brothers—declared bankruptcy. Suddenly, it became clear to lenders that lending to non-banks, even for a short time, and at very high interest rates, wasn't worth the risk. The flow of credit to non-banks ceased. Their only option to pay back debts coming due was to sell their assets at fire-sale prices, and watch their capital disappear. Of course, all the selling made asset prices fall further. Figure 6 adds these events in the shadow banking system (Boxes 3′ through 5′), showing a more complete picture of the downward spiral affecting the entire financial system.

The figure also highlights the two main ways that events in the shadow banking system infected the regular banking system. First, the non-banks held many of the same assets as the banks. This intensified the fire sales of assets (Box 6) causing their prices to fall even further (Box 2), which further worsened capital at the banks (Box 3).

Second, many banks had extended loans to the non-banks. If a major non-bank failed, then these loans—assets to the banks—might become worthless, forcing the banks into insolvency. Thus, fears that non-banks might become insolvent (Box 4′) added to the fears that banks would become insolvent (Box 4).

The interconnections between banks and non-banks were not limited to the United States; banks in England, Ireland, France, Germany, Switzerland, Iceland, and more held the same types of risky assets, and had extended loans to non-banks in the U.S. and their own countries.

Bank Failures and Government Rescue

As the crisis unfolded, it became clear that falling asset prices—especially for mortgage-backed securities—were threatening the solvency of not just the shadow banking system, but the regular banking system as well. The Federal Reserve responded in a variety of ways—including emergency loans to financial institutions, and various policies designed to boost the prices of mortgage-backed securities. We'll discuss these

Fed actions—and the logic behind them—in the next chapter. But the U.S. government responded too, with an unusual and controversial program that we turn to now.

TARP

In October 2008, Congress approved the Bush administration's request to fund the *Troubled Asset Relief Program (TARP)*. The program authorized the government to purchase $700 billion in mortgage-backed securities and similar assets (for comparison, the government's entire annual budget for national defense in 2008 was $616 billion). Purchases of these assets, it was hoped, would boost their prices, thereby increasing shareholders' equity and slowing the spread of insolvency through the financial system. If all worked as planned, the government would hold the risky assets until the crisis was over, and then sell them back to private investors, perhaps even turning a profit.

But in a controversial move, TARP was soon repurposed. The government decided it would be quicker and more effective to invest in financial institutions *directly*, by buying ownership shares in them. By boosting shareholders' equity, fears of insolvency would dissipate, renewing their ability to borrow from the private sector as their short-term loans became due. The government used TARP funds to buy shares of stock in banks, as well as a major non-bank (the insurance company AIG) and even a major automobile company (General Motors). Both the Bush administration (which initiated and repurposed TARP) and the Obama administration (which continued it) defended the program as a distasteful but necessary intervention to help prevent a global financial meltdown.

But TARP angered many Americans. The government, by borrowing from the public to purchase ownership shares in private companies, had put taxpayers at risk. If the shares declined in value, or became worthless, taxpayers would still have to pay interest on the government's debt. Moreover, TARP—and other actions by the Fed and the government—ended up helping some very wealthy investors, as well as highly-paid traders, CEOs, and other top employees of financial institutions. These were the very people whose decisions helped to create the housing bubble and bust, which led to the financial crisis and the recession.

In the end, the government used less than $400 billion of the $700 billion that had been authorized under TARP. The program's *losses* were less than this—perhaps as low as $25 billion—because most of the government's shares rose in value. Although hundreds of banks did fail, the share purchases helped restore confidence in some of the nation's largest banks and financial institutions, helped to keep the financial system running, and thus prevented the recession from being even worse than it was. But for the general public, TARP—and similar government rescues in other countries—left a bitter aftertaste, and provided the political momentum for a major overhaul of banking regulations in the U.S. and Europe.

The Dodd-Frank Act

In the U.S., the authority for new banking regulations was provided by the *Dodd-Frank Wall Street Reform and Consumer Protection Act* of 2010. A major goal of the Dodd-Frank Act was to prevent the need for another TARP-like rescue in the future. Among other changes, the Act extended the regulatory power of the Federal Reserve, and enabled it to impose minimum capital ratios on any financial institution—bank or non-bank. A new government body was created—the *Financial Stability Oversight Council*—to collect information from financial institutions, identify threats to the financial system, and formulate policies to avert them. For example, exceptionally large financial institutions, or those engaged in more risky investments, would be ordered to hold even more capital against each dollar of assets on their balance sheets, giving them an added cushion against insolvency.

The Dodd-Frank Act focused much of its attention on regular banks, which enjoy the special advantage of FDIC insurance on their deposits. In addition to raising their capital requirements, their investments would be monitored more closely than before, with new restrictions on risky lending and high-risk financial trading.

Many economists believe that Dodd-Frank was, at minimum, a step in the right direction. Extending and raising capital requirements, in particular, is a widely favored, common-sense step. But the Act itself may not be enough to prevent another financial crisis. Government or Fed officials, however well intentioned, are unable to identify every threat to the financial system in advance. More importantly, financial institutions have a history of lobbying government agencies to weaken regulations, or finding ways around them. Indeed, in late 2011—more than a year after Dodd-Frank had passed—most of the new banking regulations it authorized had still not been written, and the banking industry was working hard to shape them. As the old expression goes, the devil is in the details. And many of the details authorized by the Dodd-Frank Act had yet to appear.

SUMMARY

Money is an asset that is also widely accepted as a means of payment. In the United States, the standard measure of money includes currency, checking account balances, and traveler's checks.

Money provides three important functions. First, it provides for a generally acceptable *means of payment*. Second, it serves as a *store of value*—a way of holding wealth. Finally, it creates a unit of account that helps us compare the costs of different goods and services. In the United States, the unit of account is the dollar, and the means of payment includes dollar-denominated paper currency.

The amount of money circulating in the economy is influenced by the actions of the Federal Reserve and the banking system. The Fed influences bank behavior by altering their balance sheets. In a balance sheet, *assets* always equal *liabilities* plus *shareholders' equity* (the difference between total assets and total liabilities). A key asset is *reserves*—accounts that banks hold at the Fed or cash they hold in their vaults and ATMs. The money supply often changes when the Fed conducts *open market operations*. An *open market purchase* typically increases the money supply. The Fed pays with a check that is deposited in a bank. On the asset side of the bank's balance sheet, reserves increase; on the liabilities side, checking accounts (a form of money) increase. If the bank does not want to hold *excess reserves*, the funds lent out will end up in other banks, where they create still more checking accounts. The

money supply will increase by some *multiple* of the original injection of reserves by the Fed.

An *open market sale,* in which the Fed sells government bonds, has the opposite effect, draining reserves out of the system and decreasing the money supply.

In the simplest version, the money multiplier has the value of 1/RRR, where RRR is the *required reserve ratio*—the fraction of checking deposits that banks should hold as reserves. But the simple formula ignores changes in the public's cash holdings and banks' excess reserve holdings as the money supply changes, which reduce the money multiplier.

A *bank run* occurs when many worried depositors try to withdraw funds at the same time. A *banking panic* occurs when there is a system-wide run on many banks at the same time. Banking panics were largely eliminated in the United States and other countries by providing *deposit insurance*. But this requires government to closely regulate banks, e.g. imposing *capital requirements* that are based on a bank's total assets and their risk.

Both banks and *non-bank* financial institutions (which comprise the *shadow banking system*) have short-term liabilities and long-term assets. Banks' liabilities are largely government-guaranteed deposits, and banks are highly regulated. Non-banks' liabilities are non-guaranteed borrowing, and in the past, non-banks were very lightly regulated. The financial crisis of 2008 proved that non-bank financial institutions pose a risk to the banking system as well, resulting in new financial system regulations.

PROBLEM SET

Answers to even-numbered Problems can be found on the text Web site through www.cengagebrain.com

1. Suppose the required reserve ratio is 0.2. If an extra $20 billion in reserves is injected into the banking system through an open market purchase of bonds, by how much will the money supply increase? Would your answer be different if the required reserve ratio were 0.1?

2. If the Fed buys $50 million of government securities, by how much will the money supply increase if the required reserve ratio is 0.15? How will your answer be different if the required reserve ratio is 0.18?

3. Which of the following is considered part of the U.S. money supply? (Use the M1 measures.)
   a. A $10 bill you carry in your wallet
   b. A $100 traveler's check you bought but did not use
   c. A $100 bill in a bank's vault
   d. The $325.43 balance in your checking account
   e. A share of General Motors stock worth $40

4. Suppose a country, Zeekland, uses a unit of account called the "zeek." Its banks have no reserve requirements, but banks always want to hold 3 percent of their total checking deposits as cash, and another 2 percent as accounts with the Zeekland Central Bank. If the central bank buys 50 million zeeks worth of government bonds, by how much will the country's money supply increase?

5. Suppose accountants at Mid-Size National Bank (Table 1) discover that they've made an error: Cash in vault is only $8 million, not $10 million.
   a. Which other entries in the bank's balance sheet will change as a consequence of discovering this error?
   b. If the required reserve ratio is 0.10, does this bank now have excess reserves or deficient reserves? Of what value?

6. Suppose that Mid-Size National Bank has the balance sheet in Table 1. One day, a hurricane destroys 20 percent of its property and buildings, and its insurance covers only half this amount. Illustrate (with new entries) how its balance sheet will change.

7. Suppose that the money supply is $1 trillion. Decision makers at the Federal Reserve decide that they wish to use open market operations to reduce the money supply by $100 billion, or by 10 percent. If the required reserve ratio is 0.05, and the simple money multiplier formula applies, what does the Fed need to do to carry out the planned reduction?

8. Suppose that the money supply is $3.2 trillion. Decision makers at the Federal Reserve decide that they wish to use open market operation to increase the money supply by $500 billion. If the required reserve ratio is 0.10, what does the Fed need to do to carry out the planned increase? What if the required reserve ratio is 0.15?

9. For each of the following situations, determine whether the money supply will increase, decrease, or stay the same.
   a. Depositors become concerned about the safety of depository institutions.
   b. The Fed lowers the required reserve ratio. (Assume banks never hold excess reserves.)
   c. The economy enters a recession and banks have a hard time finding credit-worthy borrowers.
   d. The Fed sells $100 million of bonds to First National Bank of Ames, Iowa; banks never hold excess reserves; and the public doesn't change its cash holdings.
   e. The Fed buys $100 million of bonds from First National Bank of Ames, Iowa, but the interest rate banks can earn from lending is the same as the interest rate the Fed pays on reserves.

10. Suppose a bank has the following entries on its balance sheet: $20 million in property and buildings; $200 million in government bonds; $300 million in loans; $5 million cash in vault; $95 million in accounts with the Federal Reserve; $550 million in checking account liabilities. There are no other entries on the balance sheet except for shareholders' equity.
    a. What is this bank's "capital?"
    b. What is the maximum value of the bank's loans that could be "written off" due to bankruptcies before the bank would become insolvent?

More Challenging

11. Suppose that Mid-Size Bank has the balance sheet in Table 1, and is required by law to have 20 percent of its total assets as bank capital.
    a. What percentage of total assets is Mid-Size's current level of capital?
    b. Suppose Mid-Size issues new shares of stock, which it sells for $75 million. It then lends out the $75 million. Is Mid-Size meeting its capital requirement now? Why or why not?
    c. [Harder] How many dollars would Mid-Size have to raise by selling shares of stock to exactly meet its capital requirement? (Assume it will always lend out the proceeds of any stock sale.)

12. [Requires appendix.] Suppose that Mid-Size National Bank has the balance sheet in Table 1 and is required by law to have 20 percent of its total assets as bank capital.
    a. What is the maximum simple leverage ratio Mid-Size is permitted to have?
    b. What is Mid-Size's *actual* simple leverage ratio?
    c. Suppose Mid-Size decides to bring its leverage ratio down to the maximum permitted level by selling some assets and using the proceeds to pay off some of its debts and checking deposits. How much in assets would it have to sell?

13. [Requires appendix.] Suppose that Mid-Size National Bank has the balance sheet in Table 1, and one day, the value of every asset it holds (including its loans) decreases by 5 percent.
    a. What is Mid-Size's leverage ratio now?
    b. Suppose Mid-Size wants to bring its leverage ratio back to its original level, by selling assets at their current lower value, and using the proceeds to pay off its debts or reduce its deposits. How much in assets must Mid-Size sell?

If you follow discussions about the cause of the financial crisis of 2008, or proposals for reform, you'll continually hear the term *leverage*. Someone might say, "We allowed financial institutions to become too highly leveraged." Or "We don't want them to *deleverage* too rapidly." What, precisely, are they talking about?

Leverage can be measured in different ways. One basic measure is closely related to the measure you learned in the appendix to Chapter 4. In that chapter, we defined an individual's equity in an asset (such as a home) as the difference between its value and any debt associated with the asset. This equity is what the owner of the asset has at risk. Then we defined the *simple leverage ratio* as the current value of the asset divided by the owner's equity:

$$\text{Simple Leverage Ratio (for an asset owner)} = \frac{\text{Value of asset}}{\text{Equity in asset}}$$

A simple leverage ratio for a bank (or any other financial institution) can be defined in a similar way, but instead of using the value of a single asset, we look at the value of all assets together. And instead of equity in just one asset, we look at total shareholders' equity. This gives us the following measure:

$$\text{Financial Institution's Simple Leverage Ratio} = \frac{\text{Total Assets}}{\text{Shareholder's Equity}}$$

In Table 1, for example, Mid-Size National Bank has a simple leverage ratio of $1,000 million/$125 million = 8. This tells us that for each dollar of shareholders' equity—which the bank's owners have put in and have at risk—the bank has used seven of *other* people's dollars (deposits or borrowing) to buy or create the assets on its balance sheet. As you can see, the less shareholder equity a bank has relative to its assets, the greater its leverage ratio.

Why is the leverage ratio important? Remember (from Chapter 4), that the leverage ratio acts as a "rate-of-return" multiplier for an individual homeowner. The same is true for a bank. The greater the leverage ratio, the more interest-earning assets the bank can acquire with each dollar of its capital (shareholders' equity), and the greater the return it can earn for its shareholders. For example, as you can verify, if Mid-Size were to borrow another $1,000 million from others and lend out those funds, its leverage ratio would rise from 8 to 16. For each dollar the owners have put in, the bank would have twice as many dollars loaned out. Because it tends to lend long-term at high interest rates, and borrow short-term at low interest rates, higher leverage increases the owners' rate of return on their capital.

But just as greater leverage multiplies a bank's potential *profits,* it also multiplies a bank's potential *losses.* In this chapter, we mentioned that before the financial crisis began, banks had capital ratios (shareholders' equity as a percentage of total assets) of about 10 percent. Another way of saying this is that their leverage ratio was about 10. (As you can see from the equation, the simple leverage ratio is just the reciprocal of the capital ratio.)

We also mentioned that some of the larger investment banks—such as Bear Stearns and Lehman Brothers—had substantially lower capital ratios—less than 3 percent. This means they had simple leverage ratios above 33. When asset values fell, high leverage multiplied the losses, and their capital headed rapidly toward zero.

Deleveraging

Deleveraging is the process of *reducing* leverage, and therefore reducing the risk to your capital from any further declines in asset prices. During and after the financial crisis, financial institutions of all kinds wanted to deleverage. As you can see from the definition of the leverage ratio, this required the financial institution to either (1) reduce total assets or (2) increase capital.

How could each of these be accomplished? Using the first method—reducing total assets—the firm would sell off assets and use the proceeds to pay off some of its liabilities. For example, consider the financial institution with the simple balance sheet below:

Assets		Liabilities and Shareholders' Equity	
Long-term assets	$10 billion	Short-term borrowing	$ 9 billion
		Shareholders' equity	$ 1 billion
Total	$10 billion	Total	$10 billion

Total assets are $10 billion, and shareholders' equity is $1 billion, so the simple leverage ratio is 10. If the firm were to sell off $3 billion in assets and use the proceeds to pay off $3 billion in debt, its balance sheet would look like this:

Assets		Liabilities and Shareholders' Equity	
Long-term assets	$7 billion	Short-term borrowing	$6 billion
		Shareholders' equity	$1 billion
Total	$7 billion	Total	$7 billion

Notice that selling off assets at their value as stated on the balance sheet has no effect on shareholders' equity itself. But the leverage ratio falls from 10 to 7. The firm's capital is now less sensitive to fluctuations in asset prices.

In the aftermath of the financial crisis, everyone agreed that lower leverage ratios would be a good thing. The problem was how to get there. It is easy for *one* financial institution, acting alone, to sell off assets rapidly to reduce its leverage. But when many financial institutions do so at the same time, asset prices fall and bank capital declines for all of them. It was this rapid, system-wide deleveraging that contributed to the downward spiral of the financial crisis.

The second way to decrease leverage is to increase capital. A financial institution could do this by selling new shares of stock, or by earning profit over time and keeping it within the firm (rather than giving the profit to its shareholders). These methods of deleveraging may take longer and involve some costs to the firm. But they create less damage to the financial system.

© JAMES LEYNSE/CORBIS

CHAPTER 14

The Money Market and Monetary Policy

The phrase "monetary policy"—in the broadest sense—refers to the various tools the Fed can use to influence the macroeconomy. As you'll see in this chapter, the most common method used by the Fed is to change *interest rates*. By doing so, the Fed can affect aggregate expenditure and real GDP.

Our starting point is to look at supply and demand in the *money market*, where households and businesses decide how much of their wealth to hold as money, and take steps to acquire it. This will build a foundation for understanding monetary policy in a simplified economy in which there is only one interest rate, and in which the financial system is functioning normally.

Once you understand how monetary policy would work in this simple case, we'll get more realistic in two ways: First, we'll deal with the existence of *many* interest rates, and see how that complicates the Fed's job. Second, we'll look at the *unconventional* tools that the Fed can use under extraordinary circumstances.

Finally, in the Using the Theory section, we'll discuss how the Fed used both conventional and unconventional tools during the financial crisis and recession of 2008–2009, and the long slump that followed.

THE DEMAND FOR MONEY

Reread the title of this section. Does it appear strange to you? Don't people always want as much money as possible?

Indeed, they do. But when we speak about the *demand* for something, we don't mean the amount that people would desire if they could have all they wanted, without having to sacrifice anything for it. Instead, economic decision makers always face constraints: They must sacrifice one thing in order to have more of another. Thus, the *demand for money* does not mean how much money people would *like* to have in the best of all possible worlds. Rather, it means *how much money people would like to hold, given the constraints that they face.* Let's first consider the demand for money by an individual, or household, and then turn our attention to the demand for money in the entire economy.

A Household's Demand for Money

Money is one of the forms in which people hold their wealth. Unfortunately, at any given moment, the total amount of wealth we have is given; we can't just snap our fingers and have more of it. Therefore, if we want to hold more wealth in the form

393

of money, we must hold less wealth in other forms: savings accounts, money market funds, time deposits, stocks, bonds, and so on. Indeed, people exchange one kind of wealth for another millions of times a day—in banks, stock markets, and bond markets. If you sell shares in the stock market, for example, you give up wealth in the form of corporate stock and acquire money. The buyer of your stock gives up money and acquires the stock.

These two facts—that wealth at any moment is given, and that you must give up one kind of wealth in order to acquire more of another—determine an individual's **wealth constraint**. Whenever we speak about the demand for money, the wealth constraint is always in the background, as in the following statement:

Wealth constraint At any point in time, total wealth is fixed.

> *A household's quantity of money demanded is the amount of wealth that the household chooses to hold as money, rather than as other assets.*

Why do people want to hold some of their wealth in the form of money? The most important reason is that money is a *means of payment;* you can buy things with it. Other forms of wealth, by contrast, are *not* used for purchases. (For example, we can't pay for our groceries with shares of stock.) However, the other forms of wealth provide a financial return to their owners. For example, bonds, savings deposits, and time deposits pay interest, while stocks pay dividends and may also rise in value (which is called a *capital gain*). Money, by contrast, pays very little interest (some types of checking accounts) or none at all (cash and most checking accounts). Thus,

> *when you hold money, you bear an opportunity cost—the interest or other financial return you could have earned by holding other assets instead.*

Each of us must continually decide how to divide our total wealth between money and other assets. The upside to money is that it can be used as a means of payment. The more of our wealth we hold as money, the easier it is to buy things at a moment's notice, and the less often we will have to pay the costs (in time, trouble, and commissions to brokers) to change our other assets into money. The downside to money is that it pays little or no interest.

> *Households choose how to divide wealth between: (1) money, which can be used as a means of payment but earns no interest; and (2) other assets, which earn interest or other financial returns, but cannot be used as a means of payment.*

This choice involves a clear tradeoff: The more wealth we hold as money, the less often we will have to go through the inconvenience of changing our other assets into money . . . but the less interest we will earn on our wealth.

What determines how much money each of us will decide to hold? While tastes vary from person to person, 3 key variables have rather predictable impacts on most of us.

- **The price level.** The greater the number of dollars you spend in a typical week or month, the more money you will want to have on hand to make your purchases. A rise in the price level, which raises the dollar cost of your purchases, should therefore increase the amount of money you want to hold.

- **Real income.** Suppose the price level remains unchanged, but your income increases. Once again, you will spend more dollars in a typical week or month, so you will want to hold more of your wealth in the form of money.
- **The interest rate.** Interest payments and other financial returns are what you give up to hold money. In this chapter, we'll be focusing mostly on interest rates— the rate of return you earn by holding bonds, certificates of deposit, and other similar assets. The greater the interest rate, the greater the opportunity cost of holding money. Thus, a rise in the interest rate *decreases* your quantity of money demanded.

Nominal versus Real Interest Rates

The effect of the interest rate on the quantity of money demanded will play a key role in our analysis. But as you learned several chapters ago, we often need to distinguish between nominal and real interest rates. The real rate is what people care about when making decisions about spending or saving. But which interest rate tells us the opportunity cost of holding money?

Let's find the answer with an example. Imagine that you must decide whether to hold $1,000 as money or in some other asset that pays a nominal interest rate of 10%. Suppose you know that the inflation rate for the year is going to be 10%. Then the real interest rate on the other asset (calculated by subtracting the rate of inflation from the nominal interest rate) will be zero. Which interest rate—0% or 10%—is your opportunity cost for holding money?

One one hand, if you hold the $1,000 as money, at the end of the year you will have exactly $1,000, but you will have lost 10% of its purchasing power due to inflation. On the other hand, if you hold the interest-earning asset, you will have $1,100, which means your purchasing power will be the same as at the beginning of the year. That's not very good, but holding the money would have been even worse. The money leaves you with 10% less purchasing power than the interest-earning asset. As you can verify, the same would be true if the inflation rate were zero, 5%, or any other value: holding money causes you to lose 10% more of your purchasing power. So it is the *nominal* interest rate (in this case 10%) that tells us the opportunity cost of holding money.

In much of this chapter, we will be assuming either that there is no inflation, or that the inflation rate is stable. In that case, if the nominal interest rate rises by 1 percentage point, the real interest rate will rise by 1 percentage point as well. So we'll often use the phrase "change in the interest rate" without specifying nominal or real. Later in the chapter, when the distinction matters, we'll be careful to include the labels "nominal" or "real."

The Economy-Wide Demand for Money

In addition to households, money is also demanded by businesses. Stores keep some currency in their cash registers, and firms generally keep funds in business checking accounts so they can pay bills easily. And businesses face the same types of constraints as individuals: They have only so much wealth, and they must decide how much of it to hold as money rather than other assets.

The quantity of money demanded by businesses follows the same principles we have developed for households: When the price level rises, businesses want to hold more money because each transaction they engage in will involve more dollars. As real income in the economy rises, businesses want to hold more money because they will be buying and selling more goods and services each day. Finally, a rise in (nominal) interest rates will decrease businesses' demand for money, because they will prefer to hold more interest-earning assets instead.

When we combine the demand for money by all households and all businesses, we get the *total* or *economy-wide* quantity of money demanded (which we'll call simply the *quantity of money demanded*, without the qualifiers):

> *The quantity of money demanded is the amount of total wealth in the economy that all households and businesses, together, want to hold as money rather than other assets.*

The demand for money in the economy depends on the same three variables that we discussed for individual households and firms. In particular, (1) a rise in the price level will increase the demand for money; (2) a rise in real income (real GDP) will increase the demand for money; and (3) a rise in nominal interest rates will *decrease* the quantity of money demanded.

Demand for Money with a Single Interest Rate

Our first step in understanding monetary policy is to imagine an economy much simpler than our own, in which households and businesses can hold their wealth in only two types of assets: *money* or *bonds*. Money pays no interest. Bonds, on the other hand, do pay interest. To make our analysis even simpler, we'll suppose that all bonds pay the *same* interest rate. So our two-asset economy will also be a *single-interest-rate* economy.

Money demand curve A curve indicating how much money will be demanded at each nominal interest rate.

The Money Demand Curve

Figure 1 shows the economy's **money demand curve,** which tells us *the total quantity of money demanded in the economy at each (nominal) interest rate.* Notice that the curve is downward sloping. As long as the other influences on money demand don't change, a drop in the interest rate—which lowers the opportunity cost of holding money—will increase the quantity of money demanded.

Point *E,* for example, shows that when the interest rate is 6 percent, the quantity of money demanded is $1,000 billion. If the interest rate falls to 3 percent, we move to point *F,* where the quantity demanded is $1,600 billion. As we move along the money demand curve, the interest rate changes, but other determinants of money demand (such as the price level and real income) are assumed to remain unchanged.

Shifts in the Money Demand Curve

What happens when something *other* than the interest rate changes the

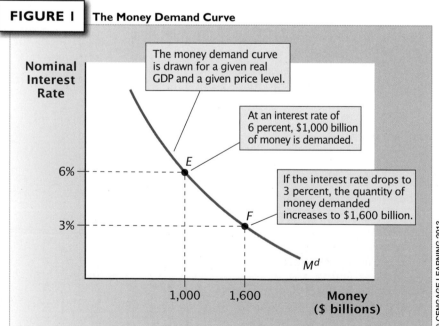

FIGURE 1   **The Money Demand Curve**

The money demand curve is drawn for a given real GDP and a given price level.

At an interest rate of 6 percent, $1,000 billion of money is demanded.

If the interest rate drops to 3 percent, the quantity of money demanded increases to $1,600 billion.

Nominal Interest Rate

6%   *E*

3%   *F*

M^d

1,000   1,600   Money ($ billions)

© CENGAGE LEARNING 2013

quantity of money demanded? Then the curve shifts. For example, suppose that real income or the price level increases. Then, at each interest rate, households and businesses will want to hold *more* of their wealth in the form of money. The entire money demand curve will shift rightward. This is illustrated in Figure 2, where the money demand curve shifts rightward from M_1^d to M_2^d. At an interest rate of 6 percent, the quantity of money demanded rises from $1,000 billion to $1,400 billion; if the interest rate were 3 percent, the amount of money demanded would rise from $1,600 billion to $2,000 billion.

In general,

> *a change in the interest rate moves us along the money demand curve. A change in money demand caused by something other than the interest rate (such as real income or the price level) will cause the curve to shift.*

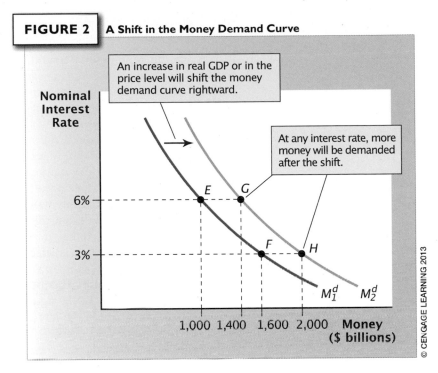

FIGURE 2 A Shift in the Money Demand Curve

An increase in real GDP or in the price level will shift the money demand curve rightward.

At any interest rate, more money will be demanded after the shift.

© CENGAGE LEARNING 2013

Figure 3 summarizes how the key variables we've discussed so far affect the demand for money.

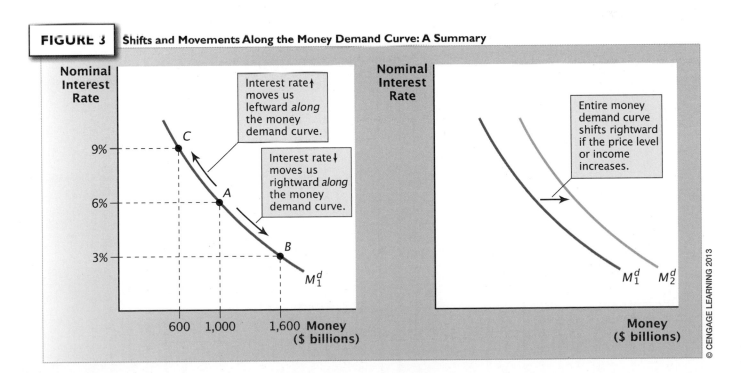

FIGURE 3 Shifts and Movements Along the Money Demand Curve: A Summary

Interest rate↑ moves us leftward *along* the money demand curve.

Interest rate↓ moves us rightward *along* the money demand curve.

Entire money demand curve shifts rightward if the price level or income increases.

© CENGAGE LEARNING 2013

THE SUPPLY OF MONEY

Just as we did for money demand, we would like to draw a curve showing the quantity of money *supplied* at each interest rate. The supply of money is the amount of money (cash and demand deposits) that the Fed and the banking system have created.

What determines this quantity? In the previous chapter, you learned how Federal Reserve actions can influence the money supply. For now, we'll go further: We'll assume that the Fed can simply set the money supply at whatever level it wishes. That is, the Fed can use open market operations to inject or withdraw reserves from the banking system, and rely on the money multiplier to do the rest. Because the Fed decides what the money supply will be, we'll treat it as a fixed amount. That is, the interest rate can rise or fall, but the money supply will remain constant unless and until the Fed decides to change it.

Money supply curve A line showing the total quantity of money in the economy at each interest rate.

Look at the vertical line labeled M_1^S in Figure 4. This is the economy's **money supply curve**, which shows the total amount of money supplied at each interest rate. The line is vertical because once the Fed sets the money supply, it remains constant until the Fed changes it. In the figure, the Fed has chosen to set the money supply at $1,000 billion. A rise in the interest rate from, say, 3 percent to 6 percent would move us from point J to point E along the money supply curve M_1^S, leaving the money supply unchanged.

Now suppose the Fed, for whatever reason, were to *change* the money supply. Then there would be a *new* vertical line, showing a different quantity of money supplied at each interest rate. For example, if the money multiplier is 10, and the Fed purchases government bonds worth $40 billion, the money supply increases by 10 × $40 billion = $400 billion. In this case, the money supply curve shifts rightward, to the vertical line labeled in the figure.

FIGURE 4   **The Supply of Money**

Once the Fed sets the money supply, it remains constant until the Fed changes it. The vertical supply curve labeled M_1^S shows a money supply of $1,000 billion, regardless of the interest rate. An increase in the money supply to $1,400 billion is depicted as a rightward shift of the money supply curve to M_2^S.

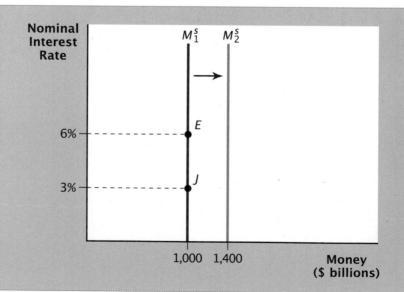

© CENGAGE LEARNING 2013

EQUILIBRIUM IN THE MONEY MARKET

Now let's combine money demand and money supply to find the *equilibrium interest rate*: the interest rate at which the quantity of money demanded and the quantity of money supplied are equal. Figure 5 combines the money supply and demand curves. Equilibrium occurs at point *E*, where the two curves intersect. At this point, the quantity of money demanded and the quantity supplied are both equal to $1,000 billion, and the equilibrium interest rate is 6 percent.

It is important to understand what equilibrium in the money market actually means. First, remember that the money supply curve tells us the quantity of money, determined by the Fed, that *actually exists* in the economy. Every dollar of this money—either in cash or in checking account balances—is held by *someone*. Thus, the money supply curve, in addition to telling us the quantity of money supplied by the Fed, also tells us the quantity of money that people *are actually holding* at any given moment. The money demand curve, on the other hand, tells us how much money people *want* to hold at each interest rate. Thus, when the quantity of money supplied and the quantity demanded are equal, all of the money in the economy is being *willingly held*. That is, people are satisfied holding the money that they are *actually* holding.

> *Equilibrium in the money market occurs when the quantity of money people are actually holding (quantity supplied) is equal to the quantity of money they want to hold (quantity demanded).*

Can we have faith that the interest rate will reach its equilibrium value in the money market, such as 6 percent in our figure? Indeed we can. In the next section, we explore the forces that drive the money market toward its equilibrium.

How the Money Market Reaches Equilibrium

To understand how the money market reaches its equilibrium, suppose that the interest rate, for some reason, were *not* at its equilibrium value of 6 percent in Figure 5. For example, suppose the interest rate were 9 percent. As the figure shows, at this interest rate the quantity of money demanded would be $600 billion, while the quantity supplied would be $1,000 billion. Or, put another way, people would *actually* be holding $1,000 billion of their wealth

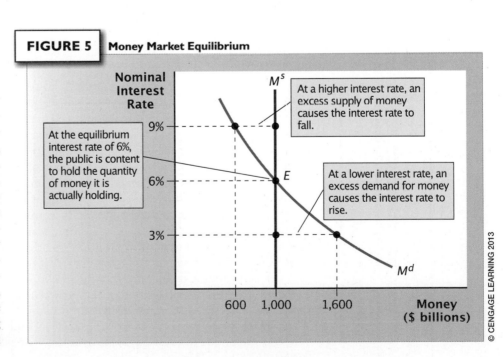

FIGURE 5 **Money Market Equilibrium**

Nominal Interest Rate

At the equilibrium interest rate of 6%, the public is content to hold the quantity of money it is actually holding.

At a higher interest rate, an excess supply of money causes the interest rate to fall.

At a lower interest rate, an excess demand for money causes the interest rate to rise.

M^s

M^d

E

9%

6%

3%

600   1,000   1,600

Money ($ billions)

© CENGAGE LEARNING 2013

Excess supply of money The amount of money supplied exceeds the amount demanded at a particular interest rate.

Excess demand for bonds The amount of bonds demanded exceeds the amount supplied at a particular interest rate.

as money, but they would *want* to hold only $600 billion as money. There would be an **excess supply of money** (the quantity of money supplied would exceed the quantity demanded) equal to $1,000 billion − $600 billion = $400 billion.

Now comes an important point. Remember that in our analysis, money and bonds are the only two assets available. If people want to hold *less* money than they are currently holding, then, by definition, they must want to hold *more* in bonds than they are currently holding—an **excess demand for bonds.**

> When there is an excess supply of money in the economy, there is also an excess demand for bonds.

To understand this more clearly, imagine that instead of the money market, which can seem rather abstract, we were discussing something more concrete: the arrangement of books in a bookcase. Suppose that you have a certain number of books, and you have only two shelves on which to place all of them: top and bottom. One day, you look at the shelves and decide that, the way you've arranged things, the top shelf has *too many* books. Then, by definition, you must also feel that the bottom shelf has *too few* books. That is, an excess supply of books on the top shelf (it has more books than you want there) is the same as an excess demand for books on the bottom shelf (it has fewer books than you want there).

A similar conclusion applies to the money market. People allocate a given amount of wealth between two different assets: money and bonds. Too much in one asset implies too little in the other.

So far, we've established that if the interest rate were 9 percent, which is higher than its equilibrium value, there would be an excess supply of money, and an excess demand for bonds. We can illustrate the steps in our analysis so far as follows:

What happens next? In order to take our story further, we first need to take a detour for a few paragraphs.

An Important Detour: Bond Prices and Interest Rates

A bond, in the simplest terms, is a promise to pay back borrowed funds at a certain date or dates in the future. There are many types of bonds. Some promise to make payments each month or each year for a certain period and then pay back a large sum at the end. Others promise to make just one big payment at some future date. When a large corporation or the government wants to borrow money, it issues a new bond and sells it in the marketplace; the amount borrowed is equal to the price of the bond.

All the bonds that have been issued in the past, and have not yet *matured* (been paid off), are held by households and businesses as part of their wealth. These bonds are bought and sold in an active market. If there is an excess demand for bonds, people will try to acquire bonds. Bonds become scarcer, so *the price of bonds will rise.*

Why does that matter? Because there is an important relationship between the *price* of any given bond and the *interest rate* it earns for its owner.

Let's consider a very simple example: a bond that promises to pay to its owner $1,000 exactly 1 year from today. Suppose that you purchase this bond for $800. What interest rate are you earning on your bond? Let's see: You will be getting back $200 more than it cost you, so $200 is your *interest payment.* The annual interest *rate* is the interest payment over the year divided by the amount you paid, or $200/$800 = 0.25 or 25 percent.

Now, what if instead of $800, you paid a price of $900 for this very same bond? The bond still promises to pay $1,000 one year from now, so your annual interest payment would now be $100, and your interest rate would be $100/$900 = 0.11 or 11 percent—a considerably lower interest rate. As you can see, the interest rate that you will earn on your bond depends entirely on the *price* of the bond. *The higher the price, the lower the interest rate.*

This general principle applies to virtually all types of bonds, not just the simple one-time-payment bond we've considered here. Bonds promise to pay various sums to their holders at different dates in the future. Therefore, the more you pay for any bond, the lower your overall rate of return, or interest rate, will be. Thus,

> *when the price of bonds rises, the interest rate falls; when the price of bonds falls, the interest rate rises.*

Now that you have a better understanding of the relationship between bond prices and interest rates, let's return to our explanation of how the money market reaches equilibrium.

Back to the Money Market

Look back at Figure 5, and let's recap what you've learned so far. If the interest rate were 9 percent, there would be an excess supply of money, and therefore an excess demand for bonds. The price of bonds would rise. Now we can complete the story. As you've just learned, a rise in the price of bonds means a *decrease* in the interest rate. The complete sequence of events is

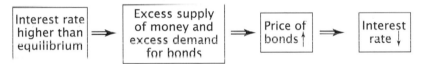

Thus, if the interest is 9 percent in our figure, it will begin to fall. Therefore, 9 percent is *not* the equilibrium interest rate.

How far will the interest rate fall? As long as there continues to be an excess supply of money, and an excess demand for bonds, the public will still be trying to acquire bonds, and the interest rate will continue to fall. But notice what happens in the figure as the interest rate falls: The quantity of money demanded *rises*. Finally, when the interest rate reaches 6 percent, the excess supply of money, and therefore the excess demand for bonds, is eliminated. At this point, there is no reason for the interest rate to fall further, so 6 percent is, indeed, our equilibrium interest rate.

> *If the interest rate is higher than the equilibrium rate, an excess supply of money (and an excess demand for bonds) causes the price of bonds to rise, so the interest rate falls.*

We can also do the same analysis from the other direction. Suppose the interest rate were *lower* than 6 percent in the figure—say, 3 percent. Then, as you can see in Figure 5, there would be an *excess demand for money,* and an *excess supply of bonds.* In this case, the following would happen:

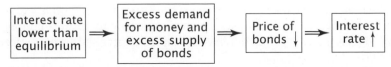

The interest rate would continue to rise until it reached its equilibrium value: 6 percent.

> *If the interest rate is lower than the equilibrium rate, an excess demand for money (and an excess supply of bonds) causes the price of bonds to fall, so the interest rate rises.*

Are There Two Theories of the Interest Rate?

Something may be bothering you about the theory of the money market and the interest rate we've been developing. After all, several chapters ago, you *already* learned a theory of how the interest rate is determined in the economy. In the classical model, the interest rate is determined in the *market for loanable funds*. In this chapter, you've learned that the interest rate is determined in the *money market,* where people make decisions about holding their wealth as money and bonds. Which theory is correct?

The answer is: Both are correct. The classical model, you remember, tells us what happens in the economy in the *long run,* with the economy operating at full-employment output. In the classical model, the *real* interest rate adjusts until new saving and new borrowing in the loanable funds market are equal in the long run.

In this chapter, we are looking at how the *nominal* interest is determined in the *short run.* So we are taking account of some short-run events that the classical model ignores. For example, the classical model ignores an important idea discussed in this chapter: that the public continuously chooses how to divide its wealth between money and bonds. In the short run, the public's preferences over money and bonds can change, and this, in turn, can change the interest rate. This idea does not appear in the classical model.

The classical model also ignores the actions of the Fed, such as open market operations. In the short run, these actions by the Fed can move the interest rate away from the long-run equilibrium rate in the loanable funds market, as you're about to see.

WHAT HAPPENS WHEN THINGS CHANGE?

Now that we have seen how the interest rate is determined in the money market, we turn our attention to *changes* in the interest rate. We'll focus on two questions: (1) What *causes* the equilibrium interest rate to change? and (2) What are the *consequences* of a change in the interest rate? As you are about to see, the Fed can change the interest rate as a matter of policy, or the interest rate can change on its own, as a by-product of other events in the economy. We'll begin with the Fed.

How the Fed Can Change the Interest Rate

Suppose the Fed wants to *lower* the interest rate. (Remember: We're assuming for now that there is just one interest rate in the economy.) Fed officials cannot just declare that the interest rate should be lower. To change the interest rate, the Fed must change the *equilibrium* interest rate in the money market, and it does this by changing the money supply.

Look at Figure 6. Initially, with a money supply of $1,000 billion, the money market is in equilibrium at point *E,* with an interest rate of 6 percent. To lower the interest rate, the Fed *increases* the money supply through open market purchases of bonds. In the figure, the Fed raises the money supply to $1,600 billion, shifting the money supply curve rightward. (This is a much greater shift than the Fed would

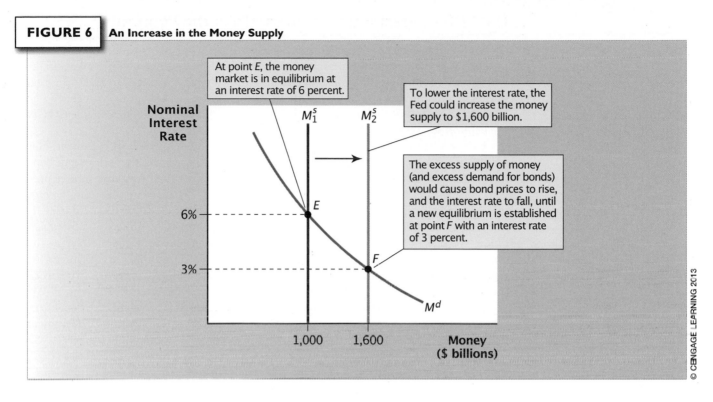

FIGURE 6 | **An Increase in the Money Supply**

At point *E*, the money market is in equilibrium at an interest rate of 6 percent.

To lower the interest rate, the Fed could increase the money supply to $1,600 billion.

The excess supply of money (and excess demand for bonds) would cause bond prices to rise, and the interest rate to fall, until a new equilibrium is established at point *F* with an interest rate of 3 percent.

ever actually engineer in practice, but it makes the graph easier to read.) At the old interest rate of 6 percent, there would be an excess supply of money and an excess demand for bonds. This will drive the interest rate down until it reaches its new equilibrium value of 3 percent, at point *F*. The process works like this:

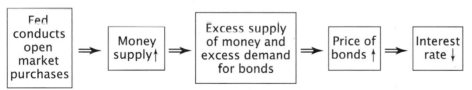

The Fed can *raise* the interest rate as well, through open market *sales* of bonds. In this case, the money supply curve in Figure 6 would shift leftward (not shown), setting off the following sequence of events:

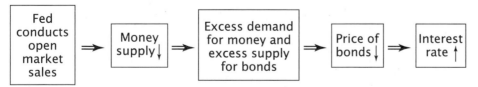

In an economy with just one interest rate, we can summarize how the Fed would control that rate as follows:

> *If the Fed increases the money supply by buying government bonds, the interest rate falls. If the Fed decreases the money supply by selling government bonds, the interest rate rises. By controlling the money supply through purchases and sales of bonds, the Fed can also control the interest rate.*

How Do Interest Rate Changes Affect the Economy?

As you've just learned, if the Fed increases the money supply through open market purchases of bonds, the nominal interest rate falls. If there is no ongoing inflation (as we've been assuming), the nominal and real interest rates are the same, so the real interest rate falls as well. But what then? How is the macroeconomy affected? The answer is: *A drop in the interest rate will boost several different types of spending in the economy.*

First, a lower interest rate stimulates business spending on plant and equipment. This idea came up a few chapters ago in the classical model, but we will go back over it here.

Remember that the interest rate is one of the key costs of any investment project. If a firm must borrow funds, it will have to pay for them at the going rate of interest—for example, by selling a new bond at the going price. If the firm uses its *own* funds, so it doesn't have to borrow, the interest rate *still* represents a cost: Each dollar spent on plant and equipment *could* have been lent to someone else at the going interest rate. (For example, the firm could have purchased a government or corporate bond with those dollars.) Thus, the interest rate is the *opportunity cost* of the firm's own funds when they are spent on plant and equipment.

A firm deciding whether to spend on plant and equipment compares the benefits of the project—the increase in future income—with the costs of the project. With a lower interest rate, the costs of funding investment projects are lower, so more projects will get the go-ahead. Other variables affect investment spending as well. But all else equal, a drop in the interest rate will cause an increase in spending on plant and equipment.

Interest rate changes also affect another kind of investment spending: spending on new houses and apartments that are built by developers or individuals. Most people borrow to buy new houses or apartments, and most developers borrow to finance their construction projects. Thus, when the Fed lowers the interest rate, families find it more affordable to buy homes, and developers find it more profitable to build them. Total investment in new housing increases.

Finally, in addition to investment spending, the interest rate affects consumption spending on big-ticket items such as new cars, furniture, and dishwashers. Economists call these *consumer durables* because they usually last several years. Spending on new cars, the most expensive durable that most of us buy, is especially sensitive to interest rate changes.

We can summarize the impact of money supply changes as follows:

> *When the Fed increases the money supply, the interest rate falls, and spending on three categories of goods increases: plant and equipment, new housing, and consumer durables (especially automobiles). When the Fed decreases the money supply, the interest rate rises, and these categories of spending fall.*

MONETARY POLICY

Monetary policy Control or manipulation of interest rates by the Federal Reserve designed to achieve a macroeconomic goal.

Two chapters ago, you learned that changes in aggregate expenditure cause changes in real GDP through the multiplier process. In this chapter, you've learned that the Federal Reserve, through its control of the money supply, can change the interest rate, and therefore influence aggregate expenditure. Thus, the Fed—through its control of the interest rate—has the power to influence real GDP. When the Fed exercises this power, it is engaging in **monetary policy.**

Let's put all the pieces of our analysis together and see how monetary policy works.

FIGURE 7   Monetary Policy and the Economy

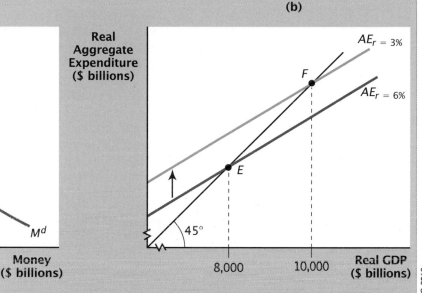

Initially, the Fed has set the money supply at $1,000 billion, so the interest rate (real and nominal) is 6% (point A). Given that interest rate, aggregate expenditure is $AE_{r=6\%}$ in panel (b), and real GDP is $8,000 billion (point E).

If the Fed increases the money supply to $1,600 billion, money market equilibrium moves to point B in panel (a). The interest rate falls to 3% (point B), stimulating interest-sensitive spending and driving aggregate expenditures upward in panel (b). Through the multiplier process, real GDP increases to $10,000 billion (point F).

How Monetary Policy Works

In Figure 7, we revisit the short-run macro model, but we now include the money market in our analysis. In panel (a), the Fed has initially set the money supply at $1,000 billion. Equilibrium is at point A, with a nominal interest rate of 6 percent. Panel (b) shows the familiar short-run aggregate expenditure diagram, with equilibrium at point E, and equilibrium GDP equal to $8,000 billion.

But notice the new labels in the figure. The aggregate expenditure line has the subscript "$r = 6\%$," Why this additional label?

Because now that we are including the effects of interest rates on spending, whenever we draw an aggregate expenditure line, it must be drawn for a particular interest rate. (More specifically, the position of the aggregate expenditure line will depend on the *real* interest rate, which we're representing with the symbol r. But for now, remember: There is no ongoing inflation, so real and nominal interest rates are the same.)

As you are about to see, a change in the (real) interest rate will cause the aggregate expenditure line to shift. Therefore, our aggregate expenditure line is drawn for a particular interest rate, the one determined in the money market, or 6%.

DANGEROUS CURVES ⚠

Shift versus movement along the AE line When thinking about the effects of monetary policy, try not to confuse movements *along* the aggregate expenditure line with *shifts* of the line itself. We move *along* the line only when a change in *income* causes spending to change. The line shifts when something *other* than a change in income causes spending to change.

When the Fed changes the interest rate, both types of changes occur, but it's important to keep the order straight. *First,* the drop in the interest rate (something other than income) causes interest-sensitive spending to change, *shifting* the aggregate expenditure line. *Then,* increases in income cause further increases in spending (through the multiplier process), moving us *along* the new aggregate expenditure line.

Now we suppose that the Fed increases the money supply to $1,600 billion. In panel (a), the money market equilibrium moves from point A toward point B, and the nominal interest rate drops to 3%. In panel (b), the real interest rate also drops to 3%. The drop in the interest rate causes planned investment spending on plant and equipment and on new housing to rise. It also causes an increase in consumption spending—especially on consumer durables like automobiles—to rise at any level of income. (This is an increase in autonomous consumption spending.) The aggregate expenditure line shifts upward, setting off the multiplier effect and increasing equilibrium GDP. The new equilibrium in the right panel is point F, with real GDP at $10,000 billion. In the end, we see that the Fed, by increasing the money supply and lowering the interest rate, has increased the level of output.

We've covered a lot of ground to reach our conclusion, so let's review the highlights of how monetary policy works. This is what happens when the Fed conducts open market purchases of bonds:

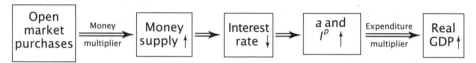

Open market *sales* by the Fed have exactly the opposite effects. In this case, the money supply curve in Figure 7 would shift leftward (not shown), driving the interest rate up. The rise in the interest rate would cause a decrease in interest-sensitive spending (a and I^p), shifting the aggregate expenditure line downward. Equilibrium GDP would fall by a multiple of the initial decrease in spending.

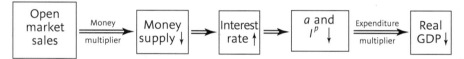

Feedback Effects?

If you've been paying close attention, you may have a question about Figure 7. We've shown how changes in the left panel (an increase in the money supply) cause changes in the right panel (equilibrium GDP rises). But what about effects that go in the other direction? Shouldn't the rise in income in the right panel increase the demand for money in the left panel?

In Figure 7, we have ignored this "feedback effect" from changes in income to changes in money demand. Including this effect would make our analysis of monetary policy a bit more complicated. But it would not alter the direction of the changes, or any of the conclusions we've reached about monetary policy. As you can verify, to achieve the 3% interest rate target when the money demand curve shifts rightward, the Fed would have to increase the money supply by a bit more than it does in Figure 7.

Targeting the Interest Rate

Let's continue to assume that there is just a single interest rate in the economy: the interest rate earned on bonds. You've just seen how changes in that rate can shift the AE line and change equilibrium GDP. During most periods, the Fed wants to prevent unnecessary fluctuations in the interest rate in order to avoid unnecessary shifts in the AE line. It can do this by *targeting* the interest rate. At other times, the Fed will want to *change* its target, to *cause* a shift in the AE line. Let's see how the Fed can, in theory, accomplish each of these goals.

| FIGURE 8 | Maintaining an Interest Rate Target |

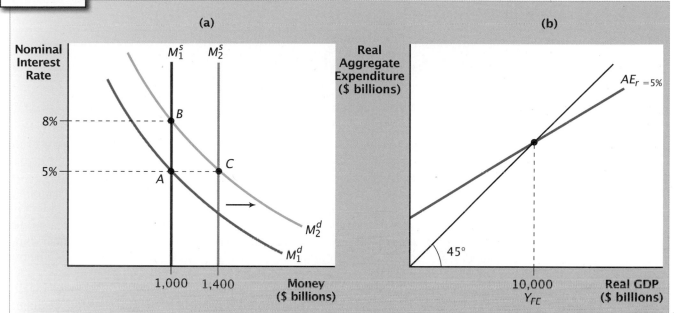

Initially, the money market in panel (a) is at point A, with the interest rate at its target of 5 percent. In panel (b), this interest rate positions the AE line to create equilibrium output of $10,000 billion, which results in full employment.

   An increase in money demand from M_1^d to M_2^d in panel (a), with no action by the Fed, would drive the interest rate up to 8 percent, and shift the AE line in panel (b) downward. To prevent this, the Fed increases the money supply from $1,000 billion ($M_1^s$) to $1,400 billion ($M_2^s$), moving the money market equilibrium to point C. This maintains the interest rate at its target of 5 percent, and prevents any change in equilibrium output in panel (b).

Maintaining an Interest Rate Target

Figure 8 shows an economy that is initially operating at full-employment output. In the left panel, the money market is in equilibrium at point A, with the interest rate at its assumed target level of 5 percent. The money supply is $1,000 billion, which is just the amount needed to maintain the target. In the right panel, the aggregate expenditure line for an interest rate of 5 percent ($AE_{r-5\%}$) intersects the 45° line to create equilibrium output of $10,000 billion. We assume that this happens to be the economy's full-employment output (Y_{FE}) as well.

   Now suppose that public preferences change: People suddenly want to hold more of their wealth in money, which means less in bonds. (Perhaps it's the holiday shopping season, and people need to hold more wealth as money because they are making more purchases. Or perhaps they suddenly view bonds as more risky than before.) Because people want to hold more money at every interest rate, the money demand curve shifts rightward. If the Fed did nothing and left the money supply unchanged, the money market equilibrium would move to point B, with an interest rate of 8 percent. But this rise in the interest rate would cause the AE line in the right panel to shift downward (not shown), and cause equilibrium GDP to fall below Y_{FE}—a recession.

   To prevent any drop in GDP, the Fed must *maintain* its target interest rate. It does so by increasing the money supply (from $1,000 billion to $1,400 billion in the figure), shifting the money supply curve rightward from M_1^s to M_2^s. After the shift, the new equilibrium in the money market occurs at point C, with the interest rate back to its target rate of 5 percent.

In general,

> to prevent fluctuations in money demand from affecting the economy, the Fed can adjust the money supply to maintain its interest rate target.

Changing the Interest Rate Target

Figure 9 illustrates a case where the Fed would want to *change* its interest rate target. Initially, things are fine: In the left panel, the Fed is maintaining a target interest rate of 5 percent, at point A. In the right panel, the aggregate expenditure line for that interest rate (AE_1) creates full-employment output of $10,000 billion.

Then something happens: Some sector of the economy reduces its spending. Perhaps pessimism about the future has caused a decrease in investment spending or autonomous consumption spending. Or perhaps the government has increased net taxes. Regardless of the cause, the aggregate expenditure line in the right panel shifts downward, to AE_2. Equilibrium output falls to $9,000 billion at point F— below potential output. We are in a recession.

The Fed knows that a lower interest rate would stimulate additional investment and consumption spending, and could shift the AE line back up to its original

| FIGURE 9 | Changing the Interest Rate Target to Prevent a Recession |

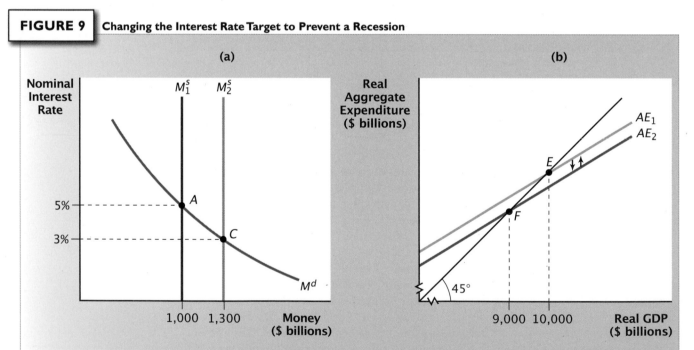

Initially, the money market in panel (a) is at point A, with the interest rate at its target of 5 percent. In panel (b), equilibrium output is $10,000 billion, which is the full-employment output level.

Then, in panel (b), the AE line shifts downward because of a decrease in some sector's spending. With no change in Fed policy, output would fall from $10,000 billion to $9,000 billion (point F). To prevent this recession, the Fed lowers its interest rate target to 3 percent in panel (a), and increases the money supply from $1,000 billion ($M_1^S$) to $1,300 billion ($M_2^S$). This moves the money market equilibrium to point C. The lower interest rate raises consumption and investment spending, shifting the AE line in panel (b) back to its original position.

position. So now the Fed will *lower* its interest rate target. For example, suppose the Fed believes an interest rate of 3 percent will move the aggregate expenditure line back to its original position. To achieve this new target, the Fed increases the money supply as necessary (to $1,300 billion in the figure).

> *To prevent or address unwanted changes in aggregate expenditure, the Fed can change its interest rate target, adjusting the money supply as needed to reach it.*

Monetary Policy with Many Interest Rates

As we've discussed, the real world economy has many different interest rates. The Fed could target *several* different interest rates at the same time, adjusting them separately. On rare occasions (as you'll see a bit later in this chapter) it has done so. But because interest rates tend to rise and fall together, targeting any one of them is usually sufficient to influence all of them. Also, by targeting just one interest rate, the Fed can allow the private market to determine differences *between* interest rates. For example, assets considered of higher-than-average risk must pay higher-than-average rates of return—otherwise, no one would be willing to hold them. But, except in unusual circumstances, the Fed lets private decision-makers gauge the riskiness of different assets, rather than asserting that it knows better.

The Federal Funds Rate

For the past couple of decades, the Fed has chosen to target the interest rate paid on loans in a market that it can very easily monitor and control, called the *federal funds market*. In this market, banks with excess reserves lend them out to other banks for very short periods, usually a day. The interest rate in the federal funds market—the Fed's target—is called the **federal funds rate.**

> **Federal funds rate** The interest rate charged for loans of reserves among banks.

Once the Fed selects its target, it can use open market operations to hit the target. For example, if the federal funds rate temporarily rises above its target level, the Fed will conduct open market purchases, adding reserves to the banking system. As the new reserves flood into the system, banks offer to lend more reserves to other banks, and the federal funds rate falls.

Although it is just an interest rate for lending among banks, many other interest rates in the economy will fall as well. For example, as the federal funds rate falls, banks will find lending in the federal funds market less attractive than before, while other assets—such as government bonds—will be more attractive. As banks try to purchase more government bonds, *their* prices will rise, so the interest rate on government bonds falls. With government bonds paying lower interest rates, *corporate* bonds will look relatively more attractive . . . and so on. In this way, changes in the federal funds rate affect all other interest rates in the economy—including those on automobile loans, business loans, mortgages, and home equity loans. They may change less or more than the federal funds rate has changed, but they usually move in the same direction.

Since 1994, the Federal Open Market Committee has formalized this practice, by publicly announcing its target for the federal funds rate[1] when it meets every six weeks or so. The FOMC then instructs its open market operations desk, operating out of the

---

[1] Even though loans in the federal funds market are very short-term—just a day or so—the federal funds rate—like most interest rates—is stated as an annual rate of return. That is, it is the percent of the loan that someone would earn in interest from lending at that same rate, day after day, for an entire year.

New York Federal Reserve Bank, to adjust the quantity of reserves in the system as needed (with open market operations) to reach and maintain the announced target.

Notice that the money supply itself plays a subservient role in the Fed's thinking about monetary policy. The Fed knows, of course, that by injecting reserves into the banking system, it will also increase the money supply through the money multiplier. But the change in the money supply is a by-product of adjusting reserves to manipulate the federal funds rate.

How does the Fed decide how *much* to change its target? Initially, it will base its decision on current economic conditions, and on research by Fed economists about how changes in the target are likely to affect spending. But in the end, the Fed often uses a trial-and-error approach. After a change in the federal funds rate, economists at the Fed will observe how other interest rates are changing, as well as the different components of aggregate expenditure. At the next meeting, these observations will help the FOMC decide whether another change in the target is warranted. This trial-and-error approach is not perfect, and the Fed has made mistakes—overshooting full employment in some periods and not quite hitting it in others. We'll explore in more detail some of the Fed's problems in guiding the macroeconomy in the next chapter.

Interest on Reserves (IOR) and the Federal Funds Rate

As discussed in the previous chapter, the Federal Reserve began paying interest on reserves (IOR) in October 2008. This has given the Fed another way to move the federal funds rate toward its target, one that does not require open market operations or changes in the money supply. This is because the IOR rate puts a *floor* on the federal funds rate.

To see how this works, imagine that the Fed has been targeting the Federal funds rate at 2.0%, and now wants to raise the target to 2.5%. It could conduct open market sales, draining reserves out of the system. Or it could instead simply announce that it is setting the IOR rate at 2.5%. No bank will lend reserves to another bank at an interest rate *less* than 2.5%, because it it can get that much by simply holding the funds in its reserve account with the Fed. As you'll see in the Using the Theory section, the IOR rate has given the Fed new flexibility to "exit" from some of the unconventional policies it adopted in 2008.

UNCONVENTIONAL MONETARY POLICY

So far, we've described how the Fed tries to guide the economy by controlling the federal funds rate and—through that rate—interest rates in general, aggregate expenditure, and real GDP. This entire process is sometimes called *conventional monetary policy*. But there are times—such as during the financial crisis that began in 2008, and the deep recession that followed—when the Fed must reach beyond its conventional tools to stabilize the economy. Any of three situations can make the Fed's *conventional* monetary policy less effective—and possibly ineffective. The conditions are:

1. Changing Interest Rate Spreads
2. The Zero Lower Bound
3. Financial Crises

As you are about to see, in each of these scenarios, the Fed can do its job using *unconventional* tools. But there are downsides to using them. Let's explore these scenarios one at a time.

Changing Interest Rate Spreads

Lending in the federal funds market is very short-term, and considered very low risk. By contrast, most borrowing done by households and businesses is long-term and considered higher risk. Therefore, these other loans—and assets backed by these loans—usually pay interest rates greater than the federal funds rate. The difference between any particular interest rate and a benchmark interest rate is often called a **spread** (more formally, an *interest rate spread*). For example, if the Federal funds rate is 2%, but the interest rate on corporate bonds is 5%, the spread between these two rates would be 3%.

Spread The difference between an interest rate and some other, benchmark interest rate.

During normal times, perceptions of risk are stable, so spreads remain more or less constant. In that case, the Fed can change interest rates on *all* types of loans by just changing the federal funds rate. In our example with corporate bonds, if the funds rate is lowered from 2% to 1%, the corporate bond rate should drop from 5% to around 4%, maintaining the spread of roughly 3% between the two rates. By maintaining or changing its federal funds target, the Fed can also maintain or change the level of *all* interest rates in the economy, and in this way it can control interest-sensitive spending in *general*.

But perceptions of risk—and the spread between the federal funds rate and other rates—can change. For example, if lenders suddenly think that mortgage loans are more risky, the spread between mortgages and the federal funds rate will rise. Facing a higher interest rate, people will take out fewer mortgage loans, and investment spending on new housing declines. If the mortgage interest rate jumps too much and too suddenly, this could set off a recession.

On the other hand, suppose that lenders suddenly think that mortgage loans are *less* risky, which causes the spread between mortgages and the federal funds rate to fall. Facing a lower interest rate, people will take out *more* mortgage loans, and investment spending on new housing rises. This could (and did) contribute to a speculative boom in housing, creating a danger of overheating the economy, or sending the economy into a tailspin when the bubble bursts.

If the Fed wants to rely on its conventional tool—the federal funds rate—as spreads are changing, it faces a dilemma. Changing that rate will do nothing about the spread, which is based on differences in risk. So the only way to influence the mortgage market using the federal funds rate is to change *all* interest rates together. This could create *too much* or *too little* lending and spending in other sectors of the economy. On the other hand, if the funds rate is *not* changed, the problem in the housing sector remains. Can the Fed do anything?

Unconventional Policy to Alter Spreads

Ordinarily, the fed injects reserves into the banking system by buying and selling government bonds. Usually, these are short-term government bonds that mature within days or weeks. But the Fed can purchase other types of assets as well. For example, if mortgage interest rates have suddenly spiked, the Fed can start buying mortgage-backed securities. This will drive up the price of existing mortgage-backed securities, as well as the prices for newly issued ones, lowering their interest rates. Ultimately, it will lower the interest rate paid on mortgages as well.

In theory, the Fed could purchase *any* type of asset to alter its rate of return—long-term government bonds, corporate bonds, shares of stock, even real estate. For some types of purchases, it would have to ask for extra powers from Congress. In other cases, it can use standing emergency authority or provide incentives for *others* to borrow from the Fed and purchase the assets in its place. This, too, will drive up their price and lower their rate of return.

DANGEROUS CURVES

Fed losses are *not* costless You might think that because the Federal Reserve can pay for assets or lend out funds by just "printing money" (actually, creating new reserves for banks in Fed accounts), no one really loses if it purchases private sector assets that later decline in value or become worthless due to a default. But in fact, losses to the Fed are actually losses to taxpayers. Why? The Fed earns interest every year on the assets it holds (including the government bonds it has acquired doing open market purchases in the past.) The Fed uses some of this interest to cover its operating expenses. But most of it goes right back to the government, where it joins the general flow of tax revenue from other sources. When the Fed's assets or loans go bad, the Fed earns less interest, so it turns over less to the government. The government must then either increase tax revenue from some other source, cut government outlays, or run a larger deficit. Each of these options creates a burden for the tax-paying public. If the Fed tried to cover the loss by creating still *more* reserves—more than called for by responsible monetary policy—it would overheat the economy and create inflation. (We'll be discussing Fed-caused inflation in the next two chapters.)

© AXL/SHUTTERSTOCK.COM

Unfortunately, there are downsides to this unconventional tool. First, by acquiring these assets the Fed would be taking on additional risk that the private sector is reluctant to bear. If, as the private market fears, the assets decline in value (the reason for their spread in the first place), the Fed's losses will ultimately be borne by taxpayers. (See the Dangerous Curves box.)

Second, by changing interest rate spreads, the Fed gets deeply involved in financial markets, deciding who should pay more for loans and who should pay less, and which assets should sell for less and which for more. It is, in effect, picking winners and losers in the financial markets. One of the major tenets of the market system is that funds are allocated most efficiently when *private* decision-makers, with their own wealth at risk—rather than government-appointed officials—determine market outcomes. Moreover, once the Fed begins using its discretion to affect individual interest rates, it becomes vulnerable to political influence. For example, legislators from automobile manufacturing states—seeing that the Fed has lowered mortgage interest rates—might want the same for automobile loans. Because Congress created the Fed—and can alter its powers—the Fed may fear that using its discretion to influence spreads could compromise its ability to conduct an independent monetary policy.

To sum up thus far:

> *While the Fed cannot change interest rate spreads with its conventional tool (adjusting the federal funds rate), it can change spreads by arranging the buying or selling of assets other than government bonds. But because of the economic and political costs, the Fed ordinarily avoids doing so.*

The Zero Lower Bound

With conventional monetary policy, if a decrease in spending causes real GDP to fall below potential, the Fed will repeatedly lower its federal funds rate target to bring real GDP back up again—cutting the target repeatedly, as needed.

But what would happen if the federal funds rate reached zero, and interest-sensitive spending was *still* not high enough? At that point, the federal funds rate cannot be lowered further. It has hit its **zero lower bound**. (This situation is sometimes called a *liquidity trap*.) Any further drop in the federal funds rate would imply a *negative* rate, which—under conventional policy—cannot occur.

Why can't the funds rate be negative? Remember that it's a *nominal* interest rate. It tells us the annual percentage a bank earns in *dollars* from lending funds to another bank. If the rate were negative, a bank would be paid back fewer dollars than the dollars it lent out to another bank. It would do better just to keep the reserves, as cash or in its federal reserve account.

But even before the rate reached zero, the Fed would confront problems. For one thing, other very-short-term lending rates—which closely track the funds rate—would also approach zero. Other parts of the financial system that make loans for short

Zero lower bound The lowest possible value (zero) for any nominal interest rate (such as the federal funds rate).

periods, such as money market accounts, would be unable to attract funds. After all, if you get virtually no interest by putting funds in a money market account, why not just hold money instead? Money market accounts might disappear, creating chaos for those who rely on them for short-term loans.

Another problem is psychological. Once the rate gets very close to zero, the media will report that the Fed is "out of ammunition." A more accurate statement would be that the Fed is out of *conventional* ammunition. It can still conduct monetary policy and stimulate GDP, using *unconventional* tools. But the public may not understand these policies as well. What are these unconventional tools?

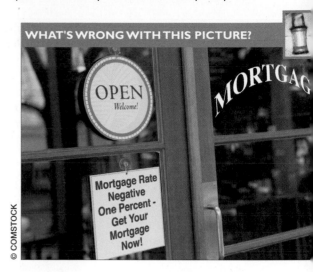

Unconventional Policy at the Zero Lower Bound

We've already discussed one unconventional tool the Fed could use at the zero lower bound: It could begin purchasing assets *other than* short-term government bonds. Remember that the federal funds rate is just one among many interest rates in the economy—usually one of the lowest rates. Even at the zero lower bound, other interest rates—such as mortgage rates—will be well above zero. By purchasing other assets (such as mortgages or mortgage-backed securities), the Fed can reduce the spread between these other rates and the (zero) funds rate.

Second, even if the Fed can't lower the *nominal* funds rate, it can still lower the *real* rate. It's the *real* rate of interest—the percentage change in *purchasing power* received by a lender and paid by a borrower—that matters for decisions to lend, borrow, and spend. Recall (from the earlier chapter on the price level and inflation) that the real rate of interest is the nominal rate minus the rate of inflation:

$$\text{real interest rate} = \text{nominal interest rate} - \text{rate of inflation}$$

This implies that the real interest rate people *expect* for a loan is the difference between the nominal interest rate and the average rate of inflation they *expect* to occur over the time of the loan:

$$\begin{aligned}\textit{expected}\ \text{real interest rate} = \\ \text{nominal interest rate} - \textit{expected}\ \text{rate of inflation}\end{aligned}$$

As you'll see over the next two chapters, the Fed can create inflation in a variety of ways, and borrowers and lenders know this. If the Fed makes clear it will *raise* the inflation rate, the *expected* inflation rate will rise too. Assuming an unchanged nominal federal funds rate (even one at zero), and unchanged spreads for other interest rates, higher expected inflation will decrease all *real* interest rates simultaneously.

For example, suppose there is no expected inflation, and the Fed has cut the funds rate almost to zero—say, to 0.01%. Then the *real* federal funds rate would be 0.01%, equal to its nominal rate. Now suppose the Fed creates expectations of 2% inflation over the next few years. Then the *real* fed funds rate drops to −1.99% (0.01% minus 2.0%). Similarly, a nominal interest rate of 7% for auto loans now becomes a 5% *real* rate. As real interest rates drop throughout the economy, aggregate expenditure increases.

Unfortunately, as with all unconventional tools, there are some downsides. First, it may not work: With higher expected inflation, lenders might demand higher *nominal* interest rates, to compensate them for the lower purchasing power of every dollar in interest they earn. And fear that the Fed might overshoot and create more inflation than it intends could raise nominal rates further, particularly on long-term loans and securities. In that case, long-term *real* interest rates might not decline at all, and could even increase, causing aggregate expenditure to fall.

Second, as you'll see in the next chapter, once higher inflation and expected inflation takes root in the economy, it can be difficult and costly to bring them back down later. The economy might then be stuck for some time with the new, higher inflation rate. This is no problem if the Fed-created inflation is low—say, a mild 2, 3, or even 4 percent. But inflation rates much higher than that would be costly for society. So the Fed has to be careful not to use this tool too aggressively.

> *Even when the federal funds rate hits the zero lower bound, the Fed still has unconventional tools to increase aggregate expenditure, including (1) purchasing assets other than short-term government bonds to reduce spreads; and (2) increasing expected inflation to reduce real interest rates. However, these policies have potential downsides.*

Financial Crises

During a financial crisis—such as the one in 2008 that you read about in the last chapter—the normal relationships between financial institutions break down. Uncertainty about which institutions are near failure can create the equivalent of bank runs. People and businesses want to hold wealth in only the safest of assets—insured deposits, government bonds, and cash—and try to get rid of those backed only by private financial institutions. If the situation is allowed to deteriorate, the normal movement of funds from one institution to another simply stops. Functions that we take for granted—businesses paying their workers, merchants honoring credit cards, insurance companies and retirement funds honoring their claims and commitments—all could be threatened. Much of economic life as we know it could come to a halt, and our living standard would plummet. This is sometimes referred to as a *financial collapse.*

> *When a financial crisis looms, the Fed's most important job—along with other government agencies—is to help stabilize the financial system itself and prevent a financial collapse.*

To some extent, the system has two conventional features that automatically help slow the downward spiral, at least within the banking system: (1) deposit insurance; and (2) the discount window, where the Fed stands ready to be the "lender of last resort" for banks. But in a financial crisis, non-banks are swept up too, and the Fed may have to expand and extend these features to institutions and investments not normally eligible for assistance. The goal is to keep the system working, prevent further panic among savers and investors, and slow the spread of insolvency throughout the system, where it can bring down institutions that would otherwise remain healthy.

A financial crisis played a key role in the early stages of the Great Depression, which began in 1929. The economy did not fully recover from the depression until World War II, more than 10 years later. The Fed at the time did not see its role as it does now, and did not take the kinds of stabilizing actions we've been discussing. In some cases, based on an apparent misunderstanding of the situation, Fed officials did the *opposite* of what modern economics suggests it should have done. For example, during the first few years of the downturn, the Fed raised the discount rate, allowed the money supply to fall and real interest rates to rise. It stood by as thousands of U.S.

commercial banks—about a fifth of the total—failed. People lost their life savings, the unemployment rate rose to roughly 25 percent, and real GDP fell by more than 25 percent. It made further mistakes a few years later, such as raising the required reserve ratio, leading to another drop in the money supply and another rise in interest rates.

In 2008, the Fed—as well as other central banks around the world—acted very differently. It helped that one of the world's leading scholars on the Great Depression—economist Ben Bernanke—was chair of the Federal Reserve Board. True, the Fed was widely criticized for its policies before the crisis: for helping to cause the housing bubble, acting too slowly as the bubble burst, and for regulatory weaknesses that left the financial system vulnerable. It was also attacked for its tepid responses during the long slump after the recession ended in 2009. But during the financial crisis of 2008, the Fed snapped into action. While some of its policy choices were controversial and came with risks and costs, most economists agreed that the Fed's actions during the crisis helped to prevent a financial collapse. We'll take a closer look in the Using the Theory section of this chapter.

USING THE THEORY

AP PHOTO/DAVID J. PHILLIP

THE RECESSION, THE FINANCIAL CRISIS, AND THE FED

As the housing boom turned into the housing bust in the second half of 2007, the Fed began to see looming problems. Falling housing prices (see Figure 15 in Chapter 4) meant falling household wealth, which generally decreases consumption spending. Higher prices for oil and gasoline were squeezing household budgets, and consumers were spending less on automobiles. The Fed had kept the federal funds rate at a relatively high 5.25 percent for more than a year, due to earlier concerns about the economy overheating. But now it appeared to the Fed that it was time to ease up and lower interest rates.

Conventional Tools in 2007 and Early 2008

Figure 10(a) illustrates the initial situation of the economy in the fourth quarter of 2007, with the AE line at AE_{2007-4} and real GDP at \$13,326 billion. Even before the AE line began shifting downward, the Fed began to lower its federal funds target rate (in September 2007), and continued to lower it for the next 15 months (panel b). Had the Fed not taken these moves in 2007 and 2008, the aggregate expenditure line would have probably shifted downward even more than it did, as illustrated by the hypothetical drop to $AE_{hypothetical}$. Because of the Fed's easing, real GDP did not decrease as much as it otherwise would have. But the Fed's policy was not enough to prevent a recession: Over the next 18 months, the AE line shifted down to AE_{2009-2}, with real GDP dropping to \$12,641 billion.

Panel (c) shows one reason that lowering the federal funds target was not enough to avoid recession: Other interest rates in the economy remained stubbornly high. Some slight downward movement occurred in some of the rates (such as on credit cards and personal loans). But for the most part, perceptions of risk and interest rate spreads were rising as the federal funds rate fell. Making matters worse, the interest rates

FIGURE 10   Conventional Monetary Policy to Fight the Recession

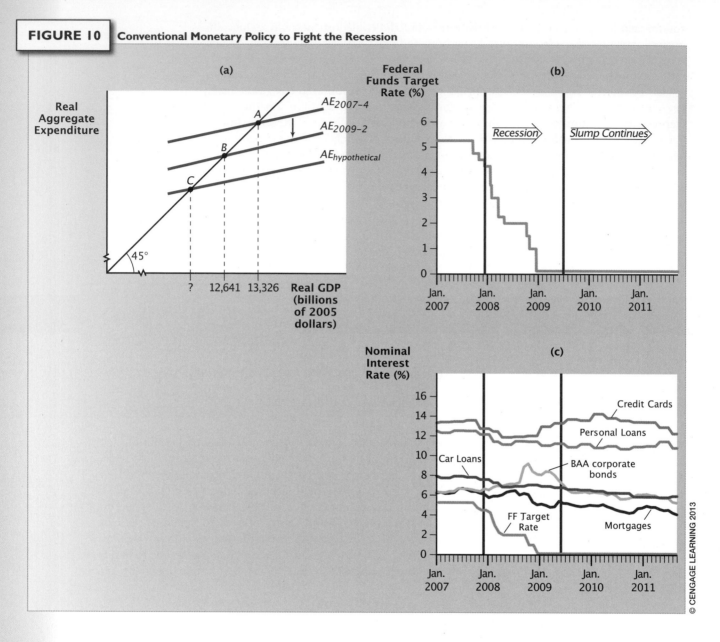

in panel (c) are all *nominal* interest rates. According to a variety of estimates, expected inflation trended steadily downward from 2007 through 2011. (Two chapters from now, you'll learn why expected inflation fell.) When expected inflation decreases, any given nominal interest rate translates to a higher expected *real* interest rate. So when the nominal interest rates are flat in the figure, the real rates associated with them were actually rising. Conventional monetary policy (lowering the federal funds rate) seemed unable to do its normal job of reducing interest rates *in general* to increase aggregate expenditure.

The Need for Unconventional Tools

As 2008 proceeded, the recession deepened, and all three conditions that require unconventional policy tools were present. First—as illustrated in Figure 10(c)—there were rising spreads. The Fed continued to lower the funds rate through 2008, but after the first months of that year, it made no further difference. Nominal and real interest rates on private sector loans and assets remained high.

Second, the federal funds rate was fast approaching the zero lower bound. By December 2008, the Fed acknowledged this, announcing that its new target rate was "between 0 and 0.25 percent."

And third, the financial crisis was worsening. To briefly review what we discussed in the last chapter: Falling housing prices and defaults on mortgages caused the prices of mortgage-backed securities to drop. Their complexity made it hard to know which financial institutions—banks and non-banks—had suffered losses sufficient to make them fail. Lending to financial institutions was sharply curtailed, which required them to sell these securities to pay their short-term debts and rebuild their capital (shareholders' equity). But selling these securities drove their prices even lower, creating a vicious cycle.

By September 2008, after several large financial institutions failed, investors suspected that others were close to failure as well. Preferences for holding wealth shifted rapidly toward safe government bonds and money, and away from the debt of financial institutions, mortgage-backed securities, or *any* asset with a whiff of risk. (In Figure 10(c), notice how the interest rate on corporate bonds rated "BAA" (somewhat risky) spiked upward from September to October 2008.) The vicious cycle accelerated, and there was a danger that the financial system—in the U.S., and in other countries experiencing similar problems—would cease to function.

How the Fed Responded

In the previous chapter, we discussed the government's major policy move during the financial crisis (TARP), overseen by the U.S. Treasury. The Fed cooperated with the Treasury's efforts in various way, but more importantly, took a series of very aggressive steps of its own. Many were aimed squarely at stopping the downward spiral of falling asset prices, especially mortgage-backed securities. If unchecked, the price drops could weaken the balance sheets of even healthy financial institutions, and increase fears of insolvency throughout the system.

In its initial efforts to address the crisis, the Fed relied on its traditional role as a lender of last resort, but put it in overdrive. As early as December 2007, it introduced a new program that made it easier for banks to borrow (anonymously, and so without stigma) for short periods. This reduced a bank's need to sell mortgage-backed securities and other risky assets when its short-term debts came due. A few months later, the Fed created incentives for other financial players to *purchase* these securities, helping to drive up their price. And when these efforts proved insufficient, the Fed announced (in November 2008) that it would purchase mortgage-backed securities on its own, buying more than $1 trillion over the next year. It paid for these assets partly by selling government bonds that it had accumulated (through open market operations in the past), and partly with newly created reserves. This unconventional policy—and others that followed—were dubbed "quantitative easing"

© AXL/SHUTTERSTOCK.COM

DANGEROUS CURVES

The Fed versus the Treasury It is easy to confuse the Federal Reserve with the U.S. Treasury, especially after their unusually close cooperation during the financial crisis of 2008–2009. But their differences are important. The Federal Reserve is an independent organization, responsible for controlling the money supply and influencing interest rates, as well as a major regulator of banks. Once appointed to their 14-year terms, Fed governors are not under the control of any government official or agency. The U.S. Treasury, by contrast, is a part of the executive branch of government, controlled directly by the President of the United States. The Treasury is responsible for collecting taxes, disbursing government outlays, and borrowing to cover the government's budget deficit. This is why government bonds are often called "treasury securities."

by the business press, perhaps because they involved an increase in the quantity of various assets held by the Fed.

By mid-2009, it seemed that the Fed (and Treasury) had largely succeeded—at least in preventing the crisis from turning into a financial collapse. And because the financial crisis was making the recession worse, these efforts also helped to stabilize the economy. But the Fed's problems were not over.

Further Moves during the Slump

As the recession and subsequent slump continued, the Fed made further unconventional moves. All were designed to reduce the stubbornly elevated spreads between the federal funds rate and other interest rates. In late 2010, the Fed announced that it would purchase $600 billion in *long-term* government bonds within the next year, paying with new reserves. With the federal funds rate already at virtually zero, the additional reserves were *not* designed to lower the federal funds rate. Instead, the goal was to drive up the price of long-term government bonds and reduce *their* interest rates, making them less attractive to banks and investors. Banks might then make more long-term loans, and investors might look for other investments, such as long-term corporate bonds.

In mid-2011, with the deep slump continuing, the Fed took another unprecedented step: It announced that it expected to keep the federal funds rate at "exceptionally low levels" for at least another two years. The goal was to convince banks and investors that interest rates were not about to rise any time soon, so banks and investors might as well lend out funds now. Finally, in September 2011, the Fed announced it would acquire another $400 billion in long-term government bonds, this time by selling an equivalent amount of short-term government bonds.

As you can see in Figure 10(c), while the Fed's unconventional policies may have helped to prevent spreads from getting larger, they remained stubbornly high. Interest rates for businesses and consumers—both nominal and real—remained high throughout the slump, and aggregate expenditure remained depressed.

Controversies

Virtually everything the Fed did as the slump continued was attacked, and from opposite sides. One side believed the Fed was doing too much, creating a danger of inflation or even hyperinflation. The other side believed the Fed was doing too little.

Attacks on the Fed for Doing Too Much

One fear—expressed by some politicians and many media personalities, but few economists—was that the Fed's policies would create hyperinflation. This criticism was based on a fact illustrated in Figure 11: the explosive growth in reserves at banks. By lowering the federal funds rate with open market purchases and by buying other assets, the Fed had injected more than $1.5 trillion of new reserves into the banking system. A common view among non-economists is that inflation is caused right away whenever "too much money is chasing too few goods." Another commonly held view is that creating new reserves is the equivalent of "printing money."

Few economists took this attack seriously, for two reasons. First, as you can see in Figure 11, the rise in reserves was almost entirely *excess* reserves, sitting idle in banks' reserve accounts at the Fed. Because these reserves were not lent out and not passed from bank to bank, they were not expanding the money supply as much as the normal money multiplier would suggest. In fact, the money multiplier during the recession and slump was unusually low.

Second, the relationship between the money supply and inflation—at least in the short run—is more complex than the common view suggests (as we'll discuss in the next two chapters). Most economists and investors saw little immediate danger of hyperinflation, or even a rise in the inflation rate.

A related criticism, however, was more sophisticated: that the Fed might not be able to prevent high inflation *later*, as the economy recovered. At that point, with confidence restored, the desire to borrow and lend would resume, and the money multiplier process would be back at work. The $1.5 trillion in excess reserves would lead to a surge of new lending and money creation, causing interest rates to plunge toward the unusually low federal funds rate.

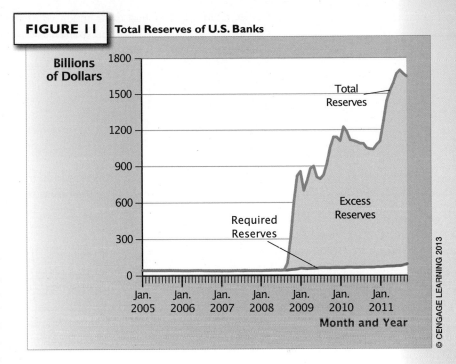

FIGURE 11   Total Reserves of U.S. Banks

© CENGAGE LEARNING 2013

What would the Fed do then? Its normal response would be to raise the federal funds rate, using open market sales of government bonds, and in the process draining the excess reserves out of the system. But the Fed might not *have* enough government bonds for this purpose, because it had exchanged so many of them for mortgage-backed securities. Would the Fed really be willing to sell these mortgage-backed securities, causing their prices to drop and mortgage interest rates to rise, just as the recovery was getting underway? Many thought the answer was no. The Fed might then be trapped into leaving hundreds of billions of dollars of excess reserves in the system, where they would be lent out, overheat the economy, and eventually lead to high inflation.

The Fed had a convincing response to this fear: It no longer needed to worry about draining reserves out of the banking system. Its new tool—the IOR (interest on reserves) rate—would enable it to slow lending to any desired level. By raising the IOR rate sufficiently high, the Fed could induce banks to hold onto their excess reserves, rather than lend them out.

A final criticism was that the Fed's emergency loans and other assistance to financial institutions—like similar steps by the Treasury—had put taxpayer dollars at risk. And while the steps may have helped prevent a financial collapse, they also preserved the investments of many wealthy and well-connected bank officials and financial traders, and enabled these firms to continue paying extremely large bonuses to their top employees. Some felt the Fed could have asked for more in return for its assistance. As a result, there was a growing call in Congress for closer supervision of the Fed, and restrictions on its ability to take similar emergency steps in the future.

Attacks on the Fed for Doing Too Little

From professional and academic economists, the most forceful criticism came from the opposite side. While the Fed may have done all the right things during the financial crisis, it had done much too little during the long slump. In this view, the Fed had all the tools needed to increase aggregate expenditure and spur a much more rapid recovery, but the Fed was not using them. One such unused tool was an aggressive Fed policy to raise expected inflation.

An increase in expected inflation would boost aggregate expenditure in at least two ways. First, it would reduce the *real* value of household debt. Most household debt is specified in nominal terms. (A typical mortgage, for example, is an agreement to pay back a certain number of *dollars*.) Inflation lowers the purchasing power of the dollars owed. Owing less in real terms, households saddled with debt would be more willing and able to spend.

Second, higher inflation would help to lower real interest rates. Ideally, it could even drive some real rates (including the federal funds rate) into negative territory. Lower real rates, as you've learned, would increase household spending on homes, automobiles, furniture, and other consumer durables, as well as business spending on capital equipment.

How would the Fed create higher inflation? We'll be discussing this over the next two chapters. For now, we'll note that merely announcing its intention to increase the inflation rate in the future would convince many households and businesses that the Fed would make good on its word.

In spite of calls from several prominent economists, the Fed resisted taking this step. It may have been concerned that inflationary expectations—once raised—could be difficult to control. For example, using this tool once could lead people to think it might be used again in the future, and that the inflation rate would continue to rise. If the Fed ended up creating greater uncertainty about future inflation, lenders might demand much higher nominal interest rates (to compensate them for the *risk* of higher inflation), causing real interest rates to rise, rather than fall as desired.

Also, the Fed knew that among much of the public, and some members of Congress, inflation is wildly unpopular, regardless of any benefits to the economy in the short run. A Fed announcement of purposely higher inflation might have unleashed a firestorm of congressional opposition. Congress might then take steps to tighten control over the Fed, making it more difficult to conduct an independent, professional monetary policy in the future.

This threat was made concrete in September, 2011, when four prominent Republican congressional leaders took an unprecedented step, writing a letter to the Fed before its upcoming FOMC meeting:

> It is our understanding that the Board Members of the Federal Reserve will meet later this week to consider additional monetary stimulus proposals. We write to express our reservations about any such measures. Respectfully, we submit that the board should resist further extraordinary intervention in the U.S. economy. . . .[2]

Congress created the Fed in 1913, and over several decades, gave it more power to guide the macroeconomy. Although not stated in the letter, it was well understood that Congress could take away that power.

---

[2] The letter was signed by Sen. Mitch McConnell, the Senate Republican leader; Sen. Jon Kyl of Arizona, the Senate Republican whip; House Speaker John Boehner of Ohio; and House Majority Leader Eric Cantor of Virginia. The full text of the letter can be found at http://blogs.wsj.com/economics/2011/09/20/full-text-republicans-letter-to-bernanke-questioning-more-fed-action/

SUMMARY

An individual's *demand for money* is the amount of wealth that person wishes to hold in the form of money. Money is useful as a means of payment, but holding money means sacrificing the interest that could be earned by holding other asssets instead. The higher the nominal interest rate, the larger the fraction of their wealth people will want to hold in the form of other assets, and the smaller the fraction they will want to hold as money.

In a simple economy with just two assets (money and bonds) and one interest rate, a rise in the interest rate will reduce the demand for money. Equilibrium in the money market occurs at the intersection of the downward-sloping money demand curve and the vertical money supply curve. The nominal interest rate adjusts so that the quantity of money demanded by households and firms just equals the quantity of money supplied by the Fed and the banking system.

A nominal interest rate above equilibrium in the money market would cause an *excess supply of money* and an *excess demand for bonds*. As people move to acquire more bonds, their price will rise and the nominal interest rate on the bonds will fall. Thus, an excess supply of money will cause the interest rate to fall. Similarly, an *excess demand for money* will cause the interest rate to rise.

The Fed can lower the nominal interest rate by increasing the money supply. With no change in expected inflation, a decrease in the nominal interest rate is also a decrease in the real interest rate. This will increase aggregate expenditure and equilibrium GDP. In theory, by targeting the nominal interest rate, the Fed can control aggregate expenditure and real GDP.

In the real world, with many assets and many interest rates, the Fed conducts conventional monetary policy by announcing a target for the *federal funds rate*—the interest rate that banks charge for lending reserves to other banks.

The Fed has traditionally used open market operations to continually adjust the money supply as needed to maintain the target, so the money supply changes as a by-product of targeting the federal funds rate. The Fed can also use a relatively new tool—the interest rate it pays on reserves (the *IOR rate*)—to put a floor under the federal funds rate.

Changes in the federal funds rate normally lead to changes in other interest rates in the economy. Lowering the federal funds rate—and other interest rates—generally shifts the aggregate expenditure line upward and raises real GDP; raising the federal funds rate has the opposite effects.

Under certain conditions (changing interest rate *spreads*, a federal funds rate approaching zero, or a financial crisis) the Fed will have to use *unconventional* tools to conduct monetary policy. Among these are emergency lending to financial institutions, interventions in specific markets for assets, and changing the expected rate of inflation. Each of these tools has costs and risks, and are only used in extraordinary circumstances.

PROBLEM SET

Answers to even-numbered Problems can be found on the text Web site through www.cengagebrain.com

1. Assume the money multiplier is 10. For each of the following, state the impact on the money supply curve (the direction it will shift, and the amount of the shift), and whether the nominal interest rate will rise or fall as a consequence.
   a. The Fed purchases bonds worth $10 billion.
   b. The Fed sells bonds worth $5 billion.

2. Assume the money multiplier is 7. For each of the following, state the impact on the money supply curve (the direction it will shift, and the amount of the shift), and whether the nominal interest rate will rise or fall as a consequence.
   a. The Fed purchases bonds worth $28 million.
   b. The Fed sells bonds worth $17 million.

3. A bond promises to pay its owner $500 one year from now. For the following prices, find the corresponding interest payments and interest rates that the bond offers.

Price	Amount Paid in 1 Year	Interest Payment	Interest Rate
$375	$500	____	____
$425	$500	____	____
$450	$500	____	____
$500	$500	____	____

As the price of the bond rises, what happens to the bond's interest rate?

4. A bond promises to pay its owner $20,000 one year from now.
   a. Complete the following chart.

Price	Amount Paid in 1 Year	Interest Payment	Interest Rate	Quantity of Money Demanded
	$2,000			$2,300 billion
	$1,500			$2,600 billion
	$1,000			$2,900 billion
	$ 500			$3,200 billion
	$ 0			$3,500 billion

b. Draw a graph of the money market, assuming that it is currently in equilibrium at an interest rate of 5.26 percent. What is the price of this bond? How large is the money supply?

c. Find the new interest rate and the new bond price if the money supply increases by $300 billion. Show this on your graph.

5. A fellow student in your economics class stops you in the hallway and says: "An increase in the demand for money causes the interest rate to rise. But a rise in the interest rate causes people to demand *less* money. Therefore, increases in money demand largely cancel themselves out, and have very little effect on the interest rate." Is this correct? Why or why not? (Hint: Draw a graph.)

6. For each of the following events, state (1) the impact on the money demand curve, and (2) whether the Fed should increase or decrease the money supply if it wants to keep the interest rate unchanged. (Hint: Assume there is just one interest rate in the economy. It will help to draw a diagram of the money market for each case.)

a. People start making more of their purchases over the Internet, using credit cards.

b. Greater fear of credit card fraud makes people stop buying goods over the Internet with credit cards, and discourages the use of credit cards in other types of purchases as well.

c. A new type of electronic account is created in which your funds are held in bonds up to the second you make a purchase. Then—when you buy something—just the right amount of bonds are transferred to the ownership of the seller. (Hint: Would you want to increase or decrease the amount of your wealth in the form of money after this new type of account were available?)

7. Suppose that you own a bond that matures in one year, and promises to pay you $1,000 at that time. The current one-year interest rate in the economy is 6 percent.

a. What is the price that someone would pay for your bond?

b. Suppose that in the next few days, you *expect* the Fed to raise its federal funds rate target, which will cause the interest rate on one-year bonds like yours to rise to 8 percent. What is the price that you *expect* someone would pay for your bond after the Fed acts?

c. If you have confidence in your expectation, which of the following will you want to do *now* (before the Fed acts): (1) acquire more bonds like the one you have; (2) sell your bond now; (3) neither? Explain briefly.

d. If most other people develop the same expectations about the Fed that you have, what will likely happen to the money demand curve *now* (before the Fed acts)?

8. Suppose that there is just one interest rate in the economy. In an attempt to prevent the economy from overheating, the Fed raises its interest rate target. Illustrate graphically, using a diagram similar to Figure 7 in this chapter, the effect on the money supply, interest rate, and GDP.

9. In a later chapter, you will learn that a drop in the interest rate has *another* channel of influence on real GDP: It causes a depreciation of the dollar (that is, it makes the dollar cheaper in terms of foreign currency), which, in turn, increases U.S. net exports.

a. When we take account of the effect on net exports, does a given change in the money supply have *more* or *less* impact on real GDP?

b. Suppose that the Fed wants to stimulate the economy using conventional tools, as it did during late 2007 and early 2008. Should the Fed lower the interest rate by more or by less when it takes the impact on net exports into account (compared to the case of no impact on net exports)? Explain.

10. In Chapter 4, you learned about the difference between flow variables and stock variables. Which theory of the interest rate (long-run/classical or the short-run theory of this chapter) relies on stock variables, and which uses flow variables? Explain briefly.

11. How would each of the following likely affect the spread (increase, decrease, or no effect) between 10-year treasury securities and moderately risky corporate bonds? Explain briefly.

a. A financial crisis develops.

b. A financial crisis ends.

c. The Fed or the Treasury guarantees all payments promised to holders of moderately risky corporate bonds.

d. Due to a rise in oil prices, there is an increased chance of a moderately risky corporation going bankrupt.

e. The government—to fund large budget deficits—offers huge amounts of additional new 10-year treasury securities for sale to the public.

More Challenging

12. As in problem 8, suppose that the Fed raises its interest rate target to prevent the economy from overheating. Illustrate graphically, using a diagram similar to Figure 7, but this time include the *feedback effects* mentioned in the chapter (the impact of rising income on the money market). To hit the same interest rate target, will the Fed have to change the money supply by more than in problem 8? By less? Explain briefly.

Aggregate Demand and Aggregate Supply

Economic fluctuations are facts of life. If you need a reminder, look back at Figure 1 in the chapter titled "Economic Fluctuations." There you can see that while potential GDP tends to move upward year after year due to economic growth, *actual* GDP tends to rise above and fall below potential over shorter periods.

But the figure also reveals another important fact about the economy: Deviations from potential output don't last forever. When output dips below or rises above potential, the economy returns to potential output after a few quarters or years. True, in some of these episodes, government policy—either fiscal or monetary—helped the economy return to full employment more quickly. But even without corrective policies—such as during long parts of the Great Depression of the 1930s—the economy shows a remarkable tendency to begin moving back toward potential output. Why? And what, exactly, is the mechanism that brings us back to our potential when we have strayed from it? These are the questions we will address in this chapter. And we'll address them by studying the behavior of a variable that we've put aside for several chapters: the price level.

The chapter begins by exploring the relationship between the price level and output. This is a two-way relationship, as you can see in Figure 1 in this chapter. On the one hand, changes in the price level can cause changes in real GDP. This causal relationship is illustrated by the *aggregate demand curve,* which we will discuss shortly. On the other hand, changes in real GDP cause changes in the price level. This relationship is summarized by the *aggregate supply curve,* to which we will turn later.

Once we've developed the aggregate demand and supply curves, we'll be able to use them to understand how changes in the price level—sometimes gently, other times more harshly—steer the economy back toward potential output.

There is one important proviso to keep in mind as you read this chapter. To keep the exposition simple, we'll assume that when the economy is in equilibrium, there is no ongoing inflation. That is, once the price level reaches its equilibrium value, it stays there until the economy is hit by some event that causes it to change. This assumption will help us develop the basics of the relationship between the price level and real GDP. But it also means that the model we'll develop is best suited for an economy with no ongoing inflation, or an inflation rate so low that it can be safely ignored. When an economy has significant ongoing inflation even when it's in equilibrium, the model needs to be adjusted. We'll discuss ongoing inflation, and some ways of adjusting the model, in the next chapter.

FIGURE 1   The Two-Way Relationship between Output and the Price Level

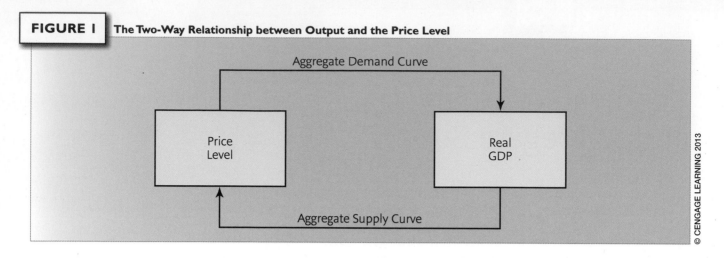

THE AGGREGATE DEMAND CURVE

The aggregate demand curve summarizes how the price level influences real GDP. But *why* would a change in the price level affect real GDP? Our first step in answering that question is to think about *money*.

The Price Level and the Money Market

People hold money because of its convenience. Each day, as we make purchases, we need cash or funds in our checking accounts to pay for them. Even if we pay by credit card, we need funds in our checking accounts to pay the bill each month. Of course, when we hold money, we give up the interest we could have earned if we were holding other assets. For now, let's use the simplest version of the money market, where we assume the economy has just *one* interest rate, and all assets (other than money) pay that rate. In that case, the money demand curve tells us how much of their wealth people want to hold as money (as opposed to other assets) at each interest rate.

What if the price level *rises,* and our average purchase is more expensive? Then we'll need to hold *more* of our wealth as money just to achieve the same level of convenience. Thus, at any given interest rate, the demand for money increases, and the money demand curve shifts rightward, as illustrated in Figure 2(a).

What happens then? That depends on how the Fed would respond. We'll be exploring possible Fed reactions to changes in the price level in the next chapter. For now, we'll assume that the Federal Reserve *does not change the money supply.*

With an unchanged money supply, the rightward shift of the money demand curve in Figure 2(a) will initially cause an excess demand for money, which—as you learned in the previous chapter—causes the interest rate to rise.

> *An increase in the price level (with no change in the money supply) shifts the money demand curve rightward, and raises the equilibrium interest rate.*

Understanding the Assumptions

Before we go further, let's spend a moment understanding some of the assumptions we're making about the money market. First, why do we assume a constant money supply? In

FIGURE 2   Deriving the Aggregate Demand Curve

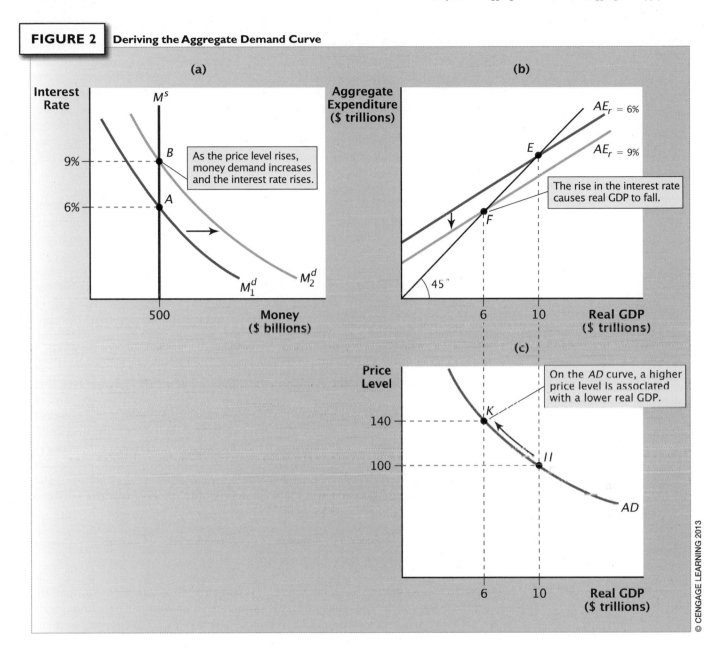

(a)

Interest Rate

M^s

9% — B

As the price level rises, money demand increases and the interest rate rises.

6% — A

M_1^d M_2^d

500   **Money ($ billions)**

(b)

Aggregate Expenditure ($ trillions)

$AE_r = 6\%$

E

$AE_r = 9\%$

The rise in the interest rate causes real GDP to fall.

F

45°   6   10   **Real GDP ($ trillions)**

(c)

Price Level

On the *AD* curve, a higher price level is associated with a lower real GDP.

140 — K

100 — II

AD

6   10   **Real GDP ($ trillions)**

© CENGAGE LEARNING 2013

large part, so we have a benchmark against which we can later compare different possible Fed responses. But the assumption also serves another purpose: It will help us understand the economy's *self-correcting mechanism*—a topic we'll discuss later in this chapter.

Assuming a constant money supply is equivalent to viewing the money supply as determined by forces *outside* of our model. (This is similar to how we assumed that tastes and technology were treated as given variables in the simple supply and demand model of Chapter 3.) The constant-money-supply assumption corresponds roughly to earlier historical periods in the U.S. and other countries, before there was a Federal Reserve (or a central bank) that would actively change the money supply to stabilize the economy. Instead, the money supply was backed by gold, which served a role very similar to bank reserves in the modern financial system.

With the gold standard, the money supply would often change, as more gold was mined, or gold flowed into or out of the country, or citizens responded to economic events by moving gold into or out of the banking system. But there was no intelligent hand adjusting the money supply or targeting the interest rate to make the economy perform at its best. Yet, even without active monetary policy, the economy tended to recover from deep recessions, and *eventually* find its way back to full employment, as the classical model predicts. So viewing the money supply as a "given" can help us understand how the economy can, over time, correct itself even without a central bank or a Fed to give it a nudge. It can also help us understand why the self-correcting process can be long and painful, and how a wise monetary policy can be helpful.

Second, note that Figure 2(a) refers to the interest rate, rather than to the *nominal* interest rate. In this chapter, nominal and real interest rates are the same, because we're assuming there is *no ongoing inflation*. So for example, when the price level rises, there is a temporary bout of inflation, but the inflation stops when the price level gets to its destination. Prices do not keep rising, nor does anyone expect them to keep rising. If no one expects continued inflation, then everyone treats the real interest rate as equal to the nominal interest rate when making decisions about spending. This is why we'll refer to *the* interest rate throughout this chapter, represented by the letter r.

Finally, in this chapter, we're discussing the economy as if there were only a single interest rate. But with many different interest rates, our story would be very much the same—as long as all interest rates move up and down together. The interest rate in Figure 2(a), for example, can represent the *average* interest rate in the economy. When the price level rises, people want to hold more wealth in the form of money at each average interest rate, and the money demand curve shifts rightward. As people try to acquire more money by selling other assets, the prices of these other assets fall, and their interest rates rise—causing the average interest rate to rise as well. The broad conclusions we'll come to in this chapter also apply when there are many interest rates, as long as they all move together.

Deriving the Aggregate Demand Curve

So far, you've seen how a change in the price level can change the interest rate in the money market. Now we'll connect the price level with equilibrium GDP. Look again at Figure 2(a), where the initial money demand curve is M_1^d. That money demand curve has been drawn for a particular price level (let's give it an arbitrary value of 100). With that price level, the money market is initially in equilibrium at point A, and the interest rate is 6 percent.

Now move to panel (b), which shows the initial position of aggregate expenditure line, $AE_{r-6\%}$, when the interest rate is 6 percent. With this aggregate expenditure line, equilibrium GDP is found at point E, with output equal to $10 trillion.

Now let's imagine a rather substantial rise in the price level, from 100 to 140. What will happen in the economy? The initial impact, as you've learned, is in the money market. The money demand curve will start to shift rightward, and the interest rate will rise. Next, in panel (b), the higher interest rate decreases interest-sensitive spending—business investment, new housing, and consumer durables. The aggregate expenditure line shifts downward, and equilibrium real GDP decreases. All of these changes continue until we reach a new, consistent equilibrium in both panels. Compared with our initial position, this new equilibrium has the following characteristics:

- The money demand curve has shifted rightward.
- The interest rate is higher.
- The aggregate expenditure line has shifted downward.
- Equilibrium GDP is lower.

Remember that all of these changes are caused by a rise in the price level.

Figure 2 shows one possible new equilibrium that meets these requirements. In panel (a), the money demand curve has shifted to M^d_2. The interest rate has risen to 9 percent. In panel (b), the aggregate expenditure line has shifted downward, to the one marked "$r = 9\%$." Finally, equilibrium output has fallen to $6 trillion.

Now recall the initial event that caused real GDP to fall: a rise in the price level. We've thus established an important principle:

> *A rise in the price level, with a constant money supply, causes a decrease in equilibrium GDP.*

In panel (c), we introduce a new curve that directly shows the negative relationship between the price level and equilibrium GDP. In this panel, the price level is measured along the vertical axis, while real GDP is on the horizontal. Point H represents our initial equilibrium, with $P = 100$ and equilibrium GDP $= $10 trillion. Point K represents the new equilibrium, with $P = 140$ and equilibrium GDP $= $6 trillion. If we continued to change the price level to other values—raising it further to 150, lowering it to 85, and so on—we would find that each different price level results in a different equilibrium GDP. This is illustrated by the downward-sloping curve in the figure, which we call the *aggregate demand curve*.

> *The **aggregate demand** (AD) curve tells us the equilibrium real GDP at any price level, with a constant money supply.*

Aggregate demand (AD) curve A curve indicating equilibrium GDP at each price level when the money supply is constant.

Understanding the AD Curve

The *AD* curve is unlike any other curve you've encountered in this text. In all other cases, our curves have represented simple behavioral relationships. For example, the demand curve for maple syrup shows us how a change in price affects the behavior of buyers in a market. Similarly, the aggregate expenditure line shows how a change in income affects total spending in the economy.

But the *AD* curve represents more than just a behavioral relationship between two variables. Each point on the curve represents a short-run *equilibrium* in the economy. For example, point H on the *AD* curve in Figure 2 tells us that when the price level is 100, *equilibrium* GDP is $10 trillion. Thus, point H doesn't just tell us that total spending is $10 trillion; rather, it tells us that when $P = 100$, spending and output are equal to each other only when they *both* are equal to $10 trillion.

⚠ DANGEROUS CURVES

Two misconceptions about the AD curve Watch out for two common mistakes. The first is thinking that the AD curve is simply a "total demand" or "total spending" curve for the economy. This is an oversimplification. Rather, the AD curve tells us the *equilibrium* real GDP at each price level. This is the level of output at which total spending *equals* total output. Thus, total spending is only part of the story behind the AD curve: The other part is the requirement that total spending and total output be equal.

A second, related mistake is thinking that the AD curve slopes downward for the same reason that a microeconomic demand curve slopes downward. This, too, is wrong. In the market for maple syrup, for example, a rise in price causes quantity demanded to decrease, mostly because people switch to *other* goods that are now relatively cheaper. But along the AD curve, a rise in the price level generally causes the prices of *all* goods to increase *together*. There are no relatively cheaper goods to switch to!

The AD curve works in an entirely different way from microeconomic demand curves. Along the AD curve, an increase in the price level raises the interest rate in the money market, which decreases spending on interest-sensitive goods, causing a drop in equilibrium GDP.

© AXL/SHUTTERSTOCK.COM

As you can see, a better name for the AD curve would be the "equilibrium-output-at-each-price-level" curve—not a very catchy name. The AD curve gets its name because it *resembles* the demand curve for an individual product. It's a downward-sloping curve, with the price level (instead of the price of a single good) on the vertical axis and *equilibrium total output* (instead of the quantity of a single good demanded) on the horizontal axis. But there the similarity ends. The AD curve is not a demand curve at all, in spite of its name.

Movements along the AD Curve

Whenever the price level changes, we move *along* the AD curve. It's important to understand what happens in the economy as we make such a move.

Look again at the AD curve in panel (c) of Figure 2. Suppose the price level rises, and we move from point H to point K along this curve. Then the following sequence of events occurs: The rise in the price level increases the demand for money, raises the interest rate, decreases autonomous consumption (a) and investment spending (I^p), and works through the multiplier to decrease equilibrium GDP. The process can be summarized as follows:

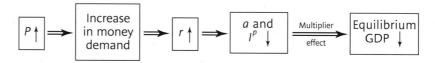

The opposite sequence of events will occur if the price level falls, moving us rightward along the AD curve:

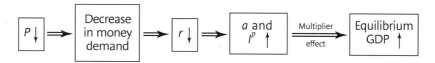

Shifts of the AD Curve

When we move along the AD curve in Figure 2, we assume that the price level changes but that other influences on equilibrium GDP are constant. When any of these other influences on GDP changes, the AD curve will shift. The distinction between movements along the AD curve and shifts of the curve itself is very important. Always keep the following rule in mind:

When a change in the price level causes equilibrium GDP to change, we move along the AD curve. Whenever anything other than the price level causes equilibrium GDP to change, the AD curve itself shifts.

What are these other influences on GDP? They are the very same changes you learned about in previous chapters. Specifically, equilibrium GDP will change whenever there is a change in any of the following:

- Government purchases
- Taxes
- Autonomous consumption spending
- Investment spending
- Net exports
- The money supply

Let's consider some examples and see how each causes the *AD* curve to shift.

An Increase in Government Purchases

In Figure 3, we assume that the economy begins at a price level of 100. In the money market (not shown), the equilibrium interest rate is 6 percent and equilibrium output—given by point *E* in panel (a)—is $10 trillion. Panel (b) shows the same equilibrium as represented by point *H* on AD_1.

Now let's repeat an experiment from an earlier chapter: We'll increase government purchases—this time by $1 trillion—and ask: What will happen to equilibrium GDP assuming *the price level remains at 100?* If the MPC is 0.6, and our simple multiplier formula applies, the value of the multiplier will be $1/(1 − 0.6) = 2.5$. Therefore, GDP will rise by $1 trillion × 2.5 = $2.5 trillion. Our new value for equilibrium GDP is $12.5 trillion. This new equilibrium is also shown in panel (a) of Figure 3. The aggregate expenditure line shifts upward

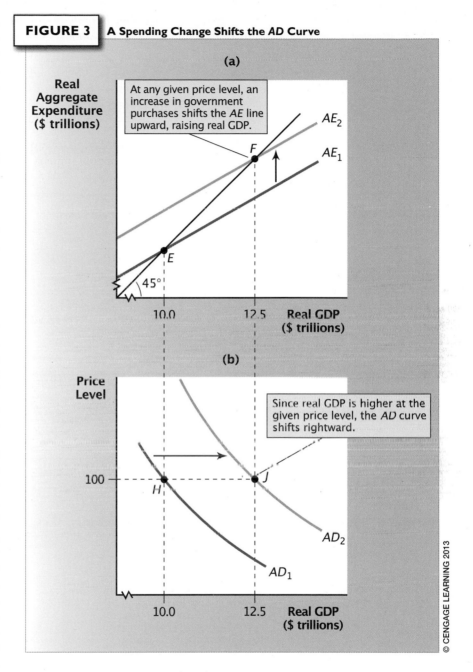

FIGURE 3   **A Spending Change Shifts the *AD* Curve**

to AE_2, and the equilibrium moves to point *F*. With the price level remaining at 100, equilibrium GDP increases.

Now look at panel (b) in Figure 3. There, the new equilibrium is represented by point *J* (*P* = 100, real GDP = $12.5 trillion). This point lies to the right of our original curve AD_1. Point *J*, therefore, must lie on a *new AD* curve—a curve that tells us equilibrium GDP at any price level *after the increase in government spending*. The new *AD* curve is the one labeled AD_2, which goes through point *J*. What about the other points on AD_2? They tell us that, if we had started at any *other* price level, an increase in government spending would have increased equilibrium GDP at that price level, too. We conclude that *an increase in government purchases shifts the entire* AD *curve rightward*.

Any other factor that initially shifts the aggregate expenditure line upward will shift the *AD* curve rightward, just as in Figure 3. More specifically,

> *the* AD *curve shifts rightward when government purchases, investment spending, autonomous consumption spending, or net exports increase, or when net taxes decrease.*

Our analysis also applies in the other direction. For example, at any given price level, a *decrease* in government spending shifts the aggregate expenditure

---

FIGURE 4   **Effects of Key Changes on the Aggregate Demand Curve**

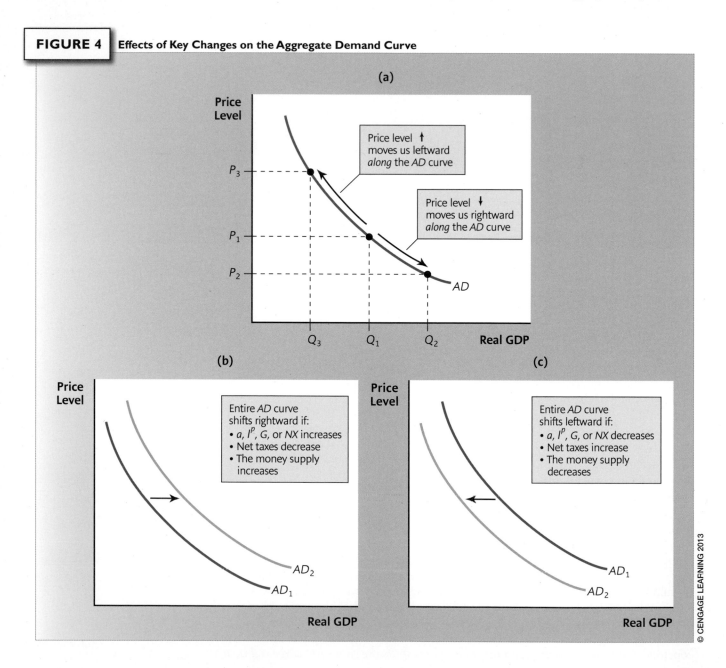

(a)

Price level ↑ moves us leftward *along* the *AD* curve

Price level ↓ moves us rightward *along* the *AD* curve

(b)

Entire *AD* curve shifts rightward if:
• *a*, I^p, *G*, or *NX* increases
• Net taxes decrease
• The money supply increases

(c)

Entire *AD* curve shifts leftward if:
• *a*, I^p, *G*, or *NX* decreases
• Net taxes increase
• The money supply decreases

© CENGAGE LEARNING 2013

line *downward,* decreasing equilibrium GDP. This in turn shifts the *AD* curve leftward.

Changes in the Money Supply

Changes in the money supply will also shift the aggregate demand curve. To see why, let's imagine that the Fed *increases* the money supply. As you learned in the previous chapter, this will cause the interest rate to decrease, increasing investment spending and autonomous consumption spending. Together, these spending changes will shift the aggregate expenditure line upward, just as in panel (a) of Figure 3, and increase equilibrium GDP. Because this change in equilibrium output is caused by something *other* than a change in the price level, the *AD* curve shifts. In this case, because the money supply *increased,* the *AD* curve shifts *rightward,* just as in panel (b) of Figure 3.

> An increase in the money supply shifts the AD *curve rightward.*

A decrease in the money supply would have the opposite effect: The interest rate would rise, the aggregate expenditure line would shift downward, and *equilibrium GDP at any price level would fall.*

Shifts versus Movements along the AD Curve: A Summary

Figure 4 summarizes how some events in the economy cause a movement along the *AD* curve, and other events shift the *AD* curve. You can use the figure as an exercise, drawing diagrams similar to Figures 2 and 3 to illustrate why we move along or shift the *AD* curve in each case.

Notice that panels (b) and (c) of Figure 4 tell us how a variety of events affect the *AD* curve, but *not* how they affect *real GDP.* The reason is that, even if we know which *AD* curve we are on, we could be at *any point* along that curve, depending on where the price level ends up.

But where will the price level end up? To answer that question, we must understand the other side of the relationship between GDP and the price level.

THE AGGREGATE SUPPLY CURVE

Look back at Figure 1, which illustrates the *two-way* relationship between the price level and output. On the one hand, changes in the price level affect output. This is the relationship, summarized by the *AD* curve, which we've just explored in the previous section. On the other hand, changes in output affect the price level. This relationship—summarized by the *aggregate supply curve*—is the focus of this section.

The effect of changes in output on the price level is complex, involving a variety of forces. Current research is helping economists get a clearer picture of this relationship. Here, we will present a simple model of the aggregate supply curve that focuses on the link between prices and costs. Toward the end of the chapter, we'll discuss some additional ideas about the aggregate supply curve.

Fast-food restaurants, like other firms in the economy, charge a markup over cost per unit. The average markup in the economy is determined by competitive conditions and tends to change slowly over time.

SUSAN VAN ETTEN

Costs and Prices

The price *level* in the economy results from the pricing behavior of millions of individual business firms. In any given year, some of these firms will raise their prices, and some will lower them. For example, in recent years, tablet computers and smart phones have come down in price, while college tuition and the prices of movies have risen. These types of price changes are subjects for *microeconomic* analysis, because they involve individual markets.

But often, all firms in the economy are affected by the same *macroeconomic* event, causing prices to rise or fall throughout the economy. This change in the price *level* is what interests us in macroeconomics.

To understand how macroeconomic events affect the price level, we begin with a very simple assumption:

> *Firms set the prices of their products as a markup over their cost per unit.*

For example, if it costs Burger King $2.50, on average, to produce a Whopper (cost per unit is $2.50), and Burger King's percentage markup is 10 percent, then it will charge $2.50 + (0.10 \times $2.50) = $2.75 per Whopper.[1]

The percentage markup in any particular industry will depend on the degree of competition there. If there are many firms competing for customers in a market, all producing very similar products, then we can expect the markup to be relatively small. Thus, we expect a relatively low markup on fast-food burgers or personal computers. In industries where there is less competition—such as daily newspapers or jet aircraft—we would expect higher percentage markups.

In macroeconomics, we are not concerned with how the markup varies among different industries, but rather with the *average percentage markup* in the economy:

> *The average percentage markup in the economy is determined by competitive conditions in the economy. The competitive structure of the economy changes very slowly, so the average percentage markup should be somewhat stable from year to year.*

In our analysis, we'll assume that there is some "normal" percentage markup in the economy, which does not change over the period of time we're considering. But a stable markup does not necessarily mean a stable price level, because unit costs can change. For example, if Burger King's markup remains at 10 percent, but the unit cost of a Whopper rises from $2.50 to $3.00, then the price of a Whopper will rise to $3.00 + (0.10 \times $3.00) = $3.30. Extending this example to all firms in the economy, we can say:

> *In the short run, the price level rises when there is an economy-wide increase in unit costs, and the price level falls when there is an economy-wide decrease in unit costs.*

---

[1] In microeconomics, you learn more sophisticated theories of how firms' prices are determined. But our simple markup model captures a central conclusion of those theories: that an increase in costs will result in higher prices.

How GDP Affects Unit Costs

In the complex real-world economy, unit costs can change for many reasons. Our primary concern in this chapter is the impact of *real GDP* on unit costs and, therefore, on the price level. Why should a change in total output affect unit costs? We'll focus on three key reasons.

As total output increases:

Greater amounts of inputs may be needed to produce a unit of output. As output increases, firms hire new, untrained workers who may be less productive than existing workers. Firms also begin using capital and land that are less well suited to their industry. As a result, greater amounts of labor, capital, land, and raw materials are needed to produce each unit of output. Even if the prices of these inputs remain the same, unit costs will rise.

For example, imagine that Intel increases its output of computer chips. Then it will have to be less picky about the workers it employs, hiring some who are less well suited to chip production than those already working there. Thus, more labor hours will be needed to produce each chip. Intel may also have to begin using older, less-efficient production facilities, which require more silicon and other raw materials per chip. Even if the prices of all of these inputs remain unchanged, unit costs will rise.

The prices of nonlabor inputs rise. In addition to needing greater quantities of inputs, firms will have to pay a higher price for them. This is especially true of inputs like land and natural resources, which may be available only in limited quantities in the short run. An increase in the output of final goods raises the demand for these inputs, causing their prices to rise. Firms that produce final goods experience an increase in unit costs, and raise their own prices accordingly.

The nominal wage rate rises. Greater output means higher employment, leaving fewer unemployed workers looking for jobs. As firms compete to hire increasingly scarce workers, they must offer higher nominal wage rates to attract them. Higher nominal wages increase unit costs, and therefore result in a higher price level. Notice that we use the nominal wage, rather than the real wage we've emphasized elsewhere in this book. That's because we are interested in explaining how firms' prices are determined. Because price is a nominal variable, it is marked up over *nominal* costs.

A decrease in output affects unit costs through the same three forces, but with the opposite result. As output falls, firms can be more selective in hiring the best, most efficient workers and in choosing other inputs, decreasing their input requirements per unit of output. Decreases in demand for land and natural resources will cause their prices to drop. And as unemployment rises, wages will fall as workers compete for jobs. Each of these forces contributes to a drop in unit costs, and a decrease in the price level.

Short Run versus Long Run

All three of our reasons are important in explaining why a change in output affects unit costs. However, they operate within different time frames. When total output increases, new, less-productive workers will be hired rather quickly. Similarly, the prices of certain key inputs—such as lumber, land, oil, and wheat—may rise within a few weeks or months.

But our third explanation—changes in the nominal wage rate—is a different story. While wages in some lines of work might respond very rapidly, we can expect wages in many industries to change very little or not at all for a year or more after a change in output. Economists sometimes refer to this phenomenon as "wage stickiness."

> *For a year or so after a change in output, nominal wages are "sticky," and are less important than other forces in changing unit costs.*

Why Are Nominal Wages Sticky?

Economists have long observed that nominal wages tend to adjust slowly after economic conditions change. We don't have to understand *why* this happens in order to use it in a macroeconomic model. But economists are very interested in understanding why wages are sticky because—as you'll see later in this chapter—they can prolong deviations from full-employment output. While there is no single, definitive explanation for sticky wages, there are a number of plausible ones, including the following:

- Many firms have union contracts that specify wages for up to three years. Although wage increases are often built into these contracts, a rise in output will not affect the amount of the wage increase. When output rises or falls, these firms continue to abide by the contract.
- Wages in many large corporations are set by slow-moving bureaucracies.
- Wage changes in either direction can be costly to firms. Higher wages to attract new workers must be widely publicized in order to raise the number of job applicants at the firm. Lower wages can reduce the morale of workers—and their productivity. Thus, when output changes, many firms delay raising or lowering wages, until they are reasonably sure that the change in output is long lasting.
- Firms may benefit from developing reputations for paying stable wages. A firm that raises wages when output is high and labor is scarce may have to lower wages when output is low and labor is plentiful. Such a firm would develop a reputation for paying unstable wages, and have difficulty attracting new workers.

Sticky Wages and the Short Run

For the next several pages, we'll be focusing exclusively on the short run—a time horizon of a year or so after a change in output. Since the average nominal wage rate changes very little over the short run, we'll make the following simplifying assumption: *The nominal wage rate is fixed in the short run.* More specifically,

> *we assume that changes in output have no effect on the nominal wage rate in the short run.*

Keep in mind, though, that our assumption of a constant wage holds only in the *short run*. As you will see later, wage changes play a very important role in the economy's adjustment over the long run.

Because we assume a constant nominal wage in the short run, a change in output will affect unit costs through the other two factors we mentioned earlier. Specifically, in the short run, a rise in real GDP raises firms' unit costs because (1) input requirements per unit of output rise, and (2) the prices of nonlabor inputs rise. In the other direction, a *drop* in real GDP lowers unit costs because (1) input requirements per unit of output fall, and (2) the prices of nonlabor inputs fall.

FIGURE 5   The Aggregate Supply Curve

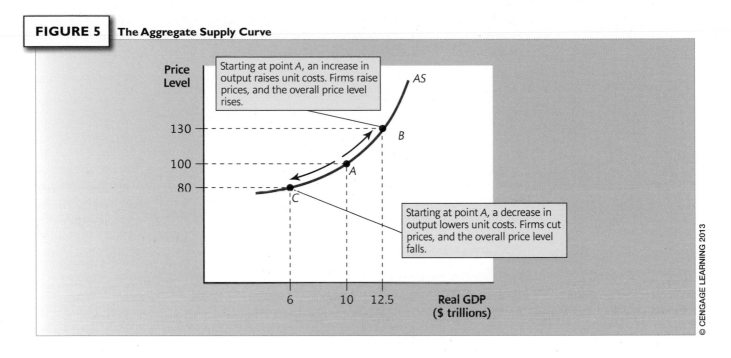

Deriving the Aggregate Supply Curve

Now we're ready to put together the two insights behind the aggregate supply curve: the impact of real GDP on unit costs, and the impact of unit costs on the price level.

> *A rise in real GDP increases unit costs, which—given a stable average markup in the economy—causes the price level to rise. A decrease in real GDP causes unit costs to fall, which—given a stable average markup in the economy— causes the price level to drop.*

Figure 5 formalizes this relationship with a graph. Suppose the economy begins at point *A*, with output at $10 trillion and the price level at 100. Now suppose that output rises to $12.5 trillion. What will happen in the short run? Even though wages are assumed to remain constant, the price level will rise because of the other forces we've discussed. In the figure, the price level rises to 130, indicated by point *B*. If, instead, output *fell* to $6 trillion, the price level would fall—to 80 in the figure, indicated by point *C*.

As you can see, each time we change the level of output, there will be a new price level in the short run, giving us another point on the figure. If we connect all of these points, we obtain the economy's *aggregate supply curve*:

> *The **aggregate supply curve** (or **AS curve**) tells us the price level that is consistent with firms' unit costs and their percentage markups at any level of output over the short run.*

Aggregate supply (AS) curve
A curve indicating the price level that is consistent with firms' unit costs and markups for any level of output over the short run.

A more accurate name for the *AS* curve would be the "short-run-price-level-at-each-output-level" curve, but that is more than a mouthful. The *AS* curve gets its name because it *resembles* a microeconomic market supply curve. Like the supply curve for maple syrup we discussed in Chapter 3, the *AS* curve is upward sloping, and it has a price variable (the price level) on the vertical axis and a quantity variable (total output) on the horizontal axis. But there the similarity ends.

Movements along the *AS* Curve

When a change in output causes the price level to change, we *move along* the economy's *AS* curve. But what happens in the economy as we make such a move?

Look again at the *AS* curve in Figure 5. Suppose we move from point *A* to point *B* along this curve in the short run. The increase in output raises the prices of raw materials and other (nonlabor) inputs and also raises input requirements per unit of output at many firms. Both of these changes increase costs per unit. As long as the markup remains somewhat stable, the rise in unit costs will lead firms to raise their prices, and the price level will increase. Thus, as we move upward along the *AS* curve, we can represent what happens as follows:

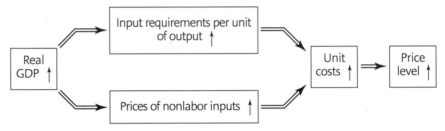

The opposite sequence of events occurs when real GDP falls, moving us downward along the *AS* curve:

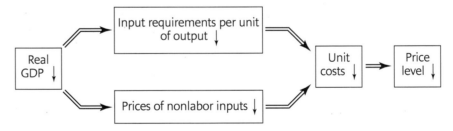

Shifts of the *AS* Curve

When we drew the *AS* curve in Figure 5, we assumed that a number of important variables remained unchanged. In particular, we assumed that the only changes in unit costs were those caused by a change in output. But in the real world, unit costs sometimes change for reasons *other* than a change in output. When this occurs, unit costs—*and* the price level—will change at *any* level of output, so the *AS* curve will shift.

In general, we distinguish between a movement along the *AS* curve, and a shift of the curve itself, as follows:

> *When a change in real GDP causes the price level to change, we move along the* AS *curve. When anything other than a change in real GDP causes the price level to change, the* AS *curve itself shifts.*

Figure 6 illustrates the logic of a shift in the *AS* curve. Suppose the economy's initial *AS* curve is AS_1. Now suppose that some economic event *other* than a change

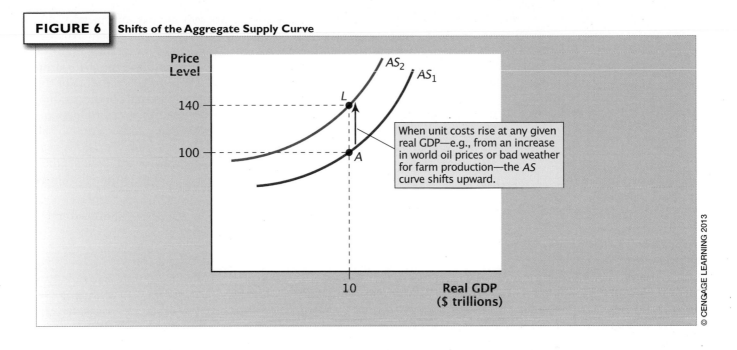

FIGURE 6   Shifts of the Aggregate Supply Curve

Price Level axis with values 140, 100. *Real GDP ($ trillions)* axis with value 10. Curves AS_2 and AS_1. Point L at (10, 140), point A at (10, 100).

Callout: When unit costs rise at any given real GDP—e.g., from an increase in world oil prices or bad weather for farm production—the *AS* curve shifts upward.

in output—for the moment, we'll leave the event unnamed—causes firms to raise their prices. Then the price level will be higher at *any* level of output we might imagine, so the *AS* curve must shift *upward*—for example, to AS_2 in the figure. At an output level of $10 trillion, the price level would rise from 100 to 140. At any other output level, the price level would also rise.

What can cause unit costs to change at any given level of output? The following are some important examples:

- *Changes in world oil prices.* Oil is traded on a world market, where prices can fluctuate even while output in the United States does not. And changes in world oil prices have often caused shifts in the *AS* curve. For example, from January 2007 to July 2008, the price of oil rose from about $60 per barrel to more than $140. (A major reason, as discussed in Chapter 3, was rapidly rising demand for oil in fast-growing economies such as China and India.) Some firms—especially those that use relatively large quantities of oil, gasoline, or jet fuel (including FedEx, UPS, and American Airlines)—raised prices right away, as did gasoline retailers. The aggregate supply curve shifted noticeably upward, and the price level (as measured by the consumer price index) shot up by about 8.6 percent over this 18-month period (much faster than it had been rising earlier).

Conversely, oil prices fell sharply during 1997 and 1998. This caused unit costs to decrease at many firms, shifting the *AS* curve downward.

DANGEROUS CURVES

A misconception about the AS curve A common mistake about the AS curve is thinking that it describes the same kind of relationship between price and quantity as a microeconomic supply curve. There are two reasons why this is wrong.

First, in our model of the AS curve, the direction of causation between price and output is reversed. For example, when we draw the supply curve for maple syrup, we view changes in the price of maple syrup as causing a change in output supplied. But along the AS curve, it's the other way around: A change in *output* causes a change in the *price level*.

Second, the basic assumption behind the AS curve is very different from that behind a single market supply curve. When we draw the supply curve for an individual product, we assume that the prices of inputs used in producing the good remain fixed. This is a sensible thing to do because an increase in production for a single good is unlikely to have much effect on input prices in the economy as a whole.

But when we draw the AS curve, we imagine an increase in *real GDP*, in which *all* firms are increasing their output. This will significantly raise the demand for inputs, so it is unrealistic to assume that input prices remain fixed. Indeed, the rise in input prices is one of the important reasons for the AS curve's upward slope.

- *Changes in the weather*. Good crop-growing weather increases farmers' yields for any given amounts of land, labor, capital, and other inputs used. This decreases farms' unit costs, and the price of agricultural goods falls. Since many of these goods are final goods (such as fresh fruit and vegetables), the price drop will contribute directly to a drop in the price level and a downward shift of the *AS* curve. Additionally, agricultural products are important inputs in the production of many other goods. (For example, corn is an input in beef production.) Good weather thus leads to a drop in input prices for many other firms in the economy, causing their unit costs, and their prices, to decrease. For these reasons, we can expect good weather to shift the *AS* curve downward. Bad weather, which decreases crop yields, increases unit costs at any level of output and shifts the *AS* curve upward.

FIGURE 7   Effects of Key Changes on the Aggregate Supply Curve

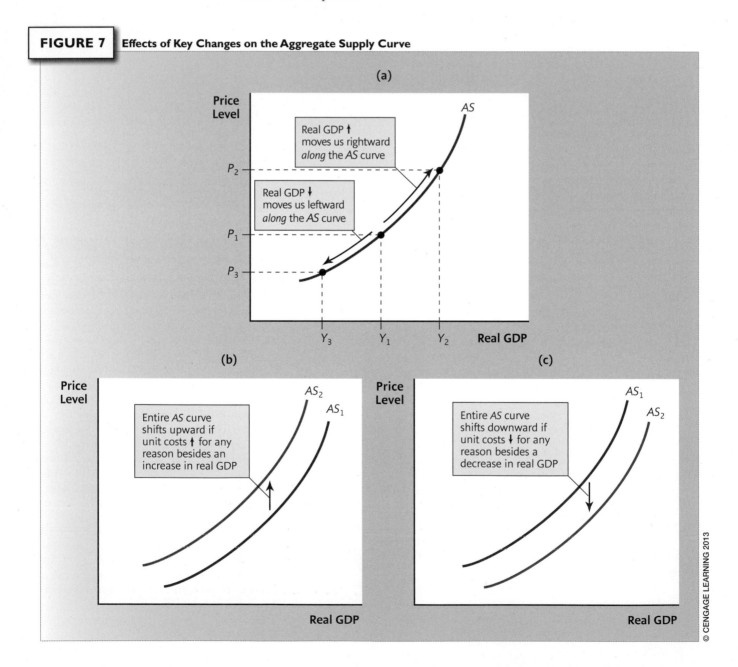

- *Technological change.* New technologies can enable firms to produce any given level of output at lower unit costs. For example, the development of the Internet, and continual improvements in its speed over the last decade, have lowered administrative and information costs for business throughout the economy. As technology improves, the *AS* curve tends to shift downward over time.
- *The nominal wage.* Remember that in our short-run analysis we're assuming the nominal wage rate does *not* change. As we move along the *AS* curve, we hold the nominal wage rate constant. But later in the chapter—when we extend our time horizon beyond a year or so—you'll see that changes in the nominal wage are an important part of the economy's long-run adjustment process. Here we just point out that, *if* the nominal wage were to increase for any reason, it would raise unit costs for firms at any level of output and therefore *shift* the *AS* curve *upward*. Similarly, *if* the nominal wage rate were to fall for any reason, it would *decrease* unit costs at any level of output and shift the *AS* curve downward. We'll come back to this important fact later.

Figure 7 summarizes how different events in the economy cause a movement along, or a shift in, the *AS* curve.

But the *AS* curve tells only half of the economy's story: It shows us the price level *if* we know the level of output. The *AD* curve tells the other half of the story: It shows us the level of output *if* we know the economy's price level. In the next section, we finally put the two halves of the story together, allowing us to determine both the price level and output.

AD AND AS TOGETHER: SHORT-RUN EQUILIBRIUM

Where will the economy settle in the short run? That is, where is our **short-run macroeconomic equilibrium?** Figure 8 shows how to answer that question, using both the *AS* curve and the *AD* curve. If you suspect that the equilibrium is at

Short-run macroeconomic equilibrium A combination of price level and GDP consistent with both the *AD* and *AS* curves.

FIGURE 8   **Short-Run Macroeconomic Equilibrium**

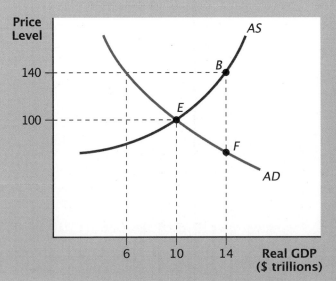

Short-run equilibrium occurs where the AD and AS curves intersect. At point E, the price level of 100 is consistent with an output of $10 trillion along the AD curve. The output level of $10 trillion is consistent with a price level of 100 along the AS curve. At any other combination of price level and output, such as point F or point B, at least one condition for equilibrium will not be satisfied.

© CENGAGE LEARNING 2013

point *E*, the intersection of these two curves, you are correct. At that point, the price level is 100 and output is $10 trillion. But it's worth thinking about *why* point *E*—and only point *E*—is our short-run equilibrium.

First, we know that in equilibrium, the economy must be at some point on the *AD* curve. For example, suppose the economy were at point *B*, which is on the *AS* curve, but lies to the right of the *AD* curve. At this point, the price level is 140 and output is $14 trillion. But the *AD* curve tells us that with a price level of 140, *equilibrium* output is $6 trillion. Thus, at point *B*, real GDP would be greater than its equilibrium value. As you learned several chapters ago, this situation cannot persist for long, since inventories would pile up and firms would be forced to cut back on their production. Thus, point *B* cannot be our short-run equilibrium.

Second, short-run equilibrium requires that the economy be operating on its *AS* curve. Otherwise, firms would not be charging the prices dictated by their unit costs and the average percentage markup in the economy. For example, point *F* lies *below* the *AS* curve. But the *AS* curve tells us that if output is $14 trillion, based on the average percentage markup and unit costs, the price level should be 140 (point *B*), not something lower. That is, the price level at point *F* is *too low* for equilibrium. This situation will not last long either, since firms will want to raise prices, causing the overall price level to rise.

We could make a similar argument for any other point that is off the *AS* curve, off the *AD* curve, or off of both curves. Our conclusion is always the same: Unless the economy is on *both* the *AS* and the *AD* curves, the price level and the level of output will change. Only when the economy is at point *E*—on *both* curves—can we have a sustainable real GDP and price level.

WHAT HAPPENS WHEN THINGS CHANGE?

Now that we know how the short-run equilibrium is determined, and armed with our knowledge of the *AD* and *AS* curves, we are ready to put the model through its paces. In this section, we'll explore how different types of events cause the short-run equilibrium to change.

Our short-run equilibrium will change when either the *AD* curve, the *AS* curve, or both, *shift*. Since the consequences for the economy are very different for shifts in the *AD* curve as opposed to shifts in the *AS* curve, economists have developed a shorthand language to distinguish between them:

Demand shock Any event that causes the *AD* curve to shift.

Supply shock Any event that causes the *AS* curve to shift.

> *An event that causes the* AD *curve to shift is called a* **demand shock.** *An event that causes the* AS *curve to shift is called a* **supply shock.**

In this section, we'll first explore the effects of demand shocks, both in the short run and during the adjustment process to the long run. Then, we'll take up the issue of supply shocks.

Demand Shocks in the Short Run

Figure 4, which lists the causes of a shift in the *AD* curve, also serves as a list of demand shocks to the economy. Let's consider some examples.

FIGURE 9   **The Effect of a Demand Shock**

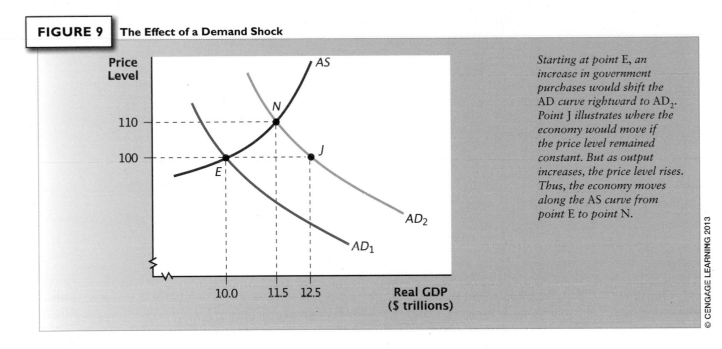

Starting at point E, an increase in government purchases would shift the AD curve rightward to AD_2. Point J illustrates where the economy would move if the price level remained constant. But as output increases, the price level rises. Thus, the economy moves along the AS curve from point E to point N.

An Increase in Government Purchases

You've learned that an increase in government purchases shifts the *AD* curve rightward. Now we can see how it affects the economy in the short run. Figure 9 shows the initial equilibrium at point *E*, with the price level equal to 100 and output at $10 trillion. Now, suppose that government purchases rise by $1 trillion, causing the *AD* curve to shift rightward. What will happen to equilibrium GDP?

Back in Figure 3, this $1 trillion rise in government purchases increased output to $12.5 trillion. But that analysis did not consider any change in the price level. Thus, the rise in output to $12.5 trillion makes sense *only if the price level does not change.* Here, in Figure 9, this *would* be a movement rightward, from point *E* to point *J*. However, *point J does not describe the economy's short-run equilibrium.* Why not? Because it ignores two facts that you've learned about in this chapter: The rise in output will change the price level, and the change in the price level will, in turn, affect equilibrium GDP.

To see this more clearly, let's first suppose that the price level did *not* rise when output increased, so that the economy actually *did* arrive at point *J* after the *AD* shift. Would we stay there? Absolutely not. Point *J* lies below the *AS* curve, telling us that when GDP is $12.5 trillion, the specific price level that is consistent with firms' unit costs and average markup must be *greater* than 100. Firms would soon raise prices, and this would cause a movement leftward along AD_2. The price level would keep rising and output would keep falling, until we reached point *N*. At that point, with output at $11.5 trillion, we would be on both the *AS* and *AD* curves, so there would be no reason for a further rise in the price level and no reason for a further fall in output.

However, the process we've just described is not entirely realistic. It assumes that when government purchases rise, *first* output increases (the move to point *J*) and *then* the price level rises (the move to point *N*). In reality, output and the price level tend to rise *together*. Thus, the economy would likely *slide along* the *AS* curve from point *E* to point *N*. As we move along the *AS* curve, output rises, increasing unit costs and the price level. At the same time, the rise in the price level *reduces equilibrium GDP* (the level of output toward which the economy is heading on the *AD* curve) from point *J* to point *N*.

We can summarize the impact of a rise in government purchases this way:

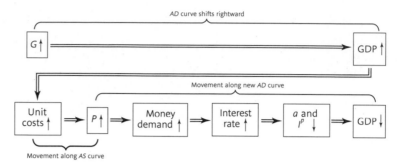

Net Effect: GDP ↑, but by less due to effect of *P* ↑

Fiscal Policy and Crowding Out

Let's step back a minute and get some perspective about this example of fiscal policy. When you first learned about fiscal policy, we used the simple multiplier formula to determine the impact of an increase in *G* on real GDP. Now you've learned that a rise in government purchases will increase the price level. With a constant money supply, the interest rate rises and crowds out some interest-sensitive spending, thus making the rise in GDP smaller than it would be otherwise.

We know that the crowding out is not *complete*, as it was in the classical model, because GDP still rises. This tells us that the drop in consumption and investment spending must be smaller than the rise in government purchases. But this partial crowding out reduces the impact of fiscal policy on GDP. When the partial crowding out of *C* and I^p is included, the expenditure multiplier will be smaller than our simple multiplier formula $[1/(1 - MPC)]$ suggests.

We can summarize the impact of price-level changes this way:

> *When government purchases increase, the horizontal shift of the* AD *curve measures how much real GDP would increase if the price level remained constant. But with a constant money supply, the rise in the price level causes real GDP to rise by less than the horizontal shift in the* AD *curve.*

Now let's switch gears into reverse: How would we illustrate the effects of a *decrease* in government purchases? In this case, the *AD* curve would shift *leftward,* causing the following to happen:

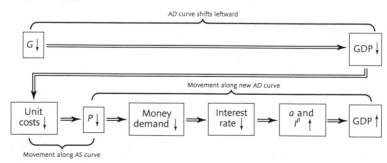

Net Effect: GDP ↓, but by less due to effect of *P* ↓

As you can see, the same sequence of events occurs in the same order, but each variable moves in the opposite direction. A decrease in government purchases decreases equilibrium GDP, but the multiplier effect is smaller because the price level falls.

An Increase in the Money Supply

Although monetary policy stimulates the economy through a different channel than fiscal policy, once we arrive at the *AD* and *AS* diagram, the two look very much alike. For example, an increase in the money supply, which reduces the interest rate, will stimulate interest-sensitive consumption and investment spending. Real GDP then increases, and the *AD* curve shifts rightward, just as in Figure 9. Once output begins to rise, we have the same sequence of events as in fiscal policy: The price level rises, so the increase in GDP will be smaller. We can represent the situation as follows:

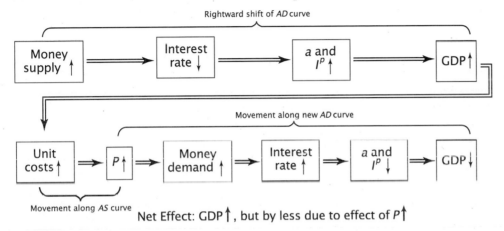

Other Demand Shocks

On your own, try going through examples of different demand shocks (see the list in Figures 4(b) and (c)) and explain the sequence of events in each case that causes output and the price level to change. This will help you verify the following general conclusion about demand shocks:

> *A positive demand shock—one that shifts the* AD *curve rightward—increases both real GDP and the price level in the short run. A negative demand shock—one that shifts the* AD *curve leftward—decreases both real GDP and the price level in the short run.*

An Example: The Great Depression

As mentioned at the beginning of the chapter, the U.S. economy collapsed far more seriously during the period 1929 through 1933—the onset of the Great Depression—than it did at any other time in the country's history. Because the price level fell during this time, we know that the contraction was caused by an adverse demand shock. (An adverse supply shock would have caused the price level to *rise* as GDP fell, as you will see in a few pages.)

What do we know about the demand shocks that caused the depression? This question has been debated by economists almost continuously over the past 70 years. The candidates are numerous, and it appears that a combination of events was responsible. The 1920s were a period of optimism, with high levels of investment by businesses and spending by families on houses and cars. The stock market soared. In the fall of 1929, the bubble of optimism burst. The stock market crashed, and investment and consumption spending plummeted. Similar events occurred in other countries, and the demand for products exported by the United States fell. The Fed—then only 16 years old—reacted by cutting the money supply sharply, which added an adverse monetary shock to all of the cutbacks in spending. Each of these events contributed to a leftward shift of the *AD* curve, causing both output and the price level to fall.

Demand Shocks: Adjusting to the Long Run

Back in Figure 9, point *N* was the new equilibrium after a positive demand shock *in the short run*—a year or so after the shock. But point *N* is not necessarily where the economy will end up in the long run. For example, suppose full-employment output is $10 trillion, and point *N*—representing an output of $11.5 trillion—is *above full-employment output*. Then, with employment unusually high and unemployment unusually low, business firms will have to compete to hire scarce workers, driving up the wage rate. It might take a year or more for the wage rate to rise significantly (recall our earlier list of reasons that wages adjust only slowly). But extending our horizon to several years or more, if output is above its potential, the wage rate will rise. Because the *AS* curve is drawn for a given wage, a rise in the wage rate will *shift* the curve upward, changing our equilibrium.

Alternatively, we could imagine a situation in which short-run equilibrium GDP was *below* its potential. In this case, with abnormally high unemployment, workers would compete to get scarce jobs, and eventually the wage rate would fall. Then the *AS* curve would shift downward, once again changing our equilibrium GDP.

> *In the short run, we treat the wage rate as given. But in the long run, the wage rate can change. When output is above full employment, the wage rate will rise, shifting the* AS *curve upward. When output is below full employment, the wage rate will fall, shifting the* AS *curve downward.*

Now we are ready to explore what happens over the long run in the aftermath of a demand shock. Figure 10 shows an economy in equilibrium at point *E*. We assume that the initial equilibrium is at full-employment output (Y_{FE}) because—as you are about to see—this is where the economy always ends up after the long-run adjustment process is complete. To make our results as general as possible, we'll use symbols, rather than numbers, to represent output and price levels.

Now suppose the *AD* curve shifts rightward due to, say, an increase in government purchases. In the short run, the equilibrium moves to point *N*, with a higher price level (P_2) and a higher level of output (Y_2). Point *N* tells us where the economy will be about a year after the increase in government purchases, before the wage rate has a chance to adjust. (Remember, along any given *AS* curve, the wage rate is assumed to be constant.)

But now let's extend our analysis beyond a year. Notice that Y_2 is greater than Y_{FE}. Eventually, the wage will begin to rise, raising unit costs at any given output level and causing firms to raise prices. In the figure, the *AS* curve would begin shifting upward. Point *K* shows where the shifting aggregate supply curve might be 2 years after the shock, after the long-run adjustment process has begun. (You might want to pencil this intermediate *AS* curve into the figure, so that it intersects AD_2 at point *K*.) At this point, output would be at Y_3, and the rise in the price level has moved us along the new aggregate demand curve, AD_2.

But point *K* cannot be our final, long-run equilibrium. At Y_3, output is *still* greater than Y_{FE}, so the wage rate will continue to rise and the *AS* curve will

FIGURE 10   Long-Run Adjustment after a Positive Demand Shock

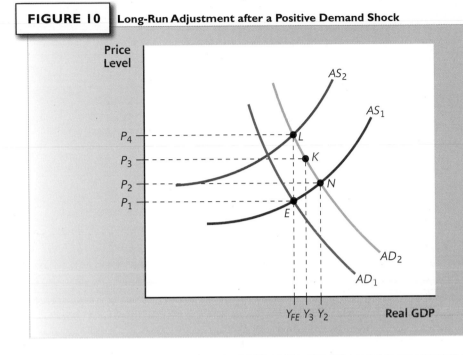

Beginning at point E, a positive demand shock would shift the aggregate demand curve to AD_2, raising both output and the price level. At point N, output is above the full-employment level, Y_{FE}. Firms will compete to hire scarce workers, thereby driving up the wage rate. The higher wage rate will shift the AS curve to AS_2. Only when the economy returns to full-employment output at point L will there be no further shifts in AS.

continue to shift upward. At point *K*, the long-run adjustment process is not yet complete. When will the process end? Only when the wage rate stops rising, that is, only when output has returned to Y_{FE}. This occurs when the *AS* curve has shifted all the way to AS_2, moving the economy to point *L*—our new, long-run equilibrium.

As you can see, the increase in government purchases has no effect on equilibrium GDP in the long run: The economy returns to full employment, which is just where it started. This is why the long-run adjustment process is often called the economy's **self-correcting mechanism.** And this mechanism applies to any demand shock, not just an increase in government purchases:

> *If a demand shock pulls the economy away from full employment, changes in the wage rate and the price level will eventually cause the economy to correct itself and return to full-employment output.*

Self-correcting mechanism The adjustment process through which price and wage changes return the economy to full-employment output in the long run.

For a positive demand shock that shifts the *AD* curve rightward, the self-correcting mechanism works like this:

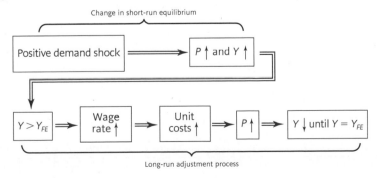

FIGURE 11   Long-Run Adjustment after a Negative Demand Shock

Starting from point E, a negative demand shock shifts the AD curve to AD$_2$, lowering GDP and the price level. At point N, output is below the full-employment level. With unemployed labor available, wages and unit costs will fall, causing firms to lower their prices. The AS curve shifts downward until full employment is regained at point M, with a lower price level.

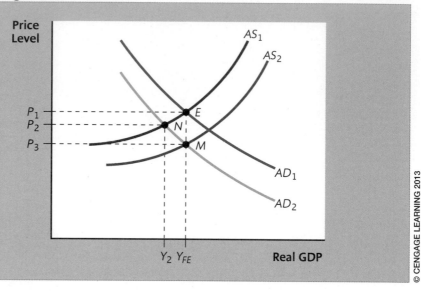

© CENGAGE LEARNING 2013

Figure 11 illustrates the case of a negative demand shock, in which the *AD* curve shifts leftward. Starting at point *E*, the short-run equilibrium moves to point *N*, with real GDP *below* Y_{FE}. Over the long run, high unemployment drives the wage rate down, shifting the *AS* curve down as well. The price level decreases, causing equilibrium GDP to rise along the *AD$_2$* curve. The process comes to a halt only when output returns to Y_{FE}. Thus, in the long run, the economy moves from point *E* to point *M*, and the negative demand shock causes no change in equilibrium GDP.

The complete sequence of events after a negative demand shock looks like this:

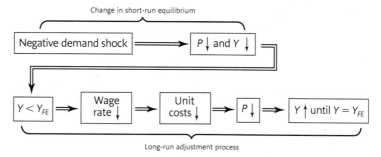

Pulling all of our observations together, we can summarize the economy's self-correcting mechanism as follows:

> *Whenever a demand shock pulls the economy away from full employment, the self-correcting mechanism will eventually bring it back. When output exceeds its full-employment level, wages will eventually rise, causing a rise in the price level and a drop in GDP until full employment is restored. When output is less than its full-employment level, wages will eventually fall, causing a drop in the price level and a rise in GDP until full employment is restored.*

Remember that, throughout this analysis, we've assumed that no government policy is helping the economy return to full employment. Specifically, we've assumed that the money supply is a given, determined by outside forces, rather than being actively managed by the Fed. (In the next chapter, we'll explore how active Federal Reserve policy can be analyzed with the *AS-AD* model.)

The Long-Run Aggregate Supply Curve

The self-correcting mechanism provides an important link between the economy's long-run and short-run behaviors. It helps us understand why deviations from full employment don't last forever. Often, however, we are primarily interested in the long-run effects of a demand shock. In these cases, we may want to skip over the self-correcting mechanism and go straight to its end result. A new version of the *AS* curve helps us do this.

Now look at Figure 12, which illustrates the impact of a positive demand shock like the one in Figure 10. The economy begins at full employment at point *E*, then moves to point *N* in the short run (before the wage rate rises), and then goes to point *L* in the long run (after the rise in wages). If we skip over the short-run equilibrium, we find that the positive demand shock has moved the economy from *E* to *L*, which is vertically above *E*. That is, in the long run, the price level rises but output remains unchanged.

FIGURE 12 The Long-Run *AS* Curve

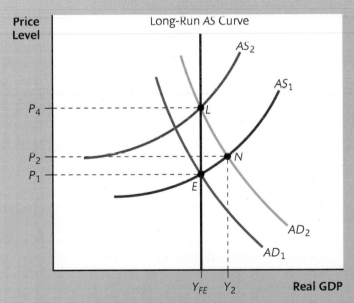

This figure, like Figure 10, illustrates a positive demand shock, but focuses on the long-run effects. The initial equilibrium is at point E, with output at full employment (Y_{FE}) and price level P_1. After the positive demand shock and all the long-run adjustments to it, the economy ends up at point L with a higher price level (P_4), but the same full-employment output level (Y_{FE}). The long-run AS curve—a vertical line—shows all possible combinations of price level and output for the economy, skipping over the short-run changes. The vertical, long-run AS curve shows that in the long run, demand shocks can affect the price level but not output.

Long-run aggregate supply curve A vertical line indicating all possible output and price-level combinations at which the economy could end up in the long run.

Now look at the vertical line in Figure 12, which shows another way of illustrating this long-run result. In the figure, the vertical line is the economy's **long-run aggregate supply curve**. It summarizes all possible output and price-level combinations at which the economy could end up in the long run. It is vertical because, in the long run, GDP will be the same—full-employment output—*regardless* of the position of the *AD* curve. The price level, however, will depend on the position of the *AD* curve. In the long run, a positive demand shock shifts the *AD* curve rightward, moving the economy from *E* to *L*: a higher price level, but the same level of output. Similarly, in Figure 11, a negative demand shock—which shifts the *AD* curve leftward—moves the economy from *E* to *M* in the long run: a lower price level with the same level of output. (You may want to pencil in a vertical long-run aggregate supply curve in Figure 11 connecting points *E* and *M* to help you see that it is the same curve as the one drawn in Figure 12.)

The Long Run and the Classical Model

The long-run aggregate supply curve tells us something very important about the economy: In the long run, after the self-correcting mechanism has done its job, *the economy behaves as the classical model predicts*. In particular, the classical model tells us that demand shocks cannot change equilibrium GDP in the long run. Figure 12 illustrates why: While demand shocks shift the *AD* curve, this only moves the economy up or down along a vertical long-run *AS* curve, leaving output unchanged.[2]

The long-run aggregate supply curve also illustrates another classical conclusion. In the classical model, an increase in government purchases causes *complete crowding out;* the rise in government purchases is precisely matched by a drop in consumption and investment spending, leaving total output and total spending unchanged. In Figure 12, the same result holds in the long run. How do we know? The figures tell us that, in the long run, the rise in government purchases causes no change in GDP. But if GDP is the same, and government purchases are higher, then other components of GDP—consumption and investment—must decrease by the amount that government purchases increased.

> *The self-correcting mechanism shows us that, in the long run, the economy will eventually behave as the classical model predicts.*

But notice the word *eventually* in the previous statement. It can take several years before the economy returns to full employment after a demand shock. The adjustment process depends on changes in the nominal wage rate, and—as we've discussed—wages are sticky, especially after a negative demand shock. This is one reason governments around the world are reluctant to rely on the self-correcting mechanism alone to keep the economy on track. Instead, they often use monetary policies—and occasionally, fiscal policy—in an attempt to return the economy to full employment more quickly.

---

[2] Of course, full-employment output can increase from year to year, as you learned in the chapter on economic growth. When potential output is growing, the long-run *AS* curve will shift rightward. In that case, the level of output at which the economy will eventually settle increases from year to year.

Supply Shocks

In recent decades, supply shocks have been important sources of economic fluctuations. The most dramatic supply shocks have resulted from sudden changes in world oil prices. As you are about to see, supply shocks affect the economy differently than demand shocks.

Short-Run Effects of Supply Shocks

Figure 13 shows an example of a supply shock: an increase in world oil prices that shifts the aggregate supply curve upward, from AS_1 to AS_2. As rising oil prices increase unit costs, firms will begin raising prices, and the price level will increase. The rise in the price level decreases equilibrium GDP along the AD curve. In the short run, the price level will continue to rise, and the economy will continue to slide upward along its AD curve, until we reach the AS_2 curve at point R. At this point, the price level is consistent with firms' unit costs and average markup (we are on the AS curve), and total output is equal to total spending (we are on the AD curve). As you can see, the short-run impact of higher oil prices is a rise in the price level and a fall in output. We call this a *negative* supply shock, because of the negative effect on output.

> In the short run, a negative supply shock shifts the AS curve upward, decreasing output and increasing the price level.

Notice the sharp contrast between the effects of negative supply shocks and negative demand shocks in the short run. After a negative demand shock (see, for example, Figure 11), both output and the price level fall. After a negative supply shock, output falls but the price level rises. Economists and journalists have coined the term **stagflation** to describe a *stag*nating economy experiencing in*flation*.

Stagflation The combination of falling output and rising prices.

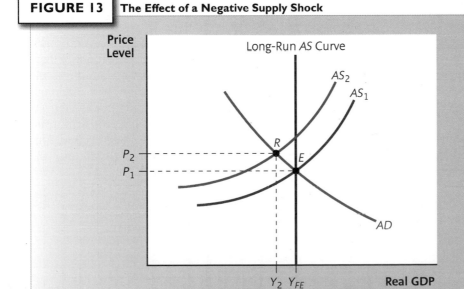

FIGURE 13   **The Effect of a Negative Supply Shock**

Price Level

Long-Run *AS* Curve

AS_2

AS_1

R

E

P_2

P_1

AD

Y_2 Y_{FE}

Real GDP

A negative supply shock would shift the AS curve upward from AS_1 to AS_2. In the short-run equilibrium at point R, the price level is higher and output is below Y_{FE}. Eventually, wages will fall, causing unit costs to fall, and the AS curve will shift back to its original position. A positive supply shock would have just the opposite effect.

> *A negative supply shock causes* stagflation *in the short run.*

Stagflation caused by increases in oil prices is not just a theoretical possibility. Three of our recessions in the last quarter century—in 1973–74, 1980, and 1990–91—followed increases in world oil prices. And each of these three recessions also saw jumps in the price level. (Our most recent recession in 2008–2009 also followed a major increase in oil prices. However, a powerful demand shock dominated the story of that recession, as you'll see in the Using the Theory section.)

A *positive supply shock* would increase output by shifting the *AS* curve *downward*. (We call it positive, because of its effect on output.) If you draw such a shift on your own, you'll see that

> *a positive supply shock shifts the* AS *curve downward, increasing output and decreasing the price level.*

Examples of positive supply shocks include unusually good weather, a drop in oil prices, and a technological change that lowers unit costs. In addition, a positive supply shock can sometimes be caused by government policy. A few chapters ago, we discussed how the government could use tax incentives and other policies to increase the rate of economic growth. These policies work by shifting the *AS* curve downward, thus increasing output while tending to decrease the price level.

Long-Run Effects of Supply Shocks

What about the effects of supply shocks in the long run? In some cases, we need not concern ourselves with this question, because some supply shocks are temporary. For example, periods of rising oil prices are often followed by periods of falling oil prices. Similarly, supply shocks caused by unusually good or bad weather, or by natural disasters, are always short-lived. A temporary supply shock causes only a temporary shift in the *AS* curve; over the long run, the curve simply returns to its initial position, and the economy returns to full employment. In Figure 13, the *AS* curve would shift back from AS_2 to AS_1, the price level would fall, and the economy would move from point *R* back to point *E*.

In other cases, however, a supply shock can last for an extended period. One example was the rise in oil prices during the 1970s, which persisted for several years. In cases like this, is there a self-correcting mechanism that brings the economy back to full employment after a long-lasting supply shock? Indeed, there is, and it is the same mechanism that brings the economy back to full employment after a demand shock.

Look again at Figure 13. At point *R*, output is below full-employment output. In the long run, as workers compete for scarce jobs, the wage rate will decline. This will cause the *AS* curve to shift *downward*. The wage will continue to fall until the economy returns to full employment, that is, until we are back at point *E*.

> *In the long run, the economy self-corrects after a long-lasting supply shock, just as it does after a demand shock. When output differs from its full-employment level, the wage rate changes, and the* AS *curve shifts until full employment is restored.*

© PETER TURNLEY/CORBIS

THE STORY OF TWO RECESSIONS

The aggregate demand and aggregate supply curves are more than just abstract graphs; they're tools to help us understand important economic events. For example, they can help us understand why the economy can react so differently in a recession, depending on the cause. To explore this further, let's use the theory to discuss two very different recessions. The first—a "supply-shock" recession—occurred in the early 1990s. The second was the demand-shock recession of 2008–2009.

The Recession of 1990–91

The story of the 1990–91 recession begins in mid-1990, when Iraq invaded Kuwait, a major oil producer. During this conflict, Kuwait's oil was taken off the world market, and so was Iraq's. The reduction in oil supplies resulted in a rapid and substantial increase in the price of oil, a key input to many industries. From the second to the fourth quarter of 1990, the price of oil doubled.

The left-hand panel of Figure 14 shows our AS–AD analysis of the shock. Initially, the economy was on both AD_{1990} and AS_{1990}. Equilibrium was at point E, and output was at the full-employment level. Then, the oil price shock shifted the AS curve upward, to AS_{1991}, while leaving the AD curve more or less unchanged. As the short-run equilibrium moved to point R, real GDP fell and the price level *rose*. Now look at the left side of the next figure (Figure 15). The upper panel shows the behavior of GDP during the period leading up to, and during, the recession. As you can see, consistent with our AS–AD analysis, real GDP fell—from a high of \$8,053 billion in the third quarter of 1990 to a low of \$7,943 billion in the first quarter of 1991 (a decrease of 1.4 percent). The lower panel shows the behavior of the Consumer Price Index (CPI). While the CPI was rising modestly before the recession began, it rose more rapidly during the second half of 1990, as the recession took hold.

FIGURE 14   **An *AD* and *AS* Analysis of Two Recessions**

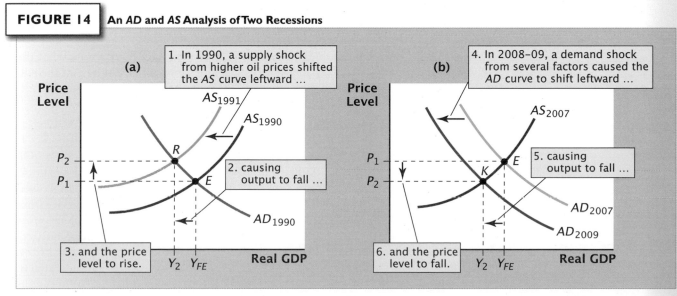

(a)

Price Level

1. In 1990, a supply shock from higher oil prices shifted the *AS* curve leftward ...

AS_{1991}

AS_{1990}

R

P_2

P_1

E

2. causing output to fall ...

AD_{1990}

3. and the price level to rise.

Y_2 Y_{FE} **Real GDP**

(b)

Price Level

4. In 2008–09, a demand shock from several factors caused the *AD* curve to shift leftward ...

AS_{2007}

P_1

E

K

5. causing output to fall ...

P_2

AD_{2007}

AD_{2009}

6. and the price level to fall.

Y_2 Y_{FE} **Real GDP**

© CENGAGE LEARNING 2013

FIGURE 15   GDP and the Price Level in Two Recessions

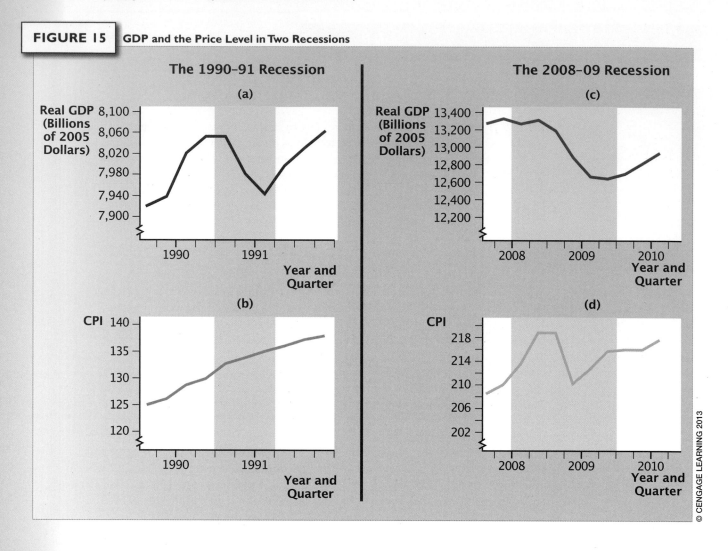

Once again, this is consistent with what our *AS–AD* analysis predicts for a negative supply shock, such as the rise in oil prices in 1990.

What about the recovery that followed this recession? Once you know what the Fed did, you have all the tools to answer this question yourself. Problem 7 at the end of this chapter takes you through the process.

The Recession of 2008–2009

The recession of 2008–2009 *began* almost identically to that of 1990–1991: Oil prices spiked through all of 2007 and into 2008, creating an adverse supply shock. But then events took a very different turn. In mid-2008, after global growth slowed dramatically, oil prices reversed course, falling back to their previous levels within about 6 months. And by this time the economy had a much bigger problem on its hands: A powerful, negative *demand* shock. Home prices began falling in mid-2006, and in 2008 they were in free fall. This, together with a similar plunge in stock prices, destroyed about $14 trillion in household wealth in a little over a year (about equal to an entire year's GDP). The result—not surprisingly—was a large drop in autonomous consumption spending. At the same time, new home construction fell rapidly—a decrease in investment spending. Previously, you learned how these events shifted the aggregate expenditure line downward and pulled the country into a serious recession. Now, we can see this from a different perspective: a leftward shift of the AD curve. Much the same was happening in most of Europe and in other countries around the world.

The right-hand panel of Figure 14 shows our AS–AD analysis of this period. Initially, the U.S. economy was on both AD_{2007} and AS_{2007}, with equilibrium at point E and output roughly at the full-employment level. Then the decrease in autonomous consumption and investment shifted the AD curve leftward, eventually reaching AD_{2009}. The AS curve, meanwhile, was more or less unchanged. As the short-run equilibrium moved to point K, real GDP fell. This is mirrored in Figure 15, where the upper right-hand panel shows the behavior of real GDP. As you can see, consistent with our AS–AD analysis, real GDP did fall in the first quarter of 2008, although it sputtered upward in the second quarter before falling again for the next four quarters.

In retrospect, the Fed responded much too slowly—resisting any drop in its target federal funds rate until September 2007, well after housing prices began falling. At that point, as we discussed in the previous chapter, the Fed began pumping reserves into the banking system and reducing its target federal funds rate, but these moves were not enough to reverse the leftward shift in the AD curve. Even the Fed's unconventional policies during the recession—while they might have prevented the AD curve from shifting even further leftward—were not sufficient to move it rightward.

Fiscal policy came into play during this period as well, as we discussed a few chapters ago. But it did not arrive until late in the period we're analyzing. Congress passed the American Reinvestment and Recovery Act—which called for $787 billion in tax cuts and increases in government outlays—only in February 2009. By the middle of 2009, less than $100 billion of the total had made its way into the economy.

And finally, before we close this chapter, there is one more thing to discuss: the *price level*. We need to recognize a slight difference between what our AS–AD analysis predicts and what actually happened. In the right panel of Figure 14, our model tells us that the price level should fall. And indeed, in the lower right panel of Figure 15, you can see that the price level eventually *did* fall—in the fourth quarter of 2008. But for much of the recession we can see that instead of the price level falling, it was rising. In part this was due to the supply shock of rising oil prices (not shown in Figure 14), which only reversed itself in the third quarter of 2008.

But there was another reason that prices continued rising—and continued rising into 2009. In the next chapter, you will learn that inflation often has some *momentum*: When it's been rising at a certain rate for some time, then—left alone—it will continue to rise at that rate. The leftward shift in the AD curve meant that inflation was *not* left alone in 2008. And, as you can see, the downward pressure on prices from the leftward-shifting AD curve (helped by oil prices that were now *falling*) eventually overcame the inflationary momentum, causing an actual drop in the price level toward the end of 2008. This is just what we'd expect from our AS–AD analysis.

SUMMARY

The model of aggregate supply and demand explains how the price level and output are determined in the short run—a period of a year or so following a change in the economy—and how the economy adjusts over longer time periods as well.

The *aggregate demand* (AD) *curve* shows how changes in the price level affect equilibrium real GDP when the money supply is held constant. A change in the price level shifts the money demand curve and alters the interest rate in the money market. The change in the interest rate, in turn, affects interest-sensitive forms of spending, shifts the aggregate expenditure curve, triggers the multiplier process, and leads to a new level of equilibrium real GDP. A lower price level means a higher equilibrium real GDP, and a higher price level means lower GDP. A change in government purchases, net taxes, autonomous consumption, planned investment, net exports, or the money supply will cause the AD curve to shift.

The *aggregate supply* (AS) *curve* summarizes the way changes in output affect the price level. To draw the AS curve, we assume that firms set the price of individual products as a markup over their costs per unit, and that the economy's average markup is determined by competitive conditions. We also assume that the nominal wage rate is fixed in the short run. As we move upward along the AS curve, a rise in real GDP, by raising unit costs, causes the price level to increase. When anything other than a change in real GDP causes the price level to change, the entire AS curve shifts.

AD and AS together determine real GDP and the price level. The economy must be on the AD curve, or real GDP would not be at its equilibrium level. It must be on the AS curve or firms would not be charging prices dictated by their unit costs and markups. Both conditions are satisfied at the intersection of the two curves.

The AD–AS equilibrium can be disturbed by a *demand shock*. An increase in government purchases, for example, shifts the AD curve rightward. As a result, the price level rises, and so does real GDP. In the long run, if GDP is above potential, wages will rise. This causes unit costs to rise and shifts the AS curve upward. Eventually, GDP will return to potential and the only long-run result of the demand shock is a higher price level. This implies that the economy's long-run aggregate supply curve is vertical at potential output.

The short-run AD–AS equilibrium can also be disturbed by a *supply shock*, such as an increase in world oil prices. With unit costs higher at each level of output, the AS curve shifts upward, decreasing real GDP and increasing the price level. Eventually, the shock will be self-correcting: With output below potential, the wage rate will fall, unit costs will decrease, and the AS curve will shift back downward until full employment is restored.

PROBLEM SET

Answers to even-numbered Problems can be found on the text Web site through www.cengagebrain.com

1. Redraw Figure 2, showing how a decrease in the price level will lead to an increase in equilibrium real GDP.

2. With a three-panel diagram—one panel showing the money market, one showing the aggregate expenditure diagram, and one showing the AD curve—show how a *decrease* in the money supply shifts the AD curve leftward.

3. Suppose firms become pessimistic about the future and consequently investment spending falls. With an AD and AS graph, describe the short-run effects on real GDP and the price level. If the AS curve was a horizontal line, how would your answer change?

4. With an AD and AS diagram only, explain the short-run and long-run effects of a decrease in the money supply on real GDP and the price level. *Assume the economy begins at full employment.*

5. Use an AD and AS graph to explain the short-run and long-run effects on real GDP and the price level of an increase in autonomous consumption spending. Assume the economy begins at full employment.

6. A new government policy successfully lowers firms' unit costs. What are the short-run and the long-run effects of such a policy? (Assume that full-employment output does not change.)

7. In 1991, the Fed lowered its interest rate target, helping to bring the recession of that year to a rapid end. Make two copies of Figure 14(a) on a sheet of paper. Add curves to illustrate your answer to question (a) on one copy and question (b) on the other:
   a. What *would* have happened in the years after 1991 if the Fed had done nothing and the economy had relied solely on the self-correcting mechanism to return to full employment?
   b. What *did* happen as a result of the Fed bringing down the interest rate to end the recession?
   c. Is there a difference in the behavior of the price level during the recovery in these two cases? Explain.

8. What would happen to the AD curve if both government purchases and net taxes were increased by the same amount? [Hint: Review the balanced budget multiplier in the fiscal policy chapter.]

9. Increased international trade has forced many U.S. firms to compete with foreign producers. The increased competition has likely affected the average markup in the U.S. economy. (How?) Use *AS* and *AD* curves to illustrate the short-run impact on the economy if, at the same time,
    a. The Fed does nothing.
    b. The Fed pursues a policy that successfully achieves the highest possible level of GDP with no rise in the price level.

10. Using *AD* and *AS* curves:
    a. Graphically show the effects of a temporary decrease in nonlabor input prices.
    b. How will your results change if this decrease lasts for an extended period?
    c. How would your results differ if the Fed intervened to keep the economy at full employment?

More Challenging

11. Suppose that wages are slow to adjust downward but rapidly adjust upward. What would the *AS* curve look like? How would this affect the economy's adjustment to demand shocks (compared to the analysis given in the chapter)?

12. During the 1990s, because of technological change, the *AS* curve was shifting downward, but—except for a few months—the price level did not fall. Why not? (Hint: What might the Fed have been doing as the economy's potential output and actual output grew?)

CHAPTER 16

Inflation and Monetary Policy

JIM WATSON/AFP/GETTY IMAGES

In the late 1970s, the annual inflation rate in the United States reached 13 percent. At the time, polls showed that the public considered inflation the most serious economic problem facing the country. From 1991 to 2008, however, the annual inflation rate averaged about 2.5%, and the problem receded as a matter of public concern. Bringing the inflation rate down, and keeping it low, was one of the solid victories of national economic policy.

From 2009 to 2011, however, the behavior of the price level was once again in the news, from two opposing points of view. On one hand, a number of economists warned about the possibility of *deflation*—a negative rate of inflation. On the other hand, television pitchmen and radio talk-show hosts were warning people to buy gold, in order to protect themselves from another episode of 1970s-style inflation. (In times of high inflation, gold's price often rises as fast as—or faster than—the price level.)

Why was the inflation rate so high in the 1970s? How did the Fed bring the rate down? Why would economists ever worry about deflation? And more generally, what principles should guide the Fed as it tries to steer the economy?

In this chapter, we'll be addressing these and other questions as we take a closer look at the Fed's management of monetary policy. A few chapters ago, when we first analyzed monetary policy, our discussion was somewhat limited, because we hadn't yet developed the tools needed to explain changes in the price level. But now that you've learned about the *AD* and *AS* curves, we can explore monetary policy more fully, incorporating changes in the price level and—later in the chapter—ongoing inflation.

THE OBJECTIVES OF MONETARY POLICY

The Fed's objectives have changed over the years. When the Fed was first established in 1913, its chief responsibility was to ensure the stability of the banking system. By acting as a *lender of last resort*—injecting reserves into the banking system in times of crisis—the Fed was supposed to alleviate financial panics.

From the 1950s until 2008, the stability of the banking system receded as a major concern, largely because deposit insurance programs had effectively elimi-nated panics. Accordingly, the Fed's objective in the 1950s and 1960s changed to keeping the interest rate low and stable. In the 1970s, the Fed's objectives shifted once again. As stated in the Federal Reserve Banking Act of 1978, which is still in force, the Fed is now responsible for achieving a low, stable rate of inflation, as well as full employment of the labor force. These two responsibilities are often called the *dual mandate* of the Fed.

During and after the financial crisis of 2008. the stability of the banking system—and the financial system in general—once again took center stage. Congress gave the Fed enhanced regulatory powers designed to help prevent another crisis (See our earlier discussion in the chapter titled Money, Banks, and the Federal Reserve.) But the Fed's primary responsibilities are still defined by the dual mandate: a low, stable inflation rate and full employment. Let's consider each of these goals in turn.

Low, Stable Inflation

Why is a low rate of inflation important? Several chapters ago, we reviewed the social costs of inflation. When the inflation rate is high, society uses up resources coping with it—resources that could have been used to produce goods and services. Among these resources are the labor needed to update prices at stores and factories, and the additional time spent by households and businesses to manage their wealth and protect it from a loss of purchasing power.

In addition to keeping the inflation rate low, the Fed tries to keep it *stable* from year to year. For example, the Fed would prefer a steady yearly inflation rate of 3 percent to an inflation rate of 5 percent half the time, and 1 percent the other half, even though the average inflation rate would be 3 percent in both cases. The reason is that unstable inflation is difficult to predict accurately; it will often turn out higher or lower than people expected. As you learned several chapters ago, an inflation rate higher than expected redistributes real income from lenders to borrowers, while an inflation rate lower than expected has the opposite effect. Thus, unstable inflation adds to the risk of lending and borrowing, and interferes with long-run financial planning.

The Fed, as a public agency, chooses its policies with the costs of inflation in mind. And the Fed has another concern: Inflation is very unpopular with the public. Surveys show that most people associate high rates of inflation with a general breakdown of government and the economy. A Fed chairman who delivers low rates of inflation is seen as popular and competent, while one who tolerates high inflation goes down in history as a failure.

Full Employment

"Full employment" means that unemployment is at normal levels. But what, exactly, is a *normal* amount of employment?

Recall that there are different types of unemployment. Some of the unemployed in any given month will find jobs after only a short time of searching. This *frictional* unemployment is part of the normal workings of the labor market and is not a serious social problem. Other job seekers will spend many months or years out of work because they lack the skills that employers require, or because they lack information about available jobs. While this *structural* unemployment is a serious social problem, it is usually addressed with *micro*economic policies, such as job-training programs or improved information flows.

Cyclical unemployment, by contrast, is a *macro*economic problem. It occurs during a recession, in which millions of workers lose their jobs and remain unemployed as they seek new ones. This is why macroeconomists use the term "full employment" to mean *the absence of cyclical unemployment*. When the economy achieves full employment according to this definition, macroeconomic policy has done all that it can do.

The Fed is concerned about cyclical unemployment for two reasons. First is its *opportunity cost:* the output that the unemployed could have produced if they were working. By maintaining full employment, the Fed can help society avoid this cost.

Second, cyclical unemployment represents a social failure, one that can cause significant hardship. In a recession, people who have the right skills and who could be working actually *lose* their jobs. Excess unemployment lingers for several years after a recession strikes. Thus, cyclical unemployment caused by a recession is a partial breakdown of the system. The economy is not doing what it should do: provide jobs for those who want to work and have the needed skills.

But why should the Fed try to eliminate only *cyclical* unemployment? Why not go further and push output above its full-employment level? After all, at higher levels of output, business firms would be more willing to hire *any* available workers. The frictionally unemployed would find jobs more easily, and some of the structurally unemployed would be hired as well. If unemployment is a bad thing, shouldn't the Fed aim for the lowest possible unemployment rate?

The answer is no. If the unemployment rate falls too low, GDP rises beyond its potential, full-employment level. As you learned in the last chapter, this causes the economy's self-correcting mechanism to kick in: The *AS* curve shifts upward, increasing the price level. Thus, unemployment that is too low compromises the Fed's other chief goal by creating inflation. And, as you will see later in the chapter, the Fed cannot keep the economy operating beyond full employment for more than a short time anyway. In the long run, its attempts to push the economy too hard would only create more inflation and would not succeed in lowering unemployment.

The Natural Rate of Unemployment

Natural rate of unemployment
The unemployment rate when there is no cyclical unemployment.

The unemployment rate at which GDP is at its full-employment level—that is, with no cyclical unemployment—is sometimes called the **natural rate of unemployment.** Using this concept, we can summarize what the *AD–AS* tells as follows:

> *When the unemployment rate is below the natural rate, GDP is greater than potential output. The economy's self-correcting mechanism will then create inflation. When the unemployment rate is above the natural rate, GDP is below potential output. The self-correcting mechanism will then put downward pressure on the price level.*

The word *natural* must be interpreted with care. The natural unemployment rate is not etched in stone, nor is it the outcome of purely natural forces that can't be influenced by public policy. But it is determined by rather slow-moving forces in the economy: how frequently workers move from job to job, how efficiently the unemployed can search for jobs and firms can search for new workers, and how well the skills of the unemployed match the skills needed by employers.

Still, the natural rate can change when any of these underlying conditions change. And it can also be influenced by government policies that provide incentives or disincentives for workers to find jobs quickly, or for employers to hire them. Indeed, economists generally believe that over the past decade, the natural rate has decreased in the United States—from 6 or 6.5 percent in the mid-1980s to around 5 percent today.

Why use the term *natural* for such a changeable feature of the economy? The term makes sense only from the perspective of *macroeconomic* policy. Simply put, there isn't much that macroeconomic policy can do about the natural rate. Stimulating the economy with fiscal or monetary policy may bring the *actual* unemployment rate down for a time, but it will not change the natural rate itself. And pushing unemployment below the natural rate would cause inflation. Thus, the natural rate

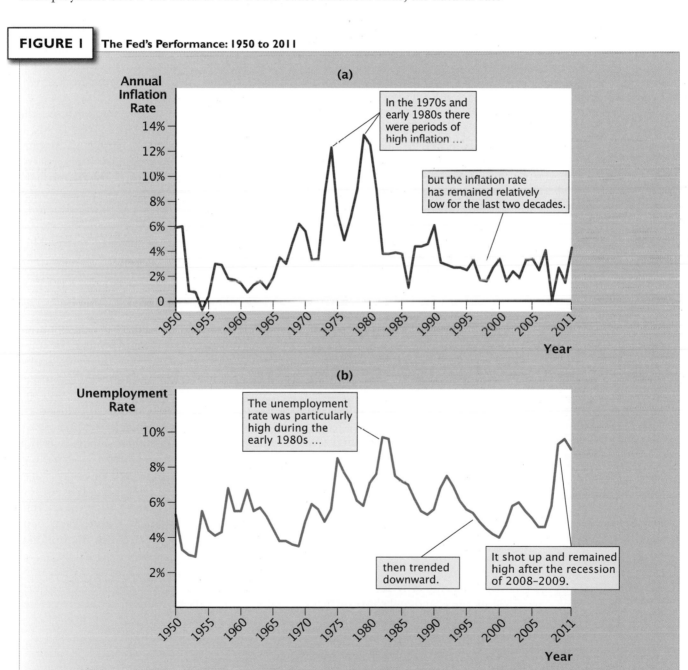

FIGURE 1   **The Fed's Performance: 1950 to 2011**

(a)

Annotations in chart:
"In the 1970s and early 1980s there were periods of high inflation …"
"but the inflation rate has remained relatively low for the last two decades."

(b)

Annotations in chart:
"The unemployment rate was particularly high during the early 1980s …"
"then trended downward."
"It shot up and remained high after the recession of 2008–2009."

Source: Bureau of Labor Statistics. Annual inflation rate—percent rise in December CPI-U from previous December. Unemployment rate—average of monthly rates for each year. Data for 2011 is annualized (inflation) and averaged (unemployment) through August 2011.

of unemployment can be seen as a kind of goalpost for the Fed. The location of the goalpost may change over the years, but during any given year, it tells us where the Fed is aiming.

The Fed's Performance

How well has the Fed achieved its goals? Panel (a) of Figure 1 shows the annual inflation rate since 1950, as measured by the Consumer Price Index. You can see that monetary policy permitted extended periods of high inflation in the 1970s and early 1980s. You can also see, as noted at the beginning of the chapter, that the Fed has achieved great success in controlling inflation since then. Indeed, over the past two decades, the inflation rate has averaged about 2.5 percent.

Panel (b) shows the average unemployment rate since 1950. As you can see, the Fed's performance regarding unemployment has been mixed. During the 1990s, it slowly inched the unemployment rate down to 4 percent *without* heating up inflation. The Fed even managed to keep the unemployment rate hovering near 4 percent for more than 2 years. But two recessions—one in 2001 and one in 2008–2009—brought the good news on unemployment to an end.

To understand why the Fed has not been completely successful in satisfying its dual mandate, we need to understand more about monetary policy—in both theory and practice.

FEDERAL RESERVE POLICY: THEORY AND PRACTICE

The Fed's job is not an easy one. It must constantly respond to macroeconomic events with its twin goals in mind: low inflation and full employment. In some cases, the correct response—at least in theory—is clear, because the same action that maintains full employment also helps maintain low inflation. But in other cases, the Fed must trade off one goal for another: Responses that maintain full employment will worsen inflation, and responses that alleviate inflation will create more unemployment.

In this section, we'll make two simplifying assumptions: (1) The Fed's goal is an inflation rate of *zero*, and (2) over the long run, the Fed succeeds in achieving this goal. There might be a temporary bout of inflation or deflation if some event causes the price level to change. But once the price level reaches its new equilibrium value, it will stay there until the economy is hit by some new event that causes it to change again. With no ongoing inflation, no one *expects* continued inflation, so everyone treats the real interest rate as equal to the nominal interest rate.

In reality, the Fed's goal is *low,* but not zero, inflation. A few pages from now, we'll discuss why the Fed prefers a low inflation rate to a zero rate, and explore how the economy behaves when the ongoing and expected inflation rate are greater than zero.

Responding to Demand Shocks

In the last chapter, you learned that a demand shock is a change in spending that shifts the economy's aggregate demand (*AD*) curve. Suppose an economy is operating at its potential output, and then it is hit with a *positive* demand shock. The shock might come from fiscal policy (an increase in government purchases or a tax cut) or from the private sector (an increase in autonomous consumption, investment, or net exports). In theory, how should the Fed respond?

Let's consider three possible responses: Maintaining the money supply, maintaining the interest rate, and neutralizing the shock. As you'll see, the first two responses would be poor choices for the Fed. The last one does the best job in achieving the Fed's goals.

Hypothetical Response: Constant Money Supply

Figure 2 illustrates an economy that is initially operating at full employment. Panel (a) shows the money market, with an equilibrium interest rate of 5 percent (point A). Panel (b) shows the aggregate demand and aggregate supply diagram. The equilibrium (point E) is a price level of 100 and an output of $10 trillion—the assumed full-employment level. Points A and E represent a *long-run* equilibrium for this economy—with output at its potential and, therefore, unemployment at its natural rate, the economy is at rest.

Then a positive demand shock (an increase in spending) hits the economy, setting off the multiplier process. The AD curve shifts rightward, from AD_1 to AD_2. At every price level, equilibrium GDP is greater than before. If, for example, the price level stayed at 100, the figure tells us that equilibrium GDP would rise to $12.5 trillion (point F). But that is not necessarily where the economy will end up; it depends on the actions of the Fed.

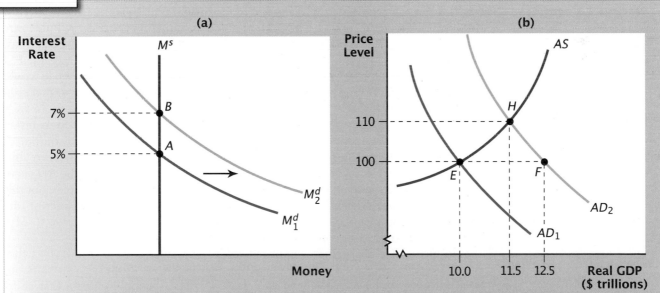

FIGURE 2 | **A Positive Demand Shock with a Constant Money Supply**

A positive demand shock would shift the AD curve rightward to AD$_2$ in panel (b), causing both the price level and output to rise. If the Fed maintains a constant money supply, the rise in the price level causes the money demand curve to shift to M$_2^d$ in panel (a), driving the interest rate (nominal and real) up from 5 percent to 7 percent. A higher interest rate causes some crowding out of consumption and investment spending, but not complete crowding out. In panel (b), output ends up higher than initially, and the price level rises as well (point H).

In the last chapter, we assumed that the money supply remained constant after a demand shock. That is not a realistic description of Fed policy, but it served as a benchmark case. In Figure 2, we once again explore this benchmark case.

In panel (b), the rise in GDP causes a movement along the economy's *AS* curve, and the price level rises. In the money market in panel (a), the rise in the price level shifts the money demand curve rightward, driving the interest rate up to 7 percent (point *B*). This crowds out some consumption and investment spending, so that GDP does not rise by as much as it otherwise would. But it still rises. In panel (b), we end up at point *H*, with the price level rising to 110, and real GDP rising to $11.5 trillion.

As you can see, the Fed would not want to respond to a positive demand shock by holding the money supply constant as in the figure. Output would rise above potential, bringing the unemployment rate below its natural rate. The price level would rise as well—to 110 in the figure. And in the long run, the price level would rise further, as the self-correcting mechanism returned the economy to full employment (by shifting the *AS* curve upward—not shown).

> *If a fully employed economy experiences a positive demand shock, and the Fed responds by holding the money supply constant, output will overshoot its potential. The price level will rise in the short run, and rise further in the long run.*

Because we are assuming, for now, that one of the Fed's goals is zero inflation, holding the money supply constant would not be an advisable response.

Hypothetical Response: Constant Interest Rate

Two chapters ago, you learned that, in practice, the Fed conducts monetary policy by setting a target for the federal funds rate. In normal times, when different interest rates in the economy move up and down together, targeting the federal funds rate is roughly equivalent to targeting the *average* level of interest rates in the economy. This is how we'll think about the "interest rate target" in this chapter. Once the Fed sets its target, it then adjusts the money supply as necessary to hit it. What would happen if the Fed, in response to a positive demand shock, chose to maintain a *constant* interest rate target?

Figure 3 provides the answer. In panel (a), the interest rate is initially at its target rate of 5 percent. In panel (b), the economy is at full employment with output of $10.0 trillion. When the positive demand shock hits, the *AD* curve begins to shift rightward in panel (b). We've included AD_2 in the figure, to show where the *AD* curve would be if the Fed did not change the money supply (as in the last example). But this time, as the money demand curve shifts rightward in panel (a), and the interest rate rises, the Fed increases the money supply (shifting the money supply curve to M_2^s). This will maintain the interest rate at its target of 5 percent (point *C*).[1]

An increase in the money supply, as you've learned, is one of the factors that shifts the *AD* curve rightward. So now, in panel (b), the *AD* curve will shift out farther than it did before—all the way to AD_3. (The spending change first shifts it to AD_2; the increase in the money supply shifts it farther, to AD_3.) In effect, by

[1] You might have noticed that, in panel (a) of Figure 3, the money demand curve shifts out farther than in Figure 2. This is because in Figure 3, the price level ends up higher, so the increase in money demand is greater.

FIGURE 3 | A Positive Demand Shock with a Constant Interest Rate

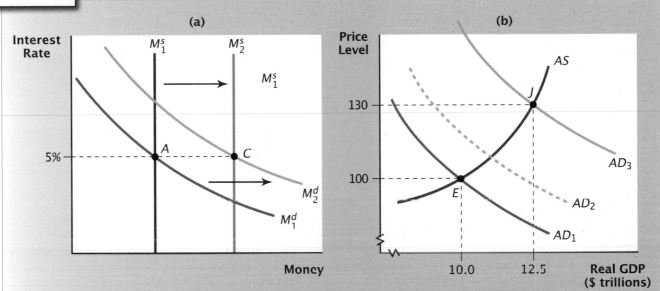

A positive demand shock initially shifts the AD curve rightward to AD₂ in panel (b), causing both the price level and output to rise. The rise in the price level shifts the money demand curve rightward to M₂ᵈ in panel (a), which would ordinarily cause the interest rate to rise. But if the Fed maintains a constant interest rate target, it will increase the money supply to prevent any rise in the interest rate. There will be no crowding out of consumption or investment spending, so the AD curve in panel (b) shifts farther rightward (to AD₃). As a result, the economy ends up at point J, with output and the price level rising by more than under a constant-money-supply policy.

maintaining the interest rate target at 5 percent, the Fed prevents *any* crowding out of consumption or investment that would otherwise result from a higher interest rate. Instead, it allows the economy to experience the full effect of the multiplier, so output rises all the way to $12.5 trillion (point *J*).

But notice the consequence: In Figure 3, the price level rises even more (in comparison with the constant-money-supply policy of Figure 2). By maintaining its interest rate target, the Fed pushes output even farther beyond its potential, causing an even greater rise in the price level both in the short run (to 130 in the figure) and in the long run (as the economy self-corrects—not shown).

> *If a fully employed economy experiences a positive demand shock, a constant interest rate creates an even greater overshooting of potential output than a constant money supply. The result is an even greater rise in the price level.*

You can see that maintaining a constant interest rate would be an even poorer choice for the Fed than maintaining a constant money supply.

Best Response: Neutralization

A third possible response to a demand shock—and the best one—is for the Fed to prevent any shift in the *AD* curve at all. That is, the Fed should completely neutralize the demand shock.

FIGURE 4   A Positive Demand Shock Neutralized by Monetary Policy

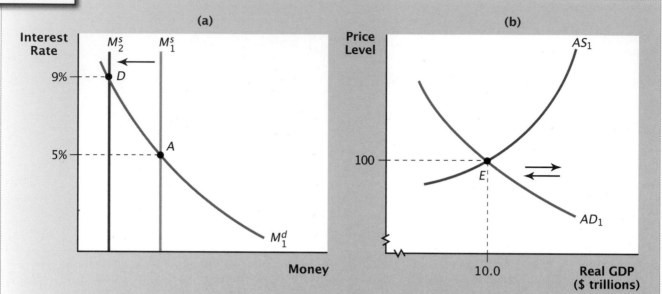

A positive demand shock begins to shift the AD curve rightward in panel (b), which would ordinarily cause both the price level and output to rise. But the Fed can neutralize the shock by increasing its interest rate target enough to cause complete crowding out of consumption and investment spending. To reach the new, higher interest rate target, the Fed must decrease the money supply in panel (a), moving the money market equilibrium to a point like D. This reverses (or prevents) the shift in the AD curve, so the economy ends up at point E in panel (b), at its initial output and price level.

This is illustrated in Figure 4. Once again, in panel (b), an increase in spending begins to shift the *AD* curve rightward (as indicated by the rightward arrow). But this time, instead of keeping the money supply constant (so the interest rate rises enough for *partial* crowding out) or keeping the interest rate constant (preventing *any* crowding out at all), the Fed now creates *complete crowding out*. That is, it raises its interest rate target by just enough to make spending fall as much as it initially rose from the demand shock. In this way, total spending remains unchanged, and the *AD* curve does not shift at all. In the figure, this is indicated by arrows showing the *AD* curve first shifts rightward, and then leftward back to its original position.

Panel (a) shows what happens in the money market as the Fed raises its interest rate target. In order to neutralize the demand shock completely, the Fed must raise the interest rate *higher* than it rose in Figure 2 (which caused only partial crowding out). In Figure 4, we assume that an interest rate of 9 percent will do the trick. The Fed shifts the money supply curve leftward, from M_1^s to M_2^s, moving the money market equilibrium to point *D*. Note that the money demand curve does not shift in this case. This is because, in the end, we are back at our original price level.

If the Fed acts quickly enough, it could prevent the demand shock from shifting the *AD* curve at all, keeping the economy at point *E* in panel (b). The Fed could thus prevent *any* rise in the price level. At the same time, it could keep the economy at full employment.

If a *negative* demand shock hits the economy, shifting the *AD* curve leftward, the Fed should respond with the opposite policy: lowering its interest rate target by *increasing* the money supply. The lower interest rate will stimulate additional consumption and investment spending, and can prevent the *AD* curve from shifting leftward.

> To maintain full employment and price stability after a demand shock, the Fed must change its interest rate target. A positive demand shock requires an increase in the target; a negative demand shock requires a decrease in the target.

In recent years, the Fed has changed its interest rate target often, attempting to keep the economy on track. If the Fed observes that the economy is overheating—and that the unemployment rate has fallen below its natural rate—it will raise its target. The Fed, believing that the *AD* curve was shifting rightward too rapidly, reacted this way from June 2004 to June 2006, raising its federal funds rate target 17 times in 2 years. When the Fed raises its target, it responds to forces that shift the *AD* curve rightward by creating an opposing force—a higher interest rate—to prevent the shift.

When the Fed observes that the economy is sluggish—and the unemployment rate has risen above its natural rate—the Fed will lower its target. The Fed began doing this in September 2007, as housing prices declined, and there were signs that investment and consumption spending were slowing. Over the next 15 months, it lowered its federal funds target 10 times (from 5.25 percent to a range between 0 and 0.25 percent), trying to create a force opposing the leftward shift of the *AD* curve. While the Fed was not able to prevent the recession, virtually all economists agreed that its actions—lowering the target rate and trying to shift the *AD* curve rightward—were the right *direction* for policy.

As you can see, demand shocks present the Fed with a no-lose situation: The same policy that helps to keep unemployment at its natural rate also helps to maintain a stable price level. However, even demand shocks present a challenge to the Fed that it doesn't face during other, less-eventful periods. To change the interest rate target by just the right amount, the Fed needs accurate information about how the economy operates. We'll return to this and other problems in conducting monetary policy a bit later.

Responding to Supply Shocks

So far in this chapter, you've seen that demand shocks, in general, present the Fed with easy policy choices. By changing its interest rate target from time to time, it can deal with demand shocks, such as those caused by changes in aggregate expenditure. For demand shocks, the very same policy that maintains a stable price level also helps to maintain full employment.

But adverse or negative *supply* shocks present the Fed with a true dilemma: If the Fed tries to preserve price stability, it will worsen unemployment; if it tries to maintain high employment, it will worsen inflation. And even though supply shocks are usually temporary, the shocks themselves—and the Fed's response—can affect the economy for several quarters or even years.

Figure 5 illustrates the Fed's dilemma when confronting an adverse supply shock. Initially, the economy is at point *E* (full employment). Then, a supply shock—say, a rise in world oil prices—shifts the *AS* curve up to AS_2. One possible response for the Fed is to keep the *AD* curve at AD_1. It would do this by holding the *money supply* constant as the price level rose, allowing the interest rate to rise (not shown) and allowing the economy to move along AD_1. The short-run

FIGURE 5 | Responding to Supply Shocks

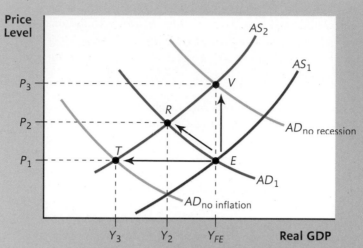

Starting at point E, a negative supply shock shifts the AS curve upward to AS$_2$. With a constant money supply, a new short-run equilibrium would be established at point R, with a higher price level (P$_2$) and a lower level of output (Y$_2$). The Fed could prevent inflation by decreasing the money supply and shifting AD to AD$_{no\ inflation}$, but output would fall to Y$_3$. At the other extreme, it could increase the money supply and shift the AD curve to AD$_{no\ recession}$. This would keep output at the full-employment level, but at the cost of a higher price level, P$_3$.

equilibrium would then move from point *E* to point *R*, and the economy would experience *stagflation*—both inflation and a recession—with output falling to Y$_2$ and the price level rising to P$_2$.

But the Fed can instead respond by *shifting* the *AD* curve, changing the money supply in order to alter the short-run equilibrium. Which policy should it choose? The answer will depend on whether it is mostly concerned about rising prices or rising unemployment. Let's start by imagining two extreme positions.

First, the Fed could prevent inflation entirely by decreasing the money supply, shifting the *AD* curve leftward to the curve labeled *AD*$_{no\ inflation}$. This would move the short-run equilibrium to point *T*. Notice, though, that while the price level remains at P$_1$, output decreases to Y$_3$, exacerbating the recession.

At the other extreme, the Fed could prevent any fall in output. To accomplish this, the Fed would *increase* the money supply and shift the *AD* curve rightward, to *AD*$_{no\ recession}$. The equilibrium would then move to point *V*, keeping output at its full-employment level. But this policy causes more inflation, raising the price level all the way to P$_3$.

In practice, the Fed is unlikely to choose either of these two extremes to deal with a supply shock, preferring instead some intermediate policy. But the extreme positions help illustrate the Fed's dilemma:

> *A negative supply shock presents the Fed with a short-run tradeoff: It can limit the recession, but only at the cost of more inflation; and it can limit inflation, but only at the cost of a deeper recession.*

The choice between the two policies is a hard one. After supply shocks, there are often debates within the Fed—and in the public arena—about how best to respond. Inflation *hawks* lean in the direction of price stability and are willing to tolerate more unemployment in order to achieve it. In the face of an adverse supply shock, hawks would prefer a response that shifts the AD curve closer to $AD_{\text{no inflation}}$, even though it means higher unemployment. Inflation *doves* lean in the direction of a milder recession, and are more willing to tolerate the cost of higher inflation. They would prefer a response that brings the AD curve closer to $AD_{\text{no recession}}$.

Choosing between Hawk and Dove Policies

When a supply shock hits, should the Fed use a hawk policy, should it employ a dove policy, or should it keep the AD curve unchanged? That depends. Over time, as the economy is hit by supply shocks, the hawk policy maintains more stability in the price level but less stability in output and employment. The dove policy gives the opposite result: more stability in output and less stability in the price level. The Fed should choose a hawkish policy if it cares more about price stability, and a dovish policy if it cares more about the stability of output and employment. Or it can pick an intermediate policy—one that balances price and employment stability more evenly.

The proper choice depends on how the Fed weights the harm caused by unemployment against the harm caused by inflation. And since the Fed is a public institution, its views should reflect the assessment of society as a whole. This is why supply shocks present such a challenge to the Fed: The public itself is divided between hawks and doves.

Both inflation and unemployment cause harm, but of very different kinds. Inflation imposes a more general cost on society: the resources used up to cope with it. If the inflation is unexpected, it will also redistribute income between borrowers and lenders. And, as you'll see in the next section, if inflation continues, people will expect it to continue into the future. At that point, prices and wages will begin to rise automatically, even if we are back at the natural rate of unemployment.

The costs of unemployment are borne largely by the unemployed themselves—who suffer the harm of job loss—but partly by taxpayers, who provide funds for unemployment insurance. Balancing the gains and losses from hawk and dove policies is no easy task.

In recent years, some officials at the Fed have argued that the dual mandate—stable prices *and* full employment—is unrealistic when there are supply shocks. They point to the European Central Bank and the Bank of England, which operate with a single mandate: Their governing statutes require them to give priority to controlling inflation. The previous chair of the Board of Governors, Alan Greenspan, asked Congress to change the Fed's mandate to one of controlling inflation, period. But it would be difficult for the Fed to ignore the costs of higher unemployment, even if it were legally permitted to do so. Others have proposed that the Fed follow a predetermined rule, spelling out just how hawkish or dovish its response to supply shocks will be. We'll come back to this controversial idea later in the chapter.

EXPECTATIONS AND ONGOING INFLATION

So far in this chapter, we've assumed that the Fed strives to maintain *zero* inflation, and that the price level remains constant when the economy reaches its long-run, full-employment equilibrium. But as we discussed earlier, this is not entirely realistic. Look again at panel (a) of Figure 1. There you can see that the U.S. economy has been characterized by *ongoing inflation*. Even in the 1990s and into early 2001— with unemployment at (or very close to) its natural rate—the annual inflation rate hovered around 2 to 3 percent. This means that, even though the economy was at full employment (so the economy's self-correcting mechanism was not operating), prices were *continually rising*.

Even when the unemployment rate is *above* its natural rate—as in 2009—prices keep rising. Why? And how does ongoing inflation change our analysis of the effects of monetary policy or the guidelines that the Fed should follow? We'll consider these questions next.

How Ongoing Inflation Arises

The best way to begin our analysis of ongoing inflation is to explore how it arises in an economy. We can do this by revisiting the 1960s, when the inflation rate rose steadily, and ongoing inflation first became a public concern.

What was special about the economy in the 1960s? First, it was a period of exuberance and optimism, for both businesses and households. Business spending on plant and equipment rose, and household spending on new homes and automobiles rose as well. At the same time, government spending rose—both military spending for the war in Vietnam and social spending on programs to help alleviate poverty. These increases in spending all contributed to rightward shifts of the *AD* curve; they were positive demand shocks. The unemployment rate fell below the natural rate— hovering around 3 percent in the late 1960s. And, as expected, the economy's self-correcting mechanism kicked in: Higher wages shifted the *AS* curve upward, causing the price level to rise.

As you've learned in this chapter, the Fed could have neutralized the positive demand shocks by raising its interest rate target (as in Figure 4), shifting the *AD* curve back to its original position. Alternatively, the Fed could have allowed the self-correcting mechanism to bring the economy back to full employment with a higher—but stable—price level. But in the late 1960s, the Fed made a different choice: It maintained its low interest rate target. This required the Fed to increase the money supply, thus adding its *own* positive demand shock to the spending shocks already hitting the economy. In Figure 3, this was the equivalent of moving the *AD* curve all the way out to AD_3, preventing any rise in interest rates but overheating the economy even more.

Why did the Fed act in this way? No one knows for sure, but one likely reason is that, in the 1960s, the Fed saw its job differently than it does today. The Fed tried to keep the interest rate stable and low, both to maintain high investment spending and to avoid instability in the financial markets. This is what it had been doing for years, with good effect: Americans had prospered in the previous decade, the 1950s, and financial markets were, indeed, stable.

But even though this policy worked well in the 1950s, it did not serve the economy well during and after the demand shocks of the 1960s. That's because the Fed's policy—year after year—prevented the self-correcting mechanism from bringing the economy back to full employment. Instead, each time the price level began rising, and the economy began to self-correct, the Fed would increase the money supply *again*, causing output to remain *continually* above its potential output. And that, in turn, meant that the price level would continue to rise, year after year.

Now comes a crucial part of the story: As the price level continued to rise in the 1960s, the public began to *expect* it to rise at a similar rate in the future. This illustrates a more general principle:

> *When inflation continues for some time, the public develops expectations that the inflation rate in the future will be similar to the inflation rates of the recent past.*

Why are expectations of inflation so important? Because when managers and workers expect inflation, it gets built into their decision-making process. Union contracts that set wages for the next 3 years will include automatic increases to compensate for the anticipated loss of purchasing power caused by future inflation. Nonunion wages will tend to rise each year as well, to match the wages in the union-ized sector. And contracts for future delivery of inputs—like lumber, cement, and unfinished goods—will incorporate the higher prices everyone expects by the date of delivery. For reasons like these,

> *a continuing, stable rate of inflation gets built into the economy. The built-in rate is usually the rate that has existed for the past few years.*

Built-In Inflation

Once there is built-in inflation, the economy continues to generate inflation even *after* the self-correcting mechanism has finally been allowed to do its job and bring us back to potential output. To see why, look at Figure 6. It shows what might

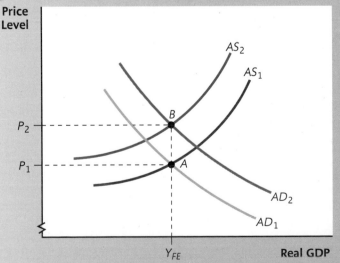

FIGURE 6 | **Long-Run Equilibrium with Built-In Inflation**

During the year, the aggregate supply curve shifts upward by the built-in rate of inflation. To keep the economy at full employment, the Fed shifts the AD curve rightward by increasing the money supply.

happen over the year in an economy with built-in inflation. In the figure, output is at its full-employment level. But over the year, the *AS* curve shifts upward and the *AD* curve shifts rightward, so the equilibrium moves from *A* to *B* and the price level rises from P_1 to P_2. Why does all this happen when there is built-in inflation?

Let's start with the reason for the upward shift of the *AS* curve. Unemployment is at its natural rate, so the self-correction mechanism is no longer contributing to any rise in wages or unit costs. But something else is causing unit costs to increase: inflationary expectations. Based on recent experience, the public expects the price level to rise as it has been rising in the past, so wages (and other input prices) will continue to increase, *even though real GDP is equal to potential output.* Thus,

> *in an economy with built-in inflation, the* AS *curve will shift upward each year, even when output is at potential and unemployment is at its natural rate. The upward shift of the* AS *curve will equal the built-in rate of inflation.*

For example, if the public expects inflation of 6 percent during the year, then contracts will call for wages and input prices to rise by 6 percent that year. This means that unit costs will increase by 6 percent. Firms—marking up prices over unit costs—will raise their prices by 6 percent as well, and the *AS* curve will shift upward by 6 percent.

Explaining why the *AS* curve shifts upward is only half the story in Figure 6. We must also explain why the *AD* curve shifts rightward. The simple answer is: The *AD* curve shifts rightward because the Fed increases the money supply. But *why* does the Fed shift the *AD* curve rightward, when it knows that doing so only prolongs inflation? One reason is that reducing inflation would be *costly* to the economy.

Imagine what would happen if the Fed decided *not* to shift the *AD* curve rightward during the year. The *AS* curve will shift upward anyway, by a percentage shift equal to the built-in rate of inflation. This will happen *no matter what the Fed does* because the shift is based on expected inflation, which, in turn, is based on past experiences of inflation. There is nothing the Fed can do today to affect what has happened in the past, so it must accept the upward shift of the *AS* curve as a given. So if, during the year, the Fed maintains the *AD* curve at AD_1, the new equilibrium (not labeled in the figure) will be at the intersection of AD_1 and AS_2. The Fed would achieve its goal of reducing inflation that year—the price level would rise from P_1 to something less than P_2 instead of all the way to P_2. But the drop in inflation would come with a cost: The economy's output will decline below Y_{FE}—a recession.

> *In the short run, the Fed can reduce the rate of inflation below the built-in rate, but only at the cost of creating a recession.*

Would the Fed ever purposely create a recession to reduce inflation? Indeed it would, and it has—more than once. By far the most important episode occurred during the early 1980s. As Figure 1 shows, annual inflation reached the extraordinary level of 13.3 percent in 1979. Soon after, with some support from the newly elected President Reagan, the Fed embarked on an aggressive campaign to bring inflation down. The Fed stopped increasing the money supply and stopped shifting the *AD* curve rightward, and a recession began in July of 1981. Unemployment peaked, as shown earlier in Figure 1, at 10.7 percent at the end of 1982. With tremendous slack in the economy, the inflation rate fell rapidly, to below 4 percent in 1982. The Fed deliberately created a serious recession, but it brought down the rate of inflation.

Creating a recession is not a decision that the Fed takes lightly. Recessions are costly to the economy and painful to those who lose their jobs. The desire to avoid a recession is one reason that the Fed tolerated ongoing inflation for years and continued to play its role by shifting the *AD* curve rightward. We'll discuss other reasons for the Fed's tolerance of ongoing inflation a bit later.

Ongoing Inflation and the Phillips Curve

Ongoing inflation changes our analysis of monetary policy. For one thing, it forces us to recognize a subtle, but important, change in the Fed's objectives: While the Fed still desires full employment, its other goal—price stability—is not zero inflation, but rather a *low and stable inflation rate*.

Another difference is in the graphs we use to illustrate the Fed's policy choices. Instead of continuing to analyze the economy with *AS* and *AD* graphs, when there is ongoing inflation, we usually use another powerful tool.

This tool is the *Phillips curve*—named after the late economist A. W. Phillips, who did early research on the relationship between inflation and unemployment. The **Phillips curve** illustrates the Fed's choices between inflation and unemployment in the short run, for a given built-in inflation rate.

Figure 7 shows a Phillips curve for the U.S. economy. The inflation rate is measured on the vertical axis; the unemployment rate on the horizontal. Point *E* shows the long-run equilibrium in the economy when the built-in inflation rate is 6 percent. At point *E*, unemployment is at its natural rate—U_N—and inflation remains constant from year to year at the built-in rate of 6 percent.

Notice that the Phillips curve is downward sloping. Why? Because it tells the same story we told earlier—with *AD* and *AS* curves—about the Fed's options in the short run. If the Fed wants to decrease the rate of inflation from 6 percent to 3 percent, it must slow the rightward shifts of the *AD* curve. This would cause a movement *along* the Phillips curve from point *E* to point *F*. As you can see, in moving to point *F*, the economy experiences a recession: Since output falls, unemployment rises above the natural rate.

Phillips curve A curve indicating the Fed's choices between inflation and unemployment in the short run.

FIGURE 7 | **The Phillips Curve**

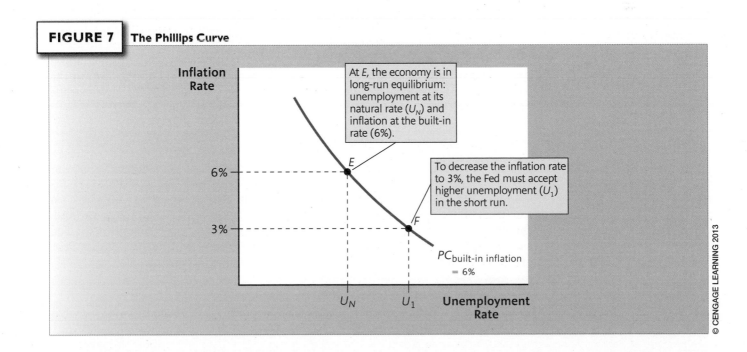

At *E*, the economy is in long-run equilibrium: unemployment at its natural rate (U_N) and inflation at the built-in rate (6%).

To decrease the inflation rate to 3%, the Fed must accept higher unemployment (U_1) in the short run.

$PC_{\text{built-in inflation}} = 6\%$

FIGURE 8 | The Phillips Curve Shifts Downward

Initially, the economy is at point E, with inflation equal to the built-in rate of 6%. If the Fed moves the economy to point F and keeps it there for some time, the public will eventually come to expect 3% inflation in the future. The built-in inflation rate will fall and the Phillips curve will shift downward to $PC_{built\text{-}in\ inflation\ =\ 3\%}$. The economy will move to point G in the long run, with unemployment at the natural rate and an actual inflation rate equal to the built-in rate of 3%.

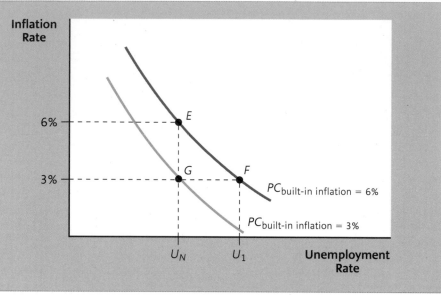

© CENGAGE LEARNING 2013

> In the short run, the Fed can move along the Phillips curve by adjusting the rate at which the AD curve shifts rightward. When the Fed moves the economy downward and rightward along the Phillips curve, the unemployment rate increases, and the inflation rate decreases.

A Downward Shift in the Phillips Curve

Suppose the Fed moves the economy downward along the Phillips curve, from point E to point F, and then keeps it at point F. In the long run, the public—observing a 3 percent inflation rate—will come to expect 3 percent inflation into the future. Thus, in the long run, 3 percent will become the economy's built-in rate of inflation. Figure 8 shows the effect on the Phillips curve. When the economy's built-in inflation rate drops from 6 percent to 3 percent, the Phillips curve shifts downward, to the lower curve. At any unemployment rate, the inflation rate will be lower, now that the public expects inflation of only 3 percent rather than 6 percent.

> In the long run, a decrease in the inflation rate leads to a lower built-in inflation rate, and the Phillips curve shifts downward.

Once the Fed has reduced the built-in inflation rate, it can locate anywhere on the new Phillips curve by adjusting how rapidly it lets the money supply grow (and, therefore, how rapidly the AD curve shifts rightward each year). Therefore, the Fed can choose to bring the economy back to full employment (point G), with a new, lower inflation rate of 3 percent rather than the previous 6 percent.

An Upward Shift in the Phillips Curve

The process we've described—moving down the Phillips curve and thereby causing it to shift downward—also works in reverse: Moving *up* the Phillips curve will,

FIGURE 9   The Phillips Curve Shifts Upward

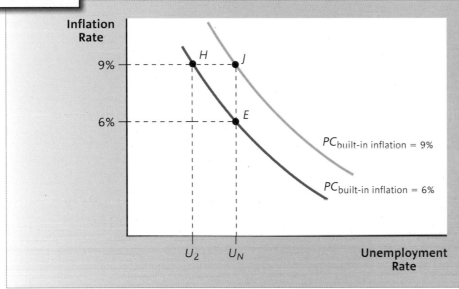

Initially, the economy is at point E, with inflation equal to the built-in rate of 6%. If the Fed moves the economy to point H and keeps it there for some time, the public will eventually come to expect 9% inflation in the future. The built-in inflation rate will rise and the Phillips curve will shift upward to $PC_{built\text{-}in\ inflation\ =\ 9\%}$. The economy will move to point J in the long run, with unemployment at the natural rate and an actual inflation rate equal to the built-in rate of 9%.

in the long run, shift the curve *upward*. Figure 9 illustrates this case. Once again, assume the economy begins at point E, with a built-in inflation rate of 6 percent and unemployment at its natural rate. Now suppose the Fed begins to increase the money supply *more rapidly* than in the past, and begins shifting the AD curve farther rightward than in Figure 6. In the short run, the economy would move *along* the Phillips curve from point E to point H in Figure 9. The inflation rate would rise to 9 percent, and the unemployment rate would fall below its natural rate—in the short run.

But suppose the Fed keeps the economy at point H for some time, continuing to shift the AD curve rightward at a faster rate than before. Then, in the long run, the public will begin to expect 9 percent inflation, and that will become the new built-in rate of inflation. The Phillips curve will then shift upward. At this point, if the Fed returns the economy to full employment, we end up at point J. The economy will be back in long-run equilibrium—but with a higher built-in inflation rate.

> *In the long run, an increase in the inflation rate leads to a higher built-in inflation rate, and the Phillips curve shifts upward.*

The Long-Run Phillips Curve

Figure 10 combines the previous two figures, showing the policy choices for the Fed and their consequences. We assume, as before, that we are initially at point E on the middle Phillips curve. The built-in inflation rate is 6 percent, and the economy is operating at full employment. In the short run, the built-in inflation rate will remain at 6 percent, so the Fed can freely move along the middle Phillips curve, say, to point H or point F. In doing so, the Fed exploits the short-run trade-off between unemployment and inflation. But in the long run—once the public's

FIGURE 10 | The Long-Run Phillips Curve

The vertical line is the economy's long-run Phillips curve, showing all combinations of unemployment and inflation the Fed can choose in the long run. The curve is vertical because in the long run, the unemployment rate must equal the natural rate. Starting at point E with 6% inflation, the Fed can choose unemployment at the natural rate with either a higher rate of inflation (point J) or a lower rate of inflation (point G). But points off of the vertical line are not sustainable in the long run.

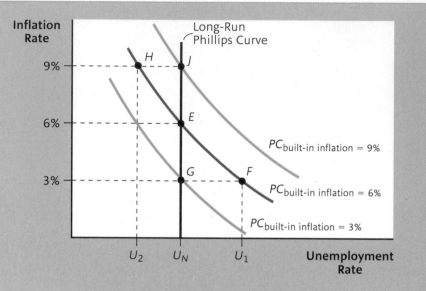

© CENGAGE LEARNING 2013

expectations of inflation adjust to the new reality—the built-in inflation rate will change, and the Phillips curve will shift. Indeed, the Phillips curve will *keep* shifting whenever the unemployment rate is kept above or below the natural rate. (To see why, ask yourself what would happen in the future if the Fed tried to keep the unemployment rate *permanently* at a level like U_2—below the natural rate.) Thus, the economy cannot be in long-run equilibrium until the unemployment rate returns to its natural rate, and output is back to its potential level. In the long run, when we are at the natural rate of unemployment, the Fed can only choose *which* Phillips curve the economy will be on.

> *In the short run, there is a tradeoff between inflation and unemployment: The Fed can choose lower unemployment at the cost of higher inflation, or lower inflation at the cost of higher unemployment. But in the long run, since unemployment always returns to its natural rate, there is no such tradeoff.*

Now look at the vertical line. It tells us how monetary policy affects the economy in the long run, without the distractions of the short-run story. The vertical line is the economy's *long-run Phillips curve*, which tells us the combinations of unemployment and inflation that the Fed can choose in the long run.

To see why, suppose the Fed moves the economy from point *E* to point *H* in the short run. Then in the long run, we will end up at point *J* on the vertical line: The economy will be back at the natural rate of unemployment, but with a higher inflation rate (9 percent). Suppose, on the other hand, the Fed moves us from point *E* to point *F* in the short run. Then in the long run, we will once again be on the vertical line, but this time at point *G*. Unemployment is at its natural rate, but with a lower inflation rate (3 percent). No matter what the Fed does, unemployment will always return to the natural rate, U_N, in the long run. However, the Fed can use monetary policy to select any rate of inflation it wants.

> *The **long-run Phillips curve** is a vertical line at the natural rate of unemployment. It shows us that, in the long run, the Fed can change the rate of inflation, but not the rate of unemployment.*

Long-run Phillips curve
A vertical line indicating that in the long run, unemployment must equal its natural rate, regardless of the rate of inflation.

Why the Fed Allows Ongoing Inflation

Because the Fed can choose any rate of inflation it wants, and because inflation is costly to society, we might think that the Fed would aim for an inflation rate of zero. But a look back at panel (a) of Figure 1 shows that this is not what the Fed has chosen to do. In recent years, with unemployment very close to its natural rate, the Fed has maintained annual inflation at around 2 or 3 percent. Why doesn't the Fed eliminate inflation from the economy entirely?

One reason is a widespread belief that the Consumer Price Index (CPI) and other measures of inflation actually *overstate* the true rate of inflation in the economy. As you've learned, many economists believe that the CPI has overstated the true annual inflation rate by 1 to 2 percent—or more—in recent decades. Although the Bureau of Labor Statistics has been working hard to correct the problem, some significant upward bias remains. Thus, if the Fed tried to get the measured inflation rate down to zero, the economy might actually be experiencing *deflation*. As you'll see in a few pages, this would be harmful to the economy.

Another reason the Fed prefers ongoing inflation (to zero inflation) is that a low, stable inflation rate makes the labor market work more smoothly. The argument goes as follows: While no one wants a cut in his or her real wage rate, people seem to react differently, depending on *how* the real wage is decreased. For example, suppose there is an excess supply of workers in some industry, and a real wage cut of 3 percent would bring that labor market back to equilibrium. Workers would strongly resist a 3 percent cut in the nominal wage. But they would more easily tolerate a freeze in the nominal wage while the price level rises by 3 percent, even though in both scenarios, the real wage falls by 3 percent.

If this argument is correct, then a low or modest inflation rate would help wages adjust in different markets, helping to ensure that workers move to industries where they would be most productive as the structure of the economy changes over time. In some labor markets, real wages can be raised by increasing nominal wages faster than prices. In other labor markets, real wages can be cut by increasing nominal wages more slowly than prices, or not at all.

Finally (and perhaps most importantly), maintaining the inflation rate at 2 or 3 percent gives the Fed more flexibility in setting interest rates. If there were no ongoing inflation, real and nominal interest rates would be equal. And because nominal interest rates cannot go below zero, real interest rates could never drop below zero either. But there are times—such as during the recession of 2008–2009—when the Fed might want real interest rates to become *negative*, in order to create a powerful boost to aggregate expenditure. With a lower bound of zero on the nominal rate, the only way to create a negative *real* interest rate is through ongoing inflation. By maintaining ongoing and expected inflation of 2 to 3 percent, the Fed maintains the ability to set the real federal funds rate at negative 2 or 3 percent, and to manipulate other interest rates lower than they could otherwise be.

> *The Fed has tolerated measured inflation at 2 to 3 percent per year because (1) it knows that the true rate of inflation is lower; (2) ongoing inflation may help labor markets adjust more easily; and (3) ongoing inflation gives the Fed more flexibility to bring down real interest rates.*

CHALLENGES FOR MONETARY POLICY

So far in this chapter, we've described some clear-cut guidelines the Fed *can* and *does* follow in conducting monetary policy. We've seen that the proper response to demand shocks is a change in the interest rate target. Dealing with a supply shock is more problematic, because it requires the Fed to balance its goal of low, stable inflation with its goal of full employment. But even here, once the Fed decides on the proper balance, its policy choice is straightforward: Shift the *AD* curve to achieve the desired combination of inflation and unemployment in the short run, and then guide the economy back to full employment in the long run.

One might almost conclude that monetary policy is akin to operating a giant machine—adjusting this or that knob, and making the occasional repair by consulting the manual. And policy making might appear rather uncontroversial, other than the occasional debate between those who favor hawkish and dovish policies toward inflation after a supply shock.

But the truth is very much the opposite. First, the Fed faces frequent criticism from members of Congress, the business community, the media, and some academic economists—over not just its policy choices but also the *way* it arrives at them. Second, the Fed, rather than operating a well-understood machine, must conduct monetary policy with highly imperfect information about the economy's course and precisely how its policies will alter that course. Let's consider some of the challenges facing the Fed.

Information Problems

The Federal Reserve has hundreds of economists carrying out research and gathering data to improve its understanding of how the economy works, and how monetary policy affects the economy. Research at the Fed is widely respected and has made great progress. But because the economy is complex and constantly changing, serious gaps remain. Two of the most important gaps concern the time lag before monetary policy affects the economy, and knowledge of the natural rate of unemployment (or—equivalently—the economy's potential output).

Changing and Uncertain Time Lags

Monetary policy works with an uncertain time lag. Even after a rise in the interest rate, business firms will likely continue to build the new plants and new homes they've already started constructing. The most powerful effects on investment spending will be the cancellation of *new* projects currently being planned—projects that *would* have entered the pipeline of new spending many months later. When the Fed lowers the interest rate, the full effects will be felt many months later, after new investment projects are planned and firms begin spending to implement them.

The time lag in the effectiveness of monetary policy can have serious consequences. Economists often use an analogy to describe this problem. Imagine that you are trying to drive a car with a special problem: When you step on the gas, the car will go forward . . . but not until 5 minutes later. Similarly, when you step on the brake, the car will slow, but also with a 5-minute lag. It would be very difficult to maintain an even speed with this car: You'd step on the gas, and when nothing happened, you'd be tempted to step on it harder. When the car finally moves, it will accelerate rapidly and speed down the road. So you try to slow down, but once again, hitting the brakes makes nothing happen. So you brake harder.

The Fed can make—and, in the past, has made—similar mistakes. When it tries to cool off an overheated economy, it may find that nothing is happening. If it hits the monetary brakes harder, it might go too far; if it doesn't, it runs the risk of continued overheating. Even worse, the time lag can change, and the Fed can never be sure how long it will take before any given policy action will affect the economy. Just when the Fed may think it has mastered the rules, the rules change.

> *Because the effects of monetary policy occur after a lag of uncertain duration, policies meant to stabilize the economy could instead destabilize it.*

Uncertainty about the Natural Rate of Unemployment

In our Phillips curve analysis, we've assumed that the Fed knows the economy's natural rate of unemployment, signified by the vertical long-run Phillips curve at some value U_N. In this case, once the economy achieved a long-run equilibrium, the Fed's job would be relatively straightforward: to shift the *AD* curve rightward by just the right amount each period to maintain the natural rate of unemployment. But while many economists believe that today the natural rate is between 4.5 and 5 percent, no one is really sure. And the natural rate can change over time.

An incorrect estimate of the natural rate can have serious consequences for the economy. For example, suppose the Fed believes the natural rate of unemployment is 5 percent, but the rate is really 4.5 percent. Then—at least for a time—the Fed will steer the economy toward an unnecessarily high unemployment rate, and society will needlessly bear the social and economic burden of higher unemployment. On the other hand, if the Fed believes the natural rate is 4.5 percent when it is really 5 percent, it will overheat the economy. This will raise the inflation rate—and a costly recession may be needed later in order to reduce it.

> *Fed policy based on an incorrect estimate of the natural rate of unemployment can be costly for the economy, creating a period of higher-than-necessary unemployment, or higher-than-desired inflation.*

Trial and error can help the Fed determine the true natural rate. If the Fed raises unemployment above the *true* natural rate, the inflation rate will drop. If unemployment falls below the *true* natural rate, the inflation rate will rise. But (as we discussed earlier) trial and error works best when there is continual and rapid feedback. It can take some time for the inflation rate to change—6 months, a year, or even longer. In the meantime, the Fed might continue to err.

Rules versus Discretion

Over the past several decades, the Federal Reserve has formulated monetary policy using *discretion*: responding to demand and supply shocks in the way that Fed officials think best at the time. In some cases, this seems to have helped the economy's performance, as when the Fed aggressively cut interest rates during 2001 and helped to make the recession that year shorter and milder.

In other cases, discretion has worked less well. Some economists believe the Fed helped create the housing bubble with its low interest rates from 2002 to 2005 and criticize the Fed for bringing rates down too slowly after the bubble burst in late

2006 and 2007. If they are right, the Fed's discretion helped to cause and exacerbate the recession and financial turmoil of 2008 and 2009. Some of the Fed's critics have suggested that its performance, on average, would be better with less discretion and more deference to predetermined rules.

The Taylor Rule

Taylor rule A proposed rule that would require the Fed to change the interest rate by a specified amount whenever real GDP or inflation deviates from its pre-announced target.

The most often discussed rule for monetary policy is the **Taylor rule,** originally proposed by economist John Taylor. Under this rule, the Fed would be required to announce a target for the inflation rate (say, 2 percent per year) and another target for real GDP (the Fed's estimate of potential GDP in that period). Then the Fed would be required to change its interest rate target by some predetermined amount whenever either output or inflation (or both) deviated from their respective targets.

For example, suppose the economy was hit by a positive demand shock. At some point either real GDP would rise above potential, or the inflation rate would rise above its target rate, or both would occur. The Fed would then be obligated to raise its interest rate target by an amount that everyone knew in advance, depending on the changes observed in output and inflation. On the other side, if a negative demand shock started to threaten a recession, changes in inflation and/or output would commit the Fed to *lower* its interest rate target and stimulate the economy back toward full employment.

What about a negative supply shock—such as a rise in oil prices—that causes the inflation rate to rise and output to fall? In this case, inflation would rise *higher* than its target and output would fall *below* it. But the rule would determine the Fed's response. It would raise or lower the interest rate target depending on which variable—output or inflation—was deviated the most, based on the rules. Thus, the hawk–dove debate that follows every supply shock would be settled—publically—in advance.

What would be the advantage of such a rule? First, it could help keep expected inflation under control. For example, when the inflation rate rises after a positive demand shock, the message from the Fed would be, "Even though the inflation rate just rose, you know the rules. We have to bring the inflation rate back down, so don't get any ideas that we're going to let this continue." Similarly, if a negative demand shock sent the economy into a recession, and the Fed began to stimulate the economy, the message would be, "Yes, we're stimulating the economy, but you needn't worry about inflation. If we go too far by mistake and overheat the economy, the rule says we'll bring the inflation rate down again."

A second advantage of the Taylor rule is political: It would give the Fed ammunition to fight inflation with a higher interest rate—even when doing so might prove unpopular at the time. The Fed would only be following the rule that everyone understood in advance. This would help discourage the sort of discretion, and political pressure, that can create ever-rising inflation, as occurred during the 1970s.

> *In theory, following a rule—such as the Taylor rule—could help the Fed manage inflationary expectations, and make it easier to take actions that, while beneficial in the long run, are unpopular in the short run.*

The Taylor rule is controversial. Opponents argue that it implies more advanced knowledge about the economy—and what an appropriate future response should be—than is realistically possible. And unless the rule was written into law—which only a few economists advocate—the Fed would not be obligated to follow it. Because the public would know this, the mere existence of the rule might not have much effect on the formation of inflationary expectations.

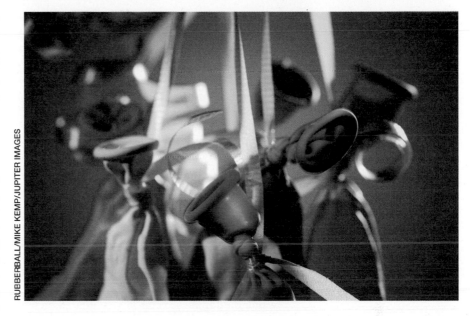

RUBBERBALL/MIKE KEMP/JUPITER IMAGES

Avoiding Deflation

During the first four years of the Great Depression, the price level fell an average of 10 percent per year—a very serious period of *deflation* (negative inflation). Since then, episodes of deflation in the U.S. have been mild and short-lived. But the Fed is always on guard against any return of prolonged or serious deflation.

What's wrong with deflation? For one thing, it can render conventional monetary policy powerless. As you've learned, the Fed controls a *nominal* interest rate (the federal funds rate). But what matters for consumption and investment spending is the *real* rate of interest—the percentage change in purchasing power that a borrower must repay. The real interest rate people expect on loans is the nominal rate minus the expected rate of inflation.

Ordinarily, the expected inflation is positive, so real interest rates are lower than nominal interest rates. In that case, the Fed can easily lower the *real* federal funds rate to any level it desires. It can even make the real federal funds rate negative. For example, if expected inflation is 3 percent, and the Fed pushes the federal funds rate down to 1 percent, then the real rate will be $1\% - 3\% = -2\%$. (Lending still occurs at a negative *real* rate because losing 2 percent of your purchasing power is better than the alternative—holding cash and losing 3 percent.)

But suppose that people expect deflation, such as an inflation rate of -5 percent. Then the real interest rate will be *higher* than the nominal rate. For example, a 1 percent nominal rate now translates to a 6 percent real rate, because $1\% - (-5\%) = 6\%$. A 1-year loan would be repaid with 1 percent *more* dollars than were borrowed, but because prices have declined by 5 percent, those dollars will have 6 percent more purchasing power than was borrowed.

Now let's put this together with something we discussed a couple of chapters ago. The nominal federal funds rate has a *zero lower bound*. (A *nominal* rate can't be negative, because that would imply people are lending out dollars for the privilege of getting back fewer dollars! Better to keep the funds as cash.) But when people expect deflation, a nominal rate at the zero lower bound translates to a *positive real* interest rate. In fact, that positive real rate will be equal to the expected rate of *de*flation. For example, if people expect deflation of 5 percent per year, then the lowest possible level for the *real* federal funds rate (when the nominal rate is zero) is *positive* 5 percent. Remember that other interest rates in the economy are *higher* than the federal funds rate. Thus, with deflation of 5 percent, the Fed will be unable to move *any* real interest rate in the economy below 5 percent. If we are in a recession, the Fed may be unable to stimulate spending with its conventional tool (the federal funds rate), and it will have to use its more controversial, *unconventional* tools to do the job.

> *Expected deflation creates a* positive *lower bound for the* real *federal funds rate—equal to the expected rate of deflation. If the Fed wants to reduce real interest rates below that lower bound, it will have to use* unconventional tools.

Moreover, once *deflation* gets going, it can feed on itself and get worse. Most debts (such as amounts owed by homeowners, students, businesses, and government agencies) are *nominal* debts. But in periods of deflation, prices and wages are falling. This means that households and businesses—while earning fewer dollars each year—must repay an unchanged number of dollars on their debts. The result is more bankruptcies, reduced spending—and possibly a worsening deflation problem. And worsening deflation will drive real interest rates even higher.

Economists at the Fed have thought hard about the appropriate response to deflation. They have pointed out that a modest deflation needn't become worse. Japan, for example, had deflation averaging roughly 1 percent per year for about a decade. While the Japanese economy stagnated, deflation never spiraled out of control.

Moreover, the Fed has made clear that it could use unconventional tools to address the problem, if it arises. One such tool is the *expected* inflation rate. The Fed can indicate—by announcing its policies in advance—that it will create positive inflation in the near future, using a variety of methods (discussed a couple of chapters ago) to stimulate new spending. A higher expected inflation rate lowers expected *real* interest rates. Finally, if the Fed proves unable to address deflation on its own, it can be assisted by *fiscal* policy, which increases spending directly, bypassing the need to reduce real interest rates.

We have one more major challenge for monetary policy to discuss: how the Fed should deal with rapidly rising asset prices. We'll explore that question next, in our Using the Theory section.

USING THE THEORY

SHOULD THE FED PREVENT (OR POP) ASSET BUBBLES?

DENNIS NOVAK/GETTY IMAGES

A central goal of the Federal Reserve in the United States and other central banks around the world, is price stability—keeping inflation rates low. But inflation, as measured by a consumer price index or the broader price index for GDP, means rising prices for *goods and services*. What about the prices of *assets,* such as shares of stock or real estate? These are not included in measures of inflation, nor should they be. If an asset (such as a share of stock) has a higher price, you will pay more when you buy it, but you will also get more when you sell it. The higher price for the share of stock does not reduce the purchasing power of your income over goods and services. And rapidly rising stock prices don't create the kinds of efficiency-costs that occur with very high rates of inflation.

Does this mean the Fed should ignore asset price "bubbles"—rapid price increases driven mostly by expectations of future price increases, rather than sustainable market forces? Or should it attempt to "pop" them before they get out of hand? This question—widely debated for more than a decade—has become a leading controversy about monetary policy after housing prices began crashing in 2007.

The argument *for* popping bubbles before they go too far is suggested by Figure 11, which shows the net worth of the household sector (along with non-profits) as a percentage of annual GDP. When wealth rises at the same percentage rate as GDP, the ratio remains unchanged. In that case, the graph would be flat. When the graph rises, it means wealth is rising by an even greater percentage than GDP.

Notice the two recent episodes where the graph rises rapidly. The first occurred during the Internet, or "dot-com," bubble of the late 1990s, with household wealth rising from 3.5 times annual GDP to 4.5 times. The driving force was excessive optimism about stock prices—particularly those in companies that seemed in any way connected to the Internet. The second episode was the recent housing boom, where household wealth rose from about 3.75 times annual GDP to 4.75 times. During four of these years (from 2002 to 2006), household wealth rose from $41 trillion to $63 trillion.

As you've learned, household wealth is one of the determinants of consumption spending. During both of these "bubble periods," consumption rose rapidly, and so did aggregate expenditure and real GDP. The economy was booming. The rapid rise in GDP during these bubbles—the denominator of the ratio—makes the rise in the ratio itself all the more remarkable.

But you can also see what happened *after* each of these episodes: a rapid *decline* in wealth relative to GDP. When the housing bubble burst, household wealth declined

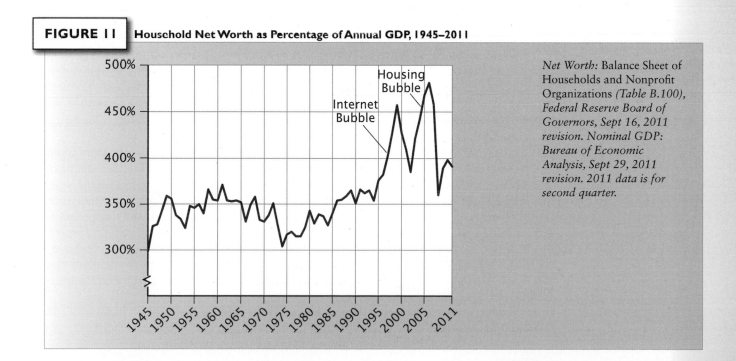

FIGURE 11 **Household Net Worth as Percentage of Annual GDP, 1945–2011**

Net Worth: Balance Sheet of Households and Nonprofit Organizations *(Table B.100), Federal Reserve Board of Governors, Sept 16, 2011 revision. Nominal GDP: Bureau of Economic Analysis, Sept 29, 2011 revision. 2011 data is for second quarter.*

by about $14 trillion. As a fraction of GDP, it ended up below its pre-bubble percentage. And such large declines in wealth and asset prices can start several vicious cycles: Falling asset prices force leveraged financial institutions and investors to sell assets, causing their prices to fall further. At the same time, falling asset prices destroy household wealth, which decreases consumption spending and real GDP. This, in turn, causes layoffs and falling profits at business firms, which prompts further asset-selling by households and businesses. The bursting of the Internet bubble was a major cause of the recession of 2001. The bursting of the housing bubble was a central cause of the severe recession of 2008–2009, and a major reason that the slump that followed was so deep and lengthy.

But where was the Fed? During both of these run-ups in asset prices, inflation in goods and services—as measured by standard price indexes—was mild. The Fed at various times expressed concern about rising stock or home prices, and occasionally raised interest rates to restrain them. But it made no strong, concerted efforts to pop either bubble, as it certainly would have if it were goods and services, rather than assets, whose prices were rising. Some economists think that was a serious mistake, and that in the future the Fed should actively try to stop bubbles from forming or at least burst them before they grow too large. Among this group, some believe that merely raising the federal funds rate would do the job; others argue for a more interventionist approach, using regulatory and other changes aimed at specific asset markets.

In retrospect, it does seem that if the Fed had stopped the housing bubble earlier, the economy could have avoided what followed: the collapse of wealth, the severe recession, and the financial crisis. But as home prices were rising, the Fed chairs—first Alan Greenspan and then Ben Bernanke—argued against aggressive intervention. Other Fed officials and research economists echoed these views. They maintained that trying to stop bubbles in their early stages has high costs and doubtful benefits, for several reasons.

First, while it is easy to identify a bubble in retrospect, it is not so easy to do so in advance. Asset prices can also rise rapidly because of fundamental market forces. For example, coastal real estate prices have risen very rapidly for decades, something that many observers in the past identified as a classic bubble. But even after the fall in housing prices nationwide, coastal real estate prices have maintained most of their decades-long gains. What seemed like a bubble at the time now seems to be a simple case of limited supply and growing demand—and sustainable high prices in the long run. The Fed may be no better at identifying bubbles than anyone else. And if the Fed thinks it sees a bubble and is wrong, it will be fighting a costly and losing battle trying to prevent asset prices from rising.

Second, *how* would the Fed burst the bubble? It generally shies away from intervening in specific asset markets except in extreme circumstances. The Fed does not believe it should be the arbiter of relative asset prices. Intervening in specific asset markets inevitably leads to political pressure and threats to the Fed's independence. For example, suppose the Fed observed that the price of farmland was rising rapidly and tried to intervene specifically in that market—say, by increasing capital requirements for banks that lend to farmland buyers. The Fed would then face pressure from senators in farm states that are temporarily booming. They might demand that the Fed mind its own business and threaten legislation to restrict the Fed's powers more broadly if it ignored them.

This leaves conventional monetary policy—raising the federal funds rate. In theory, higher interest rates might slow the borrowing that is fueling leveraged asset buying. This could slow the bubble's expansion and maybe even stop it in its tracks.

And if higher interest rates caused asset prices to plunge, at least it would happen early, before the bubble had grown large enough to bring down the entire economy.

But there's a problem with this approach. A rise in the federal funds rate drives up *all* interest rates and makes *all* borrowing in the economy more expensive. The Fed—in its effort to control the bubble—would be reining in spending *throughout* the economy, reducing output below potential. Even if the Fed was correct about the bubble, fighting it this way would entail a high cost. And if the Fed was wrong, and fundamental, sustainable forces were driving up asset prices, we would suffer a needless long period of unemployment until the Fed gave up.

Finally, it is not clear that the Fed *could* control a bubble by raising interest rates to any reasonable degree, because overly-optimistic investors might not respond. In the final stages of the Internet bubble, for example, many investors expected annual rates of return on dot-com stocks of 100 percent or more. During the housing bubble, home buyers in the hottest real estate markets—using borrowed funds to buy homes—expected similar returns. Even a relatively large hike in the federal funds rate—say, from 4 percent to 8 percent—might have been little noticed by overly-optimistic home buyers, while severely slowing the rest of the economy. Meanwhile, raising the federal funds rate that high could be devastating to the rest of the economy.

In recent years, the Fed's thinking about bubbles has centered on a "mop-up" strategy: Don't try to prevent bubbles from forming, but be prepared to mop up the damage (with lower interest rates) when they burst, so they don't bring the rest of the economy down with them. This strategy did not work well in 2007 and 2008 when—after housing prices collapsed—the Fed seemed unable to mop up in time. The result was a painful recession, and the need to reach beyond conventional policy to prevent financial collapse. The Fed, ironically, had to intervene in specific asset markets to contain the damage. This led to attacks from the media and by some in Congress, who saw the Fed as trying to rescue highly unpopular financial institutions, rather than the financial system itself. The Fed thus found itself in the midst of the type of controversy it tries so hard to avoid. As a result, Fed officials have been actively reexamining their position and reassessing the costs and benefits of trying to identify and pop bubbles in advance.

SUMMARY

As the nation's central bank, the Federal Reserve bears primary responsibility for maintaining a low, stable rate of inflation and for maintaining full employment of the labor force as the economy is buffeted by a variety of shocks.

Demand shocks can shift the *AD* curve, causing output to deviate from its full-employment level. The Fed can neutralize these shocks by adjusting its interest rate target—changing the money supply to shift the *AD* curve back to its original position.

The Fed's most difficult problem is responding to supply shocks. A negative supply shock—an upward shift of the *AS* curve—presents the Fed with a dilemma. In the short run, it must choose a point along that new *AS* curve. If it wishes to maintain price stability, it must shift the *AD* curve to the left and accept higher unemployment. If the Fed wishes to maintain full employment, it must shift the *AD* curve to the right

and accept a higher rate of inflation. A "hawk" policy puts greater emphasis on price stability, while a "dove" policy emphasizes lower unemployment.

If Fed policy leads to ongoing inflation, then businesses and households come to expect the prevailing inflation rate to continue. As a result, the *AS* curve continues to shift upward at that built-in expected inflation rate. To maintain full employment, the Fed must shift the *AD* curve rightward, creating an inflation rate equal to the expected rate.

If the Fed wishes to change the built-in inflation rate, it must first change the expected inflation rate. For example, to lower the expected inflation rate, the Fed will slow down the rightward shifts of the *AD* curve. The actual inflation rate will fall, and expectations will eventually adjust downward. While they do so, however, the economy will experience a recession. The Fed's short-run choices between inflation and unemployment can be illustrated with the Phillips curve. In the short run, the Fed can move the economy along the downward-sloping *Phillips curve* by adjusting the rate at which the *AD* curve shifts. If the Fed moves the economy to a new point on the Phillips curve and holds it there, the built-in inflation rate will eventually adjust and the Phillips curve will shift. In the long run, the economy will return to the natural rate of unemployment with a different inflation rate. The *long-run Phillips curve* is a vertical line at the natural rate of unemployment.

In conducting monetary policy, the Fed faces several challenges. It has imperfect information about the time required for its policies to affect the economy, and also about the economy's potential GDP (or its natural rate of unemployment) during any given period. The Fed often faces criticism for using discretion rather than following rigid rules, especially when the economy does not perform well. And the Fed faces a special challenge in formulating policy toward asset bubbles.

PROBLEM SET

Answers to even-numbered Problems can be found on the text Web site through www.cengagebrain.com

1. Suppose that a law required the Fed to do everything possible to keep the inflation rate equal to zero. Using *AD* and *AS* curves, illustrate and explain how the Fed would deal with (a) a negative demand shock from a decrease in investment spending and (b) an adverse aggregate supply shock. What would be costs and benefits of such a law?

2. Suppose that, in a world with *no* ongoing inflation, the government raises taxes. Using *AD* and *AS* curves, describe the effects on the economy if the Fed decides to keep the money supply constant. Alternatively, how could the Fed use active policy to neutralize the demand shock?

3. Suppose that, initially, the price level is P_1 and GDP is Y_1, with no built-in inflation. The Fed reacts to a negative demand shock by neutralizing it. The next time the Fed receives data on GDP and the price level, it finds that the price level is above P_1 and GDP is above Y_1. Give a possible explanation for this finding.

4. Suppose the economy has been experiencing a low inflation rate. A new chair of the Federal Reserve is named, and he or she is known to be sympathetic to dove policies. Explain the possible effects on the Phillips curve.

5. "The idea of the Fed having to choose between hawk and dove policies in Figure 5 is silly. All the Fed has to do is shift the *AS* curve back to its original position,

which would prevent *both* recession *and* inflation." Do you agree? Why or why not?

6. Using a graph similar to Figure 9, and some additional curves, show what would happen in the future if the Fed tried to keep the unemployment rate *permanently* at a level like U_2—below the natural rate.

More Challenging

7. Suppose the economy is experiencing ongoing inflation. The Fed wants to reduce expected inflation, so it announces that in the future it will tolerate less inflation. How does the Fed's credibility affect the success of the reduction? How can the Fed build its credibility? Are there costs to building credibility? If so, what are they?

8. This chapter mentioned what would happen if the Fed over- or underestimated the natural rate of unemployment. Using the *AD–AS* model, suppose the economy is at the true natural rate of unemployment, so that GDP is at its potential level. Suppose, too, that the Fed wrongly believes that the natural rate of unemployment is higher (potential GDP is lower) and acts to bring the economy back to its supposed potential. What will the Fed do? What will happen in the short run? If the Fed continues to maintain output below potential, what will happen over the long run?

CHAPTER 17

Exchange Rates and Macroeconomic Policy

FRANCIS JOSEPH DEAN/DEAN PICTURES

I f you've ever traveled to a foreign country, you were a direct participant in the **foreign exchange market**—a market in which one country's currency is traded for that of another. For example, if you traveled to Mexico, you might have stopped near the border to exchange some dollars for Mexican pesos.

But even if you have never traveled abroad, you've been involved, at least indirectly, in all kinds of foreign exchange dealings. For example, suppose you buy some Mexican-grown tomatoes at a store in the United States, where you pay with dollars. A Mexican farmer grew the tomatoes; Mexican truckers transported them to the distribution center in the nearest large city; and Mexican workers, machinery, and raw materials were used to package them. All of these people need to be paid in Mexican pesos, regardless of who buys the final product. After all, they live in Mexico, so they need pesos to buy things there. But you, as an American, want to pay for your tomatoes with dollars.

Let's think about this for a moment. You want to pay for the tomatoes in dollars, but the Mexicans who produced them want to be paid in pesos. How can this happen?

The answer: *Someone*, here or abroad, must use the foreign exchange market to exchange dollars for pesos. For example, it might work like this: You pay dollars to your supermarket, which pays dollars to a U.S. importer, who pays dollars to the distributor in Mexico, who—finally—turns the dollars over to a Mexican bank in exchange for pesos. Finally, the Mexican distributor uses these pesos to pay the Mexican farmer.

In this chapter, we'll look at the markets in which dollars are exchanged for foreign currency. We'll also expand our macroeconomic analysis to consider the effects of changes in exchange rates. As you'll see, what happens in the foreign exchange market affects the economy, and changes in the economy affect the foreign exchange market. This has implications for the Fed as it tries to use monetary policy to steer the economy and keep it growing smoothly. Finally, we'll turn our attention to an analysis of the large and growing U.S. trade deficit.

Foreign exchange market The market in which one country's currency is traded for another country's.

FOREIGN EXCHANGE MARKETS AND EXCHANGE RATES

Every day, all over the world, more than 100 different national currencies are exchanged for one another in banks, hotels, stores, and kiosks in airports and train stations. Traders exchange dollars for Mexican pesos, Japanese yen, European euros, Indian rupees, Chinese yuan, and so on. In addition, traders exchange each of these foreign currencies for one another: pesos for euros, yen for yuan, euros for yen. . . . There are literally thousands of combinations. How can we hope to make sense of these markets—how they operate and how they affect us?

Our basic approach is to treat each pair of currencies as a separate market. That is, there is one market in which dollars are exchanged for euros, another in which Angolan kwanzas trade for yen, and so on. The physical locations where the trading takes place do not matter: Whether you exchange your dollars for yen in France, Germany, the United States, or even in Ecuador, you are a trader in the same dollar–yen market.

Exchange rate The amount of one country's currency that is traded for one unit of another country's currency.

In any foreign exchange market, the rate at which one currency is traded for another is called the **exchange rate** between those two currencies. For example, if you happened to trade dollars for British pounds on July 28, 2006, each British pound would have cost you about $1.86. On that day, the exchange rate was 1.8629 dollars per pound.

Dollars per Pound or Pounds per Dollar?

Table 1 lists exchange rates between the dollar and various foreign currencies on a particular day in 2011. But notice that we can think of any exchange rate in two ways: as so many units of foreign currency per dollar, or so many dollars per unit of foreign currency. For example, the table shows the exchange rate between the British pound and the dollar as 0.6321 pounds per dollar, or 1.5820 dollars per pound. We can always obtain one form of the exchange rate from the other by taking its reciprocal: 1/0.6321 = 1.5820, and 1/1.5820 = 0.6321.

In this chapter, we'll always define the exchange rate as "dollars per unit of foreign currency," as in the last column of the table. That way, from the American point of view, the exchange rate is just another *price*. The same way you pay a certain number of dollars for a gallon of gasoline (the price of gas), so, too, you pay a certain number of dollars for a British pound (the price of pounds).

> *The exchange rate is the price of foreign currency in dollars.*

TABLE 1

Foreign Exchange Rates, October 14, 2011

Country	Name of Currency	Symbol	Units of Foreign Currency per Dollar	Dollars per Unit of Foreign Currency
Brazil	real	R	1.732	$0.5775
China	yuan	Y	6.379	$0.1568
European Monetary Union Countries	euro	€	0.7204	$1.3881
Great Britain	pound	£	0.6321	$1.5820
India	rupee	R	49.010	$0.0204
Japan	yen	¥	77.219	$0.0130
Mexico	peso	P	13.231	$0.0756
Russia	ruble	R	30.858	$0.0324

Sources: www.bloomberg.com and www.xe.com.

Table 1 raises some important questions: Why, in late 2011, did a pound cost $1.58? Why not $1? Or $5? Why did one Japanese yen cost about a penny? And a Russian ruble about three cents?

The answers to these questions certainly affect Americans who travel abroad. Suppose you are staying in a hotel in London that costs 100 pounds per night. If the price of the pound is $1, the hotel room will cost you $100, but if the price is $5, the room will cost you $500. And exchange rates affect Americans who stay at home, too. They influence the prices of many goods we buy in the United States, and help determine which of our industries will expand and which will contract.

How are all these exchange rates determined? In most cases, they are determined by the familiar forces of supply and demand. As in other markets, each foreign exchange market reaches an equilibrium at which the quantity of foreign exchange demanded is equal to the quantity supplied.

In the next several sections, we'll build a model of supply and demand for a representative foreign exchange market: the one in which U.S. dollars are exchanged for British pounds. Taking the American point of view, we'll call this simply "the market for pounds." The other currency being traded—the dollar—will always be implicit.

The Demand for British Pounds

To analyze the demand for pounds, we start with a very basic question: *Who* is demanding them? The simple answer is, anyone who has dollars and wants to exchange them for pounds. But the most important buyers of pounds in the pound–dollar market will be American households and businesses. When Americans want to buy things from Britain, they will need to acquire pounds. To acquire these pounds, they will need to offer U.S. dollars. To keep our analysis simple, we'll focus on just these American buyers. We'll also—for now—ignore any demand for pounds by the U.S. government.

> *In our model of the market for pounds, we assume that American households and businesses are the only buyers.*

Why do Americans want to buy pounds? There are 2 reasons:

1. *To buy goods and services from British firms.* Americans buy sweaters knit in Edinburgh, airline tickets sold by Virgin Airways, and insurance services offered by Lloyd's. American tourists also stay in British hotels, use British taxis, and eat at British restaurants. To buy goods and services from British firms, Americans need to acquire pounds in order to pay for them.
2. *To buy British assets.* Americans buy British stocks, British corporate or government bonds, and British real estate. In each case, the British seller will want to be paid in pounds, so the American buyer will have to acquire them.

The Demand for Pounds Curve

Panel (a) of Figure 1 shows an example of a **demand curve for foreign currency,** in this case, the demand curve for pounds. The curve tells us *the quantity of pounds Americans will want to buy in any given period, at each different exchange rate.* Notice that the curve slopes downward: The lower the exchange rate, the greater the quantity of pounds demanded. For example, at an exchange rate of $2.25 per pound, Americans would want to purchase £200 million (point *A*). If the exchange rate fell to $1.50 per pound, Americans would want to buy £300 million (point *E*).

Demand curve for foreign currency A curve indicating the quantity of a specific foreign currency that Americans will want to buy, during a given period, at each different exchange rate.

FIGURE I | **The Demand for British Pounds**

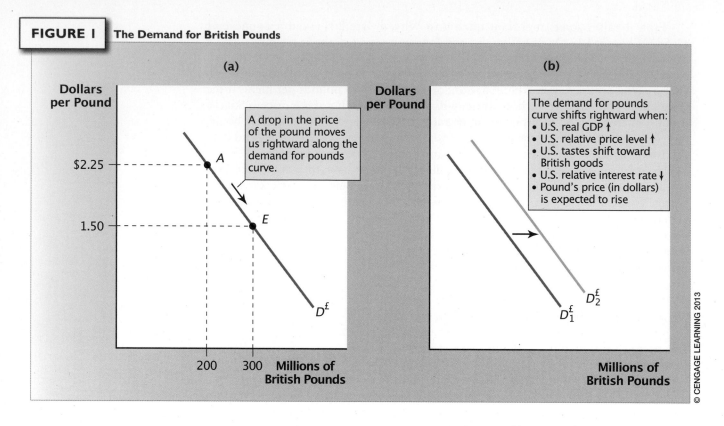

Why does a lower exchange rate—a lower price for the pound—make Americans want to buy more of them? Because the lower the price of the pound, the less expensive British goods are to American buyers. Remember that Americans think of prices in dollar terms. A British compact disc that sells for £8 will cost an American $18 at an exchange rate of $2.25 per pound, but only $12 if the exchange rate is $1.50 per pound.

Thus, as we move rightward *along* the demand for pounds curve, as in the move from point *A* to point *E*:

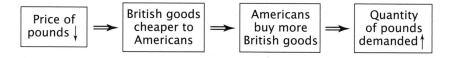

Shifts in the Demand for Pounds Curve

In panel (a), you saw that a change in the exchange rate moves us *along* the demand for pounds curve. But other variables besides the exchange rate influence the demand for pounds. If any of these other variables changes, the entire curve will shift. As we consider each of these variables, keep in mind that we are assuming that only one of them changes at a time; we suppose the rest to remain constant.

U.S. Real GDP. Suppose real GDP and real income in the United States rise— say, because of continuing economic growth or a recovery from a recession. Then, Americans will buy more of everything, including goods and services from Britain.

Thus, at any given exchange rate, Americans will demand more pounds. This is illustrated, in panel (b), as a rightward shift of the demand curve from $D_1^£$ to $D_2^£$.

Relative Price Levels. Suppose that the U.S. price level rises by 8 percent, while that in Britain rises by 5 percent. Then U.S. prices will rise *relative* to British prices. Americans will shift from buying their own goods toward buying the relatively cheaper British goods, so their demand for pounds will rise. That is, the demand for pounds curve will shift rightward.

Americans' Tastes for British Goods. All else being equal, would you prefer to drive a General Motors Corvette or a Jaguar? Do you prefer British-made films, such as *Jane Eyre* or *Harry Potter and the Deathly Hallows,* or America's offerings, such as *Moneyball* or *Bridesmaids*? These are matters of taste, and tastes can change. If Americans develop an increased taste for British cars, films, tea, or music, their demand for these goods will increase, and the demand for pounds curve will shift rightward.

Relative Interest Rates. Because financial assets must remain competitive in order to attract buyers, the rates of return on different financial assets—such as stocks and bonds—tend to rise and fall together. Thus, when one country's interest rate is high relative to that of another country, the first country's assets, *in general,* will have higher rates of return.

Now, suppose you're an American trying to decide whether to hold some of your wealth in British financial assets or in American financial assets. You will look very carefully at the rate of return you expect to earn in each country. All else being equal, a lower U.S. interest rate, relative to the British rate, will make British assets more attractive to you. Accordingly, as you and other Americans demand more British assets, you will need more pounds to buy them. The demand for pounds curve will shift rightward.

Expected Changes in the Exchange Rate. Once again, imagine you are an American deciding whether to buy an American or a British bond. Suppose British bonds pay 10 percent interest per year, while U.S. bonds pay 5 percent. All else equal, you would prefer the British bond, because it pays the higher rate of return. You would then exchange dollars for pounds at the going exchange rate and buy the bond.

But what if the price of the pound falls before the British bond becomes due? Then, when you cash in your British bond for pounds and convert the pounds back into dollars, you'll be *selling your pounds at a lower price* than you bought them for. While you'd benefit from the higher interest rate on the British bond, you'd lose on the foreign currency transaction—buying pounds when their price is high and selling them when their price is low. If the foreign currency loss is great enough, you would be better off with U.S. bonds, even though they pay a lower interest rate.

As you can see, it is not just relative interest rates that matter to wealth holders; it is also *expected changes in the exchange rate.* An expectation that the price of the pound will fall will make British assets less appealing to Americans, because they will expect a foreign currency loss. In this case, the demand for pounds curve will shift leftward.

The opposite holds as well. If Americans expect the price of the pound to *rise,* they will expect a foreign currency *gain* from buying British assets. This will cause the *demand for pounds curve to shift rightward.*

The Supply of British Pounds

The demand for pounds is one side of the market for pounds. Now we turn our attention to the other side: the supply of pounds. And we'll begin with our basic question: *Who* is supplying them?

In the real world, pounds are supplied from many sources. Anyone who has pounds and wants to exchange them for dollars can come to the market and supply pounds. But the most important sellers of pounds are British households and businesses, who naturally have pounds and need dollars in order to make purchases from Americans. To keep our analysis simple, we'll focus on just these British sellers, and we'll ignore—for now—any pounds supplied by the British government:

> *In our model of the market for pounds, we assume that British households and firms are the only sellers.*

The British supply pounds in the dollar–pound market for only one reason: because they want dollars. Thus, to ask why the British supply pounds is to ask why they want dollars. We can identify 2 separate reasons:

1. *To buy goods and services from American firms.* The British buy airline tickets on United Airlines, computers made by Hewlett-Packard and Apple, and the rights to show films made in Hollywood. British tourists stay in American hotels and eat at American restaurants. The British demand dollars—and supply pounds—for all of these purchases.
2. *To buy American assets.* The British buy American stocks, American corporate or government bonds, and American real estate. In each case, the American seller will want to be paid in dollars, and the British buyer will acquire dollars by offering pounds.

The Supply of Pounds Curve

Supply curve for foreign currency A curve indicating the quantity of a specific foreign currency that will be supplied, during a given period, at each different exchange rate.

Panel (a) of Figure 2 shows an example of a **supply curve for foreign currency**—here, British pounds. The curve tells us *the quantity of pounds the British will want to sell in any given period, at each different exchange rate.* Notice that the curve slopes upward: The higher the exchange rate, the greater is the quantity of pounds supplied. For example, at an exchange rate of $1.50 per pound, the British would want to supply £300 million (point E). If the exchange rate rose to $2.25 per pound, they would supply £400 million (point F).

Why does a higher exchange rate—a higher price for the pound—make the British want to sell more of them? Because the higher the price for the pound, the more dollars someone gets for each pound sold. This makes U.S. goods and services less expensive to British buyers, who will want to buy more of them. British buyers will need more dollars, and will supply more pounds to get those dollars.[1]

---

[1] Actually, it is not a logical necessity for the supply of pounds curve to slope upward. Why not? When the price of the pound rises, it is true that the British will buy more U.S. goods and need more dollars to buy them. However, each dollar they buy costs *fewer pounds*. It might be that, even though the British obtain more dollars, they actually supply fewer pounds to get them at the higher exchange rate. In this case, the supply of pounds curve would slope downward. Evidence suggests, however, that a downward-sloping supply curve for foreign currency—while theoretically possible—is very rare.

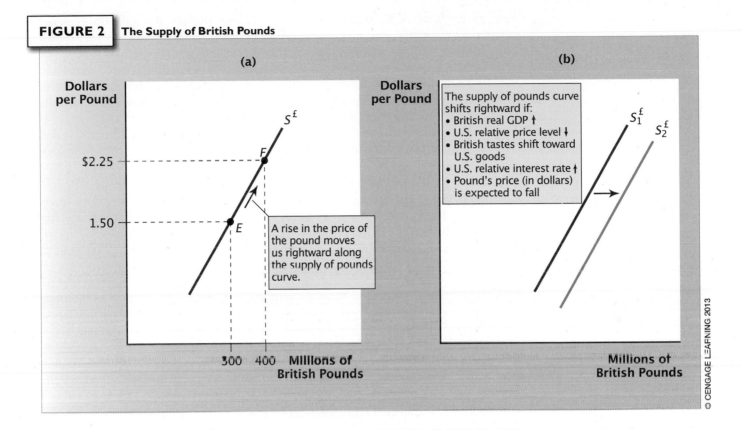

FIGURE 2   The Supply of British Pounds

To summarize, as we move rightward *along* the supply of pounds curve, such as the move from point *E* to point *F*:

Shifts in the Supply of Pounds Curve

When the exchange rate changes, we *move along* the supply curve for pounds, as in panel (a) of Figure 2. But other variables can affect the supply of pounds besides the exchange rate. When any of these variables change, the supply of pounds curve will shift, either rightward as shown in panel (b), or leftward (not shown). What are these variables?

Real GDP in Britain. If real GDP and real income rise in Britain, British residents will buy more goods and services, including those produced in the United States. Because they will need more dollars to buy U.S. goods, they will supply more pounds. In panel (b) this causes a rightward shift of the supply curve, from $S_1^£$ to $S_2^£$.

Relative Price Levels. Earlier, you learned that a rise in the relative price level in the United States makes British goods more attractive to Americans. But it also makes *American* goods *less* attractive to the British. Since the British will want to buy fewer U.S. goods, they will want fewer dollars and will supply fewer pounds. Thus, a rise in the relative U.S. price level shifts the supply of pounds curve leftward.

British Tastes for U.S. Goods. Recall our earlier discussion about the effect of American tastes on the demand for pounds. The same reasoning applies to the effect of British tastes on the *supply* of pounds. The British could begin to crave things American—or recoil from them. A shift in British tastes *toward* American goods will shift the supply of pounds curve rightward. A shift in tastes *away* from American goods will shift the curve leftward.

Relative Interest Rates. You've already learned that a rise in the relative U.S. interest rate makes U.S. assets more attractive to Americans. It has exactly the same effect on the British. As the U.S. interest rate rises, and the British buy more U.S. assets, they will need more dollars and will supply more pounds. The supply of pounds curve will shift rightward.

Expected Change in the Exchange Rate. In deciding where to hold their assets, the British have the same concerns as Americans. They will look, in part, at rates of return; but they will *also* think about possible gains or losses on foreign currency transactions. Suppose the British *expect the price of the pound to fall.* Then, by holding U.S. assets, they can anticipate a foreign currency gain—selling pounds at a relatively high price and buying them back again when their price is relatively low. The prospect of foreign currency gain will make U.S. assets more attractive, and the British will buy more of them. *The supply of pounds curve will shift rightward.*

The Equilibrium Exchange Rate

Floating exchange rate An exchange rate that is freely determined by the forces of supply and demand.

Now we will make an important—and in most cases, realistic—assumption: that the exchange rate between the dollar and the pound *floats.* A **floating exchange rate** is one that is freely determined by the forces of supply and demand, without government intervention to change it or keep it from changing. Indeed, many of the world's leading currencies, including the Japanese yen, the British pound, the 16-nation euro, and the Mexican peso, do float freely against the dollar most of the time.

In some cases, however, governments do not allow the exchange rate to float freely, but instead manipulate its value by intervening in the market, or even *fix* it at a particular value. We'll discuss government intervention in foreign exchange markets later. In this section, we assume that both the British and U.S. governments leave the dollar–pound market alone.

When the exchange rate floats, the price will settle at the level where quantity supplied and quantity demanded are equal. Here, buyers and sellers are trading British pounds, and the price is the exchange rate—the *price of the pound.*

Look at panel (a) of Figure 3. The equilibrium in the market for pounds occurs at point *E*, where the supply and demand curves intersect. The equilibrium price is $1.50 per pound. As you can verify, if the exchange rate were *higher,* say, $2.25 per pound, there would be an *excess supply* of pounds, forcing the price of the pound back down to $1.50. If the exchange rate were *lower* than the equilibrium price of $1.50, there would be an *excess demand* for pounds, driving the price back up to $1.50.

FIGURE 3   The Equilibrium Exchange Rate

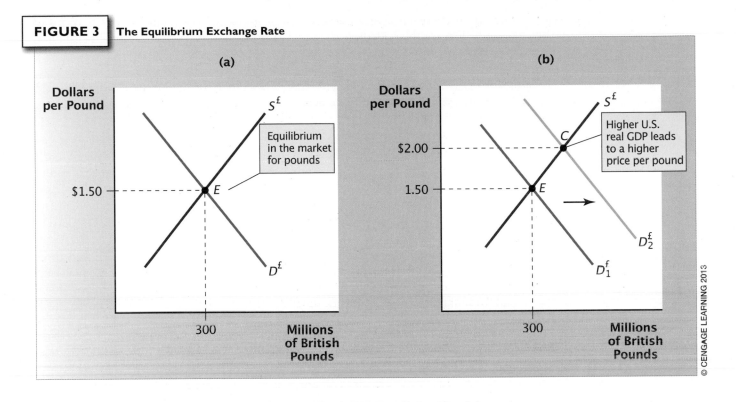

When the exchange rate floats—that is, when the government does not intervene in the foreign currency market—the equilibrium exchange rate is determined at the intersection of the demand curve and the supply curve.

WHAT HAPPENS WHEN THINGS CHANGE?

What would cause the price of the pound to rise or fall? The simple answer to this question is, anything that shifts the demand for pounds curve, or the supply of pounds curve, or both curves together. Have another look at the right-hand panels of Figures 1 and 2. They summarize the major factors that can shift the demand and supply curves for pounds and therefore change the floating exchange rate.

Let's illustrate with a simple example. In panel (b) of Figure 3, the initial equilibrium in the market for pounds is at point E, with an exchange rate of $1.50 per pound. Now suppose that real GDP rises in the United States. As you've learned (see Figure 1), this rise in U.S. GDP will shift the demand for pounds curve rightward, from $D_1^£$ to $D_2^£$ in the figure. At the old exchange rate of $1.50 per pound, there would be an excess demand for pounds, which would drive the price of the pound higher. The new equilibrium—where the quantities of pounds supplied and demanded are equal—occurs at point C, and the new equilibrium exchange rate is $2.00 per pound.

To recap, the increase in American GDP causes the price of the pound to rise from $1.50 to $2.00. When the price of any floating foreign currency rises because of a shift in the demand curve, the supply curve, or both, we call it an **appreciation** of the currency. In our example, the pound appreciates against the dollar. At the

Appreciation An increase in the price of a currency in a floating-rate system.

Depreciation A decrease in the price of a currency in a floating-rate system.

same time, there has been a **depreciation** of the dollar—a fall in its price in terms of pounds. (To see this, calculate the price of the dollar in terms of pounds before and after the shift in demand.)

> *When a floating exchange rate changes, one country's currency will appreciate (rise in price) and the other country's currency will depreciate (fall in price).*

As you've learned, there are many other variables besides U.S. GDP that can change and affect the exchange rate. We could analyze each of these changes, using diagrams similar to panel (b) of Figure 3. However, we'll organize our discussion of exchange rate changes in a slightly different way.

How Exchange Rates Change over Time

When we examine the actual behavior of exchange rates over time, we find three different kinds of movements. Look at Figure 4, which graphs hypothetical exchange rate data between the U.S. dollar and some other currency. We're using hypothetical data to make these three kinds of movements stand out more clearly than they usually do in practice.

Notice first the sharp up-and-down spikes. These fluctuations in exchange rates occur over the course of a few weeks, a few days, or even a few minutes—periods of time that we call the *very short run.*

Second, we see a gradual rise and fall of the exchange rate over the course of several months or a year or two. An example is the appreciation of the foreign currency from point *A* to *B* and its depreciation from point *B* to *C*. These are *short-run* movements in the exchange rate.

Finally, notice that while the price of the foreign currency fluctuates in the very short run and the short run, we can also discern a general *long-run* trend: This

---

FIGURE 4 | **Hypothetical Exchange Rate Data over Time**

These hypothetical data show typical patterns of exchange rate fluctuations. Over the course of a few minutes, days, or weeks, the exchange rate can experience sharp up-and-down spikes. Over several months or a year or two, the exchange rate may rise or fall, as in the appreciation of the foreign currency from points A to B and the depreciation from B to C. Over the long run, there may be a general upward or downward trend, like the depreciation of the foreign currency illustrated by the dashed line connecting points A and E.

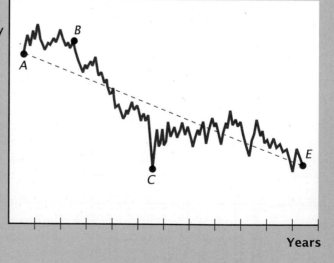

nation's currency seems to be depreciating in the figure. This long-run trend is illustrated by the dashed line connecting points *A* and *E*.

In this section, we'll explore the causes of movements in the exchange rate over all three periods: the very short run, the short run, and the long run.

The *Very* Short Run: "Hot Money"

Banks and other large financial institutions collectively have trillions of dollars worth of funds that they can move from one type of investment to another at very short notice. These funds are often called "hot money." If those who manage hot money perceive even a tiny advantage in moving funds to a different country's assets—say, because its interest rate is slightly higher—they will do so. Often, decisions to move billions of dollars are made in split seconds, by traders watching computer screens showing the latest data on exchange rates and interest rates around the world. Because these traders move such large volumes of funds, they have immediate effects on exchange rates.

Let's consider an example. Suppose that the relative interest rate in the United States suddenly rises. Then, as you've learned, U.S. assets will suddenly be more attractive to residents of both the United States and England, including managers of hot-money accounts in both countries. As these managers shift their funds from British to United States assets, they will be dumping billions of pounds on the foreign exchange market in order to acquire dollars to buy U.S. assets. This will cause a significant rightward shift of the supply of pounds curve.

In addition to affecting managers of hot-money accounts, the higher relative interest rate in the United States will affect ordinary investors. British investors will want to buy more American assets, helping to shift the supply of pounds curve further rightward. And American investors will want to buy fewer British assets than before, causing some decrease in the *demand* for pounds. Thus, in addition to the very large rightward shift in the supply of pounds, there will be a more moderate leftward shift in the demand for pounds.

Both of these shifts are illustrated in Figure 5: The supply of pounds curve shifts from $S_1^{\pounds}$ to $S_2^{\pounds}$, and the demand for pounds curve shifts from $D_1^{\pounds}$ to $D_2^{\pounds}$. The result is easy to see: The equilibrium in the market for pounds moves from point *E* to point *G*, and the price of the pound *falls* from \$1.50 to \$1.00. The pound depreciates and the dollar appreciates.

Expectations about future exchange rates can also trigger huge shifts of hot money, and Figure 5 also illustrates what would happen if American and British residents suddenly *expect* the pound to depreciate against the dollar. In this case, it would be the anticipation of foreign currency gains from holding U.S. assets, rather than a higher U.S. interest rate, that would cause the supply and demand curves to shift. As you can see in Figure 5, the expectation that the pound will depreciate actually *causes* the pound to depreciate—a self-fulfilling prophecy.

Sudden changes in relative interest rates, as well as sudden expectations of an appreciation or depreciation of a nation's currency, occur frequently in foreign exchange markets. They can cause massive shifts of hot money from the assets of one country to those of another in very short periods of time. For this reason,

relative interest rates and expectations of future exchange rates are the dominant forces moving exchange rates in the very short run.

FIGURE 5   Hot Money in the Very Short Run

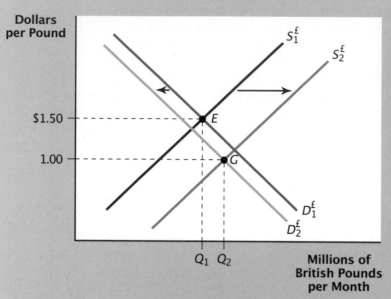

The market for pounds is initially in equilibrium at point E, with an exchange rate of $1.50 per pound. A rise in the U.S. interest rate relative to the British rate will make U.S. assets more attractive to both Americans and Britons. Hot-money managers in both countries will shift funds from British to U.S. assets, causing a rightward shift of the supply of pounds curve. American investors will want to buy fewer British assets, causing a decrease in the demand for pounds. The net effect is a lower exchange rate—$1.00 per pound at point G.

The Short Run: Macroeconomic Fluctuations

Look again at Figure 4. What explains the movements in the *short-run* rate—the changes that occur over several months or a few years? In most cases, the causes are economic fluctuations taking place in one or more countries.

Suppose, for example, that both Britain and the United States are in a recession, and the U.S. economy begins to recover, while the British slump continues. As real GDP rises in the United States, so does U.S. demand for foreign goods and services, including those from Britain. The demand for pounds curve will shift rightward, and—as shown in panel (a) of Figure 6—the pound will appreciate.

A year or so later, when Britain recovers from *its* recession, its real GDP will rise. British residents will begin to buy more U.S. goods and services, and supply more pounds so they can acquire more dollars. The supply of pounds curve will shift rightward, and—as shown in panel (b) of Figure 6—the pound will depreciate. Thus,

in the short run, movements in exchange rates are caused largely by economic fluctuations. All else equal, a country whose GDP rises will experience a depreciation of its currency. A country whose GDP falls will experience an appreciation of its currency.

FIGURE 6   **Exchange Rates in the Short Run**

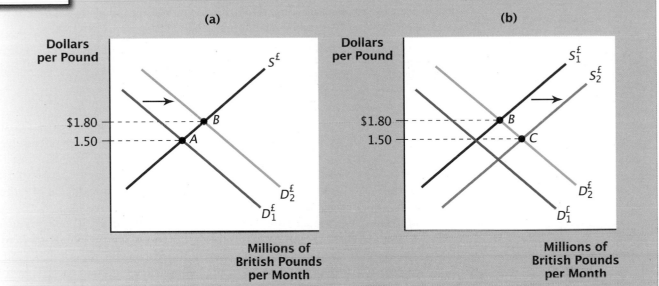

Panel (a) shows a situation in which the United States recovers from a recession first. U.S. demand for foreign goods and services increases, shifting the demand for pounds curve to the right. The equilibrium moves from A to B—an appreciation of the pound. Panel (b) shows Britain's subsequent recovery from its recession. As the British begin to buy more U.S. goods and services, the supply of pounds curve shifts rightward. The equilibrium moves from B to C, causing the pound to depreciate.

© CENGAGE LEARNING 2013

This observation contradicts a commonly held myth: that a strong (appreciating) currency is a sign of economic health and a weak (depreciating) currency denotes a sick economy. The truth may easily be the opposite. Over the course of several quarters or a few years, the dollar could appreciate because the U.S. economy is *weakening*—entering a serious recession. This would cause Americans to cut back spending on domestic *and* foreign goods, and decrease the demand for foreign currency. Similarly, a *strengthening* U.S. economy—in which Americans are earning and spending more—would increase the U.S. demand for foreign currency and (all else equal) cause the dollar to depreciate.

Keep in mind, though, that other variables can change over the business cycle besides real GDP, including interest rates and price levels in the two countries. For example, a recession can be caused by a monetary contraction that raises the relative interest rate in a country. Or a monetary stimulus in the midst of a recession could result in a relatively low interest rate. These changes, too, will influence exchange rates over the business cycle.

The Long Run: Purchasing Power Parity

In mid-1992, you could buy about 100 Russian rubles for one dollar. In mid-1998, that same dollar would get you more than 6,000 rubles—so many that the Russian government that year created a new ruble that was worth 1,000 of the old rubles. (The ruble exchange rate in Table 1 is for the new ruble.) What caused the ruble to depreciate so much against the dollar during those 6 years?

This is a question about exchange rates over many years—the long run. Movements of hot money—which explain sudden, temporary movements of exchange rates—cannot explain this kind of long-run trend. Nor can business cycles, which are, by nature, temporary. What, then, causes exchange rates to change over the long run?

In general, long-run trends in exchange rates are determined by *relative price levels* in two countries. We can be even more specific:

Purchasing power parity (PPP) theory The idea that the exchange rate will adjust in the long run so that the average price of goods in two countries will be roughly the same.

> *According to the **purchasing power parity (PPP) theory**, the exchange rate between two countries will adjust in the long run until the average price of goods is roughly the same in both countries.*

To see why the PPP theory makes sense, imagine a basket of goods that costs $750 in the United States and £500 in Britain. If the prices of the goods themselves do not change, then, according to the PPP theory, the exchange rate will adjust to $750/£500 = $1.5 dollars per pound. Why? Because at this exchange rate, $750 can be exchanged for £500, so the price of the basket is the same to residents of either country—$750 for Americans and £500 for the British.

Now, suppose the exchange rate was *below* its PPP rate of $1.50 per pound—say, $1 per pound. Then a trader could take $500 to the bank, exchange it for £500, buy the basket of goods in Great Britain, and sell it in the United States for $750. She would earn a profit of $250 on each basket of goods traded. In the process, however, traders would be increasing the demand for pounds and raising the exchange rate. When the price of the pound reached $1.50, purchasing power parity would hold, and special trading opportunities would be gone. As you can see, trading activity will tend to drive the exchange rate toward the PPP rate. (On your own, explain the adjustment process when the exchange rate starts *higher* than the PPP rate.)

The PPP theory has an important implication:

> *In the long run, the currency of a country with a higher inflation rate will depreciate against the currency of a country whose inflation rate is lower.*

Why? Because in the country with the higher inflation rate, the relative price level will be rising. As that country's basket of goods becomes relatively more expensive, only a depreciation of its currency can restore purchasing power parity. And traders—taking advantage of opportunities like those just described—would cause the currency to depreciate.

Purchasing Power Parity: Some Important Caveats

While purchasing power parity is a good general guideline for predicting long-run trends in exchange rates, it does not work perfectly. For a variety of reasons, exchange rates can deviate from their PPP values for many years.

First, some goods—by their very nature—are difficult to trade. Suppose a haircut costs £5 in London and $30 in New York, and the exchange rate is $1.50 per pound. Then British haircuts are cheaper for residents of both countries. Could traders take advantage of this? Not really. They cannot take $30 to the bank in exchange for £20, buy four haircuts in London, ship them to New York, and sell them for a total of $120 there. Haircuts and most other personal services are nontradable.

Second, high transportation costs can reduce trading possibilities even for goods that *can* be traded. Our earlier numerical example would have quite a different ending if moving the basket of goods between Great Britain and the United States involved $500 of freight and insurance costs.

Third, artificial barriers to trade, such as special taxes or quotas on imports, can hamper traders' ability to move exchange rates toward purchasing power parity.

Still, the purchasing power parity theory is useful in many circumstances. Under floating exchange rates, a country whose relative price level is rising rapidly will almost always find that the price of its currency is falling rapidly. If not, all of its tradable goods would soon be priced out of the world market.

For example, we've already mentioned the sharp depreciation of the Russian ruble from 1992 to 1998. During those 6 years, the number of rubles that exchanged for a dollar rose from around 100 to about 6,000. Over the same period, the annual inflation rate averaged about 200 percent in Russia, but only about 3 percent in the United States. And in Zimbabwe, which experienced hyperinflation from 2001 through 2008, the number of original Zimbabwe dollars that exchanged for one U.S. dollar went from 100 in 2001 to more than 10^{27} Zimbabwe dollars in 2008. (That's one billion $\times$ one billion $\times$ one billion Zimbabwe dollars per U.S. dollar.) The official currency was replaced several times along the way (to reduce the number of zeros), and by early 2009, no one was using it at all.

GOVERNMENT INTERVENTION IN FOREIGN EXCHANGE MARKETS

As you've seen, when exchange rates float, they can rise and fall for a variety of reasons. But a government may not be content to let the forces of supply and demand change its exchange rate. If the value of a country's currency rises, its goods will become more expensive to foreigners, causing harm to its export-oriented industries. If the value of its currency falls, goods purchased from other countries will rise in price, harming consumers and firms that import raw materials. Finally, if the exchange rate is too volatile, it can make trading riskier or require traders to acquire special insurance against foreign currency losses, which costs them money, time, and trouble. For all of these reasons, governments sometimes *intervene* in foreign exchange markets involving their currency.

Managed Float

Many governments let their exchange rate float *most of the time,* but will intervene on occasion when the floating exchange rate moves in an undesired direction or becomes too volatile. For example, look back at Figure 5, where the price of the British pound falls to $1 as hot money is shifted out of British assets. Suppose the British government does not want the pound to depreciate. Then its central bank—the Bank of England—could begin trading in the dollar–pound market itself. It would buy British pounds with dollars, thereby shifting the demand for pounds curve rightward. If it buys just the right amount of pounds, it can prevent the pound from depreciating at all. Alternatively, the U.S. government might not be happy with the *appreciation* of the dollar in Figure 5. In that case, the Federal Reserve can enter the market and buy British pounds with dollars, once again shifting the demand for pounds curve rightward.

The central banks of many countries—including the Federal Reserve—will sometimes intervene in this way in foreign exchange markets. When a government buys or sells its own currency or that of a trading partner to influence exchange rates, it is engaging in a "managed float" or a "dirty float."

Managed float A policy of frequent central bank intervention to move the exchange rate.

> Under a **managed float,** a country's central bank actively manages its exchange rate, buying its own currency to prevent depreciations, and selling its own currency to prevent appreciations.

Managed floats are used most often in the very short run, to prevent large, sudden changes in exchange rates. For example, in mid-2007, New Zealand's central bank sold New Zealand dollars in order to stop a rapid *appreciation* of its currency against the U.S. dollar and the Japanese yen. In the other direction, South Korea's central bank intervened to slow the *depreciation* of its currency in mid-2008, reportedly purchasing more than $10 billion worth of South Korean won in a single week.

That last example raises a question. When a country—such as South Korea—wants to prevent or slow a depreciation of its currency (the won) against the dollar, it has to buy its own currency with dollars. Where does it get those dollars? Unfortunately for South Korea, it cannot print dollars; only the U.S. Federal Reserve can do that. Instead, South Korea must use its *reserves* of dollars—the dollars its central bank keeps on hand specifically to intervene in the dollar–won market.

Almost every nation holds reserves of dollars—as well as euros, yen, and other key currencies—just so it can enter the foreign exchange market and sell them for its own currency when necessary. Under a managed float, periods of selling dollars are usually short-lived, and alternate with periods of buying dollars. Thus, countries rarely use up all of their dollar reserves when they engage in managed floats.

Managed floats are controversial. Some economists believe they help to avoid wide swings in exchange rates, and thus reduce the risks for international traders and investors. But others are critical of how managed floats often work out in practice. They point out that countries often intervene when the forces behind an appreciation or depreciation are strong. In these cases, the intervention only serves to delay inevitable changes in the exchange rate—sometimes, at great cost to a country's reserves of dollars and other key currencies.

Fixed Exchange Rates

Fixed exchange rate A government-declared exchange rate maintained by central bank intervention in the foreign exchange market.

A more extreme form of intervention is a **fixed exchange rate,** in which a government declares a particular value for its exchange rate with another currency. The government, through its central bank, then commits itself to intervene in the foreign exchange market any time the *equilibrium* exchange rate differs from the *fixed* rate.

For example, from 1987 to 1997, the government of Thailand fixed the value of its currency—the *baht*—at $0.04 per baht. The two panels of Figure 7 show the different types of intervention that might be necessary in the baht–dollar market to maintain this fixed exchange rate. Each panel shows a different set of supply and demand curves—and a different equilibrium exchange rate that might exist for the baht. Look first at panel (a). Here, we assume that the equilibrium exchange rate is $0.06 per baht, so that the fixed rate is *lower* than the equilibrium rate. At the fixed rate of $0.04 per baht, 400 million baht would be demanded each month, but only 100 million would be supplied. There would be an *excess demand* of 300 million baht, which would ordinarily drive the exchange rate back

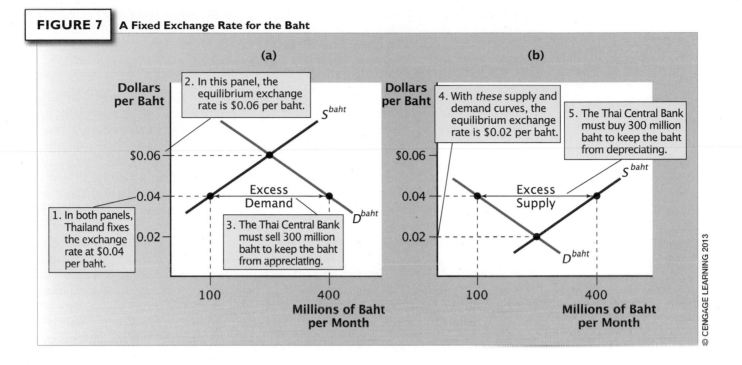

FIGURE 7 A Fixed Exchange Rate for the Baht

(a)

Dollars per Baht

2. In this panel, the equilibrium exchange rate is $0.06 per baht.

S^{baht}

$0.06

0.04

Excess Demand

D^{baht}

1. In both panels, Thailand fixes the exchange rate at $0.04 per baht.

0.02

3. The Thai Central Bank must sell 300 million baht to keep the baht from appreciating.

100   400

Millions of Baht per Month

(b)

Dollars per Baht

4. With *these* supply and demand curves, the equilibrium exchange rate is $0.02 per baht.

5. The Thai Central Bank must buy 300 million baht to keep the baht from depreciating.

$0.06

0.04

Excess Supply

S^{baht}

0.02

D^{baht}

100   400

Millions of Baht per Month

© CENGAGE LEARNING 2013

up to its equilibrium value of $0.06. But the Thai government prevents this by entering the market and *selling* just enough baht to cover the excess demand. In panel (a), the Central Bank of Thailand would sell 300 million baht per month to maintain the fixed rate.

> When a country fixes its exchange rate below the equilibrium value, the result is an excess demand for the country's currency. To maintain the fixed rate, the country's central bank must sell enough of its own currency to eliminate the excess demand.

Panel (b) shows another possibility, where the equilibrium exchange rate is $0.02, so that the same fixed exchange rate of $0.04 per baht is now *above* the equilibrium rate. There is an excess *supply* of 300 million baht. In this case, to prevent the excess supply from driving the exchange rate down, the Central Bank of Thailand must *buy* the excess baht.

> When a country fixes its exchange rate above the equilibrium value, the result is an excess supply of the country's currency. To maintain the fixed rate, the country's central bank must buy enough of its own currency to eliminate the excess supply.

Fixed exchange rates present little problem for a country as long as the exchange rate is fixed at or very close to its equilibrium rate. But when the equilibrium exchange rate moves away from the fixed rate—as in the two panels of Figure 7—governments often try to maintain their fixed rate anyway, sometimes for long periods. This can create problems, especially when the exchange rate is fixed *above* the equilibrium rate.

Foreign Currency Crises

To see how a fixed exchange rate can be problematic, look at Figure 8. Initially, the supply and demand curves for baht are given by S_1 and D_1, respectively, so that the equilibrium exchange rate, $0.04, is equal to the fixed exchange rate. At this point, the central bank is neither selling nor buying baht. Now, suppose that, for some reason (we'll be more specific in a few paragraphs), the supply and demand curves shift to S_2 and D_2, respectively. The equilibrium rate falls, so the fixed rate of $0.04 is above the equilibrium rate of $0.02. The Central Bank of Thailand must now *buy* its own currency with dollars—at the rate of 300 million baht per month. Each baht costs the central bank 4 cents, so as the months go by, its dollar reserves are being depleted at the rate of 300 million × $0.04 = $12 million per month. Once those reserves are gone, Thailand will have only two choices: to let its currency float (which means an immediate depreciation to the lower, equilibrium rate) or to declare a new, lower fixed rate—a **devaluation** of its currency.

Devaluation A change in the value of a currency from a higher fixed value to a lower fixed value.

Of course, at a certain point, foreign exchange speculators and traders would see that Thailand doesn't have many dollars left. (Most countries' central banks regularly report their holdings of key currencies, and economists can estimate the holdings of countries that don't.) Looking ahead, these speculators and traders will begin to *anticipate* a drop in the baht. And—as you've learned in this chapter—expected changes in the exchange rate *shift* supply and demand curves for foreign currency. In this case, an expected fall in the baht causes the supply curve for baht to shift farther rightward and the demand curve to shift farther leftward, as indicated by the heavy arrows in the diagram. In Figure 8, these shifts will *decrease* the

---

FIGURE 8 | **A Foreign Currency Crisis**

Initially, the baht is fixed at the equilibrium rate of $0.04. When the supply and demand curves shift to D_2 and S_2, the equilibrium exchange rate falls to $0.02. If Thailand continues to fix the rate at $0.04, it will have to buy up the excess supply of 300 million baht per month, using dollars. As its dollar reserves dwindle, traders will anticipate a drop in the value of the baht, shifting the curves out farther, as indicated by the arrows.

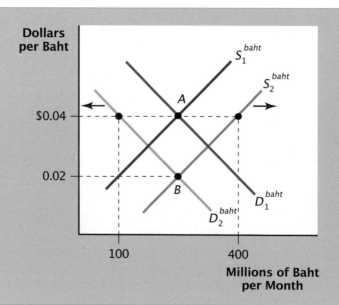

equilibrium value of the baht, increase the *excess supply* of baht, and make the fixed rate of $0.04 even harder to maintain. The country is now experiencing a *foreign currency crisis*.

> A *foreign currency crisis* arises when people no longer believe that a country can maintain a fixed exchange rate above the equilibrium rate. As a consequence, the supply of the currency increases, demand for it decreases, and the country must use up its reserves of dollars and other key currencies even faster in order to maintain the fixed rate.

Foreign currency crisis A loss of faith that a country can prevent a drop in its exchange rate, leading to a rapid depletion of its foreign currency (e.g., dollar) reserves.

Once a foreign currency crisis arises, a country typically has no choice but to devalue its currency or let it float and watch it depreciate. And ironically, because the country waited for the crisis to develop, the exchange rate may for a time drop even lower than the original equilibrium rate. For example, in Figure 8, an early devaluation to $0.02 per dollar might prevent a crisis from occurring at all. But once the crisis begins, and the supply and demand curves shift out further than S_2 and D_2, the currency will have to drop *below* $0.02 to end the rapid depletion of dollar reserves.

Our analysis of a foreign currency crisis used the example of the Thai baht for good reason. In 1997 and 1998, Thailand was at the center of a financial crisis that rocked the world.

The crisis began when a lack of confidence in Thailand's financial system led to dramatic shifts in the supply and demand curves for baht—just as in Figure 8. While the *equilibrium* exchange rate fell, Thailand continued to fix the *actual* exchange rate at $0.04 per baht, above the equilibrium rate. As a result, Thailand's central bank was depleting its reserves of dollars and other foreign currencies. This, of course, led currency traders to anticipate a devaluation, shifting the supply and demand curves even farther. Finally, in July 1997, the Thai central bank simply ran out of foreign currency reserves, and was forced to let its currency float. The baht immediately depreciated from $0.04 to $0.02.

But this was only the beginning of the story. Many of Thailand's banks—counting on the fixed exchange rate—had borrowed heavily in dollars, yen, and other foreign currencies, but then lent funds to Thai businesses in baht. Once the baht depreciated, these banks were obligated to make unchanged dollar and yen payments on their debts, while continuing to receive unchanged baht payments on the funds they had lent. The problem was that, after the depreciation, the baht coming in would no longer cover the dollars going out. Thailand's banks were in trouble.

And the trouble spread. Investors began to wonder if banks in *other* nearby countries were similarly vulnerable, and began to dump the foreign exchange of Indonesia, South Korea, Malaysia, and the Philippines. Before the crisis ended, it had even spread to several Latin American countries.

EXCHANGE RATES AND THE MACROECONOMY

Exchange rates can have important effects on the macroeconomy—largely through their effect on net exports. And although we've included net exports in our short-run macro model, we haven't yet asked how exchange rates affect them. That's what we'll do now.

Exchange Rates and Demand Shocks

Suppose that the dollar depreciates against the foreign currencies of its major trading partners. (We'll discuss *why* that might happen in a later section.) Then U.S. goods would become cheaper to foreigners, and net exports would rise at each level of output. This increase in net exports is a positive demand shock to the economy—it increases aggregate expenditure and shifts the aggregate demand curve to the right. And, as you've learned, positive demand shocks increase GDP in the short run.

> *A depreciation of the dollar causes net exports to rise—a positive demand shock that increases real GDP in the short run. An appreciation of the dollar causes net exports to drop—a negative demand shock that decreases real GDP in the short run.*

The impact of net exports on equilibrium GDP—often caused by changes in the exchange rate—helps us understand one reason why governments are often concerned about their exchange rates. An unstable exchange rate can result in repeated shocks to the economy. At worst, this can cause fluctuations in GDP; at best, it makes the central bank's job more difficult as it tries to keep the economy on an even keel.

Exchange Rates and Monetary Policy

In several earlier chapters, we've explored how the Fed tries to keep the U.S. economy on an even keel with monetary policy. Central banks around the world are engaged in a similar struggle, and face many of the same challenges as the Fed. One challenge to central banks is that monetary policy causes changes in exchange rates, and thus has additional effects on real GDP that we have not yet considered.

To understand this, let's run through an example. Suppose the United States is in a recession, and the Fed decides to increase equilibrium GDP by reducing interest rates. Interest-sensitive spending rises, and so does aggregate expenditure. When we consider the foreign exchange market, however, there is an additional effect on aggregate expenditure.

By lowering U.S. interest rates, the Fed makes *foreign* financial assets more attractive to Americans, which raises Americans' demand for foreign currency. In the market for pounds, for example, this will shift the demand for pounds curve rightward. At the same time, U.S. financial assets become less attractive to foreigners, which decreases the supply of foreign exchange (in the market for pounds, a leftward shift in the supply of pounds curve). If you sketch out these shifts right now, you'll see that, as long as the exchange rate floats, the result is a *depreciation of the dollar* against the pound.

Now let's see how the depreciation of the dollar affects the economy. With dollars now cheaper to foreigners, they will buy more U.S. goods, raising U.S. exports. At the same time, with foreign goods and services more expensive to Americans, U.S. imports will decrease. Both the increase in exports and the decrease in imports contribute to a rise in net exports, NX. This, in turn, increases aggregate expenditure.

Thus, as you can see, the expansionary monetary policy causes aggregate expenditures to rise in two ways: first, by increasing interest-sensitive spending and, second, by increasing net exports. As a result, equilibrium GDP rises by more—and monetary policy is more effective—when the effects on exchange rates are included.

The channels through which monetary policy works are summarized in the following schematic:

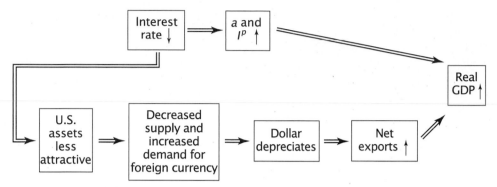

Net Effect: GDP ↑ by more when the exchange rate's effect on net exports is included

The top line shows the familiar effect on interest-sensitive spending: autonomous consumption spending (a) and investment spending (I^p). The bottom line shows the *additional* effect on net exports through changes in the exchange rate—the effects we've been discussing.

The analysis of contractionary monetary policy is the same, but in reverse. Higher interest rates not only decrease interest-sensitive spending, but also cause the dollar to appreciate and net exports to drop. Thus, it will cause equilibrium GDP to fall by more than we showed in earlier chapters, where we ignored the foreign exchange market.

The channel of monetary influence through exchange rates and the volume of trade is an important part of the full story of monetary policy in the United States. And in small countries where exports are relatively large fractions of GDP, it is the main channel through which monetary policy affects the economy.

> *Monetary policy has a stronger effect when we include the impact on exchange rates and net exports, rather than just the impact on interest-sensitive consumption and investment spending.*

EXCHANGE RATES AND THE EURO ZONE

On January 1, 2002, after years of planning, 12 European countries introduced their new common currency: the euro. The original countries included some of Europe's largest (Germany, France, Italy, and Spain). By 2011, membership had grown to 17 countries.

Countries that are part of the euro zone can no longer run their own monetary policy, because the European Central Bank (ECB) has the sole authority for changing the supply of euros. Why did these nations decide to do away with their national currencies and give up the right to run an independent monetary policy? A large part of the motivation was political: For decades, government leaders had striven to unify Europe as an antidote to centuries of war. Also, a united Europe could speak with one voice, giving it more power and influence on the world stage. But there were purely economic benefits too.

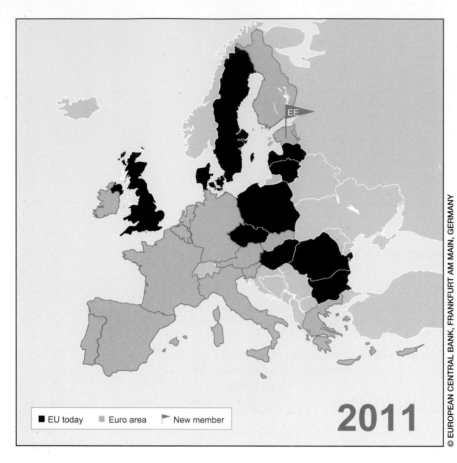

2011

■ EU today   ■ Euro area   ⚑ New member

© EUROPEAN CENTRAL BANK, FRANKFURT AM MAIN, GERMANY

Advantages of the Euro

One advantage of the euro is that European firms—when they buy or sell across borders—avoid commissions on the exchange of currency, and do not face any risk that exchange rates might change before accounts are settled. By reducing the cost of trading, the euro increases the volume of trading, which contributes to higher living standards.

Second, by eliminating exchange rate risk, the euro makes it easier for European firms to sell stocks and bonds to residents anywhere in the euro zone. This helps to channel funds to the most profitable and productive investment projects, wherever they might be located in the zone.

Finally, before the euro, some of its member countries—such as Italy—had a history of loose monetary policy that generated high and variable rates of inflation. Giving up the right to run an independent monetary policy, and leaving it to the stricter European Central Bank, would enable these countries to maintain low and more stable inflation rates, creating less inflation risk for borrowers and lenders.

Disadvantages of the Euro

Even when the euro was in the planning stages, many economists warned that it would create some serious problems. A single currency and a single monetary policy can work fine when all the countries involved are at the same stage in their business cycles. But what would happen if, say, Spain went into recession while the other euro zone countries did not? In the old days before the euro, Spain could use monetary policy to dig its way out: It could increase its money supply (Spanish pesetas), and reduce interest rates. Domestic consumption and investment spending would rise, and its currency would depreciate, increasing its net exports.

But as a euro-zone member, Spain could *not* increase its money supply to lower its interest rate; only the ECB could do that. And Spain could *not* depreciate its currency relative to its main trading partners (other euro zone countries), because all used the same currency. The ECB could depreciate the euro against other currencies (such as the U.S. dollar), but it would do so only if the rest of the euro zone (and not just Spain) were in recession too.

Deprived of monetary policy, fiscal policy would be the only recession-fighting tool. But as you've learned, countercyclical fiscal policy is fraught with problems. Moreover, the euro zone required strict fiscal discipline from all of its members. So a country in recession would not have much flexibility with fiscal policy either.

The Euro Zone Crisis of 2011

The disadvantages of the euro were apparent in 2011, when the euro zone faced a crisis that threatened to break it apart. Ironically, the crisis occurred as a result of the euro's success in achieving one of its goals: encouraging a flow of funds to countries with the most profitable and productive investment projects. Once the euro zone was established, funds from the wealthier countries (such as Germany, France, Austria, and Belgium) began flowing into what is sometimes called the *periphery* of the zone (Portugal, Italy, Ireland, Greece, and Spain), where investment opportunities abounded. The peripheral countries enjoyed an investment boom, with new homes and factories being built at a rapid pace. Unemployment fell, and incomes rose. This was a positive demand shock, which, as you've learned, causes the price level to rise. With higher prices, the peripheral countries' exports became less competitive. But the resulting decline in net exports was not a problem for total production or employment—as long as the investment boom continued.

When the global recession arrived in 2008, the peripheral countries were hit hard. The flow of investment from the wealthier countries dried up. Projects were canceled, workers lost jobs, and home prices plunged. Government debts soared. At least one country—Greece—had been running an irresponsible fiscal policy from the beginning. In the others, government debts rose because of the recession (rising transfer payments and falling tax revenue), and because governments had rescued creditors and depositors at financial institutions that failed as housing prices declined.

Was there a way out of recession for the peripheral countries?

Fiscal stimulus was out of the question. Because of rising debt ratios, lenders were already demanding very high interest rates. Fiscal stimulus—which would increase debt ratios even more—could cause interest rates to skyrocket.

What about monetary policy? Strong action by the ECB to lower interest rates might have helped in two ways. First, lower interest rates would stimulate spending throughout the euro zone, including the periphery. Second, lower interest rates would raise inflation rates throughout the euro zone, but more so in Germany and France (which were closer to full employment) than in the peripheral countries (which were suffering much deeper slumps). The difference in inflation rates would help make the peripheral countries' exports more price-competitive. And the resulting rise in net exports would increase production and employment in the periphery.

The ECB, however, did not want to raise inflation in the rest of the euro zone, so it resisted using monetary policy to pull the periphery out of recession. As a result, periphery exports could become more competitive only through deflation: lower wage rates for workers causing lower costs for producers so they, in turn, could lower the prices of their products and export more of them. But as you learned in earlier chapters, wages are sticky: It takes time for them to fall. And deflation can make things worse before it makes them better, because it forces debtors (including periphery governments) to repay unchanged nominal debts out of lower nominal incomes.

The peripheral countries did, however, have some leverage over the rest of Europe: Most of the government bonds they had issued in the past were owned by banks in the wealthier euro zone countries, especially Germany and France. A government default by any one country would lead to fears of default by the others. Peripheral government bond prices would plunge, German and French banks would fail or need government rescue, and Europe would experience a financial crisis. To avoid the crisis, the wealthier euro zone countries would have no choice but to help the periphery. And Greece—the country closest to default—was the flash point.

Toward the end of 2011, governments in the wealthier euro zone countries, as well as the ECB and international financial organizations, were struggling to delay a Greek default. They provided low-interest loans to the Greek government, and purchased Greek government bonds. These moves were extremely unpopular in the wealthier countries. Partly for this reason, the assistance was conditioned on strict fiscal austerity from Greece: less government spending and higher taxes. Austerity was required in the other peripheral countries as well. Throughout the euro zone, government officials and ordinary citizens were realizing that the creation of the euro had been, at best, a mixed blessing.

EXCHANGE RATES AND TRADE DEFICITS

A country's trade deficit is the amount by which its imports exceed its exports:

$$\text{Trade deficit} = \text{Imports} - \text{Exports}$$

On the other hand, when exports exceed imports, a nation has a trade surplus:

$$\text{Trade surplus} = \text{Exports} - \text{Imports}$$

Trade deficit The excess of a nation's imports over its exports during a given period.

Trade surplus The excess of a nation's exports over its imports during a given period.

As you can see, the trade surplus is nothing more than a nation's net exports (NX). And when net exports are negative, we have a trade deficit.

The United States has had large trade deficits with the rest of the world since the early 1980s. In 2008, the trade deficit was approximately $700 billion. Simply put, Americans bought about $700 billion more goods and services from other countries than their residents bought from the United States.

Why does the United States have a trade deficit with the rest of the world? A variety of explanations have been offered in the media, including poor U.S. marketing savvy in selling to foreigners, and a greater degree of protectionism in foreign markets.

But economists believe that there is a much more important reason.

The Origins of the U.S. Trade Deficit

To keep our analysis simple, we'll start by looking at the U.S. trade deficit with just one country—Japan—but our results will hold more generally to the trade deficit with many other countries as well.

Before we analyze the causes of the trade deficit, we need to do a little math. Let's begin by breaking down the total quantity of yen demanded by Americans $(D^{¥})$ into two components: the yen demanded to purchase Japanese goods and services (U.S. imports from Japan) and the yen demanded to buy Japanese assets:

$$D^{¥} = \text{U.S. imports from Japan} + \text{U.S. purchases of Japanese assets.}$$

Similarly, we can divide the total quantity of yen supplied by the Japanese $(S^{¥})$ into two components: the yen exchanged for dollars to purchase American goods (U.S. exports to Japan) and the yen exchanged for dollars to purchase American assets like stocks, bonds, or real estate:

$$S^{¥} = \text{U.S. exports to Japan} + \text{Japanese purchases of U.S. assets.}$$

As long as the yen floats against the dollar without government intervention—which it does during most periods—we know that the exchange rate will adjust until the quantities of yen supplied and demanded are equal, or $D^¥ = S^¥$. Substituting the foregoing breakdowns into this equation, we have

$$\left\{ \begin{array}{l} \text{U.S. imports from Japan} \\ + \text{ U.S. purchases of Japanese assets} \end{array} \right\} = \left\{ \begin{array}{l} \text{U.S. exports to Japan} \\ + \text{ Japanese purchases of U.S. assets} \end{array} \right\}.$$

Now let's rearrange this equation—subtracting U.S. exports from both sides and subtracting American purchases of Japanese assets from both sides—to get

$$\left\{ \begin{array}{l} \text{U.S. imports from Japan} \\ - \text{ U.S. exports to Japan} \end{array} \right\} = \left\{ \begin{array}{l} \text{Japanese purchases of U.S. assets} \\ - \text{ U.S. purchases of Japanese assets} \end{array} \right\}.$$

The term on the left should look familiar: It is the U.S. trade deficit with Japan. And since a similar equation must hold for every country, we can generalize it this way:

$$\left\{ \begin{array}{l} \text{U.S. imports from other countries} \\ - \text{ U.S. exports to other countries} \end{array} \right\} = \left\{ \begin{array}{l} \text{Foreign purchase of U.S. assets} \\ - \text{ U.S. purchases of foreign assets} \end{array} \right\}.$$

But what is the expression on the right? It tells us the extent to which foreigners are buying more of our assets than we are buying of theirs. It is often called the **net financial inflow** into the United States, because when the residents of other countries buy U.S. assets, funds flow into the U.S. financial market, where they are made available to U.S. firms and the U.S. government. Thus, the equation we've derived—which must hold true when exchange rates float—can also be expressed as

Net financial inflow An inflow of funds equal to a nation's trade deficit.

$$\text{U.S. trade deficit} = \text{U.S. net financial inflow}$$

Why have we bothered to derive this equation? Because it tells us two very important things about the U.S. trade deficit. First, it tells us how the trade deficit is *financed*. Think about it: If the United States is running a trade deficit with, say, Japan, it means that the Japanese are providing more goods and services to Americans— more automobiles, VCRs, memory chips, and other goods—than Americans are providing to them. The Japanese are not doing this out of kindness. They must be getting *something* in return for the extra goods we are getting, and the equation tells us just what that is: U.S. assets. This is one reason why the trade deficit concerns U.S. policy makers: It results in a transfer of wealth from Americans to foreign residents.

The second important insight provided by the equation is that a trade deficit can arise *because* of forces that cause a financial inflow. That is, if forces in the global economy make the right side of the equation positive, then the left side must be positive as well, and we will have a trade deficit.

Indeed, economists believe this is just what has happened to the United States: that the U.S. trade deficit has been caused by the desire of foreigners to invest in the United States. The result was a massive financial inflow and trade deficit that arose in the early 1980s, as illustrated in Figure 9. This financial inflow was unprecedented in size and duration, and it reversed a long-standing pattern of ownership between the United States and other countries. For decades, American holdings of foreign assets far exceeded foreign holdings of U.S. assets. But the financial inflows of the 1980s

FIGURE 9   U.S. Net Financial Inflow as a Percentage of GDP

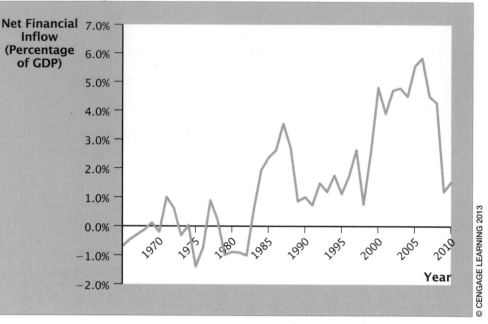

Beginning in the early 1980s, and continuing today, a massive net financial inflow has led to a U.S. trade deficit. The inflow shrank during and after the financial crisis of 2008, but it was still a significant fraction of GDP.

© CENGAGE LEARNING 2013

changed that: By 1990, foreigners held about $200 billion more in U.S. assets than Americans held in foreign assets. By 2008, the difference in asset holdings exceeded $3 trillion. The net financial inflow shrank during the global financial turmoil from 2008 to 2010. But it remained positive, and was still a significant percentage of GDP.

But how do the forces that create a financial inflow also *cause* a trade deficit?

How a Financial Inflow Causes a Trade Deficit

Figure 10 illustrates this process, using the yen–dollar market. We'll assume that, initially, neither the Japanese nor the Americans are buying *assets* from the other country. Only goods and services are traded. Point *A* shows the initial equilibrium under this special assumption. Under these circumstances, the demand curve for yen would reflect U.S. *imports* of goods and services from Japan, and the supply curve would reflect U.S. *exports* of goods and services to Japan. The exchange rate would be $0.015 per yen (one-and-a-half cents per yen), and each year, 10,000 billion yen would be traded in exchange for 10,000 × 0.015 = 150 billion dollars. Since the quantities of yen demanded and supplied are equal in equilibrium, there is no trade deficit: The United States buys $150 billion in goods from Japan, and Japan buys $150 billion in goods from the United States.

Now suppose that the Japanese start to buy U.S. stocks, bonds, and real estate. Specifically, they want to purchase 5,000 billion yen worth of these assets from Americans each year. To do so, they need dollars, so they must supply additional yen to the foreign exchange market to get them. Accordingly, the supply of yen curve shifts rightward by 5,000 billion yen. The market equilibrium moves from

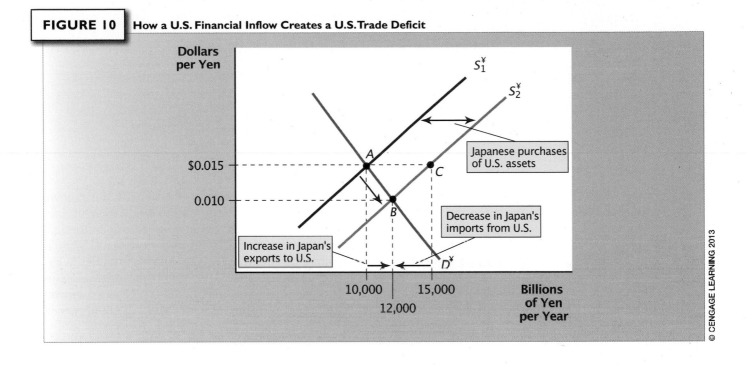

FIGURE 10   How a U.S. Financial Inflow Creates a U.S. Trade Deficit

point *A* to point *B*, and the new exchange rate is $0.01 per yen. The yen depreciates against the dollar, and the dollar appreciates against the yen.

But something interesting happens in the market as the exchange rate changes. First, there is a *movement along the demand curve* for yen, from point *A* to point *B*. Why? The yen is now cheaper, so Americans—finding Japanese goods and services cheaper—buy more of them. Thus, the movement along the demand curve represents an *increase in Japan's exports to the U.S.* (valued in yen, the units on the horizontal axis). In the figure, Japan's exports—the quantity of yen demanded—rise by 2,000 billion yen as we move from *A* to *B*.

But there is a second movement as well. After the shift in the supply curve, *and at the old exchange rate of $0.015,* the Japanese want to supply 15,000 billion yen to the market (point *C*). But as the exchange rate falls, there is a movement from point *C* to point *B*—the quantity of yen supplied decreases. Why does this happen? Because as the yen depreciates (the dollar appreciates), U.S. goods and services become more expensive to the Japanese. Accordingly, they purchase fewer U.S. goods. Assuming that the Japanese still want to purchase the same 5,000 billion yen in U.S. *assets*, the entire decrease in the quantity of yen supplied as we move from *C* to *B* represents a *decrease in Japan's imports from the United States* (valued in yen). In the figure, Japan's imports decrease by 3,000 billion yen.

Let's recap: Because the Japanese wanted to purchase 5,000 billion yen in U.S. assets (a net financial inflow to the United States of 5,000 billion yen), the yen depreciated. This, in turn, made Japanese goods cheaper for Americans—increasing Japan's exports (U.S. imports) by 2,000 billion yen per year. It also made U.S. goods more expensive in Japan, decreasing Japan's imports (U.S. exports) by 3,000 billion yen per year. Since U.S. imports have risen by 2,000 billion ¥ and U.S. exports have fallen by 3,000 billion ¥, the United States—which initially had no trade deficit with Japan at point *A*—now has a trade deficit equal to

5,000 billion yen. This is exactly equal to the financial inflow—Japan's purchases of U.S. assets.

More generally,

> *an increase in the desire of foreigners to invest in the United States contributes to an appreciation of the dollar. As a result, U.S. exports—which become more expensive for foreigners—decline. Imports—which become cheaper to Americans—increase. The result is a rise in the U.S. trade deficit.*

Explaining the Net Financial Inflow

What explains the huge financial inflow that began in the 1980s and has since grown larger? In the 1980s, an important part of the story was *a rise in U.S. interest rates relative to interest rates abroad,* which made U.S. assets more attractive to foreigners, and foreign assets less attractive to Americans. In the 1990s, however, U.S. interest rates were low relative to rates in other countries, yet the inflow continued. Why?

Even when U.S. interest rates are lower than abroad, it seems that foreign residents have a strong preference for holding American assets. In part, this is because of a favorable investment climate. The United States is a stable country with a long history of protecting individual property rights. People know that if they buy American stocks or bonds, unless they violate U.S. criminal law, the U.S. government is very unlikely to confiscate foreign-owned assets or suddenly impose punitive taxes when foreigners want to repatriate the funds to their home countries. This asymmetrical foreign preference for American assets helps explain why the U.S. net financial inflow has been *persistent.*

But why did the inflow *surge* from the mid-1990s to around 2006? One reason is that Americans were saving less, and foreigners were saving more. (In Europe and in Japan, aging populations have been saving heavily for retirement, while developing country governments have been reducing debt and building up financial reserves.) All of this new foreign wealth needed to be held in *some* country's assets, and—for reasons discussed earlier—the U.S. seemed to be the favorite.

At the same time, the *demand* for loanable funds in the U.S. was growing rapidly. Part of this greater demand for funds arose from new investment opportunities, causing business firms to issue new shares of stock and new bonds in order to finance projects. This was especially true in the late 1990s, during the Internet boom. And when the boom became a bust in the early 2000s, a new demand for funds arose from two other sources: (1) The government's need to finance large budget deficits; and (2) households' demand for mortgage loans to finance housing purchases during the housing boom. New types of mortgage-backed securities were developed that made it easier for foreigners—both private parties and governments—to lend funds to American home buyers by purchasing these securities.

Remember that, under floating exchange rates, the financial inflow equals the trade deficit. Thus, the story of the U.S. financial inflow of the 1980s, 1990s, and early 2000s is also the story of the U.S. trade deficit:

> *The rise in the U.S. trade deficit came from (1) relatively high interest rates in the 1980s; (2) a long-held preference for American assets that grew stronger in the 1990s; and (3) a growing demand for funds in the U.S. combined with high saving in other countries beginning in the late 1990s. Each contributed to a large U.S. net financial inflow, a higher value for the dollar, and a trade deficit.*

In addition to a strong desire to buy U.S. assets, a trade deficit can arise from another cause: a foreign currency fixed at an artificially low value. In the minds of many economists, this has contributed to the United States' growing trade deficit with China. We will explore the U.S. trade deficit with China in our Using the Theory section. But first, let's look at why many economists are concerned about the large U.S. trade deficit.

Concerns about the Trade Deficit

Should we be concerned about the U.S. trade deficit? To most economists, the answer is yes. But the reasons are different from those typically offered in public debate.

To many *non*-economists, the U.S. trade deficit is viewed as bad because it makes Americans poorer. We get VCRs, toys, and T-shirts from the rest of the world. But we don't pay for all of these things with our own goods and services. To make up the difference, we sell assets: We turn over ownership of our factories and real estate to the rest of the world, and also accumulate debt to them (when we sell them bonds). According to this view, the U.S. trade deficit means declining American wealth.

Although the first part of this analysis is correct (the United States *does* finance its trade deficit by selling assets to the rest of the world), it does not necessarily follow that the trade deficit makes American households poorer. That would follow if the total amount of wealth in the U.S. economy were fixed, so that any wealth sold to foreigners meant less wealth in American hands. But, in fact, total U.S. wealth tends to grow over time, as new factories and new homes are built, new intellectual property is developed, and more. And even after deducting the wealth that the rest of the world acquires, what is left in American hands has continued to grow decade by decade. True, trillions of dollars in U.S. wealth were lost during the financial crisis and recession of 2008–2009. But this hit—while massive—still left inflation-adjusted wealth per U.S. household well above its average during the 1990s. In the future, U.S. wealth will eventually catch up to the peak reached in mid-2007 and grow beyond it.

What *does* follow from this analysis is that, *because of the trade deficit, U.S. wealth owned by the U.S. public grows more slowly than it otherwise would.* Slower growing wealth is a choice made by U.S. households (choosing to buy more toys and T-shirts instead of saving more) and the U.S. government (choosing to pay for part of its expenditure by borrowing instead of taxing). Economists continue to debate the wisdom or lack of wisdom behind these choices, but slower growing wealth is not the main reason for economists' concern.

The real issue, as economists view it, is the trade deficit's *sustainability*.

Why might the trade deficit not be sustainable? As the U.S. trade deficit continues year after year, foreign holdings of U.S. assets continue to accumulate—rapidly. And the *proportion* of the rest of the world's total wealth that is held in dollar-denominated assets grows as well. At some point, the rest of the world's wealth holders may decide that their portfolios are too "dollar heavy," and that the time has come to diversify. This would mean a slowdown—or possibly a halt—in new purchases of U.S. assets. If this occurs, we can imagine two possibilities.

The Soft-Landing Scenario

In the benign, soft-landing scenario, the U.S. and world economies would gradually adjust to a slowdown in foreign purchases of U.S. assets. A decline in the demand for

U.S. assets, as you've learned, would cause the dollar to depreciate. Imports would become more expensive for U.S. residents, and U.S. exports would become cheaper to the rest of the world, so the trade deficit would gradually shrink.

At the same time, the U.S. interest rate would rise. From a long-run, loanable funds perspective, the interest rate would rise because the supply of funds to the U.S. loanable funds market is shrinking. From a short-run perspective, the Fed would raise its interest rate target to prevent the rise in net exports from overheating the U.S. economy.

The rise in the U.S. interest rate would contribute to the gradualness of the adjustment. First, a higher interest rate would mean more saving by Americans, enabling them to buy some of the assets foreigners are no longer buying. Second, higher interest rates would help make U.S. assets more attractive to foreigners.

The soft-landing scenario would not be painless. It would require structural changes in the U.S. economy as exporting and import-competing industries expanded, while interest-sensitive industries such as home building declined. But it would not be a disaster.

The Hard-Landing Scenario

The more dangerous, hard-landing scenario works much like the soft-landing scenario, except that the changes are much larger and more sudden. Once again, we start with a decline in the demand for U.S. assets by foreigners. Only this time, as the dollar begins to depreciate, foreigners anticipate *further* depreciation in the future. They begin to dump dollar-denominated assets *en masse*, before the anticipated decline in their value. Hot money flows out of the dollar and into other currencies. The dollar doesn't just depreciate—it plummets. And the more it does, the more foreign wealth holders want to get rid of their dollars.

The interest rate would rise. (See the soft-landing scenario.) But in this case, with the dollar depreciating so rapidly, substitute the word *skyrocket* for *rise*. With soaring interest rates, spending on interest-sensitive goods, such as new factories and homes, would disappear. Moreover, as you learned a few chapters ago, the rise in interest rates would cause stock and bond prices to fall—a decline in household wealth. Consumption spending would fall across the board.

In the most pessimistic form of the hard-landing scenario, the United States would experience a very serious recession—one that the Fed would be unable to prevent. If the Fed tried to lower the interest rate to prevent the recession entirely, it would have to allow the dollar to continue plummeting. This would make the price of imports rise rapidly and cause unacceptable inflation. And even if the Fed decided to take this course, the dramatic changes in the economy would make any Fed response particularly error prone.

Which of these two scenarios is most likely to occur? Economists continue to debate the probabilities. Some argue that the hard-landing scenario is unrealistic. It assumes that central banks in the rest of the world would *allow* the dollar to plummet, even though this would devastate their own export industries and decrease the value of their remaining dollar-denominated assets. Surely, so the soft-landers say, these central banks would intervene in the foreign exchange market, by purchasing dollars to prop up its value. Others are not so confident.

USING THE THEORY

THE U.S. TRADE DEFICIT WITH CHINA

The growing U.S. trade deficit with China has become one of the most controversial issues of U.S. public policy. Figure 11 shows United States imports to, and exports from, China from 1988 to 2010. (The figure excludes trade in services, but this has little impact on the numbers.) Trade in both directions expanded dramatically. But while U.S. exports to China increased by a factor of 17, U.S. *imports* from China increased 42-fold, from $8.5 billion in 1988 to $357 billion in 2010. During this period, China went from being a relatively unimportant trading partner of the United States to one of the largest. In the figure, the growing trade deficit is the increasing distance between the (higher) imports line and the (lower) exports line. In 2010, the United States had a larger trade deficit with China—$271 billion—than with any other country.

The U.S. trade deficit with China has been soaring for a variety of reasons, including special trade agreements during this period that gave China new access to U.S. markets, and Chinese trade policies that have encouraged exports and discouraged imports. But another factor, as mentioned earlier, is China's undervalued exchange rate. From 1995 to 2004 China rigidly fixed the value of its currency (the yuan) against the dollar at about $0.12 per yuan—well below the yuan's

SUSAN VAN E TEN

FIGURE 11 **The Growing U.S. Trade Deficit with China**

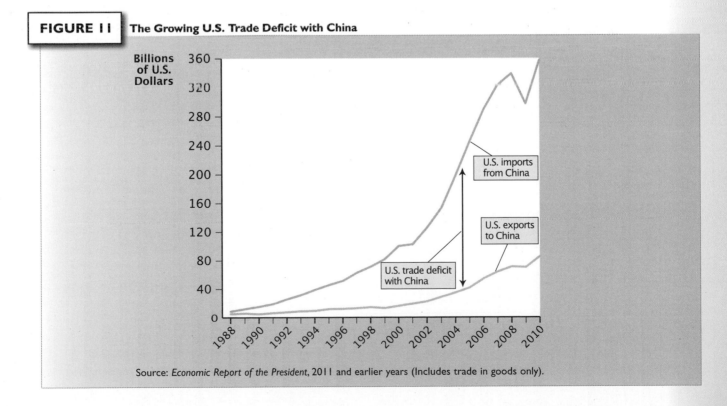

Source: *Economic Report of the President*, 2011 and earlier years (Includes trade in goods only).

equilibrium value. Beginning in 2005, China—under U.S. pressure—allowed the yuan to appreciate—modestly at first, then more slowly. Still, by 2011, China was still keeping the exchange rate well below its equilibrium value, fixing it between $0.15 and $0.16 per yuan.

Figure 12 illustrates how an undervalued yuan can create a trade deficit for the United States. In this discussion, we'll regard the exchange rate as effectively *fixed* by China at $0.15 per yuan. And we'll assume, for purposes of illustration, that if the exchange rate were floating, the market equilibrium would be at point A, with an exchange rate of $0.24 per yuan. In this case, 700 billion yuan would be exchanged for 700 × $0.24 = $168 billion dollars each year.

Now we introduce the lower, fixed exchange rate of $0.15 per yuan. Compared to the equilibrium exchange rate, the fixed exchange rate causes a movement along the *demand* for yuan curve, from point A to point C. The yuan is now cheaper, which makes Chinese goods and services cheaper to Americans, who buy more of them. Measured along the horizontal axis, *China's exports to the U.S. increase* by 300 billion yuan per year.

There is also a move from point A to point B along the *supply* curve; the quantity of yuan supplied decreases. A lower-valued yuan makes U.S. goods and services more expensive to Chinese households and businesses, so they purchase fewer of them. Along the horizontal axis, *China's imports from the U.S. decrease* by 500 billion yuan.

Because the fixed exchange rate has caused *China's imports from the U.S. to decrease* by 500 billion yuan, and *China's exports to the U.S. to increase* by 300 billion yuan, the U.S. trade deficit with China—valued in yuan—rises by 500 + 300 or 800 billion yuan per year.

But wait . . . doesn't the rise in the U.S. trade deficit have to equal the rise in the net financial inflow? Indeed it does. Figure 12 shows an *excess demand for yuan*

FIGURE 12   How an Undervalued Chinese Yuan Can Create a U.S. Trade Deficit

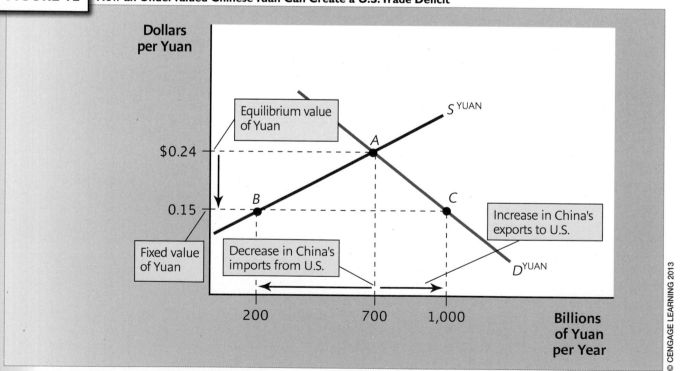

of 1,000 − 200 = 800 billion at the fixed exchange rate. The Chinese government must supply these yuan, selling them for U.S. dollars. These dollars are then used to purchase U.S. assets, contributing to the U.S. net financial inflow.

> When a U.S. trading partner fixes the dollar price of its currency below its equilibrium value, U.S. exports—which become more expensive to foreigners—decline. Imports—which become cheaper to Americans—increase. The result is a rise in the U.S. trade deficit.

Even with the fixed exchange rate, the yuan has become less undervalued in recent years, because of higher inflation in China than in the U.S. As you've learned in this chapter, when a country has relatively high inflation, the *equilibrium* price of its currency falls, which brings the equilibrium rate closer to the unchanged fixed rate. (An end-of-chapter problem will guide you through the details.)

Still, China's fixed exchange rate with the dollar remains a source of considerable tension between the two countries. On the one hand, the undervalued yuan enables Americans to purchase goods from China at even lower prices than otherwise. But rapidly growing trade with China also disrupts production in the U.S. economy, as U.S. businesses that produce sandals, shoes, suits, electronic goods, toys, and textiles are unable to compete with cheaper goods from China. A fixed, undervalued yuan gives China an even *greater* cost advantage than it would otherwise have. U.S. firms and consumers who buy Chinese goods get an even better deal. But those who compete in these markets must adjust more rapidly—and painfully—to the new pattern of international trade.

SUMMARY

When residents of two countries trade with one another, one party ordinarily makes use of the foreign exchange market to trade one national currency for another. In this market, suppliers of a currency interact with demanders to determine an *exchange rate*—the price of one currency in terms of another.

In the market for U.S. dollars and British pounds, for example, demanders are mostly Americans who wish to obtain pounds in order to buy goods and services from British firms or to buy British assets. A higher dollar price for the pound will lead Americans to demand fewer pounds—the demand curve slopes downward. Changes in U.S. real GDP, the U.S. price level relative to the British price level, Americans' tastes for British goods, interest rates in the United States relative to Britain, or expectations regarding the exchange rate can each cause the demand curve to shift.

Suppliers of pounds are mostly British residents who wish to buy American goods, services, or assets. A higher dollar price for the pound will lead Britons to supply more pounds—the supply curve slopes upward. The supply curve will shift in response to changes in British real GDP, prices in Britain relative to the United States, British tastes for U.S. goods, the British interest rate relative to the U.S. rate, and expectations regarding the exchange rate.

When the exchange rate floats, the equilibrium rate is determined where the supply and demand curves cross. If demand for a currency increases, it will *appreciate*—its price will rise. (The other country's currency will *depreciate*.) An increase in the supply of a currency will cause it to depreciate.

Governments often intervene in foreign exchange markets. Many countries manage their float, buying and selling their own currency to alter the exchange rate. Some countries fix their exchange rate to the dollar or the currency of a major trading partner.

When a currency depreciates, its net exports rise. Monetary policy, in addition to its impact on interest-sensitive spending, also changes the exchange rate and net exports, adding to changes in output. This monetary policy is more effective in changing GDP when its effects on net exports are included. The nations of the euro zone, however, have chosen to give up their ability to run their own monetary policies, which has caused problems for the euro zone.

The United States has had a persistent—and growing—*trade deficit* with the rest of the world. Much of this trade deficit can be explained by the growing U.S. *financial inflow* from the rest of the world. In addition, when an exchange rate is fixed, an under-valued foreign currency can create a U.S. trade deficit. By making the U.S. dollar artificially more expensive to residents of the foreign country, it causes U.S. exports to decline and U.S. imports to rise.

PROBLEM SET

Answers to even-numbered Problems can be found on the text Web site through www.cengagebrain.com

1. Would each of the following events, *ceteris paribus*, cause the dollar to appreciate against the euro or to depreciate?
   a. Health experts discover that red wine, especially French and Italian red wine, lowers cholesterol.
   b. GDP in nations across Europe falls.
   c. The United States experiences a higher inflation rate than Europe does.
   d. The U.S. budget deficit rises. (Hint: What happens to the U.S. interest rate?)

2. Let the monthly demand for British pounds and the monthly supply of British pounds be described by the following equations:

$$\text{Demand for pounds} = 10 - 2e$$

$$\text{Supply of pounds} = 4 + 3e$$

   where the quantities are in millions of pounds, and e is dollars per pound.
   a. Find the equilibrium exchange rate.
   b. Suppose the U.S. government intervenes in the foreign currency market and uses U.S. dollars to buy 2 million pounds each month. What happens to the exchange rate? Why might the U.S. government do this?

3. Let the demand and supply of Philippine pesos each month be described by the following equations:

$$\text{Demand for pesos} = 100 - 2000e$$

$$\text{Supply of pesos} = 20 + 3000e$$

   where the quantities are millions of pesos, and e is dollars per peso.
   a. Find the equilibrium exchange rate.
   b. Suppose the Philippine central bank wants to fix the exchange rate at 50 pesos per dollar and

keep it there. Should the Philippine central bank buy or sell its own currency? How much per month?

4. Suppose the United States and Mexico are each other's sole trading partners. The Fed, afraid that the economy is about to overheat, raises the U.S. interest rate.
   a. Will the dollar appreciate or depreciate against the Mexican peso? Illustrate with a diagram of the dollar–peso foreign exchange market.
   b. What will happen to equilibrium GDP in the United States?
   c. How would your analyses in (a) and (b) change if, at the same time that the Fed was increasing the U.S. interest rate, the Mexican central bank increased the Mexican interest rate by an equivalent amount?

5. Jordan fixes its national currency—the dinar—against the dollar. In mid-2011, the fixed rate was 1.41 dollars per dinar.
   a. Draw a diagram illustrating the market in which Jordanian dinars are traded for U.S. dollars, assuming that the equilibrium exchange rate is 1.00 dollars per dinar. (In your diagram, put the number of dinars per month on the horizontal axis.)
   b. Under the assumption in (a), would Jordan's central bank be buying or selling Jordanian dinars in this market? Indicate the number of dinars per month that the central bank must buy or sell as a distance on your graph.
   c. Based on your diagram and your answers so far, could Jordan continue to fix its currency at 1.41 dollars per dinar forever? Why or why not?

d. Suppose that foreign currency traders believe that Jordan will soon allow the dinar to float. How would this affect the current supply and demand curves for dinars? (Draw new curves to indicate the impact.)

e. How would the events in (d) affect the number of dinars that Jordan's central bank must buy or sell?

6. As in problem 5, note that Jordan fixes its national currency—the dinar—against the dollar at 1.41 dollars per dinar.

a. Draw a diagram illustrating the market in which Jordanian dinars are traded for U.S. dollars, assuming that the equilibrium exchange rate is 2.00 dollars per dinar. (Put the number of dinars per month on the horizontal axis.)

b. Under the assumption in (a), would Jordan's central bank be buying or selling Jordanian dinars in this market? Indicate the number of dinars per month that the central bank must buy or sell as a distance on your graph.

c. Based on your diagram and your answers so far, could Jordan continue to fix its currency at $1.41 per dinar forever? Why or why not?

d. Suppose that foreign currency traders believe that Jordan will soon allow the dinar to float. How would this affect the current supply and demand curves for dinars? (Draw new curves to indicate the impact.)

e. How would the events in (d) affect the number of dinars that Jordan's central bank must buy or sell?

7. Some nations that fix their exchange rates make their currency more expensive for foreigners (an overvalued currency), while others make their currency artificially cheap to foreigners (an undervalued currency).

a. Why would a country want an overvalued currency? How, specifically, would the country benefit?
Would the policy cause harm to anyone in the country? Explain briefly.

b. Why would a country want an undervalued currency? How, specifically, would the country benefit? Would the policy cause harm to anyone in the country? Explain briefly.

8. If the inflation rate in Country A is 4 percent and the inflation rate in Country B is 6 percent, explain what will happen to the relative value of each country's currency.

9. a. Use the information in the following table to find the exchange rate if the euro and the U.S. dollar are allowed to float freely.

Dollars per Euro	Quantity of Euros Demanded	Quantity of Euros Supplied
$1.20	500 million	2,600 million
$1.10	1,000 million	2,400 million
$1.00	1,500 million	2,200 million
$0.90	2,000 million	2,000 million
$0.80	2,500 million	1,800 million

b. What will happen to the exchange rate if the demand for euros rises by 700 million at each price if there is no intervention?

c. Assume that the European central bank currently owns 400 million dollars and the Fed currently owns 300 million euros. If the demand for euros rises by 700 million at each price, what would the European central bank have to do to maintain a fixed exchange rate equal to the exchange rate you found in part (a)? Is this possible?

10. Refer to Figure 10 in the chapter. Remember that there was no trade deficit at point A. What is the U.S. trade deficit with Japan in *dollars* at point B?

More Challenging

11. It is often stated that the U.S. trade deficit with Japan results from Japanese trade barriers against U.S. exports to Japan.

a. Suppose that Japan and the United States trade goods but not assets. Show—with a diagram of the dollar–yen market—that a U.S. trade deficit is impossible as long as the exchange rate floats. (Hint: With no trading in assets, the quantity of yen demanded at each exchange rate is equal in value to U.S. imports, and the quantity of yen supplied at each exchange rate is equal in value to U.S. exports.)

b. In the diagram, illustrate the impact of a reduction in Japanese trade barriers enabling an increase in U.S. exports to Japan. Would the dollar appreciate or depreciate against the yen? What would be the impact on U.S. net exports?

c. Now suppose that the United States and Japan also trade assets, but that the Japanese buy more U.S. assets than we buy of theirs. Could the elimination of Japanese trade barriers wipe out the U.S. trade deficit with Japan? Why, or why not? (Hint: What is the relationship between the U.S. trade deficit and U.S. net financial inflow?)

12. Toward the end of the Using the Theory section, you learned that higher inflation in China than in the U.S. has reduced the yuan's undervaluation in recent years. To see how this works, draw a graph similar to that in Figure 12. To keep the problem simple, suppose the price level in the U.S. does not change and the price level in China rises, while China continues to fix the exchange rate at $0.15 per yuan.

   a. What impact does the rise in China's price level have on the supply of yuan curve?

   b. What impact does the rise in China's price level have on the demand for yuan curve?

   c. What is the combined effect of the changes you found in (a) and (b) above on the *equilibrium* price of the yuan?

   d. After the changes you found above, is the yuan (fixed at $0.15 per yuan) *more* or *less* undervalued than initially? Explain briefly.

A

Absolute advantage The ability to produce a good or service, using fewer resources than other producers use.

Aggregate demand (*AD*) curve A curve indicating equilibrium GDP at each price level when the money supply is constant.

Aggregate expenditure (*AE*) The sum of spending by households, business firms, the government, and foreigners on final goods and services produced in the United States.

Aggregate production function The relationship showing how much total output can be produced with different quantities of labor, with quantities of all other resources and technology held constant.

Aggregate supply (*AS*) curve A curve indicating the price level that is consistent with firms' unit costs and markups for any level of output over the short run.

Aggregation The process of combining different things into a single category.

Alternate goods Other goods that firms in a market could produce instead of the good in question.

Alternate market A market other than the one being analyzed in which the same good could be sold.

Appreciation An increase in the price of a currency in a floating-rate system.

Automatic destabilizers A feature of the economy that increases the size of the expenditure multiplier and enlarges the impact of spending changes on real GDP.

Automatic stabilizer A feature of the economy that reduces the size of the expenditure multiplier and diminishes the impact of spending changes on real GDP.

Autonomous consumption spending The part of consumption spending that is independent of income; also the vertical intercept of the consumption function.

B

Balance sheet A financial statement showing assets, liabilities, and shareholders' equity at a point in time.

Balanced budget multiplier The multiplier for a change in government purchases that is matched by an equal change in taxes.

Bank capital Another name for shareholders' equity in a bank.

Banking panic A situation in which fearful depositors attempt to withdraw funds from many banks simultaneously.

Black market A market in which goods are sold illegally at a price above the legal ceiling.

Bond A promise to pay back borrowed funds, issued by a corporation or government agency.

Boom A period of time during which real GDP is above potential GDP.

Budget deficit The excess of government purchases over net taxes.

Budget surplus The excess of net taxes over government purchases.

Burden of the debt Interest payments on the national debt as a percentage of GDP.

Business cycles Fluctuations in real GDP around its long-term growth trend.

Business demand for funds curve Indicates the level of investment spending firms plan at various interest rates.

C

Capital A long-lasting tool that is used to produce other goods.

Capital gain The gain to the owner of an asset when it is sold for a price higher than its original purchase price.

Capital gains tax A tax on profits earned when a financial asset is sold at more than its acquisition price.

Capital loss The loss to the owner of an asset when it is sold for a price lower than its original purchase price.

Capital per worker The total capital stock divided by total employment.

Capital ratio A bank's capital (shareholders' equity) as a percentage of its total assets.

Capital stock The total amount of capital in a nation that is productively useful at a particular point in time.

Cash in the hands of the public Currency and coins held by the non-bank public.

Catch-up growth Economic growth, primarily in less-advanced countries, based on increasing capital per worker from low levels, and adopting technologies already used in more advanced countries.

Central bank A nation's principal monetary authority responsible for controlling the money supply.

Ceteris paribus Latin for "all else remaining the same."

Change in demand A shift of a demand curve in response to a change in some variable other than price.

Change in quantity demanded A movement along a demand curve in response to a change in price.

Change in quantity supplied A movement along a supply curve in response to a change in price.

Change in supply A shift of a supply curve in response to a change in some variable other than price.

Circular flow A simple model that shows how goods, resources, and dollar payments flow between households and firms.

Classical model A macroeconomic model that explains the long-run behavior of the economy.

Command or centrally planned economy An economic system in which resources are allocated according to explicit instructions from a central authority.

Comparative advantage The ability to produce a good or service at a lower opportunity cost than other producers.

Complement A good that is used together with some other good.

Complete crowding out A dollar-for-dollar decline in one sector's spending caused by an increase in some other sector's spending.

Consumer Price Index An index of the cost, through time, of a market basket of goods purchased by a typical household.

Consumption (C) The part of GDP purchased by households as final users.

Consumption function A positively sloped relationship between real consumption spending and real disposable income.

Consumption tax A tax on the part of their income that households spend.

Consumption–income line A line showing aggregate consumption spending at each level of income or GDP.

Corporate profits tax A tax on the profits earned by corporations.

Critical assumption Any assumption that affects the conclusions of a model in an important way.

Crowding out A decline in one sector's spending caused by an increase in some other sector's spending.

Cyclical unemployment Joblessness arising from changes in production over the business cycle.

D

Debt ratio Publicly held national debt as a percentage of GDP.

Deflation A decrease in the price level from one period to the next.

Demand curve A graph of a demand schedule; a curve showing the quantity of a good or service demanded at various prices, with all other variables held constant.

Demand curve for foreign currency A curve indicating the quantity of a specific foreign currency that Americans will want to buy, during a given period, at each different exchange rate.

Demand curve for housing A curve showing, at each price, the total number of homes that everyone in the market would like to own, given the constraints that they face.

Demand schedule A list showing the quantities of a good that consumers would choose to purchase at different prices, with all other variables held constant.

Demand shock Any event that causes the *AD* curve to shift.

Demand-side effects Macroeconomic policy effects on total output that work through changes in total spending.

Depreciation A decrease in the price of a currency in a floating-rate system.

Depression An unusually severe recession.

Devaluation A change in the exchange rate from a higher fixed rate to a lower fixed rate.

Discount rate The interest rate the Fed charges on loans to banks.

Discouraged workers Individuals who would like a job, but have given up searching for one.

Discovery-based growth Economic growth, primarily in advanced countries, based on technological change from new discoveries.

Disposable income Household income minus net taxes, which is either spent or saved.

E

Economic growth The increase in our production of goods and services that occurs over long periods of time.

Economics The study of choice under conditions of scarcity.

Entrepreneurship The ability and willingness to combine the other resources—labor, capital, and land—into a productive enterprise.

Equilibrium GDP In the short run, the level of output at which output and aggregate expenditure are equal.

Equilibrium price The market price that, once achieved, remains constant until either the demand curve or supply curve shifts.

Equilibrium quantity The market quantity bought and sold per period that, once achieved, remains constant until either the demand curve or supply curve shifts.

Excess demand At a given price, the amount by which quantity demanded exceeds quantity supplied.

Excess demand for bonds The amount of bonds demanded exceeds the amount supplied at a particular interest rate.

Excess reserves Reserves in excess of required reserves.

Excess supply At a given price, the amount by which quantity supplied exceeds quantity demanded.

Excess supply of money The amount of money supplied exceeds the amount demanded at a particular interest rate.

Exchange The act of trading with others to obtain what we desire.

Exchange rate The amount of one country's currency that is traded for one unit of another country's currency.

Excise tax A tax on a specific good or service.

Expansion A period of increasing real GDP.

Expenditure approach Measuring GDP by adding the value of goods and services purchased by each type of final user.

Expenditure multiplier The amount by which equilibrium real GDP changes as a result of a one-dollar change in autonomous consumption, investment spending, government purchases, or net exports.

Explicit cost The dollars sacrificed—and actually paid out—for a choice.

F

Factor payments Payments to the owners of resources that are used in production.

Factor payments approach Measuring GDP by summing the factor payments earned by all households in the economy.

Federal funds rate The interest rate charged for loans of reserves among banks.

Federal Open Market Committee (FOMC) A committee of Federal Reserve officials that establishes U.S. monetary policy.

Federal Reserve System The monetary authority of the United States, charged with creating and regulating the nation's supply of money.

Fiat money Something that serves as a means of payment by government declaration.

Final good A good sold to its final user.

Financial intermediary A business firm that specializes in brokering between savers and borrowers.

Fiscal policy A change in government purchases or net taxes designed to change total output.

Fixed exchange rate A government-declared exchange rate maintained by central bank intervention in the foreign exchange market.

Floating exchange rate An exchange rate that is freely determined by the forces of supply and demand.

Flow variable A variable representing a process that takes place over some time period.

Foreign currency crisis A loss of faith that a country can prevent a drop in its exchange rate, leading to a rapid depletion of its foreign currency (e.g., dollar) reserves.

Foreign exchange market The market in which one country's currency is traded for another country's.

Frictional unemployment Joblessness experienced by people who are between jobs or who are just entering or reentering the labor market.

Full employment A situation in which there is no cyclical unemployment.

G

GDP price index An index of the price level for all final goods and services included in GDP.

Government demand for funds curve Indicates the amount of government borrowing at various interest rates.

Government outlays Total disbursements by the government for purchases, transfer payments, and interest on the debt.

Government purchases (G) Spending by federal, state, and local governments on goods and services.

Gross domestic product (GDP) The total value of all final goods and services produced for the marketplace during a given year, within the nation's borders.

Growth equation An equation showing the percentage growth rate of real GDP per capita as the sum of the growth rates of productivity, average hours, and the employment-population ratio.

H

(Household) saving The portion of after-tax income that households do not spend on consumption.

Human capital The skills and training of the labor force.

I

Implicit cost The value of something sacrificed when no direct payment is made.

Income The amount that a person or firm earns over a particular period.

Index A series of numbers used to track a variable's rise or fall over time.

Indexed payment A payment that is periodically adjusted in proportion with a price index.

Inferior good A good that people demand less of as their income rises.

Inflation rate The percentage change in the price level from one period to the next.

Injections Spending on a country's output from sources other than its households.

Input Anything (including a resource) used to produce a good or service.

Insolvent Condition of a firm (e.g., a bank) when total assets are less than total liabilities.

Intermediate goods Goods used up in producing final goods.

Investment tax credit A reduction in taxes for firms that invest in new capital.

Involuntary part-time workers Individuals who would like a full-time job, but who are working only part time.

L

Labor The time human beings spend producing goods and services.

Labor demand curve Indicates how many workers firms will want to hire at various real wage rates.

Labor force Those people who have a job or who are looking for one.

Labor productivity The output produced by the average worker in an hour.

Labor supply curve Indicates how many people will want to work at various real wage rates.

Land The physical space on which production takes place, as well as the natural resources that come with it.

Law of demand As the price of a good increases, the quantity demanded decreases.

Law of supply As the price of a good increases, the quantity supplied increases.

Leakages Income earned by households that they do *not* spend on the country's output during a given year.

Loan An agreement to pay back borrowed funds, signed by a household or noncorporate business.

Loanable funds market The market in which savers make their funds available to borrowers.

Long-run aggregate supply curve A vertical line indicating all possible output and price-level combinations at which the economy could end up in the long run.

Long-run Phillips curve A vertical line indicating that in the long run, unemployment must equal its natural rate, regardless of the rate of inflation.

M

Macroeconomics The study of the behavior of the overall economy.

Managed float A policy of frequent central bank intervention to move the exchange rate.

Marginal propensity to consume The amount by which consumption spending rises when disposable income rises by one dollar.

Market A group of buyers and sellers with the potential to trade with each other.

Market clearing Adjustment of prices until quantities supplied and demanded are equal.

Market economy An economic system in which resources are allocated through individual decision making.

Means of payment Anything acceptable as payment for goods and services.

Microeconomics The study of the behavior of individual households, firms, and governments; the choices they make; and their interaction in specific markets.

Mixed economy A market economy in which the government also plays an important role in allocating resources.

Model An abstract representation of reality.

Monetary policy Control or manipulation of interest rates by the Federal Reserve designed to achieve a macroeconomic goal.

Money An asset widely accepted as a means of payment.

Money demand curve A curve indicating how much money will be demanded at each nominal interest rate.

Money multiplier The multiple by which the money supply changes after a change in reserves.

Money supply The total amount of money (cash, checking deposits, and traveler's checks) held by the public.

Money supply curve A line showing the total quantity of money in the economy at each interest rate.

Mortgage A loan given to a home-buyer for part of the purchase price of the home.

N

National debt The total amount the federal government still owes to the general public from past borrowing.

Natural rate of unemployment The unemployment rate when there is no cyclical unemployment.

Net exports (*NX*) Total exports minus total imports.

Net financial inflow An inflow of funds equal to a nation's trade deficit.

Net investment Investment minus depreciation.

Net taxes Government tax revenues minus transfer payments.

Nominal interest rate The annual percent increase in a lender's dollars from making a loan.

Nominal variable A variable measured without adjustment for the dollar's changing value.

Non-bank A financial intermediary less strictly regulated than a bank, and with no government-guaranteed deposits.

Nonmarket production Goods and services that are produced but not sold in a market.

Normal good A good that people demand more of as their income rises.

Normative economics The practice of recommending policies to solve economic problems.

O

Open market operations Purchases or sales of government bonds by the Federal Reserve System.

Opportunity cost What is given up when taking an action or making a choice.

P

Perfectly competitive market (informal definition) A market in which no buyer or seller has the power to influence the price.

Phillips curve A curve indicating the Fed's choices between inflation and unemployment in the short run.

Physical capital The part of the capital stock consisting of physical goods, such as machinery, equipment, and factories.

Planned investment spending Business purchases of plant and equipment.

Positive economics The study of how the economy works.

Potential output The level of output the economy could produce if operating at full employment.

Price The amount of money that must be paid to a seller to obtain a good or service.

Price ceiling A government-imposed maximum price in a market.

Price floor A government-imposed minimum price in a market.

Price level The average level of prices in the economy.

Product markets Markets in which firms sell goods and services to households.

Production possibilities frontier (PPF) A curve showing all combinations of two goods that can be produced with the resources and technology currently available.

Productively inefficient A situation in which more of at least one good can be produced without sacrificing the production of any other good.

Purchasing power parity (PPP) theory The idea that the exchange rate will adjust in the long run so that the average price of goods in two countries will be roughly the same.

Q

Quantity demanded The quantity of a good that all buyers in a market would choose to buy during a period of time, given their constraints.

Quantity supplied The specific amount of a good that all sellers in a market would choose to sell over some time period, given their constraints.

R

Real interest rate The annual percent increase in a lender's purchasing power from making a loan.

Real variable A variable adjusted for changes in the dollar's value.

Recession A period of significant decline in real GDP.

Rent controls Government-imposed maximum rents on apartments and homes.

Required reserve ratio The minimum fraction of checking account balances that banks must hold as reserves.

Required reserves The minimum amount of reserves a bank must hold, depending on the amount of its deposit liabilities.

Reserves Vault cash plus balances held at the Fed.

Resource markets Markets in which households that own resources sell them to firms.

Resources The labor, capital, land (including natural resources), and entrepreneurship that are used to produce goods and services.

Run on the bank An attempt by many of a bank's depositors to withdraw their funds.

S

Say's law The idea that total spending will be sufficient to purchase the total output produced.

Scarcity A situation in which the amount of something available is insufficient to satisfy the desire for it.

Seasonal adjustment Adjusting an economic variable to remove the effects of changes predicted to occur at that time of year.

Seasonal unemployment Joblessness related to changes in weather, tourist patterns, or other seasonal factors.

Self-correcting mechanism The adjustment process through which price and wage changes return the economy to full-employment output in the long run.

Shadow banking system The entire collection of non-bank financial intermediaries.

Shareholders' equity The difference between total assets and total liabilities.

Short side of the market The smaller of quantity supplied and quantity demanded at a particular price.

Short-run macro model A macroeconomic model that explains how changes in spending can affect real GDP in the short run.

Short-run macroeconomic equilibrium A combination of price level and GDP consistent with both the *AD* and *AS* curves.

Shortage An excess demand not eliminated by a rise in price, so that quantity demanded continues to exceed quantity supplied.

Simplifying assumption Any assumption that makes a model simpler without affecting any of its important conclusions.

Slump A period during which real GDP is below potential and/or the employment rate is below normal.

Specialization A method of production in which each person concentrates on a limited number of activities.

Spread The difference between an interest rate and some other, benchmark interest rate.

Stagflation The combination of falling output and rising prices.

Stock variable A variable representing a quantity at a moment in time.

Store of value A form in which wealth can be held.

Structural unemployment Joblessness arising from mismatches between workers' skills and employers' requirements or between workers' locations and employers' locations.

Subsidy A government payment to buyers or sellers on each unit purchased or sold.

Substitute A good that can be used in place of some other good and that fulfills more or less the same purpose.

Supply curve A graph of a supply schedule, showing the quantity of a good or service supplied at various prices, with all other variables held constant.

Supply curve for foreign currency A curve indicating the quantity of a specific foreign currency that will be supplied, during a given period, at each different exchange rate.

Supply curve for housing A vertical line showing the total number of homes in a market that are available for ownership.

Supply of funds curve Indicates the level of household saving at various interest rates.

Supply schedule A list showing the quantities of a good or service that firms would choose to produce and sell at different prices, with all other variables held constant.

Supply shock Any event that causes the *AS* curve to shift.

Supply-side effects Macroeconomic policy effects on total output that work by changing the quantities of resources available.

Surplus An excess supply not eliminated by a fall in price, so that quantity supplied continues to exceed quantity demanded.

T

Tax incidence The division of a tax payment between buyers and sellers, determined by comparing the new (after tax) and old (pretax) market equilibriums.

Tax multiplier The amount by which real GDP changes for each one-dollar change in net taxes.

Taylor rule A proposed rule that would require the Fed to change the interest rate by a specified amount whenever real GDP or inflation deviates from its pre-announced target.

Technological change The invention or discovery of new inputs, new outputs, or new production methods.

Total demand for funds curve Indicates the total amount of borrowing at various interest rates.

Trade deficit The excess of a nation's imports over its exports during a given period.

Trade surplus The excess of a nation's exports over its imports during a given period.

Traditional economy An economy in which resources are allocated according to long-lived practices from the past.

Transfer payment Any payment that is not compensation for supplying goods, services, or resources.

U

Unemployment rate The fraction of the labor force that is without a job.

Unit of account A common unit for measuring how much something is worth.

V

Value added The revenue a firm receives minus the cost of the intermediate goods it buys.

Value-added approach Measuring GDP by summing the values added by all firms in the economy.

W

Wealth The total value of everything a person or firm owns, at a point in time, minus the total amount owed.

Wealth constraint At any point in time, total wealth is fixed.

Z

Zero lower bound The lowest possible value (zero) for any nominal interest rate (such as the federal funds rate).